The Banker's Handbook on Credit Risk

The Banker's Handbook on Credit Risk
Implementing Basel II

Morton Glantz
Johnathan Mun

AMSTERDAM • BOSTON • HEIDELBERG • LONDON
NEW YORK • OXFORD • PARIS • SAN DIEGO
SAN FRANCISCO • SINGAPORE • SYDNEY • TOKYO
Academic Press is an imprint of Elsevier

Elsevier Academic Press
30 Corporate Drive, Suite 400, Burlington, MA 01803, USA
525 B Street, Suite 1900, San Diego, California 92101-4495, USA
84 Theobald's Road, London WC1X 8RR, UK

This book is printed on acid-free paper.

Library of Congress Cataloging-in-Publication Data

Glantz, Morton.
    The banker's handbook on credit risk : implementing Basel II / Morton Glantz, Johnathan Mun.
        p. cm.
    Includes index.
    ISBN 978-0-12-373666-6 (hbk. : alk. paper)   1. Bank loans—Management.
2. Asset-liability management.   3. Credit analysis.   4. Banks and banking—Risk management.
I. Mun, Johnathan.   II. Title.

    HG1641.G553 2008
    332.1068—dc22

                                                                        2007046402

British Library Cataloguing in Publication Data

A catalogue record for this book is available from the British Library

ISBN: 978-0-12-373666-6

For all information on all Elsevier Academic Press publications
visit our Web site at www.books.elsevier.com

Printed in The United States of America

08   09   10   11   12   9   8   7   6   5   4   3   2   1

This book is dedicated to Martin L. Kahn, M.D.
"Warmth, sympathy, and understanding outweigh the surgeon's knife and the chemist's drug."
—Morton Glantz

To Penny, for putting up with me these many years.
—Johnathan Mun

Contents

Preface

Much literature has been published on banking—and for bankers. The authors tell us how to derive clients' cash flows and financial needs but not how to model value drivers with the latest technology. They advise us how to analyze financial alternatives and choose what appears to be the best decision but not how to create choices that are germinal in a client's corporate data. They refer us to quantitative objective functions and many formulas. They do not give us the means to run up stochastic solutions quickly and easily, thereby improving chances of ever being able to explain, *qualitatively*, optimal objectives on which any assessment of loss reserves, risk-adjusted pricing, and capital allocation must reside. They provide macrostructures but do not show how micro processes work, such as leveraging the latest stochastic technology to improve credit decision making.

Thanks in part to Basel II, in recent years, we have seen banking evolve from a casual discipline to a rigorous science. Just over a decade or so ago, technologies in the banking business such as neural nets, stochastic optimization, simulation, fuzzy logic, and data mining were still largely exploratory and at best quite tentative. Algorithms, as a term, rested on the outskirts of financial thought. More than a few bankers had not even heard of Monte Carlo outside of casinos and travel magazines. Machine learning was in its infancy, while migration risk and default frequencies concepts were encased in the Stone Age logic of ratios, deterministic forecasts, rudimentary cash flows, and, on more than a few occasions, front-page accounting shenanigans.

Yet, the concern is that some bankers are resisting computer-actualized solutions and are under the wrong impression that the past will satisfy (Basel II) compliance. Quantitative methods, such as the use of advanced models or even the use of math, do not alarm sharp banking professionals. Modeling tools are not black boxes that ignore or inhibit wisdom or that mechanize the loan approval process. In many financial institutions, however, models and, for that matter, change may intimidate banking professionals, inhibiting technological growth and, alas, the requisite skills to participate in strategic Basel II decision making at the highest level. Otherwise capable bankers find it difficult to creatively deploy sophisticated modeling techniques to crystallize value drivers, explain optimal capital allocation strategies, and deliver the goods to their boss or to a money committee. Knowledge gaps, particularly when it involves the new world of banking, are detrimental to continued growth both within the institution and in advancing one's career.

The hands-on applications covered in this book are vast, including areas of Basel II banking risk requirements (credit risk, credit spreads, default risk, value at risk, market risk, and so forth) and financial analysis (exotic options and valuation), risk analysis (stochastic forecasting, risk-based Monte Carlo simulation, portfolio optimization), and real options analysis (strategic options and decision analysis). This book is targeted at banking practitioners and financial analysts who require algorithms, examples, models, and insights in solving more advanced and even esoteric problems. This book not only talks about modeling and illustrates some basic concepts and examples, but it is also accompanied by a DVD filled with sample modeling videos, case studies, and software applications to help the reader get started immediately. The various trial software applications included give the reader quick access to the approximately 800 modeling functions and models, as well as over 300 analytical model templates, and powerful risk-based simulation software, designed to help in the understanding and learning of the concepts covered in the book and in using the embedded functions and algorithms in their own models. In addition, the reader can get a quick start in running risk-based Monte Carlo simulations, utilize advanced forecasting methods (ARIMA, GARCH, stochastic process forecasting, and many other methods), perform optimization in a variety of situations, as well as structure, engineer, and solve customized real options and financial options problems.

Each banking and credit or market risk model found in the Basel II Modeling Toolkit software is also described in this book—in detail only when the application warrants it; otherwise this book would be at least double its current size. All of the advanced mathematical concepts, models, and analytical algorithms are embedded in the software and so will not be discussed in the book. This book is unique in that it is a handbook or application-based book, and its focus is primarily on helping the reader hit the ground running, rather than delve into the theoretical structures of the models for which there are a plethora of mathematical modeling and theory-laden books without any real hands-on applicability. The best test for a pragmatic book is to answer the following question: When the banker needs to compute the probability of default of a particular loan from a certain corporation, would the banker rely on a book showing how to run an Excel-based software that takes a minute to compute, or would the banker prefer to take weeks to understand the theory of which he or she was unsure of how to apply, let alone trying to understand the complex theoretical mathematical concepts?

Indeed, this book should help you carry out your decision-making tasks more succinctly and might even empower you to grab the modeling hardball and to pitch winning games in a domain that is hot, dynamic, complex, and often combative.

About the Authors

Professor Morton Glantz is an internationally renowned educator, author, and banker. He serves as a financial consultant, educator, and adviser to a broad spectrum of professionals, including corporate financial executives, government ministers, privatization managers, investment and commercial bankers, public accounting firms, members of merger and acquisition teams, strategic planning executives, management consultants, attorneys, and representatives of foreign governments and international banks.

Professor Morton Glantz is a principal of Real Consulting and Real Options Valuation, firms specializing in risk consulting, training, certification, and advanced analytical software in the areas of risk quantification, analysis, and management solutions.

As a senior banker of a JP Morgan Chase heritage bank, Professor Glantz built a progressive career path specializing in credit analysis and credit risk management, risk grading systems, valuation models, and professional training. He was instrumental in the reorganization and development of the credit analysis module of the Bank's Management Training Program—Finance, which at the time was recognized as one of the foremost training programs in the banking industry.

A partial list of client companies Professor Glantz has worked with includes Institutional Investor, The Development Bank of Southern Africa, CUCORP, Canada, The Bank of China, GE Capital, Cyprus Development Bank, Decisioneering, Misr Iran

Development Bank (Cairo), Gulf Bank (Kuwait), Institute for International Research (Dubai), Inter-American Investment Corporation, Ernst & Young, UAL Merchant Bank (Johannesburg), Euromoney, ICICI Bank (India), Council for Trade and Economic Cooperation (Russia), BHF Bank, and IBM Credit Corporation.

Professor Glantz is on the finance faculty of the Fordham Graduate School of Business. He has appeared in the Harvard University International Directory of Business and Management Scholars and Research, and he has earned Fordham University Deans Award for Faculty Excellence on three occasions. He is a Board Member of the International Standards Board, International Institute of Professional Education and Research (IIPER). The IIPER is a global institute with partners and offices around the world, including the United States, Switzerland, Hong Kong, Mexico, Portugal, Singapore, Nigeria, and Malaysia.

Professor Glantz is widely published in financial journals and has authored a number of books published internationally, including *Credit Derivatives: Techniques to Manage Credit Risk for Financial Professionals* (with Erik Banks and Paul Siegel), McGraw-Hill, 2006; *Optimal Trading Strategies*, AMACOM, 2003 (co-author: Dr. Robert Kissell); *Managing Bank Risk: An Introduction to Broad-Base Credit Engineering*, Academic Press/Elsevier, 2002 (RISKBOOK.COM Award: Best Finance Books of 2003; *Scientific Financial Management*, AMACOM 2000; and *Loan Risk Management*, McGraw-Hill (1995).

Prof. Dr. Johnathan C. Mun is the founder and CEO of Real Options Valuation, Inc., a consulting, training, and software development firm specializing in Basel II analytics and modeling, strategic real options, financial valuation, risk-based Monte Carlo simulation, stochastic forecasting, optimization, and risk analysis located in northern California. He is also the Chairman of the International Institute of Professional Education and Research (IIPER), an accredited global organization providing the Certified in Risk Management (CRM) designation among others, staffed by professors from named universities from around the world. He is also the creator of the *Real Options SLS Super Lattice Solver* software, *Risk Simulator* software, *Basel II Modeling Toolkit* software, and *Employee Stock Options Valuation* software showcased in this book, as well as the risk analysis Training DVD, and he holds public seminars on risk analysis and Certified in Risk Management (CRM) programs. He has authored nine other books, including *Advanced Analytical Models: 800 Applications from Basel II to Wall Street* (Wiley 2007); *Modeling Risk: Applying Monte Carlo Simulation, Real Options, Optimization, and Forecasting* (Wiley 2006); *Real Options Analysis: Tools and Techniques,* 1st and 2nd editions (Wiley, 2003 and 2005); *Real Options Analysis Course: Business Cases* (Wiley, 2003); *Applied Risk Analysis: Moving Beyond Uncertainty* (Wiley, 2003); *Valuing Employee Stock Options* (Wiley, 2004), and others. His books and software are being used at top universities around the world (including the Bern Institute in Germany, Chung-Ang University in South Korea, Georgetown University, ITESM in Mexico, Massachusetts Institute of Technology, U.S. Naval Postgraduate School, New York University, Stockholm University in Sweden, University of the Andes in Chile, University of Chile, University of Pennsylvania Wharton School, University of York in the United Kingdom, and Edinburgh University in Scotland).

Dr. Mun is also currently a finance and economics professor and has taught courses in financial management, investments, real options, economics, and statistics at the undergraduate and graduate MBA and Ph.D. levels. He has taught at universities all over the world, from the U.S. Naval Postgraduate School with the U.S. Department of Defense (Monterey, California) and University of Applied Sciences (Switzerland and Germany) as full professor, to San Francisco State University, Golden Gate University (California) and St. Mary's College (California) as adjunct professor, and he has chaired many graduate research MBA thesis and Ph.D. dissertation committees. He also teaches risk analysis, real options analysis, and risk analysis for managers' public courses where participants can obtain the Certified in Risk Management (CRM) designation upon completion of the week-long program. He is also a senior fellow at the Magellan Center and sits on the board of standards at the American Academy of Financial Management.

He was formerly the Vice President of Analytics at Decisioneering, Inc., where he headed up the development of options and financial analytics software products, analytical consulting, training, and technical support, and where he was the creator of the Real Options Analysis Toolkit software, the older and much less powerful predecessor of the Real Options Super Lattice Solver (SLS) software showcased in this book. Prior to joining Decisioneering, he was a Consulting Manager and Financial Economist in the Valuation Services and Global Financial Services practice of KPMG Consulting and a Manager with the Economic Consulting Services practice at KPMG LLP. He has extensive experience in econometric modeling, financial analysis, real options, economic analysis, and statistics. During his tenure at Real Options Valuation, Inc., Decisioneering, and at KPMG Consulting, he taught and consulted on a variety of real options, risk analysis, financial forecasting, project management, and financial valuation issues for over 100 multinational firms. Former and existing clients include 3M, Airbus, Bank of China, Boeing, BP, Chevron Texaco, Financial Accounting Standards Board, Fujitsu, GE, GE Capital, Microsoft, Motorola, Pfizer, Timken, U.S. Department of Defense, U.S. Navy, Veritas, and many others. In addition, together with Prof. Glantz, Dr. Mun has taught at, consulted for, or his software applications and algorithm techniques have been used at financial institutions and banks around the world (e.g., Alliance Bank, Bank of China, Citigroup, Dubai Islamic, Euromoney, Hong Leong, HSBC, GE Capital, Maybank, Morgan Stanley, National Bank of Dominica, OCBC, RHB, Salomon Smith Barney, UAL Merchants, and others). His experience prior to joining KPMG included Department Head of financial planning and analysis at Viking Inc. of FedEx, performing financial forecasting, economic analysis, and market research. Prior to that, he did financial planning and freelance financial consulting work.

Dr. Mun received his Ph.D. in Finance and Economics from Lehigh University, where his research and academic interests were in the areas of Investment Finance, Econometric Modeling, Financial Options, Corporate Finance, and Microeconomic Theory. He also has an MBA in business administration, an M.S. in management science, and a B.S. in Biology and Physics. He is Certified in Financial Risk Management (FRM), Certified in Financial Consulting (CFC), and Certified in Risk Management (CRM). He is a member of the American Mensa, Phi Beta Kappa Honor Society, and Golden Key Honor Society as well as several other professional organizations, including the Eastern and Southern Finance Associations, American Economic Association, and Global Association of Risk Professionals. Finally, he has written many academic articles published in the *Journal of the Advances in Quantitative Accounting and Finance,* the *Global Finance Journal,* the *International Financial Review,* the *Journal of Financial Analysis,* the *Journal of Applied Financial Economics,* the *Journal of International Financial Markets, Institutions and Money,* the *Financial Engineering News,* and the *Journal of the Society of Petroleum Engineers.*

About the DVD

The enclosed DVD contains a 30-day trial version of Real Options Valuation's **Basel II Modeling Toolkit** *software,* **SLS Super Lattice Solver** *software, and the* **Risk Simulator** *software.*

Minimum System Requirements

- Personal computer with Pentium III or higher processor (Dual Core processors recommended)
- 512 MB RAM (1 GB recommended) and 200 MB hard-disk space
- DVD-ROM drive, SVGA monitor with 256 Colors (a minimum of 1280×800 screen resolution is recommended)
- Excel XP, 2003, 2007, or later
- Windows XP or Vista
- Microsoft .NET Framework 1.1 and 2.0 (both versions are required and typically exist on most computers; they are also included in the DVD)

How to Install the Software onto Your Computer

An automated setup program is available in the DVD for the Real Options Valuation's *Basel II Modeling Toolkit, Real Options Super Lattice Solver*, and the *Risk Simulator* software. To run the setup program, do the following:

1. Insert the enclosed DVD into the DVD-ROM drive of your computer.
2. The setup program should come up automatically. If it does not, visit www.realoptionsvaluation.com (click on the **Downloads** page) to obtain the latest software versions as well as for the latest installation requirements and instructions. Detailed installation instructions are available in the DVD.
3. After installing the Basel II Modeling Toolkit, you will be prompted for a license key. Please write down the **FINGERPRINT ID** when the message appears. Then, in order to use the software immediately, enter the following user name and trial license key. This key will activate the software for 30 days. In the meantime, you can purchase the full license at www.realoptionsvaluation.com by clicking on the Purchase link.

   Name: 30 Day Trial **Key:** 4C55-0BA2-420E-CA84

Please note that the Real Options SLS software comes with a default license of 30 days and does not require any special licenses to run within this time period. For the Risk Simulator software, a 30-day trial license is available in the DVD. Simply install the software, start Excel and click on Risk Simulator, License, Install License, browse to the DVD to install your free trial license. Please review the relevant chapters in this book for details on using this software.

For obtaining a permanent license or an extended academic trial (a special offer for professors and students), please contact *admin@realoptionsvaluation.com* or visit www.realoptionsvaluation.com for details.

CHAPTER | 1

Basel II and Principles for the Management of Credit Risk

A key objective of Basel II is to revise the rules of the 1988 Basel Capital Accord in such a way as to align banks' regulatory capital more closely with risks. Progress in measuring and managing risk and the opportunities risk provides is important because Basel II implementation is a large-scale undertaking, making considerable demands on banks and regulators alike and requiring appropriate rethinking of risk analysis globally. The Bank for International Settlements, based in Basel, Switzerland, was charged with establishing a framework for setting minimum capital levels. The new accords—Basel II—go beyond Basel I minimum capital requirements, allowing lenders to use internal models to ascertain regulatory capital while seeking to ensure that banks amend and improve risk management culture from the bottom up. A strong risk management culture goes hand in hand with aligning banks' capital requirements with prevailing modern risk management practices and with ensuring that the focus on risk is elevated to supervisory levels and market discipline through enhanced risk- and capital-related disclosures.[1]

---

1. Consultative Document Overview of the New Basel Capital Accord, April 2003.

BASEL COMMITTEE ON BANKING SUPERVISION Implementation of Basel II Presentation to the IIF Asian CEO Summit

Singapore, 14 September2007

Why Basel II?

- Given rapid financial innovation, Basel I capital ratios are no longer very accurate measures of bank risk.
- Basel II more closely aligns bank capital to the actual level of risk.
- Basel II is more capable of evolving with financial innovation.
- Basel II is more closely aligned with the bank's internal risk management practices.
- Basel II is a necessary response to a complex and changing environment.
- Innovation in financial markets.
- Significant advances in technology, financial product innovation, and risk management; examples include:
  - Derivatives products (from plain vanilla to exotic).
  - Securitization (from simple risk transfer to increasing sophistication in the slicing and dicing of risk).
- Innovation continues to occur at a rapid pace.
- Shift in many banks' business models, from buy-and-hold to originate-to-distribute.
- Greater reliance on markets for risk transfer and liquidity.
- Models have generally focused on behavior under "normal" circumstances.
- Supervisory focus is on what happens under "stressed" conditions.
- New challenges for banks (and supervisors).

Features of Basel II Pillar 1[2]

The computation of minimum capital requirements includes credit, market, and operational risk. *Credit risk*, the most pervasive of banking risks—in its simplest form—arises when an obligor fails to make payments due on a loan. *Market risk* is associated with loss resulting from changes in market value of assets before positions can be offset or liquidated. *Operational risk* refers to any number of risks associated with being in business. Within Basel II such risk is defined as that of loss due to failed or inadequate internal processes, problems with people and systems, or external events. This chapter focuses on credit risk essentials.

Returning to Basel I, the minimum required capital ratio (set at 8%) was calculated as the regulatory capital divided by the risk exposure (measured by the risk-weighted assets). Under Basel I, this calculation related only to credit risk, with a calculation for market risk added in 1996. Basel II adds a further charge to allow for operational risk. One of the greatest innovations of Basel II is that it offers lenders a choice between:

1. The standardized approach: This method involves using grades provided by external organizations.
2. The Foundation Internal Ratings-Based Approach (F-IRB): This internal methodology is suitable for the financial institution regarding the evaluation of dimensions or grades, in order to measure the relative credit risk. Here, default probabilities and loss given default are imposed by regulators.

---

2. Most language, tables, and examples delineating the three Basel Principles in this chapter—Tiers One, Two, Three—were assembled from public domain documents at the Bank for International Settlements, Basel Committee, and the Federal Reserve Bank. Secondary sources are provided in chapter footnotes. Since Basel II implementation is central to this book, the authors felt that discussions of major issues should come directly from the source.

3. Advanced Internal Ratings-Based Approach (A-IRB): This methodology is similar to that of F-IRB, except that the banks control all risk components.

Standardized Approach to Credit Risk

The standardized approach is similar to "Basel I" since the method calculates risk-weighted assets by allocating assets and off-balance-sheet exposures among a fixed set of risk weights. However, the standardized approach increases risk sensitivity of the capital framework by recognizing that different counterparties within the same loan category present far different risks to banks. Thus, instead of placing all commercial loans in the 100 percent risk weight basket, the standardized approach takes account of borrowers' credit ratings. The following examples illustrate the enhanced alignment between risk capital under the standardized methodology:

- *Claims against corporations.* Assets representing claims against corporations (including insurance companies) are assigned a risk weight according to the appropriate credit rating. Credit ratings must be assigned by an external recognized rating agency (that is the key) that satisfies certain criteria. Calibration of risk-weighted assets is expressed as percentages of exposures' nominal values, which vary between zero—the highest rated exposures—and 150 percent, or more in certain cases—for credits on the lowest rating scale. For unrated exposures, the risk weight is 100 percent. The following chart correlates credit ratings with risk weights for rated exposures:

Credit Rating	AAA to AA−	A+ to A−	BBB+ to BB−	Below BB−	Unrated
Risk Weight	20 percent	50 percent	100 percent	150 percent	100 percent

- *Retail exposures* (loans to individuals and small businesses). Loans to individuals and small businesses, including credit card loans, installment loans, student loans, and loans to small business entities are risk weighted at 75 percent, if a bank supervisor determines a bank's retail portfolio is diverse.[3]
- *Residential real estate.* Prudently written residential mortgage loans are risk weighted at 35 percent. Generally, loans secured by commercial real estate are assigned to the 100 percent risk basket, but regulators have the discretion to assign mortgages on office and multipurpose commercial properties, as well as multifamily residential properties, in the 50 percent basket subject to certain prudential limits.
- *Claims against sovereign governments and central banks.* These claims are risk weighted according to the risk rating assigned to that government by recognized export credit agencies, as seen in the accompanying chart.

Credit Rating	AAA to AA−	A+ to A−	BBB+ to BB−	Below BB−	Unrated
Risk Weight	0 percent	20 percent	50 percent	150 percent	100 percent

- *Claims on banks and securities firms.* The first option risk weights claims on banks and securities firms at one risk weight category below the country's risk weight.

---

3. Basel Committee, *Basel II: International Convergence of Capital Measurement and Capital Standards: A Revised Framework*, November 2005 (www.bis.org/publ/bcbs118b.pdf).

The second option is to risk weight banks and securities firms based on an external credit assessment score, and with lower risk weights for short term obligations (originally maturity of three months or less).

- *Standardized approach to off balance sheet items.* Off-balance-sheet items, such as loan commitments and guarantees, expose a financial institution to credit risk. Both Basel I and the standardized approach recognize this credit risk by converting the off-balance-sheet item into an on-balance-sheet asset, and then placing the asset into the appropriate risk basket.

Standard Approach and Credit Risk Mitigation

Credit risk mitigation techniques, such as a third-party guaranty, generally are not recognized under Basel I. The standardized approach greatly enhances risk sensitivity by recognizing many more credit risk mitigation techniques. For example:

- *Collateral.* Banks have two options for recognizing collateral for capital purposes. Under the simple approach, the bank may adjust the risk weight for its exposure by using the appropriate risk weight for the supporting collateral instrument. The collateral must be marked-to-market and revalued at least every six months. A risk weight floor of 20 percent will also apply, unless the collateral is cash, certain government securities, or certain repo instruments. Eligible collateral includes corporate debt instruments rated BBB− or higher, equity securities traded on a main index, and government instruments. Under the second option, or "comprehensive approach," the value of the exposure is reduced by a discounted value of the collateral.

  The amount of the discount varies with the credit rating of the collateral. The standardized approach provides for the amount of the discount. For example, collateral consisting of A+ rated debt with a remaining maturity of five years or less would be discounted by 6 percent. Alternatively, the regulatory agencies may permit the banks to calculate their own discounts based on internal models that take into account market volatility, historical performance, and foreign exchange rate movement.

- *Guarantees and Credit Derivatives.* Contracts that provide equivalent protection are recognized, provided certain conditions are met—for example, the guarantee must be direct, explicit, unconditional, and irrevocable. The risk weight of the guarantor is substituted for the risk weight of the actual counterparty. Guarantors and credit protection sellers must have a credit rating of at least A−. (Basel I recognizes guarantees issued by OECD (Organization for Economic Co-operation and Development) governments and GSEs (Government Sponsored Enterprises) and by banks and securities firms chartered in OECD countries.)

Standardized Approach—Securitizations

The standardized approach permits exclusion of securitized assets from the calculation of risk-weighted assets if the credit risk associated with the assets has been transferred to third parties and the bank does not maintain effective or indirect control over the transferred exposures. The assets must be beyond the reach of the bank and its creditors. However, the transferring bank may continue to service the assets.

- *General Rule.* Banks that retain or acquire positions in a securitization, or have an off-balance-sheet exposure in a securitization, are required to hold capital with respect to these interests. The position is assigned a risk-weight basket depending on the credit rating of the exposure as follows:

Credit Rating	AAA to AA–	A+ to A–	BBB+ to BB–	Below BB-	Unrated
Risk Weight	20 percent	20 percent	100 percent	350 percent	Deduct from capital

- *Gain on sale.* Originating banks must deduct from capital any "gain on sale" that results from the transfer of the asset into the securitization pool.
- *Early amortization.* If a bank sells revolving assets (e.g., credit card receivables) into a securitization structure that contains an early amortization feature, the bank is required to hold capital against a specified percentage of assets sold (the investor's interest in the pool). The percentage increases as the excess spread account (which serves to protect security holders) declines.

Standardized Approach—Operational Risk

Another major adjustment involves capital requirements for operational risk. Operational risk is the risk of loss arising from failures or errors in the external or internal technical, procedural, or control mechanisms surrounding the processing of business. Operational risk can span many fronts, including poor credit systems (risk rating, global exposure, back office), criminal/fraudulent behavior, personnel mismanagement, unauthorized activities, transaction processing errors, technological inadequacies, and external disasters.

Credit derivative processes may be at risk to the internal front- and back-office control failures that affect other businesses, and they may be vulnerable to external disruptions that threaten market activity. For instance, some institutions lack the proper infrastructure to handle credit derivative trading, from pricing and risk management to back-office processing. The potentially large losses emanating from control failure have moved operational risk issues to the forefront in recent years, and regulators and institutions are more attuned to the need for effective operational risk management controls, including warning mechanisms, error tracking, internal audits, valuation checks, and improved technology architecture and data recovery.

Foundation Internal Ratings-Based Approach

Basel II encourages banks to initiate the internal ratings-based approach for measuring credit risks and is expected to be more capable of adopting more sophisticated techniques in credit risk management. The foundation internal ratings-based (IRB or F-IRB) approach refers to a set of credit risk-measurement techniques proposed under Basel II capital adequacy rules for banking institutions. Lenders will be able to develop their own models to determine regulatory capital requirement using the IRB approach. Banks determine their estimation for some components of risk measure, including the probability of default, exposure at default, and effective maturity.

Under this approach, the banks are allowed to develop their own empirical model[4] to estimate default probabilities but subject to approval from regulators. Under F-IRB, banks are required to use the regulator's prescribed loss given default (the book's risk rating algorithms will help you develop industry/deal ratings) and risk-weighted asset.

---

4. Many of these models appear on the DVD and are referenced at the conclusion of this chapter.

The total capital allocated is a fixed percentage of estimated risk-weighted assets. The goal is to define risk weights by determining the cutoff points between and within areas of the expected loss (EL) and the unexpected loss (UL), where the regulatory capital should be held, in the probability of default. Then, the risk weights for individual exposures are calculated based on the function provided by Basel II (see Figure 1-1).

Below are the formulas for some banks' major products: corporate, small-medium enterprise (SME), residential mortgage, and qualifying revolving retail exposure.[5] It

5. *Source: Basel II: International Convergence of Capital Measurement and Capital Standards: a Revised Framework (BCBS) (November 2005 Revision). Exhibit references:* [10]*Function is taken from paragraph 272;* [11]*Function is taken from paragraph 273;* [12]*Function is taken from paragraph 328;* [13]*Function is taken from paragraph 22.9.*

Corporate exposure[10]

$$\text{Correlation (R)} = 0.12 \times (1 - \text{EXP}(-50 \times \text{PD})) / (1 - \text{EXP}(-50)) + 0.24 \times [1 - (1 - \text{EXP}(-50 \times \text{PD}))/(1 - \text{EXP}(-50))]$$

$$\text{Maturity adjustment (b)} = (0.11852 - 0.05478 \times \ln(\text{PD}))^2$$

$$\text{Capital requirement}^{68} \text{ (K)} = [\text{LGD} \times N[(1 - R)^{-0.5} \times G(\text{PD}) + (R/(1 - R))^{0.5} \times G(0.999)] - \text{PD} \times \text{LGD}] \times (1 - 1.5 \times b)^{-1} \times (1 + (M - 2.5) \times b)$$

$$\text{Risk-weighted assets (RWA)} = K \times 12.5 \times \text{EAD}$$

Corporate exposure adjusted for SME[11]

$$\text{Correlation (R)} = 0.12 \times (1 - \text{EXP}(-50 \times \text{PD}))/(1 - \text{EXP}(-50)) + 0.24 \times [1 - (1 - \text{EXP}(-50 \times \text{PD}))/(1 - \text{EXP}(-50))] - 0.04 \times (1 - (S - 5)/45)$$

Residential mortgage exposure[12]

$$\text{Correlation (R)} = 0.15$$

$$\text{Capital requirement (K)} = \text{LGD} \times N[(1 - R)^{-0.5} \times G(\text{PD}) + (R/(1 - R))^{0.5} \times G(0.999)] - \text{PD} \times \text{LGD}$$

$$\text{Risk-weighted assets} = K \times 12.5 \times \text{EAD}$$

Qualifying revolving retail exposure[13] **(credit card product)**

$$\text{Correlation (R)} = 0.04$$

$$\text{Capital requirement (K)} = \text{LGD} \times N[(1 - R)^{-0.5} \times G(\text{PD}) + (R/(1 - R))^{0.5} \times G(0.999)] - \text{PD} \times \text{LGD}$$

$$\text{Risk-weighted assets} = K \times 12.5 \times \text{EAD}$$

PD = the probability of default
LGD = loss given default
EAD = exposure at default
M = effective maturity

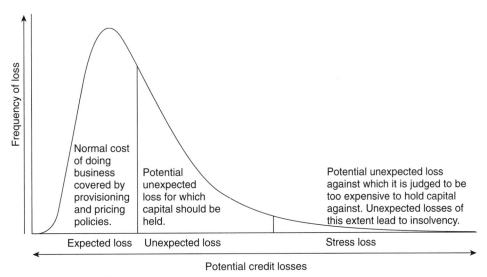

Figure 1-1 Cutoff points.

is important to note that the IRB approach differs substantially from the standardized approach in that banks' internal assessments of key risk drivers serve as primary inputs to the capital calculation. Because the approach is based on banks' internal assessments, the potential for more risk-sensitive capital requirements is substantial. However, the IRB approach does not allow banks themselves to determine all of the elements needed to calculate their own capital requirements. Instead, the risk weights and thus capital charges are determined through the combination of quantitative inputs provided by banks and formulas specified by the Basel Committee.

Corporate, Bank, and Sovereign Exposures

The IRB calculation of risk-weighted assets for exposures to sovereigns, banks, or corporate entities uses the same basic approach. It relies on four quantitative inputs:

1. *Probability of default*, which measures the likelihood that the borrower will default over a given time horizon.[6]
2. *Loss given default*, which measures the proportion of the exposure that will be lost if a default occurs.[7]
3. *Exposure at default*, which for loan commitments measures the amount of the facility that is likely to be drawn if a default occurs.
4. *Maturity*, which measures the remaining economic maturity of the exposure.

Given a value for each of these four inputs, the corporate IRB risk-weighted function produces a specific capital requirement for each exposure. In addition, for exposures to small, midsized enterprise (SME) borrowers, banks will be permitted to make use of a firm size adjustment to the corporate IRB risk-weighted formula.

---

6. Our stochastic valuation models determine the probabilities that equity value falls below zero (probabilities liabilities > assets).

7. Final risk grade–risk rating model.

Summary of the Second Pillar—Supervisory Review of Capital Adequacy

The second pillar establishes supervisory review explicitly as a central piece in the new capital allocation structure. The supervisory review process rather than being a discretionary pillar acts as a fundamental complement to both the minimum regulatory capital requirements (Pillar 1) and market discipline (Pillar 3). Supervisors need to take on an increased role, not only reviewing a bank's capital position and strategy, but also ensuring that capital is in accord with a bank's overall risk profile and, furthermore, that the bank is in compliance with regulatory capital minimums. If capital falls below threshold levels, the second pillar invites quick, early supervisory action. Following are four basic "rules" for regulators:[8]

1. Regulators will expect banks to operate above the minimum regulatory capital ratios and require banks to hold capital in excess of the minimum.
2. Banks should have processes for assessing overall capital adequacy in relation to their risk profile, as well as strategies for maintaining capital levels.
3. Supervisors should review and evaluate a bank's internal capital adequacy assessment and strategy, as well as its compliance with regulatory capital ratio.
4. Supervisors should seek to intervene at an early stage to prevent capital from falling below prudent levels.

With regard to establishing appropriate capital levels, a variety of "qualitative" factors fall in place, including:

1. Experience and quality of management and key personnel
2. Risk appetite and track record in managing risk
3. Nature of the markets in which a bank operates
4. Quality, reliability, and volatility of earnings
5. Quality of capital and its access to new capital
6. Diversification of activities and concentration of exposures
7. Liability and liquidity profile
8. Complexity of legal and organizational structure
9. Adequacy of risk management systems and controls
10. Support and control provided by shareholders
11. Degree of supervision by other supervisors

The Federal Reserve Bank (FRB) developed a framework for "a sound internal analysis of capital adequacy" (their language) calling for four fundamental elements: identifying and measuring all material risks, relating capital to the level of risk, stating explicit capital adequacy goals with respect to risk, and assessing conformity to the institution's stated objectives. Recognizing the significance of Pillar 2, we have included extracts from the FRB's four-point framework:[9]

---

8. *Source*: Federal Reserve Bank (FRB).
9. FRB Trading and Capital-Markets Activities Manual April 2000 Capital Adequacy Section 2110.1.

1. *Identifying and measuring all material risks.* A disciplined risk-measurement program promotes consistency and thoroughness in assessing current and prospective risk profiles, while recognizing that risks often cannot be precisely measured. The detail and sophistication of risk measurement should be appropriate to the characteristics of an institution's activities and to the size and nature of the risks that each activity presents. At a minimum, risk-measurement systems should be sufficiently comprehensive and rigorous to capture the nature and magnitude of risks faced by the institution, while differentiating risk exposures consistently among risk categories and levels. Controls should be in place to ensure objectivity and consistency and to provide that all material risks, both on- and off-balance-sheet, are adequately addressed. Measurement should not be oriented to the current treatment of these transactions under risk-based capital regulations.

   When measuring risks, institutions should perform comprehensive and rigorous stress tests[10] to identify possible events or changes in markets that could have serious adverse effects in the future. Institutions should also give adequate consideration to contingent exposures arising from loan commitments, securitizations programs, and other transactions or activities that may create these exposures for the bank.

2. *Relating capital to the level of risk.* The amount of capital held should reflect not only the measured amount of risk, but also an adequate "cushion" above that amount to take account of potential uncertainties in risk measurement. A banking organization's capital should reflect the perceived level of precision in the risk measures used, the potential volatility of exposures, and the relative importance to the institution of the activities producing the risk. Capital levels should also reflect the fact that historical correlations among exposures can rapidly change. Institutions should be able to demonstrate that their approach to relating capital to risk is conceptually sound and that outputs and results are reasonable. An institution could use sensitivity analysis of key inputs and peer analysis in assessing its approach.

   One credible method for assessing capital adequacy is for an institution to consider itself adequately capitalized if it meets a reasonable and objectively determined standard of financial health, tempered by sound judgment—for example, a target public-agency debt rating or even a statistically measured maximum probability of becoming insolvent over a given time horizon. In effect, this method serves as the foundation of the Basel Accord's treatment of capital requirements for market foreign-exchange risk.

3. *Stating explicit capital adequacy goals with respect to risk.* Institutions need to establish explicit goals for capitalization as a standard for evaluating their capital adequacy with respect to risk. These target capital levels might reflect the desired level of risk coverage or, alternatively, a desired credit rating for the institution that reflects a desired degree of creditworthiness and, thus, access to funding

---

10. As part of the evaluation process, rigorous stress testing is called for, centering on unexpected downturns in market conditions that might adversely impact capital. This is particularly important in the trading area to ensure that market risk is sufficiently covered by capital. Stress testing on the market side includes material interest rate positions, repricing and maturity data, principal payments, (interest) reset dates, maturities, and the rate index used for repricing and contractual interest rate ceilings or floors for adjustable-rate instruments. This assessment is based largely on the bank's own measure of *value-at-risk*.

sources. These goals should be reviewed and approved by the board of directors. Because risk profiles and goals may differ across institutions, the chosen target levels of capital may differ significantly as well. Moreover, institutions should evaluate whether their long-run capital targets might differ from short-run goals, based on current and planned changes in risk profiles and the recognition that accommodating new capital needs can require significant lead time.

An institution's internal standard of capital adequacy for credit risk could reflect the desire that capital absorb "unexpected losses"—that is, some level of potential losses in excess of that level already estimated as being inherent in the current portfolio and reflected in the allowance. In this setting, an institution that does not maintain its allowance at the high end of the range of estimated credit losses would require more capital than would otherwise be necessary to maintain its overall desired capacity to absorb potential losses. Failure to recognize this relationship could lead an institution to overestimate the strength of its capital position.

4. *Assessing conformity to the institution's stated objectives.* Both the target level and composition of capital, along with the process for setting and monitoring such targets, should be reviewed and approved periodically by the institution's board of directors.

Capital Adequacy Ratings

Regulators assign CAMELS[11] *Capital Adequacy Ratings Rating 1 and 2* when capital levels are strong relative to risk profiles or a satisfactory capital level (Rating 2). *Rating 3* is assigned to banks with less than satisfactory capital levels;[12] this rating implies a need for improvement. A 4 rating indicates deficient capital levels, while a rating of 5 is assigned to a financial institution critically deficient in regulatory capital such that "immediate assistance from shareholders or other external sources of financial support is *required.*"

A Summary of the Third Pillar—Market Discipline

The requirements for transparency under Pillar 3 should be examined in the context of increased links between banks' internal controls and accounting and the contents of banking regulation, greater reporting requirements regarding their governance, and the demands placed on their information systems. Pillar 3 addresses the issue of improving market discipline through effective public disclosure. Specifically, it presents a set of disclosure requirements that should improve the ability of market participants to assess banks' capital structures, risk exposures, risk management processes, and, hence, their overall capital adequacy.[13]

The Basel Committee has sought to encourage market discipline by developing a set of disclosure requirements that allow market participants to assess key information about a bank's risk profile and capital levels relative to risk. By bringing greater market discipline to bear through enhanced disclosures, Pillar 3 of the new capital

11. CAMELS is the Federal Reserve System Uniform Financial Institutions Rating System. "C" denotes Capital Adequacy, "A" Asset Quality, "M" Management, "E" Earnings, and "S" Sensitivity.

12. See CAMELS Rating in the DVD.

13. FRBSF Economic Letter 2003–22; August 1, 2003 Disclosure as a Supervisory Tool: Pillar 3 of Basel II.

framework can produce significant benefits in helping banks and supervisors to manage risk and improve stability. Another important consideration has been the need for the Basel II disclosure framework to align with national accounting standards.[14] One Basel II objective is to ensure that the disclosure requirements of the New Accord focus on bank capital adequacy and do not conflict with broader accounting disclosure standards with which banks must comply. This objective has been accomplished through a strong and cooperative dialogue with accounting authorities.

Principles for the Management of Credit Risk[15]

The sound practices set out in the important Adobe Document address the following areas: (1) establishing an appropriate credit risk environment; (2) operating under a sound credit-granting process; (3) maintaining an appropriate credit administration, measurement, and monitoring process; and (4) ensuring adequate controls over credit risk.

Although specific credit risk management practices may differ among banks depending on the nature and complexity of their credit activities, a comprehensive credit risk management program focuses on these four areas. These practices should also be applied in conjunction with sound practices related to the assessment of asset quality, the adequacy of provisions and reserves, and the disclosure of credit risk, all of which have been addressed in other recent Basel Committee documents. The exact approach chosen by individual supervisors will depend on a host of factors, including their on-site and off-site supervisory techniques and the degree to which external auditors are also used in the supervisory function. All members of the Basel Committee agree, however, that the principles set out in this paper should be used in evaluating a bank's credit risk management system. A summary of Part One of this document follows:

Establishing an Appropriate Credit Risk Environment

- Principle 1: The board of directors should have responsibility for approving and periodically (at least annually) reviewing the credit risk strategy and significant credit risk policies of the bank.
- Principle 2: Senior management should have responsibility for implementing the credit risk strategy approved by the board of directors and for developing policies and procedures for identifying, measuring, monitoring, and controlling credit risk.
- Principle 3: Banks should identify and manage credit risk inherent in all products and activities.

Operating under a Sound Credit Granting Process

- Principle 4: Banks must operate within sound, well-defined credit-granting criteria.
- Principle 5: Banks should establish overall credit limits at the level of individual borrowers and counterparties, and groups of connected counterparties that aggregate in comparable and meaningful manner different types of exposures, both in the banking and trading book and on and off the balance sheet.

---

14. Accounting standards are covered in Chapter 2 of the present volume.
15. The Adobe Document: Principles for the Management of Credit Risk is included on the DVD.

- Principle 6: Banks should have a clearly-established process in place for approving new credits as well as the amendment, renewal, and refinancing of existing credits.
- Principle 7: All extensions of credit must be made on an arm's-length basis.

Maintaining an Appropriate Credit Administration, Measurement, and Monitoring Process

- Principle 8: Banks should have in place a system for the ongoing administration of their various credit risk-bearing portfolios.
- Principle 9: Banks must have in place a system for monitoring the condition of individual credits, including determining the adequacy of provisions and reserves.
- Principle 10: Banks are encouraged to develop and utilize an internal risk rating system in managing credit risk.
- Principle 11: Banks must have information systems and analytical techniques that enable management to measure the credit risk inherent in all on- and off-balance-sheet activities.
- Principle 12: Banks must have in place a system for monitoring the overall composition and quality of the credit portfolio.
- Principle 13: Banks should take into consideration potential future changes in economic conditions when assessing individual credits and their credit portfolios, and should assess their credit risk exposures under stressful conditions.

Ensuring Adequate Controls over Credit Risk

- Principle 14: Banks must establish a system of independent, ongoing assessment of the bank's credit risk management processes, and the results of such reviews should be communicated directly to the board of directors and senior management.
- Principle 15: Banks must ensure that the credit-granting function is being properly managed and that credit exposures are within levels consistent with prudential standards and internal limits.
- Principle 16: Banks must have a system in place for early remedial action on deteriorating credits, managing problem credits, and similar workout situations.

The Role of Supervisors

- Principle 17: Supervisors should require that banks have an effective system in place to identify measure, monitor, and control credit risk as part of an overall approach to risk management.

Modeling Toolkit and Basel's Principles for the Management of Credit Risk

The Modeling Toolkit software comprises over 800 analytical models and functions, with 300 analytical model Excel/SLS templates and example spreadsheets covering the areas of risk analysis, simulation, forecasting, Basel II risk analysis, credit and default risk, statistical models, and much more! This toolkit contains a set of mathematically sophisticated models, written in C++ and linked into Excel spreadsheets. There are over 1000 tools, models, and functions with Excel spreadsheet and SLS software. The analytical areas covered that are most applicable to Basel II are listed below. These software can be used to run millions of transactions valuations in minutes, but for simplicity, the models presented throughout this book are run on individual models or transactions.

Specifically, Principle 13 in the Basel II accord states that banks should take into consideration "potential future changes in economic conditions when assessing individual credits and their credit portfolios, and should assess their credit risk exposures under stressful conditions." The applications in the *Banking Models* section shows economic and financial models on valuation of a firm, multiple cash flow analyses for loans, project financing, and so forth, in considering future changes in economic conditions. The *Credit Analysis and Debt Analysis* sections, coupled with the *Probability of Default* models, are used to assess individual creditworthiness and credit exposure effects. When combined into portfolios, the *Value at Risk* models can be used in concert with these credit models to determine the effects of new credit on the entire credit and debt portfolio. The applications in the *Simulation* section show how stress testing can be done through risk-based simulations of thousands and hundreds of thousands of trials and outcomes, providing a very powerful stress testing technique under real-life conditions.

As another example, Principle 9 states that banks "must have in place a system for monitoring the condition of individual credits, including determining the adequacy of provisions and reserves." This is where the models and applications in the *Probability of Default* and *Value at Risk* are most applicable. The example models for computing default probabilities are applicable for individuals as well as for private and public firms. And for the determination of capital adequacy, the applications under the *Value at Risk* sections are appropriate in determining regulatory capital requirements. In addition, Principle 10 states: "Banks are encouraged to develop and utilize an internal risk rating system in managing credit risk." This applies directly to the two risk rating models—(corporate) *Risk Rating Model* and *Project Finance Risk Rating Model*. The two rating systems will help bankers develop their own models to determine regulatory capital requirement using the approach based on foundation internal ratings.

In Principle 11, banks are required to have "information systems and analytical techniques that enable management to measure the credit risk inherent in all on- and off-balance sheet activities. The management information system should provide adequate information on the composition of the credit portfolio, including identification of any concentrations of risk." According to Principle 12, banks must have in place a system for monitoring the overall composition and quality of the credit portfolio. Again, there are multiple *Portfolio Optimization* models for risk diversification purposes and portfolio-based *Value at Risk* computations.

A further case in point is Principle 16: "Banks must have a system in place for early remedial action on deteriorating credits, managing problem credits and similar workout situations." Banking models such as Classified Breakeven Loan Inventory, Classified Loan Borrowing Base, Classified Loan Cash Budget, Valuation and Appraisal, and Overdraft Facilities will help bankers cope with problem loans. The risk weights for the parts of past-due loans that are unsecured by collateral or guarantees vary according to the proportion covered by specific provisions. The models focus on collateral. Credit risk mitigation—the reduction of credit risk through the use of collateral guarantees—is a major Basel II issue.

Banking Models
- **Audit of Construction Lending**
- **Banker's Construction Budget**

- **Classified Breakeven Loan Inventory**
- **Classified Loan Borrowing Base**
- **Classified Loan Cash Budget and Overdraft Facilities**
- **Federal Reserve CAMELS Rating System**
- **Firm in Financial Distress**
- **Project Finance Risk Rating Model**
- **Queuing Models**
- **Reconciling Enron's Cash Flow**
- **Risk Rating Model**
- **Sample Cash Flow (Gem)**
- **Stochastic Loan Pricing Model**
- **Valuation and Appraisal**

Credit Analysis
- **Credit Premium**
- **Credit Risk and Effects on Prices**
- **External Debt Rating and Spreads**
- **Internal Credit Risk Rating Model**
- **Profit Cost Analysis of New Credit**

Debt Analysis
- **Asset Equity Parity Model**
- **Cox Model on Price and Yield of Risky Debt with Mean Reverting Rates**
- **Debt Repayment and Amortization**
- **Debt Sensitivity Models**
- **Merton Price of Risky Debt with Stochastic Asset and Interest**
- **Vasicek Debt Option Valuation**
- **Vasicek Price and Yield of Risky Debt**

Exotic Options
- **American and European Options**
- **Asian Arithmetic**
- **Asian Geometric**
- **Asset or Nothing**
- **Barrier Options**
- **Binary Digital Options**
- **Cash or Nothing**
- **Commodity Options**
- **Complex Chooser**
- **Currency Options**
- **Double Barriers**
- **Exchange Assets**
- **Extreme Spread**
- **Foreign Equity Linked Forex**
- **Foreign Equity Domestic Currency**
- **Foreign Equity Fixed Forex**
- **Foreign Takeover Options**
- **Forward Start**
- **Futures and Forward Options**

- **Gap Options**
- **Graduated Barriers**
- **Index Options**
- **Inverse Gamma Out-of-the-money Options**
- **Jump Diffusion**
- **Leptokurtic and Skewed Options**
- **Lookback Fixed Strike Partial Time**
- **Lookback Fixed Strike**
- **Lookback Floating Strike Partial Time**
- **Lookback Floating Strike**
- **Min and Max of Two Assets**
- **Option Collar**
- **Options on Options**
- **Perpetual Options**
- **Simple Chooser**
- **Spread on Futures**
- **Supershares**
- **Time Switch**
- **Trading Day Corrections**
- **Two Assets Barrier**
- **Two Assets Cash**
- **Two Assets Correlated**
- **Uneven Dividends**
- **Writer Extendible**

Forecasting
- **Data Diagnostics**
- **Econometric, Correlations, and Multiple Regression Modeling**
- **Exponential J-Growth Curves**
- **Forecasting Manual Computations**
- **Linear Interpolation**
- **Logistic S-Growth Curves**
- **Markov Chains and Market Share**
- **Multiple Regression**
- **Nonlinear Extrapolation**
- **Stochastic Processes and Yield Curves (Cubic Spline, Brownian Motion, Mean Reversion, Jump Diffusion)**
- **Time-Series Analysis**
- **Time-Series ARIMA**

Optimization
- **Capital Investments (Part A)**
- **Capital Investments (Part B)**
- **Continuous Portfolio Allocation**
- **Discrete Project Selection**
- **Inventory Optimization**
- **Investment Portfolio Allocation**
- **Military Portfolio and Efficient Frontier**
- **Optimal Pricing with Elasticity**

- **Optimization of a Harvest Model**
- **Optimizing Ordinary Least Squares**
- **Stochastic Portfolio Allocation**

Options Analysis
- **Binary Digital Instruments**
- **Inverse Floater Bond Lattice Maker**
- **Options Adjusted Spreads on Debt**
- **Options on Debt**

Probability of Default
- **Empirical (Individuals)**
- **External Options Model (Public Company)**
- **Merton Internal Model (Private Company)**
- **Merton Market Options Model (Industry Comparable)**
- **Yields and Spreads (Market Comparable)**

Real Options SLS
- **Employee Stock Options—Simple American Call**
- **Employee Stock Options—Simple Bermudan Call with Vesting**
- **Employee Stock Options—Simple European Call**
- **Employee Stock Options—Suboptimal Exercise**
- **Employee Stock Options—Vesting and Suboptimal Exercise**
- **Employee Stock Options—Vesting, Blackout, Suboptimal, Forfeiture**
- **Exotic Options—American Call Option with Dividends**
- **Exotic Options—Accruals on Basket of Assets**
- **Exotic Options—American Call Option on Foreign Exchange**
- **Exotic Options—American Call Option on Index Futures**
- **Exotic Options—Barrier Option—Down and In Lower Barrier**
- **Exotic Options—Barrier Option—Down and Out Lower Barrier**
- **Exotic Options—Barrier Option—Up and In Upper Barrier**
- **Exotic Options—Barrier Option—Up and In, Down and In Double Barrier**
- **Exotic Options—Barrier Option—Up and Out Upper Barrier**
- **Exotic Options—Barrier Option—Up and Out, Down and Out Double Barrier**
- **Exotic Options—Basic American, European, versus Bermudan Options**
- **Exotic Options—Chooser Option**
- **Exotic Options—Equity Linked Notes**
- **Exotic Options—European Call Option with Dividends**
- **Exotic Options—Range Accruals**
- **Options Analysis—Plain Vanilla Call Option I**
- **Options Analysis—Plain Vanilla Call Option II**
- **Options Analysis—Plain Vanilla Call Option III**
- **Options Analysis—Plain Vanilla Call Option IV**
- **Options Analysis—Plain Vanilla Put Option**

- **Real Options—Abandonment American Option**
- **Real Options—Abandonment Bermudan Option**
- **Real Options—Abandonment Customized Option**
- **Real Options—Abandonment European Option**
- **Real Options—Contraction American and European Option**
- **Real Options—Contraction Bermudan Option**
- **Real Options—Contraction Customized Option**
- **Real Options—Dual-Asset Rainbow Option Pentanomial Lattice**
- **Real Options—Excel-based Options Models**
- **Real Options—Exotic Complex Floating American Chooser**
- **Real Options—Exotic Complex Floating European Chooser**
- **Real Options—Expand Contract Abandon American and European Option**
- **Real Options—Expand Contract Abandon Bermudan Option**
- **Real Options—Expand Contract Abandon Customized Option I**
- **Real Options—Expand Contract Abandon Customized Option II**
- **Real Options—Expansion American and European Option**
- **Real Options—Expansion Bermudan Option**
- **Real Options—Expansion Customized Option**
- **Real Options—Jump Diffusion Calls and Puts using Quadranomial Lattices**
- **Real Options—Mean Reverting Calls and Puts using Trinomial Lattices**
- **Real Options—Multiple Asset Competing Options (3D Binomial)**
- **Real Options—Multiple Phased Complex Sequential Compound Option**
- **Real Options—Multiple Phased Sequential Compound Option**
- **Real Options—Multiple Phased Simultaneous Compound Option**
- **Real Options—Simple Calls and Puts using Trinomial Lattices**
- **Real Options—Simple Two Phased Sequential Compound Option**
- **Real Options—Simple Two Phased Simultaneous Compound Option**
- **Real Options—Strategic Cases—High-Tech Manufacturing Strategy A**
- **Real Options—Strategic Cases—High-Tech Manufacturing Strategy B**
- **Real Options—Strategic Cases—High-Tech Manufacturing Strategy C**
- **Real Options—Strategic Cases—Oil and Gas—Strategy A**
- **Real Options—Strategic Cases—Oil and Gas—Strategy B**
- **Real Options—Strategic Cases—R&D Stage—Gate Process A**
- **Real Options—Strategic Cases—R&D Stage—Gate Process B**
- **Real Options—Strategic Cases—Switching Option's Strategy A**
- **Real Options—Strategic Cases—Switching Option's Strategy B**

Risk Analysis
- **Integrated Risk Analysis**
- **Interest Rate Risk**
- **Portfolio Risk and Return Profile**

Risk Hedging
- **Delta Gamma Hedge**
- **Delta Hedge**
- **Effects of Fixed versus Floating Rates**

- **Foreign Exchange Cash Flow Model**
- **Foreign Exchange Exposure Hedging**

Sensitivity
- **Greeks**
- **Tornado and Sensitivity Charts Linear**
- **Tornado and Sensitivity Nonlinear**

Simulation
- **Basic Simulation Model**
- **Correlated Simulation**
- **Correlation Effects Model**
- **Data Fitting**
- **DCF, ROI, and Volatility**
- **Debt Repayment and Amortization**
- **Demand Curve and Elasticity Estimation**
- **Retirement Funding with VBA Macros**
- **Time Value of Money**

Valuation
- **Buy versus Lease**
- **Caps and Floors**
- **Convertible Bonds**
- **Financial Ratios Analysis**
- **Financial Statements Analysis**
- **Valuation Model**
- **Valuation—Warrant—Combined Value**
- **Valuation—Warrant—Put Only**
- **Valuation—Warrant—Warrant Only**

Value at Risk
- **Optimized and Simulated Portfolio VaR**
- **Options Delta Portfolio**
- **Portfolio Operational and Capital Adequacy**
- **Right Tail Capital Requirements**
- **Static Covariance Method**

Volatility
- **EWMA Volatility Models**
- **GARCH Volatility Models**
- **Implied Volatility**
- **Log Asset Returns Approach**
- **Log Cash Flow Returns Approach Probability to Volatility**

Yield Curve
- **CIR Model**
- **Curve Interpolation BIM**
- **Curve Interpolation NS**

- **Forward Rates from Spot Rates**
- **Spline Interpolation and Extrapolation.xls**
- **Term Structure of Volatility**
- **US Treasury Risk Free Rate**
- **Vasicek Model**

CHAPTER | 2

International Financial Reporting Standards and Basel II

Banks should have methodologies that enable them to quantify the risk involved in exposures to individual borrowers or counterparties. Banks should use measurement techniques that are appropriate to the complexity and level of the risks involved in their activities, based on <u>robust</u> <u>data</u>, and subject to periodic validation.[1]

Many countries are adopting International Financial Reporting Standards (IFRSs). Since January 1, 2005, European Union public companies or firms with debt on a European exchange have been required to use IFRS.

IFRSs refer to the entire body of IASB pronouncements, including standards and interpretations approved by the IASB International Accounting Standards Board and International Accounting Standards (IASs) and IAS's Standing Interpretations Committee (SIC) interpretations approved by the predecessor International Accounting Standards Committee. Having a single set of accounting standards makes it easier to arrive at credit decisions (far easier than working through differing sets of national accounting standards). Without a single set of accounting standards, bankers spend lots of time and effort working through financials. Also, financial information that is inconsistent causes confusion; remember: bankers are outsiders and are not privy to investment budgets, inventory schedules, and so on.

---

1. *Principle 11*, in the July 1999 consultative paper, issued by the Basel Committee on Banking Supervision.

Scope of International Financial Reporting Standards (IFRSs)

1. All International Accounting Standards (IASs) and Interpretations issued by the former International Accounting Standards Committee founded in June 1973 (IASC) and SIC continue to be applicable unless and until they are amended or withdrawn.
2. IFRSs apply to general-purpose financial statements and other financial reporting by profit-oriented entities—those engaged in commercial, industrial, financial, and similar activities, regardless of their legal form.
3. Entities other than profit-oriented business organizations may also find IFRSs appropriate.
4. General-purpose financial statements are intended to meet the common needs of shareholders, creditors, employees, and the public at large for information about an entity's financial position, performance, and cash flows.
5. Other financial reporting includes information provided outside financial statements that assists interpreting a complete set of financial statements or improves users' ability to make efficient economic decisions.
6. IFRS applies to individual company and consolidated financial statements.
7. A complete set of financial statements includes a balance sheet, an income statement, a cash flow statement, a statement showing either all changes in equity or changes in equity other than those arising from investments by and distributions to owners, a summary of accounting policies, and explanatory notes.
8. If an IFRS allows both a "benchmark" and an "allowed alternative" treatment, financial statements may be described as conforming to IFRS, whichever treatment is followed.
9. In developing standards, IASB does not intend to permit choices in accounting treatment. Furthermore, IASB intends to reconsider the choices in existing IASs with a view to reducing the number of those choices.
10. IFRS will present fundamental principles in boldface type and other guidance in nonbold type (the "black-letter"/"gray-letter" distinction). Paragraphs of both types have equal authority.
11. Since IAS 1 sets out the overall framework and responsibilities for the presentation of financial statements, IAS 1 requires compliance with every applicable IAS interpretation including compliance with all IFRS pronouncements.

Under the International Accounting Standards Committee Foundation (IASCF) Constitution (included on the DVD), the objectives of the IASB are:

1. To develop, in the public interest, a single set of high-quality, understandable, and enforceable global accounting standards that require high quality, transparent, and comparable information in financial statements and other financial reporting in order to help participants in the world's capital markets and other users make economic decisions.
2. To promote the use and rigorous application of those standards.
3. To take account of, as appropriate, the special needs of small and medium-sized entities and emerging economies.

4. To bring about the convergence of national accounting standards and International Accounting Standards and International Financial Reporting Standards to high-quality solutions.

The Auditor's Role

Accounting standards, above all, apply to the preparation of independent reports based on properly conducted audits and supported by all tests necessary to verify the accuracy of data under scrutiny. While financial reports *can never* alone determine credit decisions, they play a major role within a much broader context called lending due diligence. That is because bankers need a great deal of ancillary information before they can begin to understand the borrower's *real environment*. Credit decisions are founded on real values—earning power of assets—and never just historically based financial reports. Later chapters deal with these very issues.

With IFRS, auditors bear even greater responsibility for fostering the usefulness of financial statements—to increase the reliability and usefulness of audits in two main areas: (1) statements presented in accordance with international accounting standards and (2) adequate disclosure. So as not to repeat the Enron, Tyco, and WorldCom accounting debacles, financial reports are expected to present the borrower's economic, financial, and operating condition fairly, clearly, and completely. In preparing financial reports, it is perhaps naïve to think that accounting (like any communication process) is immune to threats of bias, misinterpretation, error, and evasiveness. To minimize these dangers and to render financial statements that are industry comparable and consistent from period to period, a body of conventions are both generally accepted and universally practiced.

Despite the debate and healthy criticism surrounding accounting standards and principles, the international business community recognizes this far-reaching body of theories, methods, and practices as the fundamental bonding of three disciplines: accounting, finance, and banking. Thus, International Accounting Standards 1 (IAS 1), *Disclosure of Accounting Policies*, includes the following guidelines for financial reports:

- Fair presentation
- Accounting policies
- Going concern
- Accrual basis of accounting
- Consistency of presentation
- Materiality and aggregation
- Offsetting
- Comparative information

IAS 1 prescribes the minimum structure and content, including certain information required on the face of the financial statements:

- Balance sheet (current/noncurrent distinction is not required)
- Income statement (operating/nonoperating separation is required)
- Cash flow statement (IAS 7 sets out the details)
- Statement showing changes in equity.

Various formats are allowed:

1. The statement shows (a) each item of income and expense, gain or loss, which, as required by other IASC Standards, is recognized directly in equity, and the total of these items (examples include property revaluations (IAS 16, Property, Plant and Equipment), certain foreign currency translation gains and losses (IAS 21, The Effects of Changes in Foreign Exchange Rates), and changes in fair values of financial instruments (IAS 39, Financial Instruments: Recognition and Measurement)) and (b) net profit or loss for the period, but no total of (a) and (b). Owners' investments and withdrawals of capital and other movements in retained earnings and equity capital are shown in the notes.
2. Same as above, but with a total of (a) and (b) (sometimes called "comprehensive income"). Again, owners' investments and withdrawals of capital and other movements in retained earnings and equity capital are shown in the notes.
3. The statement shows both the recognized gains and losses that are not reported in the income statement and owners' investments and withdrawals of capital and other movements in retained earnings and equity capital. An example of this would be the traditional multicolumn statement of changes in shareholders' equity.

The report of an independent accountant may be a complete detailed audit implying attempts to verify all items and transactions—or simply a book audit, concerned only with the maintenance of mathematical accuracy in transferring the general ledger or other schedules onto reported statements. Between these extremes are special-purpose audits and limited audits. In the limited audits, the auditor's report usually indicates that some items are incorporated with insufficient verification because of restrictive circumstances or because of management's insistence that certain figures be accepted without complete checking. For a book audit in such cases, accountants protect themselves and avoid misleading users as to the extent of the verification by noting in the report's certificate limitations imposed on the examination. Accounting standards are governed by "reporting thresholds" called "opinions." Let's examine the underlying principles behind accountants' opinions.

Certified Opinions

"In the opinion of this auditor, generally accepted accounting principles have been followed, they have been applied on a basis consistent with that of the preceding year, and the financial statements present fairly the firm's financial condition." This pronouncement provides assurance that, in the absence of notice to the contrary, no changes have been made fiscal to fiscal in evaluation methods or in determining depreciation charges and reserves, and income statement items have not shifted around from one category to another. Here's an example of a short-form certificate:

> We have examined the consolidated balance sheet of A. B. Morris Textile Corporation and its subsidiary companies as of December 31, 2006 and the related consolidated statements of income, stockholders' equity, and changes in financial position for the year then ended. Our examination was made in accordance with generally accepted auditing standards, and accordingly included such tests of the accounting records and such other auditing procedures, as we considered necessary in the circumstances.

In our opinion, such financial statements present fairly the financial position of the companies at December 31, 2006 and the results of their operations and the changes in financial position for the year then ended, in conformity with generally accepted accounting principles applied on a basis consistent with that of the preceding year.

Qualified Audit

A qualified audit stipulates that overall financial statements provide a fair representation of a company's condition, but certain items need qualification. Exceptions outlined are not serious enough to negate the report; otherwise auditors render an adverse opinion. The events leading to qualified audits include the following.

1. The examination is of limited scope, or constraints are placed on the audit.
2. Financials depart from requirements to present fairly the firm's financial position or its results of operations due to a digression or lack of conformity with generally accepted accounting principles and standards or inadequate disclosure.
3. Accounting principles and standards are not consistently applied.
4. Unusual uncertainties exist concerning future developments, the effects of which cannot be reasonably estimated or otherwise resolved satisfactorily.

Adverse Opinion

An adverse opinion is required in reports in which exceptions of fair presentation are so material that a qualified opinion is not justified. Adverse opinions are rare, because most enterprises change their accounting to conform to the auditor's desires. A disclaimer of an opinion is normally issued for one of two reasons: (1) the auditor has gathered so little information on the financial statements that no opinion can be expressed, or (2) the auditor concludes on the basis of the evaluation that the company's ability to continue on a going concern basis is highly questionable because of financing or operating problems.

Compilation

A compilation is in fact management's report—auditors offer no assurance as to whether material, or significant, changes are necessary for statements to conform to accepted accounting principles (or another comprehensive basis of accounting, such as the cash or tax basis). During a compilation, auditors arrange data in conventional formats but do not probe beneath the surface unless information is in error or incomplete.

Historical Cost

Historical costs are real and once established are fixed for the life of the asset, or as long as the asset remains on the company's books. For example, when a company purchases a building, the purchase price or historical cost is recorded on the company's balance sheet. However, if that building appreciates in value, the asset is still recorded at the historical cost, less depreciation. This accounting practice often results in assets that are carried at significantly off-market prices. Bankers should note that historical costs might overstate or understate asset value.

In a slightly different context, the (accounting) principal of recording assets at historical cost may lend itself to manipulation as noted in the following trading example. A company with a trading position that is out-the-money (money is lost if the position is closed) may be inclined to roll over that position and either postpone recognizing the loss or hope the market changes and turns the position into a gain.

Accounting Standards as Applied to Revenue Realization

Revenue realization is one facet of reporting practice that gets the lender's particular attention. Revenues, cash received for merchandise sold or services rendered, are generally recorded at the time of sale or completion of the service. However, two conditions must be met before revenue can be recorded. First, the earnings process must be substantially complete, and second, the collectibility of the revenue must be estimated. The earnings process is not substantially complete if:

1. The seller and buyer have not agreed on the price of the merchandise or service.
2. The buyer does not have to pay the seller until the merchandise is resold.
3. The merchandise is stolen or physically destroyed, and the buyer does not have to pay the seller.
4. There are intercompany transactions—that is, the buyer and seller are related parties.
5. The seller must continue to provide substantial performance or services to the buyer or aid in reselling the product. If, however, substantial performance has occurred and the collectibility of the revenue can be estimated, the sale of the product or service can be recorded.

Revenue recognition, though consistent with applicable accounting standards, may be derived from sources other than operating cash flows. For example, some firms turn retiree-medical plans into a source of profit. Financial Accounting Standard 106 introduced in the early 1990s requires companies to report their total anticipated retiree health-care coverage costs. Companies had two incentives to overstate their anticipated costs: (1) excessive costs provided a rational basis to reduce employee benefits; and (2) if the excessive costs proved to be wrong, that is, excessive, then the companies could recognize a paper gain by reducing their retiree liability.

The Matching Principle

The popularity of the calendar year as a fiscal period is partly due to the collection of federal income taxes on a calendar-year basis. However, the Internal Revenue Service permits filing tax returns on the basis of a business year instead of a calendar year. Generally Acceptable Accounting Principals (GAAP) recognizes the concept of matching under the accrual method. The intention is to determine revenue first and then match appropriate costs against revenue. If a financial statement is prepared on another basis of accounting, a statement must be made that the presentation is not in conformity with GAAP. Many small businesses have chosen this method. By preparing their financial statements on an income tax basis, many of the complexities, such as calculating deferred taxes, are avoided. Thus, the cash method of accounting can be used when preparing a compilation or review of financial statements.

Consistency

While consistency means applying identical methods fiscal to fiscal, firms are free to switch from one method of accounting to another, but with restrictions. Firms and their accountants need to demonstrate to bankers and investors that the newly adopted principle is preferable to the old. And then, the nature and effect of the accounting change as well as the justification for it must be disclosed in the financial statements for the period in which the change is made.

Disclosure

Adequate disclosure calls for revealing facts significant enough to influence the judgment of the knowledgeable reader. Sufficient disclosure includes more descriptive explanations, acceptable presentation, and succinct but meaningful footnotes—for example, detailed disclosure of financial obligations, current accounts such as inventory breakdown and method of pricing, and whatever additional disclosure is required to prevent the audit from becoming a guessing game. Auditors can add one or more paragraphs to an unqualified report if they feel that the information is important for the reader to know. This addition is known as the emphasis of a matter paragraph and is usually added before the standard opinion paragraph of an unqualified report. Obviously, the paragraph should not include mention of the emphasized matter and should instead refer to the footnotes.

Objectivity

Notwithstanding an audit disclaimer, it is imperative that bankers be assured that the information in financial reports is factual and impartial. Although no disclosure is totally objective, the process must be based on the auditor's sound judgment, diagnostic good sense, and irrefutable background. Reliable estimates must be made of depreciation charges, deferrals, and accruals of cost, along with revenue items, equity earnings, restructuring charges, and deferred tax credits. Estimates are deemed objective if the audit process is founded on adequate information and data that can be authenticated by independent parties. Most importantly, if there is any doubt "objectivity" should favor conservatism. Schilit suggests that financial statement readers favor firms that present conservative accounting policies.

> Companies that fail to use conservative accounting methods might demonstrate a lack of integrity in their financial reporting process. Indeed, many analysts place a premium on companies that use conservative accounting policies. In searching for excellent companies, for example, the widely respected analyst and shenanigan buster Thornton O'Glove offers the following advice: Look for companies that use very conservative accounting principles. In my experience, if a company does not cut corners in its accounting, there's a good chance it doesn't cut corners in its operations. You know you've got your money with a high quality management.[2]

2. Howard M. Schilit, *Financial Shenanigans* (New York: McGraw-Hill, 1993).

Off-Balance-Sheet Financial Reporting

Footnotes are integral to financial statements but are often overlooked because they tend to be somewhat technical and frequently appear in small print. Footnotes are the accountant's way of disclosing details of crucial data. The restrictions imposed by footnotes provide bankers with a wealth of information for assessing the financial condition of borrowers and the quality of reported earnings.[3] Schilit reminds us that the footnotes detail such issues as "(1) accounting policies selected, (2) pending or imminent litigation, (3) long-term purchase commitments, (4) changes in accounting principles or estimates, (5) industry–specific notes, and (6) segment information showing healthy and unhealthy operations."

On the whole, credit analysts see footnote disclosure as a step above core financial data. As Kenneth Fisher Forbes notes: "The back of the report, the footnotes is where they hide the bad stuff they didn't want to disclose but had to. They bury the bodies where the fewest folks find them—in the fine print."

APB[4] in Opinion No. 22, "Disclosure of Accounting Policies," concluded that "information about the accounting policies adopted and followed by a reporting entity is essential for financial-statement users in making economic decisions."

As an integral part of financial reports, a statement identifies accounting policies that have been adopted and followed by the reporting entity. The APB believes that disclosure should be given in a separate Summary of Significant Accounting Policies preceding the notes to the financial statements or as the initial note. After reviewing the disclosure of accounting policies, wise bankers look for information such as contingencies that may negatively impact borrowers. The complete disclosure of material contingencies is an important property of financial statements according to International Accounting Standards guidelines because of the uncertainties that may exist at the conclusion of each accounting period.[5]

For example, standards governing accounting for loss contingencies require accrual and/or note disclosure when specified recognition and disclosure criteria are met. Gain contingencies generally are not recognized in financial statements but can be disclosed. Reporting criteria centers around the high probability that a change in the estimate will occur in the near term.

Here are examples of the types of situations that may require disclosure in accordance with SOP 94-6:

1. Specialized equipment subject to technological obsolescence
2. Valuation allowances for deferred tax assets based on future taxable income

3. Ibid.

4. The Auditing Practices Board (APB) was established in April 2002 and replaces a previous APB, which had been in place since 1991. APB is a part of the Financial Reporting Council. The information set out in this section documents the APB's current objectives, membership, and procedures.

The APB is committed to leading the development of auditing practice in the United Kingdom and the Republic of Ireland so as to:

- establish high standards of auditing;
- meet the developing needs of users of financial information; and
- ensure public confidence in the auditing process.

5. Financial Accounting Standards Board Statement No. 5 Accounting for Contingencies.

3. Capitalized motion picture film production costs
4. Inventory subject to rapid technological obsolescence
5. Capitalized computer software costs
6. Deferred policy acquisition costs of insurance enterprises
7. Valuation allowances for commercial and real estate loans
8. Environmental remediation-related obligations
9. Litigation-related obligations
10. Contingent liabilities for obligations of other entities
11. Amounts reported for long-term obligations like pensions
12. Expected loss on disposition of a business or assets
13. Amounts reported for long-term contracts

Under FASB Statement No. 5, an estimated loss from a loss contingency must be charged against net income as soon as the loss becomes probable and estimable. In addition, now that the use of prior-period adjustments has been extremely narrowed by FASB Statement No. 16, *Prior Period Adjustments 8*, almost all such loss accruals must be charged against current income. Another impact of FASB Statement No. 5 on earnings is that accrual of contingency losses is prohibited unless an asset has probably been impaired or a liability has been incurred and the loss is estimable. This means that firms cannot provide reserves for future losses through yearly income statement adjustments. The reason is to prevent earnings volatility, the result of guesswork.

Classification of Contingencies
1. Probable: likely to materialize
2. Reasonably possible: halfway between probable and remote
3. Remote: slight chance of materializing

To review, although some contingencies are disclosed in footnotes, bankers should recalculate certain balance sheet ratios in figuring possible losses. That's because creditors focus on possible accounting loss associated with financial instruments, including losses from the failure of another party to perform according to contract terms (credit risk), the possibility that future changes in market prices may render financial instruments less valuable (market risk), and the risk of physical loss. Similarly, a financial instrument has off-balance-sheet risk if the risk of loss exceeds the amount recognized as an asset, or if the obligation exceeds the amount recognized in the financial statements. Bankers are particularly watchful of general loss contingencies.

General Loss Contingencies

General loss contingencies may arise from risk of exposure to:

1. Product warranties or defects
2. Pending or threatened litigation
3. Risk of catastrophe (i.e., losses)
4. Direct guarantees: guarantor makes payment to creditor if debtor fails to do so
5. Claims and assessments
6. Preacquisition contingencies

Financial Instruments with Off-Balance-Sheet Risk

While management may claim that off-balance-sheet financial instruments reduce risks, these instruments can function as speculative tools. Borrowers anticipating a harsh fiscal period may capitalize on positive changes in the value of financial instruments to improve results—results unattainable through normal operating activities.

1. A recourse obligation on receivables or bills receivable (B/Rs) sold
2. Interest rate and currency swaps, caps, and floors
3. Loan commitments and options written on securities; futures contracts
4. Obligations arising from financial instruments sold short
5. Synthetic asset swap that might result in an unwind if the bond goes into default
6. Obligations to repurchase securities sold

Product Warranties or Defects

A warranty (product guarantee) is a promise, for a specific time period, made by a seller to a buyer to make good on a deficiency of quantity, quality, or performance in a product. Warranties can result in future cash outlays, *frequently significant additional outlays.* Although the future cost is indefinite as to amount, due date, and even customer, a liability—an estimate of costs incurred after sale and delivery associated with defect correction—does exist, and experienced lenders ask accountants or management to quantify the downside effect.

Litigation Contingencies

Publicly traded companies are required to disclose litigation contingencies when eventual loss from a lawsuit is possible. Studies were done on the classification of predisposition years (i.e., the years before the year of court adjudication or settlement). It was found that 47.6 percent of surveyed companies showed unsatisfactory disclosure, with no mention of the litigation in financial statements, or a strong disclaimer of liability did not accompany mention of the litigation. Legal action includes antitrust, patent infringement, fraud or misrepresentation, breach of contract, and other non-insurable suits.

The (above) survey represents a banker's bona fide red flag, if ever there was one. Contingencies such as product lawsuit losses, which can show up from nowhere, are often explosive and can finish off an otherwise profitable company in the process. The best hedge against litigation contingencies is preparation that often means a present value analysis. This means placing values on material lawsuits by determining present value. Minor lawsuits, on the other hand, are usually irrelevant; an adverse opinion will not impact on equity, debt service, or the borrower's sustainable cash flows. On the contrary, if we have a Firestone on our hands, can litigation be settled? If so when and for how much? This brings up other questions:

• If litigation cannot be settled, when will the court hear the case?
• What are the probabilities the court will render an adverse opinion?
• If the opinion is adverse, will there be grounds for appeal?
• If so, when will the appeal be heard?
• What are the probabilities that the appeal will collapse?

- Given the time value of money and the joint probabilities of adverse opinions including appeals, what is the expected present value of the product lawsuit (use face amounts, not expected reduced awards)?
- Pro forma expected losses on fiscal spreadsheets. Is the financial structure strong enough to absorb expected losses?

How do adjusted (pro forma) debt and cash flow coverage ratios stack up against the industry or benchmarks? Has the borrower's industry quartile ranking deteriorated? What is the anticipated impact on bond ratings and/or the bank's credit grade?

Environmental Contingencies

Environmental protection laws pose many dangers for unwary lenders. To avoid potentially unlimited liability that may result from environmental violations, prudent bankers try to extract out expected present values and adjust financials accordingly. Environmental troublespots include but are not restricted to:

- Transportation of hazardous substances
- Real property
- The disposition of hazardous substances
- Manufacturing processes that involve use, creation, or disposition of hazardous wastes
- Petroleum or chemicals stored on the premises
- Underground storage tanks
- Equipment used to transport hazardous materials
- Pipes leading to waterways

A few financial institutions prepare guidelines in the form of questionnaires. Here's one questionnaire dealing with potential environmental hazards:

1. *Are toxic or otherwise hazardous or regulated materials, such as used machine oil, handled at any stage of the production process?*
2. *Request a copy of the borrower's EPA plan, if any.*
3. *Does the client have above- or belowground tanks, and when were they last inspected for environmental impact purposes?*
4. *Are there paint shops on the property?*
5. *What was the previous use of the property prior to our client owning it, and how long has our client been at this property?*
6. *Have there been past or are there present EPA violations against the property? Provide copies of those violations to our marketing representative.*
7. *Are there any waterways on or near the property? If so, where are they located in proximity to the property?*
8. *What is the specific use of the property, i.e., what kind of process or processes is being done on the property?*
9. *Does our prospective client stock drums of solvents or fluids on the property? What is the exact nature of those solvents or fluids, and where are they located?*
10. *What is the nature of the uses on adjoining and neighboring properties? Do they appear to create environmental risk?*

Risk of Catastrophic Losses

It might be advisable for bankers to worry more about the possibilities that some obligors might face catastrophic loss. Two criteria must be met to classify a gain or loss as an extraordinary item (both criteria must be met before a company can classify a gain or loss as extraordinary):

Unusual—The event is one that is unrelated to the typical activities of the business. *Nonrecurring*—The event is one that management does not expect to occur again.

Natural disasters meet the definition of unusual (unrelated to the typical activities of the business). For example, a corn farmer in Kansas hit by a drought would not classify the loss as nonrecurring and thus could not be considered extraordinary. On the other hand, a flood in Phoenix would give rise to an extraordinary loss. The criteria of "unusual" and "nonrecurring" must be considered from the standpoint of the firm's geographical location and business.

Direct and Indirect Guarantees

Direct guarantees, representing a direct connection between creditor and guarantor, warrant that the guarantor will make payment to the creditor if the debtor fails to do so. In an indirect guarantee, the guarantor agrees to transfer funds to the debtor if a specified event occurs. Indirect guarantees connect directly from the guarantor to debtor but benefit the creditor indirectly.

   FASB 5 requires that the nature and amount of the guarantee be disclosed in the financial statements. Guarantees to repurchase receivables or related property, obligations of banks under letters of credit or *standby agreements,* guarantees of the indebtedness of others, and unconditional obligations to make payments are examples of the types of guarantee contingencies that must be disclosed even if they have only a *remote* possibility of materializing.

Financial Instruments with Off-Balance-Sheet Risk

Recourse Obligations on Receivables or B/Rs Sold

A widely used method of financing transactions involving small, high-ticket items, notably furs and fine jewelry, has been the presentation of bills receivable (B/Rs) or notes receivable for discount, or as security to demand loans. A B/R is an unconditional order in writing addressed by one person (or firm) to another, signed by the person giving it, requiring the person to whom it is addressed to pay on demand, or at a fixed or determinable future time, a sum certain in money to order or to bearer. A B/R evidences indebtedness arising out of the sale of goods by the bank's customer in the normal course of business. B/Rs are endorsed over to the bank with *full recourse* to the bank's customer. These are off-balance-sheet contingencies and should be "pro forma" back on the balance sheet by an amount equal to the expected loss.

Asset Securitization

Any asset that can generate cash flow can be securitized. When a company securitizes its assets, those assets are sold as a "true sale" and are no longer assets of the company.

In fact, many times that is precisely the reason many companies securitize assets—that is, to get them off their balance sheet to improve their profitability ratios. However, some have argued that securitization may inadvertently cause adverse selection for the company's remaining assets; that is, the company securitizes its best assets (the assets most marketable and easiest to securitize) and retains its poorer assets, thereby causing an adverse selection.

Creditors face little risk in the event of bankruptcy because assets can be quickly liquidated. In exchange, however, creditors receive a lower return on their investments. In addition, if these creditors liquidate the securitized assets, the company will be further unable to recover from a financial crisis and will put its general creditors at even greater risk. Other risks besides credit/default include maturity mismatch and prepayment volatility. As a side note, bankers and investors can reduce contingency risks by using computer software containing models and structural and analytical data for asset securitizations, including commercial loan securitizations, whole-loan and senior-subordinated securities, as well as home equity loans.[6]

Futures Contracts

A commodity such as copper used for production may be purchased for current delivery or for future delivery. Investing in commodity futures refers to the buying or selling of a contract to deliver a commodity in the future. In the case of a purchase contract, the buyer agrees to accept a specific commodity that meets a specified quality in a specified month. In the case of a sale, the seller agrees to deliver the specified commodity during the designated month. Hedging against unexpected increases in raw material costs is a wise move; speculating in commodity futures with the bank's money is another story. There is a large probability that the firm will suffer a loss on any particular purchase or sale of a commodity contract.

Management may purchase a contract for future delivery. This is known as a long position in which the firm will profit if the price of the commodity, say copper, rises. Also, management may enter into a contract for future delivery (a short position). These long and short positions run parallel to the long and short positions in security markets.

Pensions

Pension expense represents the amount of money management should invest at the end of the year to cover future pension payments that will be made to employees for this additional year's service. Accounting records reflect management's best guess as to real pension costs. Accountants try to measure the cost of these retirement benefits at the time the employee earns them rather than when the employee actually receives them. A multiplicity of pension assumptions needs to be compiled to come up with the required pension amount.

- Interest invested funds are expected to earn;
- Number of years an employee is expected to live after retirement
- Salary of employee at retirement
- Average years of service of an employee at retirement

6. Ron Unz, "New Software Can Provide Risk Models," *American Banker* 57, no. 164, August 25, 1992, p. 12A (1).

One should beware of unfunded projected benefit obligations because this liability indicates that pension investments fall short of future pension benefits. Borrowers that continuously fund less than current pension expense or that incorporate unrealistic assumptions in their pension plan could find themselves embedded in a thicket of thorns in the not too distant future.

Companies with defined benefit pension plans must disclose three items: (1) pension discount rate, (2) expected rate of future compensation increases, and (3) projected long-term rate of return on pension assets. Understanding what these figures mean provides insight into, for example, whether a merger candidate's pension liabilities make it worth less than meets the eye, and how companies use perfectly legal (but fairly sneaky) accounting gimmicks to inflate profits.

Discretionary Items

Some expenditures are discretionary, meaning they fall under management's control, including:

- Repair and maintenance of equipment
- Research and development
- Marketing and advertising expenditures
- New product lines, acquisitions, and divestitures of operating units

Management might forgo timely equipment repairs in order to improve earnings, but the policy could backfire over the longer term.

Research and Development

In its Statement of Financial Accounting Standards No. 2, Accounting for Research and Development Costs (October 1974), the Financial Accounting Standards Board concludes, "All research and development costs encompassed by this Statement shall be charged to expense when incurred". The FASB (Statement No. 2) and the SEC (ASR No. 178) mandated all companies to expense R&D outlays. The board reached its conclusion as a result of a reasoning process in which several preliminary premises were accepted as true.

- Uncertainty of future benefits. R&D expenditures often are undertaken whereby there is a small probability of success. The Accounting Board mentioned that the high degree of uncertainty of realizing the future benefits of individual research and development projects was a significant factor in reaching this conclusion.
- Lack of causal relationship between expenditures and benefits.
- Failure of R&D to meet the accounting concept of an asset.
- Matching of revenues and expenses.
- Relevance of resulting information for investment and credit decisions.

An incontrovertible solution for avoiding problems involved in overstating R&D expenditures is to expense costs associated with the acquisition of assets where some significant probability exists that the asset will be worth less than cost. This so-called conservative approach is consistent with guidelines dealing with expensing R&D.

A Banker's Guide: Uncovering Shenanigans

Change in Auditors

When respected auditors are frequently changed, particularly if downtiering occurs, bankers want to know why. Management may cite high auditing fees as the motive for change, but there may also be adverse credit implications foretelling lower quality disclosures, conflict of interest, and less validation effort. The downtiering in auditors may have been brought on by a difference of opinion between auditor and management regarding treatment and certification of material items. The bank may also check with other bankers sharing the credit or the firm's suppliers. At the very least one should compare the present accountant's certificate with that of the previous auditor to ensure that all variances are understood.

Creative Accounting

"Creative accounting" is any method of accounting that overstates revenues or understates expenses. For example, companies might choose to inflate income or to navigate around accounting rulings governing revenue recognition, inventory valuation, depreciation, and treatment of research and development costs, pension costs, disclosure of other income, or any number of other accounting standards. According to the Securities and Exchange Commission (SEC), there has been a marked increase in the number of large restatements of financial results because select firms and their auditors failed to heed accounting standards.[7]

Enron[8]

On October 16, 2001, Enron announced that it would take $1.01 billion in aftertax nonrecurring charges to its third-quarter earnings in order to recognize asset impairments in its water and wastewater service unit, restructuring costs in its broadband services, and losses associated with other investments including a retail energy service. These charges occurred in ventures outside its core businesses in wholesale energy and transportation and distribution services. The $644 million net loss it took for the quarter was the first reported quarterly loss since the second quarter of 1997. In a conference call from the company on October 16, Enron also revealed that it would declare a reduction to shareholder equity of $1.2 billion related to the company's repurchase of its common stock. This repurchase was tied to the performance of several special-purpose entities operated by the private investment limited partnership, LJM2 Co-Investment, L.P. (LJM2). LJM2 was formed in December 1999 and was managed until July 2001 by Enron CFO Andrew Fastow. On October 22, the SEC began an investigation of these transactions. Following an overwhelming loss of investor confidence in the company, Fastow was fired on October 24. Enron's share price declined over 80 percent for the year by the end of October.

Prompted by SEC inquiry, Enron filed a Form 8-K to the Commission on November 8, revealing that it would restate its financial statements from 1997 to the first two quarters of 2001, with net reductions totaling $569 million for the four and one-half years—roughly 16 percent of its net income over the period. Enron also announced

---

7. According to the SEC.
8. We decompose and reconstruct Enron's fiscal 2000 statement in Chapter 3.

that accounting irregularities had occurred in previous financial periods, and as a result three unconsolidated special-purpose entities (including LJM2) should have been consolidated in the financial statements pursuant to U.S. GAAP. During the initial capitalization and later in ongoing transactions with the special purpose entities (SPEs), Enron issued its own common stock in exchange for notes receivable. The company then erroneously increased both notes receivable and shareholder's equity on its balance sheet in recognition of these transactions. However, GAAP[9] requires that notes receivable culminating from transactions containing a company's capital stock be presented as deductions from stockholder's equity and not as assets, which is not how Enron and its auditor, Arthur Andersen, had booked the transactions. These overstatements happened twice: first, $1.0 billion in overstated shareholder's equity and, second, a purchase of a limited partnership's equity interest in an SPE in the third quarter of 2001, which reduced equity an additional $200 million. When combined, these two overstatements produced the $1.2 billion total reduction in shareholder's equity.

Characteristic of the firm in its prime, during which little of the company's complex financial maneuvers were adequately explained, minimal information was provided in Enron's public financial statements to indicate to investors and lenders the loss potential connected with the extensive portfolio of SPEs. Buried in the footnotes of the 1999 annual report under Related Party Transactions (which is destined to become highly popular reading for energy sector credit analysts interested in job security) is mention of the company's transactions with LJM2 partnership, of the senior member of Enron who was a managing member of LJM2, and of transactions in which Enron common stock went to a partnership in return for notes receivable. The partnership was mentioned again in the footnotes of quarterly statements and in the 2000 annual report, but few details were disclosed about the vehicles and the complicated transactions behind them.

Because LJM2 and other Enron SPEs, such as JEDI and Chewco, were considered off-balance-sheet entities, extensive financial information did not have to appear in Enron's financial statements. Among the steps satisfying GAAP requirements for off-balance-sheet treatment of the partnerships, at least 3 percent of their capital had to be contributed by outside investors; while this was originally considered to be achieved, evidently this was not the case. It was not until the filing of the 8-K on November 8, 2001, that Enron and its auditor, Arthur Andersen, determined that three unconsolidated entities were mishandled in previous financial statements and should have been consolidated. The extent of the losses associated with these vehicles, and the full scope of financing Enron used in off-balance-sheet transactions, were effectively obscured to the outside lending community until this disclosure. Meanwhile, the energy company's on-balance-sheet levels of debt, debt-to-equity, and interest expense coverage ratios did not look noticeably unhealthy before the third quarter of 2001.

Not only did Enron's accounting practices come under serious scrutiny following its meltdown, but the reputation of Andersen was demolished as well. Serving as Enron's auditors since 1985, Andersen, one of the Big Five auditing firms, stood by the financial reports of its client until November's restatements. Of particular interest

---

9. EITF Issue No. 85-1, *Classifying Notes Received for Capital Stock*, and SEC Staff Accounting Bulletin No. 40, Topic 4-E, *Receivables from the Sale of Stock*.

from an accounting standpoint was Andersen's treatment of Enron's off-balance-sheet entities and its mark-to-market accounting practices on its energy-trading contracts. Briefly, mark-to-market accounting on energy-trading contracts (whether forwards or spot-market transactions) allows companies to include earnings in current periods for contracts that have yet to be settled. Currently, GAAP does not specify how to derive the fair value of these contracts and allows energy companies ample discretion in calculating their value. Enron required substantial liquidity and an investment grade credit rating to maintain its energy-trading operations. Much of the liquidity was obtained from lenders satisfied with its impressive revenues and seemingly healthy levels of reported debt. Thus, the treatment of its off-balance-sheet debts and mark-to-marketing practices on its trading contracts was critical to the operations of the energy company. Given the extent (Enron had over 100 off-balance-sheet partnerships) and complexity of off-balance-sheet activities at Enron, it indicated Andersen was not capable of accurately and thoroughly auditing transactions that Enron conducted. In addition, Enron's method of its mark-to-market accounting, a firm that attributed over 90 percent of its earnings in 2000 to energy trading, had a major bearing on the impression of Enron's strong operating performance. Andersen's treatment of these issues and the financial data provided by its client call into question the value of Enron's financial statements, which were critical to lending decisions. Ongoing disclosures of knowledge of accounting improprieties at Enron and the destruction of Enron documents was smoking gun evidence of the increasing use of creative accounting at major U.S. corporations.

CHAPTER | 3

Decomposing Cash Flow:
A Banker's Primer

Lenders rely on cash flow statements because cash flows help measure default frequencies and represent a core ingredient of debt service. Cash flow is literally the obligor's lifeblood. The weaker, more volatile cash flows, the higher default probabilities. Looking at this from the banker's perspective, cash flow statements should be completed in sufficient detail to make it easier to measure the impact that cash and noncash investments have on financial position, external financing requirements, reasons for variances between payments and income, and the ability to fund dividends and meet obligations. Earlier accounting standards (specifically, Accounting Principles Board [APB] Opinion 19) allowed businesses to disclose information on either a working capital or cash basis. However, there are significant problems with accepting working capital as a proxy for cash. For example, working capital reports fail to take into account the composition of working capital. While absolute working capital may increase, liquidity could actually be compromised due to buildups of stale inventory.

The section on operating activities may be disclosed using either direct or indirect methods. Under either method, a reconciliation of net cash flow from operations to net income is required, and either method should result in the same cash flow from operations. The direct method focuses on cash and the impact of cash inflows/outflows on the borrower's financial condition. By checking numbers carefully and comparing cash-based numbers to accrual results, bankers walk away with a better understanding of their client's cash flow. The indirect basis starts off with net income but makes the necessary adjustments to pull out noncash and nonoperating revenue and expenses to arrive at the correct operating cash flow.

Indirect Method of Cash Reporting: The Banker's Cash Flow

Most reported cash flow statements commingle working (capital) assets/liabilities with gross operating cash flow (GOCF), which is not the best disclosure. Net operating cash flow should break out working capital and not combine income statement accounts. GOCF represents the income statement's ability to provide the primary internal cash required for future growth. Two cash sources are available to finance growth: internal and external. We associate external financing with debt or equity injections, while internal sources originate from within firms themselves, namely, from profits and net asset disposals.

For purposes of the banker's cash flow, internal cash flow or cash from the income statement is classified as gross operating cash flow; thus, GOCF is introduced to the cash flow format. Gross operating cash flow is usually compared to cash provided by debt-financing activities. This allows the lender to (1) check for any imbalance in internal versus external financing and (2) make comparisons in financial leverage trends (see Exhibit 3-1).

Exhibit 3-1 Revised "Banker's" Cash Flow

COMPANY X

For the Year Ended December 31, 2007

Increase (Decrease) in Cash and Cash Equivalents

Cash flows from operating activities:

Net income	3,040

Adjustments to reconcile net income to net cash provided by operating activities:

Depreciation and amortization	1,780
Provision for losses on accounts receivable	800
Gain on sale of facility	(320)
Undistributed earnings of affiliate	(100)
Gross operating cash flow*	**5,200**
(Inc.) Dec. in accounts receivable	(860)
(Inc.) Dec. in inventory	820
(Inc.) Dec. in prepaid expenses	(100)
Operating cash needs*	**(140)**
Inc. (Dec.) in accounts payable and accrued expenses	(1,000)
Inc. (Dec.) in interest and income taxes payable	200

Inc. (Dec.) in deferred taxes	600
Inc. (Dec.) in other current liabilities	200
Inc. (Dec.) in other adjustments	<u>400</u>
Operating cash sources*	**<u>400</u>**
Net cash provided by operating activities	**5,460**
Cash flows from investing activities:	
Proceeds from sale of facility	2,400
Payment received on note for sale of plant	600
Capital expenditures	(4,000)
Payment for purchase of Company S, net of cash acquired	<u>(3,700)</u>
Net cash used in investing activities	**(4,700)**
Cash flows from financing activities:	
Net borrowings under line of credit agreement	1,200
Principal payments under capital lease obligation	(500)
Proceeds from issuance of long term debt	<u>1,600</u>
Net cash provided by debt-financing activities*	**2,300**
Proceeds from issuance of common stock	2,000
Dividends paid	(800)
Net cash provided by other financing activities	**<u>1,200</u>**
Net increase in cash and cash equivalents	**4,260**
Cash and cash equivalents at beginning of year	2,400
Cash and cash equivalents at end of year	6,660

* Category added to complete Banker's Cash Flow Format.

Direct Method of Reporting Cash

To form a better understanding of the intricacies of the cash flow statement, let's take a look at each section individually.

Investing Activities

The Miller GAAP Guide summarizes investing activities as including the following:

> *Making and collecting loans and acquiring and disposing of debt or equity instruments and property, plant, and equipment and other productive assets; that is, assets held for or used in the production of goods or services by the enterprise (other than materials that are part of the enterprise's inventory).*

Table 3-1   Example of Investment Reconciliation

Cash flows from investing activities:

Proceeds from sale of facility	2,400
Payment received on note for sale of plant	600
Capital expenditures	(4,000)
Payment for purchase of Company S, net of cash acquired	(3,700)
Net cash used in investing activities	(4,700)

Investment activities include advances and repayments to subsidiaries, securities transactions, and investments in long-term revenue-producing assets. Cash inflows from investing include proceeds from disposals of equipment and proceeds from the sale of investment securities (see Table 3-1). Cash outflows include capital expenditures and the purchase of stock of other entities, project financing, capital and operating leases, and master limited partnerships.

Property, Plant, and Equipment (PP&E)

Cash flows associated with PP&E activities include fixed assets purchased through acquisitions and equipment purchases, capital leases, and proceeds from property disposals. Noncash transactions include translation gains and losses, transfers, depreciation, reverse consolidations, and restatements. Lenders do not usually require borrowers to break out property expenditures into expenditures for the maintenance of existing capacity and expenditures for expansion into new capacity, though this would be ideal disclosure, since maintenance and capital expenditures are nondiscretionary outlays. However, because of the difficulty (and subjectivity) involved in differentiating between maintenance outlays from expansion, amounts assigned to maintenance accounts would likely prove unreliable.

Unconsolidated Subsidiaries

When companies acquire between 20 and 50 percent of outside stock, the purchase is denoted an "investment in unconsolidated subsidiary" and is listed as an asset on the acquiring firm's balance sheet. Cash inflows/outflows include dividends, advances, repayments, and stock acquisitions and sales. Noncash events include equity earnings and translation gains and losses.

Investment Project Cash Flows and Joint Ventures

This category includes investments in joint ventures or separate entities formed for the purpose of carrying out large projects. Typically, new entities borrow funds to build plants or projects supported with debt guarantees furnished by companies forming the new entity. Cash flows generally are remitted (upstreamed) to owner firms as dividends. Bankers typically receive a through-and-through disclosure of the project's future cash flows because endeavors like construction projects are governed by explicit accounting rules. Thus, it is often difficult for bankers to untangle cash flows hidden beneath noncash events such as equity earnings. In addition, the project's projections may not be useful if cash streams are masked in joint ventures while the loan that financed the project to begin with is disclosed on the borrower's consolidated balance sheet.

Financing Activities

According to the Miller GAAP Guide, financing activities include the following:

Obtaining resources from owners and providing them with a return on, and return of, their investment; borrowing money and repaying amounts borrowed, or otherwise settling the obligation; and obtaining and paying for other resources obtained from creditors on long-term credit.

Cash inflows from financing activities include new equity infusions, treasury stock sales, and funded debt such as bonds, mortgages, notes, commercial paper, and short-term loans. Cash outflows consist of dividends, treasury stock purchases, and loan payments.

Long-Term Debt

Bond proceeds represent the amount a company actually receives from a debt issue, while increases and reductions in long-term debt include amortization of bond discounts and premiums. Amortization of a bond discount reduces earnings (noncash charge), while the bond's book value increases accordingly. No cash was received or paid out via the bookkeeping entry in Table 3-2, yet debt levels were adjusted on financial statements. Thus, bond discounts are subtracted from debt increases to determine "true" debt increases. The amortization of a bond premium is subtracted from long-term debt reductions to determine the "actual" reductions. Let's review two short examples.

In Table 3-3, the bond proceeds are $754,217 because the bond sold at a discount. Each year the unamortized discount of $245,783, a contra liability against the bond, is amortized. As a result, book value debt increases in value to $1,000,000 at maturity. The entry represents a noncash debt increase. Consider the journal entries and the effects of a bond discount on the firm's financial statements (Table 3-3 and Figure 3-1).

Now let's assume that a $50,000 discount was amortized in the following year:

Amortization of Bond Discount (noncash expense)	50,000
Unamortized Bond Discount	50,000

The amortization of bond discount reduced the unamortized bond discount to 195,783 (Table 3-4). Notice that the book value of bonds increased to 804,217.

Assume that the firm borrowed 300,000 long-term (as in the previous example) and had no other debt except for the bonds. While the increase in long-term debt is 350,000, actual proceeds are 300,000.

Table 3-2   Example of Financing Activities

Cash flows from financing activities:	
Net borrowings under line of credit agreement	1,200
Principal payments under capital lease obligation	(500)
Proceeds from issuance of long-term debt	1,600
Net cash provided by debt-financing activities	2,300
Proceeds from issuance of common stock	2,000
Dividends paid	(800)
Net cash provided by equity financing activities	1,200
Cash flows from financing activities	3,500

Table 3-3   Coupon Rate below Market Rate

Face value of bond	$1,000,000
Term	10 years
Interest paid annually coupon rate	6%
Market rate	10%
Solve for present value	754,217
Cash	754,217
Bond discount	245,783
Bonds payable	1,000,000

Assets		Liabilities	
Cash	754,217	Bonds Payable	1,000,000
		Less:	
		Unamortized Bond Discount	(245,783)
		Net Bonds	754,217

Figure 3-1   Effects of a bond discount on the firm's financial statements.

Table 3-4 Balance Sheet Effect of Bond Amortization: Year 2

Liabilities	
Bonds payable	1,000,000
Less:	
Unamortized bond discount	(195,783)
Net bonds	804,217
Debt increase	50,000

Let's examine a bond premium. Bond premiums arise when market rates are below coupon rates. Proceeds from the bond sale are 1,124,195, since the bond sold at a premium. Each year a portion of 124,195 of unamortized premium is set off as a noncash increase in income, while on the balance sheet debt is reduced (the unamortized bond premium decreases in value). At maturity, 1,000,000 will be due:

Table 3-5 Coupon Rate above Market Rate

Face value of bond	1,000,000
Term	8 years
Interest paid annually	
Coupon rate	8%
Market rate	6%
Solve for present value	1,124,195
Cash	1,124,195
Bond premium	124,195
Bonds payable	1,000,000
Assume $13,000 premium was amortized the following year:	
Unamortized bond premium (noncash income)	$13,000
Amortization of bond premium	$13,000

Table 3-6   Balance Sheet Effect of Bond Premium: Year I

Assets		Liabilities	
Cash	1,124,195	Bonds payable	1,000,000
		Plus:	
		Unamortized bond premium	124,195
		Net bonds	1,124,195

The amortization bond premium reduced the unamortized bond premium to 111,195 (Table 3-7). The book value of bonds decreased to 1,111,195. Suppose the firm paid the 125,000 long-term debt in the previous example and had no other debt except for the bonds. While reductions in long-term debt amounted to 138,000 (125,000 debt payment and 13,000 bond premium amortized), the actual cash payout was $125,000.

Keep in mind that the traditional interest-bearing bond is composed of the principal portion, which will be repaid to the holder of the bond, in full at maturity and the interest portion of the bond, consisting of coupon payments that the holder of the bond receives at regular intervals, usually every six months. In contrast, zero coupons pay "zero" coupons, deferring the interest to maturity. The amortization required, because it is so large, increases reported debt levels, but no cash payout is made until maturity. Hence, cash flow is affected only at maturity when payment is due investors. Bankers should always keep this in mind when evaluating disparate debt issues. Conversion of debt to equity normally results in a substantial noncash transaction. However, conversion eliminates interest payments while reducing financial leverage. Financing activities also include preferred and common stock issues plus treasury stock inflows/outflows and options.

Table 3-7   Journal Entries and Balance Sheet Effect of Bond Premium: Year 2

Liabilities	
Bonds payable	1,000,000
Plus:	
Unamortized bond premium	111,195
Net bonds	1,111,195
Debt issue decreased	13,000
Bonds payable (debit)	13,000
Amortization of bond premium (credit)	13,000

Dividends

Businesses grow by reinvesting current earnings. If stockholders withdraw earnings to support a lavish lifestyle, they put the cart before the horse. Most businesses experience cycles of good and bad times, growth and retraction. Without accumulating a "war chest," firms may not survive recessions or be liquid enough to repay obligations. Furthermore, without reinvesting earnings, management cannot exploit opportunities by financing expansion internally. Exhibit 3-2 is an example of the most important source of internal cash flow, operating activities.

Exhibit 3-2 Operating Activities

Cash flows from operating activities

Net income	$3,040

Adjustments to reconcile net income to net cash provided by operating activities:

Depreciation and amortization	1,780
Provision for losses on accounts receivable	800
Gain on sale of facility	(320)
Undistributed earnings of affiliate	(100)
Gross operating cash flow	**$5,200**
Increase in accounts receivable	$(860)
Decrease in inventory	820
Increase in prepaid expenses	(100)
Operating cash needs	**(140)**
Decrease in accounts payable and accrued expenses	$(1,000)
Increase in interest and income taxes payable	200
Increase in deferred taxes	600
Increase in other liabilities	200
Other adjustments	400
Operating cash sources	**400**
Net cash provided by operating activities	**5,460**

The Miller GAAP Guide defines operating activities as follows:

All transactions and other events not defined as investing or financing activities. Operating activities generally involve producing and delivering goods and providing services. Cash flows from operating activities are generally the cash effects of transactions and other events that enter into the determination of income.

Gross Operating Cash Flow

Gross operating cash flow, an important feature of the cash flow statement, equals net income plus noncash charges, less noncash credits, plus or minus nonoperating events. This section depicts cash generated by operating income, routinely the borrower's dominant source of internal financing. Noncash charges represent reductions in income that do not call for cash outlays. Depreciation and amortization, provision for deferred taxes, asset write-downs, and amortization of bond discounts, provisions, reserves, and losses in equity investments are familiar examples of noncash charges. Noncash credits increase earnings without generating cash and include equity earnings in unconsolidated investments, amortization of bond premiums, and negative deferred tax provisions. Nonoperating charges and earnings such as restructuring gains/charges and gains and losses on the sale of equipment are also adjusted, representing further refinements to reported earnings.

A typical interpretative problem area for lenders is disclosure of unconsolidated entities where cash inflows depend on dividend streams returned by projects or investment divestitures. Noncash profits can easily be managed by selecting liberal accounting methods or by simply manufacturing income. In one such case Enron, involved in a joint venture with Blockbuster, reported large profits, even though the venture never attracted more than a few customers (see Enron cash flow).

Cash generated from nonrecurring items may artificially inflate the borrower's profits, but it usually cannot be depended on to provide cash flow to support long-term financing. Included are gains and losses from the sale of business units, judgments awarded to the company, and other one-time cash inflows. One-time extraordinary expenses usually have little impact on long-term cash flows. For example, if XYZ Company settles a lawsuit over patent infringement that results in a one-time cash payout, the long-term health of the company may not be affected—that is, if XYZ Company can afford the settlement. On the other hand, consider a pharmaceutical company that loses a product liability suit, resulting in a cash settlement along with the recall of its best-selling drug. If the product is crucial to long-term survival, the borrower may end up financially distressed. Lenders should review nonrecurring items and their impact on credit decisions since it is core earnings that pay off loans, not phantom events or extraordinary income. Indeed, borrowing or capital stock issues may provide more funds than operations, but bankers count on business operations to provide the funds to finance ongoing operations, repay obligations, and distribute dividends.

Equity Earnings

Equity earnings show up on the income statement as increases to earnings. These often illusory earnings end up included in retained earnings, and because they are noncash items, leverage and coverage ratios are sometimes distorted. What's the story behind equity earning? Suppose your borrower owns between 20 and 50 percent of another firm's stock. Accountants say your borrower "influences" the firm's operations and so must include the prorated share of earnings into its financial statements. Thus, if the firm makes $1,000,000 profit, 25 percent of those profits (or $250,000) is included as equity earnings.

Suppose your borrower, company A, originally invested $1 million in company B in year 0, obtaining a 25 percent equity stake. By year 5, the value of this 25 percent stake may have grown to $2.5 million. The equity earnings from this investment would have been reflected on your borrower's (company A) income statement over the five-year period, but no cash has been received from the investment (assuming no dividends), cash that might have paid loans. To adjust for the income statement distortion, banks pull this noncash credit from cash flows. The investment may be perfectly circumspect in a number of ways, but there is the danger that the investment could pay out ill-timed dividends or otherwise set the stage for financial maneuvering—siphoning funds, for example.

Deferred Tax Credits

Deferred tax credits cause earnings to increase but may not provide cash, nor offer a sustainable source of cash. Deferred tax credits often come about when previous provisions for deferred taxes are reversed.

Operating Cash Needs

Accounts receivable and inventory are of approximately equal magnitude and typically constitute almost 80 percent of current assets for manufacturing industries. With such a large, relatively volatile working capital investment, operating cash needs deserve special attention. Accounts receivable and inventory levels reflect the borrower's marketing abilities and credit policies. Revenue from sales may have been reported for the period, but cash may have not been received. A rise in receivables represents a use of cash and is usually financed. A decrease in receivables is associated with cash inflows.

Operating Cash Sources

The right side of the balance sheet supports assets. Large increases and decreases in current accounts represent substantial inflows and outflows of cash. Operating cash sources generally include non-interest-bearing current liabilities that tend to follow sales increases. Accounts payable represent inventory purchases on credit. Increases in accounts payable are a source of cash in the sense that they delay cash outflows into the future. While the borrower has use of this cash, it can utilize it for daily needs as well as for investment purposes. Eventual payment to creditors decreases accounts payable, converting them into a use of cash. Generally, decreases from one period to the next represent an amount paid to suppliers in excess of purchases expensed. Increases in accruals and taxes payable represent sources of cash, because items such as salaries, taxes, and interest are expensed but not paid out. Thus, cash is conserved for a limited period. A decrease in accruals arises from payments in excess of costs expensed. In the current period, therefore, the decrease is subtracted from the cash flow as a use of cash.

Net Operating Cash Flow

Net operating cash flow denotes the cash available from gross operating cash flow to internally finance a borrower's future growth (after demands on working capital demands are satisfied). One of the great things about the structure of the cash flow format is how pieces of information surface to offer compelling insights about company operations. For example, if gross operating cash flow is often lower than net cash flow from operations, traditional sources of working capital, accounts payable, and accruals have completely covered traditional working capital uses, accounts receivable, inventory, and so on. As a result, precious operating cash income need not be diverted to support working capital levels and can thus be rerouted to finance "growth" strategies included in investment activities—the lifeblood of shareholder value.

Cash Flow Workshop

The cash flow analysis is not a stand-alone document. It is used in conjunction with the balance sheet and income statement. As discussed earlier, cash flow is the sum of cash flowing in and out of firms. Before beginning our workshop, we consider transactions making up sources and uses of cash and how each is derived. The statement of cash flow is directly related to the balance sheet. To illustrate, behind two fiscal balance sheets are underlying transactions that make up all operating, investment, and financing activities. Subtracting two balance sheets will make it relatively easy to classify transactions that indeed end up on the banker's cash flow statement. Let's start with the basic accounting equation given in Exhibit 3-3. Later in the chapter we will move the technique further along by decomposing and re-creating the cash flow of a front-page news firm—Enron. Enron is on the DVD and has been dismantled and re-created.

Exhibit 3-3 Steps to Derive Cash Flow Equation

DERIVATION OF CASH FLOW	NOTES
Equation One: Assets = Liabilities + Equity	Basic Accounting Equation
Equation Two: Cash + Accounts receivable + Inventory + Net fixed assets + Investments in unconsolidated subsidiaries = Accounts payable + Accruals + Short-term debt + Current portion long-term debt + Long-term debt + Equity	Extrapolate the basic accounting equation
Equation Three: Cash = Accounts payable + Accruals + Short-term debt + Current portion long-term debt + Long-term debt + Equity − Accounts receivable − Inventory − Net fixed assets − Investments in unconsolidated subsidiaries	Solve for cash
Equation Four: ΔCash = ΔAccounts payable + ΔAccruals + ΔShort-term debt + ΔCurrent portion long-term debt + ΔLong-term debt + ΔEquity − ΔAccounts receivable − ΔInventory − ΔNet fixed assets − ΔInvestments in unconsolidated subsidiaries	Multiply both sides of *Equation Three* by delta Δ
Equation Five: −ΔCash = −ΔAccounts payable − ΔAccruals − ΔShort-term debt − ΔCurrent portion long-term debt − ΔLong-term debt − ΔEquity + ΔAccounts receivable + ΔInventory + ΔNet fixed assets + ΔInvestments in unconsolidated subsidiaries	Multiply both sides of *Equation Four* by minus 1

Equations 4 and 5 show that changes in cash are exactly equal to differences between cash sources and uses. Note that assets, defined as uses of cash, depict negative deltas (Δ) preceding balance sheet changes, while liabilities and equity accounts, traditional sources of cash, are preceded by positive deltas. For example, if a borrower, say Company A, manufactures product X and sells it but has not paid for raw materials used in production, cash is conserved. As a result, there are increases in accounts payable, a source of cash. Conversely, if the firm sells on terms, no cash is received at the time of the sale, resulting in the expansion of receivables, a use of cash. Cash sources and uses appear in the following chart:

Sources of Cash	Uses of Cash
Decreases in assets ($-\Delta$)	Increases in assets ($+\Delta$)
Increases in liabilities ($+\Delta$)	Decreases in liabilities ($-\Delta$)
Increases in equity ($+\Delta$)	Decreases in equity ($-\Delta$)

Let's get started with a simple example: Gem Furniture Company. We will build up Gem's cash flow from scratch. Gem Furniture is on the DVD: in both the Excel worksheet and the solution. Four steps are involved:

1. Develop a control sheet.
2. Prepare reconciliations arising from your control sheet.
3. Complete the cash flow statement.
4. Develop your analysis.

Gem Furniture Company Fiscal Statements

Gem Furniture Co. Cash Flow

Gem Furniture Company
Balance Sheet

Assets	12/31/1989	12/31/1990	12/31/1991
Cash	15,445	12,007	11,717
Accts Receivable Net	51,793	55,886	88,571
Inventory	56,801	99,087	139,976
Total Current Assets	**124,039**	**166,980**	**240,264**
Plant & Equipment	53,283	60,301	68,621
Accumulated Deprec	(8,989)	(13,961)	(20,082)
Net Plant & Equip.	44,294	46,340	48,539
Total Assets	**168,333**	**213,320**	**288,803**
Short Term Borrowings	9,562	15,300	54,698
Accounts Payable	20,292	31,518	59,995
Accruals	10,328	15,300	21,994
Curr Portion Debt	500	500	500
Total Current Liabilities	**40,682**	**62,618**	**137,187**
Senior Long Term Debt	27,731	36,491	35,706
Total Liabilities	**68,413**	**99,109**	**172,893**
Common Stock	69,807	69,807	69,807
Retained Earnings	30,113	44,404	46,103
Total Owner's Equity	**99,920**	**114,211**	**115,910**
Total Liabilities and Equity	**168,333**	**213,320**	**288,803**

Gem Furniture Company
Income Statement

	_12/31/1989_	_12/31/1990_	_12/31/1991_
Net Sales	512,693	553,675	586,895
Cost of Goods Sold	(405,803)	(450,394)	(499,928)
Depreciation Expense	(4,781)	(4,973)	(6,120)
Gross Profit	**102,109**	**98,308**	**80,847**
S G & A Expense	(38,369)	(46,034)	(50,643)
Miscellaneous Expenses	(6,082)	(10,672)	(17,174)
Net Operating Profit	**57,658**	**41,602**	**13,030**
Interest Expense	(3,648)	(5,258)	(8,974)
Pre Tax Profit	**54,010**	**36,344**	**4,056**
Tax Expense	(26,068)	(17,589)	(2,091)
Net Profit	27,942	18,755	1,965

Additional Financial Information—2007

Capital Expenditures	8319
Dividends	266
Long Term Debt Increase	0
Long Term Debt Decrease	785

First Step: Develop the Control Sheet for Gem Furniture

We simply subtract Gem's balance sheet: fiscal 2006 from fiscal 2007.
Exhibit 3-4:

Exhibit 3-4 Gem Furniture 12/31/2007 Control Sheet

Control Sheet

	Increase	**Decrease**
Cash		(290)
	Source	**Use**
Accts Receivable Net		32,685
Inventory		40,889
Net Plant & Equip.		2,199
Short Term Borrowings	39,398	
Accounts Payable	28,477	
Accruals	6,694	
Curr Portion Debt	0	
Senior Long Term Debt		785
Retained Earnings	1,699	
Total	**76,268**	**76,558**
Change in cash and marketable securities	**(290)**	

1. Calculate year-to-year balance sheet changes.
2. Decide whether an item is a source or use of cash. For example, Gem's accounts receivable increased by $32,683, a use of cash.
3. Total columns to identify the cash change. The change in cash is equal to the difference between sources and uses of cash.

The change in fixed assets is hardly meaningful, and so we must break out reconciliation accounts, deriving transactions that contributed to change. One of the most important benefits of reconciliations is that they determine "information gaps"—differences between derived and ending balances on important reconciliations.

Decide what parts of the control sheet need to be reconciled. Some reconciliations are nondiscretionary, whereas others are discretionary. Nondiscretionary reconciliations include net fixed assets, equity, long-term debt, investments in unconsolidated subsidiaries, deferred taxes, and, importantly, any bizarre or unusual item that appears on the balance sheet. Discretionary reconciliations include goodwill and intangibles.

Second Step: Complete Reconciliations

Net Fixed Asset Reconciliation

Included are capital expenditures, depreciation, acquisitions, capital leases, proceeds from disposals of property, unrealized translation gains and losses, and transfers. Adding book gains or subtracting book losses derives proceeds from disposals. Translation gains and losses (FASB 52) earmark currency holding gains and losses. They are included so that bankers may distinguish between realized and unrealized fixed asset transactions.

Exhibit 3-5 Example of the Fixed Asset Reconciliation

Net PP&E	(prior period)
Less: Depreciation and amortization of net fixed assets	(current period)
Less: Proceeds from disposals	(current period)
Less: Losses on sale of fixed assets	(current period)
Plus: Gain on sale of fixed assets	(current period)
Plus: Capital expenditures	(current period)
Plus: Acquired fixed assets	(current period)
Plus/(Less) Translation Gains (Losses)	(current period)
= Derived Net Property Plant and Equipment	(current period)
Less: Actual Net Property Plant and Equipment	(current period)
= Increase/Decrease Net Property Plant and Equipment	(current period) INFORMATION GAP

Gem Furniture Fixed Asset Reconciliation

Property Plant & Equipment:	Amount
Beg. Balance	46,340
Less: Depreciation	(6,120)
Plus: Capital Exp.	8,319
Derived Ending Balance	48,539
Balance Sheet End	48,539
(Inc)Dec Fixed Assets	0 No Information Gap: Derived
Ending Balance = Ending Balance (Sheet)	

The Equity Reconciliation

Comprehensive equity reconciliations are frequently organized in annual report footnotes and the cash flow statement. The equity reconciliation is completed as follows:

- Equity accounts and opening balances appear as headings with total equity the last column.
- Listed down columns are transactions corresponding to their respective equity account. Totals for each transaction along the row are recorded in the total equity column.
- After transactions are recorded, each column is totaled identifying the ending balance for each equity account. The ending balance equals year-end account balances.
- Total equity column should reconcile to the sum of the account balances across the bottom, thus maintaining the self-proving nature of the system.
- Transactions not affecting cash cancel out so that numbers are not carried to the total column and will not appear on the cash flow statement.

Examples include net income, cash dividends, proceeds from stock sale, exercise of stock options, cumulative translation adjustments, and purchases and sales of treasury stock. Cash transactions affecting equity are carried to the cash flow statement. Equity transfers, like stock dividends, are excluded.

Gem Furniture Reconcilliation of Equity Accounts

	Common Stock	Retained Earnings	Total
Equity Accounts			
Beginning Balance	69,807	44,404	114,211
Net Income (Loss)		1,965	1,965
Cash Dividends		(266)	(266)
Ending Balance	69,807	46,103	115,910

Exhibit 3-6 Long-Term Debt Reconciliation

Current portion	(prior year)
Plus: noncurrent portion	(prior year)

Plus: increase in long-term debt (current year derived from the issue-by-issue breakdown in the footnotes)	(current year)
Less: noncurrent portion	(current year)
= Reductions in long-term debt	(current year)

Gem Furniture Long-Term Debt Reconcillation

Current Portion Long-Term Debt 1990	500
Non Current Long-Term Debt 1990	36,491
Plus: New Debt Issue	0
Less Current Portion Long-Term Debt 1991	(500)
Less Non Current Portion Long-Term Debt 1991	(35,706)
= Long Term Decreases 1991	785

Other Significant Reconciliations (Absent from Gem Furniture Corporation)

Investment Reconciliation

Equity investment transactions include equity earnings, dividends from subsidiaries, advances and repayments, purchase and sale of securities, translation gains/losses, consolidations, and deconsolidations. A summary financial statement may be included in the footnotes if the auditor determines that a more detailed explanation is warranted. Equity earnings are sometimes netted out against dividends. Dividends can be pulled out as the difference between undistributed equity and equity earnings. Project finance activities can also show up in investment schedules. See Exhibit 3-7.

Exhibit 3-7 Example: Investment Reconciliation

Investment in unconsolidated subsidiaries	(prior period)
Plus: Equity earnings	(current period)
Less: Cash dividends from subsidiaries	(current period)
Plus: Advances to subsidiaries	(current period)
Less: Repayment of loans	(current period)
Plus: Translation gains (FASB 52)	(current period)
Less: Translation losses (FASB 52)	(current period)
= Derived investment in unconsolidated. subsidiaries	(current period)
Less: Actual investment in unconsolidated. subsidiaries	(current period)
= Inc/Dec investment in unconsolidated. subsidiaries	(current period)

Deferred Tax Reconciliation (Exhibit 3-8)

Tax expense includes both current and deferred taxes. Deferred taxes arise because of "timing differences"—for example, when income/expenses reported on financial statements differ from taxes reported to the IRS. Common factors that cause timing dissimilarities include different depreciation methods for financial statement and tax purposes, and recognition of income in different periods for book and tax purposes. If taxable income exceeds book income (this occurs when prepaid cash is booked such as a subscription), deferred taxes are recorded as an asset. A negative provision increases income and reduces the deferred tax liability. Information on deferred tax is usually found in the tax footnote.

Exhibit 3-8 Deferred Tax Reconciliation

Deferred taxes	(prior period)
Plus: Deferred tax provision	(current period)
Less: Deferred tax credits	(current period)
= Derived deferred taxes	(current period)
Less: Actual deferred taxes	(current period)
= Increase/decrease deferred taxes	(current period)

Intangible Reconciliation

Goodwill and intangible reconciliations are required when amortization of goodwill or intangibles are disclosed in the annual report.

The Intangible Reconciliation

Balance sheet beginning balance	(prior year)
Plus: amortization of intangibles	(current year)
Plus: acquired intangibles	(current year)
Derived intangibles	(current year)
Balance sheet ending balance	(current year)
Increase/decrease Intangibles	(current year)

Minority Interest Reconciliation (Exhibit 3-9)

Claims on the parent's income by minority shareholders is recognized as minority interest in earnings (income statement) and minority interest (balance sheet).

Exhibit 3-9 Minority Interest Reconciliation

Balance sheet beginning balance	(prior year)
Plus: Minority interest in earnings	(current year)
Less: Dividends to minority interest	(current year)
Derived minority interest	(current year)
Increase/decrease in minority interest	(current year)

Third Step: Complete Cash Flow Statement for Gem Furniture (see the GemCF Answer Excel Spreadsheet on the DVD)

First, set up labels, leaving enough space to include transfers from the control sheet and reconciliations, as follows:

1. Gross Operating Cash Flow
2. Operating Cash Needs
3. Operating Cash Sources
4. Net Cash Flow From Operations

5. Investment Activities
6. Financing Activities

Next: Transfer directly to the cash flow all control sheet items that did not require a reconciliation: accounts receivable, inventory, and so on. Transfer them exactly as they appear on the control sheet: A source of cash on the control sheet is a source of cash on the banker's cash flow statement.

Next: Transfer all items within reconciliations and determine whether the items about to be transferred are sources or uses of cash.

Finally: Sum the cash flow and make sure you have included subtotals. The change in cash should prove.

Gem Furniture Company		
Cash Flow		
Cash Flow Accounts		
Net Income	1,965	
Plus/Less: Non-cash Items		
Depreciation	<u>6,120</u>	
GROSS OPERATING CASH FLOW		**8,085**
(Inc.)/Dec. Net A/R	(32,685)	
(Inc.)/Dec. Inventory	<u>(40,889)</u>	
Operating Cash Needs		**(73,574)**
(Inc.)/Dec. Net A/P	28,477	
(Inc.)/Dec. Accruals	<u>6,694</u>	
Operating Cash Sources		<u>**35,171**</u>
Net Cash Provided By Operating Activities		**(30,318)**
Capital Expenditures	<u>(8,319)</u>	
Net Cash Used In Investing Activities		(8,319)
Long Term Debt Increases	0	
Long Term Debt Payments	(785)	
Short Term Debt	<u>39,398</u>	
Cash Flows From Interest Bearing Debt		**38,613**
Cash Dividends	<u>(266)</u>	
Cash Flows From Equity		**(266)**
NET CHANGE IN CASH ITEMS		**(290)**

Fourth Step: Develop Your Analysis: Bullets and Points for Completing the Cash Flow Statement

Gross Operating Cash Flow

- Merchandise is sometimes shipped out at the end of the year to window-dress the financials. Be on the lookout for the following warning signs: unearned income; shifting sales to future periods via reserves; income-smoothing gimmicks; creating gains and losses by selling or retiring debt; hiding losses inside discontinued operations; selling assets after pooling; moving current expenses to later periods by improperly capitalizing costs; amortizing costs too slowly; and failing to write off worthless assets.

- Analyze the quality, magnitude, and trend of earnings. Check quality of earnings in such areas as adequacy of reserves, nonrecurring items, and cash versus accrual-based income.

- When you analyze earnings trends, pay particular attention to the contribution of income to overall financing. If income is contributing less and less to overall financing, go back and check the strategic plans.

- Compare net income and dividends to each other. Are dividends large in proportion to net income? If so, why are they upstreamed?

- Compare depreciation with capital expenditures. If depreciation is greater than capital expenditures, assets may be running below optimal levels. Although reserves and write-downs such as inventory are add-backs to gross operating cash flow, they should be fully investigated.

Operating Cash Uses

- Beware of the following red flags: large overdue receivables; overdependence on one or two customers; related-party receivables; slow receivables turnover (annualize this frequently); right of return; changes in terms, credit standards, discounts or collections, or creating receivables through distortive accounting. For example, Enron issued its common stock in exchange for notes receivable. The company then increased both notes receivable and shareholder's equity in recognition of these transactions. However, accounting convention requires that notes receivable culminating from transactions containing a company's capital stock be presented as deductions from stockholder's equity and not as assets, which is not how Enron and its auditor, Arthur Andersen, had booked the transactions.

- If the average collection period has increased, determine the reason(s). The Average Collection Period (ACP) measures the time it takes to convert receivables into cash. Accounts receivable policy is closely allied to inventory management, since these represent the two largest current asset accounts. Of approximately equal magnitude, together they comprise almost 80 percent of current assets and over 30 percent of total assets for manufacturing industries. The ACP is influenced partly by economic conditions and partly by a set of controllable factors, which are called internal (management) factors. Internal factors include credit policy variables (liberal, balanced, or conservative credit policy), credit terms, sales discounts, and collection.

- Large increase when sales are flat; slow inventory turnover; faddish inventory; inventory collateralized without your signature; watch unjustified last in, first out (LIFO) to first in, first out (FIFO) changes; insufficient insurance; change in divisional inventory valuation methods; increase in the number of LIFO pools; unreasonable intercompany profits; inclusion of inflation profits in inventory; large, unexplained increase in inventory; gross profit trends bad but no markdowns; inclusion of improper costs in inventory; capitalized instead of flow-through.

- Be sure to write down inventory if losses are sizable.

- Develop a pro forma analysis to figure out the cash loss that resulted because of poor receivable management. The difference between receivables that borrowers should have on their fiscal statements and actual receivables represents the loss in cash flow that bankers must now replace. An example follows.

Accounts Receivable Fiscal
Sales   2,856.000
ACP   50
ACP Industry   32

Cash Flow Analysis: Operating Cash Needs

Accounts Receivable = ACP(Sales)/365

	1989	1990
Accounts Receivable	27,400	388,000

Accounts Receivable Pro forma
    = 32(2,865,000)/365 =   250,389
Accounts Receivable Fiscal   388,000
Delayed Cash (Use of Cash)   **137,611**

Increase in AR	110,600
Increase AR: Normal	**NONE**
Expansion of AR	
Increase AR: Mismanaged	**137,611**
AR	

A small change in the average collection period has a profound effect on Oscar's liquidity positon.

= IF(J79>E80, J79-E80, "NONE")

Inventory Pro forma = Cost of Goods Sold/Inventory
Turnover Industry
            = 2,284,800/7   **326,400**
Inventory Fiscal   **826,200**
Inventory That Did Not Convert To   **499,800**
Receivables

Operating Cash Sources

- The spread between loan pricing and an annualized 37 percent return associated with anticipating 2/10 net 30 terms multiplied by the payable is desirable. Check to see if the payables manager takes advantage of trade discounts.
- Operating cash flow should be compared with accounts payable. A "bulge" in payables may indicate late payments, particularly if gross operating cash flow is not making an adequate contribution to investment activities, or the operating unit is highly leveraged.
- Determine if the cash conversion cycle contributes to increased payables balances and late payments.

Net Cash Provided by Operating Activities

- Net cash provided by operating activities is the line in the cash flow statement that provides cash to primary expenditures after working capital coverage.
- Working capital requirements can pull large amounts of cash from the business. This can cut into capital expansion programs, particularly if operating cash flow falls significantly below expectations.
- One of the best ways to check the quality of earnings is to compare net income to net cash flow from operations. For example, if earnings consistently reach high levels but little remains to cover investment activities, then what good is net income availability to pay debt service? For example, has net income been distorted and/or cannibalized by noncash credits, uncollectible receivables, or

increases in unsalable inventory? If so, little income will be left to finance both new investments and loan reductions.

Investment Activities

- Companies with volatile cash flow histories tend to invest less on the average than firms with smoother cash flows. They may also face stiffer costs when seeking funds from external capital markets.
- For firms with volatile cash flow patterns, business decisions are compounded by a higher tendency to have periods of low internal cash flows that can distract managers and cause them to throw out budgets, delay debt repayments, and defer capital expenditures.
- Investment activities can be categorized into two groups: discretionary and non-discretionary. Nondiscretionary investment activities refer to outlays required to keep a healthy gross margin on the operating-unit level. Say, for example, non-discretionary investments are covered by the borrower's internal cash flow. From this you can assume that financing activities are discretionary and the firm has better control of its capital structure.
- Assets require continuous replacement and upgrading to ensure efficient operations. When depreciation expenses consistently exceed capital expenditures over time, this is an indication of a declining operation. Eventually, this will lead to a fall in earnings and profitability. Capital expenditures represent major non-discretionary outlays.
- Watch out for outdated equipment and technology, high maintenance and repair expense, declining output level, inadequate depreciation charges, changes in depreciation method, lengthening depreciation period, decline in the depreciation expense, and large write-off of assets. Also watch out for distortions regarding currency translations.
- Check to see if deferred taxes are running off. Deferred taxes usually increase when capital expenditures accelerate. Download the most recent capital budgeting schedule. Focus on project cost, net present values (NPVs), and internal rate of return (IRR).
- Be alert to sharp increases in fixed asset turnover (sales/net fixed assets). This ratio measures the turnover of plant and equipment in relation to sales. The fixed asset/turnover ratio is really a measure of cash flow efficiency since it indicates how well fixed assets are being utilized.
- Determine if backlogs are increasing without a large pickup in sales. Unresolved backlogs usually occur only once, and then customers go elsewhere.
- Determine if work-in-process inventory ties into a sharply deteriorating inventory turnover.
- Make sure the gross margin has not trended down over the past few years due to increased labor costs and decreased operating leverage.
- Always use real options tools when applicable.

Investment Project Cash Flows and Joint Ventures

- Once the financial merits of a project have been examined, a judgment should be made as to whether the project's cash flow is reasonably understood. For example, if XYZ division fails to maintain property, plant, and equipment, a series of problems could easily ensue. The unit's aging or outmoded machinery would increasingly experience longer periods of downtime and goods produced could be defective. The operating unit will begin to fall behind its competitors from both a technological and an opportunity cost standpoint. Worse, customers may perceive its products as inferior, of lower quality, or old-fashioned compared to those of its competitors.

- From a summary of IAS 31, a joint venture is a contractual arrangement subject to joint control. There are three types of joint ventures: jointly controlled operations, jointly controlled assets, and jointly controlled entities.

- The venture should recognize jointly controlled operations by including the assets and liabilities it controls, the expenses it incurs, and its share of the income that it earns from the sale of goods or services by the venture. Jointly controlled assets should be recognized on a proportional basis, and jointly controlled entities should be recognized in consolidated financial statements, as outlined in the text box.

- The cost of capital should be appropriate. If it is artificially low, the project's NPV will be inflated.

- Look for a slow amortization period, a lengthening amortization period, a high ratio of intangibles to total assets and capital, and a large balance in goodwill, even though profits are weak.

- Make sure the time frame set out to complete the project is realistic. Projects that take longer to complete than projected will invariably cost more than budgeted. This will lower the project's NPV and may lead to an eventual cash crunch for the company.

- Determine what, if any, contingencies the company has made in the event that project costs or completion time exceed the original estimate. If the business can raise additional capital without difficulty, this is a very positive factor from a lender's point of view.

- Watch for switching between current and noncurrent classifications, investments recorded in excess of costs, and investments.

- Determine the real value of projects and not just book values.

- Never stop questioning clients on off-balance-sheet projects that are not fully understood. Enron's Raptor partnerships were used to exaggerate profits by $1 billion over a period of months. Aggressive cash flow due diligence by bankers may have extracted this shenanigan from its Alice-in-wonderland milieu.

- Always examine increases in long-term debt on a specific issue basis in order to ensure optimal financing.

- Optimal financing means financing that minimizes the cost of capital, maximizes equity value, and perhaps prevents your borrower's credit grade or bond rating from downtiering.

- Make sure you distinguish real debt increases from accounting debt increases on the cash flow statement. For example, as we saw earlier, amortization of bond discount results in debt increases, but no cash inflow is involved.

- Decreases in long-term debt should be matched against increases in long-term debt, along with the magnitude of gross operating cash flow. For example, in an expanding business, increases in long-term debt may exceed reductions. As long as leverage is within acceptable levels, internal cash flow is probably contributing its fair share to the overall financing of the business.

- Amortization of bond premiums distorts actual debt reductions. Find cash decreases by separating bond premiums from debt payments.
- Look for long-term debt conversions to equity. Conversion to equity may represent a substantial noncash exchange.

Equity and Other Financing Activities

- Review dividends to determine whether they are tied to income or are relatively constant.
- Examine financial leverage as well to verify that dividends are reasonable in light of future prospects. Determine whether an established partner exists in the business's capital expenditure program.

Final Points about Cash Flow Analysis

1. Cash flow statements retrace all firms' financing and investment activities for a given period of time. This includes the extent to which cash has been generated and absorbed.
2. Today more and more lenders rely on the statement of cash flows as a measure of corporate performance because it "images" the probability distribution of future cash flows in relation to debt capacity.
3. The greater and more certain the cash flows, the greater the debt capacity of the firm.
4. SFAS 95 mandates segregating the borrower's business activities into three classifications: operating, financing, and investing activities. The operating activities section may be presented using either a direct or an indirect presentation.
5. The direct method focuses on cash and the impact of cash on the business's financial condition.
6. Investing activities involve making and collecting loans and acquiring and disposing of debt or equity instruments and property, plant, and equipment, and other productive assets—that is, assets held for or used in the production of goods or services by the enterprise.
7. Cash flows from unconsolidated subsidiaries include dividends from subsidiaries, advances and repayments, and the acquisition or sale of securities of subsidiaries. Noncash transactions include equity earnings, translation gains and losses, and consolidations.
8. Prudent bankers must obtain a full disclosure concerning the project's future cash flows since construction projects may report noncash earnings—construction accounting or equity earnings.
9. Investing activities involve obtaining resources from owners and providing them with a return on, and return of, their investment; borrowing money and repaying amounts borrowed or otherwise settling the obligation; and obtaining and paying for other resources obtained from creditors on long-term credit.
10. Operating activities include all transactions and other events that are not defined as investing or financing activities. Operating activities generally involve producing and delivering goods and providing services. Cash flows from operating

activities are generally the cash effects of transactions and other events that enter into the determination of income.

11. Gross operating cash flow is often the most important line in the cash flow statement, representing net income plus all noncash charges less all noncash credits, plus or minus all nonoperating transactions.

12. Cash generated from nonrecurring items may artificially inflate earnings for a period, but it cannot be depended on to provide cash flow to support long-term financing.

13. Net income must be the predominant source of a firm's funds in the long run.

14. For the most part, current assets represent more than half the total assets of many businesses. With such a large, relatively volatile cash investment connected to optimizing shareholder value, current assets merit financial management's undivided attention.

15. Net operating cash flow denotes the cash available from gross operating cash flow to internally finance a firm's future growth after working capital demands have been satisfied.

16. Sources of cash include decreases in assets, increases in liabilities, and increases in equity. Uses of cash include increases in assets, decreases in liabilities, and decreases in equity.

17. The control sheet shows that the change in the cash account is always equal to the difference between sources and uses of cash.

18. Sources and uses of cash are usually net changes, meaning the end result of many different transactions. Thus, reconciliations lie at the core of cash flow analysis.

19. The quality, magnitude, and trend of operating cash flow must be examined carefully since it should contribute a reasonable amount to financing. This is readily determined by the composition of the gross operating cash flow.

20. When depreciation expenses consistently exceed capital expenditures over time, this is an indication of a business in decline. Eventually, it will lead to a reduction in earnings and profitability.

21. If investment in unconsolidated subsidiaries represents a large item on the balance sheet, lenders should ask for financial statements of the unconsolidated subsidiary—or at least a full financial summary.

It is now time to put our most important tool, cash flow, to use. We shall take the complex cash flow of Enron 2000 fiscal and reconstruct it into a banker's format.

Enron Cash Flow Decomposition

Each credit proposal should be subject to careful analysis by a credit analyst with expertise commensurate with the size and complexity of the transaction. An effective evaluation process establishes minimum requirements for the information on which the analysis is to be based. There should be policies in place regarding the information and documentation needed to approve new credits, renew existing credits, and/or change the terms and conditions of previously approved credits. The information received will be the basis for any internal evaluation or rating assigned to the credit, and its accuracy and adequacy is critical to management making appropriate judgments about the acceptability of the credit.[1]

Cash Flow Reconstruction

Generally, the weaker the credit, the more due diligence—it's as simple as that. Please open the Excel files Enron Cash Flow on the DVD. Below is a brief listing of each worksheet in the Enron Cash Flow workbook and description:

Table 3-8

Worksheet	Summary Description
Enron 10-K	Enron's Securities and Exchange from 10-K Fiscal 2000
EnronCFOrig	Copy of Original Cash Flow Statement from Enron's Fiscal 2000 10-K. Check subtotal and total columns.
Income	Copy of Original Income Statement from Enron's Fiscal 2000 10-K. Subtotal and total all columns.
BSReconcil	Copy of Balance Sheet from fiscal 2000 10-K. Subtotal and total all columns. Set up control sheet and complete reconciliations.
CF Worksheet	Prepare Enron's Preliminary Bankers Cash Flow using information gathered in CF Reconciliation Section. Label cash flow categories: for example, gross operating cash flow . . . Transfer entries from reconciliations and control sheet to the appropriate section in the preliminary cash flow. Add up subtotal and total columns. Make sure the cash flow balances.
FinalProforma	To set up Enron Corp.'s Pro forma Bankers Fiscal 2000 Cash Flow, copy the preliminary cash flow from the CFWorksheet into the new worksheet named FinalProForma. Adjust the cash flow with offsetting entries including misleading disclosure, inappropriately liberal accounting, or incorrect or misleading account classification. Cross-reference offsetting adjustments using sequential superscripted numbers, 1, 2, etc. The resulting cash flow approximates a more realistic document. While offsetting entries were driven by reports in the media, in real life alert bankers actualize their own "media." They receive explanations for questions dealing with aggressive or confusing financial statement disclosure. After you record an offsetting entry, check the change in cash. If the number changes, undo the entry and correct your error.

[1]From Basel Committee principles, number 6, point 44. The Adobe Document Principles for the Management of Credit Risk can be found on the DVD.

Table 3-8 (*Continued*)

Worksheet	Summary Description
Comparison	We insert a new and final worksheet called Comparison. Compare the Bankers 2000 fiscal submitted by Arthur Andersen. Match key groupings and take note of differences.
ProfomaInvest	Finally, we adjust Enron's balance sheet consolidating the following investments and eliminating "Investments in and advances to unconsolidated equity affiliates": Azurix Corp., Bridgeline Holdings, Citrus Corp., Dabhol Power Company, Joint Energy Development Investments L.P. (JEDI)(b), Joint Energy Development Investments II L.P. (JEDI II)(b), SK-Enron Co. Ltd., Transportadora de Gas del Sur S.A, Whitewing Associates, L.P.(b), and others.

CHAPTER 4

Step-by-Step in Getting Started with the Modeling Toolkit and Risk Simulator Software Applications

The Risk Simulator and Basel II Modeling Toolkit software has over 300 different analytical Excel/SLS model templates and over 800 Excel functions and models. Only some of the key models that pertain to credit risk and market risks are covered in this book, and this chapter provides a good primer on getting started in using Risk Simulator. At first glance, this chapter has little to do with credit or market risk analysis, but in reality, the materials covered in this chapter provide the critical building blocks for advanced credit and market risk in banks presented in later chapters. Trial versions of these software applications are included in the book's DVD or can be downloaded directly from the Web at www.realoptionsvaluation.com. Readers who are currently expert users of the Modeling Toolkit software and Risk Simulator software may skip this section and move directly into the models in the text.

Introduction to the Modeling Toolkit Software

At the time of writing, the Modeling Toolkit software incorporated about 800 different advanced analytical models and 300 Excel/SLS model templates in a variety of industries and applications. To obtain the detailed listing of models and functions, first install the software and then click on **Start | Programs | Real Options Valuation | Modeling Toolkit | Model & Function List**. We will focus on the Excel-based version of the software for the purposes of this book (running smaller models with a few transactions at a time) instead of the server and database version (capable of running millions of transactions per second) as the methodologies and algorithms are similar.

To install this software for a trial period of 30 days, insert the DVD that comes with the book or visit www.realoptionsvaluation.com and click on **Downloads**. Look for the Modeling Toolkit software. You will need to be online to download the latest installation file. This software works on Windows XP, Vista, or later and requires Excel XP, 2003, 2007, or later to run. Downloading from the Web will ensure that the latest version is installed.

After installing the Basel II Modeling Toolkit, you will be prompted for a license key. Please write down the **FINGERPRINT ID** when the message appears. Then, in order to use the software immediately, enter the following user name and license key. You will need this Fingerprint ID to purchase a permanent license later, from www.realoptionsvaluation.com.

To start the software, click on **Start | Programs | Real Options Valuation | Modeling Toolkit | Modeling Toolkit**. This action will start Excel. Inside Excel, you will

---

Name: 30 Day Trial   **Key:** 4C55-0BA2-420E-CA84

---

notice a new menu item called **Modeling Toolkit** (this will appear under the Add-Ins tab in certain Excel 2007 configurations). This menu is self-explanatory as the models are categorized by application domain, and the key credit and market risk models are described in more detail in this book. Please note that this software uses Excel macros. If you receive an error message on macros, it is because your system is set to a high security level and you need to first fix this by starting Excel XP or 2003 and clicking on **Tools | Macros | Security | Medium** and restarting the software. If you are using Excel 2007, you can simply click on **Enable Macros** when prompted (or reset your security settings when in Excel 2007 by clicking on the **Office** button located at the top left of the screen and selecting **Excel Options | Trust Center | Trust Center Settings | Macro Settings | Enable All Macros**).

Note that the trial version will expire in 30 days. To obtain a full corporate license, please contact the author's firm, Real Options Valuation, Inc., at admin@realoptions valuation.com or visit the company's Web site mentioned above. Finally, notice that after the expiration of the software, some of the models that depend on Risk Simulator or Real Options SLS software will still function until their expiration dates. In addition, after the expiration date, these worksheets will still be visible, but the analytical results and functions will return null or error values. Finally, software versions continually change and improve, and the best recommendation is to visit the aforementioned Web site for any new versions or details on installation and licensing.

Introduction to Risk Simulator

This chapter also introduces the novice risk analyst to the Risk Simulator software for performing Monte Carlo simulation, stochastic forecasting, portfolio optimization, and general statistical analysis, where a 30-day trial version of the software is included in the book's DVD. This section starts off by illustrating what Risk Simulator does and what steps are taken in a Monte Carlo risk-based simulation, as well as some of the more basic elements in a simulation analysis. This chapter then continues with how to interpret the results from a simulation and ends with a discussion of correlating variables in a simulation as well as applying precision and error control. Because software versions with new enhancements are continually released, review the software's user manual and the software download site (www.realoptionsvaluation.com) for more up-to-date details on using the latest version of the software. For more technical details on using Risk Simulator, see *Modeling Risk: Applying Monte Carlo Simulation, Real Options Analysis, Stochastic Forecasting, and Portfolio Optimization* (Wiley, 2007) also by the author.

Risk Simulator is a Monte Carlo simulation, forecasting, optimization, and statistical analysis software. It is written in Microsoft .NET C# and functions together with Excel as an add-in, and it can also be used as an OEM or integration into other existing software and database products. Risk Simulator is also compatible and often used with the Real Options SLS software introduced in Appendix 1. The different functions or modules in both software applications are briefly described next:

- The *Simulation Module* allows you to run simulations in your existing Excel-based models, generate and extract simulation forecasts (distributions of results and forecasts, Value at Risk computations, risk quantification), perform distributional fitting (automatically finding the best-fitting statistical distribution and historical simulation), compute correlations (maintain relationships among simulated random variables and particularly useful in portfolio analysis), identify sensitivities (creating tornado and sensitivity charts), test statistical hypotheses (finding statistical differences between pairs of forecasts), run bootstrap simulation (testing the robustness of result statistics and great for stress testing results), and run custom and nonparametric simulations (simulations using historical data without specifying any distributions or their parameters for forecasting without data or applying expert opinion forecasts).

- The *Forecasting Module* can be used to generate automatic time-series forecasts (with and without seasonality and trend), multivariate regressions (modeling relationships among variables), nonlinear extrapolations (curve fitting), stochastic processes (random walks, mean-reversions, jump-diffusion, and mixed processes for forecasting stock prices, interest rates, inflation rates, and commodity prices), maximum likelihood estimators (probabilities of default in credit risk applications), and Box-Jenkins ARIMA (Auto Regressive Integrated Moving Average econometric forecasts).

- The *Optimization Module* is used for optimizing multiple decision variables subject to constraints to maximize or minimize an objective, and it can be run as a static optimization, as a dynamic optimization under uncertainty together with Monte Carlo simulation, or as a stochastic optimization (useful for optimizing portfolios of assets and liabilities, reducing risk through diversification). The software can handle linear and nonlinear optimizations with integer and continuous variables.

- The *Statistical Analysis Module* provides multiple types of business statistical analysis tools such as a statistical analysis tool (which analyzes data and returns results from simple descriptive statistics to calibration of stochastic process inputs) and data diagnostics (which test historical data used for forecasts in terms of its forecastability characteristics such as heteroskedasticity, multicollinearity, and nonlinearity).

To install the software, insert the accompanying DVD, click on the Install Risk Simulator link, and follow the onscreen instructions. You will need to be online to download the latest version of the software. The software requires that Windows XP or Vista, administrative privileges, and Microsoft .Net Framework 1.1 and 2.0 be installed on the computer. Most new computers come with Microsoft .NET Framework 1.1 and 2.0 preinstalled. However, if an error message pertaining to requiring .NET Framework 1.1 occurs during the installation of Risk Simulator, exit the installation. Then, install the relevant .NET Framework software, which is also included in the DVD (found in the *Required Software* folder). Complete the .NET installation, restart the computer, and then reinstall the Risk Simulator software. Version 1.1 of the Framework is required even if your system has version 2.0/3.0 as they work independent of each other. You may also download this software on the aforementioned Web site's Download page.

Once installation is complete, start Microsoft Excel, and if the installation was successful, you should see an additional *Simulation* item on the menu bar in Excel and a new icon bar as seen in Figure 4-1. Figure 4-2 shows the icon toolbar in more detail. You are now ready to start using the software. The following sections provide step-by-step instructions for using the software. As the software is continually updated and improved, the examples in this book might be slightly different from the latest version downloaded from the Internet.

A 30-day trial license file comes with the software and is located on the DVD. To obtain a full corporate license, please contact the author's firm, Real Options Valuation, Inc. at admin@realoptionsvaluation.com or visit the Web site www.realoptionsvaluation.com.

To install a trial or permanent license, simply start Excel, click on **Risk Simulator and License**, then **Install License**, and browse to the newly acquired license file or to the DVD for your extended 30-day trial license. If you are using Windows Vista, make sure to disable User Access Control before installing the license (click on **Start | Control Panel | Classic View [on the left panel] | User Accounts | Turn User Account Control On or Off** and uncheck the option, **Use User Account Control (UAC)**, and restart the computer). When restarting the computer, you will get a message that UAC is turned off. You can turn this message off by going to the **Control Panel | Security Center | Change the Way Security Center Alerts Me | Don't Notify Me and Don't Display the Icon**. Please watch the getting started videos in the DVD for a quick primer on how to use these software tools. These videos will complement the materials covered in this chapter. For additional free modeling videos, visit the download site listed above.

Running a Monte Carlo Simulation

Typically, to run a simulation in your existing Excel model, the following steps have to be performed:

1. Start a new or open an existing simulation profile.
2. Define input assumptions in the relevant cells.
3. Define output forecasts in the relevant cells.
4. Run simulation.
5. Interpret the results.

If desired, and for practice, open the example file called **Basic Simulation Model** and follow along the examples below on creating a simulation. The example file can be found on the menu at **Risk Simulator | Examples**.

1. *Starting a New Simulation Profile*

To start a new simulation, you must first create a simulation profile. A simulation profile contains a complete set of instructions on how you would like to run a simulation, that is, all the assumptions, forecasts, simulation run preferences, and so forth. Use of profiles facilitates creating multiple scenarios of simulations; that is, by using the same exact model, several profiles can be created, each with its own specific simulation assumptions, forecasts, properties, and requirements. The same analyst can

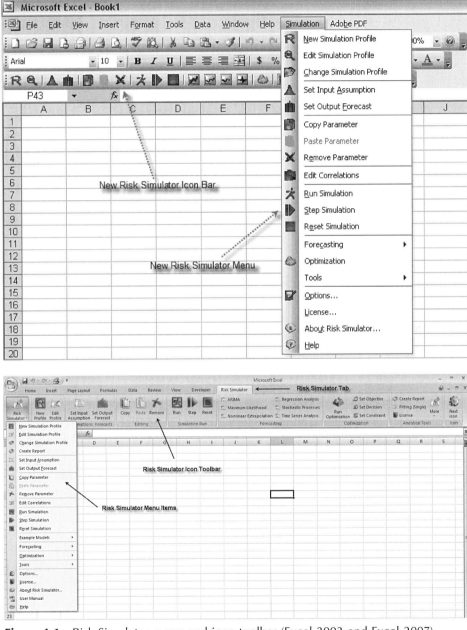

Figure 4-1   Risk Simulator menu and icon toolbar (Excel 2003 and Excel 2007).

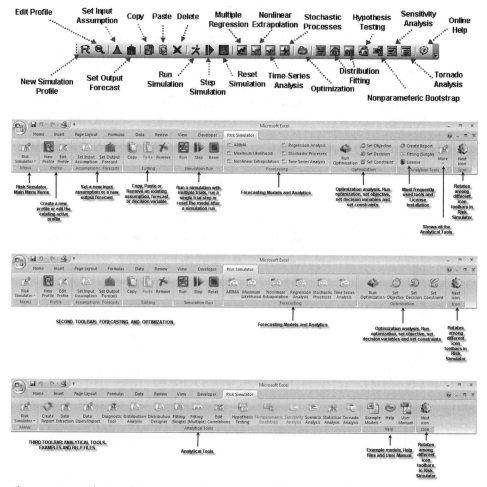

Figure 4-2   Risk Simulator icon toolbar (Excel 2003 and Excel 2007).

create different test scenarios using different distributional assumptions and inputs, or multiple users can test their own assumptions and inputs on the same model. Instead of having to make duplicates of the same model, the same model can be used, and different simulations can be run through this model *profiling* process.

The following list provides the procedure for starting a new simulation profile:

- **Start Excel** and create a new or open an existing model (you can use the Basic Simulation Model example to follow along: **Risk Simulator | Examples | Basic Simulation Model**).
- Click on **Risk Simulator | New Simulation Profile**.
- Enter a title for your simulation including all other pertinent information (Figure 4-3).

The following are the elements in the new simulation profile dialog (Figure 4-3):

- *Title*: Specifying a simulation profile name or title allows you to create multiple simulation profiles in a single Excel model, which means that you can now save

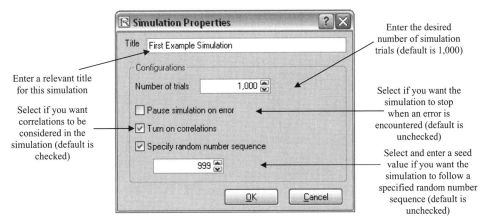

Enter a relevant title for this simulation

Enter the desired number of simulation trials (default is 1,000)

Select if you want correlations to be considered in the simulation (default is checked)

Select if you want the simulation to stop when an error is encountered (default is unchecked)

Select and enter a seed value if you want the simulation to follow a specified random number sequence (default is unchecked)

Figure 4-3   New simulation profile.

different simulation scenario profiles within the same model without having to delete existing assumptions and changing them each time a new simulation scenario is required.

- *Number of trials*: The number of simulation trials required is entered, that is, running 1,000 trials means that 1,000 different iterations of outcomes based on the input assumptions will be generated. You can change this number as desired, but the input has to be positive integers. The default number of runs is 1,000 trials.

- *Pause on simulation error*: If checked, the simulation stops every time an error is encountered in the Excel model; that is, if your model encounters a computation error (e.g., some input values generated in a simulation trial may yield a divide-by-zero error in one of your spreadsheet cells), the simulation stops. This feature is important to help audit your model to make sure there are no computational errors in your Excel model. However, if you are sure the model works, then this preference need not be checked.

- *Turn on correlations*: If checked, correlations between paired input assumptions will be computed. Otherwise, correlations will all be set to zero and a simulation will be run assuming no cross-correlations between input assumptions. As an example, applying correlations will yield more accurate results if indeed correlations exist and will tend to yield a lower forecast confidence if negative correlations exist.

- *Specify random number sequence*: By definition, simulation yields slightly different results every time it is run by virtue of the random number generation routine in Monte Carlo simulation. This is a theoretical fact in all random number generators. However, when making presentations, sometimes you may require the same results (especially when the report being presented shows one set of results and during a live presentation you would like to show the same results being generated, or when you are sharing models with others and would like the same results to be obtained every time); then check this preference and enter in an initial seed number. The seed number can be any positive integer. Using the same initial seed value, the same number of trials, and the same input assumptions will always yield the same sequence of random numbers, guaranteeing the same final set of results.

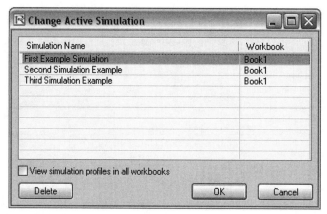

Figure 4-4   Change active simulation.

Note that once a new simulation profile has been created, you can come back later and modify these selections. In order to do so, make sure that the current active profile is the profile you wish to modify; otherwise, click on **Risk Simulator | Change Simulation Profile**, select the profile you wish to change, and click on **OK**. (Figure 4-4 shows an example where there are multiple profiles and how to activate, duplicate, or delete a selected profile.) Then, click on **Risk Simulator | Edit Simulation Profile** and make the required changes.

2. *Defining Input Assumptions*

The next step is to set input assumptions in your model. Note that assumptions can only be assigned to cells without any equations or functions (i.e., typed-in numerical values that are inputs in a model), whereas output forecasts can only be assigned to cells with equations and functions (i.e., outputs of a model). Recall that assumptions and forecasts cannot be set unless a simulation profile already exists. Follow this procedure to set new input assumptions in your model:

- Select the cell you wish to set an assumption on (e.g., cell G8 in the Basic Simulation Model example).
- Click on **Risk Simulator | Set Input Assumption** or click on the set assumption icon in the Risk Simulator icon toolbar.
- Select the relevant distribution you want, enter the relevant distribution parameters, and hit **OK** to insert the input assumption into your model (Figure 4-5).

Several key areas are worthy of mention in the Set Assumption dialog. Figure 4-6 shows the different areas:

- *Assumption Name:* This optional area allows you to enter in unique names for the assumptions to help track what each of the assumptions represents. Good modeling practice is to use short but precise assumption names.
- *Distribution Gallery:* This area to the left shows all of the different distributions available in the software. To change the views, right click anywhere in the gallery and select large icons, small icons, or list. More than two dozen distributions are available.

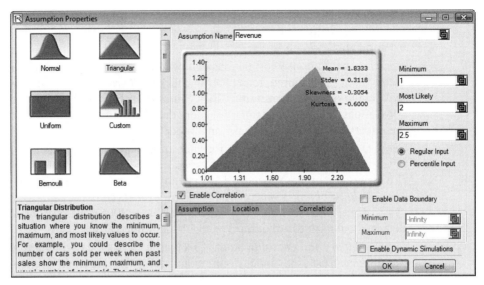

Figure 4-5   Setting an input assumption.

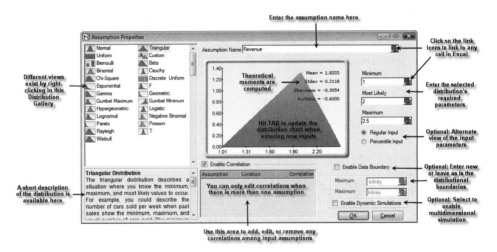

Figure 4-6   Assumption properties.

- *Input Parameters:* Depending on the distribution selected, the required relevant parameters are shown. You may either enter the parameters directly or link them to specific cells in your worksheet (click on the link icon to link an input parameter to a worksheet cell). Hard coding or typing the parameters is useful when the assumption parameters are assumed not to change. Linking to worksheet cells is useful when the input parameters need to be visible on the worksheets themselves or are allowed to be changed as in a dynamic simulation (where the input parameters themselves are linked to assumptions in the worksheets, creating a multidimensional simulation or simulation of simulations).

- *Data Boundary:* Distributional or data boundaries truncation are typically not used but exist for truncating the distributional assumptions. For instance, if a normal distribution is selected, the theoretical boundaries are between negative infinity and positive infinity. However, in practice, the simulated variable exists only within some smaller range, and this range can then be entered to truncate the distribution appropriately.

- *Correlations:* Pairwise correlations can be assigned to input assumptions here. If assumptions are required, remember to check the *Turn on Correlations* preference by clicking on **Risk Simulator | Edit Simulation Profile**. See the discussion on correlations later in this chapter for more details about assigning correlations and the effects correlations will have on a model.

- *Short Descriptions:* These exist for each distribution in the gallery and explain when a certain distribution is used as well as the input parameter requirements. See the section in the Appendix, Understanding Probability Distributions, in *Modeling Risk: Applying Monte Carlo Simulation, Real Options Analysis, Stochastic Forecasting, and Portfolio Optimization* (Wiley, 2006), also by the author, for details about each distribution type available in the software.

- *Regular Input and Percentile Input:* This option allows the user to perform a quick due diligence test of the input assumption. For instance, if you are setting a normal distribution with some mean and standard deviation inputs, you can click on the percentile input to see what the corresponding 10th and 90th percentiles are.

- *Enable Dynamic Simulation:* This option is unchecked by default, but if you wish to run a multidimensional simulation (i.e., if you link the input parameters of the assumption to another cell that is itself an assumption, you are simulating the inputs or simulating the simulation), then remember to check this option. Dynamic simulation will not work unless the inputs are linked to other changing input assumptions.

Note: If you are following along with the example, continue by setting another assumption on cell G9. This time use the Uniform distribution with a minimum value of 0.9 and a maximum value of 1.1. Then proceed to defining the output forecasts in the next step.

3. *Defining Output Forecasts*

The next step is to define output forecasts in the model. Forecasts can only be defined on output cells with equations or functions.

Use the following procedure to define the forecasts:

- Select the cell on which you wish to set an assumption (e.g., cell G10 in the Basic Simulation Model example).
- Click on **Risk Simulator | Set Output Forecast** or click on the set forecast icon on the Risk Simulator icon toolbar.
- Enter the relevant information and click on **OK**.

Figure 4-7 illustrates the set forecast properties.

- *Forecast Name:* Specify the name of the forecast cell. This is important because when you have a large model with multiple forecast cells, naming the forecast cells individually allows you to access the right results quickly. Do not underestimate the importance of this simple step. Good modeling practice is to use short but precise assumption names.

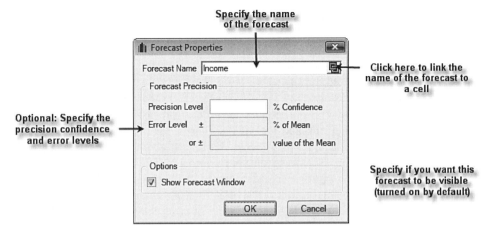

Figure 4-7   Set output forecast.

- *Forecast Precision:* Instead of relying on a guesstimate of how many trials to run in your simulation, you can set up precision and error controls. When an error-precision combination has been achieved in the simulation, the simulation will pause and inform you of the precision achieved, making the number of simulation trials an automated process and not making you rely on guesses of the required number of trials to simulate. Review the section on error and precision control for more specific details.
- *Show Forecast Window:* This property allows the user to show or not show a particular forecast window. The default is to always show a forecast chart.

4. *Run Simulation*

If everything looks right, simply click on **Risk Simulator | Run Simulation** or click on the Run icon on the Risk Simulator toolbar, and the simulation will proceed. You may also reset a simulation after it has run to rerun it (**Risk Simulator | Reset Simulation** or click the reset icon on the toolbar). Also, the step function (**Risk Simulator | Step Simulation** or the step icon on the toolbar) allows you to simulate a single trial, one at a time, which is useful for educating others on simulation (i.e., you can show that at each trial, all the values in the assumption cells are being replaced and the entire model is recalculated each time).

5. *Interpreting the Forecast Results*

The final step in Monte Carlo simulation is to interpret the resulting forecast charts. Figures 4-8 to 4-15 show the forecast chart and the corresponding statistics generated after running the simulation. Typically, the following sections on the forecast window are important in interpreting the results of a simulation:

- **Forecast Chart:** The forecast chart shown in Figure 4-8 is a probability histogram that shows the frequency counts of values occurring and the total number of trials simulated. The vertical bars show the frequency of a particular *x* value occurring out of the total number of trials, while the cumulative frequency (smooth line) shows the total probabilities of all values at and below *x* occurring in the forecast.

- **Forecast Statistics:** The forecast statistics shown in Figure 4-9 summarizes the distribution of the forecast values in terms of the four moments of a distribution. You can rotate between the histogram and statistics tab by depressing the space bar.

- **Preferences:** The preferences tab in the forecast chart (Figure 4-10) allows you to change the look and feel of the charts. For instance, if *Always Show Window on Top* is selected, the forecast charts will always be visible regardless of what other software is running on your computer. The *Semitransparent When Inactive* is a powerful option used to compare or overlay multiple forecast charts at once (e.g., enable this option on several forecast charts and drag them on top of one another to visually see the similarities or differences). *Histogram Resolution* allows you to change the number of bins of the histogram, anywhere from 5 bins to 100

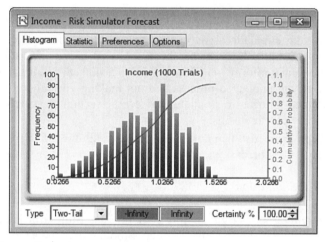

Figure 4-8 Forecast chart.

Statistics	Result
Number of Trials	1000
Mean	0.8381
Median	0.8772
Standard Deviation	0.3131
Variance	0.0980
Coefficient of Variation	0.3736
Maximum	1.5208
Minimum	-0.0133
Range	1.5341
Skewness	-0.3070
Kurtosis	-0.6117
25% Percentile	0.6131
75% Percentile	1.0652
Percentage Error Precision at 95% Confidence	2.3154%

Figure 4-9 Forecast statistics.

bins. Also, the *Update Data Interval* section allows you to control how fast the simulation runs versus how often the forecast chart is updated. That is, if you wish to see the forecast chart updated at almost every trial, this will slow down the simulation as more memory is being allocated to updating the chart versus running the simulation. This is merely a user preference and does in no way change the results of the simulation, just the speed of completing the simulation.

● **Options:** This forecast chart option allows you to show all the forecast data or to filter in or out values that fall within some specified interval, or within some standard deviation that you choose. Also, the precision level can be set here for this specific forecast to show the error levels in the statistics view. See the section on precision and error control for more details. You can also elect to show some additional lines such as the location of the mean, median, first, and third quartiles.

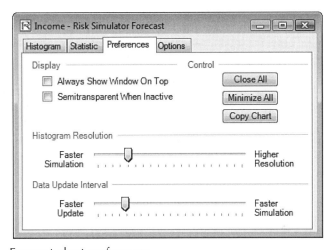

Figure 4-10 Forecast chart preferences.

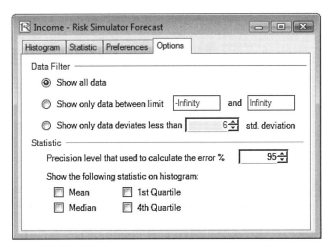

Figure 4-11 Forecast chart options.

Using Forecast Charts and Confidence Intervals

After running a simulation in forecast charts, you can determine the probability of occurrence called *confidence intervals*; that is, given two values, what are the chances that the outcome will fall between these two values? Figure 4-12 illustrates that there is a 90 percent probability that the final outcome (in this case, the level of income) will be between $0.2781 and $1.3068. The two-tailed confidence interval can be obtained by first selecting *Two-Tail* as the type, entering the desired certainty value (e.g., 90), and hitting **Tab** on the keyboard. The two computed values corresponding to the certainty value will then be displayed. In this example, there is a 5 percent probability that income will be at or below $0.2781 and another 5 percent probability that income will be at or above $1.3068; that is, the two-tailed confidence interval is a symmetrical interval centered on the median or 50th percentile value. Thus, both tails will have the same probability.

Alternatively, a one-tail probability can be computed. Figure 4-13 shows a *Left-Tail* selection at 95 percent confidence (i.e., choose *Left-Tail* as the type, enter 95 as the certainty level, and hit *Tab* on the keyboard). This means that there is a 95 percent probability that the income will be below $1.3068 (i.e., 95% on the left tail of $1.3068) or a 5% probability that income will be at or above $1.3068, corresponding perfectly with the results seen in Figure 4-12.

In addition to evaluating the confidence interval (i.e., given a probability level and finding the relevant income values), you can determine the probability of a given income value (Figure 4-14). For instance, what is the probability that income will be less than $1? To do this, select the *Left-Tail* probability type, enter 1 into the value input box, and hit **Tab**. The corresponding certainty will then be computed (in this case, there is a 64.80% probability that income will be below $1).

For the sake of completeness, you can select the *Right-Tail* probability type and enter the value 1 in the value input box, and hit **Tab** (Figure 4-15). The resulting probability indicates the right-tail probability past the value 1, that is, the probability

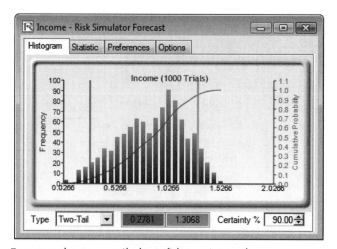

Figure 4-12   Forecast chart two-tailed confidence interval.

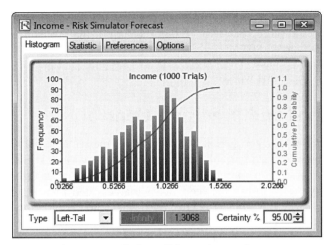

Figure 4-13   Forecast chart one-tailed confidence interval.

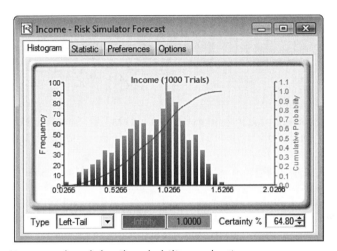

Figure 4-14   Forecast chart left tail probability evaluation.

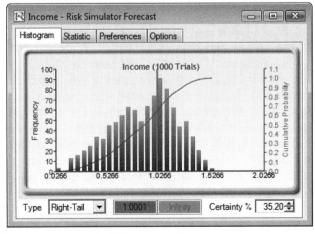

Figure 4-15   Forecast chart probability evaluation.

of income exceeding \$1 (in this case, we see that there is a 35.20% probability of income exceeding \$1). Notice that the sum of the probabilities has to be 100% (i.e., 35.20% and 64.80%).

Note that the forecast window is resizable by clicking on and dragging the bottom right corner of the forecast window.

Correlations and Precision Control

The correlation coefficient is a measure of the strength and direction of the relationship between two variables and can take on any values between -1.0 and $+1.0$; that is, the correlation coefficient can be decomposed into its direction or sign (positive or negative relationship between two variables) and the magnitude or strength of the relationship (the higher the absolute value of the correlation coefficient, the stronger the relationship).

The correlation coefficient can be computed in several ways. The first approach is to manually compute the correlation coefficient r of a pair of variables x and y using:

$$r_{x,y} = \frac{n\sum x_i y_i - \sum x_i \sum y_i}{\sqrt{n\sum x_i^2 - \left(\sum x_i\right)^2}\sqrt{n\sum y_i^2 - \left(\sum y_i\right)^2}}$$

The second approach is to use Excel's *CORREL* function. For instance, if the 10 data points for *x* and *y* are listed in cells A1 : B10, then the Excel function to use is *CORREL (A1 : A10, B1 : B10)*.

The third approach is to run Risk Simulator's *Multi-Variable Distributional Fitting Tool,* and the resulting correlation matrix will be computed and displayed.

Correlation does not imply causation. Two completely unrelated random variables might display some correlation, but this does not imply any causation between the two (e.g., sunspot activity and events in the stock market are correlated, but there is no causation between the two).

There are two general types of correlations: parametric and nonparametric correlations. Pearson's correlation coefficient is the most common correlation measure and is usually referred to simply as the correlation coefficient. However, Pearson's correlation is a parametric measure, which means that it requires both correlated variables to have an underlying normal distribution and that the relationship between the variables is linear. When these conditions are violated, which is often the case in Monte Carlo simulation, the nonparametric counterparts become more important. Spearman's rank correlation and Kendall's tau are the two nonparametric alternatives. The Spearman correlation is most commonly used and is most appropriate when applied in the context of Monte Carlo simulation—there is no dependence on normal distributions or linearity, meaning that correlations between different variables with different distribution can be applied. In order to compute the Spearman correlation, first rank all the *x* and *y* variable values and then apply the Pearson's correlation computation.

In the case of Risk Simulator, the correlation used is the more robust nonparametric Spearman's rank correlation. However, to simplify the simulation process and to be consistent with Excel's correlation function, the correlation user inputs required are the Pearson's correlation coefficient. Risk Simulator will then apply its own algorithms to convert them into Spearman's rank correlation, thereby simplifying the process.

Applying Correlations in Risk Simulator

Correlations can be applied in Risk Simulator in several ways, as long as there is more than one simulation assumption:

- When defining assumptions, simply enter the correlations into the correlation grid in the Distribution Gallery.
- With existing data, run the Multi-Variable Distribution Fitting tool to perform distributional fitting and to obtain the correlation matrix between pairwise variables. If a simulation profile exists, the assumptions fitted will automatically contain the relevant correlation values.
- With the use of a direct-input correlation matrix, click on **Risk Simulator | Edit Correlations** to view and edit the correlation matrix used in the simulation.

Note that the correlation matrix must be positive definite. That is, the correlation must be mathematically valid. For instance, suppose you are trying to correlate three variables: grades of graduate students in a particular year, the number of beers they consume a week, and the number of hours they study a week. One would assume that the following correlation relationships exist:

Grades and Beer: −   *The more they drink, the lower the grades (no show on exams)*
Grades and Study: +   *The more they study, the higher the grades*
Beer and Study: −   *The more they drink, the less they study (drunk and partying all the time)*

However, if you input a negative correlation between Grades and Study and assume that the correlation coefficients have high magnitudes, the correlation matrix will be nonpositive definite. It would defy logic, correlation requirements, and matrix mathematics. However, smaller coefficients can sometimes still work even with the bad logic. When a nonpositive definite or bad correlation matrix is entered, Risk Simulator automatically informs you of the error and offers to adjust these correlations to something that is semipositive definite while still maintaining the overall structure of the correlation relationship (the same signs as well as the same relative strengths).

The Effects of Correlations in Monte Carlo Simulation

Although the computations required to correlate variables in a simulation are complex, the resulting effects are fairly clear. Figure 4-16 shows a simple correlation model (Correlation Risk Effects Model in the example folder). The calculation for revenue is simply price multiplied by quantity. The same model is replicated for no correlations, positive correlation (+0.9), and negative correlation (−0.9) between price and quantity.

The resulting statistics are shown in Figure 4-17. Notice that the standard deviation of the model without correlations is 0.1450, compared to 0.1886 for the positive cor-

Correlation Model

	Without Correlation	Positive Correlation	Negative Correlation
Price	$2.00	$2.00	$2.00
Quantity	1.00	1.00	1.00
Revenue	$2.00	$2.00	$2.00

Figure 4-16   Simple correlation model.

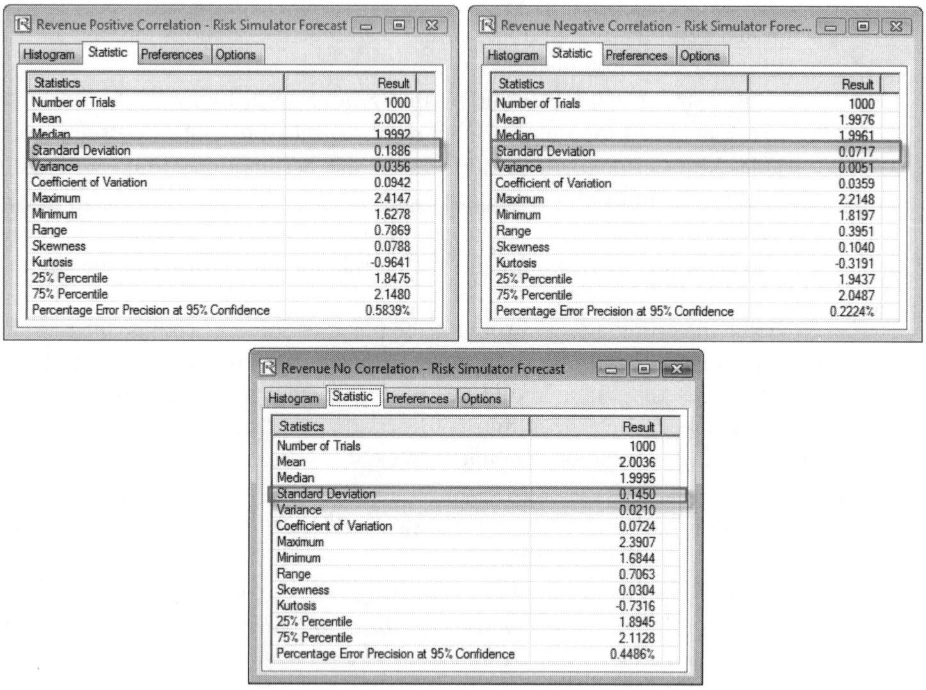

Revenue Positive Correlation - Risk Simulator Forecast

Histogram | Statistic | Preferences | Options

Statistics	Result
Number of Trials	1000
Mean	2.0020
Median	1.9992
Standard Deviation	0.1886
Variance	0.0356
Coefficient of Variation	0.0942
Maximum	2.4147
Minimum	1.6278
Range	0.7869
Skewness	0.0788
Kurtosis	-0.9641
25% Percentile	1.8475
75% Percentile	2.1480
Percentage Error Precision at 95% Confidence	0.5839%

Revenue Negative Correlation - Risk Simulator Forec...

Histogram | Statistic | Preferences | Options

Statistics	Result
Number of Trials	1000
Mean	1.9976
Median	1.9961
Standard Deviation	0.0717
Variance	0.0051
Coefficient of Variation	0.0359
Maximum	2.2148
Minimum	1.8197
Range	0.3951
Skewness	0.1040
Kurtosis	-0.3191
25% Percentile	1.9437
75% Percentile	2.0487
Percentage Error Precision at 95% Confidence	0.2224%

Revenue No Correlation - Risk Simulator Forecast

Histogram | Statistic | Preferences | Options

Statistics	Result
Number of Trials	1000
Mean	2.0036
Median	1.9995
Standard Deviation	0.1450
Variance	0.0210
Coefficient of Variation	0.0724
Maximum	2.3907
Minimum	1.6844
Range	0.7063
Skewness	0.0304
Kurtosis	-0.7316
25% Percentile	1.8945
75% Percentile	2.1128
Percentage Error Precision at 95% Confidence	0.4486%

Figure 4-17   Correlation results.

relation and 0.0717 for the negative correlation; that is, for simple models with positive relationships (e.g., additions and multiplications), negative correlations tend to reduce the average spread of the distribution and create a tighter and more concentrated forecast distribution as compared to positive correlations with larger average spreads. However, the mean remains relatively stable. This implies that correlations do little to change the expected value of projects but can reduce or increase a portfolio's risk. Recall in financial theory that negatively correlated variables, projects, or assets when combined in a portfolio tend to create a diversification effect where the overall risk is reduced. Therefore, we see a smaller standard deviation for the negatively correlated model.

In a positively related model (e.g., $A + B = C$ or $A \times B = C$), a negative correlation reduces the risk (standard deviation and all other second moments of the distribution) of the result (C), whereas a positive correlation between the inputs (A and B) will increase the overall risk. The opposite is true for a negatively related model (e.g., $A - B = C$ or $A/B = C$), where a positive correlation between the inputs will reduce the risk and a negative correlation increases the risk. In more complex models, as is

Spearman's Nonlinear Rank Correlation on Raw Data Extracted from Simulation

Price Negative Correlation	Quantity Negative Correlation	Correlation	Price Positive Correlation	Quantity Positive Correlation	Correlation
676	145	-0.90	102	158	0.89
368	452		461	515	
264	880		515	477	
235	877		874	833	
122	711		769	792	
490	641		481	471	
336	638		627	446	
495	383		82	190	
241	568		659	674	
651	571		188	286	
854	59		458	439	
66	950		981	972	
707	262		528	569	
943	186		865	812	

Figure 4-18 Correlations recovered.

often the case in real-life situations, the effects will be unknown *a priori* and can only be determined after a simulation is run.

Figure 4-18 illustrates the results after running a simulation, extracting the raw data of the assumptions, and computing the correlations between the variables. The figure shows that the input assumptions are recovered in the simulation; that is, you enter +0.9 and −0.9 correlations, and the resulting simulated values have the same correlations. Clearly, there will be minor differences from one simulation run to another, but when enough trials are run, the resulting recovered correlations approach those that were inputted. In order to obtain such accurate resulting correlations, some advanced algorithms employing multidimensional copulas were used. The specifics will not be discussed here as they are outside the scope of this chapter.

Tornado and Sensitivity Tools in Simulation

One of the powerful simulation tools, tornado analysis, captures the static impacts of each variable on the outcome of the model; that is, the tool automatically perturbs each variable in the model a preset amount, captures the fluctuation on the model's forecast or final result, and lists the resulting perturbations ranked from the most significant to the least. Figures 4-19 through 4-24 illustrate the application of a tornado analysis. For instance, Figure 4-19 is a sample discounted cash flow model where the input assumptions in the model are shown. The question is what are the critical success drivers that affect the model's output the most? That is, what really drives the net present value of $96.63, or which input variable impacts this value the most?

The tornado chart tool can be obtained through **Risk Simulator | Tools | Tornado Analysis**. To follow along the first example, open the **Tornado and Sensitivity Charts (Linear)** file in the examples folder (**Risk Simulator | Examples**). Figure 4-20 shows this sample model where cell G6 containing the net present value is chosen as the target result to be analyzed. The target cell's precedents in the model are used in creating the tornado chart. Precedents are all the input variables that affect the

Discounted Cash Flow Model

Base Year	2005	Sum PV Net Benefits	$1,896.63
Market Risk-Adjusted Discount Rate	15.00%	Sum PV Investments	$1,800.00
Private-Risk Discount Rate	5.00%	Net Present Value	$96.63
Annualized Sales Growth Rate	2.00%	Internal Rate of Return	18.80%
Price Erosion Rate	5.00%	Return on Investment	5.37%
Effective Tax Rate	40.00%		

	2005	2006	2007	2008	2009
Product A Avg Price/Unit	$10.00	$9.50	$9.03	$8.57	$8.15
Product B Avg Price/Unit	$12.25	$11.64	$11.06	$10.50	$9.98
Product C Avg Price/Unit	$15.15	$14.39	$13.67	$12.99	$12.34
Product A Sale Quantity ('000s)	50.00	51.00	52.02	53.06	54.12
Product B Sale Quantity ('000s)	35.00	35.70	36.41	37.14	37.89
Product C Sale Quantity ('000s)	20.00	20.40	20.81	21.22	21.65
Total Revenues	$1,231.75	$1,193.57	$1,156.57	$1,120.71	$1,085.97
Direct Cost of Goods Sold	$184.76	$179.03	$173.48	$168.11	$162.90
Gross Profit	$1,046.99	$1,014.53	$983.08	$952.60	$923.07
Operating Expenses	$157.50	$160.65	$163.86	$167.14	$170.48
Sales, General and Admin. Costs	$15.75	$16.07	$16.39	$16.71	$17.05
Operating Income (EBITDA)	$873.74	$837.82	$802.83	$768.75	$735.54
Depreciation	$10.00	$10.00	$10.00	$10.00	$10.00
Amortization	$3.00	$3.00	$3.00	$3.00	$3.00
EBIT	$860.74	$824.82	$789.83	$755.75	$722.54
Interest Payments	$2.00	$2.00	$2.00	$2.00	$2.00
EBT	$858.74	$822.82	$787.83	$753.75	$720.54
Taxes	$343.50	$329.13	$315.13	$301.50	$288.22
Net Income	$515.24	$493.69	$472.70	$452.25	$432.33
Noncash: Depreciation Amortization	$13.00	$13.00	$13.00	$13.00	$13.00
Noncash: Change in Net Working Capital	$0.00	$0.00	$0.00	$0.00	$0.00
Noncash: Capital Expenditures	$0.00	$0.00	$0.00	$0.00	$0.00
Free Cash Flow	$528.24	$506.69	$485.70	$465.25	$445.33
Investment Outlay	$1,800.00				

Financial Analysis

Present Value of Free Cash Flow	$528.24	$440.60	$367.26	$305.91	$254.62
Present Value of Investment Outlay	$1,800.00	$0.00	$0.00	$0.00	$0.00
Net Cash Flows	($1,271.76)	$506.69	$485.70	$465.25	$445.33

Figure 4-19   Sample discounted cash flow model.

outcome of the model. For instance, if the model consists of $A = B + C$, and where $C = D + E$, then B, D, and E are the precedents for A. (C is not a precedent inasmuch as it is only an intermediate calculated value.) Figure 4-20 also shows the testing range of each precedent variable used to estimate the target result. If the precedent variables are simple inputs, then the testing range will be a simple perturbation based on the range chosen (e.g., the default is ± 10% but can be changed). Each precedent variable can be perturbed at different percentages if required. A wider range is important because it is better able to test extreme values rather than smaller perturbations around the expected values. In certain circumstances, extreme values may have a larger, smaller, or unbalanced impact (e.g., nonlinearities may occur where increasing or decreasing economies of scale and scope creep in for

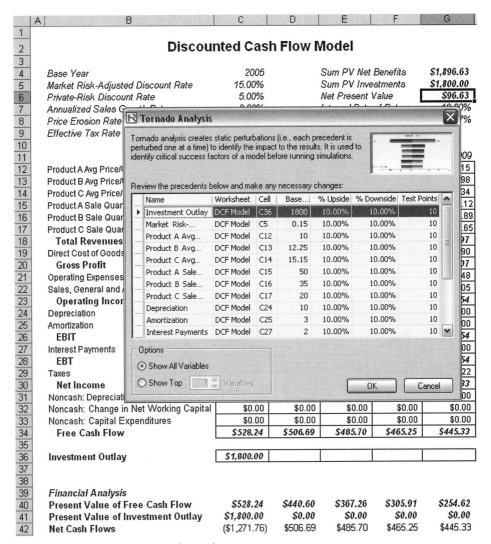

Figure 4-20   Running a tornado analysis.

larger or smaller values of a variable), and only a wider range will capture this non-linear impact.

Procedure

Use the following steps to create a tornado analysis:

- Select the single output cell (i.e., a cell with a function or equation) in an Excel model (e.g., cell G6 is selected in our example).
- Select **Risk Simulator | Tools | Tornado Analysis**.
- Review the precedents and rename them as appropriate (renaming the precedents to shorter names allows a more visually pleasing tornado and spider chart) and

click on **OK**. Alternatively, click on **Use Cell Address** to apply cell locations as the variable names.

Interpretation of Results

Figure 4-21 shows the resulting tornado analysis report, which indicates that capital investment has the largest impact on net present value (NPV), followed by tax rate, average sale price and quantity demanded of the product lines, and so forth. The report contains four distinct elements:

Tornado and Spider Charts

Statistical Summary

One of the powerful simulation tools is the tornado chart—it captures the static impacts of each variable on the outcome of the model. That is, the tool automatically perturbs each precedent variable in the model a user-specified preset amount, captures the fluctuation on the model's forecast or final result, and lists the resulting perturbations ranked from the most significant to the least. Precedents are all the input and intermediate variables that affect the outcome of the model. For instance, if the model consists of $A = B + C$, where $C = D + E$, then B, D, and E are the precedents for A (C is not a precedent as it is only an intermediate calculated value). The range and number of values perturbed is user-specified and can be set to test extreme values rather than smaller perturbations around the expected values. In certain circumstances, extreme values may have a larger, smaller, or unbalanced impact (e.g., nonlinearities may occur where increasing or decreasing economies of scale and scope creep occurs for larger or smaller values of a variable) and only a wider range will capture this nonlinear impact.

A tornado chart lists all the inputs that drive the model, starting from the input variable that has the most effect on the results. The chart is obtained by perturbing each precedent input at some consistent range (e.g.,±10% from the base case) one at a time, and comparing their results to the base case. A spider chart looks like a spider with a central body and its many legs protruding. The positively sloped lines indicate a positive relationship, while a negatively sloped line indicates a negative relationship. Further, spider charts can be used to visualize linear and nonlinear relationships. The tornado and spider charts help identify the critical success factors of an output cell in order to identify the inputs to simulate. The identified critical variables that are uncertain are the ones that should be simulated. Do not waste time simulating variables that are neither uncertain nor have little impact on the results.

Result

	Base Value: 96.6261638553219			Input Changes		
Precedent Cell	Output Downside	Output Upside	Effective Range	Input Downside	Input Upside	Base Case Value
Investment	$276.63	($83.37)	360.00	$1,620.00	$1,980.00	$1,800.00
Tax Rate	$219.73	($26.47)	246.20	36.00%	44.00%	40.00%
A Price	$3.43	$189.83	186.40	$9.00	$11.00	$10.00
B Price	$16.71	$176.55	159.84	$11.03	$13.48	$12.25
A Quantity	$23.18	$170.07	146.90	45.00	55.00	50.00
B Quantity	$30.53	$162.72	132.19	31.50	38.50	35.00
C Price	$40.15	$153.11	112.96	$13.64	$16.67	$15.15
C Quantity	$48.05	$145.20	97.16	18.00	22.00	20.00
Discount Rate	$138.24	$57.03	81.21	13.50%	16.50%	15.00%
Price Erosion	$116.80	$76.64	40.16	4.50%	5.50%	5.00%
Sales Growth	$90.59	$102.69	12.10	1.80%	2.20%	2.00%
Depreciation	$95.08	$98.17	3.08	$9.00	$11.00	$10.00
Interest	$97.09	$96.16	0.93	$1.80	$2.20	$2.00
Amortization	$96.16	$97.09	0.93	$2.70	$3.30	$3.00
Capex	$96.63	$96.63	0.00	$0.00	$0.00	$0.00
Net Capital	$96.63	$96.63	0.00	$0.00	$0.00	$0.00

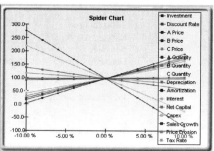

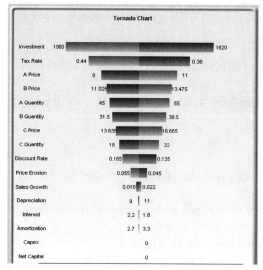

Figure 4-21   Tornado analysis report.

- Statistical summary listing the procedure performed.
- The Sensitivity table (Figure 4-22) shows the starting NPV base value of $96.63 and how each input is changed (e.g., Investment is changed from $1,800 to $1,980 on the upside with a +10% swing, and from $1,800 to $1,620 on the downside with a −10% swing). The resulting upside and downside values on NPV are −$83.37 and $276.63, with a total absolute value change of $360, making it the variable with the highest impact on NPV. The precedent variables are ranked from the highest impact to the lowest impact.
- The spider chart (Figure 4-23) illustrates these effects graphically. The y-axis is the NPV target value, whereas the x-axis depicts the percentage change on each of the precedent value (the central point is the base case value at $96.63 at 0% change from the base value of each precedent). Positively sloped lines indicate a

	Base Value: 96.6261638553219			Input Changes		
Precedent Cell	*Output Downside*	*Output Upside*	*Effective Range*	*Input Downside*	*Input Upside*	*Base Case Value*
Investment	$276.63	($83.37)	360.00	$1,620.00	$1,980.00	$1,800.00
Tax Rate	$219.73	($26.47)	246.20	36.00%	44.00%	40.00%
A Price	$3.43	$189.83	186.40	$9.00	$11.00	$10.00
B Price	$16.71	$176.55	159.84	$11.03	$13.48	$12.25
A Quantity	$23.18	$170.07	146.90	45.00	55.00	50.00
B Quantity	$30.53	$162.72	132.19	31.50	38.50	35.00
C Price	$40.15	$153.11	112.96	$13.64	$16.67	$15.15
C Quantity	$48.05	$145.20	97.16	18.00	22.00	20.00
Discount Rate	$138.24	$57.03	81.21	13.50%	16.50%	15.00%
Price Erosion	$116.80	$76.64	40.16	4.50%	5.50%	5.00%
Sales Growth	$90.59	$102.69	12.10	1.80%	2.20%	2.00%
Depreciation	$95.08	$98.17	3.08	$9.00	$11.00	$10.00
Interest	$97.09	$96.16	0.93	$1.80	$2.20	$2.00
Amortization	$96.16	$97.09	0.93	$2.70	$3.30	$3.00
Capex	$96.63	$96.63	0.00	$0.00	$0.00	$0.00
Net Capital	$96.63	$96.63	0.00	$0.00	$0.00	$0.00

Figure 4-22 Sensitivity table.

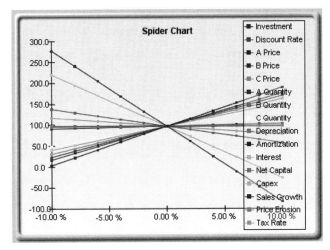

Figure 4-23 Spider chart.

positive relationship or effect, while negatively sloped lines indicate a negative relationship (e.g., investment is negatively sloped, which means that the higher the investment level, the lower the NPV, as discussed in the Sensitivity table above). The absolute value of the slope indicates the magnitude of the effect computed as the percentage change in the result given a percentage change in the precedent (a steep line indicates a higher impact on the NPV y-axis, given a change in the precedent x-axis).

● The tornado chart (Figure 4-24) illustrates the results in another graphical manner, where the highest impacting precedent is listed first. The x-axis is the NPV value, with the center of the chart being the base case condition. Green (lighter) bars in the chart indicate a positive effect, while red (darker) bars indicate a negative effect. Therefore, for investments, the red (darker) bar on the right side indicates a negative effect of investment on higher NPV—in other words, capital investment and NPV are negatively correlated. The opposite is true for price and quantity of products A to C (their green or lighter bars are on the right side of the chart).

Notes

Remember that tornado analysis is a *static* sensitivity analysis applied on each input variable in the model—that is, each variable is perturbed individually and the resulting effects are tabulated. This makes tornado analysis a key component to execute before

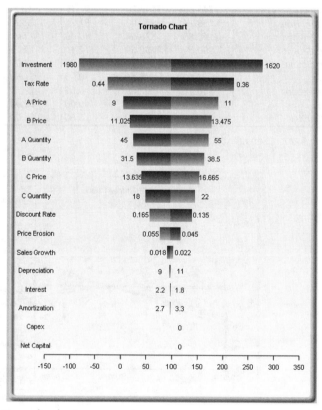

Figure 4-24 Tornado chart.

running a simulation. One of the very first steps in risk analysis is to capture and identify which are the most important impact drivers in the model. The next step is to identify which of these important impact drivers are uncertain. These uncertain impact drivers are the critical success drivers of a project, where the results of the model depend on these critical success drivers. These variables are the ones that should be simulated. Do not waste time simulating variables that are either uncertain or have little impact on the results. Tornado charts assist in identifying these critical success drivers quickly and easily. Following this example, price and quantity might have to be simulated, assuming that both the required investment and effective tax rate are known in advance and unchanging.

Although the tornado chart is easier to read, the spider chart is important in determining whether there are any nonlinearities in the model. For instance, Figure 4-25 shows another spider chart where nonlinearities are fairly evident (the lines on the graph are not straight but curved). The example model used is **Tornado and Sensitivity Charts (Nonlinear)**, which applies the Black-Scholes option pricing model. Such nonlinearities can also be ascertained from a tornado chart (the tornado chart will no longer be symmetrical) but can sometimes be more difficult to identify than using a spider chart. Nonlinearity may be important information in the model or provide decision makers important insight into the model's dynamics. For instance, in this Black-Scholes model, it is important to know that stock price and strike price are nonlinearly related to the option value. This characteristic implies that option value will not increase or decrease proportionally to the changes in stock or strike price, and that there might be some interactions between these two prices as well as other variables. As another example, an engineering model depicting nonlinearities might indicate that a particular part or component, when subjected to a high enough force or tension, will break. Clearly, it is important to understand such nonlinearities.

Sensitivity Analysis

A related feature is sensitivity analysis. Whereas tornado analysis (tornado charts and spider charts) applies static perturbations *before* a simulation run, sensitivity analysis

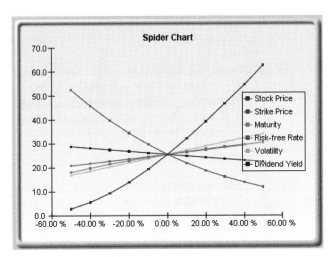

Figure 4-25   Nonlinear spider chart.

applies dynamic perturbations created *after* the simulation run. Tornado and spider charts are the results of static perturbations, meaning that each precedent or assumption variable is perturbed a preset amount one at a time, and the fluctuations in the results are tabulated. In contrast, sensitivity charts are the results of dynamic perturbations in the sense that multiple assumptions are perturbed simultaneously and their interactions in the model and correlations among variables are captured in the fluctuations of the results. Tornado charts therefore identify which variables drive the results the most and hence are suitable for simulation, whereas sensitivity charts identify the impact to the results when multiple interacting variables are simulated together in the model. This effect is clearly illustrated in Figure 4-26. Notice that the ranking of critical success drivers is similar to the tornado chart in the previous examples. However, if correlations are added between the assumptions, Figure 4-27 shows a very different picture. Notice, for instance, that price erosion had little impact on NPV, but when some of the input assumptions are correlated, the interaction that exists between these correlated variables increases the impact of price erosion. Note that tornado analysis cannot capture these correlated dynamic relationships. Only after a simulation is run will such relationships become evident in a sensitivity analysis. A tornado chart's presimulation critical success factors will therefore sometimes be different from a

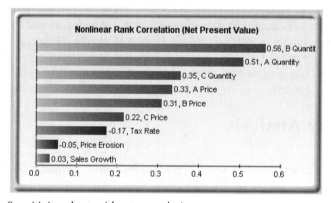

Figure 4-26   Sensitivity chart without correlations.

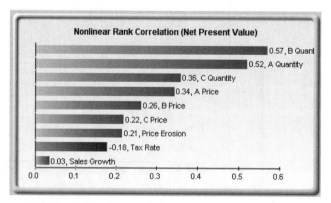

Figure 4-27   Sensitivity chart with correlations.

sensitivity chart's postsimulation critical success factor. The postsimulation critical success factors should be the ones that are of interest as these more readily capture the model precedents' interactions. Another difference is that tornado analysis is run before a simulation and tests all precedent variables, whereas sensitivity is a dynamic simultaneous analysis and is performed after a simulation, and only variables set as simulation assumptions can be tested, not all precedent variables.

Procedure

Use the following steps to create a sensitivity analysis:

- Open or create a model, define assumptions and forecasts, and run the simulation; the example here uses the Tornado and Sensitivity Charts (Linear) file.
- Select **Risk Simulator | Tools | Sensitivity Analysis**.
- Select the forecast of choice to analyze and click on **OK** (Figure 4-28).

Note that sensitivity analysis cannot be run unless assumptions and forecasts have been defined and a simulation has been run.

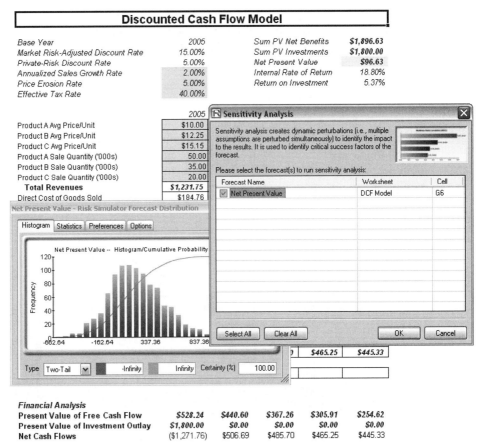

Figure 4-28   Running sensitivity analysis.

Interpretation of Results

The results of the sensitivity analysis comprise a report and two key charts. The first is a nonlinear rank correlation chart (Figure 4-29) that ranks the assumption-forecast correlation pairs from highest to lowest. These correlations are nonlinear and nonparametric, making them free of any distributional requirements (i.e., an assumption with a Weibull distribution can be compared to another with a beta distribution). The results from this chart are fairly similar to that of the tornado analysis seen previously (of course, without the capital investment value, which we decided was a known value and hence was not simulated), with one special exception. Tax rate was relegated to a much lower position in the sensitivity analysis chart (Figure 4-29) as compared to the tornado chart (Figure 4-24). This is because by itself, tax rate will have a significant impact, but once the other variables are interacting in the model, it appears that tax rate has less of a dominant effect. (This is because tax rate has a smaller distribution as historical tax rates tend not to fluctuate too much, and also because tax rate is a straight percentage value of the income before taxes, where other precedent variables have a larger effect on NPV.) This example proves that it is important to perform sensitivity analysis after a simulation run in order to ascertain if there are any interactions in the model and if the effects of certain variables still hold. The second chart (Figure 4-30) illustrates the percentage variation explained; that is, of the fluctuations in the forecast, how much of the variation can be explained by each of the assumptions after accounting for all the interactions among variables? Notice that the sum of all variations explained is usually close to 100 percent (sometimes other elements impact the model but they cannot be captured here directly), and if correlations exist, the sum may sometimes exceed 100 percent (due to the interaction effects that are cumulative).

Notes

Tornado analysis is performed before a simulation run, whereas sensitivity analysis is performed after a simulation run. Spider charts in tornado analysis can consider nonlinearities while rank correlation charts in sensitivity analysis can account for nonlinear and distribution-free conditions.

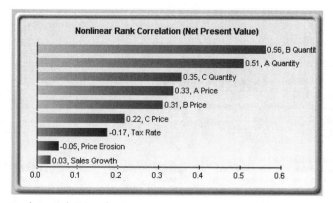

Figure 4-29 Rank correlation chart.

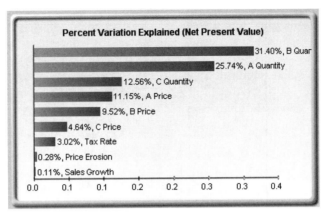

Figure 4-30 Contribution to variance chart.

Distributional Fitting: Single Variable and Multiple Variables

Another powerful simulation tool is distributional fitting; that is, which distribution does an analyst or engineer use for a particular input variable in a model? What are the relevant distributional parameters? If no historical data exist, then the analyst must make assumptions about the variables in question. One approach is to use the Delphi method where a group of experts are tasked with estimating the behavior of each variable. For instance, a group of mechanical engineers can be tasked with evaluating the extreme possibilities of a spring coil's diameter through rigorous experimentation or guesstimates. In this case, you can use the **Custom Distribution**, that is, a non-parametric simulation using the actual raw data as the simulation parameters (see the Risk Simulator user manual for details on creating and simulating this distribution). These values can be used as the variable's input parameters (e.g., uniform distribution with extreme values between 0.5 and 1.2). When testing is not possible (e.g., market share and revenue growth rate), management can still make estimates of potential outcomes and provide the best-case, most-likely case, and worst-case scenarios, whereupon a triangular or custom distribution can be created.

If reliable historical data are available, however, distributional fitting can be accomplished. Assuming that historical patterns hold and that history tends to repeat itself, then historical data can be used to find the best-fitting distribution with their relevant parameters to better define the variables to be simulated. Figures 4-31 through 4-33 illustrate a distributional-fitting example. The following illustration uses the *Data Fitting* file in the examples folder.

Procedure

Use the following steps to perform a distributional fitting model:

- Open a spreadsheet with existing data for fitting (e.g., use the Data Fitting example file).
- Select the data you wish to fit, not including the variable name (data should be in a single column with multiple rows).
- Select **Risk Simulator | Tools | Distributional Fitting (Single-Variable)**.

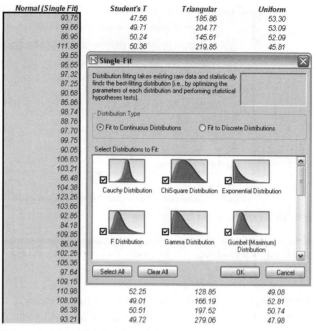

Normal (Single Fit)	Student's T	Triangular	Uniform
93.75	47.56	185.86	53.30
99.66	49.71	204.77	53.09
86.95	50.24	145.61	52.09
111.86	50.36	219.85	45.81
99.55			
95.55			
97.32			
87.25			
90.68			
85.86			
98.74			
88.76			
97.70			
99.75			
90.05			
106.63			
103.21			
66.48			
104.38			
123.26			
103.65			
92.85			
84.18			
109.85			
86.04			
102.26			
105.36			
97.64			
109.15			
110.98	52.25	128.85	49.08
108.09	49.01	166.19	52.81
95.38	50.51	197.52	50.74
93.21	49.72	279.06	47.98

Figure 4-31   Single variable distributional fitting.

- Select the specific distributions you wish to fit to or keep the default where all distributions are selected and click on **OK** (Figure 4-31).
- Review the results of the fit, choose the relevant distribution you want, and click on **OK** (Figure 4-32).

Interpretation of Results

The null hypothesis (H_o) being tested is such that the fitted distribution is the same distribution as the population from which the sample data to be fitted comes. Thus, if the computed p-value is lower than a critical alpha level (typically 0.10 or 0.05), then the distribution is the wrong distribution. Conversely, the *higher the p-value, the better the distribution fits the data.* Roughly, you can think of p-value as a *percentage explained;* that is, if the p-value is 1.00 rounded (Figure 4-32), then setting a normal distribution with a mean of 100.67 and a standard deviation of 10.40 explains close to about 100 percent of the variation in the data, indicating an especially good fit. The data were from a 1,000-trial simulation in Risk Simulator based on a normal distribution with a mean of 100 and a standard deviation of 10. Because only 1,000 trials were simulated, the resulting distribution is fairly close to the specified distributional parameters, and in this case, about a 99.99 percent precision.

Both the results (Figure 4-32) and the report (Figure 4-33) show the test statistic, p-value, theoretical statistics (based on the selected distribution), empirical statistics (based on the raw data), the original data (to maintain a record of the data used), and the assumption complete with the relevant distributional parameters (i.e., if you selected the option to automatically generate assumption and if a simulation profile already exists). The results also rank all the selected distributions and how well they fit the data.

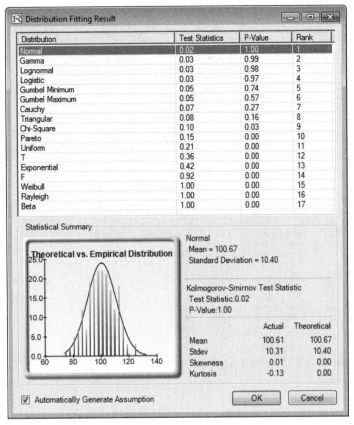

Figure 4-32   Distributional fitting result.

Bootstrap Simulation

Bootstrap simulation is a simple technique that estimates the reliability or accuracy of forecast statistics or other sample raw data. It can be used to answer a lot of confidence and precision-based questions in simulation. For instance, if an identical model (with identical assumptions and forecasts but without any random seeds) is run by 100 different people, the results will clearly be slightly different. The question is, if we collected all the statistics from these 100 people, how would the mean be distributed, or the median, or the skewness, or excess kurtosis? Suppose one person has a mean value of say, 1.50 and another 1.52. Are these two values statistically significantly different from one another, or are they statistically similar and the slight difference is due entirely to random chance? What about 1.53? So, how far is far enough to say that the values are statistically different? In addition, if a model's resulting skewness is −0.19, is this forecast distribution negatively skewed, or is it statistically close enough to zero to state that this distribution is symmetrical and not skewed? Thus, if we bootstrapped this forecast 100 times, that is, ran a 1,000-trial simulation for 100 times and collected the 100 skewness coefficients, the skewness distribution would indicate how far zero is away from −0.19. If the 90% confidence on the bootstrapped skewness distribution contains the value zero, then we can state

Statistical Summary

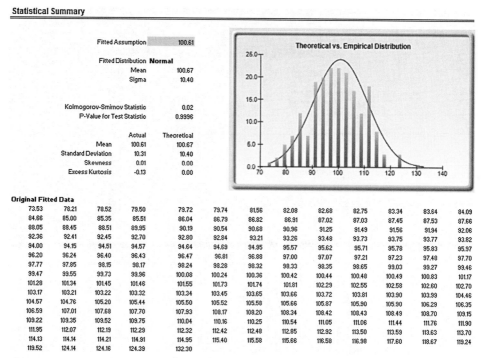

Original Fitted Data

73.53	78.21	78.52	79.50	79.72	79.74	81.56	82.08	82.68	82.75	83.34	83.64	84.09
84.66	85.00	85.35	85.51	86.04	86.79	86.82	86.91	87.02	87.03	87.45	87.53	87.66
88.05	88.45	88.51	89.95	90.19	90.54	90.68	90.96	91.25	91.49	91.56	91.94	92.06
92.36	92.41	92.45	92.70	92.80	92.84	93.21	93.26	93.48	93.73	93.75	93.77	93.82
94.00	94.15	94.51	94.57	94.64	94.69	94.95	95.57	95.62	95.71	95.78	95.83	95.97
96.20	96.24	96.40	96.43	96.47	96.81	96.88	97.00	97.07	97.21	97.23	97.48	97.70
97.77	97.85	98.15	98.17	98.24	98.28	98.32	98.33	98.35	98.65	99.03	99.27	99.46
99.47	99.55	99.73	99.96	100.08	100.24	100.36	100.42	100.44	100.48	100.49	100.83	101.17
101.28	101.34	101.45	101.46	101.55	101.73	101.74	101.81	102.29	102.55	102.58	102.60	102.70
103.17	103.21	103.22	103.32	103.34	103.45	103.65	103.66	103.72	103.81	103.90	103.99	104.46
104.57	104.76	105.20	105.44	105.50	105.52	105.58	105.66	105.87	105.90	105.90	106.29	106.35
106.59	107.01	107.68	107.70	107.93	108.17	108.20	108.34	108.42	108.43	108.49	108.70	109.15
109.22	109.35	109.52	109.75	110.04	110.16	110.25	110.54	111.05	111.06	111.44	111.76	111.90
111.95	112.07	112.19	112.29	112.32	112.42	112.48	112.85	112.92	113.50	113.59	113.63	113.70
114.13	114.14	114.21	114.91	114.95	115.40	115.58	115.66	116.58	116.98	117.60	118.67	119.24
119.52	124.14	124.16	124.39	132.30								

Figure 4-33   Distributional fitting report.

that on a 90% confidence level, this distribution is symmetrical and not skewed, and the value −0.19 is statistically close enough to zero (i.e., if the bootstrapped skewness distribution's 90% confidence interval is between −0.3 and +0.3, the value zero falls inside this interval, and we can state that there is no statistically significant skew). Otherwise, if zero falls outside of this 90% confidence area, then this distribution is negatively skewed. The same analysis can be applied to excess kurtosis and other statistics.

Essentially, bootstrap simulation is an empirical hypothesis testing tool. Classical methods used in the past relied on mathematical formulas to describe the accuracy of sample statistics by employing theoretical hypothesis tests. These methods assume that the distribution of a sample statistic approaches a normal distribution (a theoretical assumption), making the calculation of the statistic's standard error or confidence interval relatively easy. However, when a statistic's sampling distribution is not normally distributed or easily found, these classical methods are difficult to use (e.g., we do not know what distribution these 100 skewness coefficients follow). In contrast, bootstrapping analyzes sample statistics empirically by repeatedly sampling the data and creating distributions of the different statistics from each sampling. The classical methods of hypothesis testing are also available in Risk Simulator and are explained in the next section. Classical methods provide higher power in their tests but rely on normality assumptions and can only be used to test the mean and variance of a distribution, as compared to bootstrap simulation, which provides lower power but is nonparametric and distribution-free, and can be used to test any distributional statistic.

Procedure

- Run a simulation with assumptions and forecasts.
- Select **Risk Simulator | Tools | Nonparametric Bootstrap**.
- Select only *one* forecast to bootstrap, select the statistic(s) to bootstrap, and enter the number of bootstrap trials and click on **OK** (Figure 4-34).

Interpretation of Results

Figure 4-35 illustrates some sample bootstrap results. The example file used was *Hypothesis Testing and Bootstrap Simulation*. For instance, the 90 percent confidence for the skewness statistic is between −0.0189 and 0.0952, such that the value 0 falls within this confidence, indicating that on a 90 percent confidence, the skewness of this forecast is not statistically significantly different from zero, or that this distribution can be considered as symmetrical and not skewed. Conversely, if the value 0 falls outside of this confidence, then the opposite is true: the distribution is skewed (positively skewed if the forecast statistic is positive, and negatively skewed if the forecast statistic is negative).

Notes

The term *bootstrap* comes from the saying, "to pull oneself up by one's own bootstraps," and is applicable because this method uses the distribution of statistics themselves to analyze the statistics' accuracy. Nonparametric simulation is simply randomly

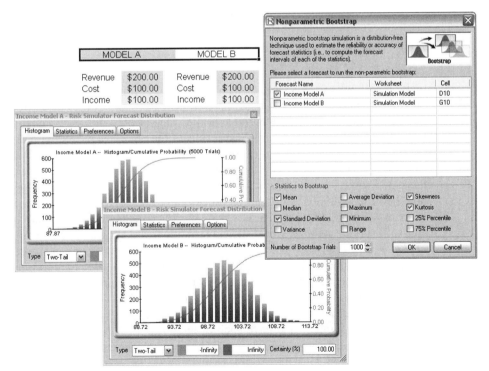

Figure 4-34 Nonparametric bootstrap simulation.

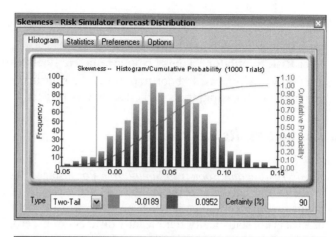

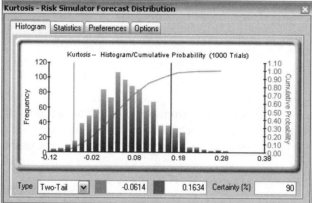

Figure 4-35 Bootstrap simulation results.

picking golf balls from a large basket with replacement where each golf ball is based on a historical data point. Suppose there are 365 golf balls in the basket (representing 365 historical data points). Imagine that the value of each golf ball picked at random is written on a large whiteboard. The results of the 365 balls picked with replacement are written in the first column of the board with 365 rows of numbers. Relevant statistics (e.g., mean, median, mode, standard deviation, and so forth) are calculated on these 365 rows. The process is then repeated, say, 5,000 times. The whiteboard will now be filled with 365 rows and 5,000 columns. Hence, 5,000 sets of statistics (that is, there will be 5,000 means, 5,000 medians, 5,000 modes, 5,000 standard deviations, and so forth) are tabulated, and their distributions are shown. The relevant *statistics of the statistics* are then tabulated, where from these results one can ascertain how confident the simulated statistics are. Finally, bootstrap results are important because according to the *Law of Large Numbers* and *Central Limit Theorem* in statistics, the mean of the sample means is an unbiased estimator and approaches the true population mean when the sample size increases. Another way to look at it is that you call up your 5,000 best friends and have each of them run the same simulation, then collect the statistics (mean, standard deviation, skewness coefficient, and kurtosis) from each of them, and you plot the results to determine the confidence intervals of each statistic.

Hypothesis Testing

A hypothesis test is performed when the means and variances of two distributions are tested to determine if they are statistically identical or statistically different from one another—that is, to see if the differences between the means and variances of two different forecasts that occur are based on random chance or if they are, in fact, statistically significantly different from one another.

This analysis is related to bootstrap simulation with several differences. Classical hypothesis testing uses mathematical models and is based on theoretical distributions. This means that the precision and power of the test are higher than bootstrap simulation's empirically based method of simulating a simulation and letting the data tell the story. However, the classical hypothesis test is only applicable for testing two distributions' means and variances (and by extension, standard deviations) to see if they are statistically identical or different. In contrast, nonparametric bootstrap simulation can be used to test for any distributional statistics, making it more useful, but the drawback is its lower testing power. Risk Simulator provides both techniques from which to choose.

Procedure

- Run a simulation.
- Select **Risk Simulator | Tools | Hypothesis Testing**.
- Select the two forecasts to test, select the type of hypothesis test you wish to run, and click on **OK** (Figure 4-36).

Interpretation of Results

A two-tailed hypothesis test is performed on the null hypothesis (H_o) such that the population means of the two variables are statistically identical to one another. The alternative hypothesis (H_a) is such that the population means are statistically different

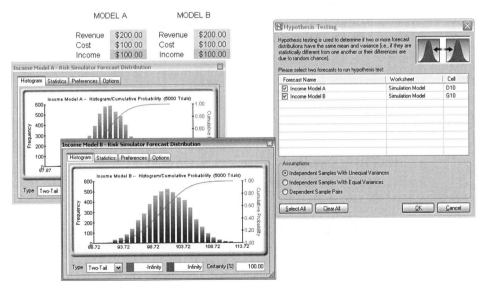

Figure 4-36 Hypothesis testing.

from one another. If the calculated p-values are less than or equal to 0.01, 0.05, or 0.10 alpha test levels, it means that the null hypothesis is rejected, which implies that the forecast means are statistically significantly different at the 1, 5, and 10 percent significance levels. If the null hypothesis is not rejected when the p-values are high, the means of the two forecast distributions are statistically similar to one another. The same analysis is performed on variances of two forecasts at a time using the pairwise F-test. If the p-values are small, then the variances (and standard deviations) are statistically different from one another; otherwise, for large p-values, the variances are statistically identical to one another. The example file used was *Hypothesis Testing and Bootstrap Simulation.* Note that the Modeling Toolkit software has multiple hypothesis test routines (e.g., analysis of variance or ANOVA, single and paired t-tests, F-tests, and nonparametric tests such as the chi-square test, Lilliefor's test, Friedman's test, and many more).

Notes

The two-variable *t*-test with unequal variances (the population variance of forecast 1 is expected to be different from the population variance of forecast 2) is appropriate when the forecast distributions are from different populations (e.g., data collected from two different geographical locations, or two different operating business units, and so forth). The two-variable *t*-test with equal variances (the population variance of forecast 1 is expected to be equal to the population variance of forecast 2) is appropriate when the forecast distributions are from similar populations (e.g., data collected from two different engine designs with similar specifications, and so forth). The paired dependent two-variable *t*-test is appropriate when the forecast distributions are from exactly the same population and subjects (e.g., data collected from the same group of patients before an experimental drug was used and after the drug was applied, and so forth).

Data Extraction, Saving Simulation Results, and Generating Reports

A simulation's raw data can be very easily extracted using Risk Simulator's *Data Extraction* routine. Both assumptions and forecasts can be extracted, but a simulation must first be run. The extracted data can then be used for a variety of other analyses, and the data can be extracted to different formats—-for use in spreadsheets, databases, and other software products.

Procedure

- Open or create a model, define assumptions and forecasts, and run the simulation.
- Select **Risk Simulator | Tools | Data Extraction**.
- Select the assumptions and/or forecasts you wish to extract the data from and click on **OK.**

The simulated data can be extracted to an Excel worksheet, a flat text file (for easy import into other software applications), or as risksim files (which can be reopened as Risk Simulator forecast charts at a later date). Finally, you can create a simulation report of all the assumptions and forecasts in the model by going to **Risk Simulator | Create Report**.

Regression and Forecasting Diagnostic Tool

This advanced analytical tool in Risk Simulator is used to determine the econometric properties of your data. The diagnostics include checking the data for heteroskedasticity, nonlinearity, outliers, specification errors, micronumerosity, stationarity and stochastic properties, normality and sphericity of the errors, and multicollinearity. Each test is described in more detail in their respective reports in the model.

Procedure

To run the analysis follow these instructions:

1. Open the example model (**Risk Simulator | Examples | Regression Diagnostics**) and go to the *Time-Series Data* worksheet and select the data including the variable names (cells **C5 : H55**).
2. Click on **Risk Simulator | Tools | Diagnostic Tool**.
3. Check the data and select the *Dependent Variable Y* from the drop down menu. Click **OK** when finished (Figure 4-37).

Spend some time reading through the reports generated from this diagnostic tool.

A common violation in forecasting and regression analysis is heteroskedasticity; that is, the variance of the errors increases over time (see Figure 4-38 for test results using the diagnostic tool). Visually, the width of the vertical data fluctuations increases or fans out over time, and typically, the coefficient of determination (R-squared coef-

Multiple Regression Analysis Data Set

Dependent Variable Y	Variable X1	Variable X2	Variable X3	Variable X4	Variable X5
521	18308	185	4.041	79.6	7.2
367	1148	600	0.55	1	8.5
443	18068	372	3.665	32.3	5.7
365	7729				
614	100484				
385	16728				
286	14630				
397	4008				
764	38927				
427	22322				
153	3711				
231	3136				
524	50508				
328	28886				
240	16996				
286	13035				
285	12973				
569	16309				
96	5227				
498	19235				
481	44487				
468	44213				
177	23619				
198	9106	134	2.573	54.9	8.6
458	24917	189	5.117	74.3	6.6
108	3872	196	0.799	5.5	6.9
246	8945	183	1.578	20.5	2.7
291	2373	417	1.202	10.9	5.5
68	7128	233	1.109	123.7	7.2

Diagnostic Tool

This tool is used to diagnose forecasting problems in a set of multiple variables.

Dependent Variable   Dependent Variable Y

Dependent Variable Y	Variable X1	Variable X2	Variable X3	Variab
521	18308	185	4.041	79.6
367	1148	600	0.55	1
443	18068	372	3.665	32.3
365	7729	142	2.351	45.1
614	100484	432	29.76	190.8
385	16728	290	3.294	31.8
286	14630	346	3.287	678.4
397	4008	328	0.666	340.8
764	38927	354	12.938	239.6
427	22322	266	6.478	111.9

OK   Cancel

Figure 4-37   Running the data diagnostic tool.

Diagnostic Results

Variable	Heteroskedasticity		Micronumerosity	Outliers			Nonlinearity	
	W-Test p-value	Hypothesis Test result	Approximation result	Natural Lower Bound	Natural Upper Bound	Number of Potential Outliers	Nonlinear Test p-value	Hypothesis Test result
Y			no problems	-7.86	671.70	2		
Variable X1	0.2543	Homoskedastic	no problems	-21377.95	64713.03	3	0.2458	linear
Variable X2	0.3371	Homoskedastic	no problems	77.47	445.93	2	0.0335	nonlinear
Variable X3	0.3649	Homoskedastic	no problems	-5.77	15.69	3	0.0305	nonlinear
Variable X4	0.3066	Homoskedastic	no problems	-295.96	628.21	4	0.9298	linear
Variable X5	0.2495	Homoskedastic	no problems	3.35	9.38	3	0.2727	linear

Figure 4-38 Results from tests of outliers, heteroskedasticity, micronumerosity, and nonlinearity.

ficient) drops significantly when heteroskedasticity exists. If the variance of the dependent variable is not constant, then the error's variance will not be constant. Unless the heteroskedasticity of the dependent variable is pronounced, its effect will not be severe: the least squares estimates will still be unbiased, and the estimates of the slope and intercept will either be normally distributed if the errors are normally distributed, or at least normally distributed asymptotically (as the number of data points becomes large) if the errors are not normally distributed. The estimate for the variance of the slope and overall variance will be inaccurate, but the inaccuracy is not likely to be substantial if the independent-variable values are symmetric about their mean.

If the number of data points is small (micronumerosity), it may be difficult to detect assumption violations. With small sample sizes, assumption violations such as non-normality or heteroskedasticity of variances are difficult to detect even when they are present. With a small number of data points, linear regression offers less protection against violation of assumptions. With few data points, it may be hard to determine how well the fitted line matches the data, or whether a nonlinear function would be more appropriate. Even if none of the test assumptions are violated, a linear regression on a small number of data points may not have sufficient power to detect a significant difference between the slope and zero, even if the slope is nonzero. The power depends on the residual error, the observed variation in the independent variable, the selected significance alpha level of the test, and the number of data points. Power decreases as the residual variance increases, decreases as the significance level is decreased (i.e., as the test is made more stringent), increases as the variation in observed independent variable increases, and increases as the number of data points increases.

Values may not be identically distributed because of the presence of outliers. Outliers are anomalous values in the data. Outliers may have a strong influence over the fitted slope and intercept, giving a poor fit to the bulk of the data points. Outliers tend to increase the estimate of residual variance, lowering the chance of rejecting the null hypothesis, that is, creating higher prediction errors. They may be due to recording errors, which may be correctible, or they may be due to the dependent-variable values not all being sampled from the same population. Apparent outliers may also be due to the dependent-variable values being from the same, but nonnormal, population. However, a point may be an unusual value in either an independent or dependent variable without necessarily being an outlier in the scatter plot. In regression analysis, the fitted line can be highly sensitive to outliers. In other words, least squares regression is not resistant to outliers; thus, neither is the fitted-slope estimate. A point vertically removed from the other points can cause the fitted line to pass close to it, instead of following the general linear trend of the rest of the data, especially if the point is relatively far horizontally from the center of the data. However, great care should be taken when deciding if the outliers should be removed. Although in most cases when outliers are removed, the regression results look better, a priori justification must first exist. For instance, if one is regressing the performance of a particular firm's stock returns, outliers caused by downturns in the stock market should be included; these are not truly outliers as they are inevitabilities in the business cycle. Forgoing these outliers and using the regression equation to forecast one's retirement fund based on the firm's stocks will yield incorrect results at best. In contrast, suppose the outliers are caused by a single nonrecurring business condition (e.g., merger and acquisition) and such business structural changes are not forecast to recur, then these outliers should be removed and the data cleansed prior to running a regression analysis. The analysis here only identifies outliers, and it is up to the user to determine if they should remain or be excluded.

Sometimes, a nonlinear relationship between the dependent and independent variables is more appropriate than a linear relationship. In such cases, running a linear regression will not be optimal. If the linear model is not the correct form, then the slope and intercept estimates and the fitted values from the linear regression will be biased, and the fitted slope and intercept estimates will not be meaningful. Over a restricted range of independent or dependent variables, nonlinear models may be well approximated by linear models (this is in fact the basis of linear interpolation), but for accurate prediction a model appropriate to the data should be selected. A nonlinear transformation should first be applied to the data before running a regression. One simple approach is to take the natural logarithm of the independent variable (other approaches include taking the square root or raising the independent variable to the second or third power) and run a regression or forecast using the nonlinearly-transformed data.

Another typical issue when forecasting time-series data is whether the independent-variable values are truly independent of each other or are they dependent. Dependent variable values collected over a time series may be autocorrelated. For serially correlated dependent-variable values, the estimates of the slope and intercept will be unbiased, but the estimates of their forecast and variances will not be reliable, and hence the validity of certain statistical goodness-of-fit tests will be flawed. For instance, interest rates, inflation rates, sales revenues, and many other time-series data are typically autocorrelated, where the value in the current period is related to the value in a previous period, and so forth (clearly, the inflation rate in March is related to February's level, which in turn, is related to January's level, and so forth). Ignoring such blatant relationships will yield biased and less accurate forecasts. In such events, an autocorrelated regression model or an ARIMA model may be better suited (**Risk Simulator | Forecasting | ARIMA**). Finally, the autocorrelation functions of a series that is nonstationary tend to decay slowly (see Nonstationary report in the model). If autocorrelation $AC(1)$ is nonzero, it means that the series is first order serially correlated. If $AC(k)$ dies off more or less geometrically with increasing lag, it implies that the series follows a low-order autoregressive process. If $AC(k)$ drops to zero after a small number of lags, it implies that the series follows a low-order moving-average process. Partial correlation $PAC(k)$ measures the correlation of values that are k periods apart after removing the correlation from the intervening lags. If the pattern of autocorrelation can be captured by an autoregression of order less than k, then the partial autocorrelation at lag k will be close to zero. Ljung-Box Q-statistics and their p-values at lag k has the null hypothesis that there is no autocorrelation up to order k. The dotted lines in the plots of the autocorrelations are the approximate two standard error bounds. If the autocorrelation is within these bounds, it is not significantly different from zero at the 5 percent significance level. Autocorrelation measures the relationship to the past of the dependent Y variable to itself. Distributive Lags, in contrast, are time-lag relationships between the dependent Y variable and different independent X variables. For instance, the movement and direction of mortgage rates tend to follow the Federal Funds Rate but at a time lag (typically 1 to 3 months). Sometimes, time lags follow cycles and seasonality (e.g., ice cream sales tend to peak during the summer months and are hence related to last summer's sales, 12 months in the past). The distributive lag analysis (Figure 4-39) shows how the dependent variable is related to each of the independent variables at various time lags, when all lags are considered simultaneously, to determine which time lags are statistically significant and should be considered.

Another requirement in running a regression model is the assumption of normality and sphericity of the error term. If the assumption of normality is violated or outliers are present, then the linear regression goodness-of-fit test may not be the most powerful or informative test available, and this could mean the difference between detecting a linear fit or not. If the errors are not independent and not normally distributed, it may indicate that the data might be autocorrelated or suffer from nonlinearities or other more destructive errors. Independence of the errors can also be detected in the heteroskedasticity tests (Figure 4-40).

The Normality test on the errors performed is a nonparametric test, which makes no assumptions about the specific shape of the population from which the sample is drawn, allowing for smaller sample datasets to be analyzed. This test evaluates the null hypothesis of whether the sample errors were drawn from a normally distributed population, versus an alternative hypothesis that the data sample is not normally distributed. If the calculated D-Statistic is greater than or equal to the D-Critical values

Autocorrelation

Time Lag	AC	PAC	Lower Bound	Upper Bound	Q-Stat	Prob
1	0.0580	0.0580	-0.2828	0.2828	0.1786	0.6726
2	-0.1213	-0.1251	-0.2828	0.2828	0.9754	0.6140
3	0.0590	0.0756	-0.2828	0.2828	1.1679	0.7607
4	0.2423	0.2232	-0.2828	0.2828	4.4865	0.3442
5	0.0067	-0.0078	-0.2828	0.2828	4.4890	0.4814
6	-0.2654	-0.2345	-0.2828	0.2828	8.6516	0.1941
7	0.0814	0.0939	-0.2828	0.2828	9.0524	0.2489
8	0.0634	-0.0442	-0.2828	0.2828	9.3012	0.3175
9	0.0204	0.0673	-0.2828	0.2828	9.3276	0.4076
10	-0.0190	0.0865	-0.2828	0.2828	9.3512	0.4991
11	0.1035	0.0790	-0.2828	0.2828	10.0648	0.5246
12	0.1658	0.0978	-0.2828	0.2828	11.9466	0.4500
13	-0.0524	-0.0430	-0.2828	0.2828	12.1394	0.5182
14	-0.2050	-0.2523	-0.2828	0.2828	15.1738	0.3664
15	0.1782	0.2089	-0.2828	0.2828	17.5315	0.2891
16	-0.1022	-0.2591	-0.2828	0.2828	18.3296	0.3050
17	-0.0861	0.0808	-0.2828	0.2828	18.9141	0.3335
18	0.0418	0.1987	-0.2828	0.2828	19.0559	0.3884
19	0.0869	-0.0821	-0.2828	0.2828	19.6894	0.4135
20	-0.0091	-0.0269	-0.2828	0.2828	19.6966	0.4770

Distributive Lags

P-Values of Distributive Lag Periods of Each Independent Variable

Variable	1	2	3	4	5	6	7	8	9	10	11	12
X1	0.8467	0.2045	0.3336	0.9105	0.9757	0.1020	0.9205	0.1267	0.5431	0.9110	0.7495	0.4016
X2	0.6077	0.9900	0.8422	0.2851	0.0638	0.0032	0.8007	0.1551	0.4823	0.1126	0.0519	0.4383
X3	0.7394	0.2396	0.2741	0.8372	0.9808	0.0464	0.8355	0.0545	0.6828	0.7354	0.5093	0.3500
X4	0.0061	0.6739	0.7932	0.7719	0.6748	0.8627	0.5586	0.9046	0.5726	0.6304	0.4812	0.5707
X5	0.1591	0.2032	0.4123	0.5599	0.6416	0.3447	0.9190	0.9740	0.5185	0.2856	0.1489	0.7794

Figure 4-39 Autocorrelation and distributive lag results.

Test Result

		Errors	Relative Frequency	Observed	Expected	O-E
Regression Error Average	0.00					
Standard Deviation of Errors	141.83	-219.04	0.02	0.02	0.0612	-0.0412
D Statistic	0.1036	-202.53	0.02	0.04	0.0766	-0.0366
D Critical at 1%	0.1138	-186.04	0.02	0.06	0.0948	-0.0348
D Critical at 5%	0.1225	-174.17	0.02	0.08	0.1097	-0.0297
D Critical at 10%	0.1458	-162.13	0.02	0.10	0.1265	-0.0265
Null Hypothesis: The errors are normally distributed.		-161.62	0.02	0.12	0.1272	-0.0072
		-160.39	0.02	0.14	0.1291	0.0109
Conclusion: The errors are normally distributed at the		-145.40	0.02	0.16	0.1526	0.0074
1% alpha level.		-138.92	0.02	0.18	0.1637	0.0163
		-133.81	0.02	0.20	0.1727	0.0273
		-120.76	0.02	0.22	0.1973	0.0227
		-120.12	0.02	0.24	0.1985	0.0415

Figure 4-40   Test for normality of errors.

at various significance values, then reject the null hypothesis and accept the alternative hypothesis (the errors are not normally distributed). Otherwise, if the D-Statistic is less than the D-Critical value, do not reject the null hypothesis (the errors are normally distributed). This test relies on two cumulative frequencies: one derived from the sample dataset, and the second from a theoretical distribution based on the mean and standard deviation of the sample data.

Sometimes, certain types of time-series data cannot be modeled using any other methods except for a stochastic process, because the underlying events are stochastic in nature. For instance, you cannot adequately model and forecast stock prices, interest rates, price of oil, and other commodity prices using a simple regression model, because these variables are highly uncertain and volatile, and do not follow a pre-defined static rule of behavior; in other words, the process is not stationary. Stationarity is checked here using the Runs Test, while another visual clue is found in the Autocorrelation report (the autocorrelation function (ACF) tends to decay slowly). A stochastic process is a sequence of events or paths generated by probabilistic laws. That is, random events can occur over time but are governed by specific statistical and probabilistic rules. The main stochastic processes include Random Walk or Brownian Motion Mean-Reversion, and Jump-Diffusion. These processes can be used to forecast a multitude of variables that seemingly follow random trends but restricted by probabilistic laws. The process-generating equation is known in advance, but the actual results generated are unknown (Figure 4-41).

The Random Walk Brownian Motion process can be used to forecast stock prices, prices of commodities, and other stochastic time-series data, given a drift or growth rate and volatility around the drift path. The Mean-Reversion process can be used to reduce the fluctuations of the Random Walk process by allowing the path to target a long-term value, making it useful for forecasting time-series variables that have a long-term rate such as interest rates and inflation rates (these are long-term target rates by regulatory authorities or the market). The Jump-Diffusion process is useful for forecasting time-series data when the variable can occasionally exhibit random jumps, such as oil prices or price of electricity (discrete exogenous event shocks can make prices jump up or down). These processes can also be mixed and matched as required.

Multicollinearity exists when there is a linear relationship between the independent variables. When this occurs, the regression equation cannot be estimated at all. In near

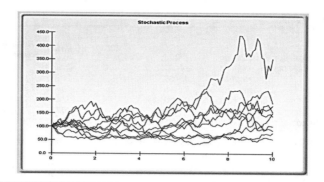

Statistical Summary

The following are the estimated parameters for a stochastic process given the data provided. It is up to you to determine if the probability of fit (similar to a goodness-of-fit computation) is sufficient to warrant the use of a stochastic process forecast, and if so, whether it is a random walk, mean-reversion, or a jump-diffusion model, or combinations thereof. In choosing the right stochastic process model, you will have to rely on past experiences and *a priori* economic and financial expectations of what the underlying data set is best represented by. These parameters can be entered into a stochastic process forecast (**Simulation | Forecasting | Stochastic Processes**).

Periodic

Drift Rate	-1.48%	Reversion Rate	283.89%	Jump Rate	20.41%
Volatility	88.84%	Long-Term Value	327.72	Jump Size	237.89

Probability of stochastic model fit: 46.48%
A high fit means a stochastic model is better than conventional models.

Runs	20	Standard Normal	-1.7321
Positive	25	P-Value (1-tail)	0.0416
Negative	25	P-Value (2-tail)	0.0833
Expected Run	26		

A low p-value (below 0.10, 0.05, 0.01) means that the sequence is not random and hence suffers from stationarity problems, and an ARIMA model might be more appropriate. Conversely, higher p-values indicate randomness and stochastic process models might be appropriate.

Figure 4-41   Stochastic process parameter estimation.

collinearity situations, the estimated regression equation will be biased and provide inaccurate results. This situation is especially true when a stepwise regression approach is used, where the statistically significant independent variables will be thrown out of the regression mix earlier than expected, resulting in a regression equation that is neither efficient nor accurate. One quick test of the presence of multicollinearity in a multiple regression equation is that the R-squared value is relatively high while the *t*-statistics are relatively low.

Another quick test is to create a correlation matrix between the independent variables. A high cross-correlation indicates a potential for autocorrelation. The rule of thumb is that a correlation with an absolute value greater than 0.75 is indicative of severe multicollinearity. Another test for multicollinearity is the use of the Variance Inflation Factor (VIF), obtained by regressing each independent variable to all the other independent variables, obtaining the R-squared value and calculating the VIF. A VIF exceeding 2.0 can be considered as severe multicollinearity. A VIF exceeding 10.0 indicates destructive multicollinearity (Figure 4-42).

The Correlation Matrix lists the Pearson's Product Moment Correlations (commonly referred to as the Pearson's R) between variable pairs. The correlation coefficient ranges between −1.0 and +1.0 inclusive. The sign indicates the direction of association between the variables, while the coefficient indicates the magnitude or strength of association. The Pearson's R only measures a linear relationship and is less effective in measuring nonlinear relationships.

Correlation Matrix

CORRELATION	X2	X3	X4	X5
X1	0.333	0.959	0.242	0.237
X2	1.000	0.349	0.319	0.120
X3		1.000	0.196	0.227
X4			1.000	0.290

Variance Inflation Factor

VIF	X2	X3	X4	X5
X1	1.12	12.46	1.06	1.06
X2	N/A	1.14	1.11	1.01
X3		N/A	1.04	1.05
X4			N/A	1.09

Figure 4-42   Multicollinearity errors.

To test whether the correlations are significant, a two-tailed hypothesis test is performed, and the resulting p-values are listed above. P-values less than 0.10, 0.05, and 0.01 are highlighted in blue to indicate statistical significance. In other words, a p-value for a correlation pair that is less than a given significance value is statistically significantly different from zero, indicating that there is significant a linear relationship between the two variables.

The Pearson's Product Moment Correlation Coefficient (R) between two variables (x and y) is related to the covariance (cov) measure where $R_{x,y} = \dfrac{COV_{x,y}}{s_x s_y}$.

The benefit of dividing the covariance by the product of the two variables' standard deviation (s) is that the resulting correlation coefficient is bounded between -1.0 and $+1.0$ inclusive. This makes the correlation a good relative measure to compare among different variables (particularly with different units and magnitude). The Spearman rank-based nonparametric correlation is also included below. The Spearman's R is related to the Pearson's R in that the data is first ranked and then correlated. The rank correlations provide a better estimate of the relationship between two variables when one or both of them are nonlinear.

It must be stressed that a significant correlation does not imply causation. Associations between variables in no way imply that the change of one variable causes another variable to change. When two variables that are moving independently of each other, but in a related path, they may be correlated but their relationship might be spurious (e.g., a correlation between sunspots and the stock market might be strong, but one can surmise that there is no causality and that this relationship is purely spurious).

Statistical Analysis Tool

Another very powerful tool in Risk Simulator is the Statistical Analysis Tool, which determines the statistical properties of the data. The diagnostics run include checking the data for various statistical properties, from basic descriptive statistics to testing for and calibrating the stochastic properties of the data.

Procedure

To run the analysis, follow these instructions:

1. Open the example model (**Risk Simulator | Examples | Statistical Analysis**) and go to the *Data* worksheet and select the data including the variable names (cells **C5:E55**).
2. Click on **Risk Simulator | Tools | Statistical Analysis** (Figure 4-43).
3. Check the *data type*, whether the data selected is from a single variable or multiple variables arranged in rows. In our example, we assume that the data areas selected are from multiple variables. Click on **OK** when finished.
4. Choose the *statistical tests* you wish to perform. The suggestion (and by default) is to choose all the tests. Click on **OK** when finished (Figure 4-44).

Spend some time going through the reports generated to get a better understanding of the statistical tests performed (sample reports are shown in Figures 4-45 through 4-48).

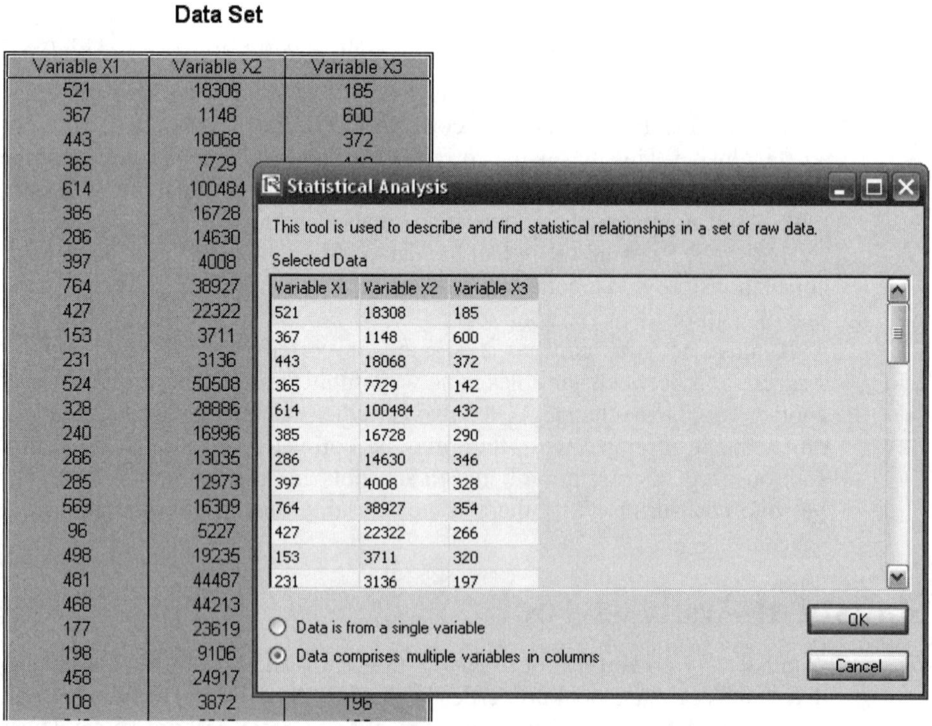

Figure 4-43   Running the statistical analysis tool.

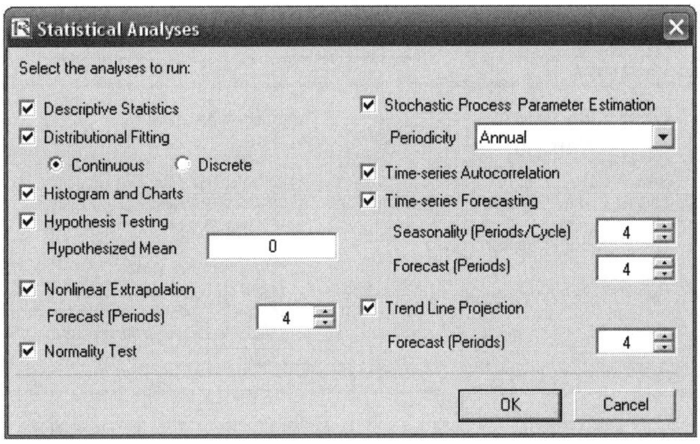

Figure 4-44   Statistical tests.

Descriptive Statistics

Analysis of Statistics

Almost all distributions can be described within 4 moments (some distributions require one moment, while others require two moments, and so forth). Descriptive statistics quantitatively capture these moments. The first moment describes the location of a distribution (i.e., mean, median, and mode) and is interpreted as the expected value, expected returns, or the average value of occurrences.

The Arithmetic Mean calculates the average of all occurrences by summing up all of the data points and dividing them by the number of points. The Geometric Mean is calculated by taking the power root of the products of all the data points and requires them to all be positive. The Geometric Mean is more accurate for percentages or rates that fluctuate significantly. For example, you can use Geometric Mean to calculate average growth rate given compound interest with variable rates. The Trimmed Mean calculates the arithmetic average of the data set after the extreme outliers have been trimmed. As averages are prone to significant bias when outliers exist, the Trimmed Mean reduces such bias in skewed distributions.

The Standard Error of the Mean calculates the error surrounding the sample mean. The larger the sample size, the smaller the error such that for an infinitely large sample size, the error approaches zero, indicating that the population parameter has been estimated. Due to sampling errors, the 95% Confidence Interval for the Mean is provided. Based on an analysis of the sample data points, the actual population mean should fall between these Lower and Upper Intervals for the Mean.

Median is the data point where 50% of all data points fall above this value and 50% below this value. Among the three first moment statistics, the median is least susceptible to outliers. A symmetrical distribution has the Median equal to the Arithmetic Mean. A skewed distribution exists when the Median is far away from the Mean. The Mode measures the most frequently occurring data point.

Minimum is the smallest value in the data set while Maximum is the largest value. Range is the difference between the Maximum and Minimum values.

The second moment measures a distribution's spread or width, and is frequently described using measures such as Standard Deviations, Variances, Quartiles, and Inter-Quartile Ranges. Standard Deviation indicates the average deviation of all data points from their mean. It is a popular measure as is associated with risk (higher standard deviations mean a wider distribution, higher risk, or wider dispersion of data points around the mean) and its units are identical to original data set's. The Sample Standard Deviation differs from the Population Standard Deviation in that the former uses a degree of freedom correction to account for small sample sizes. Also, Lower and Upper Confidence Intervals are provided for the Standard Deviation and the true population standard deviation falls within this interval. If your data set covers every element of the population, use the Population Standard Deviation instead. The two Variance measures are simply the squared values of the standard deviations.

The Coefficient of Variability is the standard deviation of the sample divided by the sample mean, proving a unit-free measure of dispersion that can be compared across different distributions (you can now compare distributions of values denominated in millions of dollars with one in billions of dollars, or meters and kilograms, etc.). The First Quartile measures the 25th percentile of the data points when arranged from its smallest to largest value. The Third Quartile is the value of the 75th percentile data point. Sometimes quartiles are used as the upper and lower ranges of a distribution as it truncates the data set to ignore outliers. The Inter-Quartile Range is the difference between the third and first quartiles, and is often used to measure the width of the center of a distribution.

Skewness is the third moment in a distribution. Skewness characterizes the degree of asymmetry of a distribution around its mean. Positive skewness indicates a distribution with an asymmetric tail extending toward more positive values. Negative skewness indicates a distribution with an asymmetric tail extending toward more negative values.

Kurtosis characterizes the relative peakedness or flatness of a distribution compared to the normal distribution. It is the fourth moment in a distribution. A positive Kurtosis value indicates a relatively peaked distribution. A negative kurtosis indicates a relatively flat distribution. The Kurtosis measured here has been centered to zero (certain other kurtosis measures are centered around 3.0). While both are equally valid, centering across zero makes the interpretation simpler. A high positive Kurtosis indicates a peaked distribution around its center and leptokurtic or fat tails. This indicates a higher probability of extreme events (e.g., catastrophic events, terrorist attacks, stock market crashes) than is predicted in a normal distribution.

Summary Statistics

Statistics	Variable X1		
Observations	50.0000	Standard Deviation (Sample)	172.9140
Arithmetic Mean	331.9200	Standard Deviation (Population)	171.1761
Geometric Mean	281.3247	Lower Confidence Interval for Standard Deviation	148.6090
Trimmed Mean	325.1739	Upper Confidence Interval for Standard Deviation	207.7947
Standard Error of Arithmetic Mean	24.4537	Variance (Sample)	29899.2588
Lower Confidence Interval for Mean	283.0125	Variance (Population)	29301.2736
Upper Confidence Interval for Mean	380.8275	Coefficient of Variability	0.5210
Median	307.0000	First Quartile (Q1)	204.0000
Mode	47.0000	Third Quartile (Q3)	441.0000
Minimum	764.0000	Inter-Quartile Range	237.0000
Maximum	717.0000	Skewness	0.4838
Range		Kurtosis	-0.0952

Figure 4-45   Sample Statistical Analysis tool report.

Hypothesis Test (t-Test on the Population Mean of One Variable)

Statistical Summary

Statistics from Dataset:		*Calculated Statistics:*	
Observations	50	t-Statistic	13.5734
Sample Mean	331.92	P-Value (right-tail)	0.0000
Sample Standard Deviation	172.91	P-Value (left-tailed)	1.0000
		P-Value (two-tailed)	0.0000
User Provided Statistics:			
		Null Hypothesis (Ho):	μ = Hypothesized Mean
Hypothesized Mean	0.00	Alternate Hypothesis (Ha):	μ < > Hypothesized Mean

Notes: "<>" denotes "greater than" for right-tail, "less than" for left-tail, or "not equal to" for two-tail hypothesis tests.

Hypothesis Testing Summary

The one-variable t-test is appropriate when the population standard deviation is not known but the sampling distribution is assumed to be approximately normal (the t-test is used when the sample size is less than 30 but is also appropriate and in fact, provides more conservative results with larger data sets). This t-test can be applied to three types of hypothesis tests: a two-tailed test, a right-tailed test, and a left-tailed test. All three tests and their respective results are listed below for your reference.

Two-Tailed Hypothesis Test

A two-tailed hypothesis tests the null hypothesis Ho such that the population mean is statistically identical to the hypothesized mean. The alternative hypothesis is that the real population mean is statistically different from the hypothesized mean when tested using the sample dataset. Using a t-test, if the computed p-value is less than a specified significance (typically 0.10, 0.05, or 0.01), this means that the population mean is statistically significantly different than the hypothesized mean at 10%, 5% and 1% significance value (or at the 90%, 95%, and 99% statistical confidence). Conversely, if the p-value is higher than 0.10, 0.05, or 0.01, the population mean is statistically identical to the hypothesized mean and any differences are due to random chance.

Right-Tailed Hypothesis Test

A right-tailed hypothesis tests the null hypothesis Ho such that the population mean is statistically less than or equal to the hypothesized mean. The alternative hypothesis is that the real population mean is statistically greater than the hypothesized mean when tested using the sample dataset. Using a t-test, if the p-value is less than a specified significance amount (typically 0.10, 0.05, or 0.01), this means that the population mean is statistically significantly greater than the hypothesized mean at 10%, 5% and 1% significance value (or 90%, 95%, and 99% statistical confidence). Conversely, if the p-value is higher than 0.10, 0.05, or 0.01, the population mean is statistically similar or less than the hypothesized mean.

Left-Tailed Hypothesis Test

A left-tailed hypothesis tests the null hypothesis Ho such that the population mean is statistically greater than or equal to the hypothesized mean. The alternative hypothesis is that the real population mean is statistically less than the hypothesized mean when tested using the sample dataset. Using a t-test, if the p-value is less than a specified significance amount (typically 0.10, 0.05, or 0.01), this means that the population mean is statistically significantly less than the hypothesized mean at 10%, 5%, and 1% significance value (or 90%, 95%, and 99% statistical confidence). Conversely, if the p-value is higher than 0.10, 0.05, or 0.01, the population mean is statistically similar or greater than the hypothesized mean and any differences are due ti random chance.

Because the t-test is more conservative and does not require a known population standard deviation as in the Z-test, we only use this t-test.

Figure 4-46 Sample Statistical Analysis tool report (hypothesis testing of one variable).

Test for Normality

The Normality test is a form of nonparametric test, which makes no assumptions about the specific shape of the population from which the sample is drawn, allowing for smaller sample data sets to be analyzed. This test evaluates the null hypothesis of whether the data sample was drawn from a normally distributed population, versus an alternate hypothesis that the data sample is not normally distributed. If the calculated p-value is less than or equal to the alpha significance value then reject the null hypothesis and accept the alternate hypothesis. Otherwise, if the p-value is higher than the alpha significance value, do not reject the null hypothesis. This test relies on two cumulative frequencies: one derived from the sample data set, the second from a theoretical distribution based on the mean and standard deviation of the sample data. An alternative to this test is the Chi-Square test for normality. The Chi-Square test requires more data points to run compared to the Normality test used here.

Test Result

			Data	Relative Frequency	Observed	Expected	O-E
Data Average	331.92		47.00	0.02	0.02	0.0497	-0.0297
Standard Deviation	172.91		68.00	0.02	0.04	0.0635	-0.0235
D Statistic	0.0859		87.00	0.02	0.06	0.0783	-0.0183
D Critical at 1%	0.1150		96.00	0.02	0.08	0.0862	-0.0062
D Critical at 5%	0.1237		102.00	0.02	0.10	0.0918	0.0082
D Critical at 10%	0.1473		108.00	0.02	0.12	0.0977	0.0223
Null Hypothesis: The data is normally distributed.			114.00	0.02	0.14	0.1038	0.0362
			127.00	0.02	0.16	0.1180	0.0420
Conclusion: The sample data is normally distributed at			153.00	0.02	0.18	0.1504	0.0296
the 1% alpha level.			177.00	0.02	0.20	0.1851	0.0149
			186.00	0.02	0.22	0.1994	0.0206
			188.00	0.02	0.24	0.2026	0.0374
			198.00	0.02	0.26	0.2193	0.0407
			222.00	0.02	0.28	0.2625	0.0175
			231.00	0.02	0.30	0.2797	0.0203
			240.00	0.02	0.32	0.2975	0.0225
			246.00	0.02	0.34	0.3096	0.0304
			251.00	0.02	0.36	0.3199	0.0401
			265.00	0.02	0.38	0.3494	0.0306
			280.00	0.02	0.40	0.3820	0.0180
			285.00	0.02	0.42	0.3931	0.0269
			286.00	0.04	0.46	0.3953	0.0647
			291.00	0.02	0.48	0.4065	0.0735
			303.00	0.02	0.50	0.4336	0.0664
			311.00	0.02	0.52	0.4519	0.0681

Figure 4-47   Sample Statistical Analysis tool report (normality test).

Stochastic Process - Parameter Estimations

Statistical Summary

A stochastic process is a sequence of events or paths generated by probabilistic laws. That is, random events can occur over time but are governed by specific statistical and probabilistic rules. The main stochastic processes include Random Walk or Brownian Motion, Mean-Reversion, and Jump-Diffusion. These processes can be used to forecast a multitude of variables that seemingly follow random trends but yet are restricted by probabilistic laws. The process-generating equation is known in advance but the actual results generated is unknown.

The Random Walk Brownian Motion process can be used to forecast stock prices, prices of commodities, and other stochastic time-series data given a drift or growth rate and a volatility around the drift path. The Mean-Reversion process can be used to reduce the fluctuations of the Random Walk process by allowing the path to target a long-term value, making it useful for forecasting time-series variables that have a long-term rate such as interest rates and inflation rates (these are long-term target rates by regulatory authorities or the market). The Jump-Diffusion process is useful for forecasting time-series data when the variable can occasionally exhibit random jumps, such as oil prices or price of electricity (discrete exogenous event shocks can make prices jump up or down). Finally, these three stochastic processes can be mixed and matched as required.

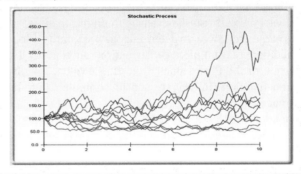

Statistical Summary

The following are the estimated parameters for a stochastic process given the data provided. It is up to you to determine if the probability of fit (similar to a goodness-of-fit computation) is sufficient to warrant the use of a stochastic process forecast, and if so, whether it is a random walk, mean-reversion, or a jump-diffusion model, or combinations thereof. In choosing the right stochastic process model, you will have to rely on past experiences and a priori economic and financial expectations of what the underlying data set is best represented by. These parameters can be entered into a stochastic process forecast (Simulation | Forecasting | Stochastic Processes).

(Annualized)

Drift Rate	5.86%	Reversion Rate	N/A	Jump Rate	16.33%
Volatility	7.04%	Long-Term Value	N/A	Jump Size	21.33

Probability of stochastic model fit: 4.63%

Figure 4-48   Sample Statistical Analysis tool report (stochastic parameter estimation).

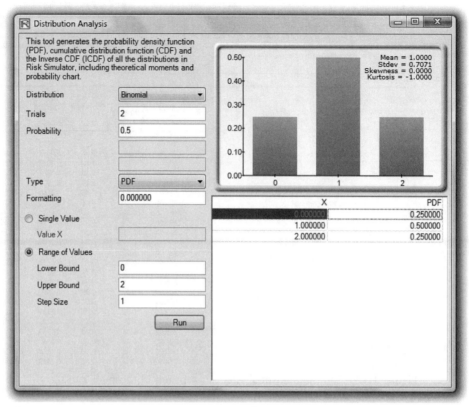

Figure 4-49   Distributional Analysis Tool (Binomial Distribution with 2 Trials).

Distributional Analysis Tool

The Distributional Analysis tool is a statistical probability tool in Risk Simulator that is useful in a variety of settings and can be used to compute the probability density function (PDF). It is also called the probability mass function (PMF) for discrete distributions (we will use these terms interchangeably), where given some distribution and its parameters, we can determine the probability of occurrence given some outcome x. In addition, the cumulative distribution function (CDF) can also be computed, which is the sum of the PDF values up to this x value. Finally, the inverse cumulative distribution function (ICDF) is used to compute the value x given the probability of occurrence.

This tool is accessible via **Risk Simulator | Tools | Distributional Analysis**. As an example, Figure 4-49 shows the computation of a binomial distribution (i.e., a distribution with two outcomes, such as the tossing of a coin, where the outcome is either Heads or Tails, with some prescribed probability of heads and tails). Suppose we toss a coin two times and set the outcome Heads as a success. We then use the binomial distribution with Trials = 2 (tossing the coin twice) and Probability = 0.50 (the probability of success, of getting Heads). Selecting the PDF and setting the range of values x as from 0 to 2 with a step size of 1 (this means we are requesting the values 0, 1, 2 for x), we find that the resulting probabilities are provided in the table

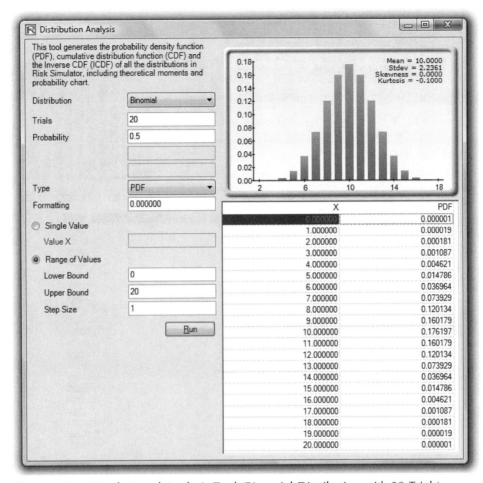

Figure 4-50 Distributional Analysis Tool (Binomial Distribution with 20 Trials).

and graphically, as well as the theoretical four moments of the distribution. As the outcomes of the coin toss are Heads-Heads, Tails-Tails, Heads-Tails, and Tails-Heads, the probability of getting exactly no Heads is 25%, one Heads is 50% percent, and two Heads is 25%.

Similarly, we can obtain the exact probabilities of tossing the coin, say 20 times, as seen in Figure 4-50. The results are presented in both table and graphical formats.

Figure 4-51 shows the same binomial distribution, but now the CDF is computed. The CDF is simply the sum of the PDF values up to the point x. For instance, in Figure 4-50, we see that the probabilities of 0, 1, and 2 are 0.000001, 0.000019, and 0.000181, whose sum is 0.000201, which is the value of the CDF at $x = 2$ in Figure 4-51. Whereas the PDF computes the probabilities of getting 2 Heads, the CDF computes the probability of getting no more than 2 Heads (or probabilities of 0, 1, and 2 Heads). Taking the complement (i.e., 1−0.00021 obtains 0.999799 or 99.9799%) provides the probability of getting at least 3 Heads or more.

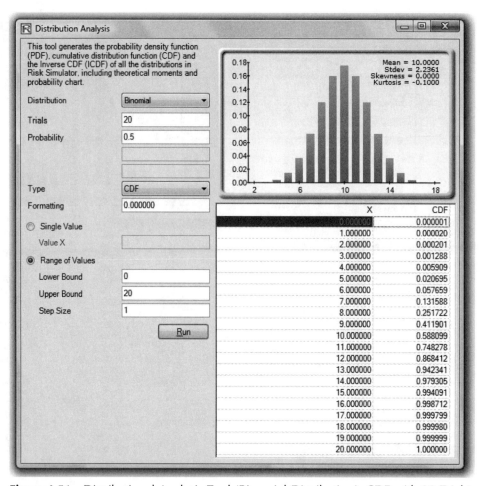

Figure 4-51   Distributional Analysis Tool (Binomial Distribution's CDF with 20 Trials).

Using this Distributional Analysis tool, even more advanced distributions can be analyzed, such as the gamma, beta, negative binomial, and many others in Risk Simulator. As further example of the tool's use in a continuous distribution and the ICDF functionality, Figure 4-52 shows the standard normal distribution (normal distribution with a mean of zero and standard deviation of one), where we apply the ICDF to find the value of x that corresponds to the cumulative probability of 97.50% (CDF). That is, a one-tail CDF of 97.50% is equivalent to a two-tail 95% confidence interval (there is a 2.50% probability in the right tail and 2.50% in the left tail, leaving 95% in the center or confidence interval area, which is equivalent to a 97.50% area for one tail). The result is the familiar Z-Score of 1.96. Therefore, using this Distributional Analysis tool, the standardized scores for other distributions, the exact and cumulative probabilities of other distributions can all be obtained quickly and easily.

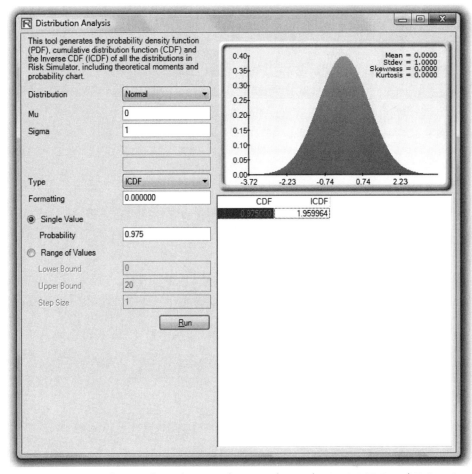

Figure 4-52   Distributional Analysis Tool (Normal Distribution's ICDF and Z-Score).

CHAPTER 5

Analytical Forecasting and Cash Flow Projections

One crucial issue in risk management deals with analyzing what could go wrong with individual credits and portfolios, and factoring this information into the analysis of risk-adjusted returns, capital adequacy, and loan provisions. "What-if" analysis can unveil previously uncovered areas of credit risk exposures and plays the vital role of locking into areas of potential problems.[1] This chapter deals with processing scenarios through various forecasting techniques ranging from modified percentage of sales to advance stochastic optimization analysis. With regard to forecasting, the Basel Committee on Banking Supervision states that "[i]n the final analysis banks should attempt to identify the types of situations, such as economic downturns, both in the whole economy or in particular sectors, higher than expected levels of delinquencies and defaults, or the combinations of credit and market events, that could produce substan-

---

[1] *"Many banks do not take sufficient account of business cycle effects in lending. As income prospects and asset values rise in the ascending portion of the business cycle, credit analysis may incorporate overly optimistic assumptions. Industries such as retailing, commercial real estate and real estate investment trusts, utilities, and consumer lending often experience strong cyclical effects. Sometimes the cycle is less related to general business conditions than the product cycle in a relatively new, rapidly growing sector, such as health care and telecommunications. Effective stress testing which takes account of business or product cycle effects is one approach to incorporating into credit decisions a fuller understanding of a borrower's credit risk."*

—Basel Committee

tial losses or liquidity problems. Stress test analyses should also include contingency plans regarding actions management might take given certain scenarios."

The emphasis on bank forecasts developed as loan demand increased to fund large and complex credits, including mergers and acquisitions. These new deals represented a new class of borrowers who pushed their financial structure to exceedingly high debt levels. As a result, lenders began to work with a new breed of sophisticated forecasting and valuation models that were able to predict expected default, financial needs, and shareholder value with much more accuracy and insight. Building projected financial statements around a set of critical assumptions or value drivers involves research, logic, and up-to-date predictive software—computers after all do not make credit decisions. They merely quantify assumptions about the future, serving as another tool, albeit an important one, in the loan decision-making process. The real value of computers is their ability to facilitate rapid analysis of many alternatives, mimicking a realistic environment as much as possible. When appropriate, the bank will run a "sensitivity analysis" examining the effect of changing key assumptions in any number of combinations in order to construct a range of outcomes from pessimistic to optimistic. We will see that simulation and optimization analysis are far more advanced methods of stress testing than is running a borrower's forecast through various "sensitivities." In determining the most suitable forecasting technique for a given situation, one of the first checks is comparability between forecast methods used and complexity of data or, for that matter, the deal. From the start lenders should be aware of both the benefits and pitfalls of each forecasting method before one is chosen. Under certain conditions, a preferred forecasting method may offer incomplete, inaccurate results in one situation while producing "OK" results in a similar analysis.

Availability of comprehensive, historical data is the standard prerequisite for developing forecasts. Since different forecasting methods generally require various amounts of historical data, requirements for data quality (and quantity) may vary as well. The next prerequisite is accuracy—triple A-rated firms require little data, with accuracy hardly an issue, while B-rated customers may require plenty of verifiable information. In the former case, risks are insignificant, financial statements are strong, and the firm operates in nonvacillating surroundings. A forecast error of 30 percent or more is irrelevant, whereas a forecast error of 100 basis points may be enough to spell disaster for a borrower with a low rating.

Advanced Analytical Forecasting with Risk Simulator

Forecasting is the act of predicting the future, whether it is based on historical data or speculation about the future when no history exists. When historical data do exist, a quantitative or statistical approach is best, but if there are no such data, then a qualitative or judgmental approach is usually the only recourse. Figure 5.1 lists the most common methodologies for analytical forecasting. The other approaches for forecasting are listed in Chapter 15 of the present volume, where more advanced techniques such as the generalized autoregressive conditional heteroskedasticity (GARCH) model, interpolation, spline extrapolation, and yield curve fitting and forecasting are discussed and applied using the Modeling Toolkit.

Different Types of Forecasting Techniques

Forecasting can be divided into quantitative and qualitative approaches. Qualitative forecasting is used when little to no reliable historical, contemporaneous, or compa-

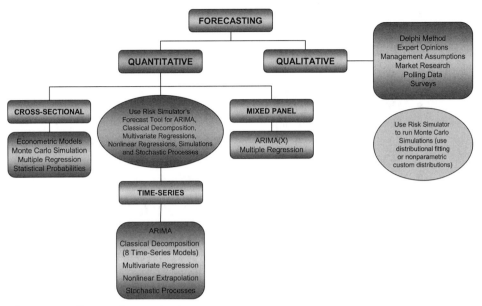

Figure 5-1   Forecasting methods.

rable data exists. Qualitative methods include the Delphi or expert opinion approach (a consensus-building forecast by field experts, marketing experts, or internal staff members), management assumptions (target growth rates set by senior management), as well as market research or external data or polling and surveys (data obtained through third-party sources, industry and sector indexes, or active market research). These estimates can be either single-point estimates (an average consensus) or a set of prediction values (a distribution of predictions). Prediction values can be entered into Risk Simulator as a custom distribution, and the resulting predictions can be simulated; that is, a nonparametric simulation can be run using the prediction data points as the custom distribution.

For quantitative forecasting, available data or data that needs to be forecasted can be divided into time-series (values that possess a time element, such as revenues at different years, inflation rates, interest rates, market share, and failure rates); cross-sectional (values that are time-independent, such as the grade point average of sophomore students across the nation in a particular year, given each student's levels of SAT scores, IQ, and number of alcoholic beverages consumed per week); or mixed panel (mixture between time-series and panel data, e.g., predicting sales over the next 10 years given budgeted marketing expenses and market share projections, which means that the sales data is considered time-series but exogenous variables such as marketing expenses and market share exist to help to model the forecast predictions).

The Risk Simulator software provides the user with several forecasting methodologies, notably:

- Autoregressive integrated moving average (ARIMA)
- Auto ARIMA Models
- Basic Econometric Models
- Cubic Spline Interpolation and Extrapolation

- Data Diagnostics for Forecast Modeling
- GARCH Volatility
- J-S Curves
- Markov Chains
- Maximum Likelihood Estimation
- Multivariate Regression
- Nonlinear Extrapolation
- Stochastic Process Forecasting (Brownian Motion random walk, mean-reversion, jump-diffusion)
- Time-series Decomposition and Forecasting

Running the Forecasting Tool in Risk Simulator

To create forecasts, several quick steps are required:

- Start Excel and enter in or open existing historical data.
- Select the data and click on **Risk Simulator | Forecasting**.
- Select the relevant sections (Box-Jenkins ARIMA, Time-series Analysis, Multivariate Regression, Stochastic Forecasting, or Nonlinear Extrapolation, etc.) and enter the relevant inputs.

Figure 5-2 illustrates the Forecasting tool and the various methodologies available in Risk Simulator.

Following is a quick review of each methodology and several quick "getting started" examples for using the software. The example data files used to create these examples are included in the Risk Simulator software and can be accessed through **Risk Simulator | Examples**.

Time-series Analysis

Theory

Figure 5-3 lists the eight most common time-series models, segregated by seasonality and trend. For instance, if the data variable has no trend or seasonality, then a single moving-average model or a single exponential-smoothing model will suffice. However, if seasonality exists but no discernible trend is present, either a seasonal additive or a seasonal multiplicative model would be better, and so forth.

Procedure

- Start Excel and type in or open an existing spreadsheet with the relevant historical data (the following example uses the Time-series Forecasting file in the examples folder).

Figure 5-2   Risk Simulator's forecasting methods.

- Make sure that you start a new simulation profile or that there is an existing profile in the model if you want the forecast results to automatically generate Monte Carlo assumptions.
- Select the historical data not including the variable name (data should be listed in a single column).
- Select **Risk Simulator | Forecasting | Time-series Analysis**.
- Choose the model to apply, enter the relevant assumptions, and click on **OK**.

To follow along in this example, choose Auto Model Selection, enter 4 for seasonality periods per cycle, and forecast for 4 periods. See Figure 5-4.

	No Seasonality	With Seasonality
No Trend	Single Moving Average	Seasonal Additive
	Single Exponential Smoothing	Seasonal Multiplicative
With Trend	Double Moving Average	Holt-Winter's Additive
	Double Exponential Smoothing	Holt-Winter's Multiplicative

Figure 5-3   The eight most common time-series methods.

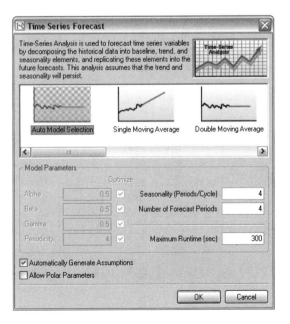

Historical Sales Revenues

Year	Quarter	Period	Sales
2000	1	1	$684.20
2000	2	2	$584.10
2000	3	3	$765.40
2000	4	4	$892.30
2001	1	5	$885.40
2001	2	6	$677.00
2001	3	7	$1,006.60
2001	4	8	$1,122.10
2002	1	9	$1,163.40
2002	2	10	$993.20
2002	3	11	$1,312.50
2002	4	12	$1,545.30
2003	1	13	$1,596.20
2003	2	14	$1,260.40
2003	3	15	$1,735.20
2003	4	16	$2,029.70
2004	1	17	$2,107.80
2004	2	18	$1,650.30
2004	3	19	$2,304.40
2004	4	20	$2,639.40

Figure 5-4   Time-series analysis.

Interpretation of Results

Figure 5-5 illustrates the sample results generated by using the Forecasting tool. The model used was a Holt-Winters multiplicative model. Notice that in Figure 5-5, the model-fitting and forecast chart indicates that the trend and seasonality are picked up nicely by the Holt-Winters multiplicative model. The time-series analysis report provides the relevant optimized alpha, beta, and gamma parameters, the error measurements, fitted data, forecast values, and forecast-fitted graph. The parameters are simply for reference. *Alpha* captures the memory effect of the base-level changes over time, *beta* is the trend parameter that measures the strength of the trend, while *gamma* measures the seasonality strength of the historical data. The analysis decomposes the historical data into these three elements and then recomposes them to forecast the future. The fitted data illustrates the historical data as well as the fitted data using the recomposed model and shows how close the forecasts are in the past (a technique called backcasting). The forecast values are either single-point estimates or assumptions (if the automatically generated assumptions option is chosen and if a simulation

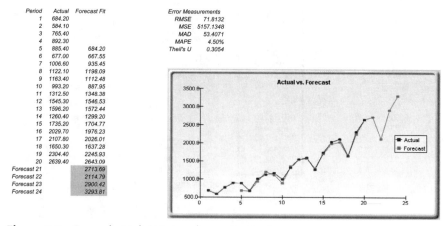

Holt-Winter's Multiplicative

Summary Statistics

Alpha, Beta, Gamma	RMSE	Alpha, Beta, Gamma	RMSE
0.00, 0.00, 0.00	914.824	0.00, 0.00, 0.00	914.824
0.10, 0.10, 0.10	415.322	0.10, 0.10, 0.10	415.322
0.20, 0.20, 0.20	187.202	0.20, 0.20, 0.20	187.202
0.30, 0.30, 0.30	118.795	0.30, 0.30, 0.30	118.795
0.40, 0.40, 0.40	101.794	0.40, 0.40, 0.40	101.794
0.50, 0.50, 0.50	102.143		

The analysis was run with alpha = 0.2429, beta = 1.0000, gamma = 0.7797, and seasonality = 4

Time-Series Analysis Summary

When both seasonality and trend exist, more advanced models are required to decompose the data into their base elements: a base-case level (L) weighted by the alpha parameter; a trend component (b) weighted by the beta parameter; and a seasonality component (S) weighted by the gamma parameter. Several methods exist but the two most common are the Holt-Winters' additive seasonality and Holt-Winters' multiplicative seasonality methods. In the Holt-Winter's additive model, the base case level, seasonality, and trend are added together to obtain the forecast fit.

The best-fitting test for the moving average forecast uses the root mean squared errors (RMSE). The RMSE calculates the square root of the average squared deviations of the fitted values versus the actual data points.

Mean Squared Error (MSE) is an absolute error measure that squares the errors (the difference between the actual historical data and the forecast-fitted data predicted by the model) to keep the positive and negative errors from canceling each other out. This measure also tends to exaggerate large errors by weighting the large errors more heavily than smaller errors by squaring them, which can help when comparing different time-series models. Root Mean Square Error (RMSE) is the square root of MSE and is the most popular error measure, also known as the quadratic loss function. RMSE can be defined as the average of the absolute values of the forecast errors and is highly appropriate when the cost of the forecast errors is proportional to the absolute size of the forecast error. The RMSE is used as the selection criteria for the best-fitting time-series model.

Mean Absolute Percentage Error (MAPE) is a relative error statistic measured as an average percent error of the historical data points and is most appropriate when the cost of the forecast error is more closely related to the percentage error than the numerical size of the error. Finally, an associated measure is the Theil's U statistic, which measures the naivety of the model's forecast. That is, if the Theil's U statistic is less than 1.0, then the forecast method used provides an estimate that is statistically better than guessing.

Period	Actual	Forecast Fit
1	684.20	
2	584.10	
3	765.40	
4	892.30	
5	885.40	684.20
6	677.00	667.55
7	1006.60	935.45
8	1122.10	1198.09
9	1163.40	1112.48
10	993.20	887.95
11	1312.50	1348.38
12	1545.30	1546.53
13	1596.20	1572.44
14	1260.40	1299.20
15	1735.20	1704.77
16	2029.70	1976.23
17	2107.80	2026.01
18	1650.30	1637.28
19	2304.40	2245.93
20	2639.40	2643.09
Forecast 21		2713.69
Forecast 22		2114.79
Forecast 23		2900.42
Forecast 24		3293.81

Error Measurements

RMSE	71.8132
MSE	5157.1348
MAD	53.4071
MAPE	4.50%
Theil's U	0.3054

Figure 5-5 Example Holt-Winters forecast report.

profile exists). The graph in the generated report illustrates the historical, fitted, and forecast values. The chart is a powerful communication and visual tool to see how good the forecast model is.

Notes

This time-series analysis module contains the eight time-series models seen in Figure 5-3. You can choose the specific model to run based on the trend and seasonality criteria, or you can choose the Auto Model Selection, which will automatically iterate through all eight methods, optimize the parameters, and find the best-fitting model for your data. Alternatively, if you choose one of the eight models, you can also deselect the *optimize* checkboxes and enter your own alpha, beta, and gamma parameters. In addition, you will need to enter the relevant seasonality periods if you choose the Auto Model Selection or any of the seasonal models. The seasonality input must be a positive integer (e.g., if the data is quarterly, enter 4 as the number of seasons or cycles a year, or enter 12 if monthly data, or any other positive integer representing the data periods of a full cycle). Next, enter the number of periods to forecast. This value also has to be a positive integer. The maximum runtime is set at 300 seconds. Typically, no changes are required. However, when forecasting with a significant amount of historical data, the analysis might take slightly longer; if the processing time exceeds this runtime, the process will be terminated. You can also elect to have the forecast automatically generate assumptions; that is, instead of single-point estimates, the forecasts will be assumptions. However, to automatically generate assumptions, a simulation profile must first exist. Finally, the polar parameters option allows you to optimize the alpha, beta, and gamma parameters to include zero and one. Certain forecasting software allows these polar parameters while others do not. Risk Simulator allows you to choose which to use. Typically, there is no need to use polar parameters. See Chapter 9 of Johnathan Mun's *Modeling Risk* (Wiley, 2006) for the technical details on time-series forecasting using the eight decomposition methods.

Multivariate Regression

Theory

It is assumed that the user is sufficiently knowledgeable about the fundamentals of regression analysis. The general bivariate linear regression equation takes the form of $Y = \beta_0 + \beta_1 X + \varepsilon$ where β_0 is the intercept, β_1 is the slope, and ε is the error term. It is bivariate because there are only two variables—a Y or dependent variable, and an X or independent variable, where X is also known as the regressor (sometimes a bivariate regression is also known as a univariate regression since there is only a single independent variable X). The dependent variable is so-named because it *depends* on the independent variable; for example, sales revenue depends on the amount of marketing costs expended on a product's advertising and promotion, making the dependent variable sales and the independent variable marketing costs. An example of a bivariate regression is seen as simply inserting the best-fitting line through a set of data points in a two-dimensional plane as seen on the left panel in Figure 5-6. In other cases, a multivariate regression can be performed, where there are multiple or k number of independent X variables or regressors and where the general regression equation will now take the form of $Y = \beta_0 + \beta_1 X_1 + \beta_2 X_2 + \beta_3 X_3 \ldots + \beta_k X_k + \varepsilon$. In this case, the best-fitting line will be within a $k + 1$ dimensional plane.

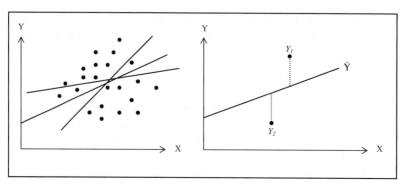

Figure 5-6   Bivariate regression.

Fitting a line through a set of data points in a scatter plot as in Figure 5-6 may result in numerous possible lines. The best-fitting line is defined as the single unique line that minimizes the total vertical errors—that is, the sum of the absolute distances between the actual data points (Y_i) and the estimated line ($\hat{Y}$) as shown on the right-hand panel of Figure 5-6. To find the best-fitting unique line that minimizes the errors, a more sophisticated approach is applied, using regression analysis. Regression analysis therefore finds the unique best-fitting line by requiring that the total errors be minimized, or by calculating

$$Min \sum_{i=1}^{n} \left(Y_i - \hat{Y}_i\right)^2$$

where only one unique line minimizes this sum of squared errors. The errors (vertical distances between the actual data and the predicted line) are squared to prevent the negative errors from canceling out the positive errors. Solving this minimization problem with respect to the slope and intercept requires calculating first derivatives and setting them equal to zero:

$$\frac{d}{d\beta_0} \sum_{i=1}^{n} \left(Y_i - \hat{Y}_i\right)^2 = 0 \text{ and } \frac{d}{d\beta_1} \sum_{i=1}^{n} \left(Y_i - \hat{Y}_i\right)^2 = 0$$

which yields the bivariate regression's least squares equations:

$$\beta_1 = \frac{\sum_{i=1}^{n}(X_i - \bar{X})(Y_i - \bar{Y})}{\sum_{i=1}^{n}(X_i - \bar{X})^2} = \frac{\sum_{i=1}^{n} X_i Y_i - \dfrac{\sum_{i=1}^{n} X_i \sum_{i=1}^{n} Y_i}{n}}{\sum_{i=1}^{n} X_i^2 - \dfrac{\left(\sum_{i=1}^{n} X_i\right)^2}{n}}$$

$$\beta_0 = \bar{Y} - \beta_1 \bar{X}$$

For multivariate regression, the analogy is expanded to account for multiple independent variables, where $Y_i = \beta_1 + \beta_2 X_{2,i} + \beta_3 X_{3,i} + \varepsilon_i$ and the estimated slopes can be calculated by

$$\hat{\beta}_2 = \frac{\sum Y_i X_{2,i} \sum X_{3,i}^2 - \sum Y_i X_{3,i} \sum X_{2,i} X_{3,i}}{\sum X_{2,i}^2 \sum X_{3,i}^2 - \left(\sum X_{2,i} X_{3,i}\right)^2}$$

$$\hat{\beta}_3 = \frac{\sum Y_i X_{3,i} \sum X_{2,i}^2 - \sum Y_i X_{2,i} \sum X_{2,i} X_{3,i}}{\sum X_{2,i}^2 \sum X_{3,i}^2 - \left(\sum X_{2,i} X_{3,i}\right)^2}$$

In running multivariate regressions, great care must be taken to set up and interpret the results. For instance, a good understanding of econometric modeling is required (e.g., identifying regression pitfalls such as structural breaks, multicollinearity, heteroskedasticity, autocorrelation, specification tests, nonlinearities, and so forth) before a proper model can be constructed.

Procedure

- Start Excel and type in or open your existing dataset.
- Make sure that the data is arranged in columns, select the data, including the variable headings, and click on **Risk Simulator | Forecasting | Multiple Regression**.
- Select the dependent variable, check the relevant options (lags, stepwise regression, nonlinear regression, and so forth), and click on **OK** (Figure 5-7).

Interpretation of Results

Figure 5-8 illustrates a sample report of a multivariate regression result. The report contains all the results for the regression, analysis of variance, fitted chart, and hypothesis test. See Chapter 9 of Johnathan Mun's *Modeling Risk* (Wiley, 2006) for the technical details of interpreting regression analysis results.

Stochastic Forecasting

Theory

A stochastic process is simply a mathematically defined equation that can create a series of outcomes over time; these outcomes are not deterministic in nature; that is, an equation or process that does not follow any simple discernible rule such as price will increase X percent every year or revenues will increase by this factor of X plus Y percent. A stochastic process is by definition nondeterministic, and one can plug numbers into a stochastic process equation and obtain different results every time. For instance, the path of a stock price is stochastic in nature, and one cannot reliably predict the exact stock price path with any certainty. However, the price evolution over time is enveloped in a process that generates these prices. *The process is fixed and predetermined, but the outcomes are not.* Hence, by stochastic simulation we create multiple pathways of prices, obtain a statistical sampling of these simulations, and make inferences on the potential pathways that the actual price may undertake given the nature and parameters of the stochastic process used to generate the time series. Four stochastic processes are included in Risk Simulator's Forecasting tool,

Multiple Regression Analysis Data Set

Aggravated Assault	Bachelor's Degree	Police Expenditure Per Capita	Population in Millions	Population Density (Persons/Sq Mile)	Unemployment Rate
521	18308	185	4.041	79.6	7.2
367	1148	600	0.55	1	8.5
443	18068	372	3.665	32.3	5.7
365	7729	142	2.351	45.1	7.3
614	100484	432	29.76	190.8	7.5
385	16728	290	3.294	31.8	5
286	14630				
397	4008				
764	38927				
427	22322				
153	3711				
231	3136				
524	50508				
328	28886				
240	16996				
286	13035				
285	12973				
569	16309				
96	5227				
498	19235				
481	44487				
468	44213				
177	23619				
198	9106				
458	24917				
108	3872				
246	8945				
291	2373				
68	7128				
311	23624				
606	5242				
512	92629				
426	28795				
47	4487				
265	48799				
370	14067				
312	12693	288	2.842	29.6	6
222	62184	229	11.882	265.1	6.9
280	9153	287	1.003	960.3	8.5
759	14250	224	3.487	115.8	6.2
114	3680	161	0.696	9.2	3.4
419	18063	221	4.877	118.3	6.6
435	65112	237	16.987	64.9	6.6
186	11340	220	1.723	21	4.9
87	4553	185	0.563	60.8	6.4
188	28960	260	6.187	156.3	5.8
303	19201	261	4.867	73.1	6.3
102	7533	118	1.793	74.5	10.5
127	26343	268	4.892	90.1	5.4
251	1641	300	0.454	4.7	5.1

Multiple Regression Analysis

Multiple Regression Analysis can be used to run linear regressions with multiple independent variables. These variables can be applied through a series of lags, nonlinear transformations or regressed in a stepwise fashion starting with the most correlated variable.

Multivariate Regression Y = F(X)

Dependent Variable   Aggravated Assault

Aggravated Assault	Bachelor's Degree	Police Expenditure Pe...
521	18308	185
367	1148	600
443	18068	372
365	7729	142
614	100484	432
385	16728	290
286	14630	346
397	4008	328
764	38927	354

Options
☐ Lag Regressors [1] Period(s)   ☐ Stepwise Regression
☐ Non-linear Regression   ☐ Show All Steps

OK   Cancel

Figure 5-7   Running a multivariate regression.

including Geometric Brownian motion or random walk, which is the most common and prevalently used process due to its simplicity and wide-ranging applications. The other three stochastic processes are mean-reversion, jump-diffusion, and mixed.

Interestingly, historical data are not required for stochastic process simulation; that is, the model does not have to fit any set of historical data. One simply computes the expected returns and the volatility of the historical data or estimates them using comparable external data or makes assumptions about these values.

Procedure

- Start the module by selecting **Risk Simulator | Forecasting | Stochastic Processes**.
- Select the desired process, enter the required inputs, click on update chart a few times to make sure the process is behaving the way you expect it to, and click on **OK** (Figure 5-9).

Regression Analysis Report

Regression Statistics

R-Squared (Coefficient of Determination)	0.5541
Adjusted R-Squared	0.4527
Multiple R (Multiple Correlation Coefficient)	0.7444
Standard Error of the Estimates (SEy)	14.7150
nObservations	28

The R-Squared or Coefficient of Determination indicates that of the variation in the dependent variable can be explained and accounted for by the independent variables in this regression analysis. However, in a multiple regression, the Adjusted R-Squared takes into account the existence of additional independent variables or regressors and adjusts this R-Squared value to a more accurate view of the regression's explanatory power. Hence, only of the variation in the dependent variable can be explained by the regressors.

The Multiple Correlation Coefficient (Multiple R) measures the correlation between the actual dependent variable (Y) and the estimated or fitted (Y) based on the regression equation. This is also the square root of the Coefficient of Determination (R-Squared).

The Standard Error of the Estimates (SE_y) describes the dispersion of data points above and below the regression line or plane. This value is used as part of the calculation to obtain the confidence interval of the estimates later.

Regression Results

	Intercept	X1	X2	X3	X4	X5
Coefficients	8.0795	-0.2446	0.1659	-0.0095	0.0178	0.4952
Standard Error	8.1593	0.4730	0.3061	0.1122	0.0418	1.6267
t-Statistic	0.9902	-0.5171	0.5418	-0.0848	0.4259	0.3044
p-Value	0.3328	0.6103	0.5934	0.9332	0.6743	0.7637
Lower 5%	-8.8419	-1.2256	-0.4690	-0.2422	-0.0688	-2.8783
Upper 95%	25.0009	0.7365	0.8007	0.2232	0.1044	3.8687

Degrees of Freedom		Hypothesis Test	
Degrees of Freedom for Regression	5	Critical t-Statistic (99% confidence with df of 22)	2.8188
Degrees of Freedom for Residual	22	Critical t-Statistic (95% confidence with df of 22)	2.0739
Total Degrees of Freedom	27	Critical t-Statistic (90% confidence with df of 22)	1.7171

The Coefficients provide the estimated regression intercept and slopes. For instance, the coefficients are estimates of the true population ¬ values in the following regression equation: $Y = \hat{\beta}_0 + \hat{\beta}_1 X_1 + \hat{\beta}_2 X_2 + ... + \hat{\beta}_n X_n$. The Standard Error measures how accurate the predicted Coefficients are, and the t-Statistics are the ratios of each predicted Coefficient to its Standard Error.

The t-Statistic is used in hypothesis testing, where we set the null hypothesis (Ho) such that the real mean of the Coefficient = 0, and the alternate hypothesis (Ha) such that the real mean of the Coefficient is not equal to 0. A t-test is performed and the calculated t-Statistic is compared to the critical values at the relevant Degrees of Freedom for Residual. The t-test is very important as it calculates if each of the coeffients is statististically significant in the presence of the other regressors. This means that the t-test statistically verifies whether a regressor or independent variable should remain in the regression or it should be dropped.

The Coefficient is statistically significant if its calculated t-Statistic exceeds the Critical t-Statistic at the relevant degrees of freedom (df). The three main confidence levels used to test for significance are 90%, 95% and 99%. If a Coefficient's t-Statistic exceeds the Critical level, it is considered statistically significant. Alternatively, the p-Value calculates each t-Statistic's probability of occurrence, which means that the smaller the p-Value, the more significant the Coefficient. The usual significant levels for the p-Value are 0.01, 0.05, and 0.10, corresponding to the 99%, 95%, and 99% confidence levels.

The Coefficients with their p-Values highlighted in blue indicate that they are statistically significant at the 95% confidence or 0.05 alpha level, while those highlighted in red indicate that they are not statistically significant at any of the alpha levels.

Analysis of Variance

	Sums of Squares	Mean of Squares	F-Statistic	P-Value	Hypothesis Test	
Regression	5919.2453	1183.8491	5.4673	0.0020	Critical F-statistic (99% confidence with df of 4 and 3)	3.9880
Residual	4763.7189	216.5327			Critical F-statistic (95% confidence with df of 4 and 3)	2.6613
Total	10682.9643				Critical F-statistic (90% confidence with df of 4 and 3)	2.1279

The Analysis of Variance (ANOVA) table provides an F-test of the regression model's overall statistical significance. Instead of looking at individual regressors as in the t-test, the F-test looks at all the estimated Coefficients' statistical properties. The F-statistic is calculated as the ratio of the Regression's Mean of Squares to the Residual's Mean of Squares. The numerator measures how much of the regression is explained, while the denominator measures how much is unexplained. Hence, the larger the F-statistic, the more significant the model. The corresponding p-Value is calculated to test the null hypothesis (Ho) where all the estimated Coefficients are simultaneously equal to zero, versus the alternate hypothesis (Ha) that they are all simultaneously different from zero, indicating a significant overall regression model. If the p-Value is smaller than the 0.01, 0.05, or 0.10 alpha significance, then the regression is significant. The same approach can be applied to the F-statistic by comparing the calculated F-statistic with the critical F values at various significance levels.

Forecasting

Period	Actual (Y)	Forecast (F)	Error (E)
1	10	16.7176	(6.7176)
2	13	18.1252	(5.1252)
3	14	19.9657	(5.9657)
4	15	22.1958	(7.1958)
5	18	23.6613	(5.6613)
6	6	24.8487	(18.8487)
7	87	24.7268	62.2732
8	21	24.9410	(3.9410)
9	23	25.9599	(2.9599)
10	34	25.8248	8.1752
11	26	27.1239	(1.1239)
12	28	27.9043	0.0957
13	29	31.0906	(2.0906)
14	30	34.3457	(4.3457)
15	33	28.9797	4.0203
16	23	36.2009	(13.2009)
17	39	37.2167	1.7833
18	44	46.1075	(2.1075)
19	44	43.8360	0.1640
20	46	48.3004	(2.3004)
21	48	48.3328	(0.3328)
22	55	53.6713	1.3287
23	57	54.3234	2.6766
24	66	67.1361	(1.1361)
25	48	48.3328	(0.3328)
26	55	53.6713	1.3287
27	57	54.3234	2.6766
28	66	67.1361	(1.1361)

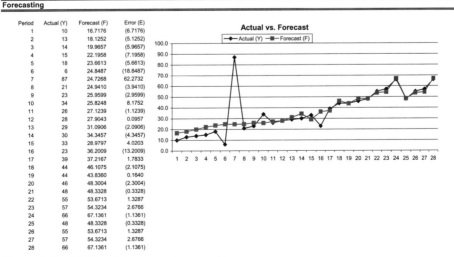

Figure 5-8　Multivariate regression results.

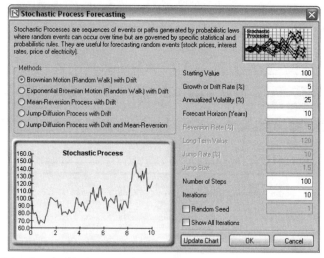

Figure 5-9   Stochastic process forecasting.

Interpretation of Results

Figure 5-10 presents the results of a sample stochastic process. The chart shows a sample set of the iterations, while the report explains the basics of stochastic processes. In addition, the forecast values (mean and standard deviation) for each time period are provided. Using these values, you can decide which time period is relevant to your analysis, and set assumptions based on these mean and standard deviation values using the normal distribution. These assumptions can then be simulated in your own custom model.

Notes

The Brownian Motion Random Walk Process

The Brownian motion random walk process takes the form of $\dfrac{\delta S}{S} = \mu(\delta t) + \sigma \varepsilon \sqrt{\delta t}$ for regular options simulation, or a more generic version takes the form of $\dfrac{\delta S}{S} = (\mu - \sigma^2/2)\delta t + \delta \varepsilon \sqrt{\delta t}$ for a geometric process. For an exponential version, we simply take the exponentials, and as an example, we have $\dfrac{\delta S}{S} = \exp\left[\mu(\delta t) + \delta \varepsilon \sqrt{\delta t}\right]$

where

S is the variable's previous value

δS is the change in the variable's value from one step to the next

μ is the annualized growth or drift rate

σ is the annualized volatility

Stochastic Process Forecasting

Statistical Summary

A stochastic process is a sequence of events or paths generated by probabilistic laws. That is, random events can occur over time but are governed by specific statistical and probabilistic rules. The main stochastic processes include Random Walk or Brownian Motion, Mean-Reversion, and Jump-Diffusion. These processes can be used to forecast a multitude of variables that seemingly follow random trends but yet are restricted by probabilistic laws.

The Random Walk Brownian Motion process can be used to forecast stock prices, prices of commodities, and other stochastic time-series data given a drift or growth rate and a volatility around the drift path. The Mean-Reversion process can be used to reduce the fluctuations of the Random Walk process by allowing the path to target a long-term value, making it useful for forecasting time-series variables that have a long-term rate such as interest rates and inflation rates (these are long-term target rates by regulatory authorities or the market). The Jump-Diffusion process is useful for forecasting time-series data when the variable can occasionally exhibit random jumps, such as oil prices or price of electricity (discrete exogenous event shocks can make prices jump up or down). Finally, these three stochastic processes can be mixed and matched as required.

The results on the right indicate the mean and standard deviation of all the iterations generated at each time step. If the Show All Iterations option is selected, each iteration pathway will be shown in a separate worksheet. The graph generated below shows a sample set of the iteration pathways.

Stochastic Process: Brownian Motion (Random Walk) with Drift

Start Value	100	Steps	50.00	Jump Rate	N/A	
Drift Rate	5.00%	Iterations	10.00	Jump Size	N/A	
Volatility	25.00%	Reversion Rate	N/A	Random Seed	1720050445	
Horizon	5	Long-Term Value	N/A			

Time	Mean	Stdev
0.0000	100.00	0.00
0.1000	106.32	4.05
0.2000	105.92	4.70
0.3000	105.23	8.23
0.4000	109.84	11.18
0.5000	107.57	14.67
0.6000	108.63	19.79
0.7000	107.85	24.18
0.8000	109.61	24.46
0.9000	109.57	27.99
1.0000	110.74	30.81
1.1000	111.53	35.05
1.2000	111.07	34.10
1.3000	107.52	32.85
1.4000	108.26	37.38
1.5000	106.36	32.19
1.6000	112.42	32.16
1.7000	110.08	31.24
1.8000	109.64	31.87
1.9000	110.18	36.43
2.0000	112.23	37.63
2.1000	114.32	33.10
2.2000	111.14	38.42
2.3000	111.03	37.69
2.4000	112.04	37.23
2.5000	112.98	40.84
2.6000	115.74	43.69
2.7000	115.11	43.64
2.8000	114.87	43.70
2.9000	113.28	42.25
3.0000	115.72	43.43
3.1000	120.05	50.48
3.2000	116.69	42.61
3.3000	118.31	45.57
3.4000	116.35	40.82
3.5000	115.71	40.33
3.6000	118.69	41.45
3.7000	121.66	45.34
3.8000	121.40	45.03
3.9000	125.19	48.19
4.0000	129.65	55.44
4.1000	129.61	53.82
4.2000	125.86	49.68
4.3000	125.70	53.79
4.4000	126.72	49.70
4.5000	129.52	50.28
4.6000	132.28	49.70
4.7000	138.47	56.77
4.8000	139.69	66.32
4.9000	140.85	65.95
5.0000	143.61	68.65

Figure 5-10   Stochastic forecast result.

To estimate the parameters from a set of time-series data, the drift rate and volatility can be found by setting μ to be the average of the natural logarithm of the relative returns $ln\dfrac{S_t}{S_{t-1}}$ while σ is the standard deviation of all $ln\dfrac{S_t}{S_{t-1}}$ values.

Mean-Reversion Process

The following describes the mathematical structure of a mean-reverting process with drift: $\dfrac{\delta S}{S} = \eta\left(\overline{S}e^{\mu(\delta t)} - S\right)\delta t + \mu(\delta t) + \sigma\varepsilon\sqrt{\delta t}$. In order to obtain the rate of reversion and long-term rate, using the historical data points, run a regression such that $Y_t - Y_{t-1} = \beta_0 + \beta_1 Y_{t-1} + \varepsilon$. We therefore find that $\eta = -\ln[1 + \beta_1]$ and $\overline{S} = -\beta_0/\beta_1$

where

η is the rate of reversion to the mean

$\overline{S}$ is the long-term value the process reverts to

Y is the historical data series

β_0 is the intercept coefficient in a regression analysis

β_1 is the slope coefficient in a regression analysis

Jump-Diffusion Process

A jump-diffusion process is similar to a random walk process, but there is a probability of a jump at any point in time. The occurrences of such jumps are completely random, but their probability and magnitude are governed by the process itself.

$$\frac{\delta S}{S} = \eta\left(\bar{S}e^{\mu(\delta t)} - S\right)\delta t + \mu(\delta t) + \sigma\varepsilon\sqrt{\delta t} + \theta F(\lambda)(\delta t) \text{ for a jump-diffusion process}$$

where

θ is the jump size of S

$F(\lambda)$ is the inverse of the Poisson cumulative probability distribution

λ is the jump rate of S

The jump size can be found by computing the ratio of the post-jump to the pre-jump level, and the jump rate can be imputed from past historical data. The other parameters are found in the same way as above.

Nonlinear Extrapolation

Theory

Extrapolation involves making statistical forecasts by using historical trends that are projected for a specified period of time into the future. It is only used for time-series forecasts. For cross-sectional or mixed panel data (time-series with cross-sectional data), multivariate regression is more appropriate. This methodology is useful when major changes are not expected (i.e., causal factors are expected to remain constant) or when the causal factors of a situation are not clearly understood. It also helps discourage the introduction of personal biases into the process. Extrapolation is fairly reliable, relatively simple, and inexpensive. However, extrapolation, which assumes that recent and historical trends will continue, produces large forecast errors if discontinuities occur within the projected time period. That is, pure extrapolation of time series assumes that all we need to know is contained in the historical values of the series being forecasted. If we assume that past behavior is a good predictor of future behavior, extrapolation is appealing. This makes it a useful approach when all that is needed are many short-term forecasts.

This methodology estimates the $f(x)$ function for any arbitrary x value by interpolating a smooth nonlinear curve through all the x values, and, using this smooth curve, extrapolates future x values beyond the historical dataset. The methodology employs either the polynomial functional form or the rational functional form (a ratio of two polynomials). Typically, a polynomial functional form is sufficient for well-behaved data; however, rational functional forms are sometimes more accurate (especially with polar functions, i.e., functions with denominators approaching zero).

Procedure

- Start Excel and enter your data or open an existing worksheet with historical data to forecast (the illustration shown next uses the file Nonlinear Extrapolation from the examples folder).
- Select the time-series data and select **Risk Simulator | Forecasting | Nonlinear Extrapolation**.
- Select the extrapolation type (automatic selection, polynomial function, or rational function are available, but in this example, use automatic selection), enter the number of forecast period desired (Figure 5-11), and click on OK.

Interpretation of Results

Figure 5-12 presents the extrapolated forecast values, the error measurements, and the graphical representation of the extrapolation results. The error measurements should be used to check the validity of the forecast and are especially important when used to compare the forecast quality and accuracy of extrapolation versus time-series analysis.

Notes

When the historical data is smooth and follows some nonlinear patterns and curves, extrapolation is better than time-series analysis. However, when the data patterns follow seasonal cycles and a trend, time-series analysis will provide better results. It is always advisable to run both time-series analysis and extrapolation and compare the results to determine which has a lower error measure and a better fit.

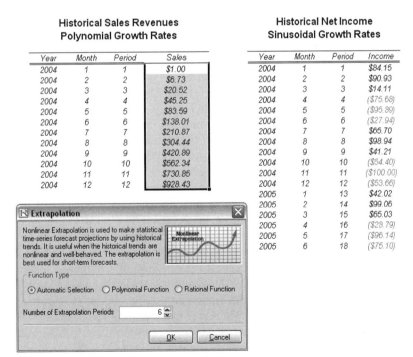

Figure 5-11   Running a nonlinear extrapolation.

Nonlinear Extrapolation

Statistical Summary

Extrapolation involves making statistical projections by using historical trends that are projected for a specified period of time into the future. It is only used for time-series forecasts. For cross-sectional or mixed panel data (time-series with cross-sectional data), multivariate regression is more appropriate. This methodology is useful when major changes are not expected, that is, causal factors are expected to remain constant or when the causal factors of a situation are not clearly understood. It also helps discourage introduction of personal biases into the process. Extrapolation is fairly reliable, relatively simple, and inexpensive. However, extrapolation, which assumes that recent and historical trends will continue, produces large forecast errors if discontinuities occur within the projected time period. That is, pure extrapolation of time series assumes that all we need to know is contained in the historical values of the series that is being forecasted. If we assume that past behavior is a good predictor of future behavior, extrapolation is appealing. This makes it a useful approach when all that is needed are many short-term forecasts.

This methodology estimates the f(x) function for any arbitrary x value, by interpolating a smooth nonlinear curve through all the x values, and using this smooth curve, extrapolates future x values beyond the historical data set. The methodology employs either the polynomial functional form or the rational functional form (a ratio of two polynomials). Typically, a polynomial functional form is sufficient for well-behaved data, however, rational functional forms are sometimes more accurate (especially with polar functions, i.e., functions with denominators approaching zero).

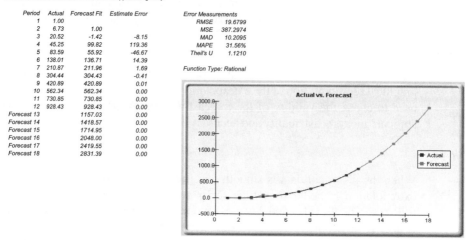

Period	Actual	Forecast Fit	Estimate Error
1	1.00		
2	6.73	1.00	
3	20.52	-1.42	-8.15
4	45.25	99.82	119.36
5	83.59	55.92	-46.67
6	138.01	136.71	14.39
7	210.87	211.96	1.69
8	304.44	304.43	-0.41
9	420.89	420.89	0.01
10	562.34	562.34	0.00
11	730.85	730.85	0.00
12	928.43	928.43	0.00
Forecast 13		1157.03	0.00
Forecast 14		1418.57	0.00
Forecast 15		1714.95	0.00
Forecast 16		2048.00	0.00
Forecast 17		2419.55	0.00
Forecast 18		2831.39	0.00

Error Measurements

RMSE	19.6799
MSE	387.2974
MAD	10.2095
MAPE	31.56%
Theil's U	1.1210

Function Type: Rational

Figure 5-12   Nonlinear extrapolation results.

Box-Jenkins ARIMA Advanced Time Series

Theory

One very powerful advanced times-series forecasting tool is the ARIMA or *Auto Regressive Integrated Moving Average* approach, which assembles three separate tools into a comprehensive model. The first tool segment is the autoregressive or AR term, which corresponds to the number of lagged values of the residual in the unconditional forecast model. In essence, the model captures the historical variation of actual data to a forecasting model and uses this variation or residual to create a better predicting model. The second tool segment is the integration order or the I term. This integration term corresponds to the number of differencings that the time series to be forecasted goes through to make the data stationary. This element accounts for any nonlinear growth rates existing in the data. The third tool segment is the moving average or MA term, which is essentially the moving average of lagged forecast errors. By incorporating lagged forecast errors, the model in essence learns from its forecast errors or mistakes and corrects for them through a moving-average calculation. The ARIMA model follows the Box-Jenkins methodology, with each term representing steps taken in the model construction until only random noise remains. Also, ARIMA modeling uses correlation techniques in generating forecasts. ARIMA can be used to model patterns that may not be visible in plotted data. In addition, ARIMA models can be mixed with exogenous variables, but one should ensure that the exogenous variables have enough data points to cover the additional number of periods to forecast. Finally, remember that ARIMA cannot and should not be used to forecast sto-chastic processes or time-series data that are stochastic in nature; instead, use the Stochastic Process module for forecasting.

An ARIMA model is superior to common time-series analysis and multivariate regressions for several reasons. The common finding in time-series analysis and mul-tivariate regression is that the error residuals are correlated with their own lagged values. This serial correlation violates the standard assumption of regression theory that disturbances are not correlated with other disturbances. The primary problems associated with serial correlation are as follows:

- Regression analysis and basic time-series analysis are no longer efficient linear estimators. However, because the error residuals can help to predict current error residuals, we can take advantage of this information to produce a better prediction of the dependent variable using ARIMA.
- Standard errors computed using the regression and time-series formula are not correct and are generally understated. If lagged dependent variables are set as the regressors, regression estimates are biased and inconsistent but can be fixed using ARIMA.

Autoregressive Integrated Moving Average or ARIMA(p,d,q) models are the exten-sion of the AR model that uses three components for modeling the serial correlation in the time-series data. The first component is the autoregressive (AR) term. The AR(p) model uses the p lags of the time series in the equation. An AR(p) model has the form: $y_t = a_1 y_{t-1} + \ldots + a_p y_{t-p} + e_t$. The second component is the integration (d) order term. Each integration order corresponds to differencing the time series. I(1) means differencing the data once. I (d) means differencing the data d times. The third component is the moving average (MA) term. The MA(q) model uses the q lags of the forecast errors to improve the forecast. An MA(q) model has the form: $y_t = e_t + b_1 e_{t-1} + \ldots + b_q e_{t-q}$. Finally, an ARMA(p,q) model has the combined form: $y_t = a_1 y_{t-1} + \ldots + a_p y_{t-p} + e_t + b_1 e_{t-1} + \ldots + b_q e_{t-q}$.

Procedure

- Start Excel and enter your data or open an existing worksheet with historical data to forecast (the illustration shown next uses the example file Time-series Forecasting).
- Click on **Risk Simulator | Forecasting | ARIMA** and select the time-series data.
- Enter the relevant P, D, and Q parameters (positive integers only), enter the number of forecast periods desired, and click on **OK.**

Interpretation of Results

In interpreting the results of an ARIMA model, most of the specifications are identical to the multivariate regression analysis. However, there are several additional sets of results specific to the ARIMA analysis, as seen in Figure 5-13. The first is the addition of the Akaike Information Criterion (AIC) and the Schwarz Criterion (SC), which are often used in ARIMA model selection and identification. That is, AIC and SC are used to determine if a particular model with specific set of p, d, and q parameters is a good statistical fit. SC imposes a greater penalty for additional coefficients than the AIC, but generally, the model with the lowest AIC and SC values should be chosen.

Finally, the ARIMA report provides an additional set of results called the autocorrelation (AC) and partial autocorrelation (PAC) statistics.

For instance, if autocorrelation AC(1) is nonzero, it means that the series is first order serially correlated. If AC dies off more or less geometrically with increasing lags, it implies that the series follows a low-order autoregressive process. If AC drops to zero after a small number of lags, it implies that the series follows a low-order moving-average process. In contrast, PAC measures the correlation of values that are k periods apart after removing the correlation from the intervening lags. If the pattern

ARIMA (Autoregressive Integrated Moving Average)

Regression Statistics

R-Squared (Coefficient of Determination)	0.7708	Akaike Information Criterion (AIC)	14.2506
Adjusted R-Squared	0.7573	Schwarz Criterion (SC)	14.3500
Multiple R (Multiple Correlation Coefficient)	0.8779	Log Likelihood	-133.3807
Standard Error of the Estimates (SEy)	580.9368	Durbin-Watson statistic	2.3576
Observations	19	Number of Iterations	0

Autoregressive Integrated Moving Average(ARIMA(p,d,q)) models are the extension of the AR model that use three components for modeling the serial correlation in the time series data. The first component is the autoregressive(AR) term. The AR(p) model uses the p lags of the time series in the equation. An AR(p) model has the form: y(t)=a(1)*y(t-1)+...+a(p)*y(t-p)+e(t).The second component is the integration(d) order term. Each integration order corresponds to differencing the time series. I(1) means differencing the data once. I(d) means differencing the data d times.The third component is the moving average(MA) term. The MA(q) model uses the q lags of the forecast errors to improve the forecast. An MA(q) model has the form: y(t)=e(t)+b(1)*e(t-1)+...+b(q)*e(t-q).Finally, an ARMA(p,q) model has the combined form: y(t)=a(1)*y(t-1)+...+a(p)*y(t-p)+e(t)+b(1)*e(t-1)+...+b(q)*e(t-q).

The R-Squared or Coefficient of Determination indicates that of the variation in the dependent variable can be explained and accounted for by the independent variables in this regression analysis. However, in a multiple regression, the Adjusted R-Squared takes into account the existence of additional independent variables or regressors and adjusts this R-Squared value to a more accurate view the regression's explanatory power. Hence, only of the variation in the dependent variable can be explained by the regressors. However, under some circumstances, it tends to be unreliable.

The Multiple Correlation Coefficient (Multiple R) measures the correlation between the actual dependent variable (Y) and the estimated or fitted (Y) based on the regression equation. This is also the square root of the Coefficient of Determination (R-Squared).

The Standard Error of the Estimates (SEy) describes the dispersion of data points above the below the regression line or plane. This value is used as part of the calculation to obtain the confidence interval of the estimates later.

The AIC and SC are often used in model selection. SC imposes a greater penalty for additional coefficients. Generally, the user should select a model with the lowest value of the AIC and SC.

The Durbin-Watson statistic measures the serial correlation in the residuals. Generally, DW less than 2 implies positive serial correlation.

Regression Results

	Intercept	Y(-1)
Coefficients	116.3328	0.9895
Standard Error	179.9049	0.1309
t-Statistic	0.6466	7.5604
p-Value	0.5265	0.0000
Lower 5%	-263.2333	0.7134
Upper 95%	495.8989	1.2656

Degrees of Freedom		**Hypothesis Test**	
Degrees of Freedom for Regression	1	Critical t-Statistic (99% confidence with df of 17)	63.6567
Degrees of Freedom for Residual	17	Critical t-Statistic (95% confidence with df of 17)	2.1098
Total Degrees of Freedom	18	Critical t-Statistic (90% confidence with df of 17)	1.7341

The Coefficients provide the estimated regression intercept and slopes. For instance, the coefficients are the b values in the following regression equation: Y = b(0) + b(1)X(1) + b(2)X(2) + ... + b(n)X(n). The Standard Errors measure how accurate the predicted Coefficients are, and the t-Statistics are the ratios of each predicted Coefficient to its Standard Error.

The t-Statistic is used in hypothesis testing, where we set the null hypothesis (Ho) such that the real mean of the Coefficient = 0, and the alternate hypothesis (Ha) such that the real mean of the Coefficient is not equal to 0. A t-test is is performed and the calculated t-Statistic is compared to the critical values at the relevant Degrees of Freedom for Residual. The t-test is very important as it calculates if each of the coefficents is statistically significant in the presence of the other regressors. This means that the t-test statistically verifies whether a regressor or independent variable should remain in the regression or it should be dropped.

The Coefficient is statistically significant if its calculated t-Statistic exceeds the Critical t-Statistic at the relevant degrees of freedom (df). The three main confidence levels used to test for significance are 90%, 95% and 99%. If a Coefficient's t-Statistic exceeds the Critical level, it is considered statistically significant. Alternatively, the p-Value calculates each t-Statistic's probability of occurrence, which means that the smaller the p-Value, the more significant the Coefficient. The usual critical levels for the p-Value are 0.01, 0.05, and 0.10, corresponding to the 99%, 95%, and 99% confidence levels.

The Coefficients with their p-Values highlighted in blue indicate that they are statistically significant at the 95% confidence or 0.05 alpha level, while those highlighted in red indicate that they are not statistically significant at any of the alpha levels.

Analysis of Variance

	Sums of Squares	Mean of Squares	F-Statistic	P-Value	**Hypothesis Test**	
Regression	4682238.0689	4682238.0689	57.1604	0.0000	Critical F-statistic (99% confidence with df of 1 and 17)	8.3997
Residual	1392538.5521	81914.0325			Critical F-statistic (95% confidence with df of 1 and 17)	4.4513
Total	6074776.6211	4764152.1014			Critical F-statistic (90% confidence with df of 1 and 17)	3.0262

The Analysis of Variance (ANOVA) table provides an F-test of the regression model's overall statistical significance. Instead of looking at individual regressors as in the t-test, the F-test looks at all the estimated Coefficient's statistical properties. The F-statistic is calculated as the ratio of the Regression's Mean of Squares to the Residual's Mean of Squares. The numerator measures how much of the regression is explained, while the denominator measures how much is unexplained. Hence, the larger the F-statistic, the more significant the model. The corresponding P-Value is calculated to test the null hypothesis (Ho) where all the Coefficients are simultaneously equal to zero, versus the alternate hypothesis (Ha) that they are all simultaneously different from zero, indicating a significant overall regression model. If the P-Value is smaller than the 0.01, 0.05, or 0.10 alpha significance, then the regression is significant. The same approach can be applied to the F-statistic.

Figure 5-13   Box Jenkins ARIMA forecast report.

Autocorrelation

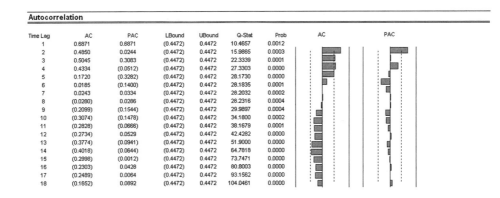

Time Lag	AC	PAC	LBound	UBound	Q-Stat	Prob
1	0.6871	0.6871	(0.4472)	0.4472	10.4657	0.0012
2	0.4850	0.0244	(0.4472)	0.4472	15.9865	0.0003
3	0.5045	0.3083	(0.4472)	0.4472	22.3339	0.0001
4	0.4334	(0.0512)	(0.4472)	0.4472	27.3303	0.0000
5	0.1720	(0.3282)	(0.4472)	0.4472	28.1730	0.0000
6	0.0185	(0.1400)	(0.4472)	0.4472	28.1835	0.0001
7	0.0243	0.0334	(0.4472)	0.4472	28.2032	0.0002
8	(0.0280)	0.0286	(0.4472)	0.4472	28.2316	0.0004
9	(0.2099)	(0.1544)	(0.4472)	0.4472	29.9897	0.0004
10	(0.3074)	(0.1478)	(0.4472)	0.4472	34.1800	0.0002
11	(0.2828)	(0.0666)	(0.4472)	0.4472	38.1679	0.0001
12	(0.2734)	0.0529	(0.4472)	0.4472	42.4282	0.0000
13	(0.3774)	(0.0941)	(0.4472)	0.4472	51.9000	0.0000
14	(0.4018)	(0.0644)	(0.4472)	0.4472	64.7818	0.0000
15	(0.2998)	(0.0012)	(0.4472)	0.4472	73.7471	0.0000
16	(0.2303)	0.0428	(0.4472)	0.4472	80.8003	0.0000
17	(0.2489)	0.0064	(0.4472)	0.4472	93.1562	0.0000
18	(0.1652)	0.0892	(0.4472)	0.4472	104.0461	0.0000

If autocorrelation AC(1) is nonzero, it means that the series is first order serially correlated. If AC(k) dies off more or less geometrically with increasing lag , it implies that the series follows a low-order autoregressive process. If AC(k) drops to zero after a small number of lags, it implies that the series follows a low-order moving-average process. Partial correlation PAC(k) measures the correlation of values that are k periods apart after removing the correlation from the intervening lags. If the pattern of autocorrelation can be captured by an autoregression of order less than k, then the partial autocorrelation at lag k will be close to zero. Ljung-Box Q-statistics and their p-values at lag k has the null hypothesis that there is no autocorrelation up to order k. The dotted lines in the plots of the autocorrelations are the approximate two standard error bounds. If the autocorrelation is within these bounds, it is not significantly different from zero at (approximately) the 5% significance level.

Forecasting

Period	Actual (Y)	Forecast (F)	Error (E)
1	584.1000	793.3540	(209.2540)
2	765.4000	694.3043	71.0957
3	892.3000	873.7021	18.5979
4	885.4000	999.2706	(113.8706)
5	677.0000	992.4430	(315.4430)
6	1,006.6000	786.2296	220.3704
7	1,122.1000	1,112.3713	9.7287
8	1,163.4000	1,226.6595	(63.2595)
9	993.2000	1,267.5262	(274.3262)
10	1,312.5000	1,099.1119	213.3881
11	1,545.3000	1,415.0618	130.2382
12	1,596.2000	1,645.4192	(49.2192)
13	1,260.4000	1,695.7852	(435.3852)
14	1,735.2000	1,363.5084	371.6916
15	2,029.7000	1,833.3267	196.3733
16	2,107.8000	2,124.7368	(16.9368)
17	1,650.3000	2,202.0173	(551.7173)
18	2,304.4000	1,749.3175	555.0825
19	2,639.4000	2,396.5546	242.8454
20		2,728.0397	
21		2,815.7494	

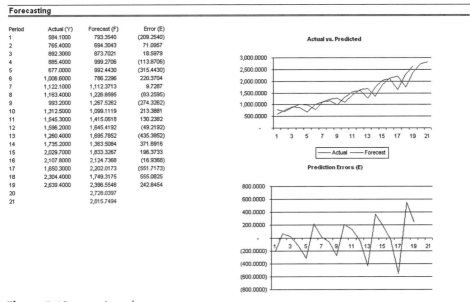

Figure 5-13   continued.

of autocorrelation can be captured by an autoregression of order less than k, then the partial autocorrelation at lag k will be close to zero. The Ljung-Box Q-statistics and their p-values at lag k are also provided, where the null hypothesis being tested is such that there is no autocorrelation up to order k. The dotted lines in the plots of the auto-correlations are the approximate two standard error bounds. If the autocorrelation is within these bounds, it is not significantly different from zero at approximately the 5 percent significance level. Finding the right ARIMA model takes practice and experience. These AC, PAC, SC, and AIC statistics are highly useful diagnostic tools to help identify the correct model specification. Finally, the ARIMA parameter results are obtained using sophisticated optimization and iterative algorithms. This means that, although the functional forms look like those of a multivariate regression, they are not the same. ARIMA is a much more computationally intensive and advanced econometric approach.

"Sensitivity" Financial Forecasting

Modified Percent of Sales Method

Historical relationships that hold firm generally will not change much at least into the near term. Finding relationships in historical statements will improve forecast accuracy—it's as simple as that. If historical relationships, say accounts receivables to revenue, were to change significantly, your ability to predict results would become murky until you identified and justified the new relationship—that is where forecasting financial statements come in; this is arguably the best way to complement and/or reinforce statistical methods.

One widely used method is *modified percent of sales*. The rationale behind this method is based on the premise that the balance sheet is correlated with changes in sales. Whether a firm restructures or just grows normally, variations in revenue generally require asset/liabilities adjustments. The "sensitivity" approach to forecasting is an efficient method to develop strategic plans. In the process of developing a forecast, you will work with two important equations: Financial Needs Formula (F) and Projected Percent of Sales Externally Financed Formula (E):

$$F = A/S \, (\Delta S) + \Delta NFA - L_1/S \, (\Delta S) - P(S)(1 - d) + R$$

The F formula determines the external financing needs of the firm. If used in conjunction with the percent of sales method, both techniques render the same answer. The formulas are easy to enter into the HP 19II's solver.

$$E = (A/S - L_1/S) - (P/g)(1 + g)(1 - d) + R/\Delta S$$

Equation Variables

A = Projected Spontaneous Assets

D = Dividend Payout Rate

E = Projected Percent of Sales Growth Externally Financed

F = Cumulative Financial Needs   (−F = Surplus)

F_1 = Incremental Financial Needs   (−F_1 = Incremental Surplus)

L_1 = Spontaneous Liabilities

P = Projected Profit Margin

R = Debt Maturities

ΔS = Change in Sales

The E formula identifies the percentage of sales growth requiring external financing. The two equations are interconnected since both are derived from the popular IAS and FAS cash flow statement. For example, firms with high-growth potential create shareholder value. That aphorism is ancient, and yet, a high-growth firm running on high octaine fixed assets can push the firm to the brink.

Setting up the Percent of Sales Method: Do Financial Statements Make Sense?

Because balance sheet changes follow the income statement, the income statement is a logical point of departure. Internally generated sources of cash (payables, accruals, retained earnings, and so on) appearing on the balance sheet are influenced by revenue and margin assumptions. Assets, uses of cash, are also tied to the income statement. A good test of income statement credibility is the comparison of pure output variables (POVs), projected pretax margins, aftertax margins, and return on total assets with historical levels. Consider the Boston Widget financial statements and the analysis, which follow:

Boston Widget Co. Inc.
Balance Sheet and Income Statement
Year Ended December 31

Assets	2005	2006	2007
Cash	$15,445	$12,007	$11,717
Receivables	$51,793	$55,886	$88,571
Inventory	$56,801	$99,087	$139,976
Current Assets	$124,039	$166,980	$240,264
Fixed Assets	$44,294	$46,340	$48,539
Total Assets	$168,333	$213,320	$288,803
Liabilities and Equity			
Short Term Debt	$9,562	$15,300	$54,698
Payables	$20,292	$31,518	$59,995
Accruals	$10,328	$15,300	$21,994
Current Maturities	$500	$500	$500
Current Liabilities	$40,682	$62,618	$137,187
Long Term Debt	$27,731	$36,491	$35,706
Total Liabilities	$68,413	$99,109	$172,893
Common Stock	$69,807	$69,807	$69,807
Retained Earnings	$30,113	$44,404	$46,103
Total Liabilities and Equity	$168,333	$213,320	$288,803
* Includes and new additional financing required because of changes to historical information.			$8,205
			$35,214
Annual Sales	$512,693	$553,675	$586,895
Cost of Goods Sold	$405,803	$450,394	$499,928
Gross Profit	$106,890	$103,281	$86,967
Profits	$28,240	$19,005	$2,265
Dividends	$7,060	$4,764	$566

INPUT SCREEN: PROJECTION ASSUMPTIONS

	2008	2009	2010	2011	2012
Cash	2.0%	2.0%	2.0%	2.0%	2.0%
Receivables	15.1%	15.1%	15.1%	15.1%	15.1%
Inventory	23.9%	23.9%	23.9%	23.9%	23.9%
Fixed Assets	8.3%	8.3%	8.3%	8.3%	8.3%
Accounts Payable	10.2%	10.2%	10.2%	10.2%	10.2%
Accruals	3.7%	3.7%	3.7%	3.7%	3.7%
Sales Growth Rate	6.0%	6.0%	6.0%	6.0%	6.0%
Profit Margin	1.0%	1.0%	1.0%	1.0%	1.0%
Dividend Payout	25.0%	25.0%	25.0%	25.0%	25.0%
Loan Amortization	$500.0	$500.0	$500.0	$500.0	$500.0

Current assets proportional (or spontaneous) to sales include cash, receivables, prepaid expenses, and inventory. For instance, if accounts receivable historically run 30 percent of sales and next year's sales are forecasted to be $100 million, accounts receivable will be projected at $30 million. Fixed assets do not generally correlate precisely with sales.

On the right side of the balance sheet, spontaneous liabilities-accounts payable and accruals move in tandem with sales. Liabilities independent of sales—all the funded ones representing financing activities—are excluded. Equity including preferred and common are financing activities and are not directly derived from variations in sales. Retained earnings is calculated by deducting the dividend payout from net profits. Before we go further, another important point to make is that it is also necessary to identify and estimate noncritical variables (not included in this exercise). This is accomplished by extrapolating historical patterns or adjusting historical trends. Examples of noncritical variables are various prepaid assets and disposals.

Applying modified sales percentage method to Boston's 2007 financial statements, we see that the following accounts have been calculated as a percentage of 2008 sales and will be used as projection assumptions for the company's original five year strategic plan:

Boston Widget Co. Inc.
Projected Statements
Year Ended December 31
   ** Note: calculation carried out 5 decimal places to generate this projection
INCOME STATEMENT:

		2008	2009	2010	2011	2012
Sales: 2008 Sales = 2007 Sales (.06)		$622,108.7	$659,435.2	$699,001.3	$740,941.4	$785,397.9
Profits	[.01 ($622,108.7)]	$6,221.1	$6,594.4	$6,990.0	$7,409.4	$7,854.0
Dividends	[.25 ($6,221.1)]	$1,555.3	$1,648.6	$1,747.5	$1,852.4	$1,963.5

BALANCE SHEET:

Cash	[.02 ($622,108.7)]	$12,442.2	$13,165.2	$13,955.1	$14,792.4	$15,680.0
Receivables	[.151 ($622,108.7)]	$93,885.3	$99,518.4	$105,489.5	$111,818.8	$118,528.0

Inventory	[.239 ($622,108.7)]	$148,374.6	$157,277.0	$166,713.7	$176,716.5	$187,319.5
Current Assets		$254,702.0	$269,960.6	$286,158.3	$303,327.8	$321,527.4
Fixed Assets	[.083 ($622,108.7)]	$51,451.3	$54,538.4	$57,810.7	$61,279.4	$64,956.1
Total Assets		$306,153.3	$324,499.1	$343,969.0	$364,607.1	$386,483.6
Liabilities, Financial Needs and Equity						
Short Term Debt	[not tied to slaes]	$54,698.0	$54,698.0	$54,698.0	$54,698.0	$54,698.0
Accounts Payables	[.102 ($622,108.7)]	$63,594.7	$67,410.4	$71,455.0	$75,742.3	$80,286.8
Accruals	[.037 ($622,108.7)]	$23,313.6	$24,712.5	$26,195.2	$27,766.9	$29,432.9
Current Maturity	[not tied to sales]	$500.0	$500.0	$500.0	$500.0	$500.0
Current Liab.		$142,106.3	$147,320.8	$152,848.2	$158,702.2	$164,917.8
Long Term Debt	[not tied to sales]	$35,206.0	$34,706.0	$34,206.0	$33,706.0	$33,206.0
Common Stock	[not tied to sales]	$69,807.0	$69,807.0	$69,807.0	$69,807.0	$69,807.0
Retained Earn	[1998 R/E + $6221.1 − $1555.3]	$50,768.8	$55,714.6	$60,957.1	$66,514.2	$72,404.6
Financial Needs	** [Plug]	**$8,265.2**	**$16,950.6**	**$26,150.7**	**$35,872.8**	**$46,148.2**
Liabilities and Equity		$306,153.3	$324,499.1	$343,969.0	$364,607.1	$386,483.6

You can see that Boston requires additional debt or equity funding to meet sales targets in each of the four years projected.

Reintroducing the F and E equations, we can draw conclusions that go beyond the yields provided by a simple accounting projection. Let's begin by first examining the F equation.

$$F = A/S \ (\Delta S) + \Delta NFA - L_l/S \ (\Delta S) - P(S)(1 - d) + R$$

$$F = .4094 \ (35214) + 2912.3 - .1397 \ (35214) - .01 \ (622109) \ (1 - .25) + 500 = 8244$$

The results approximate (rounding) the same financial needs as the projected financial statements above:

We see the effect independent (X) variables have on Boston's (Y), that is, financial needs after adjustments. The first test involves changes in spontaneous asset levels. Currently, Boston's asset investments are projected at 49.2 percent of sales. If, for example, spontaneous assets levels decrease, the overall effect on financial needs or F will also be a decrease. Since inventory and accounts receivable usually make up 80 percent of current assets, it may be best to hold the line to minimum levels in order to maintain optimal levels of working capital. When current assets operate at optimal points, the cash cycles becomes smooth and clean.

Another sensitivity variable is *spontaneous liabilities*. If Boston's spontaneous liabilities increase from its current level of 14 percent, financial needs will decrease. For example, by increasing accruals (a source of cash), financial needs will decrease as assets levels are approached or surpassed. What would be the overall effect if sales decreased? It makes sense that reduced sales projections require less financing and result in reduced external support. The same theory holds true for the dividend rate. By lowering the dividend payout ratio, additional funds will be funneled back into the company (retained earnings). With additional internal funds available to support future needs, cash requirements are reduced along with unsystematic risk. And so stakeholders relax a bit. Now let us look at E.

$$E = (A/S - L_1/S) - (P/g)(1 + g)(1 - d) + (R/\Delta S)$$

$$E = .492122 - .1397 - .01/.06 (1 + .06)(1 - .25) + .014 = .234$$

where

E = Projected % of Sales Growth Externally Financed

G = Growth Rate

Thus, 23.4 percent of Boston's sales growth will be generated by external financing, with 76.6 percent generated by internal cash flow (.234 × 35213 = 8244, same answer as above).

Deriving Financial Needs Using The "F" and "E" Equations

Boston Widget Co. Inc.: Base Case Projection
Financial Needs (F): (Note: Fixed Assets are included in A/S)

F = A/S(ΔS) – L$_1$/S(ΔS) – P(S)(1 – d) + R [Program this formula into the HP-19BII calculator]

F = .4094 (35214) + 2912.3 – .1397 (35214) – .01 (622109) (1 – .25) + 500 = 8244

		2008	2009	2010	2011	2012
F1	=	8,244.3	8,707.6	9,200.1	9,722.1	10,275.4
F	=	8,244.3	16,951.9	26,151.9	35,874.0	46,149.4
A/S	=	49.2%	49.2%	49.2%	49.2%	49.2%
T	=	6.0%	6.0%	6.0%	6.0%	6.0%
L$_1$/S	=	14.0%	14.0%	14.0%	14.0%	14.0%
R/ΔS	=	1.4%	1.3%	1.3%	1.2%	1.1%
L	=	153.9%	158.5%	163.0%	167.5%	171.8%

Percent of Sales Externally Financed:

E = (A/S-L$_1$/S) – (P/G)(1 + G)(1d) + R/ΔS [Program this formula into the HP-19BII]

E = .492122 – .1397 – .01/.06 (1 + .06)(1 – .25) + 0.14 = .234

		2008	2009	2010	2011	2012
E	=	23.4%	23.3%	23.3%	23.2%	23.1%

23.4% of Boston's sales growth will be financed externally.

And so, .23412 (35214) = 8244 which is exactly the financial needs using the "F" formula

PROOF:		2008	2009	2010	2011	2012
E * ΔS	=	8,244.3	8,707.6	9,200.1	9,722.1	10,275.4
CUMULATIVE		8,244.3	16,951.9	26,151.9	35,874.0	46,149.4

As the formula implies, the E equation determines how much sales growth requires external financing. If E reaches 95 percent in the projection period, only 5 percent of sales growth will be internally financed; this is an immediate storm signal, especially if the base-year leverage is excessive.

Setting E to zero and solving for G, the Sales Growth Rate, will give you a fast reading on the quality and magnitude of cash flows. Say, E is set to zero and G falls somewhere in the first industry quartile. This means sales growth rates are not only strong but can be financed with internal cash flow. Take another example. Let us assume that base-year leverage is high and you want to reduce leverage by internal financing levels set at 40 percent. Set the equation at 60 percent and solve for the capital output ratio required to make your strategy work. If embedded ratios (receivables, inventory, and fixed assets) are below industry or benchmarks, call a meeting of the department heads and read them the riot act.

The Cash Deficit Identifying the Borrower's Need

The Cash Deficit is the amount of external cash required from any source, bank or nonbank. The bank reviews the cash deficit to determine its causes. The deficit may be caused by growth core assets and capital expenditures; by nonproductive uses such as dividends and treasury stock purchases; or by large debt maturities. Most companies will show a combination of these uses.

Can the Borrower Afford to Grow?

Are leverage, coverage, and liquidity ratios at reasonable levels, even during periods of financial stress? Coverage ratios may indicate that margins are too slim to support increased volume.

Table 5-1 Projections Methods Summary

Summary			"F"	"F"
Method	System	Advantages	First Year	Cumulative
Projected Financial Statements	Computer	Provides forecasted financial statements	8,265.2	46,149.4
"F" Equation	Financial Calculator	Derives financial needs quickly and allows bankers to perform sensitivity analysis	8,244.3	46,149.4
"E" Equation	Financial Calculator	Used with "F" equation determines if borrower is providing sufficient internally generated funds	8,244.3	46,149.4

Use of Forward-Looking Tools in the Approval Process

Formal presentation of financial projections or other forms of forward-looking analysis of the borrower are important in making explicit the conditions required for a loan to perform and in communicating the vulnerabilities of the transaction to those responsible for approving loans.[2] Technology-driven projections rather than only describing single sets of "most likely" scenarios, characterize the kind of real-world events that might impair the loan. Confidence levels set around probabilities that operating cash flows will fail to cover debt service and probabilities that a borrower's capital structure will fail represent two major determinants of loan performance. Rigorous forecasting tools are central to initial approvals and to determining the adequacy of provisions and reserves.

Although it may be tempting to avoid running up simulations and optimizations for smaller borrowers, such as middle-market firms, these customers may collectively represent a significant portion of the institution's loan portfolio. Applying formal forward-looking analysis even on a basic level will help the institution identify and manage overall portfolio risk and pass the scrutiny of regulators with flying colors.

Regulators stress that banks understand their customers' financial condition, ensure that credits are in compliance with existing covenants, corroborate that projected cash flows on major credits meet debt-servicing requirements, affirm that in secured deals, collateral provides adequate coverage, and that problem loans are classified on a timely basis. A common problem among troubled banks was their failure to monitor borrowers, to obtain periodic financial information, and to stress testing data sufficiently with modern tools. These banks failed to recognize early signs that loan quality was deteriorating, and they missed the opportunity to work with borrowers to stem their financial deterioration. As a result of their poor, often naive loan monitoring, bank management was faced with a costly process to determine the dimension and severity of problem loans, and so large write-offs were the ultimate consequence.

---

2. FRB, Division of Banking Supervision and Regulation, Sr 00-7 (Sup) May 2, 2000, Subject: Lending Standards for Commercial Loans.

CHAPTER 6

Using Risk Simulator Optimization Procedures and Basel II Modeling Toolkit's Corporate Valuation Model

Companies restructure their product mix to boost sales and profits, increase shareholder value, or survive when the corporate structure becomes impaired. In successful restructurings, management not only actualizes lucrative new projects, but also abandons existing projects when they no longer yield sufficient returns, thereby channeling resources to more value creating uses.

At one level restructuring can be viewed as changes in financing structures and management. At another level, it may be operational—in response to production overhauls, market trends, technology, and industry or macroeconomic disturbances. It is often the essence of strategy formulation—that is, management's response to changes in the environment to creatively deploy internal resources that improve the firm's competitive position. Indeed, changing operating and financial structures in pursuit of a long-run strategy is a key corporate goal, representing the most direct path to shareholder value.

For banks called on to finance corporate restructurings, things are a bit different. For example, most loans provide a fixed return over fixed periods that are dependent on interest rates and the borrower's ability to pay. A good loan will be repaid on time and in full. Hopefully, the bank's cost of funds will be low, with the deal providing attractive risk adjusted returns. If the borrower's business excels, *the bank will not participate in upside corporate values* (except for a vicarious pleasure in the firm's success). However, if a borrower ends up financially distressed, lenders share much and perhaps most of the pain.

Two disparate goals—controlling default (credit) risk, the bank's objective, and value maximization, a traditional corporate aspiration—are often at odds, particularly if borrowers want term money to finance excessively aggressive projects. In the vast majority of cases traditional credit analysis, where the spotlight focuses on deterministically drawn projections, hidden risks are often exceedingly difficult to uncover. Devoid of viable projections, bankers will time and again fail to bridge gaps between their agendas and client aspirations.

This chapter offers ways for bankers to advance both their analytics and their communication skills; senior bank officials and clients alike, to "get the deal done" and ensure risk/reward agendas, are set in equilibrium. Undeniably, the direct way to achieve results is to take a stochastic view of strategic plans rather than rely inappropriately on deterministic base case /conservative scenarios. Let's start with the following fundamentals:

- Stochastically driven optimization models allow bankers to more realistically represent the flow of random variables.
- In negotiating restructuring loans, borrowers (and bankers) can determine under stochastic assumptions optimal amounts to invest in and/or borrow to finance projects.
- McKinsey & Company, Inc[1] suggests that business units should be defined and separated into lines of business. Business units should be broken down into the smallest components and analyzed at the base level first.
- Consolidating financials, rather than consolidated reports, should be used to perform business-unit valuations.
- In this post-Enron/WorldCom age, bankers will likely think twice before failing to look beyond consolidated financials to take care of restructuring or project finance deals, especially if the credit grade is weak.
- Knowing the market value and volatility of the borrower's assets is crucial in determining the probability of default.
- A firm's leverage has the effect of magnifying its underlying asset volatility. As a result, industries with low asset volatility can take on larger amounts of leverage while industries with high asset volatility tend to take on less.
- After restructuring is optimized at the unit stage, unit-level valuations are linked to the borrower's consolidated worksheet to process corporate valuations.

Mini Case

Consider the data in Excel spreadsheets depicted in Figures 6-1, 6-2, and 6-3. The worksheets depict management's original restructuring plan, and the model can be found in the Modeling Toolkit under **Optimization | Investment Capital Allocation (Part A)**. ABC Bank is asked to approve a $3,410,000 loan facility for the hypothetical firm RI Furniture Manufacturing LTD. Management wants to restructure four of its operating subsidiaries. In support of the facility, the firm supplied the bank with deterministic base-case and conservative consolidating and consolidated projections—income statement, balance sheet, and cash flows.

The deterministic or static forecasts tendered the bank limited the variability of outcomes. From a banker's perspective, it is often difficult to single out which of a

---

1. Tom Copeland et al., *Valuation*, 3rd ed. (New York: John Wiley & Sons, 2000)

	Distribution	Operating Profit Margin Range	Operating Profit Margin Most Likely
All Weather Resin Wicker Sets	Triangular	0.085 - 0.115	0.097
Commuter Mobile Office Furniture	Triangular	0.066 - 0.086	0.076
Specialty Furniture	Normal	Mean = 0.035	SD = 0.0035
Custom Built Furniture	Uniform	0.045 - 0.055	None

Figure 6-1   Product line assumptions.

Product Line	Lower Bound	Upper Bound
All Weather Resin Wicker Sets	1,000,000	1,250,000
Commuter Mobile Office Furniture	600,000	1,000,000
Specialty Furniture	570,000	1,100,000
Custom Built Furniture	400,000	900,000

Figure 6-2   Investment boundaries.

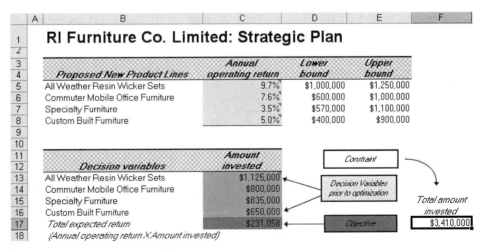

Figure 6-3   Investment model.

series of strategic options the borrower should pursue if the bank fails to understand differences in the range and distribution shape of possible outcomes and the most likely result associated with each option. Indeed, an overly aggressive restructuring program might reduce the firm's credit grade and increase default probabilities. We will not let this happen. Undeniably, this deal deserves stochastic analytics rather than a bread basket consisting of outdated deterministic tools.

On the basis of (deterministic) consolidating projections, bankers developed the stochastic spreadsheet depicted in Figure 6-3. This spreadsheet included maximum/minimum investments ranges supporting restructuring in each of four product lines. Using Risk Simulator along with the Basel II Modeling Toolkit (Corporate Valuation models), the firm's bankers came up with a stochastic solution. On a unit level, they developed a probability distribution assigned to each uncertain element in the forecast, established an optimal funding array for the various business combinations, and held cash flow volatility to acceptable levels, preserving the credit grade (again at the unit level). Finally, the last optimization (worksheet) was linked to the consolidating/consolidated discounted cash flow (DCF) valuation worksheets. The firm's bankers then determined postrestructuring equity values, specific confidence levels, and probabilities of asset values falling below debt values.

Business History

RI Furniture started operations in 1986 and manufactures a full line of indoor/outdoor furniture. Operating subsidiaries targeted for restructuring, depicted below, represent approximately 65 percent of consolidated operations.

All-Weather Resin Wicker Sets

This furniture features a complete aluminum frame with hand-woven polypropylene resin produced to resist weather. Operating profit margin distributions and investment ranges for each subsidiary are shown in Figures 6-1 to 6-3.

Commuter Mobile Office Furniture

The Commuter rolls from its storage location to any work area and sets up in minutes. It integrates computer peripherals (monitor, CPU tower, keyboard, and printer) in a compact, secure mobile unit.

Specialty Furniture

After restructuring, this business segment will include production of hotel reception furniture, cafe furniture, canteen furniture, restaurant seating, and banqueting furniture.

Custom-Built Furniture

Furniture will be custom built in the firm's own workshop or sourced from a host of reputable manufacturers both at home and abroad.

In the first optimization run (Run 1), there is a constraint on $3,410,000 investment —that is, the bank's facility cannot exceed $3,410,000. Later. we place an additional constraint: the forecast variable's risk (measured in terms of volatility).

Risk Simulator Optimization Procedures

The model is already set up with optimization and simulation assumptions and can be run by simply clicking on the **Risk Simulator | Optimization | Run Optimization**. The procedures used in setting up the optimization model from scratch are as follows:

1. Create a new profile by starting the model and clicking on **Risk Simulator | New Profile**, and give it a name. By creating a new profile, you can now set up different simulation assumptions and optimization parameters in the same Excel model, without having to create multiple models.

Note: In this example write-up, we selected the "Specify a random number sequence" seed value of 123456.

2. Select cell C5 and click on **Risk Simulator | Set Input Assumption**, and enter in the relevant assumptions (Figure 6-4 illustrates an assumption):

    All-Weather Resin Wicker Sets (C5):

    Triangular Distribution: Min 8.5%, Most Likely 9.7% and Max 11.5%

    Commuter Mobile Office Furniture (C6):

    Triangular Distribution: Min 6.6%, Most Likely 7.6% and Max 8.6%

    Specialty Furniture (C7):

    Normal Distribution: Mean 3.5%, Standard Deviation 0.35%

    Custom-Built Furniture (C8):

    Uniform Distribution: Min 4.5% and Max 5.5%

3. Set the Objective of the optimization. Select cell **C17** and click on **Risk Simulator | Optimization | Set Objective** (or click on the **O** icon in the Risk Simulator toolbar), and select **MAX** (see Figure 6-5).

4. Set the Decision Variables. Select cell **C13** and click on **Risk Simulator | Optimization | Set Decision Variable** (or click on the **D** icon in the Risk Simulator

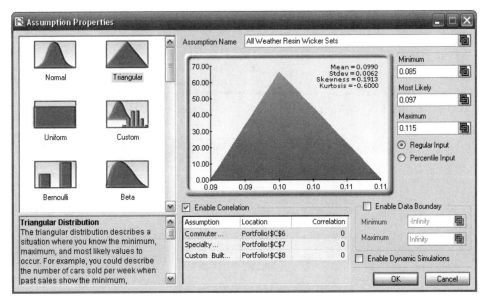

Figure 6-4   Setting input assumptions.

toolbar). Then, select **Continuous** as the decision type, and you can either enter in the lower and upper bound values (**1000000** and **1250000**) or simply click on the link icon and link it to the relevant cells (D5 and E5) as shown in Figure 6-6. Repeat for cells **C14** to **C16** with the relevant upper and lower bounds:

	Lower Bound	Upper Bound
All-Weather Resin Wicker Sets	$1,000,000	$1,250,000
Commuter Mobile Office Furniture	$600,000	$1,000,000
Specialty Furniture	$570,000	$1,100,000
Custom-Built Furniture	$400,000	$900,000

Note: Clicking on the link icon (Figure 6-6) will allow you to link the lower and upper bounds to specific cells instead of typing it in. The benefit of linking is that you can do a simple Risk Simulator Copy/Paste to replicate the decision variables on other cells.

5. Set the Constraint. Click on **Risk Simulator | Optimization | Set Constraint** (or click on the C icon in the Risk Simulator toolbar) and click on ADD to add a constraint. Then, click on the link icon to link it to cell **F17** and set it to be <= (less than or equal to) **3410000** (Figure 6-7).

6. Run the Optimization. Click on **Risk Simulator | Optimization | Run Optimization** or click on the Run Optimization icon. You may now click on **OK** to run the optimization, or review the model setup by reviewing all the tabs (Figure 6-8).

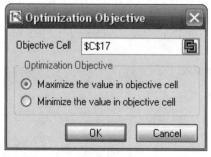

Figure 6-5   Setting the optimization objective.

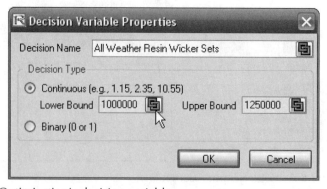

Figure 6-6   Optimization's decision variables.

7. Interpret the results. Notice that after the optimization, the **Total Expected Return** has increased from $231,058 to $246,072, creating a higher level of expected total returns. In both cases, the total amount invested remains the same at $3,410,000 (Figure 6-9).

8. You may now run a simulation on both the unoptimized and the optimized portfolios (simply click on **Risk Simulator | Run Simulation**). The results are shown in Figures 6-10 and 6-11. Note that the expected value increased for the optimized portfolio but that the risk is slightly higher, as measured by the standard deviation. However, the proportional increase in risk is very minimal as measured by the Coefficient of Variation (the standard deviation divided by mean), which is a measure of return to risk ratio, and can also be interpreted as the volatility of the investment returns. Therefore, the optimized portfolio is significantly better by returning over $15,000 without much change to the relative risk to returns ratio.

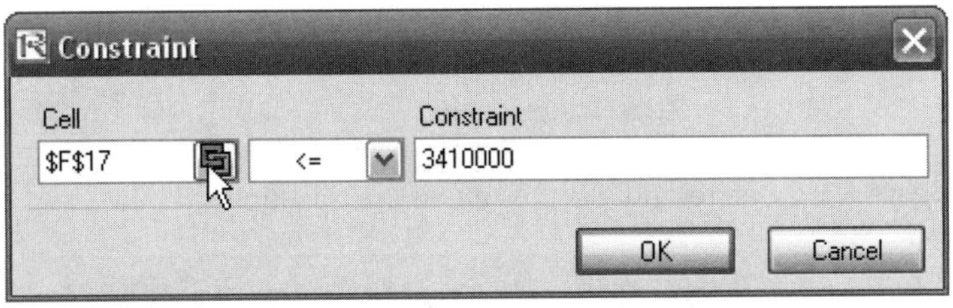

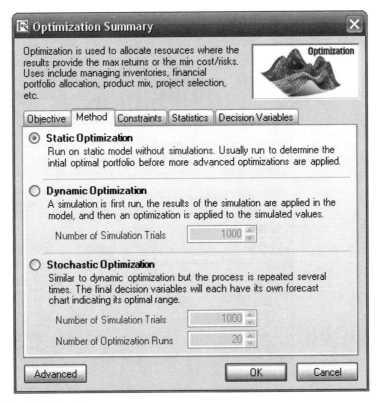

Figure 6-7   Setting a constraint.

Figure 6-8   Optimization summary.

BEFORE OPTIMIZATION:

Decision variables	Amount invested
All Weather Resin Wicker Sets	$1,125,000
Commuter Mobile Office Furniture	$800,000
Specialty Furniture	$835,000
Custom Built Furniture	$650,000
Total expected return	$231,058
(Annual operating return X Amount invested)	

AFTER OPTIMIZATION:

Decision variables	Amount invested
All Weather Resin Wicker Sets	$1,250,000
Commuter Mobile Office Furniture	$1,000,000
Specialty Furniture	$570,000
Custom Built Furniture	$590,000
Total expected return	$246,072
(Annual operating return X Amount invested)	

Figure 6-9   Before and after results of optimization.

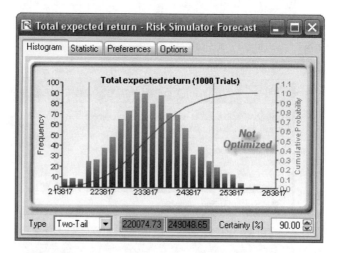

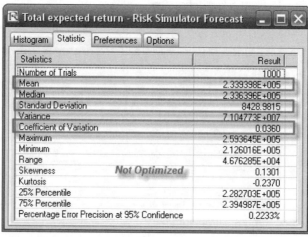

Figure 6-10   Not optimized simulation results.

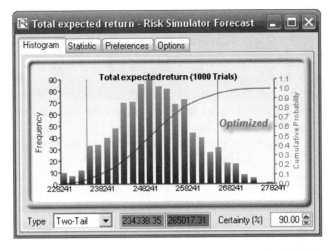

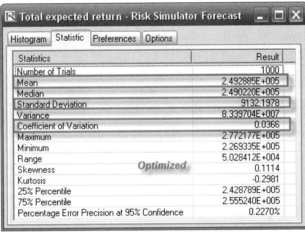

Figure 6-11   Optimized simulation results.

Analytical Note: You will see that the expected value (mean) from the simulation may be slightly different from the single-point estimates in the model (cell C17). This is because the simulated forecast results are based on thousands of scenarios as well as on the input assumptions set in the model. If asymmetrical assumptions are set, the results may be slightly different than the single point results.

Risk Simulator Optimization Procedures Volatility and Optimization

CLIENT'S AGENDA	BANKER'S AGENDA
Maximize Shareholder Value (Goal: Profit Maximization)	Prevent client's risk rating (debt rating) from migrating beyond a predetermined value (Goal: Risk Reduction)
Minimize Cost of Capital	

The volatility of operating results affects the volatility of assets. This point is crucial in the banking business. Suppose we determine the market value of a corporation's assets along with the volatility of that value using Risk Simulator. Volatility measures the propensity of asset values to change within a given time period. For example, Moody's KMV demonstrates volatility correlates with default probabilities. For instance, assume corporate asset market value is $150 million, while $75 million debt is due in one year. If asset volatility causes current asset market value to fall below $75 million, default will occur.

Thus, as a prudent next step, bankers discuss the first optimization run with management on three levels: (1) maximum expected return, (2) optimal investments/loan facility and, (3) volatility of expected return. If volatility is unacceptable, the standard deviation must be reduced to preserve credit grade integrity.

The model we use next is Part B of the Furniture Optimization model found in the Modeling Toolkit (**Modeling Toolkit | Optimization | Capital Investments—Part B**). To get started, review Part A of the model before attempting to run this follow-up model. This follow-up model looks at a twist at the optimization procedures performed in Part A by now incorporating risk and the return to risk ratio (Sharpe Ratio, a Nobel Prize–winning concept). Notice some updated information in this model, complete with risk measures (volatilities of cash flow returns) as well as other added results from the Markowitz Efficient Frontier.

In this model, instead of simply maximizing returns in the portfolio (Opt Run 1 in the Part A model), which, by definition, will create a potentially higher risk portfolio (high risk equals high return), we may also want to maximize the Sharpe Ratio (portfolio returns to risk ratio). This will in turn provide the maximum levels of return subject to the least risk, or for the same risk, provide the highest returns, yielding an optimal point on the Markowitz Efficient Frontier for this portfolio (Opt Run 2 in the Part B model).

As can be seen in the optimization results table in Figure 6-13, Opt Run 1 provides the highest returns ($246,072) as opposed to the original value of $231,058. Nonetheless, in Opt Run 2, where we maximize the Sharpe Ratio instead, we get a slightly

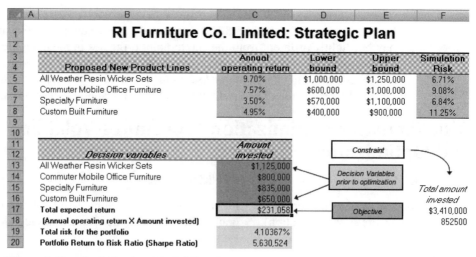

Figure 6-12 Optimization Model Part B.

lower return ($238,816), but the total risk for the entire portfolio is reduced to 4.055% instead of 4.270% . This illustrates the concept of high risk equals high return.

A simulation is run on the original investment allocation, Opt Run 1, and Opt Run 2, and the results are shown in Figures 6-14 to 6-16. Here, we clearly see that the slightly smaller returns provide a reduced level of risk, which is good for the bank.

	Original	Opt Run 1	Opt Run 2
All Weather Resin Wicker Sets	$1,125,000	$1,250,000	$1,250,000
Commuter Mobile Office Furniture	$800,000	$1,000,000	$924,636
Specialty Furniture	$835,000	$570,000	$570,000
Custom Built Furniture	$650,000	$590,000	$665,364
Objective to Maximize		Returns	Returns/Risk
Total expected return	$231,058	$246,072	$238,816
Total risk for the portfolio	4.104%	4.270%	4.055%
Portfolio Return to Risk Ratio (Sharpe Ratio)	5630524	5762758	5889030

Figure 6-13   Sample optimization results.

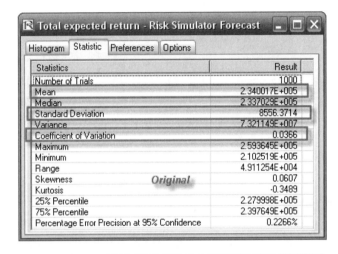

Figure 6-14   Simulation results of original investment values.

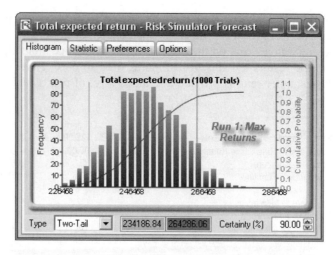

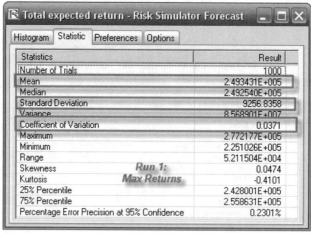

Figure 6-15   Simulation results of optimization Run 1.

To run this predefined optimization model, simply click on **Risk Simulator |
Optimization | Run Optimization** and click on **OK**. To change the objective from
Maximizing Returns to Risk to Maximizing Returns, simply click on the Objective O
icon in the Risk Simulator toolbar or click on **Risk Simulator | Optimization | Set
Objective** and link it to either cell **C20** for Sharpe Ratio or **C17** for Returns, and then
run the optimization.

To set up the optimization from scratch, please refer to the instructions for Model
A or Part I of this exercise.

In addition, the total investment budget allowed can be changed to analyze what
happens to the returns and risk of the portfolio. For instance, Figure 6-17 illustrates
the results from such an analysis and the resulting expected risk and return values. In
order to better understand the risk structure of each point, an optimization is carried
out and a simulation is run. Figures 6-18 and 6-19 show two sample extreme cases
where $2.91M versus $3.61M are lent. From the results, one can see that the higher
the risk (higher range of outcomes), the higher the returns (expected values are higher
and the probability of beating the original expected value is also higher). Such analyses will enable the bank to better analyze the risk-return characteristics of the deal.

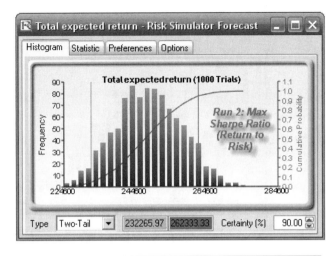

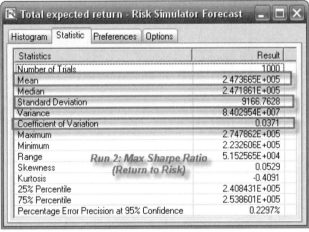

Figure 6-16   Simulation results of optimization Run 2.

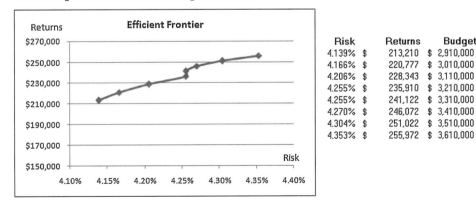

Figure 6-17   Efficient frontier of lending.

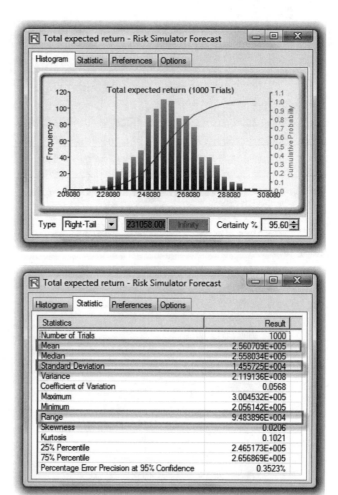

Figure 6-18   Sample simulation results with a budget of $3.61M.

A lot of additional analyses can be applied in this model. For instance, we can apply the Probability of Default computations of implied Asset Value and Implied Volatility to obtain the Cumulative Default Probability, so that the bank can understand the risk of this deal and, based on the portfolio of deals, decide what the threshold of lending should be. For instance, if the bank does not want anything above a 3.5% probability of default for a 5-year cumulative loan, then $3.41M is the appropriate loan value threshold. Figure 6-20 illustrates this situation.

In addition, Value at Risk (VaR) for a portfolio of loans (Figure 6-21) can also be determined both before and after this new loan, so that the bank can decide if absorbing this new loan is possible, and to gauge the effects to the entire portfolio's VaR valuation and capital adequacy. The following shows some existing loans (grouped by tranches and types) and the new loan request. It is up to management to decide if the additional hit to capital requirements is reasonable. For more specific details about VaR and default probability computations, please see Chapter 7 of the present volume.

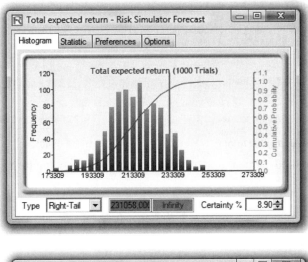

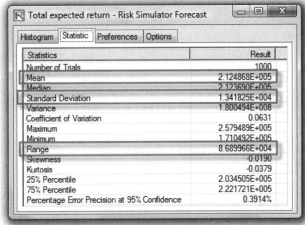

Figure 6-19   Sample simulation results with a budget of $2.91M.

The story does not end here; our analysis up to now has been restricted to the unit level—that is, business segments involved in the restructuring. While the model shown has worked its stochastic wonders, it must now link to consolidating and consolidated DCF valuation worksheets.

Consolidated discounted cash flow valuations provide a "going concern" value—the value driven by a company's future economic strength. RI Furniture Ltd. value is determined by the present value of future cash flows for a specific forecast horizon (projection period), plus the present value of cash flow *beyond* the forecast horizon (residual or terminal value). In other words, the firm's value depends on cash flow potential and the risks (threats) of those future cash flows. It is these perceived risks or threats that help define the discounting factor used to measure cash flows in present value terms. Cash flow depends on the industry and the economic outlook for the RI Furniture's products, current and future competition, sustainable competitive advantage, projected changes in demand, and this borrower's capacity to grow in light of its past financial and operating performance. Among the risk factors the

Probability of Default Analysis to Determine Lending Threshold

Total Investment/Loan Required ($000)	$3,410	$2,910	$3,610
Other Liabilities and Debt ($000)	$3,512	$3,512	$3,512
Total Equity Value ($000)	$1,200	$1,200	$1,200
Equity Volatility	20.00%	20.00%	20.00%
Maturity of New Debt	5	5	5
Riskfree Rate	5.00%	5.00%	5.00%
Implied Asset Value	**$6,583.56**	**$6,196.20**	**$6,738.31**
Implied Asset Volatility	**4.75%**	**4.82%**	**4.73%**
Probability of Default	**3.3649%**	**2.6577%**	**3.6890%**

Figure 6-20   Probability of default tied into the lending threshold.

Value at Risk Contribution Analysis to the Bank's Portfolio of Holdings

	Daily Volatilities	Amounts
Existing Loan (Tranche 1)	0.1254%	$5,410,000
Existing Loan (Tranche 2)	0.3255%	$4,450,000
Existing Loan (Tranche 3)	0.1444%	$3,410,000
Existing Loan (Tranche 4)	0.1854%	$3,410,000
Existing Loan (Tranche 5)	0.2654%	$3,410,000
New Loan Addition	0.2163%	$3,410,000

Correlation Matrix	Existing Loan (Tranche 1)	Existing Loan (Tranche 2)	Existing Loan (Tranche 3)	Existing Loan (Tranche 4)	Existing Loan (Tranche 5)	New Loan Addition
Existing Loan (Tranche 1)	1.0000	0.2500	-0.1540	0.0250	0.0140	0.0200
Existing Loan (Tranche 2)	0.0000	1.0000	-0.1335	0.0020	0.1500	-0.1200
Existing Loan (Tranche 3)	0.0000	0.0000	1.0000	0.0255	0.0480	-0.1700
Existing Loan (Tranche 4)	0.0000	0.0000	0.0000	1.0000	0.0560	-0.2600
Existing Loan (Tranche 5)	0.0000	0.0000	0.0000	0.0000	1.0000	0.2500
New Loan Addition	0.0000	0.0000	0.0000	0.0000	0.0000	1.0000

Holding Days	365
Percentile	99.95%

Value at Risk of Portfolio Before New Loan	**$1,318,330**
Value at Risk of Portfolio After New Loan	**$1,378,376**

Figure 6-21   New loan's effects on Value at Risk.

firm's bankers will examine carefully are their borrower's financial condition, quality, magnitude, and volatility of cash flows, financial and operating leverage, and management's capacity to sustain operations on a profitable basis. These primary attributes cannot be ignored when bankers determine distributions associated with assumption variables.

Embedding Risk Simulator in powerful valuation models provides an intuitive advantage; it is a decidedly efficient and precise way to get deals analyzed, done, and sold.

In summary, note a few suggestions:

1. Use consolidating financials to determine valuation building blocks intrinsic to the operating segments you are analyzing. Consolidated statements alone do not provide sufficient answers.

2. Employ the Risk Simulator and Basel II Modeling Toolkit software programs (specifically, use the Corporate Valuation model included in the toolkit). The model contains preformatted financial statements and analytical reports for evaluating performance and valuing projected performance using both the Enterprise DCF and Economic Profit approaches.

3. Enter the borrower's most likely projections adding residual period and cost of capital assumptions.

4. Open Risk Simulator and determine value drivers (assumption variables) and distributions, first on the unit level and then use results to refine consolidating/consolidated valuations.

5. On the consolidated valuation, select a forecast cell—Equity Value, Operating Value, or Enterprise Value.

6. Run a simulation. Determine the forecast variable's value within a confidence level. Then find probabilities that equity value falls below zero. The last step is quite illuminating since *within the universe and/or constraints* of your valuation model, this is the expected default probability.

7. Run a report. Finally, if borrowers or colleagues are unfamiliar with Risk Simulator report statistics, take time to explain the key numbers.

CHAPTER | 7

Analytical Techniques for Modeling Probability of Default, Loss Given Default, Economic Capital, Value at Risk, Portfolio Optimization, Hurdle Rates, and Rates of Return

With the new Basel II Accord, internationally active banks are now allowed to compute their own risk capital requirements using the internal ratings-based or internal risk-based (IRB) approach. Not only is adequate risk capital analysis important as a compliance obligation, but it gives banks the ability to optimize capital through the ability to compute and allocate risks, perform performance measurements, execute strategic decisions, increase competitiveness, and enhance profitability. This chapter discusses the various *scientific risk management* approaches required to implement an IRB method, as well as the step-by-step models and methodologies used in implementing and valuing economic capital, Value at Risk (VaR), probability of default, and loss given default, the key ingredients of an IRB approach, through the use of advanced analytics such as Monte Carlo and historical risk simulation, portfolio optimization, stochastic forecasting, and options analysis. This chapter also shows the use of Risk Simulator and the Modeling Toolkit (Basel II Toolkit) software in computing and calibrating these critical input parameters. Instead of dwelling on theory or revamping what has already been written many times over, this chapter focuses solely on the practical modeling applications of the key ingredients to the Basel II Accord. Specifically, the following topics will be addressed:

● Probability of Default (structural and empirical models for commercial versus retail banking)

- Loss Given Default and Expected Losses
- Economic Capital and Portfolio Value at Risk (structural and risk-based simulation)
- Portfolio Optimization (risk reduction and diversification)
- Hurdle Rates and Required Rates of Return

To guide the analyses in this chapter, we assume that the reader already has **Risk Simulator®**, **Real Options SLS®**, and the **Basel II Modeling Toolkit™** installed and is somewhat familiar with the basic functions of each software program. If not, please refer to www.realoptionsvaluation.com (click on the Downloads link or use the enclosed CD-ROM) and watch the getting started videos, read some of the getting started case studies, or install the latest trial versions of these software programs. Alternatively, refer to Chapter 4 to obtain a primer on using these software programs. Each topic discussed will start with some basic introduction to the methodologies that are appropriate, followed by some practical hands-on modeling approaches and examples. In addition, for the best hands-on learning result, it is highly recommended that the Excel models be reviewed together with this chapter.

Probability of Default

Probability of default measures the degree of likelihood that the borrower of a loan or debt (the obligor) will be unable to make the necessary scheduled repayments on the debt, thereby defaulting on the debt. Should the obligor be unable to pay, the debt is in default, and the lenders of the debt have legal avenues to attempt a recovery of the debt, or at least partial repayment of the entire debt. The higher the default probability a lender estimates a borrower to have, the higher the interest rate the lender will charge the borrower as compensation for bearing the higher default risk.

Probability of default models are categorized as structural or empirical. Structural models look at a borrower's ability to pay based on market data such as equity prices, market and book values of asset and liabilities, as well as the volatility of these variables, and hence, are used predominantly to estimate the probability of default of *companies* and *countries*, most applicable within the areas of commercial and industrial banking. In contrast, empirical models or credit scoring models are used to quantitatively determine the probability that a loan or loan holder will default, where the loan holder is an individual, by looking at historical portfolios of loans held, where individual characteristics are assessed (e.g., age, educational level, debt to income ratio, and so forth). Therefore, this second approach is more applicable to the retail banking sector.

Structural Models of Probability of Default

Probability of default models is a category of models that assesses the likelihood of default by an obligor. They differ from regular credit scoring models in several ways. First, credit scoring models are usually applied to smaller credits—individuals or small businesses—whereas default models are applied to larger credits—corporations or countries. Credit scoring models are largely statistical, regressing instances of default against various risk indicators, such as an obligor's income, home renter or owner status, years at a job, educational level, debt to income ratio, and so forth, something that will be shown later in this chapter. In contrast, structural default models directly model the default process and are typically calibrated to market variables, such as the obligor's stock price, asset value, book value of debt, or credit spread on its bonds. Default models have many applications within financial institutions. They are used to support credit analysis and to find the probability that a firm will default, to value counterparty credit risk limits, or to apply financial engineering techniques in developing credit derivatives or other credit instruments.

The example presented next uses the Merton probability of default model. This model is used to solve the probability of default of a publicly traded company with equity and debt holdings and to account for its volatilities in the market (Figure 7-1). This model is currently used by KMV and Moody's to perform credit risk analysis. This approach assumes that the book value of asset and asset volatility are unknown and solved in the model, and that the company is relatively stable and the growth rate of the company's assets are stable over time (e.g., not in startup mode). The model uses several simultaneous equations in options valuation theory, coupled with optimization, to obtain the implied underlying asset's market value and volatility of the asset in order to compute the probability of default and distance to default for the firm.

Illustrative Example: Structural Probability of Default Models on Public Firms

It is assumed that the reader is now well versed in running simulations and optimizations in Risk Simulator (if not, please refer to Chapter 4). The example model used is the Probability of Default—External Options Model and can be accessed through **Modeling Toolkit | Prob of Default | External Options Model (Public Company)**.

To run this model (Figure 7-1), enter in the required inputs such as the market value of equity (obtained from market data on the firm's capitalization, i.e., stock price times number of shares outstanding), equity volatility (computed in the Volatility or LPVA worksheets in the model), book value of debt and liabilities (the firm's book value of all debt and liabilities), the risk-free rate (the prevailing country's risk-free interest rate for the same maturity as the debt), the anticipated growth rate of the company (the expected cumulative annualized growth rate of the firm's assets, which can be estimated using historical data over a long period of time, making this approach more applicable to mature companies than to startups), and the debt maturity (the debt maturity to be analyzed, or enter 1 for the annual default probability). The comparable option parameters are shown in cells G18 to G23. All these comparable inputs are computed except for Asset Value (the market value of asset) and Volatility of Asset. You will need to input some rough estimates as a starting point so that the analysis can be run. The rule of thumb is to set the volatility of the asset in G22 to be one-fifth to half of the volatility of equity computed in G10, and the market value of asset (G19) to be approximately the sum of the market value of equity and book value of liabilities and debt (G9 and G11).

An optimization then needs to be run in Risk Simulator in order to obtain the desired outputs. To do this, set Asset Value and Volatility of Asset as the decision variables (make them continuous variables with a lower limit of 1% for volatility and $1 for asset, as both these inputs can only take on positive values). Set cell G29 as the objective to minimize as this is the absolute error value. Finally, the constraint is such that cell H33, the implied volatility in the default model, is set to exactly equal the numerical value of the equity volatility in cell G10. Run a static optimization using Risk Simulator.

If the model has a solution, the absolute error value in cell G29 will revert to zero (Figure 7-2). From here, the probability of default (measured in percent) and distance to default (measured in standard deviations) are computed in cells G39 and G41.

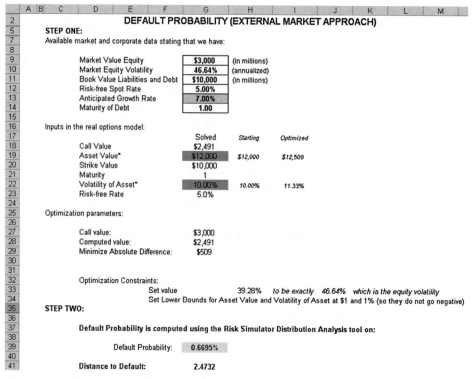

Figure 7-1 Default probability model setup.

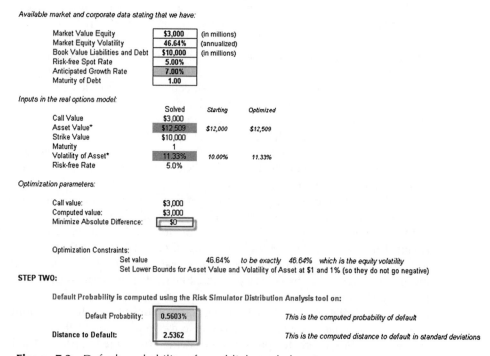

Figure 7-2 Default probability of a publicly traded entity.

CREDIT RISK DEFAULT PROBABILITY (OPTIONS APPROACH)

VALUING DEFAULT PROBABILITY AND DISTANCE TO DEFAULT BASED ON OPTIONS MODELING OF INTERNAL DEBT

Input Assumptions

Asset Book Value	$12.0000
Debt Book Value	$10.0000
Maturity	1.0000
Risk-Free Rate	5.00%
Volatility of Asset	10.00%
Anticipated Growth Rate	7.00%

Probability of Default	**0.6695%**
Distance to Default	**2.4732**

Figure 7-3   Default probability of a privately held entity.

Using the resulting probability of default, the relevant credit spread required can be determined using the Credit Analysis—Credit Premium model or some other credit spread tables (such as using the Internal Credit Risk Rating model).

The results indicate that the company has a probability of default at 0.56% with 2.54 standard deviations to default, indicating good creditworthiness (Figure 7-2).

Illustrative Example: Structural Probability of Default Models on Private Firms

Several other structural models exist for computing a firm's probability of default. Specific models are used depending on the need and availability of data. In the previous example, the firm is a publicly traded firm, with stock prices and equity volatility that can be readily obtained from the market. In this next example, we assume that the firm is privately held, meaning that no market equity data would be available. It essentially computes the probability of default or the point of default for the company when its liabilities exceed its assets, given the asset's growth rates and volatility over time (Figure 7-3). It is recommended that before using this model, the previous model on external publicly traded company first be reviewed. Similar methodological parallels exist between these two models, whereby this example builds on the knowledge and expertise of the previous example.

In Figure 7-3, the example firm with an asset value of $12M and a book value of debt at $10M with significant growth rates of its internal assets and low volatility returns a 0.67% probability of default. In addition, instead of relying on the valuation of the firm, external market benchmarks can be used if such data is available. In Figure 7-4, we see that additional input assumptions such as market fluctuation (market returns and volatility) and relationship (correlation between the market benchmark and the company's assets) are required. The model used is the Probability of Default – Merton Market Options Model accessible from **Modeling Toolkit | Prob of Default | Merton Market Options Model (Industry Comparable)**.

Empirical Models of Probability of Default

As mentioned previously, empirical models of probability of default are used to compute an individual's default probability, applicable within the retail banking arena, where empirical or actual historical or comparable data exists on past credit defaults. The dataset in Figure 7-5 represents a sample of several thousand previous loans, credit, or debt issues. The data shows whether or not each loan had defaulted (0 for no default and 1 for default), as well as the specifics of each loan applicant's age, education level (1–3 indicating high school, university, or graduate professional education), years with current employer, and so forth. The idea is to model these empirical data to see which variables affect the default behavior of individuals, using Risk Simulator's Maximum Likelihood Estimation (MLE) tool. The resulting model will help the bank or credit issuer compute the expected probability of default of an individual credit holder.

MERTON MODEL OF DEBT DEFAULT PROBABILITY
VALUING THE PROBABILITY OF DEFAULT BASED ON MARKET RELATIONSHIPS

Input Assumptions

Asset Value	$100.0000
Debt Value	$50.0000
Time to Maturity	1.00
Riskfree Rate	5.00%
Volatility of Asset	20.00%
Market Volatility	10.00%
Market Return	8.00%
Correlation	0.00

Probability of Default   0.0150%

Figure 7-4 Default probability of a privately held entity calibrated to market fluctuations.

PROBABILITY OF DEFAULT (EMPIRICAL USING MAXIMUM LIKELIHOOD)

Defaulted	Age	Education Level	Years with Current Employer	Years at Current Address	Household Income (Thousands $)	Debt to Income Ratio (%)	Credit Card Debt (Thousands $)	Other Debt (Thousands $)
1	41	3	17	12	176	9.3	11.36	5.01
0	27	1	10	6	31	17.3	1.36	4
0	40	1	15	14	55	5.5	0.86	2.17
0	41	1	15	14	120	2.9	2.66	0.82
1	24	2	2	0	28	17.3	1.79	3.06
0	41	2	5	5	25	10.2	0.39	2.16
0	39	1	20	9	67	30.6	3.83	16.67
0	43	1	12	11	38	3.6	0.13	1.24
1	24	1	3	4	19	24.4	1.36	3.28
0	36	1	0	13	25	19.7	2.78	2.15
0	27	1	0	1	16	1.7	0.18	0.09
0	25	1	4	0	23	5.2	0.25	0.94
0	52	1	24	14	64	10	3.93	2.47
0	37	1	6	9	29	16.3	1.72	3.01
0	48	1	22	15	100	9.1	3.7	5.4
1	36	2	9	6	49	8.6	0.82	3.4
1	36	2	13	6	41	16.4	2.92	3.81
0	43	1	23	19	72	7.6	1.18	4.29
0	39	1	6	9	61	5.7	0.56	2.91
0	41	3	0	21	26	1.7	0.1	0.34
0	39	1	22	3	52	3.2	1.15	0.51
0	47	1	17	21	43	5.6	0.59	1.82

Figure 7-5 Empirical analysis of probability of default.

Illustrative Example of Applying Empirical Models of Probability of Default

The example file is *"Probability of Default – Empirical"* and can be accessed through **Modeling Toolkit | Prob of Default | Empirical (Individuals)**. To run the analysis, select the dataset (include the headers) and make sure that the data have the same length for all variables, without any missing or invalid data points. Then, using Risk Simulator, click on **Risk Simulator | Forecasting | Maximum Likelihood Models**. A sample set of results are provided in the MLE worksheet, complete with detailed instructions on how to compute the expected probability of default of an individual.

The MLE approach applies a modified binary multivariate logistic analysis to model dependent variables in order to determine the expected probability of success of belonging to a certain group. For instance, given a set of independent variables (e.g., age, income, education level of credit card or mortgage loan holders), we can model the probability of default using MLE. A typical regression model is invalid because the errors are heteroskedastic and nonnormal, and the resulting estimated probability forecast will sometimes be above 1 or below 0. MLE analysis handles these problems using an iterative optimization routine. The computed results show the coefficients of the estimated MLE intercept and slopes.[1]

The coefficients estimated are actually the logarithmic odds ratios, and cannot be interpreted directly as probabilities. A quick but simple computation is first required. The approach is simple. To estimate the probability of success of belonging to a certain group (e.g., predicting if a debt holder will default given the amount of debt he or she holds), simply compute the estimated Y value using the MLE coefficients. Figure 7-6

MLE Results

Log Likelihood Value	-200.51				
Variable	Coefficients	Standard Error	Z-Statistic	p-Value	Sample Inputs
Intercept	-1.7003	0.7512	-2.2634	0.0236	
Age	0.0279	0.0205	1.3588	0.1742	
Education Level	0.0728	0.1447	0.5028	0.6151	
Years with Current Emplc	-0.2528	0.0391	-6.4644	0.0000	8.000
Years at Current Address	-0.0952	0.0271	-3.5064	0.0005	8.000
Household Income (Thou	0.0009	0.0125	0.0754	0.9399	
Debt to Income Ratio (%,	0.0750	0.0396	1.8934	0.0583	3.000
Credit Card Debt (Thous·	0.5521	0.1324	4.1697	0.0000	2.000
Other Debt (Thousands $	0.0461	0.1005	0.4592	0.6461	

	Log Odds Ratio	-3.1549
	Default Probability	4.09%

Figure 7-6 MLE results.

1. For instance, the coefficients are estimates of the true population β values in the following equation: $Y = \beta_0 + \beta_1 X_1 + \beta_2 X_2 + \ldots + \beta_n X_n$. The standard error measures how accurate the predicted coefficients are, and the Z-statistics are the ratios of each predicted coefficient to its standard error. The Z-statistic is used in hypothesis testing, where we set the null hypothesis (Ho) such that the real mean of the coefficient is equal to zero, and the alternate hypothesis (Ha) such that the real mean of the coefficient is not equal to zero. The Z-test is very important as it calculates whether each of the coefficients is statistically significant in the presence of the other regressors. This means that the Z-test statistically verifies whether a regressor or independent variable should remain in the model or whether it should be dropped. That is, the smaller the p-value, the more significant the coefficient. The usual significant levels for the p-value are 0.01, 0.05, and 0.10, corresponding to the 99, 95, and 90 percent confidence levels.

illustrates that an individual with 8 years at a current employer and current address, a low 3% debt to income ratio, and $2,000 in credit card debt has a log odds ratio of −3.1549. Then, the inverse antilog of the odds ratio is obtained by computing:

$$\frac{\exp(estimated\ Y)}{1+\exp(estimated\ Y)} = \frac{\exp(-3.1549)}{1+\exp(-3.1549)} = 0.0409$$

Thus, such a person has a 4.09% chance of defaulting on the new debt. Using this probability of default, you can then use the Credit Analysis—Credit Premium model to determine the additional credit spread to charge this person, given this default level and the customized cash flows anticipated from this debt holder.

Loss Given Default and Expected Losses

As shown previously, probability of default is a key parameter for computing the credit risk of a portfolio. In fact, the Basel II Accord requires the probability of default, as well as other key parameters such as the loss given default (LGD) and exposure at default (EAD), be reported as well. The reason is that a bank's expected loss is equivalent to:

Expected Losses = (Probability of Default) × (Loss Given Default) × (Exposure at Default) or simply: $EL = PD \times LGD \times EAD$

PD and LGD are both percentages, whereas EAD is a value. As we have shown how to compute PD in the previous section, we will now revert to some estimations of LGD. Again, several methods can be used to estimate LGD. The first is through a simple empirical approach where we set $LGD = 1 - Recovery\ Rate$. That is, whatever is not recovered at default is the loss at default, computed as the charge off (net of recovery) divided by the outstanding balance:

$$LGD = 1 - Recovery\ Rate$$
or
$$LGD = \frac{Charge\ Offs\ (Net\ of\ Recovery)}{Outstanding\ Balance\ at\ Default}$$

Therefore, if market data or historical information is available, LGD can be segmented by various market conditions, types of obligor, and other pertinent segmentations. LGD can then be easily read off a chart.

A second approach to estimate LGD is more attractive in that if the bank has available information it can attempt to run some econometric models to create the best-fitting model under an ordinary least squares approach. By using this approach, a single model can be determined and calibrated; this same model can be applied under various conditions, and no data mining is required. However, in most econometric models, a normal transformation will have to be performed first. Suppose the bank has some historical LGD data (Figure 7-7); the best-fitting distribution can be found using Risk Simulator by first selecting the historical data and then clicking on **Risk Simulator | Tools | Distributional Fitting (Single Variable)** to perform the fitting routine. The example's result is a beta distribution for the thousands of LGD values. The p-value can also be evaluated for the goodness of fit of the theoretical distribution.

Past LGD Normalized

Past LGD	Normalized
49.69%	28.54%
25.76%	18.27%
14.61%	11.84%
26.91%	18.83%
18.47%	14.33%
21.29%	15.95%
26.00%	18.39%
11.84%	9.76%
51.85%	29.41%
19.35%	14.84%
24.74%	17.76%
15.68%	12.57%
14.35%	11.66%
21.36%	15.98%
35.31%	22.65%
50.71%	28.95%
28.58%	19.63%
5.96%	3.77%
3.84%	0.38%
21.70%	16.17%
71.28%	37.64%
23.49%	17.12%
20.25%	15.36%
44.01%	26.26%
31.27%	20.87%
40.86%	24.98%
26.54%	18.65%
25.29%	18.04%
28.51%	19.60%
55.40%	30.84%
31.57%	21.00%
16.30%	12.98%
24.37%	17.57%
8.46%	6.70%
77.08%	40.52%

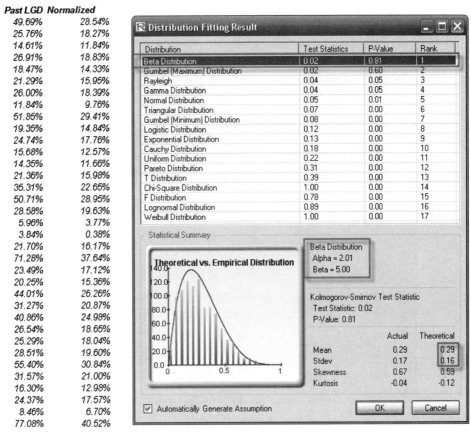

Figure 7-7   Fitting historical LGD data.

That is, the higher the p-value, the better the distributional fit, so in this example, the historical LGD fits a beta distribution 81% of the time, indicating a good fit.

Next, using the Distribution Analysis tool in Risk Simulator, obtain the theoretical mean and standard deviation of the fitted distribution (Figure 7-8). Then, transform the LGD variable using the *B2NormalTransform* function in the Modeling Toolkit software. For instance, the value 49.69% will be transformed and normalized to 28.54%. Using this newly transformed dataset, you can now run some nonlinear econometric models to determine LGD.

The following is a partial list of independent variables that might be significant for a bank, in terms of determining and forecasting the LGD value:

- Debt to capital ratio
- Profit margin
- Revenue
- Current assets to current liabilities
- Risk rating at default done a year before default
- Industry
- Authorized balance at default
- Collateral value
- Facility type
- Tightness of covenant

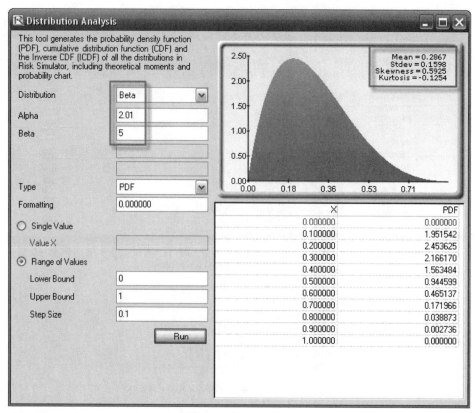

Figure 7-8   Distributional analysis tool.

- Seniority of debt
- Operating income to sales ratio (and other efficiency ratios)
- Total asset, total net worth, total liabilities

Economic Capital and Value at Risk

Economic capital is critical to a bank as it links a bank's earnings and returns to risks that are specific to a business line or business opportunity. In addition, these economic capital measurements can be aggregated into a portfolio of holdings. Value at Risk or (VaR) is used in trying to understand how the entire organization is affected by the various risks of each holding as aggregated into a portfolio, after accounting for their cross-correlations among various holdings. VaR measures the maximum possible loss given some predefined probability level (e.g., 99.90%) over some holding period or time horizon (e.g., 10 days). The selected probability or confidence interval is typically a decision made by senior management at the bank and reflects the board's risk appetite. Stated another way, we can define the probability level as the bank's desired probability of surviving per year. In addition, the holding period is usually chosen so that it coincides with the time period it takes to liquidate a loss position.

VaR can be computed in several ways. Two main families of approaches exist: structural closed-form models and Monte Carlo risk simulation approaches. We will showcase both methods in this chapter, starting with the structural models.

The second and much more powerful approach is the use of Monte Carlo risk simulation. Instead of simply correlating individual business lines or assets in the structural models, entire probability distributions can be correlated using more advanced mathematical copulas and simulation algorithms in Monte Carlo simulation methods, by using Risk Simulator. In addition, tens to hundreds of thousands of scenarios can be generated using simulation, providing a very powerful stress testing mechanism for valuing VaR. Distributional fitting methods are applied to reduce the thousands of data points into their appropriate probability distributions, allowing their modeling to be handled with greater ease.

Illustrative Example: Structural VaR Models

The first VaR example model shown is the Value at Risk—Static Covariance Method, accessible through **Modeling Toolkit | Value at Risk | Static Covariance Method.** This model is used to compute the portfolio's VaR at a given percentile for a specific holding period, after accounting for the cross-correlation effects between the assets (Figure 7-9). The daily volatility is the annualized volatility divided by the square root of trading days per year. Typically, positive correlations tend to carry a higher VaR compared to zero correlation asset mixes, whereas negative correlations reduce the total risk of the portfolio through the diversification effect (Figures 7-9 and 7-10). The approach used is a portfolio VaR with correlated inputs, where the portfolio has multiple asset holdings with different amounts and volatilities. Each asset is also correlated to each other. The covariance or correlation structural model is used to compute the VaR given a holding period or horizon and percentile value (typically 10 days at 99% confidence). Of course, the example only illustrates a few assets or business lines or credit lines for simplicity's sake. Nonetheless, using the functions in the Modeling

VALUE AT RISK (VARIANCE-COVARIANCE METHOD)

Asset Allocation	Amount	Daily Volatility
Asset A	$1,000,000.00	1.20%
Asset B	$2,000,000.00	2.00%
Asset C	$3,000,000.00	1.89%
Asset D	$4,000,000.00	3.25%
Asset E	$5,000,000.00	4.20%

Correlation Matrix	Asset A	Asset B	Asset C	Asset D	Asset E
Asset A	1.0000	0.1000	0.1000	0.1000	0.1000
Asset B	0.1000	1.0000	0.1000	0.1000	0.1000
Asset C	0.1000	0.1000	1.0000	0.1000	0.1000
Asset D	0.1000	0.1000	0.1000	1.0000	0.1000
Asset E	0.1000	0.1000	0.1000	0.1000	1.0000

Horizon (Days)	10
Percentile	99.00%

Value at Risk (Daily)	**$655,915.30**
Value at Risk (Horizon)	**$2,074,186.30**

Daily Value at Risk (Positive Correlations)	**$2,074,186.30**
Daily Value at Risk (Zero Correlations)	**$1,889,345.26**
Daily Value at Risk (Negative Correlations)	**$1,684,340.28**

Figure 7-9 Computing Value at Risk using the structural covariance method.

Correlation Matrix	Asset A	Asset B	Asset C	Asset D	Asset E
Asset A	1.0000	0.1000	0.1000	0.1000	0.1000
Asset B	0.1000	1.0000	0.1000	0.1000	0.1000
Asset C	0.1000	0.1000	1.0000	0.1000	0.1000
Asset D	0.1000	0.1000	0.1000	1.0000	0.1000
Asset E	0.1000	0.1000	0.1000	0.1000	1.0000

Correlation Matrix	Asset A	Asset B	Asset C	Asset D	Asset E
Asset A	1.0000	0.0000	0.0000	0.0000	0.0000
Asset B	0.0000	1.0000	0.0000	0.0000	0.0000
Asset C	0.0000	0.0000	1.0000	0.0000	0.0000
Asset D	0.0000	0.0000	0.0000	1.0000	0.0000
Asset E	0.0000	0.0000	0.0000	0.0000	1.0000

Correlation Matrix	Asset A	Asset B	Asset C	Asset D	Asset E
Asset A	1.0000	-0.1000	-0.1000	-0.1000	-0.1000
Asset B	-0.1000	1.0000	-0.1000	-0.1000	-0.1000
Asset C	-0.1000	-0.1000	1.0000	-0.1000	-0.1000
Asset D	-0.1000	-0.1000	-0.1000	1.0000	-0.1000
Asset E	-0.1000	-0.1000	-0.1000	-0.1000	1.0000

Figure 7-10   Different correlation levels.

Toolkit, many more lines, assets, or businesses can be modeled (the function B2VaRCorrelationMethod is used in this example).

Illustrative Example: VaR Models Using Monte Carlo Risk Simulation

The model used is Value at Risk—Portfolio Operational and Capital Adequacy and is accessible through **Modeling Toolkit | Value at Risk | Portfolio Operational and Capital Adequacy**. This model shows how operational risk and credit risk parameters are fitted to statistical distributions and how their resulting distributions are modeled in a portfolio of liabilities to determine the Value at Risk (e.g., 99.50th percentile certainty) for the capital requirement under Basel II requirements. It is assumed that the historical data of the operational risk impacts (*Historical Data* worksheet) are obtained through econometric modeling of the *Key Risk Indicators*.

The *Distributional Fitting Report* worksheet is a result of running a distributional fitting routine in Risk Simulator to obtain the appropriate distribution for the operational risk parameter. Using the resulting distributional parameters, we model each liability's capital requirements within an entire portfolio. Correlations can also be inputted if required, between pairs of liabilities or business units. The resulting Monte Carlo simulation results show the VaR capital requirements.

Note that an appropriate empirically based historical VaR cannot be obtained if distributional fitting and risk-based simulations were not first run. Only by running simulations will the VaR be obtained. To perform distributional fitting, follow the steps below:

1. In the *Historical Data* worksheet (Figure 7-11), select the data area (cells **C5: L104**) and click on **Risk Simulator | Tools | Distributional Fitting (Single Variable)**.

2. Browse through the fitted distributions and select the best-fitting distribution (in this case, the exponential distribution with a particularly high p-value fit, as shown in Figure 7-12) and click on **OK**.

Basel II - Credit Risk and Capital Requirement (Portfolio-Based)

This model applies the Basel II requirements on capital adequacy and modeling the operational risk of probability of default on 100 loans as well as the loss given default. These values are fitted based on the bank's historical loss data (Historical Data and Distributional Fitting Report sheets) using Risk Simulator. Then, the relevant historical simulation assumptions are set in this model (Credit Risk sheet) and a Monte Carlo risk-based simulation was run in Risk Simulator to determine the expected capital required and 99.50% Value at Risk (VaR). A simulation has to be run in order to determine the VaR.

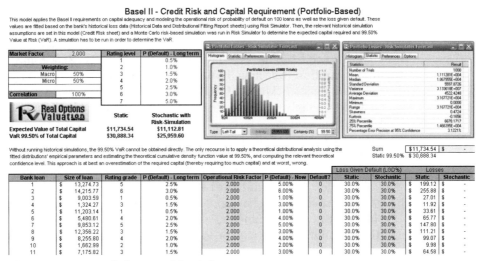

Market Factor	2.000

Weighting:	
Macro	50%
Micro	50%

Correlation	100%

Rating level	P (Default) - Long term
1	0.5%
2	1.0%
3	1.5%
4	2.0%
5	2.5%
6	3.0%
7	5.0%

	Static	Stochastic with Risk-Simulation
Expected Value of Total Capital	$11,734.54	$11,112.81
VaR 99.50% of Total Capital	$30,888.34	$25,959.60

Without running historical simulations, the 99.50% VaR cannot be obtained directly. The only recourse is to apply a theoretical distributional analysis using the fitted distributions' empirical parameters and estimating the theoretical cumulative density function value at 99.50%, and computing the relevant theoretical confidence level. This approach is at best an overestimation of the required capital (thereby requiring too much capital) and at worst, wrong.

		Sum	$11,734.54	$ -
		Static 99.50%	$30,888.34	

Bank loan	Size of loan	Rating grade	P (Default) - Long term	Operational Risk Factor	P (Default) - Now	Default?	Loss Given Default (LGD%) Static	Loss Given Default (LGD%) Stochastic	Losses Static	Losses Stochastic
1	$ 13,274.73	5	2.5%	2.000	5.00%	0	30.0%	30.0%	$ 199.12	$ -
2	$ 14,215.77	6	3.0%	2.000	6.00%	0	30.0%	30.0%	$ 255.88	$ -
3	$ 9,003.59	1	0.5%	2.000	1.00%	0	30.0%	30.0%	$ 27.01	$ -
4	$ 1,324.27	3	1.5%	2.000	3.00%	0	30.0%	30.0%	$ 11.92	$ -
5	$ 11,203.14	1	0.5%	2.000	1.00%	0	30.0%	30.0%	$ 33.61	$ -
6	$ 5,480.61	4	2.0%	2.000	4.00%	0	30.0%	30.0%	$ 65.77	$ -
7	$ 9,853.12	5	2.5%	2.000	5.00%	0	30.0%	30.0%	$ 147.80	$ -
8	$ 12,356.22	3	1.5%	2.000	3.00%	0	30.0%	30.0%	$ 111.21	$ -
9	$ 8,255.80	4	2.0%	2.000	4.00%	0	30.0%	30.0%	$ 99.07	$ -
10	$ 1,662.99	2	1.0%	2.000	2.00%	0	30.0%	30.0%	$ 9.98	$ -
11	$ 7,175.82	3	1.5%	2.000	3.00%	0	30.0%	30.0%	$ 64.58	$ -

Figure 7-11   Sample historical bank loans.

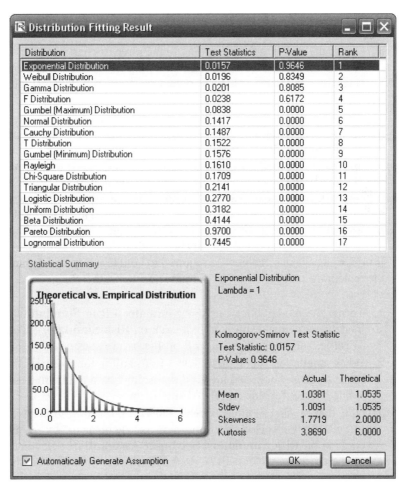

Figure 7-12   Data fitting results.

3. You may now set the assumptions on the *Operational Risk Factors* with the exponential distribution (fitted results show *Lambda* = 1) in the Credit Risk worksheet. Note that the assumptions have already been set for you in advance. You may set it by going to cell **F27** in the worksheet and clicking on **Risk Simulator | Set Input Assumption**, selecting **Exponential** distribution and entering **1** for the *Lambda* value, and clicking on **OK**. Continue this process for the remaining cells in column F or simply perform a **Risk Simulator Copy** and **Risk Simulator Paste** on the remaining cells:

    a. Note that since the cells in column F have an assumptions set, you will first have to clear them if you wish to reset and copy/paste parameters. You can do so by first selecting cells **F28:F126** and clicking on the **Remove Parameter** icon or select **Risk Simulator | Remove Parameter**.

    b. Then select cell **F27**, click on the **Risk Simulator Copy** icon or select **Risk Simulator | Copy Parameter**, and then select cells **F28:F126** and click on the **Risk Simulator Paste** icon or select **Risk Simulator | Paste Parameter**.

4. Next, additional assumptions can be set such as the probability of default using the Bernoulli distribution (column H) and *Loss Given Default* (column J). Repeat the procedure in Step 3 if you wish to reset the assumptions.

5. Run the simulation by clicking on the **Run** icon or clicking on **Risk Simulator | Run Simulation**.

6. Obtain the Value at Risk by going to the forecast chart once the simulation is done running and selecting **Left-Tail** and typing in **99.50**. Hit **Tab** on the keyboard to enter the confidence value and obtain the VaR of $25,959 (Figure 7-13).

Another example of VaR computation is presented next, where the model Value at Risk—Right Tail Capital Requirements is used and is available through **Modeling Toolkit | Value at Risk | Right Tail Capital Requirements**.

This model shows the capital requirements per Basel II requirements (99.95th percentile capital adequacy based on a specific holding period's Value at Risk). Without running risk-based historical and Monte Carlo simulation using Risk Simulator, the required capital is $37.01M (Figure 7-14) as compared to only $14.00M required using a correlated simulation (Figure 7-15). This is due to the cross-correlations between assets and business lines and can only be modeled using Risk Simulator. This lower VaR is preferred as banks can now be required to hold less required capital and can reinvest the remaining capital in various profitable ventures, thereby generating higher profits.

1. To run the model, click on **Risk Simulator | Run Simulation** (if you had other models open, make sure you first click on **Risk Simulator | Change Simulation | Profile**, and select the *Tail VaR* profile before starting).

2. When simulation is complete, select **Left-Tail** in the forecast chart, enter in **99.95** in the *Certainty* box, and hit **TAB** on the keyboard to obtain the value of $14.00M Value at Risk for this correlated simulation.

3. Note that the assumptions have already been set for you in advance in the model in cells *C6:C15*. However, you may set them again by going to cell **C6** and clicking on **Risk Simulator | Set Input Assumption**, selecting your distribution of choice or use the default *Normal Distribution* or perform a distributional fitting on historical data and click on **OK**. Continue this process for the remaining cells in column C. You may also decide to first *Remove Parameters* of these cells in

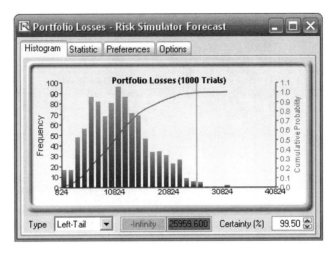

Figure 7-13   Simulated forecast results and the 99.50% Value at Risk value.

TAIL VALUE AT RISK MODEL (BASEL II REQUIREMENT)

Line of Business	Mean Required Capital	99.95th Percentile	Capital Required	Allocation Weights	Minimum Allowed	Maximum Allowed	
Business 1	$10.50	$36.52	$26.01	10.00%	5.00%	15.00%	3.48
Business 2	$11.12	$47.52	$36.39	10.00%	5.00%	15.00%	4.27
Business 3	$11.77	$48.99	$37.22	10.00%	5.00%	15.00%	4.16
Business 4	$10.77	$37.34	$26.56	10.00%	5.00%	15.00%	3.47
Business 5	$13.49	$49.52	$36.03	10.00%	5.00%	15.00%	3.67
Business 6	$14.24	$55.59	$41.35	10.00%	5.00%	15.00%	3.91
Business 7	$15.60	$60.24	$44.64	10.00%	5.00%	15.00%	3.86
Business 8	$14.95	$64.69	$49.74	10.00%	5.00%	15.00%	4.33
Business 9	$14.15	$61.02	$46.87	10.00%	5.00%	15.00%	4.31
Business 10	$10.08	$35.37	$25.29	10.00%	5.00%	15.00%	3.51
Portfolio Total	$12.67	$49.68	$37.01	100.00%			
Total Capital Required			$14.00				

Correlation Matrix

	1	2	3	4	5	6	7	8	9	10
1										
2	-0.20									
3	-0.13	0.35								
4	-0.05	0.01	0.00							
5	0.23	0.50	0.15	0.00						
6	0.00	0.00	-0.15	0.00	0.03					
7	0.25	0.00	-0.26	0.01	0.10	-0.10				
8	0.36	-0.25	-0.60	-0.30	0.00	0.00	-0.15			
9	-0.01	-0.20	0.16	0.04	-0.01	0.01	0.00	0.00		

Figure 7-14   Right-tail VaR model.

column C and set your own distributions. Furthermore, correlations can be set manually when assumptions are set (Figure 7-16) or by going to **Simulation | Edit Correlations** (Figure 7-17) after all the assumptions are set.

If risk simulation was not run, the VaR or economic capital required would have been $37M, as opposed to only $14M. And all cross-correlations between business

Figure 7-15 Simulated results of the portfolio VaR.

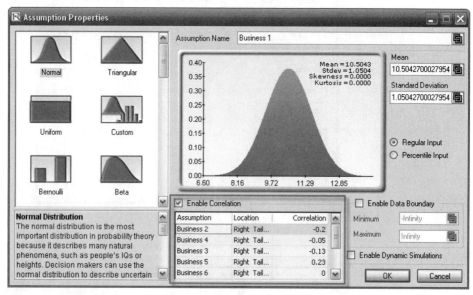

Figure 7-16 Setting correlations one at a time.

lines have been modeled, as are stress and scenario tests, and thousands and thousands of possible iterations are run. Individual risks are now aggregated into a cumulative portfolio level VaR.

Efficient Portfolio Allocation and Economic Capital VaR

As a side note, by performing portfolio optimization, a portfolio's VaR can actually be reduced. We start by first introducing the concept of stochastic portfolio optimization through an illustrative hands-on example. Then, using this portfolio optimization technique, we apply it to four business lines or assets to compute the VaR or an unoptimized versus an optimized portfolio of assets, and see the difference in computed VaR. You will note that, at the end, the optimized portfolio bears less risk and has a lower required economic capital.

Illustrative Example: Stochastic Portfolio Optimization

The optimization model used to illustrate the concepts of stochastic portfolio optimization is Optimization—Stochastic Portfolio Allocation and can be accessed via **Modeling Toolkit | Optimization | Stochastic Portfolio Allocation**. This model shows four asset classes with different risk and return characteristics. The idea here is to find the best portfolio allocation such that the portfolio's bang-for-the-buck or returns to risk ratio is maximized, that is, to allocate 100% of an individual's investment among several different asset classes (e.g., different types of mutual funds or investment styles: growth, value, aggressive growth, income, global, index, contrarian, momentum, and so forth). This model is different from others in that several simulation assumptions (risk and return values for each asset) exist, as seen in Figure 7-18. That is, a simulation is run, then optimization is executed, and the entire process is repeated multiple times to obtain distributions of each decision variable. The entire analysis can be automated using stochastic optimization.

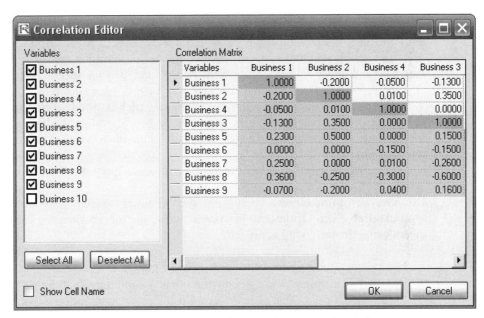

Figure 7-17 Setting correlations using the correlation matrix routine.

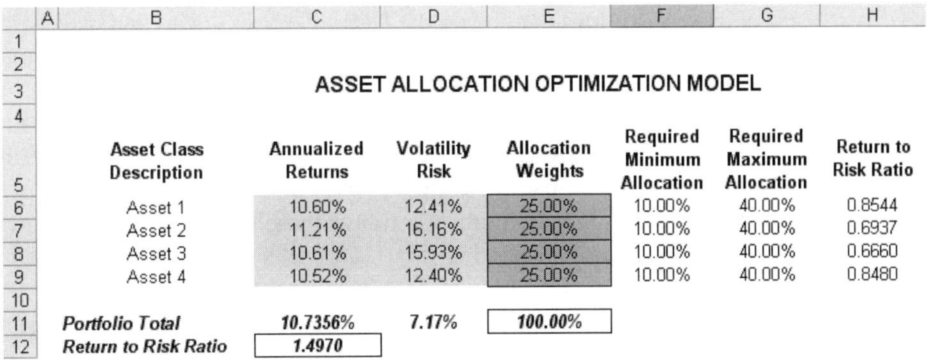

	Asset Class Description	Annualized Returns	Volatility Risk	Allocation Weights	Required Minimum Allocation	Required Maximum Allocation	Return to Risk Ratio
	ASSET ALLOCATION OPTIMIZATION MODEL						
6	Asset 1	10.60%	12.41%	25.00%	10.00%	40.00%	0.8544
7	Asset 2	11.21%	16.16%	25.00%	10.00%	40.00%	0.6937
8	Asset 3	10.61%	15.93%	25.00%	10.00%	40.00%	0.6660
9	Asset 4	10.52%	12.40%	25.00%	10.00%	40.00%	0.8480
11	*Portfolio Total*	*10.7356%*	*7.17%*	*100.00%*			
12	*Return to Risk Ratio*	*1.4970*					

Figure 7-18 Asset allocation model ready for stochastic optimization.

In order to run an optimization, several key specifications on the model have to first be identified:

Objective: Maximize Return to Risk Ratio (C12)
Decision Variables: Allocation Weights (E6:E9)
Restrictions on Decision Variables: Minimum and Maximum Required (F6:G9)
Constraints: Portfolio Total Allocation Weights 100% (E11 is set to 100%)
Simulation Assumptions: Return and Risk Values (C6:D9)

The model shows the various asset classes, and each asset class has its own set of annualized returns and annualized volatilities. These return and risk measures are annualized values such that they can be consistently compared across different asset classes. Returns are computed using the geometric average of the relative returns, while the risks are computed using the logarithmic relative stock returns approach.

The Allocation Weights in column E hold the decision variables, which are the variables that need to be tweaked and tested such that the total weight is constrained at 100% (cell E11). Typically, to start the optimization, we will set these cells to a uniform value, where in this case, cells E6 to E9 are set at 25% each. In addition, each decision variable may have specific restrictions in its allowed range. In this example, the lower and upper allocations allowed are 10% and 40%, as seen in columns F and G. This setting means that each asset class may have its own allocation boundaries.

Next, column H shows the return to risk ratio, which is simply the return percentage divided by the risk percentage, where the higher this value, the higher the bang-for-the-buck. The remaining model shows the individual asset class rankings by returns, risk, return to risk ratio, and allocation. In other words, these rankings show at a glance which asset class has the lowest risk or the highest return, and so forth.

Running an optimization: To run this model, simply click on **Risk Simulator | Optimization | Run Optimization**. Alternatively, and for practice, you can set up the model using the following approach.

1. Start a new profile (**Risk Simulator | New Profile**).
2. For stochastic optimization, set distributional assumptions on the risk and returns for each asset class. That is, select cell **C6** and set an assumption (**Risk Simulator | Set Input Assumption**) and make your own assumption as required. Repeat for cells **C7** to **D9**.
3. Select cell **E6**, and define the decision variable (**Risk Simulator | Optimization | Decision Variables** or click on the *Define Decision icon*) and make it a **Continuous Variable** and then link the decision variable's name and minimum/maximum required to the relevant cells (**B6, F6, G6**).
4. Then use the **Risk Simulator Copy** on cell **E6**, select cells **E7 to E9**, and use **Risk Simulator's Paste (Risk Simulator | Copy Parameter)** and **Simulation | Paste Parameter** or use the copy and paste icons).
5. Next, set up the optimization's constraints by selecting **Risk Simulator | Optimization | Constraints**, selecting **ADD**, and selecting the cell **E11**, and making it equal **100%** (total allocation, and do not forget the % sign).
6. Select cell **C12**, the objective to be maximized, and make it the objective: **Risk Simulator | Optimization | Set Objective** or click on the **O** icon.

7. Run the simulation by going to **Risk Simulator | Optimization | Run Optimization**. Review the different tabs to make sure that all the required inputs in steps 2 and 3 above are correct. Select **Stochastic Optimization** and let it run for 500 trials repeated 20 times (Figure 7-19 illustrates these setup steps).

You may also try other optimization routines where:

Static Optimization is an optimization that is run on a static model, where no simulations are run. This optimization type is applicable when the model is assumed to be known and no uncertainties exist. Also, a static optimization can be first run to determine the optimal portfolio and its corresponding optimal allocation of decision variables before more advanced optimization procedures are applied. For instance, before running a stochastic optimization problem, a static optimization is first run to determine if there exist solutions to the optimization problem before a more protracted analysis is performed.

Dynamic Optimization is applied when Monte Carlo simulation is used together with optimization. Another name for such a procedure is Simulation-Optimization. In other words, a simulation is run for N trials, and then an optimization process is run for M iterations until the optimal results are obtained or an infeasible set is found. That is, using Risk Simulator's optimization module, you can choose which forecast and assumption statistics to use and replace in the model after the simulation is run. Then, these forecast statistics can be applied in the optimization process. This approach is useful when you have a large model with many interacting assumptions and forecasts, and when some of the forecast statistics are required in the optimization.

Stochastic Optimization is similar to the dynamic optimization procedure with the exception that the entire dynamic optimization process is repeated T times. The results will be a forecast chart of each decision variable with T values. In other words, a simulation is run, and the forecast or assumption statistics are used in the optimization model to find the optimal allocation of decision variables. Then, another simulation is run, generating different forecast statistics, and these new updated values are then optimized, and so forth. Hence, the final decision variables will each have its own forecast chart, indicating the range of the optimal decision variables. For instance, instead of obtaining single-point estimates in the dynamic optimization procedure, you can now obtain a distribution of the decision variables, and, hence, a range of optimal values for each decision variable, also known as a stochastic optimization.

Viewing and interpreting forecast results: Stochastic optimization is performed when a simulation is first run, and then the optimization is run. The whole analysis is repeated multiple times. The result is a distribution of each decision variable rather than a single point estimate (Figure 7-20). This means that instead of saying you should invest 30.57% in Asset 1, the optimal decision is to invest between 30.10% and 30.99% as long as the total portfolio sums to 100%. It thereby provides management or decision makers a range of flexibility in the optimal decisions. Refer to Chapter 11 of Dr. Johnathan Mun's *Modeling Risk: Applying Monte Carlo Simulation, Real Options Analysis, Forecasting, and Optimization* for more detailed explanations of this model, the different optimization techniques, as well as an interpretation of the

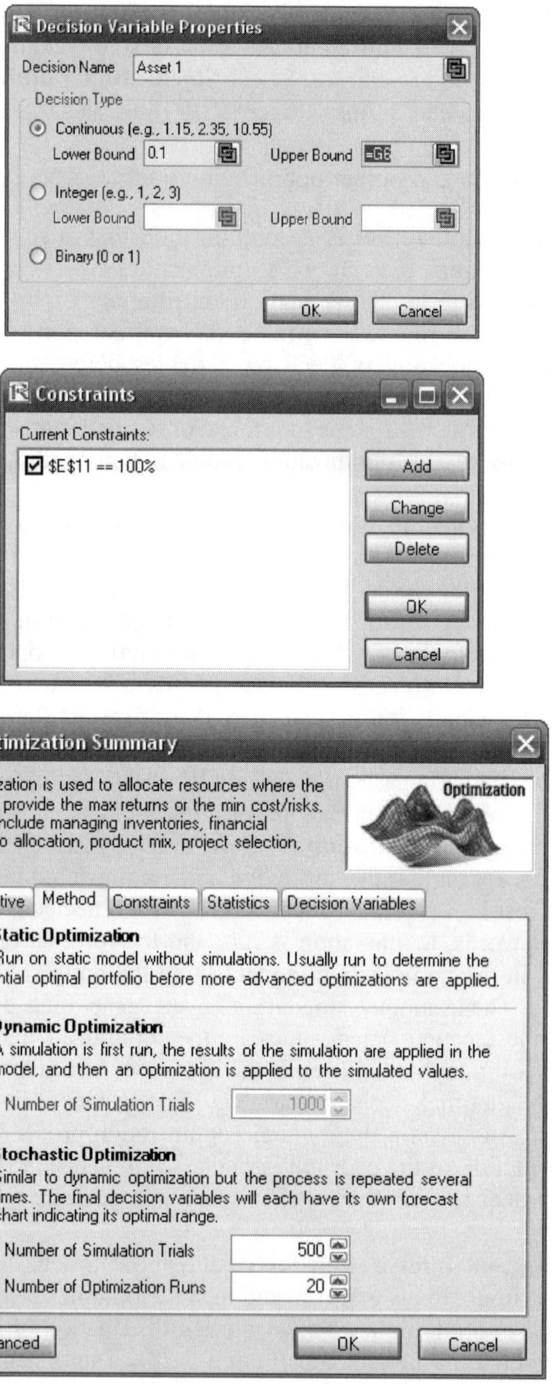

Figure 7-19 Setting up the stochastic optimization problem.

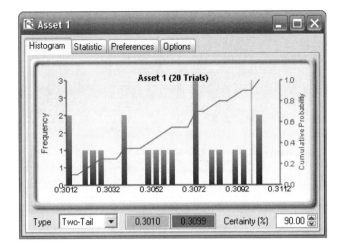

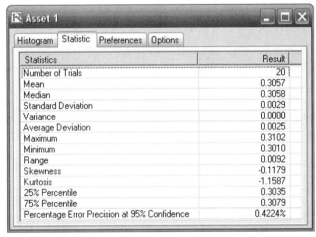

Figure 7-20 Simulated results from the stochastic optimization approach.

results. The appendix to Mun's chapter also details how the risk and return values are computed.

Illustrative Example: Portfolio Optimization and Portfolio VaR

Now that we understand the concepts of optimized portfolios, let us now examine the effects on computed economic capital through the use of a correlated portfolio VaR. This model uses Monte Carlo simulation and optimization routines in Risk Simulator to minimize the VaR of a portfolio of assets (Figure 7-21). The file used is *Value at Risk—Optimized and Simulated Portfolio VaR*, which is accessible via **Modeling Toolkit I Value at Risk I Optimized and Simulated Portfolio VaR**. In this example model, we intentionally used only four asset classes to illustrate the effects of an optimized portfolio, whereas in real life, we can extend this to cover a multitude of asset classes and business lines. In addition, we now illustrate the use of a left-tail VaR, as opposed to a right-tail VaR, but the concepts are similar.

First, simulation is used to determine the 90% left-tail VaR (this means that there is a 10% chance that losses will exceed this VaR for a specified holding period). With

VALUE AT RISK WITH ASSET ALLOCATION OPTIMIZATION MODEL

Asset Class Description	Annualized Returns	Volatility Risk	Allocation Weights	Required Minimum Allocation	Required Maximum Allocation
S&P 500	7.10%	9.80%	10.00%	10.00%	40.00%
Small Cap	9.51%	14.35%	27.30%	10.00%	40.00%
High Yield	15.90%	22.50%	22.70%	10.00%	40.00%
Govt Bonds	4.50%	7.25%	40.00%	10.00%	40.00%
		Total Weight:	*100.00%*		

Correlation Matrix	S&P 500	Small Cap	High Yield	Govt Bonds
S&P 500	1.0000	0.7400	0.6500	0.5500
Small Cap	0.7400	1.0000	0.4200	0.3100
High Yield	0.6500	0.4200	1.0000	0.2300
Govt Bonds	0.5500	0.3100	0.2300	1.0000

Covariance Matrix	S&P 500	Small Cap	High Yield	Govt Bonds
S&P 500	0.0096	0.0104	0.0143	0.0039
Small Cap	0.0104	0.0206	0.0136	0.0032
High Yield	0.0143	0.0136	0.0506	0.0038
Govt Bonds	0.0039	0.0032	0.0038	0.0053

Starting Value	$1,000,000.00
Term (Years)	5.00

Annualized Return	8.72%	**Profit/Loss**	$87,151.94
Portfolio Risk	9.84%	**Return to Risk Ratio**	88.59%
Ending Value	$1,087,151.94		

Specifications of the optimization model:

Objective:	*Maximize Return to Risk Ratio (E28)*
Decision Variables:	*Allocation Weights (E6:E9)*
Restrictions on Decision Variables:	*Minimum and Maximum Required (F6:G9)*
Constraints:	*Portfolio Total Allocation Weights 100% (E10 is set to 100%)*

Figure 7-21 Computing Value at Risk (VaR) with simulation.

an equal allocation of 25% across the 4 asset classes, the VaR is determined using simulation (Figure 7-22). The annualized returns are uncertain and hence simulated. The VaR is then read off the forecast chart. Then, optimization is run to find the best portfolio subject to the 100% allocation across the 4 projects that will maximize the portfolio's bang-for-the-buck (returns to risk ratio). The resulting optimized portfolio is then simulated once again, and the new VaR is obtained (Figure 7-23). The VaR of this optimized portfolio is a lot less than the not optimized portfolio. That is, the expected loss is $35.8M instead of $42.2M, which means that the bank will have a lower required economic capital if the portfolio of holdings is first optimized.

Hurdle Rates and Required Rate of Return

Another related item in the discussion of risk in the context of Basel II Accords is the issue of hurdle rates or the required rate of return on investment that is sufficient to justify the amount of risk undertaken in the portfolio. There is a nice theoretical connection among uncertainty and volatility whereby the discount rate of a specific risk portfolio can be obtained. In a financial model, the old axiom of *high risk, high return*

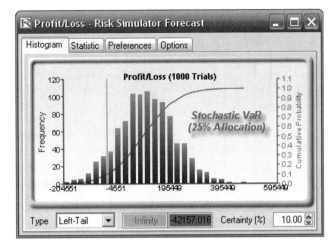

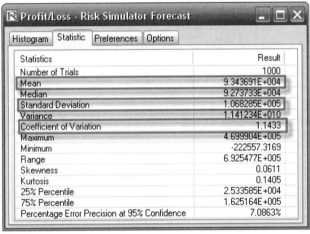

Figure 7-22 Nonoptimized Value at Risk.

is seen through the use of a discount rate. That is, the higher the risk of a project, the higher the discount rate should be to risk-adjust this riskier project so that all projects are comparable on a risk-adjusted basis.

Two methods can be used to compute the hurdle rate. The first is an internal model, where the VaR or Value at Risk of the portfolio is first computed. This economic capital is then compared to the market risk premium. That is, we have

$$\text{Hurdle Rate} = \frac{\text{Market Return} - \text{Riskfree Return}}{\text{Risk Capital}}$$

Assuming that a similar set of comparable investments is obtained in the market, based on tradable assets, the market return is determined, and using the bank's internal cash flow models, all future cash flows can be discounted at the risk-free rate, in order to determine the risk-free return. Finally, the difference is then divided into the VaR risk capital to determine the required hurdle rate. This concept is similar to the capital

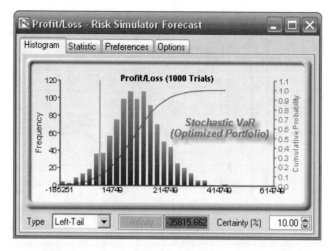

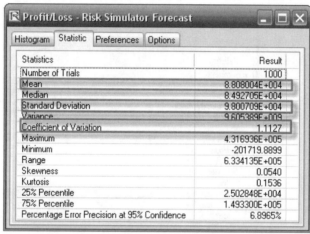

Figure 7-23   Optimal portfolio's Value at Risk through optimization and simulation.

asset pricing model (CAPM), which is often used to compute the appropriate discount rate for a discounted cash flow model. (Weighted average cost of capital, hurdle rates, multiple asset pricing models, and arbitrage pricing models are the other alternatives but are based on similar principles.) The second approach is clearly the use of the CAPM to determine the hurdle rate.

CHAPTER | 8

Portfolio Optimization

The concept of portfolio optimization is critical under the Basel II Accords. Below are several excerpts from the Basel Committee on Banking Supervision's June 2004 publication "International Convergence of Capital Measurement and Capital Standards: A Revised Framework" (Bank of International Settlements), which points to the need for analysis in terms of portfolios.

Section 232. The exposure must be one of a large pool of exposures, which are managed by the bank on a <u>pooled basis</u>. Furthermore, it must not be managed individually in a way comparable to corporate exposures, but rather as <u>part of a portfolio segment or pool of exposures with similar risk characteristics for purposes of risk assessment and quantification</u>.

Section 527 (a). <u>The capital charge is equivalent to the potential loss on the institution's equity portfolio arising from an assumed instantaneous shock equivalent to the 99th percentile</u>, one-tailed confidence interval of the difference between quarterly returns and an appropriate risk-free rate computed over a long-term sample period.

Section 527 (c). However, the model used must be able to adequately capture all of the material risks embodied in equity returns including both the general market risk and specific risk exposure of the <u>institution's equity portfolio</u>.

Section 528 (a). Internal models should be fully integrated into the institution's risk management infrastructure including use in: (i) establishing invest-

ment hurdle rates and evaluating alternative investments; (ii) measuring and assessing equity portfolio performance (including the risk-adjusted performance); and (iii) allocating economic capital to equity holdings and evaluating overall capital adequacy as required under Pillar 2.

Table 3 (b). Capital requirements for credit risk include portfolios subject to standardized or simplified standardized approach, disclosed separately for each portfolio; portfolios subject to the IRB approaches, disclosed separately for each portfolio under the foundation IRB approach and for each portfolio under the advanced IRB approach.

Not only is portfolio-level analysis required by the Basel II Accord, but it actually makes sense for the bank to manage its investment/loans portfolios: an optimal portfolio can generate added profits and lower expenses and required economic capital for the bank. In this chapter, we will detail some additional applications of portfolio optimization and showcase step-by-step methodologies on how to set up and run a portfolio optimization using Risk Simulator and the Basel II Modeling Toolkit software.

What Is an Optimization Model?

In today's competitive global economy, banks face many difficult decisions, such as allocating financial resources, building or expanding facilities, managing investments, and determining product-mix (the different types of loans) strategies. Such decisions might involve thousands or millions of potential alternatives. Considering and evaluating each of them would be impractical or even impossible. A simulation risk-based optimization model can provide valuable assistance in incorporating relevant variables when analyzing decisions and finding the best solutions for making decisions. An optimization model has three major elements: decision variables, constraints, and an objective. In short, the optimization methodology finds the best combination or permutation of decision variables (e.g., what investments or loans to hold) in every conceivable way such that the objective is maximized (e.g., revenues and net income) or minimized (e.g., risk and costs) while still satisfying the constraints (e.g., portfolio totals, budget or resources).

Obtaining optimal values generally requires an iterative or ad hoc search. This search involves running one iteration for an initial set of values, analyzing the results, changing one or more values, rerunning the model, and repeating the process until a satisfactory solution is found. This process can be very tedious and time consuming even for small models, and often it is not clear how to adjust the values from one iteration to the next.

A more rigorous method systematically enumerates all possible alternatives. This approach guarantees optimal solutions if the model is correctly specified. Suppose that an optimization model depends on only two decision variables. If each variable has 10 possible values, trying each combination requires 100 iterations or 10^2 alternatives. If each iteration is very short (e.g., 2 seconds), the entire process could be done in approximately three minutes of computer time.

Instead of two decision variables, however, consider six, and then consider that trying all combinations requires 1,000,000 iterations or 10^6 alternatives. It is easily possible for the complete enumeration process to take weeks, months, or even years to carry out.

The Traveling Financial Planner

A very simple example is in order. Figure 8-1 illustrates the traveling financial planner problem. Suppose the traveling financial planner has to make three sales trips to New York, Chicago, and Seattle. Further suppose that the order of arrival at each city is irrelevant. All that is important in this simple example is to find the lowest total cost possible to cover all three cities. Figure 8-1 also lists the flight costs from these different cities.

The problem here is cost minimization, suitable for optimization. One basic approach to solving this problem is through an ad hoc or brute force method. That is, manually list all six possible permutations of itineraries as seen in Figure 8-2. Clearly, the cheapest itinerary is going from the east coast to the west coast, from New York

Traveling Financial Planner Problem

- You have to travel and visit clients in New York, Chicago, and Seattle
- You may start from any city and you will stay at your final city, that is, you will need to purchase three airline tickets
- Your goal is to travel as cheaply as possible given these rates.

Route	Airfare
Seattle - Chicago	$325
Chicago - Seattle	$225
New York - Seattle	$350
Seattle - New York	$375
Chicago - New York	$325
New York - Chicago	$325

- How do you solve the problem?
  - Ad hoc approach–start trying different combinations
  - Enumeration–look at all possible alternatives

Figure 8-1 Traveling Financial Planner problem.

Multiple Combinations

Seattle-Chicago-New York	$325 + $325 =	**$650**
Seattle-New York-Chicago	$375 + $325 =	**$700**
Chicago-Seattle-New York	$225 + $375 =	**$600**
Chicago-New York-Seattle	$325 + $350 =	**$675**
New York-Seattle-Chicago	$350 + $325 =	**$675**
New York-Chicago-Seattle	$325 + $225 =	**$550**

Additionally, say you want to visit San Antonio and Denver

For the five cities to visit (Seattle, Chicago, New York, San Antonio, and Denver) you now have:

$5! = 5 \times 4 \times 3 \times 2 \times 1 = 120$ possible combinations

What about 100 different cities?

$100! = 100 \times 99 \times 98 \ldots \times 1 =$
93,326,215,443,944,200,000,000,000,000,000,000,000,00
0,000,000,000,000,000,000,000,000,000,000,000,000,000
,000,000,000,000,000,000,000,000,000,000,000,000,000,
000,000,000,000,000,000,000,000,000,000,000,000,000

or 9.3×10^{157} different combinations

Figure 8-2 Multiple combination of the Traveling Financial Planner problem.

to Chicago, and finally on to Seattle. Here, the problem is simple and can be calculated manually, as there were three cities and hence six possible itineraries (i.e., $3! = 3 \times 2 \times 1 = 6$ permutations). However, add two more cities, and the total number of possible itineraries jumps to 120 (i.e., $5! = 5 \times 4 \times 3 \times 2 \times 1 = 120$ permutations). Performing an ad hoc calculation will be fairly intimidating and time consuming. On a larger scale, if we suppose there are 100 cities on the salesman's list, the possible itineraries will be as many as 9.3×10^{157}. The problem will take many, many years to enumerate, even on a supercomputer, which is where optimization software and smart algorithms step in, automating the search for the optimal itinerary, without having to enumerate all possible outcomes.

The example illustrated up to now is a deterministic optimization problem; that is, the airline ticket prices are known ahead of time and are assumed to be constant. Now suppose the ticket prices are not constant but are uncertain, following some probability distribution (e.g., a ticket from Chicago to Seattle averages $325 but is never cheaper than $300 and usually never exceeds $500). The same uncertainty applies to tickets for the other cities. The problem now becomes an *optimization under uncertainty*. Ad hoc and brute force approaches simply do not work. Software such as Risk Simulator can take over this optimization problem and automate the entire process seamlessly. The next section discusses the terms required in an optimization under uncertainty, followed by several additional cases and models with step-by-step instructions on setting up and running a portfolio optimization problem.

The Language of Optimization

Before embarking on solving an optimization problem, it is vital to understand the terminology of optimization—the terms used to describe certain attributes of the optimization process. These words include decision variables, constraints, and objectives.

Decision Variables are quantities over which you have control—for example, the amount of a banking product to sell, the number of dollars or percentage to allocate among different investments or loans, or which projects to select from among a limited set. As an example, portfolio optimization analysis includes a go or no-go decision on particular projects. In addition, the dollar or percentage budget allocation across multiple projects or investments also can be structured as decision variables.

Constraints describe relationships among decision variables that restrict their values. For example, a constraint might ensure that the total amount of money allocated among various investments not exceed a specified amount, or at most one project from a certain group can be selected or other items such as budget constraints, timing restrictions, minimum returns, or risk tolerance levels.

The *Objective* of the optimization is a mathematical representation of the model's desired outcome, such as maximizing profit or minimizing cost, in terms of the decision variables. In financial analysis, for example, the objective may be to maximize returns while minimizing risks (maximizing the Sharpe Ratio or return to risk ratio).

Optimization Procedures

Many algorithms exist to run optimization, and many different procedures exist when optimization is coupled with Monte Carlo simulation. In Risk Simulator, there are three distinct optimization procedures and optimization types as well as different decision variable types. For instance, Risk Simulator can handle **Continuous Decision**

Variables (1.2535, 0.2215, and so forth), *Integers Decision Variables* (e.g., 1, 2, 3, 4, and so forth), *Binary Decision Variables* (1 and 0 for go and no-go decisions), and *Mixed Decision Variables* (both integers and continuous variables). In addition, Risk Simulator can handle *Linear Optimization* (i.e., when both the objective and constraints are all linear equations and functions) and *Nonlinear Optimizations* (i.e., when the objective and constraints are a mixture of linear and nonlinear functions and equations).

With regard to the optimization process, Risk Simulator can be used to run a *Static Optimization*, that is, an optimization that is run on a static model, where no simulations are run. In other words, all the inputs in the model are static and unchanging. This optimization type is applicable when the model is assumed to be known and no uncertainties exist. Also, a static optimization can first be run to determine the optimal portfolio and its corresponding optimal allocation of decision variables before more advanced optimization procedures are applied. For instance, before running a stochastic optimization problem, a static optimization is first run to determine whether solutions to the optimization problem exist before a more protracted analysis is performed.

Next, *Dynamic Optimization* is applied when Monte Carlo simulation is used together with optimization. Another name for such a procedure is *Simulation-Optimization*. That is, a simulation is first run, then the results of the simulation are applied in the Excel model, and finally an optimization is applied to the simulated values. In other words, a simulation is run for N trials, and then an optimization process is run for M iterations until the optimal results are obtained or an infeasible set is found. Using Risk Simulator's optimization module, you can choose which forecast and assumption statistics to use and replace in the model after the simulation is run. Then, these forecast statistics can be applied in the optimization process. This approach is useful when you have a large model with many interacting assumptions and forecasts, and when some of the forecast statistics are required in the optimization. For example, if the standard deviation of an assumption or forecast is required in the optimization model (e.g., computing the Sharpe Ratio in asset allocation and optimization problems where we have mean divided by standard deviation of the portfolio), then this approach should be used.

In contrast, the *Stochastic Optimization* process is similar to the dynamic optimization procedure with the exception that the entire dynamic optimization process is repeated T times. That is, a simulation with N trials is run, and then an optimization is run with M iterations to obtain the optimal results. Next the process is replicated T times. The results will be a forecast chart of each decision variable with T values. In other words, a simulation is run, and the forecast or assumption statistics are used in the optimization model to find the optimal allocation of decision variables. Then, another simulation is run, generating different forecast statistics, and these new updated values are optimized, and so forth. Hence, the final decision variables will each have their own forecast chart, indicating the range of the optimal decision variables. For instance, instead of obtaining single-point estimates in the dynamic optimization procedure, you can now obtain a distribution of the decision variables, hence, a range of optimal values for each decision variable, also known as a stochastic optimization.

Finally, an Efficient Frontier optimization procedure applies the concepts of marginal increments and shadow pricing in optimization. That is, what would happen to the results of the optimization if one of the constraints were relaxed slightly? Say, for instance, if the budget constraint were set at $1 million, what would happen to the portfolio's outcome and optimal decisions if the constraint were now $1.5 million, or

$2 million, and so forth? This is the concept of the Markowitz Efficient Frontier in investment finance, where if the portfolio standard deviation were allowed to increase slightly, what additional returns would the portfolio generate? This process is similar to the dynamic optimization process, with the exception that *one* of the constraints is allowed to change, and with each change, the simulation and optimization process is run. This process is best applied manually using Risk Simulator. Run a dynamic or stochastic optimization, then rerun another optimization with a new constraint, and repeat that procedure several times. This manual process is important, for by changing the constraint, the analyst can determine whether the results are similar or different, and hence, whether it is worthy of any additional analysis, or to determine how far a marginal increase in the constraint should be to obtain a significant change in the objective and decision variables. This is done by comparing the forecast distribution of each decision variable after running a stochastic optimization.

One item is worthy of consideration. Other software products exist that supposedly perform stochastic optimization, but, in fact, they do not. For instance, after a simulation is run, *one* iteration of the optimization process is generated, and then another simulation is run, then the *second* optimization iteration is generated, and so forth. This process is simply a waste of time and resources; that is, in optimization, the model is put through a rigorous set of algorithms, where multiple iterations (ranging from several to thousands of iterations) are required to obtain the optimal results. Hence, generating *one* iteration at a time is a waste of time and resources. The same portfolio can be solved using Risk Simulator in under a minute as compared to multiple hours using such a backward approach. Also, such a simulation-optimization approach will typically yield bad results and is not a stochastic optimization approach. Be extremely careful of such methodologies when applying optimization to your models.

Illustrative Example: Optimization—Continuous Portfolio Allocation

- **File Name:** *Optimization—Continuous Portfolio Allocation*
- **Location:** *Modeling Toolkit | Optimization | Continuous Portfolio Allocation*
- **Brief Description:** *This model illustrates how to run an optimization on continuous decision variables, viewing and interpreting optimization results*
- **Requirements:** *Modeling Toolkit, Risk Simulator*

This model shows 10 asset classes with different risk and return characteristics (Figure 8-3). The idea here is to find the best portfolio allocation such that the portfolio's bang-for-the-buck or return to risk ratio is maximized. That is, to allocate 100 percent of an investment portfolio among several different asset classes (e.g., different types of mutual funds or investment styles: growth, value, aggressive growth, income, global, index, contrarian, momentum, and so forth). In order to run an optimization, several key specifications on the model have to be identified first:

- **Objective:**
  Maximize Return to Risk Ratio (C18)
- **Decision Variables:**
  Allocation Weights (E6:E15)
- **Restrictions on Decision Variables:**
  Minimum and Maximum Required (F6:G15)

– **Constraints:**
Portfolio Total Allocation Weights 100% (E17 is set to 100%)

The model shows the 10 asset classes, and each asset class has its own set of annualized returns and risks, measured by annualized volatilities (Figure 8-3). These return and risk measures are annualized values such that they can be consistently compared across different asset classes. Returns are computed using the geometric average of the relative returns, while the risks are computed using the annualized standard deviation of the logarithmic relative historical stock returns approach using the Basel II Modeling Toolkit.

The allocation weights in column E holds the decision variables, which are the variables that need to be tweaked and tested such that the total weight is constrained at 100 percent (cell E17). Typically, to start the optimization, we will set these cells to a uniform value, where in this case, cells E6 to E15 are set at 10 percent each. In addition, each decision variable may have specific restrictions in its allowed range. In this example, the lower and upper allocations allowed are 5 percent and 35 percent, as seen in columns F and G. This setting means that each asset class may have its own allocation boundaries (Figure 8-3).

Next, column H shows the return to risk ratio, which is simply the return percentage divided by the risk percentage, where the higher this value, the higher the bang-for-the-buck. The remaining model shows the individual asset class rankings by returns, risk, return to risk ratio, and allocation. In other words, these rankings show at a glance which asset class has the lowest risk, or the highest return, and so forth.

Running an Optimization

To run this model, simply click on **Risk Simulator | Optimization | Run Optimization**. Alternatively, for practice, you can try to set up the model again by doing the following (the steps are illustrated in Figure 8-4):

1. Start a new profile (**Risk Simulator | New Profile**) and give it a name.
2. Select cell **E6**, and define the decision variable (**Risk Simulator | Optimization | Decision Variables** or click on the *Define Decision D* icon) and make it a *Con-*

ASSET ALLOCATION OPTIMIZATION MODEL

Asset Class Description	Annualized Returns	Volatility Risk	Allocation Weights	Required Minimum Allocation	Required Maximum Allocation	Return to Risk Ratio
Asset Class 1	10.54%	12.36%	10.00%	5.00%	35.00%	0.8524
Asset Class 2	11.25%	16.23%	10.00%	5.00%	35.00%	0.6929
Asset Class 3	11.84%	15.64%	10.00%	5.00%	35.00%	0.7570
Asset Class 4	10.64%	12.35%	10.00%	5.00%	35.00%	0.8615
Asset Class 5	13.25%	13.28%	10.00%	5.00%	35.00%	0.9977
Asset Class 6	14.21%	14.39%	10.00%	5.00%	35.00%	0.9875
Asset Class 7	15.53%	14.25%	10.00%	5.00%	35.00%	1.0898
Asset Class 8	14.95%	16.44%	10.00%	5.00%	35.00%	0.9094
Asset Class 9	14.16%	16.50%	10.00%	5.00%	35.00%	0.8584
Asset Class 10	10.06%	12.50%	10.00%	5.00%	35.00%	0.8045
Portfolio Total	12.6419%	4.58%	100.00%			
Return to Risk Ratio	2.7596					

Figure 8-3 Asset allocation optimization model.

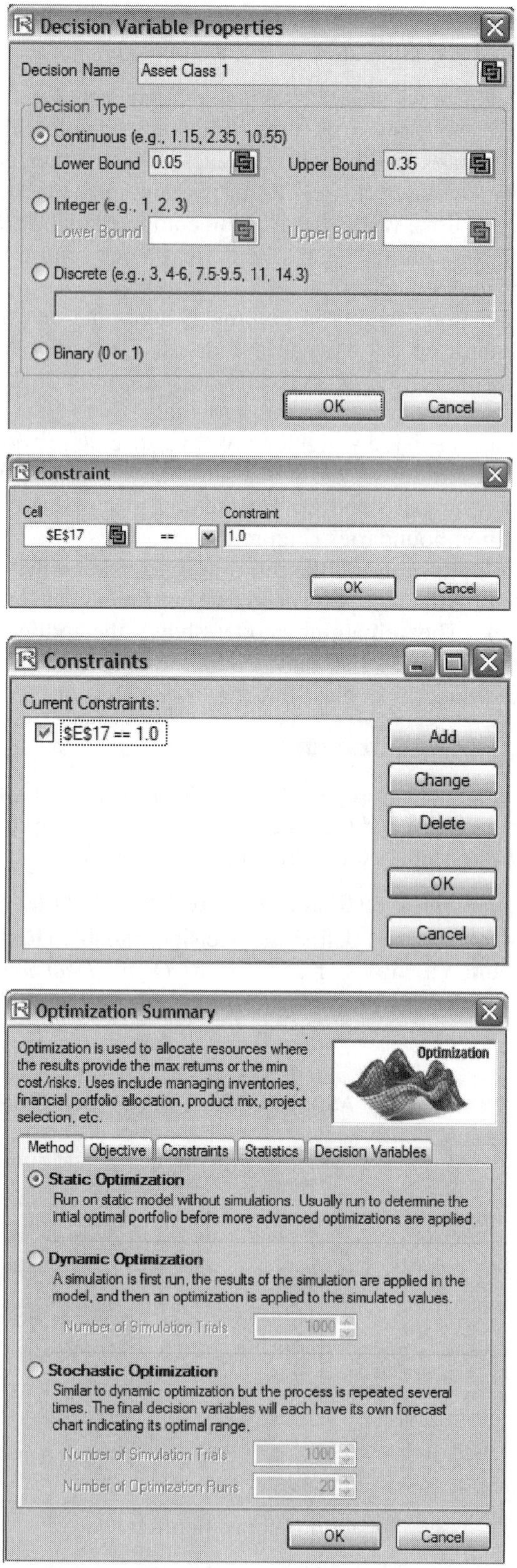

Figure 8-4   Optimization model setup.

ASSET ALLOCATION OPTIMIZATION MODEL

Asset Class Description	Annualized Returns	Volatility Risk	Allocation Weights	Required Minimum Allocation	Required Maximum Allocation	Return to Risk Ratio	Returns Ranking (Hi-Lo)	Risk Ranking (Lo-Hi)	Return to Risk Ranking (Hi-Lo)	Allocation Ranking (Hi-Lo)
Asset Class 1	10.54%	12.36%	11.09%	5.00%	35.00%	0.8524	9	2	7	4
Asset Class 2	11.25%	16.23%	6.87%	5.00%	35.00%	0.6929	7	8	10	10
Asset Class 3	11.84%	15.64%	7.78%	5.00%	35.00%	0.7570	6	7	9	9
Asset Class 4	10.64%	12.35%	11.22%	5.00%	35.00%	0.8615	8	1	5	3
Asset Class 5	13.25%	13.28%	12.08%	5.00%	35.00%	0.9977	5	4	2	2
Asset Class 6	14.21%	14.39%	11.04%	5.00%	35.00%	0.9875	3	6	3	5
Asset Class 7	15.53%	14.25%	12.30%	5.00%	35.00%	1.0898	1	5	1	1
Asset Class 8	14.95%	16.44%	8.90%	5.00%	35.00%	0.9094	2	9	4	7
Asset Class 9	14.16%	16.50%	8.37%	5.00%	35.00%	0.8584	4	10	6	8
Asset Class 10	10.06%	12.50%	10.35%	5.00%	35.00%	0.8045	10	3	8	6

Portfolio Total	12.6920%	4.52%	100.00%
Return to Risk Ratio	2.8091		

Figure 8-5   Optimization results.

tinuous Variable and then link the decision variable's name and minimum/maximum required to the relevant cells (**B6, F6, G6**).

3. Then use the **Risk Simulator Copy** on cell **E6**, select cells **E7 to E15**, and use **Risk Simulator's Paste** (**Risk Simulator I Copy Parameter** and **Risk Simulator I Paste Parameter** or use the *copy and paste icons*). To rerun the optimization, type in **10 percent** for all decision variables.

4. Next, set up the optimization's constraints by selecting **Risk Simulator I Optimization I Constraints**, selecting **ADD**, and selecting the cell **E17**, and making it (= =) equal **100 percent** (for total allocation, and remember to insert the % sign, or you can also use 1.0 as an alternative).

5. Select cell **C18** as the objective to be maximized (**Risk Simulator I Optimization I Objective**).

6. Select **Risk Simulator I Optimization I Run Optimization**. Review the different tabs to make sure that all the required inputs in steps 2–4 are correct.

7. You may now select the optimization method of choice and click on **OK** to run the optimization.

Note: Remember that if you are to run either a dynamic or stochastic optimization routine, make sure that you have assumptions first defined in the model. That is, make sure that some of the cells in C6:D15 are assumptions. No assumptions are required if running a static optimization. The model setup is illustrated in Figure 8-4.

Interpretation of Results

Briefly, the optimization results show the percentage allocation for each asset class (or projects or business lines, et cetera) that would maximize the bang-for-buck of the portfolio, that is, the allocation that would provide the highest returns subject to the least amount of risk. In other words, for the same amount of risk, what is the highest amount of returns that can be generated, or for the same amount of returns, what is the least amount of risk that can be obtained (Figure 8-5)? This is the concept of the Markowitz efficient portfolio analysis.

Illustrative Example: Optimization—Discrete Project Selection

- **File Name:** *Optimization—Discrete Project Selection*
- **Location:** *Modeling Toolkit I Optimization I Discrete Project Selection*

- **Brief Description:** *This next model illustrates how to run an optimization on discrete integer decision variables in project selection in order to choose the best projects in a portfolio given a large variety of project options, subject to risk, return, budget, and other constraints*
- **Requirements:** *Modeling Toolkit, Risk Simulator*

This model shows 12 different projects with different risk and return characteristics. The idea here is to find the best portfolio allocation such that the portfolio's total strategic returns are maximized. That is, it is used to find the best project mix in the portfolio that maximizes the total returns after considering the risks and returns of each project, subject to the constraints of number of projects and the budget constraint. Figure 8-6 illustrates the model.

- **Objective:**
  Maximize Total Portfolio Returns (C17) or Sharpe Ratio return to risk ratio (C19)
- **Decision Variables:**
  Allocation or Go/No-Go Decision (I4:I15)
- **Restrictions on Decision Variables:**
  Binary decision variables (0 or 1)
- **Constraints:**
  Total Cost (D17) is less than $5000 and less than or equal to 6 projects selected (I17)

Running an Optimization

To run this preset model, simply run the optimization (**Risk Simulator | Optimization | Run Optimization**) or for practice, set up the model yourself:

	Credit Line	ENPV	Cost	Risk $	Risk %	Return to Risk Ratio	Profitability Index	Selection
4	Project 1	$458.00	$1,732.44	$54.96	12.00%	8.33	1.26	1.0000
5	Project 2	$1,954.00	$859.00	$1,914.92	98.00%	1.02	3.27	1.0000
6	Project 3	$1,599.00	$1,845.00	$1,551.03	97.00%	1.03	1.87	1.0000
7	Project 4	$2,251.00	$1,645.00	$1,012.95	45.00%	2.22	2.37	1.0000
8	Project 5	$849.00	$458.00	$925.41	109.00%	0.92	2.85	1.0000
9	Project 6	$758.00	$52.00	$560.92	74.00%	1.35	15.58	1.0000
10	Project 7	$2,845.00	$758.00	$5,633.10	198.00%	0.51	4.75	1.0000
11	Project 8	$1,235.00	$115.00	$926.25	75.00%	1.33	11.74	1.0000
12	Project 9	$1,945.00	$125.00	$2,100.60	108.00%	0.93	16.56	1.0000
13	Project 10	$2,250.00	$458.00	$1,912.50	85.00%	1.18	5.91	1.0000
14	Project 11	$549.00	$45.00	$263.52	48.00%	2.08	13.20	1.0000
15	Project 12	$525.00	$105.00	$309.75	59.00%	1.69	6.00	1.0000
17	Total	$17,218.00	$8,197.44	$7,007				12
18	Goal:	MAX	< =$5000					<=6
19	Sharpe Ratio	2.4573						

ENPV is the expected NPV of each credit line or project, while Cost can be the total cost of administration as well as required capital holdings to cover the credit line, and Risk is the Coefficient of Variation of the credit line's ENPV.

Figure 8-6 Discrete project selection model.

1. Start a new profile (**Risk Simulator | New Profile**) and give it a name.

2. In this example, all the allocations are required to be binary (0 or 1) values, so, first select cell **I4** and make this a decision variable in the Integer Optimization worksheet and select cell **I4** and define it as a decision variable (**Risk Simulator | Optimization | Decision Variables** or click on the *Define Decision icon*) and make it a **Binary Variable** (this setting automatically sets the minimum to 0 and maximum to 1 and can only take on a value of 0 or 1). Then use the **Risk Simulator Copy** on cell **I4**, select cells **I5 to I15**, and use **Risk Simulator's Paste** (**Risk Simulator | Copy Parameter** and **Risk Simulator | Paste Parameter** or use the *Risk Simulator copy* and *paste icons*, not the Excel copy/paste).

3. Next, set up the optimization's constraints by selecting **Risk Simulator | Optimization | Constraints**, and selecting **ADD**. Then link to cell **D17**, make it <= **5000**, select **ADD** one more time, and click on the link icon and point to cell **I17** and set it to <= **6**.

4. Select cell **C19**, the objective to be maximized, and select **Risk Simulator | Optimization | Run Optimization**. Review the different tabs to make sure that all the required inputs in steps 2 and 3 above are correct.

5. You may now select the optimization method of choice and click **OK** to run the optimization.

Note: Remember that if you are to run either a dynamic or stochastic optimization routine, make sure first that you have assumptions defined in the model; that is, make sure that some of the cells in C4:C15 are assumptions. The suggestion for this model is to run a Discrete Optimization.

The model setup is illustrated in Figure 8-7.

Viewing and Interpreting Forecast Results

In addition, you can create a Markowitz Efficient Frontier by running the optimization, then resetting the budget to a higher level, and rerunning the optimization. You can do this several times to obtain the risk-return efficient frontier. For a more detailed example, see the Military Portfolio model in the Modeling Toolkit software (see the software's user manual for technical details and procedures).

Illustrative Example: Optimization—Investment Portfolio Allocation

- **File Name:** *Optimization—Investment Portfolio Allocation*
- **Location:** *Modeling Toolkit | Optimization | Inventory Optimization*
- **Brief Description:** *This sample model illustrates how to run an optimization on investment decision variables in project allocation and new product mix*
- **Requirements:** *Modeling Toolkit, Risk Simulator*

This model looks at a set of new product lines that a company is thinking of investing in and at the respective decisions on amounts to be invested to maximize profits (Figure 8-8). Each proposed new product line has its own estimated operating net returns and allowed investment range (lower and upper bounds). The idea is to maximize the total expected returns on the portfolio of investments subject to some budget constraint. See the instructions in the model for details on running this optimization model.

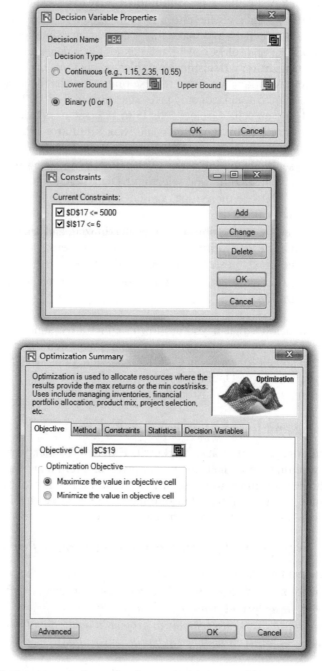

Figure 8-7   Setting up a project selection optimization problem.

Illustrative Example: Optimization—Stochastic Portfolio Allocation

- **File Name:** *Optimization—Stochastic Portfolio Allocation*
- **Location:** *Modeling Toolkit | Optimization | Stochastic Portfolio Allocation*

Strategic Investment Allocation

Proposed New Product Lines	Annual operating return	Lower bound	Upper bound
All Weather Resin Wicker Sets	19.40%	$1,000,000	$1,250,000
Commuter Mobile Office Furniture	19.27%	$600,000	$1,000,000
Specialty Furniture	19.95%	$570,000	$1,100,000
Custom Built Furniture	21.51%	$400,000	$900,000

Decision variables	Amount invested		
All Weather Resin Wicker Sets	$1,000,000		*Constraint*
Commuter Mobile Office Furniture	$600,000		*Decision Variables*
Specialty Furniture	$570,000		
Custom Built Furniture	$830,000		Total amount invested
Total expected return	$601,827		*Objective* $3,000,000
(Annual operating return X Amount invested)			Less than $3,000,000

Figure 8-8   Investment allocation model.

- **Brief Description:** *This sample model illustrates how to run a stochastic optimization on continuous decision variables with simulation and interpreting optimization results*
- **Requirements:** *Modeling Toolkit, Risk Simulator*

This model shows four asset classes with different risk and return characteristics. The idea here is to find the best portfolio allocation such that the portfolio's bang-for-the-buck or return to risk ratio is maximized. That is, to allocate 100 percent of an investment portfolio among several different asset classes (e.g., different types of mutual funds or investment styles: growth, value, aggressive growth, income, global, index, contrarian, momentum, and so forth). This model is different from others in that there are several simulation assumptions (risk and return values for each asset), as seen in Figure 8-9.

That is, a simulation is run, then portfolio optimization is executed, and the entire process is repeated multiple times to obtain distributions of each decision variable. The entire analysis can be automated using Stochastic Optimization.

In order to run an optimization, several key specifications on the model have to be identified first:

- Objective: Maximize Return to Risk Ratio (C12)
- Decision Variables: Allocation Weights (E6:E9)
- Restrictions on Decision Variables: Minimum and Maximum Required (F6:G9)
- Constraints: Portfolio Total Allocation Weights 100% (E11 is set to 100%)
- Simulation Assumptions: Return and Risk Values (C6:D9)

This model shows the various asset classes, and each asset class has its own set of annualized returns and annualized volatilities. These return and risk measures are annualized values such that they can be consistently compared across different asset classes. Returns are computed using the geometric average of the relative returns, whereas the risks are computed using the logarithmic relative stock returns approach.

The Allocation Weights in column E holds the decision variables, which are the variables that need to be tweaked and tested such that the total weight is constrained at **100%** (cell E11). Typically, to start the optimization, we will set these cells to a

	Asset Class Description	Annualized Returns	Volatility Risk	Allocation Weights	Required Minimum Allocation	Required Maximum Allocation	Return to Risk Ratio
	ASSET ALLOCATION OPTIMIZATION MODEL						
Asset 1		10.60%	12.41%	25.00%	10.00%	40.00%	0.8544
Asset 2		11.21%	16.16%	25.00%	10.00%	40.00%	0.6937
Asset 3		10.61%	15.93%	25.00%	10.00%	40.00%	0.6660
Asset 4		10.52%	12.40%	25.00%	10.00%	40.00%	0.8480
Portfolio Total		10.7356%	7.17%	100.00%			
Return to Risk Ratio		1.4970					

Figure 8-9 Asset allocation model ready for stochastic optimization.

uniform value, where in this case, cells E6 to E9 are set at **25%** each. In addition, each decision variable may have specific restrictions in its allowed range. In this example, the lower and upper allocations allowed are **10%** and **40%**, as seen in columns F and G. This setting means that each asset class may have its own allocation boundaries.

Next, column H shows the return to risk ratio, which is simply the return percentage divided by the risk percentage, where the higher this value, the higher the bang-for-the-buck. The remaining model shows the individual asset class rankings by returns, risk, return to risk ratio, and allocation. In other words, these rankings show at a glance which asset class has the lowest risk, or the highest return, and so forth.

Running an Optimization

To run this model, simply click on **Risk Simulator | Optimization | Run Optimization**. Alternatively, and for practice, you can set up the model using the following steps.

1. Start a new profile (**Risk Simulator | New Profile**), and give it a name.
2. For stochastic optimization, set distributional assumptions on the risk and returns for each asset class. That is, select cell **C6** and set an assumption (**Risk Simulator | Set Input Assumption**) and make your own assumption as required. Repeat for cells **C7** to **D9**. For practice, use any distributional assumption (in real life, you can use historical data to perform a distributional fitting routine to obtain the correct distributional assumptions to use).
3. Select cell **E6**, and define the decision variable (**Risk Simulator | Optimization | Decision Variables** or click on the *Define Decision D icon*) and make it a **Continuous Variable** and then link the decision variable's name and minimum/maximum required to the relevant cells (**B6, F6, G6**).
4. Then use the **Risk Simulator copy** on cell **E6**, select cells **E7 to E9**, and use **Risk Simulator's paste** (**Risk Simulator | Copy Parameter** and **Risk Simulator | Paste Parameter** or use the red copy and paste icons).
5. Next, set up the optimization's constraints by selecting **Risk Simulator | Optimization | Constraints**, selecting **ADD**, and selecting the cell **E11**, and making it equal **100%** (total allocation, and do not forget the % sign).
6. Select cell **C12**, the objective to be maximized and make it the objective: **Risk Simulator | Optimization | Set Objective** or click on the red **O** icon.

7. Run the simulation by going to **Risk Simulator | Optimization | Run Optimization**. Review the different tabs to make sure that all the required inputs in steps 2 and 3 above are correct. Select **Stochastic Optimization** and let it run for 500 trials repeated 20 times (Figure 8-10 illustrates these setup steps).

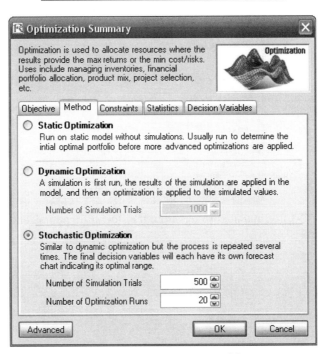

Figure 8-10   Setting up the stochastic optimization problem.

Viewing and Interpreting Forecast Results

Stochastic optimization is performed when a simulation is first run and then the optimization is run. Then the whole analysis is repeated multiple times. The result is a distribution of each decision variable rather than a single-point estimate (Figure 8-11). This means that instead of saying you should invest 30.57 percent in Asset 1, the optimal decision is to invest between 30.10 and 30.99 percent as long as the total portfolio sums to 100 percent. This way, it gives management or decision makers a range of flexibility in the optimal decisions.

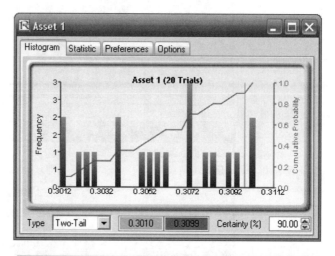

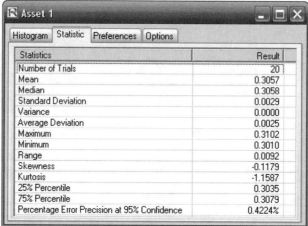

Figure 8-11   Simulated results from the stochastic optimization approach.

CHAPTER | 9

Loan Pricing and Pricing Model Construction

Methods used to include risk in loan pricing range from simple risk spreads and allocations of loan loss reserves to complex assessment of capital allocation, estimates of default frequency, loss given default, and loss volatility. Developments in quantitative credit and portfolio risk measurement vastly improve a bank's ability to measure and price risk, help facilitate capital management, and determine allowance for loan losses.

Loan Pricing Models

Assumptions include spreads, facility fees, fees in lieu of balances, fixed and variable service costs, and other variables. Forecast variables consist of Return on Assets (ROA), Return on Equity (ROE), and Risk-Adjusted Return on Capital (RAROC). Pricing models should be substantially trouble-free to install, use, and administer. They should be available on a wide variety of platforms, determine risk-adjusted returns and yields-to-maturity, and provide multi-period analysis. Finally, pricing models support the negotiating process, offer full relationship profitability, and provide comprehensive context-sensitive help.

203

Stochastic Net Borrowed Funds Pricing Model

This model is available in Modeling Toolkit under **Valuation 1 Stochastic Loan Pricing Model**. Second City Bank prices an unsecured $1,000,000 line of credit to Picnic Furniture Manufacturing Co. Details of the transaction follow:

Input Screen

STOCHASTIC PRICING MODEL
DEVELOPED BY PROF. MORTON GLANTZ DR. JOHNATHAN MUN

Facility Information
Borrower Picnic Furniture Manufacturing Co
Lenders: Second City Bank
Amount: $1,000,000 Five Year Unsecured Facility
Purpose: Expansion
Bank ROA Guideline: 1.15%

Facility Information

Enter Unsecured Line of Credit (Assumed To Be Fully Utilized)	**1,000,000**	
Enter 12 Month Average Balances (Assume Balances Not Free)	**50,000**	
Enter Base Rate (Prime or LIBOR) Rate	**10.5%**	
Enter Spread Over Base	**1.75%**	
Enter % Facility Fees (Not Connected To Balances)	**2.00%**	
Enter Funding Costs	**8.43%**	
Enter Servicing: Enter % or complete Schedule Two	**2.70%**	
Enter Loan loss expense (Applied To Income Statement)	**1.50%**	**Function of *Expected* Risk**
Enter % Equity Reserve Requirement (Function of Unexpected Risk)	**9.00%**	**Function of *Unexpected* Risk**
Enter Taxes	**35%**	

Deposit Information

12 month average balances	50,000
Enter Activity costs as a percent of balances	**4.09%**
Enter Balance Requirement	**8.75%**
Net Borrowed Funds	950,000
Interest rate: Prime + 1.5%	12.21%
Fees in lieu of balances	7.673

Schedule One Types of Facility Fees
Agent Fees
Management Fees
Compensation Balances—See Schedule Two
Fees In Lieu of Balances—See Sehedule Two

Schedule Two—Servicing Costs (See Definitions)
Do Not Complete Schedule If % Was Entered

Direct Variable	0
Allocated Variable	0
Direct fixed	0
Allocated fixed	0
Total Servicing Costs	0

Schedule Three (Complete Schedule If Applicable)
Fees In Lieu Of Balances
(1) Percent of Base Rate (Prime or LIBOR) Fee   Balances on deposit at the
Federal Reserve

(2) Line Facility Fee

**Percent of Prime fee = *(Balances Arrangement) (1 − Reserve Requirement)*
(cost of Funds) Prime Rate**

To Determine Percent of Prime Fee
Enter The Following Information

Balance Requirements as % of Facility	**10.00%**
Reserve as % of Facility	7.00%
**Cost of Funds as %	8.25%
LIBOR (Prime) Rate	10.50%
Facility Amount	1,000,000

OUTPUT

Facility	1,000,000	
% Balance Requirement	10.00%	
Balances Required	100000	
% of LIBOR (Prime) Fee	7.31%	
Fee In Lieu Of Balances	**7672.50**	**Facility Amount X % Of LIBOR (Prime) Fee X LIBOR (Prime Rate)**

Line Facility Fee

**Line Facility Fee = (Balance Arrangement) (1 = Reserve Requirement)
(cost of Funds)**

To Determine Line Facility Fee
Enter The Following Information

Balance Requirement as % of Facility	10.00%
Loan Loss Reserve as % of Facility	7.00%
**Cost of Funds as %	8.25%
Facility Amount	1,000,000

OUTPUT

Facility	1,000,000	
% Balance Requirement	10.00%	
% Line Facility Fee	0.7673%	
Line Facility Fee	**7672.50**	**Facility Amount X Line Facility Fee**

Glossary of Terms: Stochastic Pricing Model—Input Screen
Fees in Lieu of Balances

Compensating balance requirements, sometimes consigned to loan agreements, obligate the borrower to hold demand or low-interest deposits as additional compensation for the loan. Balances can be expressed as a component of the loan commitment, a portion of the actual amount borrowed, or a fixed dollar amount. Fees are paid in advance or in arrears. Since it is part of the pricing mechanism, deficiency fees are charged retroactively if the agreed upon balance arrangement is not honored. Deficient balances are treated as borrowed funds, and the fee is calculated like interest usually at the borrowing rate or earnings credit rate.

Compensating balances have been criticized as being an inefficient pricing mechanism because, though they lower effective borrowing costs, banks must hold idle reserves against the additional deposits and, therefore, cannot fully invest them in earning assets. Among banks that moved toward unbundled and explicit pricing, balance requirements obscure (loan) returns, which are one reason fees in lieu of balances or simply higher loan rates have replaced balances requirements. Since balances effectively replace funds the bank would otherwise purchase, balances "earn" income at cost of funds rate. As the cost of funds fluctuates with market rates, balances are worth more if cost of funds increases and less when funding costs declines.

Although fees in lieu of balances should reflect these changing rates, it is impracticable to reprice a loan every time the bank's funding costs change. Thus, the interest rate environment influences the setting of fees. Fees in lieu of balances are expressed as a *percent of prime fee, line fee,* or *facility fee.* Since the prime rate includes a spread over the lender's cost of funds, *percent of prime fee* in lieu of balances will keep the bankers "whole" despite fluctuations in the cost of funds. Therefore, the primary contribution of customer-supplied balances (net of effects of the reserve requirement) is reduced funding costs. As long as the balances are provided at a rate that is less than other funds available from the market, they will reduce funding costs.

The *line/facility fee* may undercompensate lenders if interest rates rise, since the fee was calculated based on a lower cost of funds. Schedule Three illustrates and compares the percent of prime fee to the line facility fee. You will see that both fees prove to the identical number.

Rates

Prime Rate

At one time approximately 90 percent of loans were linked to the prime rate. Today most banks employ a money market base. Prime is simply a benchmark by which rates for other borrowers are set and are the least complicated for both borrower and bank. Prime is a floating rate, and the pricing spread is already included in the rate. Market fluctuations during a loan's term are passed to the borrower. Additional increments added or subtracted from prime reflect a borrower's creditworthiness—the higher the credit risk, the higher the spread.

A bank's pricing decision should not be driven solely by the prime rate or any other base rate benchmark, because the whole notion of loan pricing involves complex decision making with a multiplicity of factors at play. The myth of prime (rate) lending has come to us from the misconstrued notion that prime is the lowest rate available to the bank's best corporate customers.

The standard procedure calls for an additive—that is, borrowers are quoted something like "prime + 2," which means prime plus 200 basis points. An alternative to prime-plus pricing is prime times pricing, calling for a multiplicative formula rather than an additive one. This pricing is expressed as Quoted rate = Multiplicative Adjustment Factor × Prime Rate, where the adjustment factor can be greater (premium) or less than (discount). For example, if the prime is 8.5 percent and the adjustment factor is 1.35, then the borrower is quoted a rate of 11.475 percent (8.5% times 1.35).

Some banks abandoned prime because of publicity from court cases challenging this rate and associated lending practices during the early and mid-1980s. Plaintiffs claimed that banks misled customers by implying that the prime rate was the interest rate charged to their most creditworthy customers, when in fact some loans were actually made below the prime rate.

LIBOR

Floating rates are based on the London Interbank Offering Rate (LIBOR), a widely quoted rate on short-term European money market credits. For some time, it has influenced the overseas lending rates of large U.S. banks, particularly when the spread between U.S. money market base rates and LIBOR rates favor the latter. Also, access to overseas sources of funds has recently made LIBOR an increasingly popular base rate among borrowers of regional and smaller banks.

Based on demand for alternative pricing structures, many corporate borrowers now have the option of tying their loan rates to the Eurodollar market. Eurodollars are U.S. dollar deposits held anywhere outside of the United States (actually, the Eurodollar market gives rise to LIBOR). LIBOR is an index or snapshot of the Eurodollar market at a particular point of time. At each business day at 11:00 A.M. London time, London's major banks are asked where Eurodollars are trading. These rates become LIBOR. After LIBOR is set, Eurodollars continue to trade freely, above and below LIBOR. LIBOR more accurately reflects the bank's marginal cost of funds than prime. However, as with prime loans, an incremental percentage above or below LIBOR is usually assessed to address the relative creditworthiness of the borrower.

EXAMPLE A manufacturer of plumbing equipment negotiates with its bank a $10 million loan that can be priced at either prime + 50 basis points or at 3-month LIBOR + 250 basis points. Assume that at current levels switching to a LIBOR-based facility reduces the borrower's loan costs by 25 basis points. Why would the prime option be higher in this case? A number of factors are in play. First, LIBOR fluctuates along with uncertainties inherent in the market, while prime is an administered rate, unresponsive to whims and rumors. LIBOR fluctuates on either side of 25 basis points while prime holds constant.

Should LIBOR options be selected simply because the rate is comparably low? Although prime-based loans carry higher pricing, rates offer flexibility, increasing (loan) exposure or paying down credit lines when cash flows permit. This is not true of LIBOR-based deals as banks cannot set pricing unilaterally but must negotiate with borrowers until parties mutually accept a structure and settle on a price.

Types of Facility Fees

Commitment Fee

When a bank makes commitments to lend funds or issue credit facilities, customers are charged commitment fees. This per annum fee is charged (usually quarterly or at time of interest collection) from the time of acceptance of the commitment until drawdown/issuance and on the unused portion of the commitment. A commitment fee is applied to the unused amount of the available portion (the portion that is periodically designated available or the amount the company projects it will need during a specified period). A lower commitment fee is applied to the unavailable portion.

Commitment fees on the unused portion of the loan are usually assessed in each accounting period (monthly or yearly) by calculating the average usage rate. Because the bank must set aside capital in support of the unused credit line, commitment fees should be set high enough to generate a desirable return on capital should the credit line not be fully used and to otherwise encourage use.

Facility Fee

This fee is charged to customers for making a credit facility available. Unlike the commitment fee, the facility fee applies to the entire facility regardless of usage. Facility fees are frequently used in lieu of balance arrangements and as a way to increase the overall yield on the facility. Facility fees and commitment fees are usually disclosed explicitly in the loan agreement. For profitability analysis and pricing, facility fees are generally amortized over the life of the loan according to FASB 91.

Prepayment Penalty Fee

This fee is charged if a loan is partially or entirely repaid before the scheduled maturity. Prepayments, if permitted at all, can be subject to potentially costly premiums. Since an existing agreement cannot be opened up and increased, customers wanting to increase outstandings must enter into new LIBOR agreements. LIBOR loan facilities more so than prime-based facilities may subject borrowers to prepayment premiums if loans are prepaid in whole or in part prior to maturity. Premiums are often calculated by comparing the interest banks would have earned if loans were not prepaid to the interest earned from reinvesting prepaid amounts at current market rates.

Agent's Fee

For its efforts and expense in packaging a credit and performing loan-servicing duties, a principal bank in a multibank credit charges an agent's fee. The fee may be stated as either a dollar amount or a percentage of the facility.

Management Fee

Banks designated as managing banks in a syndicated credit collect this fee.

Miscellaneous Fees

Special financing transactions such as leveraged buyouts, acquisition financing, or tax-exempt financing often warrant charging fees for the extra costs involved in structuring the deal.

Up Front Fees, Arrangement Fees, Closing Fees, and Fees Certain

These fees are collected whether or not the loan is closed. They are common fees collected for complex deals. They may be flat fees or a percentage of the loan, and they can be collected in advance or over the life of the loan.

Cost of Funds

Cost of funds reflects the *marginal* cost of all funds used to support loans. Conventional wisdom defines the incremental cost of funds as the rate paid on capital used for funding the loan. Some bankers believe this definition is narrow, underestimating the true cost of funds (rate). According to one viewpoint, the incremental cost of funds (rate) should be identified as the total incremental expense incurred in gathering $1 of investable funds. For example, some banks with a significant amount of demand deposits and branch networks might have higher operating costs, deposit insurance costs, and reserve requirements. These costs must be included in the cost of funds.

Service and Administrative Costs

Measuring overhead and administrative costs is more complicated, than—for example—funding costs because banks traditionally have not had strong cost accounting systems. In addition, it can be difficult to measure common services with differing or ambiguous values to each user (what, for example, is the dollar value of loan review?). An additional and often ignored cost of risk is risk-related overhead. Riskier loans tend to have higher administrative expenses because of incremental monitoring requirements, together with the increased involvement of credit administration and supervisory personnel required on these deals.

Collection and loan workout areas, and a portion of legal costs represent risk-related expenses, and their costs can be apportioned to loans based on the relative risks. It is unfortunate that some banks approve poorly priced loans when they cannot or are unwilling to allocate their cost base accurately.

If a bank cannot allocate costs, then it will make no distinction between the cost of lending to borrowers that require little investment in recourses and the cost of lending to borrowers that require a considerable amount of analysis and follow-up. As a result, commercial lenders have generally understood the need to reduce costs and redesign the credit process to improve efficiency, recognizing that the market will not permit a premium for inefficiency.

Service and administrative costs are based on functional-cost data, cost accounting figures allocated to average assets, or the bank's best estimates of the costs. These costs are as follows:

1. Direct variable
   Expenses charged to the profit/cost center that are directly associated with the loan. Direct variable expense can easily be estimated either from the loan proposal or by the loan department.
2. Allocated variable
   Allocated expenses are the expenses incurred by other cost centers in support of a product. These expenses can usually be derived from a bank's cost accounting system that includes variable support expenses for data processing, the customer phone center, and other support departments.

3. Allocated fixed
   Direct and allocated fixed expenses are calculated according to the total capacity of each operation (cost center) rather than using the fully loaded costs. Otherwise, as volume rises, per-unit fixed costs will be overstated. These calculations are usually based on an operation research and capacity/unit cost study.
4. Direct fixed and Allocated overhead
   Allocated overhead is the portion of the bank's total overhead that should be considered supportive of this particular product.

Hurdle Rate

While operating expenses factor into the pricing arithmetic, loan pricing involves three essential steps:

1. A minimum target or hurdle rate must be estimated. The appropriate hurdle rate incorporates both the funding costs and a specified profit target.
2. Estimate income, expenses, and yield associated with the loan.
3. Compare the estimated yield with the target or hurdle rate to determine loan profitability. If the yield is less than the hurdle rate, the loan should be either rejected or restructured so that it meets the target.

Output Screen and Yield Calculation

The underlying algorithms used to compute loan yields should be reliable and support a bank's strategic objectives. Efficient pricing should compute yields to maturity, from inception to maturity. For example, interest rates for purchased funds can change frequently, money borrowed fluctuates over time, deposit balances vary with the borrower's cash position, and administrative costs change and so on. Changes, especially in a volatile market, affect yields and must be factored into pricing. Pricing models must respond to frequent changes in the negotiating environment and include variables affecting profitability (even factors not at issue with the customer). A lending officer cannot possibly track all pricing variables; all fluctuate over time, which is one good reason computer-based loan pricing is sine qua non.

Output Screen

Yield Calculation

Interest	122,081		*Loan X Interest Rate*
Fees in lieu of balances	7,673		
Other facility Fees	20,000		*Fees X Interest Rate*
Total Loan Revenue		*149,753*	
Expenses Before Funding Costs			
Loan Servicing Costs	(27,000)		*Loan X Servicing %*
Loan Service From Schedule B	0		*From Schedule B*
Loan Loss expense	(15,000)		*Loan X Loan Loss Expense*

Annual activity costs	(2,000)		*12 month average balances X % Activity Cost*
Total Expenses		*(44,000)*	
Income Before Funding Costs		*105,753*	

Yield Calculation-Net Borrowed Funds Basis

Income Before Funding Costs	105,753	
Net Borrowed Funds	950,000	*Loan Less Balances*
Yield	11.132%	*Income Before Funding Costs/Net Borrowed Funds*

Net Income Before Funding Costs	105.753		
Funding Costs	(84,294)		*Funding Cost as % of Loan (Line Fully Utilized)*
Taxes	(7,511)		
Net Income		*13,948*	

Return on Assets Calculation

Loan Amount	1,000,000	
Net Income	13,948	
Return on Assets	1.395%	*Forecast Cell*

Return on Risk Adjusted Capital Calculation

% Equity Reserve Requirement (Function of Unexpected Risk)	9.00%	
Loan Amount	1,000,000	
$ Amt Equity Reserve Allocation (Function of Unexpected Risk)	90,000	*Unexpected Risk Not Derived In This Model*
Net Income	13,948	*But If It Were, You Would Reference The RAROC*
BAROC	15.50%	*Worksheet. See Unexpected Worksheet For Study*

Summary: Base Case
Borrower Picnic Furniture Manufacturing Co
Lenders: Second City Bank

Loan Revenue	149,753

Facility	1,000,000
Net Income	13,948
ROA	1.395%
Facility ROA Hurtle Rate	**1.15%**
Facility Internal Rate of Return (See Brady Worksheet)	
Option Pricing Generated Hurtle Rate (OptionPr Worksheet)	
RAROC	**15.50%**

In the unchanged scenario of the pricing model, the bank's 1.395 percent return on assets (ROA) is higher than the facility ROA hurdle rate of 1.15 percent. The higher the ROA over the hurdle rate, the more profitable the bank will be within its desired level of risk. The estimated loan revenue is comprised of fees in lieu of balances and facility fees. Facility is the face value amount of the loan being borrowed. Net income is income after all funding costs and administrative expenses. ROA is Net Income/ Loan Amount. Because the ROA hurdle rate is 1.15 percent and the actual ROA is 1.395 percent, the bank will accept this loan provided that the RAROC and credit grade are acceptable for the bank's loan portfolio risk profile.

Moving from Deterministic Pricing to Stochastic Pricing Solution

Recall Chapter 5 where deterministic models are described as relying on single sets of assumptions that lead to limited outcomes. Risk Simulator stochastic software yield an entire range of results and confidence levels realistic for any pricing run. Risk Simulator (Monte Carlo) simulation fosters realistic loan pricing, capturing elements of uncertainty that are too complex to be solved with deterministic pricing models. Stochastic models, as we have seen, necessitate a random number generator set against key variables in the pricing program, creating a series of loan pricing outcomes over time, outcomes that are not deterministic in nature. That is, loan pricing—ROA, ROE, or RAROC—will change by x percent if loan spreads, or allocated variable cost of the loan changes by a specific factor. Stochastic pricing is nondeterministic. By offering a stochastic simulation, we create multiple pathways and obtain a statistical sampling of these simulations.

Before starting with simulation, we first need to identify which of the variables in the model are considered critical success factors—that is, automatically performing a static perturbation of all the input variables in the model and ranking the input assumptions with the highest impact to the least impact, so that we can determine which of these precedent variables have the greatest impact on return on asset. Then, from this list, we can select the variables that are also uncertain and apply simulation assumptions on them. Do not waste time with inputs that have very little impact on ROA or are simply known or contractually set in advance. The resulting static sensitivity table and Tornado chart from Risk Simulator are presented in Table 9-1 and Figure 9-1 (we only set the software to show the top 10 impact variables).

Armed with this information and determining which variables are indeed known or unchanged, we set input assumptions of the critical key variables and the simulation is run. The report shown next (Figure 9-2), produced by Risk Simulator, shows that a 15 percent probability deal pricing falls below the 1.15 percent ROA hurdle rate set

Table 9-1   Static Sensitivity Table

| Precedent Cell | Base Value: 0.0139484609812889 | | | Input Changes | | |
	Output Downside	Output Upside	Effective Range	Input Downside	Input Upside	Base Case Value
Base Rate (Prime or LIBOR)	0.0071507	0.0207462	0.01	9.4%	11.5%	10.5%
Funding Costs	0.0194276	0.0084694	0.01	7.59%	9.27%	8.43%
Servicing	0.0157035	0.0121935	0.00	2.43%	2.97%	2.70%
% Facility Fees	0.0126485	0.0152485	0.00	1.80%	2.20%	2.00%
Spread Over Base	0.012811	0.015086	0.00	1.58%	1.93%	1.75%
Loan Loss Expense	0.0149235	0.0129735	0.00	1.35%	1.65%	1.50%
Enter Taxes	0.0146995	0.0131974	0.00	32%	39%	35%
Balance Requirement	0.0134497	0.0144472	0.00	9.00%	11.00%	10.00%
Facility Amount	0.0134497	0.0144472	0.00	900,000	1,100,000	1,000,000
Cost of Funds	0.0134497	0.0144472	0.00	7.43%	9.08%	8.25%
Unsecured Line of Credit	0.0143581	0.0136133	0.00	900,000	1,100,000	1,000,000
Annual Activity Costs	0.0140785	0.0138185	0.00	(1,800)	(2,200)	(2,000)
Reserve % Facility	0.013986	0.0139109	0.00	6.30%	7.70%	7.00%
Allocated Variable	0.0139485	0.0139485	0.00	0	0	0
Direct fixed	0.0139485	0.0139485	0.00	0	0	0
Cost of Funds	0.0139485	0.0139485	0.00	7.43%	9.80%	8.25%
Direct Variable	0.0139485	0.0139485	0.00	0	0	0
Balance Requirement	0.0139485	0.0139485	0.00	9.00%	11.00%	10.00%
Loan Loss Reserve % Facility	0.0139485	0.0139485	0.00	6.30%	7.70%	7.00%
Allocated fixed	0.0139485	0.0139485	0.00	0	0	0
LIBOR (Prime) Rate	0.0139485	0.0139485	0.00	9.45%	11.55%	10.50%
Facility Amount	0.0139485	0.0139485	0.00	900,000	1,100,000	1,000,000

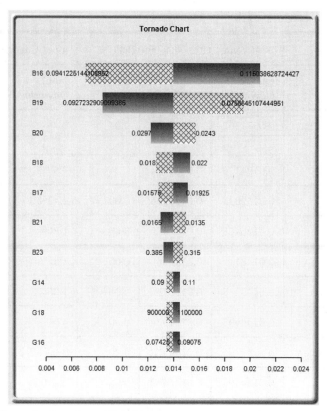

Figure 9-1 Tornado chart from Risk Simulator.

by the profit center. We are, however, 100 percent certain that ROA range will fall between 2.48 and 0.71 percent. The median return is 1.47 percent.

Risk Simulator also produced a Statistical Summary including sensitivity charts. Sensitivity charts are dynamic perturbations created after the return on assets simulation run; they are dynamic perturbations in the sense that multiple assumptions are perturbed simultaneously and their interactions are captured in the fluctuations of the results. Sensitivity charts identify the impact to the forecast variable—ROA when multiple interacting assumptions in our pricing model are simulated together. The Nonlinear Rank Correlation charts (shown below) indicate the rank correlations between each pricing assumption and our target forecast, and they are depicted from the highest to the lowest absolute value. Positive correlations are shown in solid texture, and negative correlations are shown crosshatched. Rank correlation is used instead of a regular correlation coefficient because it captures nonlinear effects between variables. In contrast, the Percent Variation Explained computes how much of the variation in the forecast variable can be explained by the variations in each assumption by itself in a dynamic simulated environment. These charts show the sensitivity of the target forecast to the simulated assumptions. (see Figures 9-3 and 9-4).

The Nonlinear Rank Correlation (Return on Assets) and Percent Variation Explained (Return on Assets) demonstrate that pricing is more sensitive to loan-servicing costs than loan spreads. This last statement is noteworthy because the bank may benefit

Simulation - Pricing Model B

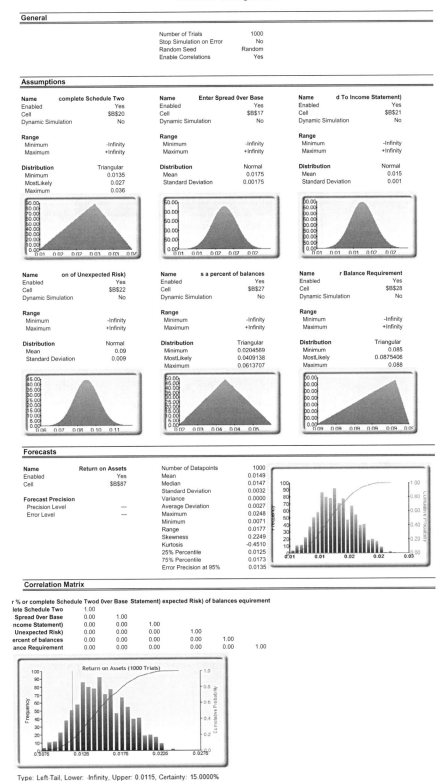

Figure 9-2   Report produced by Risk Simulator.

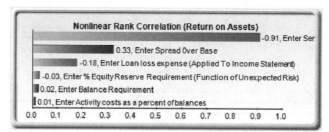

Figure 9-3 Chart showing the sensitivity of the target forecast to the simulated assumptions.

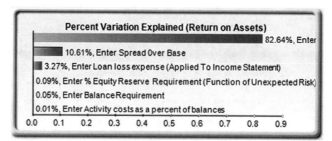

Figure 9-4 Chart showing the sensitivity of the target forecast to the simulated assumptions.

from a substantial, profitable relationship worldwide. If a profit center were required to lower spreads over base because global relationships are immensely profitable, a pricing rebate—on the one deal—would be in order. However, if loan returns are time and again unsatisfactory because costs of managing a profit center are out of control, no compensation from head office can be expected to save the day.

CHAPTER | 10

Banker's Primer on Shareholder Value

This chapter gives credit professionals the financial tools and methodology that helps determine equity value, distance to default, default probabilities, and loan value.[1] Market values validate projections, identify leveraged buyout and restructuring opportunities, and determine values in partnership buyout agreements. Bear in mind that market value, more so than book value, defines loan value: an obligor's asset value, (asset) volatility, and financial obligations link directly to distance to default and default frequencies.[2] We can decide market values and volatility of privately owned firms employing the Corporate Valuation Model[3] in the Modeling Toolkit. Our valuation model is used for developing financial statements, enterprise value, equity values, value gaps, volatility, default probabilities, earnings per share, economic profit, and other financial metrics.

1. *"Internal audits of the credit risk processes should be conducted on a periodic basis to determine that credit activities are in compliance with the bank's credit policies and procedures, that credits are authorized within the guidelines established by the bank's board of directors, and that the existence, quality, and value of individual credits are accurately being reported to senior management. Such audits should also be used to identify areas of weakness in the credit risk management process, policies and procedures as well as any exceptions to policies, procedures and limits."*—Consultative Paper Issued by the Basel Committee 2000.

2. Probabilities market equity falls below zero—given volatility—usually translates into probabilities of default.

3. Real Options Valuation Inc.

Value is composed of future cash flow potential and risks (threats) to those cash flows. These perceived risks or threats define market value of assets (before adjustments), asset volatility, equity values, distance to default, and default probabilities. Bankers looking beyond risk to business development opportunities will use valuation techniques to determine value gaps (difference between the market stock price and the stock's unrealized value).

Methods to Determine Value

Book Values Reflect the Past

Book values, based on accounting numbers, reflect historical costs yielding only vague approximations of real economic value. Moreover, book values are affected by management decisions including choices: depreciation/amortization rates, capitalization or expensing costs, perceived asset impairment. Say a firm purchases a truck and after depreciating it over a period of time records it with zero book value. When the truck is sold, the company receives cash as long as the truck operates. Hence there may be little connection between book and market values. Book value ignores asset price fluctuations—real estate, timberland, and intangibles: goodwill, trademarks, franchise licenses, and patents—all of which can produce strong cash flows.

Transaction Multiples

The fair market value of public companies is determined through decisions made by buyers and sellers. Since there are generally similar public companies (to any given private company), the market values of fair public companies can generally be compared to those of private companies.

Firms whose equity recently sold in a market priced transaction can provide a measure of minority interest (value). If a private company is similar, performance indicators of the recently sold firm are reviewed to estimate a "pro forma" market value together with an added premium for control. The problem with transaction multiples is difficulty locating comparable companies. Some firms may be diversified —operating with different product lines.

PricewaterhouseCoopers suggests that value using transaction multiples are as good as comparability from which analysis is based. High correlations with peer groups add credibility. Comparability indicators include[4]:

1. Product type
2. Market segment to which the product is sold
3. Geographic area of operation
4. Positioning in marketplace
5. Influence of buyers/suppliers
6. Growth, historical and projected
7. Profitability
8. Leverage and liquidity
9. Diversification

---

4. PricewaterhouseCoopers and Leveraged Buyouts; Solutions for Business.

Noteworthy adjustments PricewaterhouseCoopers identify include:[5]

- Extraordinary and nonrecurring items inventory policy: FIFO vs. LIFO
- Revenue recognition policy
- Nonoperating assets
- Excess marketable securities and cash
- Contingent liabilities
- Pension and other postemployment benefits funding and expense policy

Price Earnings

The price/earnings (P/E) ratio divides stock price by the last four quarters' earnings. For instance, if a firm traded at $10, with $1 in earnings per share, P/E is 15X:

$$\$15 \text{ share price}/\$1.00 \text{ EPS} = 15 \text{ P/E}$$

Keep in mind that market "price" depicts performance expectations, whereas earnings are historical. There are many permutations of P/Es using forecasted or trailing 12 months' earnings. A further complication arises using comparable P/Es for valuation purposes; a particular market sector may be temporarily mispriced by overly optimistic/ pessimistic investors.

Firms may report low earnings, yet produce impressive values because they focus on research and product development or are recent entrants in high-growth industries. For valuation purposes we look at average industry P/E ratios to benchmark if comparatives are homogeneous. Beware that earnings are sometimes window dressed by changing accounting practices or are manipulated.

Price/Sales

Price/sales takes current market capitalization and divides by the past 12 months trailing revenues. Market capitalization is current market value—that is, current share price times shares outstanding.

Liquidation Valuation Approach

Management's decision to divest business units is related to spreads between cash flow and liquidation values. Hax and Majluf[6] suggest that operating units destroy value when discounted cash flow hits a critically low mass, tying resources that otherwise could be put to better use. Operating segments that cannibalize cash flow are known as "cash traps" that produce deficit cash flows, diminishing contributions of positive cash flow businesses. Here, divestiture is usually the logical choice. Liquidation is determined by (asset) appraisals—tangible and intangible—including real estate, machinery, equipment, inventory, trademarks, patents, customer lists, proprietary systems, and customer contracts. Normally, three values are measured:

5. Ibid.

6. Arnoldo Hax and Nicolas Majluf, *The Strategy Concept and Process: A Pragmatic Approach*, 2nd ed. (New York: Prentice Hall, 1996).

1. Orderly liquidation value: the amount assets will produce if disposed of in the normal course net of liabilities. Typical equipment disposals are examples of orderly liquidation value.
2. Not so orderly liquidation based on auction: associated with forced sales of company assets (and expenses) at auction liquidation prices.
3. Replacement Value (or cost approach): the amount it would cost potential buyers to duplicate the firm's assets at current market prices.

Valuation Based on Dividends

This value is best applied to securities whose earnings and dividends are expected to increase each year. The stock price is determined by a dividend's expected future cash flow stream. Thus, intrinsic value equals the present value of expected future dividends.

Discounted Cash Flow Approach (Going Concern)

Discounted Cash Flow, the most frequently used valuation method, determines "going concern" values—that is, asset/equity economic worth driven by an obligor's economic muscle. We establish asset market values (known also as the value of a firm) by adding the present value of future cash flows over a discrete forecast horizon (projection period) to the present value of cash flow *beyond* the forecast horizon (residual or terminal value). Then we include unrealized and/or nonoperating asset values net of the expected value of contingencies. Subtracting the two will yield equity value.

We estimate three "building blocks" of value:

1. Free cash flow within a discrete projection horizon
2. Residual period or long-term horizon
3. Risk and time value of money

Free Cash Flow

By concentrating on forecasting the company's free or operating cash flow, we are able to make a distinction between the operating and financing decisions of the firm. Once cash flow is estimated, we can then take risk into account, discounting those cash flows by the cost of capital (more on cost of capital later). The estimation of cash flow involves the employment of forecast techniques to include the best possible information. When estimating company cash flow, it is not practical to estimate discrete cash flow to infinity for a going concern. Therefore, we make simplifying assumptions to estimate cash flow value after a discrete time horizon (or "forecast period"). Instead of considering value equal to the present value of a single stream of cash flow, think of value as the sum of the present value of cash flow within a discrete forecast horizon, plus the present value of a "residual" value estimate.

Choosing the Length of the Forecast Horizon

The length of the forecast horizon is not simply a "convenient" period of time in which management feels comfortable in estimating financial performance (i.e., the typical long-range planning period is three years), but a period tied to economics of the company and industry. We refer to this time horizon as the value growth duration

(VGD). Porter (1985) emphasized that, in a competitive market with free entry, firms cannot earn returns substantially greater than the cost of capital (hurdle rate) for long periods because that encourages competitors to enter, driving down prices and thus returns.[7] Normal accounting profits are just enough to pay capital costs and compensate owners for the *unique* inputs to production (e.g., management expertise) that they provide.

When estimating the appropriate VGD, management considers industry dynamics affecting the firm's competitive position.[8] Following is a short list of factors that affect that position and the relevant effect on VGD:

EXISTENCE OF	EFFECT ON VGD
Proprietary Technologies	Lengthen
Patented Products	Lengthen

We discuss length of the forecast horizon in more detail later on.

Residual Value

Residual value is cash flow value that we reasonably expect beyond a forecast horizon. Known as the terminal value, residual value is determined by multiplying cash flow at the end of the forecast horizon (the first day of the residual period is the last day of the forecast horizon) by a multiple. Selected multiples commonly use a median of total invested capital to the Earnings Before Interest Taxes Depreciation Amortization (EBITDA) of the firm or comparable companies. The selected multiple may be discounted to reflect the company's performance or size characteristics relative to comparable companies. This method is similar to dividing the cash flow by the weighted average cost of capital and including a growth factor.

Once we estimate a discrete forecast horizon, a simplifying assumption is made—cash flow after the discrete forecast period. Investment rates of return for new investments made during the VGD are assumed to be greater than the cost of capital and contributes to positive net present value (NPV). Beyond the forecast period average rates of return—new investments—will tend to equal capital costs. This is not necessarily a no-growth state; rather, the implication is that postforecast period growth is not expected to increase shareholder value since rate of returns on these new investments equal the discount rate (i.e., cost of capital). In any way of speaking, this is the same as a no-growth state.

7. Michael Porter, *Competitive Advantage* (New York: Free Press, 1985). Porter's strategic system consists primarily of a five forces analysis: strategic groups (also called strategic sets); the value chain; the generic strategies of cost leadership, product differentiation, and focus; the market positioning strategies of variety-based, needs-based, and access-based market positions; and clusters of competence for regional economic development.

8. Porter provides a detailed methodology to estimate a company's competitive position; see Michael E. Porter, *Competitive Strategies: Techniques for Analyzing Industries and Competitors* (New York: The Free Press, 1980).

The assumptions supporting the use of operating profit (aftertax) as the perpetuity cash flow instead of operating cash flow are as follows:

1. In growing capital-intensive firms, capital expenditures in any given year will be greater than depreciation expense.
2. Incremental fixed capital investment (the amount above depreciation expense necessary for new growth) and incremental working capital investment have already been determined to return only the cost of capital and therefore would not have any effect on the NPV of the firm if included. Therefore, they are excluded to simplify the calculation.

The perpetuity method of calculating residual value is suggested in most instances because it provides a methodology consistent with the shareholder value approach applied during the discrete forecast period. Of course, in some instances a more aggressive assumption regarding the value impact from new investments is appropriate. Variations of the perpetuity method can be made to accommodate these alternate situations.

Market Signals Analysis

In order to estimate what the specific VGD should be for a given company (instead of speaking in relative terms), we try to understand what the stock market estimates to be the end of the forecast horizon. Using market signals analysis, we gain that insight. Having a reasonable handle on a company's forecasted cash flow and risk (i.e., cost of capital), we "solve" for the known stock price. If our discrete period cash flow forecast earns rates of returns above the cost of capital, we know that our value estimate will increase if we extend the forecast horizon. This, in essence, delays the time when residual value assumptions (new investments earning only the cost of capital) will kick in.

For purposes of comparing estimated value to stock market value, this method obviously requires a publicly traded company. Privately held companies (or divisions of public companies, for the matter) can estimate their VGDs by performing similar analysis on publicly traded peer companies. When estimating shareholder value, it may be helpful for you to think about the three "building blocks" of value (i.e., cash flow, time horizon, and risk) in terms of what Rappaport calls value drivers.[9] Reducing an unnecessarily detailed discounted cash flow analysis to a set of observable value drivers accomplishes two objectives. First, it simplifies the analysis without cutting any corners with regard to the estimation of the key determinants of value; and second, it allows for an understanding of the key aspects of a business most responsible for value creation (or value impact). This second point is important. Knowing what value driver has the biggest impact on the business's value gives management a basis for formulating strategy to maximize the value of the firm. There are eight observable value drivers:

1. Revenue growth rates
2. Operating profit margin (alternatively, Gross Profit Margin)
3. Working Capital (Receivables and Inventory Assumptions)

9. Alfred Rappaport, *Creating Shareholder Value: The New Standard for Business Performance* (New York: The Free Press, 1986).

4. Capital Spending
5. Cost of Capital
6. Length of Forecast (VGD)
7. Residual Period Assumptions
8. Cost of Capital

The Importance of Cost of Capital in the Valuation Process

The proper discount rate (weighted average cost of capital) is often a highly significant value driver. Because the present value of cash flows changes inversely with increases in the discount rate, it is critical to the valuation process to properly assess the company's inherent risk and thus its cost of capital. If the firm hedges interest rates—thus reducing interest rate volatility—this should be considered. Most importantly, the cost of capital must be consistent with the overall valuation approach and should reflect the riskiness of the firm's operating and financial strategies, consistent with expected industry conditions. Basically,

1. Creditors and shareholders need compensation for the opportunity cost of investing funds in one particular business instead of others with equivalent risk.
2. The cost of capital is a hurdle rate because the only way to create value is to earn returns in excess of the cost of capital.

To be consistent with the free cash flow approach to valuation, the cost of capital:

1. Must comprise the weighted cost of all sources of capital, debt, equity, and the like since free cash flow represents cash available to all providers of capital.
2. Must be computed after tax since free cash flow is stated after tax.
3. Must employ market rates, not book for each financing element because the market reflects the true economic claims of each type of financing outstanding. Book value does not.
4. May be subject to change across the forecast period because of expected changes in inflation, systematic risk, or capital structure. In most cases, however, the cost of capital assigned to the first projection period is left unchanged.

Steps to Develop the Weighted Average Cost of Capital
1. Establish target market value weights for capital structure. Future financing levels could be different from current or past levels. Estimate the current market value capital structure of the company. Review capital structure of comparable companies. Review management's approach to financing the business.
2. Estimate cost of nonequity financing.
3. Recognize that non-interest-bearing liability such as accounts payable are excluded from the calculation of the weighted average cost of capital in order to avoid inconsistencies and simplify the valuation process. Non-interest-bearing liabilities have cost of capital like other forms of debt, but this cost is implied in the price paid for goods and thus is recorded in operating costs and free cash flows.
4. Include payment schedule, interest, coupon, short term debt, and leases.
5. Estimate cost of equity financing. If market exists, the calculation is stock price X outstanding shares. It is better to use the current market price than book value or average of past market values.

Table 10-1   Cost of Capital Calculation

Cost of Capital Calculation

Instrument	Before tax	After tax	Percent	Product
Short-term debt	9.90%	5.94%	1.01%	0.06%
Long-term debt	10.50%	6.30%	22.75%	1.43%
Equity (CAPM)	13.00%	13.00%	76.24%	9.91%
Weighted cost of capital				11.40%

Cost of capital components:

Cost of equity X percent equity to total capital = product

Cost of debt X percent of debt to total capital = product

Weighted average cost of capital = sum

A value-maximizing firm will establish its optimal or target capital structure and raise new capital, which will keep the capital structure on target over the projection horizon to satisfy its goals of value maximization. The Capital Asset Pricing Model and Arbitrage Pricing Theory estimate the cost of equity capital—the required return demanded by shareholders equates to the cost of risk-free debt plus an additional risk premium appropriate to the company. This infers that investors have alternative investment opportunities and will bid on investments, yielding the highest return with the lowest risk (trade-off between risk and return).

The concept of terminal value, introduced earlier and expanded here, depends on the underlying assumptions and the length of the projection period, in addition to the specifics of the business. Projection periods that are short place more emphasis on residual value. The reverse is true for longer projection periods. The common methods of estimating residual value include:

1. Liquidation value
2. Book value
3. Income capitalization
4. Market multiple techniques

Liquidation value and book value are typically employed when firms have determinate life horizons or a company's ability to continue operations beyond a projection period is dubious. Income capitalization methods divide net income or cash flow by an appropriate residual (period) discount rate (capital cost rate), the key assumption being that net income will either remain constant or will increase at a constant rate beyond the last projection year. For example, assume a five-year projection horizon with the residual period starting in year 6. Assume also that income in year 6 is $2,000,000 and that the cost of capital is fixed at 12 percent. The residual value before

Assumptions

Base Year (Valuation Year)	2008	
Start of Forecast Year	2008	
Years to Forecast	5	

Real Options Valuation
www.realoptionsvaluation.com

Discounting: Discrete End-of-Year Discounting ▼

	0	1	2	3	4	5
Forecast Year						
Year	2008	2009	2010	2011	2012	2013
Weighted Average Cost of Capital	15.00%	15.00%	15.00%	15.00%	15.00%	15.00%

Currency Units (e.g., in $000's)	1000
Equity Starting Value	129567
Marginal Tax Rate	35%
Return on Invested Capital	10%
Assumed Terminal WACC	10.00%
Assumed Terminal Growth Rate	5.00%
Current Stock Price	10.00

This is the Corporate Valuation Model used for developing financial statements as well as for enterprise valuation, and computing the total enterprise value, earnings per share, economic profit, and other financial metrics. The inputs are the boxed cells. You can extend the model to additional years by first entering the Years to Forecast (cell E7) and typing in the various required values in these future years (the boxes will automatically appear).

	0	1	2	3	4	5
Revenues	678023	711924	747520	784896	824141	865348
Revenue: % Growth		5.00%	5.00%	5.00%	5.00%	5.00%
Other Operating Revenues	14554	17465	20958	25149	30179	36215
Other Operating Revenues: % Growth		20.00%	20.00%	20.00%	20.00%	20.00%
Cost of Goods Sold	180054	194458	210015	226816	244961	264558
Cost of Goods Sold: % Growth		8.00%	8.00%	8.00%	8.00%	8.00%
Selling, Gen & Admin Expenses	385447	393156	401019	409039	417220	425565
Selling, Gen & Admin Expenses: % Growth		2.00%	2.00%	2.00%	2.00%	2.00%
Non-Operating Income	7345	8080	8887	9776	10754	11829
Non-Operating Income: % Growth		10.00%	10.00%	10.00%	10.00%	10.00%
Interest Expense	23190	24350	25567	26845	28188	29597
Interest Expense: % Growth		5.00%	5.00%	5.00%	5.00%	5.00%
Cash	12826	14109	15519	17071	18779	20656
Cash: % Growth		10.00%	10.00%	10.00%	10.00%	10.00%
Accounts Receivable	24611	27072	29779	32757	36033	39636
Accounts Receivable: % Growth		10.00%	10.00%	10.00%	10.00%	10.00%
Inventories	16080	17688	19457	21402	23543	25897
Inventories: % Growth		10.00%	10.00%	10.00%	10.00%	10.00%
Other Current Assets	5692	6546	7528	8657	9955	11449
Other Current Assets: % Growth		15.00%	15.00%	15.00%	15.00%	15.00%
Wages and Accounts Payable	28738	30175	31684	33268	34931	36678
Wages and Accounts Payable: % Growth		5.00%	5.00%	5.00%	5.00%	5.00%
Other Current Liabilities	50915	56007	61607	67768	74545	81999
Other Current Liabilities: % Growth		10.00%	10.00%	10.00%	10.00%	10.00%

DCF Valuation

Free Cash Flow	14854	64498	68498	79699	91261	103502
Discount Factor	1.0000	0.8696	0.7561	0.6575	0.5718	0.4972
Present Value of Operations	**278774**					
Computed Terminal NOPAT	114450					
Continuing Value	1201729					
Present Value of Continuing Value	**60086**					
Total Enterprise Value	**338860**					

Projected EPS	1.32	1.83	2.12	2.46	2.85	3.29
Projected Stock Price	10.00	13.81	16.03	18.61	21.58	24.87

Note that this model uses a growth rate approach where starting values are entered and the subsequent annualized growth rates of the variables are entered and the model computes the future values of these variables. You can override any of the assumption cells above by simply typing over the values (changing growth rates over time or using actual values rather than growth rates). In addition, some sample input assumptions have been set up (cells in green) and an example simulation was run. The following illustrates the same results from the simulation, indicating that there is a 12.90% chance that the stock price at the end of 5 years will fall below $23 per share, and the total enterprise value at the worst case scenario (5th percentile) Value at Risk is $309,892,000. You may override these input assumptions as required to create your own valuation model.

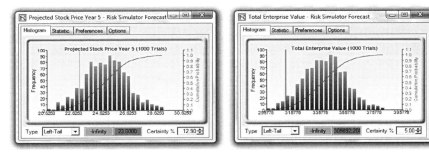

Figure 10-1 The Real Options Valuation Corporate Valuation Model.

Statement of Cash Flows

Cash Flow from Operations	2008	2009	2010	2011	2012	2013
EBITA	85755.00	103506.24	117415.89	132666.11	149343.30	167564.17
Depreciation	41321.00	38268.45	40028.18	41523.96	42795.36	43876.06
EBITDA	127076.00	141774.69	157444.07	174190.06	192138.66	211440.23
Change in Investment of Working Capital	13585.00	-6205.52	711.92	747.52	784.90	824.14
Change of Foreign Exchange Translation Effects	0.00	0.00	0.00	0.00	0.00	0.00
Cash Flow from Operations	140661.00	135569.17	158156.00	174937.58	192923.56	212264.37
Less Tax Paid	21896.00	29482.68	34234.42	39743.46	46093.21	53113.78
Cash Flow from Operations After Taxes (Addition to Cash Flow)	118765.00	106086.49	123921.58	135194.12	146830.35	159150.59
Cash Flow from Capital Investments						
Less Change in Capital Expenditures	56011.00	50000.00	50000.00	50000.00	50000.00	50000.00
Less Change in Investment	5777.00	1000.00	1000.00	1000.00	1000.00	1000.00
Less Change in Goodwill and Intangibles Acquired	3178.00	3177.00	3177.00	3177.00	3177.00	3177.00
Less Change in Other Operating Assets/Liabilities	23402.00	4000.00	4000.00	4000.00	4000.00	4000.00
Total Cash Flow from Capital Investments (Reduction of Cash Flow)	88368.00	58177.00	58177.00	58177.00	58177.00	58177.00
Cash Flow from Financing						
Interest Income (After Tax)	0.00	0.00	0.00	334.16	1868.21	3726.46
Interest Expense	23190.00	24349.50	25566.98	26845.32	28187.59	29596.97
New Debt Raised	0.00	0.00	0.00	0.00	0.00	0.00
Old Debt Repaid	0.00	0.00	0.00	0.00	0.00	0.00
Less Preferred Dividends Paid	0.00	0.00	0.00	0.00	0.00	0.00
New Preferred Issued	0.00	0.00	0.00	0.00	0.00	0.00
Old Preferred Redeemed	0.00	0.00	0.00	0.00	0.00	0.00
Less Dividends Paid	1000.00	1000.00	1000.00	1000.00	1000.00	1000.00
New Equity Raised	0.00	0.00	0.00	0.00	0.00	0.00
Old Equity Redeemed	0.00	0.00	0.00	0.00	0.00	0.00
Total Cash Flow from Financing (Addition to Cash Flow)	-24190.00	-25349.50	-26566.98	-27511.17	-27319.38	-26870.51
Total Cash Flow from Non-Operating Net Income (Addition to Cash Flow)	0.00	0.00	0.00	0.00	0.00	0.00
Total Cash Flow Payments to Reserves and Minorities (Reduction of Cash Flow)	0.00	0.00	0.00	0.00	0.00	0.00
Net Cashflow	6207.00	22559.99	39177.60	49505.95	61333.97	74103.08
NOPLAT						
EBITA	85755.00	103506.24	117415.89	132666.11	149343.30	167564.17
Adjustments (Operating Leases, Retirement Liabilities, Ongoing Provisions)	2672.00	0.00	0.00	0.00	0.00	0.00
Adjusted EBITA	88427.00	103506.24	117415.89	132666.11	149343.30	167564.17
Tax on EBT	21896.00	29482.68	34234.42	39743.46	46093.21	53113.78
Tax Shield on Interest Exp	0.00	0.00	0.00	0.00	0.00	0.00
Tax Shield on Operating Lease Interest	0.00	0.00	0.00	0.00	0.00	0.00
Tax Shield on Retirement Rel. Liab.	0.00	0.00	0.00	0.00	0.00	0.00
Tax on Interest Income	0.00	0.00	0.00	0.00	0.00	0.00
Tax on Non-operating Income	0.00	0.00	0.00	0.00	0.00	0.00
Change in Deferred Taxes	0.00	0.00	0.00	0.00	0.00	0.00
Taxes on EBITA	21896.00	29482.68	34234.42	39743.46	46093.21	53113.78
NOPLAT	66531.00	74023.56	83181.47	92922.64	103250.09	114450.39
FREE CASH FLOW						
NOPLAT	66531.00	74023.56	83181.47	92922.64	103250.09	114450.39
Depreciation	41321.00	38268.45	40028.18	41523.96	42795.36	43876.06
Gross Cash Flow	107852.00	112292.01	123209.65	134446.60	146045.45	158326.45
Change in Capital Expenditures	56011.00	50000.00	50000.00	50000.00	50000.00	50000.00
Change in Investment of Working Capital	13585.00	-6205.52	711.92	747.52	784.90	824.14
Change in Other Operating Assets/Liabilities	23402.00	4000.00	4000.00	4000.00	4000.00	4000.00
Operating Leases	0.00	0.00	0.00	0.00	0.00	0.00
Total Investments on Working Capital	36987.00	-2205.52	4711.92	4747.52	4784.90	4824.14
Gross Investments	92998.00	47794.48	54711.92	54747.52	54784.90	54824.14
Free Cash Flow Excl. Goodwill	14854.00	64497.52	68497.73	79699.08	91260.55	103502.31
Investment in Goodwill and Intangibles	0.00	0.00	0.00	0.00	0.00	0.00
Free Cash Flow Incl. Goodwill	14854.00	64497.52	68497.73	79699.08	91260.55	103502.31
Interest Income (After Tax)	0.00	0.00	0.00	334.16	1868.21	3726.46
Decreases in Excess Marketable Securities	0.00	0.00	0.00	0.00	0.00	0.00
Foreign Exchange Translation Effects	0.00	0.00	0.00	0.00	0.00	0.00
Non-Operating Cash Flow	0.00	0.00	0.00	0.00	0.00	0.00
Extraordinary Items	1003.00	0.00	0.00	0.00	0.00	0.00
Cash Flow Available to Investors	15857.00	64497.52	68497.73	80033.23	93128.77	107228.77
ECONOMIC PROFIT						
Operating Working Capital	-23008.00	-23330.90	-23571.56	-23711.74	-23730.29	-23602.59
Net Property Plant and Equipment	255123.00	266854.55	276826.37	285302.41	292507.05	298630.99
Other Assets Net of Other Liabilities	5553.00	9553.00	13553.00	17553.00	21553.00	25553.00
Value of Operating Leases	0.00	0.00	0.00	0.00	0.00	0.00
Total Invested Capital	237668.00	253076.65	266807.81	279143.67	290329.76	300581.41
Return on Invested Capital	27.99%	29.25%	31.18%	33.29%	35.56%	38.08%
Weighted Average Cost of Capital	15.00%	15.00%	15.00%	15.00%	15.00%	15.00%
Spread	12.99%	14.25%	16.18%	18.29%	20.56%	23.08%
Economic Profit (Before Goodwill)	30880.80	36062.06	43160.30	51051.09	59700.62	69363.18

Figure 10-1 (*Continued*)

Financial Ratios	2008	2009	2010	2011	2012	2013
Common Financial Ratios						
Earnings Per Share (EPS)	1.3220	1.8251	2.1192	2.4602	2.8533	3.2879
Dividends Per Share (DPS)	0.0333	0.0333	0.0333	0.0333	0.0333	0.0333
Book Value Per Share	7.4571	8.8650	10.4642	12.2738	14.3251	16.6573
Market Value Added	76289000	34051237	-13926389	-68217497	-129757609	-199725635
Price to Earnings Ratio (PE)	7.5644	5.4793	4.7188	4.0647	3.5047	3.0415
Market to Book Ratio	1.3410	1.1280	0.9556	0.8147	0.6981	0.6003
Equity Multiplier	2.3387	2.0525	1.8715	1.7711	1.6868	1.6149
Debt to Equity Ratio	84.57%	62.65%	47.69%	40.39%	34.37%	29.36%
Debt Ratio	57.24%	52.47%	47.60%	44.37%	41.36%	38.54%
Current Ratio	0.5597	0.5820	0.6037	0.6248	0.6452	0.6648
Quick Ratio	0.3915	0.4071	0.4223	0.4371	0.4513	0.4651
Inventory Turnover	42.1656	40.2490	38.4195	36.6732	35.0062	33.4150
Days Sales Outstanding	13.2488	13.8797	14.5407	15.2331	15.9585	16.7184
Fixed Asset Turnover	2.6576	2.6678	2.7003	2.7511	2.8175	2.8977
Total Asset Turnover	1.2959	1.3042	1.2723	1.2035	1.1369	1.0722
Debt to Asset Ratio	57.24%	52.47%	47.60%	44.37%	41.36%	38.54%
Times Interest Earned (TIE)	3.6979	4.2509	4.5925	4.9419	5.2982	5.6615
Net Profit Margin (NPM)	5.85%	7.69%	8.51%	9.40%	10.39%	11.40%
Basic Earning Power (BEP)	0.1639	0.1896	0.1998	0.2034	0.2060	0.2076
Return on Asset (ROA)	7.58%	10.03%	10.82%	11.32%	11.81%	12.22%
Return on Equity (ROE)	17.73%	20.59%	20.25%	20.04%	19.92%	19.74%
Return on Equity (ROE)	17.73%	20.59%	20.25%	20.04%	19.92%	19.74%
Adjusted EBITA / Revenues						
Cost of Goods Sold / Revenues	26.56%	27.31%	28.09%	28.90%	29.72%	30.57%
SGA Costs / Revenue	56.85%	55.22%	53.65%	52.11%	50.62%	49.18%
EBITDA / Revenue	18.74%	19.91%	21.06%	22.19%	23.31%	24.43%
Depreciation / Revenues	6.09%	5.38%	5.35%	5.29%	5.19%	5.07%
EBITA / Revenues	12.65%	14.54%	15.71%	16.90%	18.12%	19.36%
Return on Invested Capital						
Net PPE / Revenues	37.63%	37.48%	37.03%	36.35%	35.49%	34.51%
Working Capital / Revenues	-3.39%	-3.28%	-3.15%	-3.02%	-2.88%	-2.73%
Return on Invested Capital ROIC	27.99%	29.25%	31.18%	33.29%	35.56%	38.08%
Gross Investment / NOPLAT	1.3978	0.6457	0.6577	0.5892	0.5306	0.4790
Growth Rates						
Revenue Growth Rate		5.00%	5.00%	5.00%	5.00%	5.00%
EBITA Growth Rate		20.70%	13.44%	12.99%	12.57%	12.20%
NOPLAT Growth Rate		11.26%	12.37%	11.71%	11.11%	10.85%
Total Invested Capital Growth Rate		6.48%	5.43%	4.62%	4.01%	3.53%
Net Income Growth Rate		38.05%	16.12%	16.09%	15.98%	15.23%
Financing						
EBIT / Interest Payable	3.6979	4.2509	4.5925	4.9419	5.2982	5.6615
EBITA / Interest Payable	5.4798	5.8225	6.1581	6.4887	6.8164	7.1440
Cash Coverage (Net Cash Flow / Interest Payable)	0.2677	0.9265	1.5324	1.8441	2.1759	2.5037
Valuation indicators						
Enterprise Value / Net Income	8.5439	6.1888	5.3298	4.5910	3.9586	3.4353
Enterprise Value / EBITA	3.9515	3.2738	2.8860	2.5542	2.2690	2.0223
Enterprise Value / Revenues	0.4998	0.4760	0.4533	0.4317	0.4112	0.3916

Figure 10-1 (*Continued*)

discounting is the perpetuity: $2,000,000/ .12 = $16,000,000. Thus, $16,000,000 residual value was assumed to be six years hence, and the weighted average cost of capital for the residual period (steady state) 12 percent, the residual's present value becomes:

$$\$16,000,000 / (1 + .12)^6 = \$8,106,098$$

Strategic planning helps to organize the combined disciplines of risk and valuation, responding to changes in the external environment and creatively deploying internal resources to improve the competitive position of firms.[10] Management's failure to

---

10. Arnoldo C. Hax, Professor of Management; Sloan School of Management, MIT.

recognize changes—measuring and implementing economic, competitive, technological, and financial factors—retards growth, reduces profitability, puts debt service at risk, and compromises equity values. Aware of these consequences, resourceful managers keep themselves analytically current with concepts such as simulation, stochastic optimization, statistics, and real options, to name a few. In this way, they dramatically shift their own corporate culture and, in turn, influence bankers to cross into new methodological disciplines.

Valuation Software

Modeling Toolkit and Risk Simulation

Without simulation, revenue changes reveal only a single outcome—generally the most likely or average scenario—defining possible values for revenues over a discrete projection horizon with a probability distribution. The type of distribution selected is based on the conditions surrounding that variable or series of variables that combine to form one's assumption. To add this sort of function to an Excel spreadsheet, you would need to know the equation that represents the firm's revenue distribution. With Risk Simulator, these equations are automatically calculated for you, since the product can even fit a distribution to any historical data that you might have. The Real Options Valuation Corporate Valuation Model used for developing financial statements as well as for enterprise valuations, and computing the total enterprise value, earnings per share, economic profit, and other financial metrics (Figure 10-1).

CHAPTER | 11

Banker's Guide: Valuation Appraisal of Business Clients

Valuation appraisals help bankers understand whether borrowers are creditworthy. Appraisals are used for many reasons—for determining acquisition prices of consolidated businesses made up of numerous, separate units; carrying out bankruptcy liquidations/restructurings; establishing values of stand-alone businesses; conducting cost studies; handling estate planning; comprehending borrowers' strategic plans; completing insurance loss settlement; performing finance mergers and acquisitions; and helping to settle taxation issues.

Bank Loans and Other Financing

When considering a commercial loan (involving mainly new clients), loan officers may ask for valuation appraisals. A methodical, competent valuation can make a difference between obtaining a loan or being rejected.

Financing Acquisitions, Divestitures, and Restructurings

Bankers rely on valuation appraisals to establish a reasonable asking or offering price. Business units are valued as stand-alone entities and are then valued as if combined, using anticipated synergies from acquisitions, restructurings. Valuation appraisals help bankers determine financing and fair market price.

Partnership/Shareholder Agreements (Buy/Sell)

Buy-sell agreements should be founded on business appraisals. Valuations are finalized when shareholders buy into or exit businesses.

Financing Employee Stock Ownership Plans (ESOPs)

Employee Stock Ownership Plans (ESOPs) transfer a portion or all of the ownership of a business to employees. When dealing with an ESOP, stock must be valued by independent business appraisers annually.

Litigation Issues involving Economic/Financial Reparations

Such cases often require valuation appraisals to decide economic damages. Businesses are usually valued twice: both before and after actions that initiated damages. The spread between before and after typically represents economic damages.

Estate Planning

Bankers serving high net worth clients who have interests in closely held businesses are often called upon to oversee estate planning. Valuation appraisals are normally required and must be included in gift or estate tax returns. Since tax authorities closely examine these business valuation reports, it is important to retain a highly qualified business appraiser to prepare the needed company valuation. Bankers should have contact or be familiar with estate planning appraisers.

Liquidation vs. Restructuring Decisions

Management's decision to divest a business unit is quantified by spreads between Market Value/Liquidation Value. Why is a low ratio significant? It means a firm is likely to have more value liquidating than trying to stay in business preserving "cash traps." Cash traps are associated with sustainable negative cash flow that siphons cash from successful operating units.

S Corporation Elections

Some firms find that they can reduce tax burdens by changing from a C-Corporation to a Subchapter S Corporation. This election often eliminates corporate income taxes paid at the business level. When the election is made, appraisals may be required if assets are sold.

Eminent Domain Actions

Governments frequently invoke laws of eminent domain, which require sale or relocation of businesses. If banks are asked to help with financing, it is essential to work with competent valuations in order to establish fair prices.

Intangible Assets and Goodwill Impairment (SFAS 141 & 142)

Statement of Financial Accounting Standard (SFAS) 141 on Business Combinations requires that intangible assets be valued and recorded on a borrower's financial statement. SFAS 142 states that goodwill must be balance sheet tested at least annually for impairment.

Incentive or Employee Stock Options (ISOs and ESOs)

Incentive stock options are an important component of employee, board, investor, or advisor compensation. Rule 409A changed the rules for issuing incentive stock options.

Strategic Planning

Far-sighted financial, operational, and strategic management requires knowledge of the business and the valuation methodology. The value of a firm rises and declines over discrete time horizons and for a number of reasons: management actions, or changes in economic or industry conditions, for example. With these changes, optimal strategies will make course corrections.

Valuation Appraisals—Documents and Information

A. Financial statements (for up to the last five fiscal years if available)
1. Primary Financial Statements (Statements should cover a *relevant period,* that is, a period over which the statements represent the company's general operations, leading up to and including the valuation date.)
    i. Balance sheets
        a. If the company has significantly changed its operations a few years before the valuation date, only the last three or four years' statements may be relevant to the valuation. But if the business has a long history and some or all recent years were abnormal in some way (such as during a cyclical peak or trough in the company's industry), statements for the past seven, ten, or more years may constitute a relevant period for valuing it.
    ii. Income statements
    iii. Cash flows
    iv. Statement of stockholders equity or partners' capital accounts
2. Income tax returns for the same years
    i. A convenient summary of differences between tax return and income statement reporting is found in the schedule, "Reconciliation of Income per Books with Income per Return." In general, the statements that most closely conform to industry practices would most fairly represent the company's financial position and earning power. *The financial data and ratios derived from tax return data normally would not be relied on when comparing the company to the price/earnings or price/ book value ratios derived from publicly traded comparatives.*
3. Latest interim statements if valuation date is three months or more beyond the end of the last fiscal year and interim statement for the comparable period the year before
4. List of subsidiaries and/or financial interest in other companies with relevant financial statements
5. Off-balance-sheet assets or liabilities
    i. As we saw in Chapter 2, financial events (contingencies) may significantly affect an obligor firm's value, events that do not appear as line items on the balance sheet—lawsuits, for example.

   ii. An important category of off-balance-sheet liabilities is the potential cost
       of compliance with environmental or other government requirements.

   iii. Product liability and liability for warranties are other significant items.

6. Fiscal projections (five years)

7. Short-term cash budgets

B. Other financial data

   1. Equipment list and depreciation schedules

      i. Lists of property owned should include the acquisition date, a description
         adequate for identifying each piece or group, the original cost, the depre-
         ciation method and life used, and the net depreciated value. The totals of
         such schedules should reconcile with line items in the financial statements.
         For real estate, the schedule should show the size (acres of land and dimen-
         sions and square feet of floor space of buildings), with a brief description
         of the construction and any special features. It should also indicate the
         dates and costs of additions and remodeling.

   2. Lease agreements

      i. Leases may be favorable or unfavorable. A long-term lease costing the
         company less than the current market value adds to value; being saddled
         with a long-term lease on inadequate quarters for which the company
         cannot find an alternative tenant is anything but favorable. Lease renewal
         terms about to expire are also important considerations, above all if the
         lease is not renewable or is renewable only at a significantly increased
         cost. For companies that have many leased outlets, such as retail chains, we
         may want to prepare a list of leases with a summary of their provisions.

   3. Real and personal property tax assessments

      i. Tax assessments may not be the best yardstick of asset values, but they
         are almost always readily available. Most tax-assessed values are lower
         than replacement costs, although they may be well above liquidating
         value, especially those for personal property.

      ii. We usually can obtain local information on the broad relationship between
          tax-assessed values and market values for a particular jurisdiction. In
          many jurisdictions, the tax-assessed value purports to represent not market
          value but some fixed percentage of market value, such as 30 percent. Of
          course, in those instances we need to adjust the figures upward to the
          market value directly implied by the tax-assessed value before making
          further adjustments, if any, for whatever systematic biases are perceived
          as prevailing in the particular jurisdiction.

   4. Insurance appraisals

      i. Unlike tax appraisals, insurance appraisals tend to overvalue property,
         primarily as a means of ensuring that the insurance will be adequate to
         cover any potential loss.

   5. Independent appraisal reports

      i. An independent appraisal by a qualified practitioner, if available, usually
         is a more reliable guide to asset value than either a tax assessment or
         insurance appraisal. Such appraisals generally specify the approach taken,
         the assumptions made, and some guidance for appropriate interpretation
         and use of the appraisal. A replacement cost or depreciated replacement
         cost appraisal, for example, normally will differ significantly from a liq-

uidation value appraisal, and none of those may be appropriate for appraising assets being used in a specific ongoing business situation.

6. Capital requirements
   i. Capital requirements can arise from many sources, including catching up on deferred maintenance (a common need in small and medium-sized companies), increasing working capital needs, or making capital expenditures

7. Aged accounts receivable list
   i. The *aged receivables list* (aged list) can yield insight into the company's profitability, and even viability. The statement lists the accounts alphabetically, sometimes categorized into customer groups. The spreadsheet is laid out with columns for the total amount due, the current portion, and the portions over 30 days, 60 days, 90 days, and 120 days past due. Unusual circumstances regarding a specific account should be noted somewhere on the statement, perhaps as footnotes. Any notes or other receivables besides normal trade receivables should be listed separately, with enough detail to permit evaluation. The statement date should be as of the latest annual or interim financial statement, so that the total on the balance sheet will reconcile with the amount on the aged list.

8. Customer base
   i. The fewer customers the company relies on for its market, the more important an analysis of the customer base becomes. A convenient way to compile the customer base information is in simple tabular form. We list, in order of size of billings, the 10 to 20 largest customers in the latest year or fiscal period and the dollar amounts of billings and the percentage of total billings for each. This information should be shown for several periods in the past as well as for the latest period. The columns for the past years should also show any customers that accounted for a significant proportion of the billings at that time, even if they are not current customers. A budgeted figure for each customer for the current or forthcoming year is helpful, if available.

9. Customer contracts
   i. Customer contracts are significant items for some companies, such as a manufacturer whose customers lease rather than buy its equipment. Contracts to obtain key raw materials may be significant for some firms. An analysis of the terms and strengths of such contracts can be an important consideration in valuing the business.

10. Aged accounts payable list

11. List of prepaid expenses

12. Inventory list with any necessary information on inventory accounting policies (including work in process, if applicable). Raw material inventory replacement costs (i.e., cotton).
   i. The amount of detail desired in the inventory list will vary greatly from one appraisal to another, depending on the inventory's importance in the valuation and the extent to which inventory accounting methods tend to differ within the particular industry. In any case, the total should be reconcilable with the inventory as shown on the financial statements, using whatever adjustments conform to the company's method of inventory valuation.

13. Order backlog
    i. If the company's order backlog is significant, one should compare the backlog on the valuation date with that on one or more past dates. Such a comparison, especially with the backlog a year prior to the valuation date, is one indication of the company's future prospects that is solidly based on its past record.
14. Supplier list
    i. Like the customer base, the *supplier list* becomes more important with fewer suppliers. It also becomes more important if the future availability of certain supplies is uncertain enough to increase the company's risk. If future sources of supply are a critical factor, the appraiser should compile a list of sources other than those currently being used. The supplier list could take the same format as the customer base.
15. Any other existing contracts (employment agreements, covenants not to compete, supplier and franchise agreements, customer agreements, royalty agreements, equipment lease or rental contracts, loan agreements, labor contracts employee benefits plans, and so on)
16. Loan agreements
    i. Most loan agreements contain various requirements and restrictive covenants. One reason for reading the loan agreements is to check whether the company is in danger of defaulting on any requirement. Another consideration is the effect of any loan agreement restrictions on the company's ability to pay dividends and/or transfer stock ownership.
17. List of stockholders or partners, with number of shares owned by each or percentage of each partner's interest in earnings and capital
    i. The *stockholder list* should include each stockholder's name and number of shares held. If there is more than one class of stock, it should show the stockholders' holdings in each class. It should also identify any family or other relationships among the stockholders. This list will be examined by the IRS and the courts if they are involved.
18. Compensation schedule for owners, including all benefits and personal expenses (we should compare this information to the industry averages).
    i. An *officers' and directors' compensation schedule* usually should be prepared for the same number of years as the financial statements. It may provide a basis for adjustments to the income statements, offering evidence of the company's earning capacity.
    ii. These benefits would include base salary; bonuses or commissions; amount paid into pension, profit sharing, or other employee benefit funds; and other employee benefits. It also should include compensation other than cash, such as stock or options, company cars, or other property used, and any significant expenses paid or reimbursed for business activities performed by the employee.
    iii. We should be aware of the fact that the IRS sometimes attempts to depict compensation to owners of closely held businesses as excessive so as to get dividend tax treatment for a portion of it.
19. Dividend Schedule
    i. The *dividend schedule* normally should cover the same time period that the financial statements do. It should show the date of each dividend payment and the per-share amount for each class of stock.

      ii. Dividend paying capacity, one criterion of the value of a business interest, represents a competing use of capital, and each company must decide whether to retain cash with which to carry out needed purchases or distribute its earnings to stockholders.

20. Schedule of "key man" insurance in force

      i. In many closely held companies, the loss of a single key individual can have a significant impact on the company's operations. It is always desirable to know how much of this risk is covered by life insurance. This insurance may have to be considered as part of the company's value.

C. Company and other documents relating to rights of owners

1. Articles of incorporation, by-laws, any amendments to either, and corporate minutes

      i. The official documents of a corporation or partnership often hold facts that significantly affect the entity's valuation. The articles of incorporation, along with any amendments, and documents specifying rights attaching to each class of stock outstanding provide information that is particularly important for companies with more than one class of stock. Other information in the articles or by-laws may be relevant to the value. Certain items in the board of directors' and stockholders' minute books may also be important, especially if transactions with parties related to the company have occurred. In a partnership, the partners' rights and obligations should be contained in the articles of partnership.

2. Any existing buy-sell agreements, options to purchase stock or other documents affecting the ownership rights of the interest being valued

      i. To the extent that past transactions in the stock were at arm's length, they provide objective evidence of value. Even if not accepted, a bona fide offer, particularly if submitted in writing, can at least corroborate the value. In preparing the record of past transactions or offers, it is important to list any relationships among the parties in order to determine whether each transaction was at arm's length. The transaction record usually should go as far back as the number of years of financial statements used. On this basis, past transaction prices can be compared with the current book values, earnings, or other relevant variables.

      ii. Buy-sell or repurchase agreements with major stockholders may contain provisions that can affect the company's shares to which they apply and, in many cases, all the outstanding stock as well. Provisions in such agreements may address the question of value directly or may impose restrictions on transferability, which may bear on the value of the affected shares. If the company has an Employee Stock Ownership Plan (ESOP), the terms of the buyback provisions have a major bearing on the marketability of the shares involved and thus must be considered when valuing ESOP shares.

3. Employment and *Noncompete Agreements*

      i. Employment agreements with key personnel may affect the company's value, as may important agreements not to compete. These agreements could have either a positive or negative effect on value depending on the relationship between the cost and the value to the company.

D. Other information

1. Brief history, including how long in business and details of any changes in ownership and/or bona fide offers received

    i. We need to set the stage for placing the company in the context of its industry, especially its competition, as well as in the general economy. A relatively brief history will suffice in most cases. The history should indicate how long the company has been in business and some chronology of major changes, such as form of organization, controlling ownership, location of operations, and lines of business. Sometimes predecessor companies are a relevant part of the background. Some companies have relatively complex histories, requiring detailed explanations of transactions that have fundamentally contributed to the company's composition as of the valuation date.

2. Brief description of business, including position relative to competition and any factors that make the business unique

3. Organization chart

4. Information on related party transactions

5. Marketing literature (catalogs, brochures, advertisements)

    i. Having a set of the firm's sales materials, such as brochures, catalogs, and price lists, is helpful. These items will enable one to become familiar with the company's products, services, and pricing and to evaluate the written sales materials.

6. List of locations where company operates, with size and whether owned or leased

7. List of states in which licensed to do business

8. List of competitors, with location, relative size, and other relevant factors

9. Resumes of, or list of, key personnel with age, position, compensation, length of service, education, and prior experience (much of this can be obtained from a D&B report)

10. Relevant trade or government publications

11. Trade associations and industry sources

    i. It is helpful to obtain a list of trade associations to which the company belongs, or is eligible to belong, along with the name and address of the executive director of each. If necessary, one can then contact the trade association for industry information. Many industries have other trade sources, such as trade journals or sources of composite data. The company may be able to furnish a list of such sources and often can supply copies of relevant publications.

12. Any existing indicators of asset values, including latest property tax assessments and any appraisals that have been done

13. List of patents, copyrights, trademarks, and other intangible assets

    i. A list of patents, copyrights, and trademarks should include the items covered and relevant issue and/or expiration dates. It should have at least a brief description and enough information to permit understanding of the items. The importance of these items and the degree of detail necessary vary greatly from one situation to another.

14. Contractual Agreements and Obligations

    i. We should evaluate all significant contractual obligations for their potential positive or negative effect on the company's value. Contracts that may be significant for the value of a business or business interest can cover a wide variety of subjects.

15. Any filings or correspondence with regulatory agencies

> *If the standard of value is derived from a statute or regulation, the exact source of the governing standard of value needs to be referenced. For example, we need to include the eight factors listed in Revenue Ruling 59–60 if the valuation is for gift or estate taxes, an ESOP, or some other tax related matter.*

> *Introduction is brief and may cover any or all of half a dozen key points in summary form.*

> *The scope and organization of the appraisal report must be tailored to the purpose of the valuation. Formats or variations will differ depending on purpose.*

> *The scope and content of valuation report can vary considerably depending on the size and complexity of the firm and the use or uses to which the report will be put.*

Valuation Appraisal Outline

I. Purpose of the valuation report
   A. Taxes; estate tax purposes
      1. Address factors enumerated in Revenue Ruling 50-60
   B. ESOP
      1. Department of Labor Regulations
   C. Lawsuit
      1. Issues raised in relevant case law precedents.
   D. Strategic planning
      1. Maximize shareholder value
      2. Understand the mechanics of wealth creation
      3. Identify and sell off unprofitable business units
         i. Liquidation vs. cash flow value
      4. Purchase business
   E. Respond to offer to buy business
   F. Bank loan facilities

II. Scope and content of the valuation report
   A. Audience
      1. Prospective parties at interest and their beneficiaries
         i. Internal use by officers and directors
            a. Description of the company may be unnecessary or may allude only to certain salient points that directly affect the valuation of the firm.
            b. If audience is financially sophisticated, we can assume some knowledge of finance and accounting.
      2. Representatives of any regulatory authorities involved
      3. Judge and jury if there is existing or potential litigation

III. Organization
   A. Introduction
      1. Description of the assignment
         i. Who was retained by whom to do the appraisal?
            a. Appraiser's statement of qualifications
            b. Reviewer's judgments; for example, "have I adequately and convincingly supported the use of each discount rate, capitalization rate, and multiple used in the valuation? Is the conclusion

consistent with the economic, industry, and financial statement analysis presented? Is the analysis and conclusion consistent with the stated purpose of the appraisal and standard of value, including any statutory, regulatory, or other legal requirements?"

    ii.   Definition of the property being valued

    iii. Effective date of the appraisal

    iv. Purpose of the valuation

2. Summary description of the company

    i.   For the reader's convenience, it us useful to include in the introduction a brief statement of a firm's business, location, some idea of its size and possibly one or two salient or unique aspects of the company

3. Capitalization and ownership

    i.   Class or classes of stock and the distribution of ownership

4. Applicable standard of value (if appropriate)

    i.   Internal Revenue Service Ruling 59-60 outlines the valuation of closely held stocks and includes the following:

       a. Nature of business and history of enterprise

       b. Economic outlook and outlook of the specific industry

       c. Book value and financial condition

       d. Earning capacity

       e. Dividend-paying capacity

       f. Intangibles, including goodwill

       g. Stock sales and size of the block to be valued

       h. Market price of publicly traded stock in same or similar lines of business

    ii.   Statutes governing dissolution or dissenting stockholder actions (if any)

       a. Statement to that effect or summary statement of interpretation of the case law from a financial analysis point of view

> *Generalized list of the sources of information used. The degree of detail that is appropriate depends on the purpose and audience.*

5. Sources of information used in the appraisal

    i.   List of financial statements and supporting schedules that were examined, including the years studied for each statement

       a. Statement as to accountant's opinion

    ii.   Corporate tax returns (if appropriate)

    iii. Internally prepared budgets for the next six to twelve months

    iv. Facilities visited

    v.   Equipment list and depreciation schedule (if appropriate)

    vi. Inventory lists and receivables aging (if appropriate)

    vii. Stockholders' list as of last fiscal date

    viii. Schedule of total owners' compensation (if appropriate)

    ix. Copies of leases

    x.   Articles of incorporation and by-laws

    xi. Industry information and periodicals

    xii. Information on comparative publicly traded companies from S&P Corporation Records and SEC 10-K's. Various brokers' reports on these companies

6. Valuation approach and conclusion

    i.   Broad criterion or criteria used in reaching the valuation conclusion

    ii.   Brief statement of the conclusion

B. Description of the company
   1. Background

This section should be descriptive and analytical, allowing one to understand the firm and make qualitative judgments on the positive and negative aspects of the company that bear on its value.

Industry growth rate may be measured using any indicator relevant to the industry, including revenues, units shipped or produced, and assets. Appropriate benchmarks include real GDP growth, PCE (consumer spending), and S&P 500 growth.

   2. Physical facilities
   3. Product and/or services
   4. Distribution channels
   5. Sources of supply
   6. Labor/capital intensive; operating leverage
   7. Management
   8. Capitalization and ownership
   9. Seasonality (if any)
C. Industry data
   1. Size of firm relative to competitors
   2. Specialized segments of the market the firm serves
   3. Competitive strengths and weaknesses
   4. Technology and production
   5. Regulation
   6. Industry phase
      i. Mature phase: Product technology well established, markets saturated, long-term growth in line with general economy. Companies compete for market share on price basis
      ii. Price/earnings ratio is down; therefore, the equity market is less attractive to the company. Generally reduced need for financing
   7. Cyclicality
      i. Should be compared to a benchmark such as real GDP growth and should consider both industry-specific cycles and economic cycles.
   8. Entry barriers
      i. Economies of scale and other cost advantages, capital requirements, intensity, product differentiation, access to distribution channels, and regulations.
   9. Cost structure
      i. Labor cost, material cost, capital intensity, economies of scale, technological advantages/disadvantages, operating leverage
D. Economic data
   1. Aspects of economic conditions that may have a bearing on the firm's prospects
      i. Identify clearly macroeconomic variables that affect the firm's sales and gross profit margin
E. Financial analysis
   1. Analysis of the latest fiscal year
      i. Income statement, balance sheet, cash flow, and ratios
      ii. Industry comparatives
   2. Deterministic projections and analysis
      i. Most likely projections; ratio, cash flow, financial needs, and debt capacity analysis. Analysis will show the firm has financial resources available and is viable

        ii.   Conservative (worst-case) projection highlights
            a. Sales growth and gross margin pegged to historical five-year lows. Average collection and holding periods set at historical five-year highs
            b. Analysis reinforces firm's viability given worst-case scenario
      3. Stochastic projection and analysis
   F. Valuation analysis
      1. Approaches
        i.   Price: revenue multiples
        ii.   Capitalization of five-year average earnings
       iii. Capitalization of projected earnings
       iv. Market capitalization: book capitalization multiples

> *Stochastic projections: likely projections should be supported by simulations set at 5000 trials and a 95% certainty level.*
>
> *RISK SIMULATOR AND REAL OPTIONS SUPER LATTICE SOLVER SOFTWARE*

        v.   Price/earnings and price book
        vi.   Transaction multiple approach
       vii. Liquidation value
      viii. Dividend model
        ix.   Cash flow (While we will construct a weighted average, discounted free cash flow model will carry a substantial weight.)
        x. The forecast horizon

> *The length of the forecast horizon is not simply a convenient period of time in estimating financial performance, but a period based on the economics of the company and its industry.*

            a. Points we need to discuss to determine this extremely important valuation determinant
            b. Proprietary technologies
            c. Limited product life cycle
            d. Distribution channels
            e. Industrywide price competition
      2. Residual value
        i.   Once the discrete forecast horizon cash flows have been estimated, we can make a simplifying assumption regarding the cash flow generated after the forecast period.
      3. Cost of capital.
        i.   Use an appropriate industry beta.
        ii.   We need to discuss the cost of debt, applying the cost of debt to the firm's tax rate.
      4. Value driver analysis
        i.   Sales growth rate
        ii.   Incremental working capital investment
       iii. Incremental fixed capital investment
       iv. Cash tax rate
        v.   Cost of capital
      5. Relative impact of key variables on shareholder value
      6. Analysis of valuation ratios
            a. Market value/book value
            b. Liquidation value/market value
  G. Simulations: "Proving the valuation is right on target"
      1. Defining assumptions
        i.   Understanding and working with value drivers

          ii.   Selecting the right distribution to fit data
               a. Fitting distributions to data
          iii.   Correlating between independent variables and/or between independent variable(s) and the forecast variable
               a. Responding to problems with correlated assumptions
      2. Defining forecast
          i.   Determining the certainty level
               a. Finding the probability that valuation falls within specific ranges
      3. Developing a sensitivity check and work with sensitivity charts
      4. Creating reports
    H. Strategic planning: optimizing the company's value
      1. Setting up and optimizing the linear programming model (**Risk Simulator**)
          i.   Defining decision variables and selecting decision variables to optimize
          ii.   Specifying constraints (value drivers' limitations)
          iii.   Selecting the forecast objective: maximize shareholder value by linear programming changes to value drivers
          iv.   Perform sensitivity analysis

IV. Conclusion
    A. Summary of the valuation appraisal and recommendations

Valuation Appraisal Toolkit

The Modeling Toolkit software includes several valuation models that can be used to perform valuation appraisals of clients. For instance, under **Modeling Toolkit | Valuation | Valuation Appraisal Model** you will see the valuation appraisal model. The cells in boxes are the required inputs, and the results are displayed throughout various worksheets in the model.

The Corporate Valuation Model presented in Figure 11-1 is used for developing financial statements as well as for evaluating enterprise and computing the total enterprise value, earnings per share, economic profit, and other financial metrics. The inputs are the boxed cells. You can extend the model to additional years by first entering the Years to Forecast and typing in the various required values in these future years (the boxes will automatically appear). The model returns a set of financial statements such as the balance sheet, income statement, statement of cash flows, as well as the resulting computations of NOPAT (net operating profits after taxes), which is then used in computing free cash flows to the firm and the resulting economic profit analysis and valuation of the company. See Figure 11-2. In addition, the market approach ratios analysis is also included in the model, as a way of calibrating the valuation results.

Note that this model uses a growth rate approach where starting values and the subsequent annualized growth rates of the variables are entered and the model computes the future values of these variables. You can override any of the assumption cells by simply typing over the values (changing growth rates over time or using actual values rather than growth rates). In addition, some sample input assumptions have been set up (cells in green), and an example simulation was run. Figure 11.3

Assumptions

Base Year (Valuation Year)	2008
Start of Forecast Year	2008
Years to Forecast	5

Real Options Valuation
www.realoptionsvaluation.com

Discounting: Discrete End-of-Year Discounting

Forecast Year	0	1	2	3	4	5
Year	2008	2009	2010	2011	2012	2013
Weighted Average Cost of Capital	15.00%	15.00%	15.00%	15.00%	15.00%	15.00%

Currency Units (e.g., in $000's)	1000
Equity Starting Value	129567
Marginal Tax Rate	35%
Return on Invested Capital	10%
Assumed Terminal WACC	10.00%
Assumed Terminal Growth Rate	5.00%
Current Stock Price	10.00

This is the Corporate Valuation Model used for developing financial statements as well as for enterprise valuation, and computing the total enterprise value, earnings per share, economic profit, and other financial metrics. The inputs are the boxed cells. You can extend the model to additional years by first entering the Years to Forecast (cell E7) and typing in the various required values in these future years (the boxes will automatically appear).

Revenues	678023	711924	747520	784896	824141	865348
Revenue: % Growth		5.00%	5.00%	5.00%	5.00%	5.00%
Other Operating Revenues	14554	17465	20958	25149	30179	36215
Other Operating Revenues: % Growth		20.00%	20.00%	20.00%	20.00%	20.00%
Cost of Goods Sold	180054	194458	210015	226816	244961	264558
Cost of Goods Sold: % Growth		8.00%	8.00%	8.00%	8.00%	8.00%
Selling, Gen & Admin Expenses	385447	393156	401019	409039	417220	425565
Selling, Gen & Admin Expenses: % Growth		2.00%	2.00%	2.00%	2.00%	2.00%
Non-Operating Income	7345	8080	8887	9776	10754	11829
Non-Operating Income: % Growth		10.00%	10.00%	10.00%	10.00%	10.00%
Interest Expense	23190	24350	25567	26845	28188	29597
Interest Expense: % Growth		5.00%	5.00%	5.00%	5.00%	5.00%
Cash	12826	14109	15519	17071	18779	20656
Cash: % Growth		10.00%	10.00%	10.00%	10.00%	10.00%
Accounts Receivable	24611	27072	29779	32757	36033	39636
Accounts Receivable: % Growth		10.00%	10.00%	10.00%	10.00%	10.00%
Inventories	16080	17688	19457	21402	23543	25897
Inventories: % Growth		10.00%	10.00%	10.00%	10.00%	10.00%

Figure 11-1 Corporate Valuation model.

NOPLAT

EBITA	85755.00	69007.08	75352.45	82897.22	91753.69	119875.66
Adjustments (Operating Leases, Retirement Liabilities, Ongoing Provisions)	2672.00	0.00	0.00	0.00	0.00	0.00
Adjusted EBITA	88427.00	69007.08	75352.45	82897.22	91753.69	119875.66
Tax on EBT	24676.00	22743.41	25834.11	29233.67	33136.98	37675.09
Tax Shield on Interest Exp	0.00	0.00	0.00	0.00	0.00	0.00
Tax Shield on Operating Lease Interest	0.00	0.00	0.00	0.00	0.00	0.00
Tax Shield on Retirement Rel. Liab.	0.00	0.00	0.00	0.00	0.00	0.00
Tax on Interest Income	0.00	0.00	0.00	0.00	0.00	0.00
Tax on Non-operating Income	0.00	0.00	0.00	0.00	0.00	0.00
Change in Deferred Taxes	0.00	0.00	0.00	0.00	0.00	0.00
Taxes on EBITA	24676.00	22743.41	25834.11	29233.67	33136.98	37675.09
NOPLAT	63751.00	46263.66	49518.34	53663.55	58616.71	82200.57

FREE CASH FLOW

NOPLAT	63751.00	46263.66	49518.34	53663.55	58616.71	82200.57
Depreciation	41321.00	38268.45	40028.18	41523.96	42795.36	43876.06
Gross Cash Flow	105072.00	84532.11	89546.52	95187.51	101412.07	126076.62
Change in Capital Expenditures	56011.00	50000.00	50000.00	50000.00	50000.00	50000.00
Change in Investment of Working Capital	13585.00	-6205.52	711.92	747.52	784.90	824.14
Change in Other Operating Assets/Liabilities	23402.00	4000.00	4000.00	4000.00	4000.00	4000.00
Operating Leases	0.00	0.00	0.00	0.00	0.00	0.00
Total Investments on Working Capital	36987.00	-2205.52	4711.92	4747.52	4784.90	4824.14
Gross Investments	92998.00	47794.48	54711.92	54747.52	54784.90	54824.14
Free Cash Flow Excl. Goodwill	12074.00	36737.63	34834.60	40439.99	46627.18	71252.48
Investment in Goodwill and Intangibles	0.00	0.00	0.00	0.00	0.00	0.00
Free Cash Flow Incl. Goodwill	12074.00	36737.63	34834.60	40439.99	46627.18	71252.48
Interest Income (After Tax)	0.00	0.00	0.00	334.16	1868.21	3726.46
Decreases in Excess Marketable Securities	0.00	0.00	0.00	0.00	0.00	0.00
Foreign Exchange Translation Effects	0.00	0.00	0.00	0.00	0.00	0.00
Non-Operating Cash Flow	0.00	0.00	0.00	0.00	0.00	0.00
Extraordinary Items	1003.00	0.00	0.00	0.00	0.00	0.00
Cash Flow Available to Investors	13077.00	36737.63	34834.60	40774.14	48495.39	74978.94

ECONOMIC PROFIT

Operating Working Capital	-23008.00	-16802.48	-17514.41	-18261.93	-19046.82	-19870.97
Net Property Plant and Equipment	255123.00	266854.55	276826.37	285302.41	292507.05	298630.99
Other Assets Net of Other Liabilities	5553.00	9553.00	13553.00	17553.00	21553.00	25553.00
Value of Operating Leases	0.00	0.00	0.00	0.00	0.00	0.00
Total Invested Capital	237668.00	259605.07	272864.96	284593.48	295013.23	304313.03
Return on Invested Capital	26.82%	17.82%	18.15%	18.86%	19.87%	27.01%
Weighted Average Cost of Capital	15.00%	15.00%	15.00%	15.00%	15.00%	15.00%
Spread	11.82%	2.82%	3.15%	3.86%	4.87%	12.01%
Economic Profit (Before Goodwill)	28100.80	7322.90	8588.60	10974.53	14364.73	36553.61

Figure 11-2 NOPAT Model

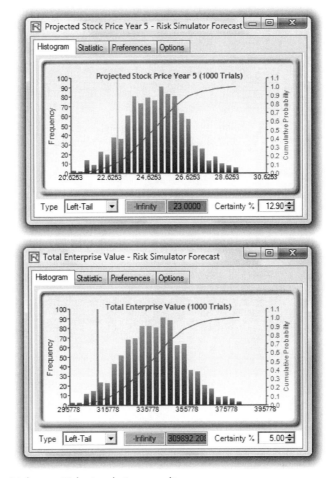

Figure 11-3   Value at Risk simulation results.

illustrates the same results from the simulation, indicating that there is a 12.90 percent chance that the stock price at the end of five years will fall below $23 per share, and the total enterprise value at the worst case scenario (5th percentile) Value at Risk is $309,892,000 (Figure 11-3). You may override these input assumptions as required to create your own valuation model.

CHAPTER | 12

Constructing Industry-Specific Credit Rating Systems

To qualify for the internal ratings-based approach, highlighted in this chapter, regulators must be convinced that a financial institution meets preset minimum requirements (see Chapter 2). The purpose of these requirements is to make sure that banks' rating systems are precise, that they demonstrate integrity, and importantly, that default frequency, loss given default, and loss reserves estimates are comparable over time and across banks.

> Internal risk ratings are an important tool in monitoring credit risk. Internal risk ratings should be adequate to support the identification and measurement of risk from all credit exposures, and should be integrated into an institution's overall analysis of credit risk and capital adequacy. The ratings system should provide detailed ratings for all assets, not only for criticized or problem assets. Loan loss reserves should be included in the credit risk assessment for capital adequacy.[1]

Credit risk rating allows a customized and elastic approach to loan pricing, loan loss reserves, and estimating default probabilities and loss given default. Robust computer-

---

1. *Core Principles for Effective Banking Supervision,* Basel Committee on Banking Supervision (September 1997), and *Core Principles Methodology,* Basel Committee on Banking Supervision (October 1999).

driven, interactive models track and rate changes in product and operational strategies, credit quality, market variables, economic environment, and operational risk (loan documentation and auditing issues). The degree by which risk models have been incorporated into credit management and economic capital allocation processes varies among banks. The use of credit risk models offers banks a framework for examining this risk in a timely manner, centralizing data on global exposures (see Chapter 13), and analyzing marginal and absolute contributions to risk. These properties contribute to the ability to identify measure and manage risk.

Under Foundation IRB or F-IRB, the *foundation internal ratings-based approach* proposed under Basel II, financial institutions will be able to develop their own models to determine regulatory capital requirement. Before a bank can start thinking of adhering to capital requirements for credit risk as outlined in Basel II, essential support systems are required, including: credit rating systems for banks adopting the IRB approach; credit risk models for banks adopting the advanced IRB approach, collateral management system, and credit limits system (see the next chapter, Chapter 13).

The Basel Committee also believes that banks' internal rating systems should accurately and consistently differentiate between different degrees of risk. The challenge is for banks to define clearly and objectively the criteria for their rating categories in order to provide meaningful assessments of both individual credit exposures and ultimately an overall risk profile. A strong control environment is another important factor for ensuring that banks' rating systems perform as intended and that the resulting ratings are accurate. An independent ratings process, internal review, and transparency are control concepts addressed in the minimum IRB standards.

An internal rating system is only as good as its inputs. Accordingly, banks using the IRB approach will need to be able to measure the key drivers of credit risk—obligor financial measures, subject measures, industry, country risk, facility risk, and so on. The minimum Basel II standards provide banks with the flexibility to rely on data derived from their own experience,[2] or from external sources as long as the bank can demonstrate the relevance of such data to its own exposures. In practical terms, banks will be expected to have in place a process that enables them to collect, store, and utilize loss statistics over time in a reliable manner.

Indeed, the principles underlying a risk rating system represent a common framework for assessing risk with a high degree of uniformity and providing a way to distinguish between levels of risk. Many of the world's leading financial institutions have developed sophisticated rating systems to quantify credit risk across geographical and product lines. The initial interest in credit risk models stemmed from the desire to develop more rigorous quantitative estimates of credit migrations, loss reserves, and economic capital required to support risk. Credit migration or transition matrices, for instance, which distinguish previous changes in obligor credit quality, are fundamental output of the risk rating models in this book and basic to many risk management applications, including portfolio risk assessment, negotiating and structuring loan facilities, pricing credit derivatives, and assigning regulatory capital. Basel II capital requirements are determined

---

2. Risk systems should have strong, subjective elements—relationship managers, who know obligors best and are not driven by statistics alone.

in part by ratings migration. Their accurate estimation is therefore crucial to compliance.

Rating systems should take proper account of gradations in risk and the overall composition of portfolios in originating new loans, assessing overall portfolio risks and concentrations, and reporting on risk profiles to directors and management. Moreover, such rating systems also should play an important role in establishing an appropriate level for the allowance for loan and lease losses, conducting internal bank analysis of loan and relationship profitability, assessing capital adequacy.[3]

The principles underlying a risk rating system are to:

- Establish a common framework for assessing risk
- Establish uniformity throughout the bank's units, divisions, and affiliates
- Establish compatibility to regulatory definitions, which distinguish various levels of "poor" credit risk
- Distinguish various levels of "satisfactory" credit risk
- Determine credit migrations and downgrades in debt ratings
- Promote common training through expanded definitions and risk rating guides
- Initiate and maintain ratings on a continuous basis
- Set criteria for review of ratings by the bank's auditing department to verify accuracy, consistency, and timeliness
- Institute a systematic methodology for uniformly analyzing risk across the loan portfolio.

We define risk as the probability that an exposure loss will be sustained. Credit risk ratings reflect not just likelihood or severity of loss but variability of loss over time, particularly as this relates to fluctuations in the business cycle. Linkage to these measurable outcomes gives greater clarity to risk rating analysis and allows for more consistent evaluation of obligor performance against relevant benchmarks.

Commercial loans expose banks to two types of risk: obligor risk and facility (or transaction) risk. Obligor risk is related to economic and industry risks, industry structure risks, customer-specific risks, and the ever-present operating risks inherent in the lending business. Facility risks are risks inherent in an instrument or facility. If a bank feels that combined risk levels are unacceptable, it might sell the exposure or acquire other deals that are less exposed to these forces, thus reducing the risk of the portfolio. Ratings begin with obligor risk and then combine risks associated with particular transactions—that is, variables that increase or reduce risk: collateral, guarantees, terms, and tenor and portfolio impact. The risk rating is the "key" rating, for it is the risk of the facility or transaction. A single borrower would have only one

---

3. Quote for FRB Memo.

obligor rating but might have several different facilities with different facility ratings, depending on terms, collateral, and so on.

The Structure of a Credit Risk Grading System

Table 12-1   Comparing the Credit Grade to the Bond Rating and Expected Default Frequency

Credit Grade	Bond Rating	Key Words	EDF High in bp	EDF Mean in bp	EDF Low in bp
1	AAA to AA–	World Class Organization	0.02	0.02	0.02
2	AA to A–	Excellent Access to Capital Markets	0.13	0.02	0.02
3	A+ to BBB+	Cash Flow Trends Generally Positive	0.27	0.06	0.03
4	BBB+ to BBB	Leverage, Coverage Somewhat Below Industry Average	0.87	0.16	0.08
5	BBB to BBB–	Lower Tier Competitor; Limited Access to Public Debt Markets	1.62	0.25	0.24
6	BBB– to BB–	Narrow Margins; Fully Leveraged; Variable Cash Flow	2.65	0.52	0.24
7	B	Cash Flow Vulnerable to Downturns; Strained Liquidity; Poor Coverage	5.44	1.89	0.64
8	C	Special Mention (1)	19.06	2.89	2.85
9	D	Substandard (2)			
10	D	Doubtful (3)			

Table 12-2   Definitions of Poor Credit Grades by the Authorities

Definitions Issued by the Regulatory Bodies as of June 10, 1993	Comptroller of the Currency Federal Deposit Insurance Corporation Federal Reserve Board Office of Thrift Supervision
Special Mention	A special mention asset has potential weaknesses that deserve management's close attention. If left uncorrected, these potential weaknesses may result in deterioration of the repayment prospects for the asset or damage to the institution's credit position at some future date. Special mention assets are not adversely classified and do not expose an institution to sufficient risk to warrant adverse classification.
Substandard Assets	A substandard asset is inadequately protected by the current sound worth and paying capacity of the obligor or of the collateral pledged, if any. Assets so classified must have a well-defined weakness or weaknesses that jeopardize the liquidation of the debt. They are characterized by the distinct possibility that the firm will sustain some loss if the deficiencies are not corrected.
Doubtful Assets	An asset classified as doubtful has all the weaknesses inherent in an asset classified as substandard, with the added characteristic that the weaknesses make collection or liquidation in full, on the basis of currently existing facts, conditions, and values, highly questionable and improbable.
Loss Assets	Assets classified as loss are considered uncollectible and of such little value that their continuance as viable assets is not warranted. This classification does not mean that the asset has absolutely no recovery or salvage value; it means rather that it is not practical or desirable to defer writing off this basically worthless asset, even though partial recovery may be affected in the future.

Risk Rating Computer Tutorial for Risk Rating Model.xls

The Risk Rating Model.xls risk rating tutorial is a 10-point interactive system *xls Industrial and Commercial Risk Grading* worksheet designed to reinforce concepts in this chapter. You may navigate throughout the system by simply clicking **Risk** on the main menu. The workbook is menu driven containing interactive dialog boxes that pop on the screen. A dialog appears where initiating information is entered. The tutorial also includes caption call-outs that reinforce concepts and help you traverse the various worksheets. The tutorial includes an extensive system of supporting macros that makes it relatively simple to adapt the model to your bank's portfolio system.

Getting Started

Open Risk Rating Model.xls. A dialog appears. The banker working a full-scale version (although this tutorial roughly reaches that level) selects industry group, facility, maximum exposure, his/her name, name of the borrower, maximum exposure, facility amount, previous credit grade (if any), and date. The Risk Rating Model tutorial shows how other macros work, is responsive to guarantees, and guarantees or collateral support the credit. Please check the box labeled *Guarantees?* and/or *Collateral?* If guarantees or collateral are not checked, they disappear from the system. If you are reviewing the guarantor, don't check the guarantee box. Complete other information the dialog requests. Enter individual credit grade for each category. The system will compute cumulative grades. Cumulative grades involve a weighting system devised by management, industry specialists, and other responsible parties. Weights differ from industry to industry. See Excel formulas.

Obligor Grades

Module 1: Obligor Financial Measures and Subjective Measures—OFM Worksheet

Examine each of the definitions corresponding to the columns (Grade, Bond Rating, and Expected Default Factor) and decide where borrowers fit. Enter individual risks grades: *Operating Cash Flows; Debt Capacity and Financing Flexibility; Asset/ Liability Quality; Valuation Measures; Contingencies; Financial Reporting and Management.*

Table 12-3   Breakdowns of Category, Cumulative Risk Grade, and Option to Accept or Override Preset Cumulative Grade Weights

	Operating Cash Flows	Debt Capacity and Financing Flexibility	Asset/Lability Quality	Valuation Measures
CATEGORY RISK GRADE	3	4	4	4
CUMULATIVE RISK GRADE	3.00	3.33	3.43	3.71
ACCEPT/OVERRIDE				

First column: earnings and operating cash flow
1. Are earnings stable, growing, and of high quality?
2. Are margins solid compared to the industry?
3. Is cash flow magnitude sufficient to fund growth internally?

4. Is operating cash flow strong in relation to present and anticipated debt?
5. Is Net Cash Flow from Operations sufficient to cover most nondiscretionary outlays?

Cash Flow	
Category Risk Grade	3
Cumulative Risk Grade	3.00

If the category risk grade is worse than 5, a "Warning" appears on the page: "Warning / Grade Worse than 5 / View EssarCash Flow Below / Is your Cash flow as Detailed?"

Debt capacity and financial flexibility
1. Are leverage and coverage within the first quartile of the industry peer group?
2. What alternative sources of debt and capital exist?
3. Does the borrower have solid investment grade ratings?
4. Can the borrower weather economic downturns?
5. Are debt maturities manageable?

Debt Capacity	
Category Risk Grade	4
Cumulative Risk Grade	3.33

Balance sheet quality and structure
1. Are assets solid and fairly valued?
2. Does the liability structure match the asset structure?
3. Do assets show concentration of location or use?
4. Are liquidity margins narrow?
5. Have asset turnover ratios been evaluated: average collection period, inventory turnover, and fixed asset turnover?
6. Is the bank lending where the assets are, and do we have access to them?

Asset Quality	
Category Risk Grade	4
Cumulative Risk Grade	3.43

Valuation

1. Do you develop a shareholder valuation from client projections? *The Toolkit includes a comprehensive valuation model.*
2. Is there a healthy spread between the obligor's asset values—that is, cash flow value or *economic value*—of assets (value of the firm) and the market value of debt?
3. What is the spread between the obligor's operating profit margin and the threshold margin? The threshold margin is the minimum profit margin required to increase shareholder value.
4. Does the obligor have hidden liabilities that may result in a significant erosion of shareholder value?
5. What are the probabilities that shareholder value will below zero?
6. Is liquidation value of the borrower's assets below shareholder value?

Valuation	
Category Risk Grade	4
Cumulative Risk Grade	3.71

Contingencies

1. Are contingencies limited and easily controlled?
2. Is potential impact on tangible new worth negligible?
3. Is the expected value of contingencies certain?
4. Are you familiar with the accounting for contingencies: SFAS No. 5, APB Opinion No. 22, "Disclosure of Accounting Policies," SEC requirements, FIN No. 34, The SEC's Financial Reporting Release (FRR) No. 23, SFAS No. 112, "Employers Accounting for Post retirement Benefits," and other accounting pronouncements?
5. Have you determined the amount to accrue for a loss contingency involving litigation?
6. Have you checked the nature and amount of large guarantees?
7. What are the borrower's obligations related to product liabilities, warranties, and catastrophic losses?
8. Have you assessed the probability that other parties will be able to pay their share of any apportioned liability?
9. Did you discount any long-term contingent liabilities net of related recoveries?
10. Did the borrower fail to record the costs of rectifying environmental problems?

Contingencies	
Category Risk Grade	5
Cumulative Risk Grade	3.71

Financial reporting

1. Does a reputable firm regularly complete an audit?
2. Are financial reports promptly issued?
3. Are statements accurate and complete?
4. Have you analyzed business segments having a significant impact on the consolidated entity?
5. Did you verify the reliability of information in business reporting?
6. Did you check the accountant's file, and can you confirm that past audits received passed the test of reliability and comparability?
7. How does the company and/or its auditors assess whether significant estimates and assumptions are based on the best information available?
8. Does the company use independent specialists or sophisticated quantitative techniques to validate or develop key estimates and assumptions?
9. What negative events or unsatisfactory outcomes occurred during the year, and how are those presented in the financial statements?
10. How do the company's accounting policies, disclosures, format of financial statements, and other financial communications compare to the company's competitors?
11. What changes, if any, have there been in the company's accounting policies or in management's application of the policies and the use of estimates and judgments?
12. Does the audit contain significant disclaimers or an adverse opinion?
13. Is the timeliness of statements problematic?
14. Did you review the borrower's business plan carefully in terms of consistency with independent audits?

Financial Reporting	
Category Risk Grade	4
Cumulative Risk Grade	3.71

Management and controls

1. Is management capable, tried, and tested now and for the foreseeable future?
2. Are strong operating and financial controls in place?
3. Does management have broad industry experience, along with good continuity and depth?
4. Do senior managers keep changing?
5. Is there a succession plan in place?
6. In the case of a closely held firm, is there a buy/sell agreement to facilitate ownership transfer upon the death of a principal?
7. Have the owners and managers taken salary cuts during difficult times?
8. Is management meeting customer or marketplace expectations?
9. How efficiently is management running the firm's operations?
10. Does management set goals providing a context for achieving them?

Management	
Category Risk Grade	4
Cumulative Risk Grade	3.71

Using weights to determine cumulative obligor financial measures
Weights assigned in Module 1 set in default mode for illustration (Cell OPM1!L107).
The system arrives at the cumulative grade using a weighting system set by management and influenced by the industry and loan facility. The weights can change from
default if the situation warrants it. The formula for the cumulative grade at this point
is:

$$IF(L106 = 0,0,IF(OR(L106 > 10,L106 = 0), \text{``ERROR''}$$
$$(Y3*\$F\$106 + Y4*\$H\$106 + Y5*\$J\$106 + Y6*\$L\$106)/(Y3 + Y4 + Y5 + Y6)))$$

In reality, algorithms programmed in the weighting grid are industry- and facility-
specific and are designed to arrive at accurate obligor cumulative grades (see
Weights!A1 and Table 12-4). However, you may "call the shots" and enter cumulative
grades directly to the worksheet, bypassing grids.

EXAMPLE 1 Assume Operating Cash Flow Grade is 3 while Debt Capacity grade is 4.
You feel that default weights in column B (7 and 2) reflect the importance of cash flow
to debt capacity, since much of the borrower's financing capacity is derived from cash
flow. If weights are accepted, the cumulative grade is (7 * 3 + 2 * 4)/(7 + 3) = 2.9.

Table 12-4   Weights to determine cumulative obligor financial measure grades.

General Corporate: Cumulative Grade Weights

Basic Materials Combination cash flow and refinancing (no assets)

Operating Cash Flows	1	2	4	4
Debt Capacity and Financing Capacity		1	2	5
Asset/Liability Quality			1	3
Valuation				2
Management Depth/Accept or Enter	6	6:1 Means Relationship Between Cumulative Grade and Management Depth		

EXAMPLE 2 Assume Operating Cash Flow Grade is 2, Debt Capacity grade is 3, and Asset/Liability Quality grade is 4. You argue that the default weights in column C (5, 3, and 9) reflect the importance of Operating Cash Flow, Debt Capacity to Asset/Liability. If weights are accepted, the cumulative grade is $(5 * 2 + 3 * 3 + 9 * 4)/(5 + 3 + 9) = 3.24$.

Module 2: Financial Situations and Recent Developments— Worksheet FinDev

This module considers important recent changes that affect the obligor financial measures grade that for good reason did not factor into previous grades. The obligor grade adjustment and reason for the adjustment is carried over to the summary page. In our practice session, we assume no change to this module.

Module 3: Industry Grade—Worksheet Indus

1. Does the borrower operate in a strong and growing industry?
2. Is the borrower a significant factor in the industry or market?
3. Are legal or regulatory climates favorable?
4. Is industry cyclically minimal?
5. Is the industry vulnerable to sudden economic or technological change?
6. Is industry operating leverage modest?
7. Are labor problems minimal?
8. Is regulatory environment satisfactory?
9. Are long-term prospects favorable?
10. Does the borrower rank in the first tier of the industry?
11. Is the borrower industry "focused," enjoying a meaningful market share?
12. Are performance ratios generally better than industry peers?

CATEGORY RISK GRADE (WORKSHEET)		5.00	4.00
CUMULATIVE RISK GRADE	3.71	3.71	3.71

ACCEPT/OVERRIDE

RISK CATEGORY		INDUSTRY SEGMENT	POSITION WITHIN INDUSTRY

Module 4: Country Risk—Worksheet COUNTRYRISK

Cross-border risks usually include but are not restricted to:

1. *Economic Risk*: the significant change in the economic structure or growth rate that produces a major change in the expected return of an investment.

2. *Transfer Risk*: the risk arising from a decision by a foreign government to restrict capital movements. Restrictions could make it difficult to repatriate profits, dividends, or capital.

3. *Exchange Risk*: an unexpected adverse movement in the exchange rate. Exchange risk includes an unexpected change in currency regime such as a change from a fixed to a floating exchange rate.

4. *Location Risk*: the spillover effects caused by problems in a region, in a country's trading partner, or in countries with similar perceived characteristics.

5. *Sovereign Risk*: deals with whether a government will be unwilling or unable to meet its loan obligations, or is likely to renege on loans it guarantees. Sovereign risk can relate to transfer risk in that a government may run out of foreign exchange due to unfavorable developments in its balance of payments.

6. *Political Risk*: risk of a change in political institutions stemming from a change in government control, social fabric, or other noneconomic factor. This category covers the potential for internal and external conflicts, expropriation risk, and traditional political analysis.

The Federal Reserve Bank has defined substandard country risk whereby (1) a country is not complying with its external service obligations, as evidenced by arrears, (2) the country is not in the process of adopting any other suitable economic adjustment program, and (3) the country and its bank creditors have not negotiated a viable rescheduling and are unlikely to do so in the near future. The designation Value Impaired, according to the Federal Reserve Board's audit guidelines, signifies that (1) the country has not met rescheduling terms for over one year and (2) the country shows no definite prospects for an orderly restoration of debt service in the near future.

When completing the rating in this module consider:

1. What is Country Investment Ranking?
2. What is the Interagency Country Exposure Review Committee (ICERC) rating?
3. Has the ICERC rating improved or deteriorated over the past six months?
4. What are the country's resource base in terms of (1) natural resources, (2) human resources, and (3) financial resources?
5. What is the outlook for domestic political stability?
6. What is the quality of economic and financial management? Does the leadership have the political strength to implement decisions, particularly if these decisions involve austerity measures?
7. What is the country's long-run development strategy?
8. Is industrial development based on efficiency or in support of prestige projects or the economic interests of politically powerful groups?
9. Is economic growth financed largely by domestic revenues and savings or through foreign speculative investments?
10. Is inflation under control?
11. Are wage and price policies in line with productivity growth?
12. In looking at the outlook for the balance of payments, what is the prognosis of current account, capital account, and debt service account improvements?
13. How are capital account deficits financed? World Bank or bilateral aid programs? Bank loans?

14. Does the bank regularly gather information as to the company's risk exposure in each country and compare this with the country limits?

15. Is there action to eliminate any exposure in excess of a particular country limit?

The cumulative grade assigned to cell F107 is set by the formula: =IF(F106 > 5,F106,D107). If the category risk grade: Country/Transfer Risk is worse than 5, the cumulative grade defaults to the country grade; otherwise the original grade stands.

Country Risk	
Category Risk Grade	1
Cumulative Risk Grade	3.71

Facility Grades

Facility risk refers to risks associated with the individual facility or deal structure itself—the credit product, tenor/maturity (long versus short), collateral and support, guarantees, purpose of facility, documentation quality and verification, and portfolio.

Module 5: Documentation Matrix—Worksheet Docum6

There is no faster way for disaster to strike than for bankers to ignore periodic and thorough reviews of loan documentation. This means knowing the obligor and guarantor in terms of decimation, reviewing covenants and recent compliance or violations, checking and updating subordination agreements and corporate resolutions, and insuring that collateral and documents supporting collateral are current. A fail-safe rule to follow is: *Risk rating is not considered complete until the banker physically reviews loan documentation under his or her jurisdiction.*

Consider these facility downgrades: Documentation may not conform to normal standards; updates are past due and may not be valid (Uniform Commercial Code (UCC) filings, etc.), resulting in a downgrade from +1 to +2. Cases where documentation does not conform to normal standards will lead to a downgrade ranging from +3 to +8. An example is an unsecured loan to a Latin American blue chip company to bridge capital markets transaction with repayment expected in 60 to 180 days. Financials are unaudited and are provided from a prospectus with information that is somewhat dated and incomplete. Documentation is satisfactory, but it lacks meaningful covenants. You decide that −1 grade improvement is justified reflecting the short loan duration.

Documentation Adjustment to Grade	0
Cumulative Risk Grade	3.71

Module 6: Guarantees—Worksheet GUAR3

A guarantee is a written contract, agreement, or undertaking involving three parties. The first party, the *Guarantor*, agrees to see that the performance of the second party, the *Guarantee*, is fulfilled according to the terms of the contract, agreement, or under-taking. The third party is the *Creditor*, or the party that benefits by the performance. If the Guarantee is less than 100 percent, bankers can complete a risk rating form or check the guarantor's bond rating before completing the guarantee worksheet. *Note:* If the loan is not supported by a guarantee, Excel removes the worksheet GUAR3 [guarantee? box not checked off on the opening page].

For partial guarantees, the worksheet calculates a weighted risk rating. The weigh-ted risk rating depends on (a) prorating credit responsibility and (b) determining the expected default frequency for the obligor and guarantor.

The expected default frequency of the obligor in basis points corresponds to the cumulative risk grade you determined thus far. You will need to enter the guarantor's grade, assumed to be 2 in Table 12-5, and the percentage of the facility under the guarantor's responsibility, 70 percent. The program derives the obligor's share of responsibility, 30 percent; the expected default factors of guarantor and obligor, 6 and 37; the combined EDF, 15.09; and the weighted grade, 3.50. Guarantees should be unconditional and uncontested for them to be acceptable at full value. At full value bankers will consider substituting the guarantor's credit grade for the obligor's credit. Coverage may include a few conditions, may be very conditional, or may be of such limited value that grade improvement is not possible.

Guarantees are only as good as their supporting documents and thus must be reviewed by (legal) counsel. The system includes a column so that bankers can deter-mine whether documentation is perfected and uncontestable, and lacks strength, if serious deficiencies exist or if documentation has no value.

Module 7: Collateral Matrix—Worksheet Coll4

A thorough review of collateral should be performed before the banker completes the risk grading process, more frequently for credits that are either heavily reliant on col-lateral or are secured by unique collateral. For example, the bank's Uniform Com-mercial Code financing statements and security agreements should be valid, up to date, and consistent with approval documentation. Risk rating time is the time to make sure your collateral is properly secured.

Table 12-5 Sample Cells in the GUAR3 Worksheet

Guarantors Grade	2	
Enter % Obligation: Guarantor	70%	
Obligors % of Obligation	30%	
Expected Default Factor/Guarantor	6	
Expected Default Factor/Obligor	37	15.09
OBLIGORS CUMULATIVE GRADE	4	
TRANSACTION WEIGHTED GRADE	3.50	

Collateral is defined as property pledged as security for the satisfaction of a debt or other obligation. The Credit Grade assigned to secured loans will depend on, among other things, the degree of coverage, the economic life cycle of the collateral versus the term of the loan, possible constraints of liquidating the collateral, and the bank's ability to skillfully and economically monitor and liquidate collateral. For the purposes of risk grading, collateral is separated into three classification tiers. Classification I includes highly liquid and readily attainable collateral with difference secured by other less liquid assets. Classification I collateral includes cash, certificate of deposits, bankers' acceptances, and commercial paper or prime investment grade bonds.

Classification II represents independent audit/valuation required security, including highest accounts receivable quality/liquid and diversified, highest inventory quality/ liquid and diversified, fixed assets—prime and readily marketable real estate— commercial, and collateral easily accessible by assignees or participants' voting rights on collateral not abridged. Classification III, or other collateral, includes leasehold improvements, stock of subsidiaries, stock on pink sheets, receivables: concentrated/ questionable quality, inventory: concentrated/questionable quality and real estate: questionable quality and marketability.

Many lenders consider the following before they complete the collateral facility page:[4]

1. What is its value compared to credit exposure?
2. What is its liquidity, or how quickly may its value be realized and with what certainty?
3. Is negotiable collateral held under joint custody?
4. Has the customer obtained and filed for released collateral sign receipts?
5. Are securities and commodities valued and margin requirements reviewed at least monthly?
6. When the support rests on the cash surrender value of insurance policies, is a periodic accounting received from the insurance company and maintained with the policy?
7. Is a record maintained for entry to the collateral vault?
8. Has the bank instituted a system ensuring that security agreements are filed, that collateral mortgages are properly recorded, that title searches and property appraisals are performed in connection with collateral mortgages, and that insurance (including loss payee clause) is in effect on property covered by collateral mortgages?
9. In mortgage warehouse financing, does the bank hold the original mortgage note, trust deed, or other critical document, releasing only against payment?
10. Have standards been set for determining percentage advance to be made against acceptable receivables?
11. Are acceptable receivables defined?
12. Has the bank established minimum requirements for verification of borrower's accounts receivable and established minimum standards for documentation?

---

4. *Source*: FRB Commercial Bank Examination Manual.

13. Have accounts receivable financing policies been reviewed at least annually to determine whether they are compatible with changing market conditions?
14. Have loan statements, delinquent accounts, collection requests, and past-due notices been checked to the trial balances that are used in reconciling subsidiary records of accounts receivable financing loans with general ledger accounts?
15. Have inquiries about accounts receivable financing loan balances been received and investigated?
16. Were payments from customers scrutinized for differences in invoice dates, numbers, terms, and so on?
17. Do bank records show, on a timely basis, a first lien on the assigned receivables for each borrower?
18. Do loans granted on the security of the receivables also have an assignment of the inventory?
19. Does the bank verify the borrower's accounts receivable or require independent verification on a periodic basis?
20. Does the bank require the borrower to provide aged accounts receivable schedules on a periodic basis?

Collateral Effect on Grade	−1
Cumulative Risk Grade	2.5

Module 8: Purpose—Worksheet PURPOSE

Classification standards
1. Facility appropriate for business
2. Match funding appropriate
3. Financing strategy not appropriate for obligor
4. Obligor borrowing short term to finance capital requirements
5. Facility used to finance excessive dividends
6. Unsecured facility while other lenders have the best collateral
7. Bank is subordinated lender
8. Poor loan structure

Purpose Adjustment to Grade	0
Cumulative Risk Grade	2.50

Module 9: Tenor—Worksheet Tenor

From time to time and for various reasons, a bank may extend credit on terms or for a tenor that for a given borrower subjects the bank to a greater level of risk than indicated by the obligor rating. The Federal Reserve Bank audit guidelines, for example, look to establish maximum maturities for various types of loans. Tenor incremental risk should be reflected in a poorer risk rating. For example, an unsecured line of credit to a company with a obligor rating of 4 would not usually warrant a change in grade . the grade may actually improve in some cases with maturities under one year (see Tenor Matrix). However, a term loan that is longer than usual tenor or with a bullet maturity or a weak loan agreement may warrant a 5 or worse. Generally, for higher grades, term loans that amortize with equal installments up to three years will carry the same rating as the borrower. Bullet and balloon term loans of the same tenor might be one grade worse. Ratings in lower tiers migrate down at an accelerated pace the farther out the tenor.

Ratings migration risk

Moody's dropped its rating on Monsanto's long-term debt to A2 from A1. The ratings affect $5 billion in debt. The downgrade reflects the stressed nature of the firm's balance sheet due to debt incurred primarily to finance acquisitions.

Sample Credit Rating Transition Matrix
(probability of migrating to another rating within one year, percent)

		Credit Rating One-year in the Future							
		AAA	AA	A	BBB	BB	B	CCC	Default
	AAA	87.74	10.93	0.45	0.63	0.12	0.10	0.02	0.02
	AA	0.84	88.23	7.47	2.16	1.11	0.13	0.05	0.02
Current	A	0.27	1.59	89.05	7.40	1.48	0.13	0.06	0.03
Credit	BBB	1.84	1.89	5.00	84.21	6.51	0.32	0.16	0.07
Rating	BB	0.08	2.91	3.29	5.53	74.68	8.05	4.14	1.32
	B	0.21	0.36	9.25	8.29	2.31	63.89	10.13	5.58
	CCC	0.06	0.25	1.85	2.06	12.34	24.86	39.97	18.60

Source: Greg M. Gupton, Christopher C. Finger, and Mickey Bhatia, *CreditMetrics -- Technical Document*, New York: Morgan Guaranty Trust Co., April 1997, p. 76.

Figure 12-1 Example: Credit Rating Transition Matrix.

Table 12-6 Sample Credit Rating Transition Matrixes

TENOR ADJUSTMENT TO GRADE		1
CUMULATIVE RISK GRADE	2.50	3.50

Module 10: Portfolio Risk and Investment Factors—Worksheet Portfolio

Two main issues in this module are (1) will the facility have a neutral effect on the bank's portfolio and (2) will the facility provide adequate opportunities in the secondary market? Small banks and banks located in industry/economic pockets (the Midwest's agriculture belt, for example) may not post exposure concentrations within specific industries. A concentration of credit generally consists of direct or indirect (1) extensions of credit and (2) contingent obligations exceeding 25 percent of the capital structure (tier 1 plus loan loss reserves). This definition does not just refer to loans, but also includes aggregates of all types of exposures: loans and discounts, overdrafts, cash items, securities purchased outright or under resale agreements, sale of federal funds, suspense assets, leases, acceptances, letters of credit, placements, loans endorsed, guaranteed or subject to repurchase agreements, and any other actual or contingent liability.

Limitations imposed by bank management and regulators are meant to prevent obligors from borrowing undue amounts—action that is detrimental to optimally balancing loan portfolios. Bankers generally recognize various types of concentrations[5]:

1. Loans dependent on a particular agricultural crop or livestock herd. Banking institutions located in farming, dairying, or livestock areas may grant substantially all their loans to individuals or concerns engaged in and dependent on the agricultural industry. A concentration of this type is commonplace and may be necessary if the bank is to perform the function for which it was chartered.

2. The aggregate amount of interim construction loans that do not have firm, permanent takeout commitments. In the event that permanent financing is not obtainable, the bank will have to continue financing the project. This longer term financing subjects the bank to additional liquidity and possibly interest rate risks as well as those risks associated with the real estate itself.

3. Loans to groups of borrowers who handle the product from the same industry. Although the borrowers may appear to be independent of one another, their financial conditions may act in similar ways if there is a situation that results in a slowdown of that economic sector.

4. Concentrations located in towns economically dominated by one or a few business enterprises. Such banks may extend a substantial amount of credit to the company and to a large percentage of the company's employees.

If exposure concentrations are material, the appropriateness of concentrations should be verified before or during the risk grading process. Concentrations that involve excessive or undue risks require close scrutiny by the bank and should be reduced over a reasonable period of time. Banks use credit derivatives, loan securitizations, and loan sales to help reduce concentrations.

---

5. Source: Commercial Bank Examination Manual.

Loan portfolio management: federal reserve loan examination guidelines

1. Establish geographic limits for loans.
2. Establish suggested guidelines for aggregate outstanding loans in relation to other balance sheet categories.
3. Establish loan authority of committees and individual lending officers.
4. Define acceptable types of loans.
5. Establish maximum maturities for various types of loans.
6. Establish loan pricing.
7. Establish appraisal policy.
8. Establish minimum financial information required at inception of credit.
9. Establish limits and guidelines for purchasing paper.
10. Establish collection procedures.
11. Define the duties and responsibilities of loan officers and loan committees.
12. Outline loan portfolio management objectives that acknowledge concentrations of credit within specific industries.
13. Review loan portfolio management policies and objectives reviewed at least annually to determine if they are compatible with changing market conditions.

The Summary Page

The summary page (see Table 12-8) summarizes the entire risk rating process and is usually the document attached to a facility sheet or credit review, or is otherwise reported through the system to senior officials.

Table 12-7   Sample Cells from the PORTFOLIO Worksheet

Module10

PORTFOLIO RISK AND INVESTMENT FACTORS

CLASSIFICATION STANDARDS		*MAXIMUM EFFECT ON GRADE*
FACILITY HAS A NEUTRAL EFFECT ON ROBFELL'S PORTFOLIO		NONE
FACILITY PROVIDES ADEQUATE OPPORTUNITIES IN THE SECONDARY MARKET		
FACILITY HAS A NEUTRAL OR POSITIVE EFFECT ON ROBFEL		FROM 0 TO −2
FACILITY PROVIDES EXCELLENT OPPORTUNITIES IN THE SECONDARY LOAN MARKET		
FACILITY SIGNIFICANTLY INCREASES PORTFOLIO'S EXPOSURE TO SYSTEMATIC RISK		FROM +1 TO +8
FACILITY REPRESENTS AN ILLIQUID ASSET PROVIDING FEW OPPORTUNITIES IN THE SECONDARY LOAN MARKET		
PORTFOLIO ADJUSTMENT TO GRADE	0	
CUMULATIVE RISK GRADE	3.50	3.50	

Cumulative Grades

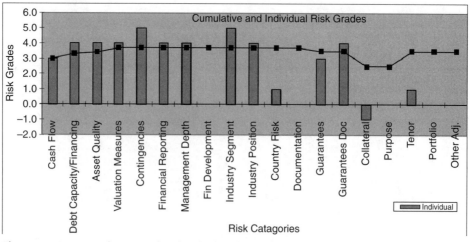

Figure 12-2   Cumulative and Individual Risk Grades.

Table 12-8 Summary Page Highlights: Individual Grades, Cumulative Grades, and Changes

SUMMARY RISK RATING

Company:	Great CoupleDesign, Inc.	Category:	General Corporate	Analyst:	John Smith
Address:	123 Success Court	Max Exposure	80,000	Credit Area:	Global Credit Co.
City/State/Zip:	Old Westbury, NY	Facility Type:	Senior	Data Source:	Audited
Date:	July 5, 2001	Classification:	Bridge	Audit Date:	6/30/2001

Weights

Weights		
Operating Cash Flows	29%	4.0
Debt Capacity and Financing Capacity	36%	5.0
Asset/Liability Quality	21%	3.0
Valuation	14%	2.0

Credit Rating

Credit Rating	
Obligor Grade:	3.7
System Grade:	3.5
Final Grade:	4.0

Obligor Financial Measure

Industry Specific Cumulative Grade Weights

OBLIGOR GRADES	Unit Grade	Change	Cumulative Grade
Cash Flow	3.0		3.0
Debt Capacity/ Financing Flexibility	4.0	0.3	3.3
Asset Quality	4.0	0.1	3.4
Valuation Measures	4.0	0.3	3.7
Contingencies	5.0	0.0	3.7
Financial Reporting	4.0	0.0	3.7
Management Depth	4.0	0.0	3.7
Fin Development	0.0	0.0	3.7
Industry Segment	5.0	0.0	3.7
Industry Position	4.0	0.0	3.7
Country Risk	1.0	0.0	3.7

FACILITIES GRADES

FACILITIES GRADES			
Documentation	0.0	0.0	3.7
Guarantees	3.0	−0.2	3.5
Guarantee Documentation	4.0	0.0	3.5
Collateral	−1.0	−1.0	2.5
Purpose	0.0	0.0	2.5
Tenor	1.0	1.0	3.5
Portfolio	0.0	0.0	3.5

Previous Rating

Previous Rating		
Previous Risk Grade2	2	1/1/2000
Previous Risk Grade	3	1/1/2001
Industry SIC Code		12345
S&P Debt Rating		AAA
Shadow Debt Rating		1001
KMV Default		
Secondary Mk Liquidity		Not Liquid
Total Debt/EBITDA		12345.0x
Interest Coverage		100000.0x

Summary Rating	Grade	Change
Obligor Only Grade	3.7	NA
Facility Risk Grade Adjustme	−0.2	−3.9
System Risk (Rounded)	3.5	3.7

Adjustments (Comments Below):		
Financial Development	0	
Other		
Final Adjusted Rating	4	

Determining Loan Loss Reserves

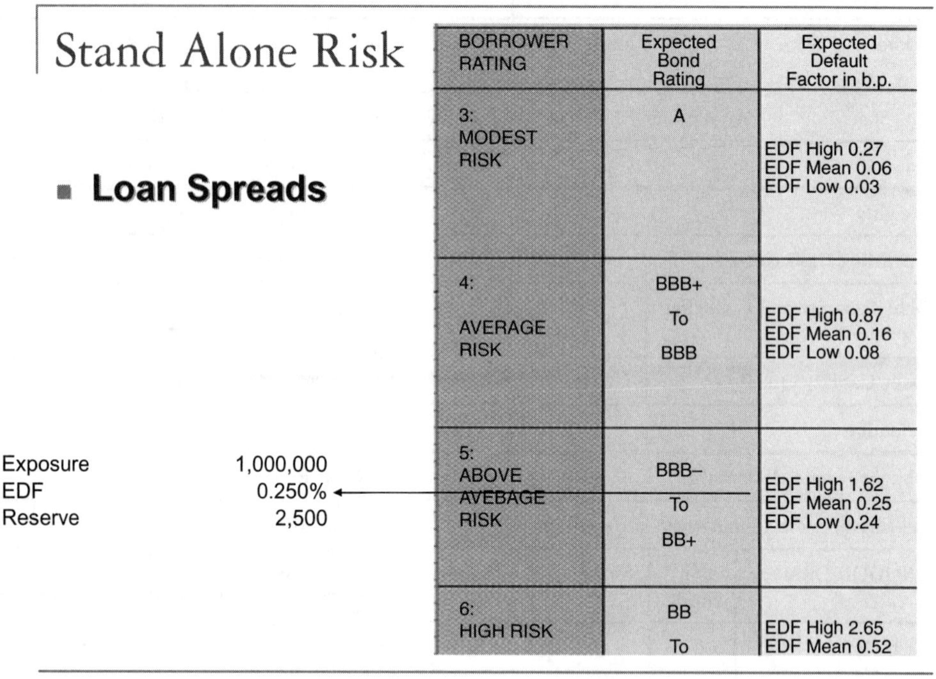

Stand Alone Risk	BORROWER RATING	Expected Bond Rating	Expected Default Factor in b.p.
	3: MODEST RISK	A	EDF High 0.27 EDF Mean 0.06 EDF Low 0.03
■ **Loan Spreads**	4: AVERAGE RISK	BBB+ To BBB	EDF High 0.87 EDF Mean 0.16 EDF Low 0.08
Exposure 1,000,000 EDF 0.250% ◄ Reserve 2,500	5: ABOVE AVEBAGE RISK	BBB– To BB+	EDF High 1.62 EDF Mean 0.25 EDF Low 0.24
	6: HIGH RISK	BB To	EDF High 2.65 EDF Mean 0.52

Figure 12-3   Loan Loss Reserve.

Thus, if loss given default is 25 bp and the amount at risk is 1,000,000, the loan loss reserve on this exposure is 2,500.

Building Industry-Specific/Risk-Specific Corporate Risk Rating Models

The algorithms built into the Excel workbook, *Risk Rating Systems,* allow you to build industry-specific risk rating models. Simply follow these steps:

1. Open the workbook and enable the macros. Click on **Click to Start Tutorial Rating**.
2. The "Guarantees?" and "Collateral?" dialog boxes are checked. Uncheck the "Guarantees" box and then click on **OK**. The Worksheet GUAR3 disappears from the system. However, the cumulative grade in the worksheet GUAR will link flawlessly to worksheet COLL4.
3. Return to INTRO and again click on **Click to Start Tutorial Rating**. Uncheck both "Guarantees?" and "Collateral?" boxes. The Worksheet GUAR3 disappears from the system. However, all cumulative grades in the system link flawlessly to arrive at a final grade. How is this accomplished? Approximately 1,700 lines of coding appear in the worksheet "MACROS." You can select macros that hide worksheets and make them appear. We will now move worksheets around:

4. The following worksheets are industry-specific:
   - Module 1 *Obligor Financial Measures and Subjective Measures*
   - Module 3 *Industry and Borrower's Industry Position*
   - Module 8 *Tenor*

5. The following worksheets tend to be nonspecific:
   - Module 2: *Financial Situations and Recent Developments*
   - Module 4: *Country Risk*
   - Module 5: *Documentation Matrix*
   - Module 6: *Guarantees*
   - Module 7: *Collateral Matrix*
   - Module 8: *Purpose*
   - Module *10: Portfolio Risk and Investment Factors*

6. Set up industry-specific modules: (1) obligor financial measures and subjective measures; (2) industry and borrower's position in the industry; and (3) tenor. The airline industry's cash flow measures, financial reporting, debt capacity, and so on differ from the textile industry. Consider airline financial reporting. The Accounting Policy Task Force of the International Air Transport Association has issued a number of airline accounting guidelines and liaises with standard-setting bodies on issues for the industry.
   - Translation of long-term foreign currency borrowings
   - Frequent flyer program accounting
   - Components of fleet acquisition cost and associated depreciation
   - Recognition of revenue
   - Accounting for maintenance costs
   - Accounting for leases of aircraft fleet assets
   - Segmental reporting

   Consider the mining industry. This industry includes thousands of companies engaged in an array of products, including precious metals, base metals, coal, uranium, and other industrial minerals. Cash flow, financial reporting, and so on differ as much from the airline industry risk characteristics than airlines differ from utilities. For example:
   - Accounting for and disclosure of mineral reserves
     - How should the costs of acquiring mineral rights or properties be accounted for, given these acquisitions may take the form of taking title to properties, obtaining mineral and mining rights, leases, patents, and so on?
     - How should generally accepted principles for determination of the impairment of such costs capitalized be determined?
     - What financial information should be disclosed to investors that will provide relevant, comparable, and transparent disclosures of mineral reserves?
   - Accounting for development activities performed contemporaneous to production
     i. Specify that costs incurred at an operating mine, excluding costs included in inventory, should not be deferred.
     ii. Provide guidance as to when a mine is under construction versus when it is in production.
     iii. Owing to the nature of the business, specify which, if any, mine development costs incurred prior or subsequent to commercial production commencing should be capitalized.

- Accounting for operating activities
  i.   Define when it would be appropriate for inventories of precious and base metals appropriately to be recorded at other than cost.
  ii. Provide guidance about common revenue recognition matters unique to the industry.

Building Specialized Lending Risk Rating Models

It is a good idea to make sure that your model is strongly influenced by regulatory compliance issues and structure. Open the Excel workbook—*Project Finance Risk Rating Model*. We built this sophisticated risk model after researching documents at the Bank for International Settlements. See link that follows: Basel Committee on Banking Supervision working paper on the internal ratings-based approach to specialized lending exposures: http://www.oenb.at/en/img/wp_irba_splend_tcm16-15490.pdf

Brief Review of Project Finance

Historical Perspective

A great variety of investments have been project financed, notably, pipelines, refineries, electric power generating facilities, hydroelectric projects, dock facilities, mines, mineral processing facilities, and many others. Project finance holds great promise as a means of financing projects designed to help meet the enormous infrastructure needs that exist in developed countries and especially in emerging markets. It involves lending to a single-purpose entity for the acquisition and /or construction of a revenue-generating asset with limited or no recourse to the sponsor. Repayment of the loan is solely from revenues generated from operation of the asset owned by the entity.

Steps to Completing Deal
- Project identification and resource allocation
- Risk allocation and project structuring
- Bidding and mandating contracts
- Due diligence and documentation
- Execution and monitoring
- Construction monitoring
- Term loan conversion and ongoing monitoring

The Rationale for Project Financing
- Reallocating free cash flow
- More efficient structuring of debt contracts
- More effective corporate organization and management
- The size and term of the initial forward commitments required to ensure that sufficient funds are available to complete the project
- The degree of sophistication needed to understand the complex security arrangements typically involved in a project financing
- Lenders' reluctance to provide funds for a project that is not expected to be profitable

- Expected rate of return on assets sufficient to cover its debt service requirements and provide an acceptable rate of return to the project's equity investors
- Lenders reluctant to lend unless they are comfortable that the project can service its debt in a timely manner
- Lenders' requirement of project sponsors to commit sufficient equity to make project creditworthy
- Interest rate high enough to attract the substantial commitments required to complete the financing and to compensate lenders fully for the default and illiquidity risk they must bear

Analysis of Project Viability
- Technical feasibility
- Economic viability
- Creditworthiness
- Assessing project risks
- Completion risk
- Technological risk
- Raw material supply risk
- Economic risk
- Financial risk
- Currency risk
- Political risk
- Environmental risk

Annex 4[6]

Table 12-9 Supervisory Slotting Criteria for Specialized Lending

Financial Strength	Strong	Good	Satisfactory	Weak
Market conditions	Few competing suppliers OR substantial and durable advantage in location, cost. or technology. Demand is strong and growing.	Few competing suppliers OR better than average location, cost, or technology but this situation may not last. Demand is strong and stable.	Project has no advantage in location, cost, or technology. Demand is adequate and stable.	Project has worse than average location, cost, or technology. Demand is weak and declining.
Financial ratios (e g., debt service coverage ratio (DSCR), loan life coverage ratio (LLCR), project life coverage ratio (PLCR), and debt-to-equity ratio.)	Strong financial ratios considering the level of project risk; very robust economic assumptions.	Strong to acceptable financial ratios considering the level of project risk: robust project economic assumptions.	Standard financial ratios considering the level of project risk.	Aggressive financial ratios considering the level of project risk.
Stress analysis	The project can meet its financial obligations under sustained, severely stressed economic or sectoral conditions.	The project can meet its financial obligations under normal stressed economic or sectoral conditions. The project is only likely to default under severe economic conditions	The project is vulnerable to stresses that are not uncommon through an economic cycle, and may default in a normal downturn.	The project is likely to default unless conditions improve soon.

6. Annex 4: Basel Committee on Banking Supervision Working Paper on the Internal Ratings-Based Approach to Specialized Lending Exposures.

Open *Project Finance Risk Rating Model on the DVD.*

Supervisory Rating Grades for Project Finance Exposures: Basel April, 2003

MODULE 4   SECURITY PACKAGE

PROJECT RATING	ASSIGNMENT OF CONTRACT AND ACCOUNTS	PLEDGE OF ASSETS (TAKING INTO ACCOUNT QUALITY, VALUE AND LIQUIDITY OF ASSETS)	LENDER'S CONTROL OVER CASH FLOW (E.G. CASH SWEEPS, INDEPENDENT ESCROW ACCOUNTS)	STRENGTH OF THE COVENANT PACKAGE (MANDATORY PREPAYMENTS, PAYMENT DEFERRALS, PAYMENT CASCADE, DIVIDEND RESTRICTIONS)	RESERVE FUNDS (DEBT SERVICE, O&M, RENEWAL AND REPLACEMENT, UNFORESEEN EVENTS, ETC)
1: STRONG	Fully comprehensive	First perfected security interest in all project assets, contracts, permits and accounts necessary to run the project	Strong	Covenant package is strong for this type of project. Project may issue unlimited additional debt	Longer than average coverage period, all reserve funds fully funded in cash or letters "of credit from highly rated bank
2: GOOD	Comprehensive	Perfected security interest in all project assets, contracts, permits and accounts necessary to run the project	Satisfactory	Covenant package is satisfactory for this type of project. Project may issue limited additional debt	Average coverage period, all reserve funds fully funded.
3: HIGH SATISFACTORY	Acceptable	Acceptable security interest in all project assets, contracts. Permits and accounts necessary to run the project	Fair	Covenant package is fair for this type of project. Project may issue extremely limited additional debt	
4: LOW SATISFACTORY					
5: WEAK	Weak	Little security or collateral for lenders; -weak negative pledge clause	Weak	Covenant package is Insufficient for this type of project. Project may issue no additional debt	Shorter than average coverage period, reserve funds funded from operating cash flows
MODULE 2 CATEGORY RISK GRADE	2	3	5	4	2
MODULE 2 CUMULATIVE RISK GRADE	2.00	2.33	2.71	3.00	3.18
	ASSIGNMENT OF CONTRACT AND ACCOUNTS	PLEDGE OF ASSETS	LENDER'S CONTROL OVER CASH FLOW	STRENGTH OF THE COVENANT PACKAGE	RESERVE FUNDS

Module 4 Security Package   The Crucial Weights

Assignment of Contracts and Accounts	1	2.00	4.00	8.00	4.00	Assignment of Co
Pledge of Assets		1.00	2.00	5.00	5.00	Pledge of Assets
Lender's Control Over Cash Flow			1.00	3.00	3.00	Lender's Control
Strength of the Covenant Package				2.00	3.00	Strength of the C
Reserve Funds					2.00	Reserve Funds

Figure 12-4   Supervisory Rating Grades for Project Finance Exposures: Security Package.

Supervisory Rating Grades for Project Finance Exposures: Basel April, 2003
Module 5 Composite Rating

PROJECT RATING	S&P Credit Assessment (Moody's)	S&P Assessment 20-Year Average Of Three-Year Cumulative Default Rate (CDR)	Basel Proposed Three-Year CDR Benchmarks MONITORING Level	Basel Proposed Three-Year CDR TRIGGER Level
1: STRONG	AAA AA (Aaa-Aa)	0.10%	0.80%	1.20%
2: GOOD	A (A)	0.25%	1.00%	1.30%
3: HIGH SATISFACTORY	BBB BB+	1.00%	2.40%	3.00%
4: LOW SATISFACTORY	BB BB-	7.50%	11.00%	12.40%
5: WEAK	B C	20.00%	28.60%	35.00%

Module 5 Composite Rating	Module Cumulative Grade	Weight Module 1,2,3,4
Project Financial Measures (5 = Override)	2.53	2.00
Political/ Legal Environment	5.00	10.00
Transaction	3.14	2.00
Security	3.18	10.00
Sum of Weights		24.00

Final Project Grade Before Override	3.88
Rating (Include: See Chart)	
S&P Credit Assessment (Include: See Chart)	
S&P Assessment 20 Yr Avg. 3 Yr. CDR (Include: See Chart)	7.50%
Basel Proposed 3 Yt. CDR Benchmarks Monitoring Level (Include: See Chart)	
Basel Proposed 3 Yt. CDR BenchmarksTrigger Level (Include: See Chart)	

Stress Analysis Override	
Project Grade After Stress Override, Before Government Override	3.88
Government Support Override	no
Project Grade After Stress And Government Override, Before Contract Enforcibility Overide	3.88
Contract Enforcibility and Permit Requirement Overide	yes
Project Grade After Override	2.00

FINAL PROJECT GRADE	3.88

Example of A Rated Basel Proposed 3 Year Monitoring Level	
Project Loan Face Value	25,000,000
Less Recoveries	(9,000,000)
Amount at Risk	16,000,000
S&P Assessment 20 Yr Avg. 3 Yr. CDR	7.50%
Reserve For Project Writeoff - Discussion	1,200,000

Figure 12-5   Supervisory Rating Grades for Project Finance Exposures: Composite Rating.

CHAPTER | 13

Building Integrated Exposure Systems

In the risk management area, the focus is on bank exposures to credit risk, market risk, risk from equity positions, and operational risk. For credit risk, which is defined as the potential losses arising from borrowers not repaying their debts, banks must provide a qualitative discussion of their risk management policies, the key definitions and statistical methods used in their risk analysis, and information on their supervisor's acceptance of their approach. The quantitative disclosures include total gross credit risk exposures after accounting for offsets and without taking account of credit risk mitigation efforts. These exposures also must be reported in disaggregated form by exposure type (such as loans or off-balance-sheet exposures), by geographic region, by industry or counterparty type, and by residual contractual maturity. Impaired loans and past-due loans also must be reported by geographic region and industry type.[1]

Global exposure risk monitoring systems (GESs) are essential to portfolio risk management, facilitating loan approvals and providing information for the entire range of credit-related products. Bank managers employ exposure systems to approve facility limits, decide credit policy, review targets and controls, allocate capital, and settle on deal pricing. Sadly, credit information and monitoring systems at some banks have not kept pace with technology and Basel II. The most common causes of bank failures are unsatisfactory credit quality, inadequate management information systems, and inferior portfolio controls.

1. FRBSF Economic Letter 2003-22; August 1, 2003, Disclosure as a Supervisory Tool: Pillar 3 of Basel II.

Failure to identify and recognize deterioration in credit quality in a timely manner can aggravate and prolong the problem."[2]

Unless deterioration is identified and losses recognized by the establishment of adequate allowances or charge-offs in a timely manner, a bank might well persist in highly risky lending strategies or practices and thus accumulate significant loan losses, possibly resulting in failure. From a safety and soundness perspective, therefore, it is important that both exposure data gathering capabilities and accounting principles capture and reflect realistic measurements of assets, liabilities, equity, derivative contracts, off-balance sheet commitments, and related profits and losses. . . . Insufficient disclosure the result of poor exposure information systems increases chances that misleading or wrong information is passed along to senior officials setting exposure limits.[3]

Strategic Planning for the Loan Portfolio[4]

(Portfolio) strategies should be consistent with the strategic direction and risk tolerance of the institution. They should be developed with a clear understanding of their risk/reward consequences. They also should be reviewed periodically and modified as appropriate. In drawing up strategic objectives, management and the board should focus on the following:

- What percentage of a bank's balance sheet the loan portfolio should comprise
- Goals for loan quality
- Goals for portfolio diversification
- How much the portfolio should contribute to the bank's financial objectives
- Loan product mix
- Loan growth targets by product, market, and portfolio segment
- Product specialization
- What the bank's geographic markets should be
- Targeted industries and market share
- Community needs and service
- General financial objectives (e.g., increase fee income)

Global risk monitoring can be structured by partitioning systems into three "responsibility tiers": (1) customer responsibility, (2) family responsibility, and (3) facility responsibility. Data flow begins at the customer (unit) relationship level, combines at the "family level"—parent and subsidiaries/affiliates, completing the process at the senior coordination level—senior management, who actually sets family, industry, and cross border facility limits.

First Tier: Customer Responsibility (Coordination) Units

Gathering and processing obligors' loan information represents the core of any exposure information system, and it begins at home with relationship managers. If, for example, a multinational client has a thousand operations worldwide and deals with

2. The Basel Committee on Bank Supervision.

3. Ibid. (Emphasis added).

4. Comptroller of the Currency Administrator of National Banks; Loan Portfolio Management Comptroller's Handbook, April 1998 A-LPM.

200 relationship managers, it is conceivable that hundreds, if not thousands of facility exposure data sheets flow in a steady stream into the system.

Basic Information
– Name of relationship manager:
– Location/ Division/Credit Area:
– Statements received:
– Memo distributed:
– Maximum exposure, including derivatives and letter of credit exposures:
– Amount of facility requested and facility type:
– Outstandings:
– Terms:
– Last credit committee review including date, committee, and summary:

Company Background
– Customer:
– Address:
– Form of organization:
– Established:
– Customer since:
– Name and address or parent (if any)
– Name and address of guarantor (if any):
– Industry code (SIC):
– Geographic market area:
– Market strategy/niche:
– Major competitors:
– Industry/Economic summary:
– Assessment of principal customers, suppliers, and product lines:
– Competition:
– Problems to which this company is most vulnerable:
– Fiscal sales and profits: dollar and percentage change from last year:
– Key "payback" ratios—cash flow coverage and leverage:
– Management summary principal/officers:
– S&P (or similar) debt rating:
– Name and address of accountant:
– Accounting changes or qualifications:
– Fiscal date:

Other Information Supporting Facility
– Guarantors (if any):
– Collateral (if any):
– Date previous credit review filed:
– Previous risk grade:
– Loan pricing:
– Risk adjusted return on capital (RAROC):

- Documentation on file and updated:
- Subordination agreements, uniform commercial code filings, etc.:
- Total bank lines: $
- Lead bank:
- Other lenders:
- Present rating:
- Recommended rating:
- Report including Dun and Bradstreet, TRW, and Litigation Records:
- Trade experience:

Outside of optional data that banks chose to include (above), the Federal Reserve has established the minimum documentation required on bank examination reports. The following information (data) is normally entered onto computer-based loan review systems[5].

- Name and location of borrower:
- Notation if the borrower is an insider or a related interest of an insider:
- Business or occupation:
- Purpose of loan:
- Repayment source:
- Collateral summary and value:
- Loan officer assigned to the credit and internal rating of the credit:
- Total commitment and total outstanding balances:
- Examination date:
- Past-due/nonaccrual status:
- Amounts previously classified:
- Loan disposition (pass, special mention, or adverse classification):
- Rationale for examiner's conclusions (preferably in bullet form):
- Name or initials of the examiner reviewing the credit:
- Any significant comments by, or commitments from, management (including management's disagreement with the disposition of the loan, if applicable):
- Any noted documentation exceptions or loan administration policy or procedural weaknesses and any contravention of law, regulation, or policy

Second Tier: Family Responsibility (Coordination) Unit

This head office group, typically referred to as Family Responsibility (Coordination) Area, pools/decomposes family exposures—parent or holding company, subsidiaries, and affiliates. For purposes of establishing aggregate family, total (credit) exposure is expressed as (1) *primary* and (2) *settlement*. Primary exposures include direct exposures and indirect exposures, with direct exposures further categorized into full value and replacement (Figure 13-1).[6]

---

5. *Source*: Memo to the Officer in Charge of Supervision at Each Federal Reserve Bank: April 4, 1996, Subject Minimum Documentation Standards for Loan Line Sheets; Richard Spillenkothen, Director.

6. This section serves as an example, keeping in mind that GES perspectives can differ.

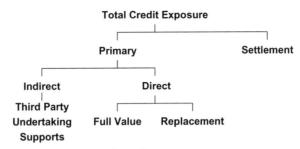

Figure 13-1 GES perspectives: total credit exposure.

Primary/Direct/Full Value Exposures

Examples of full value exposures include, but are not restricted to:

- *Own paper borrowing:* short-term unsecured borrowings not falling under a line of credit.
- *Lines of credit*: short-term lines usually established with a bank letter stating the approved advances and maximum amount allowed.
- *Joint credit lines:* the parent, together with each of its subsidiaries, may borrow singly or collectively, so that the aggregate amount of loans outstanding does not exceed the confirmed line.
- *Overlines*: a line of credit granted to a correspondent bank's customer.
- *Revolving Commitments:* legally binding obligations to extend credit for which a fee or other compensation is received. The credit risk of loan commitments stems from the possibility that the creditworthiness of the customer will deteriorate between the times the commitment is made and the loan takedown occurs.
- *Term loans*: nonrevolving commitments with maturities beyond one year. These loans generally contain periodic (annual, semiannual, or quarterly) amortization provisions.
- *Check or business credit*: credit services provided by three basic methods: overdraft system, cash reserve system, and special draft system.
- *Commercial letters of credit*: Letters of Credit are the written undertakings by a bank, made at the request of applicants, to honor drafts or other demands for payment to beneficiaries for merchandise shipped or services performed.
- *Acceptances*: exposures arising when letters of credit (L/Cs) mature but have not been retired.
- *Discounted bills or notes receivable (B/Rs):* loans are reduced at the time of each collection and liquidated when all the B/Rs are collected.
- *Construction loans:* loans for construction projects for a designated time period, with repayment contingent on the borrower obtaining permanent financing.
- *Secured loans*: factoring, loans secured with accounts receivables, inventory, or marketable securities.

Primary/Direct/Replacement

Replacement exposure (or fractional exposure) represents the unhedged cost of replacing defaulted parties when banks guarantee performance under derivative contracts.

In a manner of speaking, replacement exposure represents maximum loss possible on these contracts. For example, consider a simple (vanilla) interest rate swap. There are two ways of looking at default risk: (1) *actual exposure*—the measure of the loss if the counterparty were to default. Actual exposure is based on the movement in swap market rates between the inception of the agreement and the current date; and (2) *potential exposure*—based on a forecast of how market conditions might change between the present and the swap's maturity date, including in some manner the probability of default by the counterparty. Exposures on derivatives and similar contracts are managed so that they generally net out at day's end.

With traditional instruments—loans typically—the amount the counterparty is obliged to repay is the full or principal amount of the instrument. For these instruments, the amount at risk equals the principal amount. Derivatives are different. Because they derive value from an underlying asset or index, credit risk is not equal to the principal amount of the trade, but rather to the cost of replacing the contract if the counterparty defaults. This replacement value fluctuates over time and is made up of current replacement and potential replacement costs.

Others dealing in derivatives champion Monte Carlo simulation, probability analysis, and option valuation models as the best ways to derive potential replacement cost. Their analysis generally involves modeling the volatility of underlying variables and their effect on the value of the derivative contracts. These methods, drawing on data stored within a GES warehouse (discussed later in this chapter), can be used to derive average or "expected" exposure and maximum or "worst-case" exposure.

Primary/Indirect/Third-Party Undertaking, Supports

Indirect exposures include loans or obligations endorsed, guaranteed, or subject to repurchase agreements. Bank guarantees might be in the form of standby letters of credit, or commercial paper backup lines. They may be negotiated to cover performance under construction contracts, or they may serve as assurance that obligations will be honored under warranties.

Total Credit Exposure/Settlements

Settlement risk is the risk that a settlement in a transfer system fails to take place as expected. Three examples of settlement risk are foreign exchange, securities settlements, and over-the-counter derivatives. The risk that transactions cannot be settled can affect almost any type of asset (and instrument) requiring a transfer from one party to another. Settlement risk figures most prominently in currency trading because the daily settlement flows in foreign exchange clearing dwarfs just about any other exposure risk.

Since each trade involves two or more payments, daily settlement flows are likely to amount, in aggregate, to a multiple of this figure especially on standard expiration dates. Significantly, a report prepared by the Committee on Payment and Settlement Systems (CPSS) of the central banks of the G-10 countries maintains that a bank's maximum foreign-exchange settlement exposure could equal, or even surpass, the amount receivable for three days' worth of trades, so that at any point in time, the amount at risk to even a single counterparty *could exceed a bank's capital.*

GES and Loan Concentrations

Loans within the system are grouped so that exposures that have similar risk characteristics are combined. In addition to establishing strategic objectives for loan portfolios, senior management is charged with setting risk limits on lending activities. Exposure limits factor in historical loss experience, ability to absorb losses, and desired portfolio risk-adjusted return on capital. Exposure limits may be set in various ways, individually and in combination.[7] For example, limits may be set to individual loans, to geographical regions, to the volume of a particular segment of the loan portfolio, or to the structure of the portfolio as a whole. Risk concentrations are arguably the single most important cause of major problems in banks.[8]

1. A risk concentration is any single exposure or group of exposures with the potential to produce losses large enough (relative to a bank's capital, total assets, or overall risk level) to threaten a bank's health or ability to maintain its core operations.

2. Risk concentrations can arise in a bank's assets, liabilities, or off-balance-sheet items through the execution or processing of transactions (either product or service) or through a combination of exposures across these broad categories. Because lending is the primary activity of most banks, credit risk concentrations are often the most material risk concentrations within a bank.

3. Credit risk concentrations, by their nature, are based on common or correlated risk factors, which, in times of stress, have an adverse effect on the creditworthiness of each of the individual counterparties making up the concentration. Such concentrations are not addressed in the Pillar 1 capital charge for credit risk.

4. Banks should have in place effective internal policies, systems, and controls to identify, measure, monitor, and control their credit risk concentrations. Banks should explicitly consider the extent of their credit risk concentrations in their assessment of capital adequacy under Pillar 2. These policies should cover the different forms of credit risk concentrations to which a bank may be exposed. Concentrations include:
   a. Significant exposures to an individual counterparty or group of related counterparties. In many jurisdictions, supervisors define a limit for this kind of exposure, commonly referred to as a large exposure limit. Banks might also establish an aggregate limit for the management and control of all of its large exposures as a group.[9]
   b. Credit exposures to counterparties in the same economic sector or geographic region.
   c. Credit exposures to counterparties whose financial performance is dependent on the same activity or commodity.
   d. Indirect credit exposures arising from a bank's credit risk management activities (e.g., exposure to a single collateral type or to credit protection provided by a single counterparty).

---

7. Comptroller of the Currency Administrator of National Banks; Loan Portfolio Management Comptroller's Handbook, April 1998 A-LPM.

8. Ibid.

9. Ibid.

5. A bank's framework for managing credit risk concentrations should be clearly documented and should include a definition of the credit risk concentrations relevant to the bank and a discussion of how these concentrations and their corresponding limits are calculated. Limits should be defined in relation to a bank's capital, total assets or, where adequate measures exist, its overall risk level.

6. A bank's management should conduct periodic stress tests of its major credit risk concentrations and review the results of those tests to identify and respond to potential changes in market conditions that could adversely impact the bank's performance.

7. In the course of their activities, supervisors should assess the extent of a bank's credit risk concentrations, the way they are managed, and the degree to which the bank considers them in its internal assessment of capital adequacy under Pillar 2. Such assessments should include reviews of the results of a bank's stress tests. Supervisors should take appropriate actions.[10]

GES and Assessment of Capital Adequacy

Capital adequacy levels are tracked by exposure systems and reviewed by senior management to make sure that capital is appropriate for the nature and scale of a bank's business. Internal and outside auditors also consider the extent to which banks provide for unexpected events by setting appropriate capital levels. Basel's position is that capital ratios should be backed by enough (and accurate!) information, so that regulators are not faced with serious (Basel II) Pillar II issues. Banks are classified as "adequately capitalized" if they meet Basel requirements, but additional distinctions are made among levels of capital. Ratios implicitly or explicitly linked to capital adequacy include:

1. Return on assets
2. Return on equity
3. Loan loss coverage
4. Net charge-offs to loans
5. Equity capital to assets
6. Valuation reserve to loans
7. Ratio of provision for loan losses to net charge-offs
   a. This indicates whether provisions are in line with actual charge-offs.
8. Ratio of nonperforming assets to total loans and other real estate loans.
   a. This ratio indicates the proportion of total loans in default and the amount of real estate that had to be foreclosed and assumed. Some banks do not include loans until they are 90 or even more days in default.
9. Ratio of long-term subordinated debt to total capital accounts
   a. For "all insured commercial banks" the ratio is very low, since large banks usually sell these debt issues.
10. Earnings per share
11. Ratio of cash and U.S. government securities to assets and deposits
12. Ratio of capital accounts and equity accounts to assets and deposits
13. Ratio of capital accounts to loans (risk assets)

10. Ibid.

Liquidity Concerns

GES is an integral part of sound funds (liquidity) control, helping to ensure that liquidity requirements are continuously monitored. Thus, senior management can then take corrective action under preestablished guidelines.[11]

1. Limits on the loan to deposit ratio
2. Limits on the loan to capital ratio
3. General limits on the relationship between anticipated funding needs and available sources for meeting those needs (e.g., the ratio of anticipated needs/primary sources shall not exceed a certain percent)
4. Quantification of primary sources for meeting funding needs
5. Limits on the dependence on individual customers or market segments for funds in liquidity position calculations
6. Flexible limits on the minimum/maximum average maturity for different categories of liabilities (e.g., the average maturity of negotiable certificates of deposit shall not be less than a preordained period)
7. Minimum liquidity provision to be maintained to sustain operations while necessary longer-term adjustments are made.

Customer Relationship and Marketing

Customer information data banks include outstandings under credit lines, loan high points, fees paid for cash management services, average deposit balances, outstanding letters of credits and acceptances, profitability analyses, and affiliated data such as customers' personal loans and investments. The immediate benefits derived from information systems are obvious to lenders preparing client calls: bank customers are alert to bankers who are taking time to become familiar with their business. Clients exhort lenders to provide real-time information *accessible on laptops*—not just on loans serviced, but also on the aggregate account relationship, often globally. And to think that only a short time ago, lenders had to rifle through paper files or ask colleagues in other departments to obtain customer information.

GES and Disclosure to Outsiders

Banks are, of course, charged with proper disclosure to certain outsiders, mainly regulators and auditors of impaired and past-due loans. Examples of important disclosure include but are not restricted to[12]

1. Information dealing with accounting policies and methods used to document loans and allowance for impairment
2. Disclosure regarding methods used to determine specific along with general allowances and key assumptions
3. Information on significant concentrations of credit risk
4. Loan balances when interest accruals in accordance with the terms of the original loan agreement have ceased due to deterioration in credit quality

---

11. *Source*: FRB.
12. *Source:* FRB.

5. Reconciliations of movements in the allowance for loan impairment ("continuity schedule") showing separately various types of allowances
6. Balances and other information when loans have been restructured
7. Contractual obligations with respect to recourse arrangements and the expected losses under those arrangements

Exception Reports

In addition to constituents forming the foundation for sound lending policies, banks often place in service GES processes that target exceptions to that policy. Before a bank grants credit, GES source information, reports, established line limits, and a host of other credit communiqués are disseminated at appropriate levels. If requisite information is missing or loan data systems are incapable of providing management with enough information—and a loan is granted nonetheless—examiners will assuredly cite the "guilty" party.

Regulatory Reporting and GES

Submitting accurate, complete reports to regulators is serious business. Accordingly, regulators expect banks to develop quality systems and procedures required to prepare accurate detailed regulatory reports and maintain clear, concise records with emphasis on documenting adjustments.[13]

Consolidated Financial Statements for Bank Holding Companies (FR Y-9C)

- The FR Y-9C is the Consolidated Financial Statements for the Bank Holding Companies report. In general, the panel consists of all domestic bank holding companies with total consolidated assets of $500 million or more and all multibank holding companies with debt outstanding to the general public or engaged in certain nonbanking activities. The Y-9C is filed quarterly as of the last calendar day of March, June, September, and December.

Parent Company Only Financial Statements for Large Bank Holding Companies (FR Y-9LP)

- The FR Y-9LP report is the Parent Company Only Financial Statements for Large Bank Holding Companies. This report is filed by all domestic bank holding companies that file the FR Y-9C. If the top-tiered bank holding company files the FR Y-9C, then each bank holding company in a multitiered organization must also file a separate FR Y-9LP. The Y-9LP is filed quarterly as of the last calendar day of March, June, September, and December.

Parent Company Only Financial Statements for Small Bank Holding Companies (FR Y-9SP)

- The FR Y-9SP is the Parent Company Only Financial Statements for Small Bank Holding Companies. The panel consists of all domestic bank holding companies

---

13. Exposures arising from new bank products are automatically updated on advanced GES in real time.

with consolidated assets of less than $500 million and with only one subsidiary bank and multibank holding companies with consolidated assets of less than $500 million, without debt outstanding to the general public and not engaged in certain nonbanking activities. This report is filed semiannually at the end of June and December.

Bank Holding Company Performance Report (BHCPR)

- The BHCPR is designed to assist financial analysts and bank examiners in determining a bank holding company's financial condition and performance based on financial statements, comparative ratios, trend analyses, and percentile ranks relative to those of its peers. It is a computer-generated report of current and historical financial information produced quarterly for top-tier bank holding companies with consolidated assets of $500 million or more. The BHCPR is calculated for top-tier multibank holding companies engaged in a nonbank activity involving financial leverage or engaged in credit extending activities; or with outstanding debt to the general public. This report is filed quarterly as of the last calendar day of March, June, September, and December.

Report of Assets and Liabilities of U.S. Branches and Agencies of Foreign Banks (FFIEC 002)

- The FFIEC 002 is the Report of Assets and Liabilities of U.S. Branches and Agencies of Foreign Banks. This report is filed quarterly, as of the last calendar day of March, June, September, and December; however, supervisory agencies reserve the right to specify an alternative date at their option.

GES and Reports to the Board of Directors

The bank should establish an adequate system for monitoring and reporting risk exposures and assessing how the bank's changing risk profile affects the need for capital. The bank's senior management or board of directors should, on a regular basis, receive reports on the bank's risk profile and capital needs. These reports should allow senior management to:

- Evaluate the level and trend of material risks and their effect on capital levels;
- Evaluate the sensitivity and reasonableness of key assumptions used in the capital assessment measurement system;
- Determine that the bank holds sufficient capital against the various risks and is in compliance with established capital adequacy goals; and
- Assess its future capital requirements based on the bank's reported risk profile and make necessary adjustments to the bank's strategic plan accordingly.[14]

The board generally approves the *Annual Schedule for Loan Review* during the first meeting of each year. The schedule documents loan size, structure, performance,

---

14. *Core Principles for Effective Banking Supervision,* Basel Committee on Banking Supervision (September 1997), and *Core Principles Methodology,* Basel Committee on Banking Supervision (October 1999).

and type of loan, borrower affiliations and portfolio concentrations. Information must be complete enough to enable the board to draw conclusions concerning the portfolio's quality, along with the capital adequacy needed to cushion unexpected losses. The schedule for loan review allows sufficient time to prepare reports so that information gained from the loan review is available to management. Let's review other GES actualized and accounting reports that bank board of directors typically address.[15]

1. A monthly statement of balance condition and statement of income. Such statements, according to regulators, should be in reasonable detail, and compared to the prior month, the same month of a prior year and to the budget. The directors should receive explanations for all large variances, very difficult to attain without proper information systems.

2. Monthly statements of changes in all capital and reserve accounts. These statements should again detail variances.

3. Investment reports, which group the securities by classifications, reflect the book value, market value, yield, and a summary of purchases and sales.

4. Loan reports, which list significant past-due loans, trends in delinquencies, rate reductions, non-income-producing loans, and large new loans granted since the last report.

5. Audit and examination reports. Deficiencies in those reports should produce a prompt and efficient response from the board. The reports reviewed and actions taken should be reflected in the minutes of the board of director's meetings.

6. A full report of all new executive officer borrowing at any bank.

7. A monthly listing of type and amount of borrowing by the bank.

8. An annual presentation of bank insurance coverage.

9. All correspondence addressed to the board of directors from the Federal Reserve and any other source.

10. A monthly analysis of the bank's liquidity position.

11. An annual projection of the bank's capital needs.

12. A listing of any new litigation and a status report on existing litigation and potential exposure.

Cross-Border Exposure Reporting

The expansion of international lending has made an analysis of country risk an essential element in the overall evaluation of portfolio risk and the capital assigned to protect. Evaluating international exposures/concentrations requires lots of attention because adverse economic, social, or political developments in a country may prevent that country, its businesses, and other local borrowers from making timely payment of interest or principal to cross-border creditors. A constituent of country risk is "transfer risk," which arises when borrowers incur debt denominated in the currencies of other countries. Government policies, general economic conditions, and changes

---

15. *Source:* FRB: Duties and Responsibilities of Directors: Examination Procedures.

in the international environment may prevent borrowers from obtaining foreign currencies needed to service debt. Whatever the cause, foreign currency may not be sufficiently available to permit the government and other entities of a country to service foreign debt.

Exhibit 13-1 Country Exposure Information Report[16]

PART A—Information on exposure (as defined for Column 4) to any country that exceeds 1 percent of the reporting institution's total assets or 20 percent of its total capital, whichever is less.

Country	Amount of Cross-border Claims Outstanding After Mandated Adjustments for Transfer of Exposure (excluding derivative products)	Amount of Net Local Country Claims (Including derivative products)	Amount of Cross-border Claims Outstanding from Derivative Products after Mandated Adjustments for Transfer of Exposure	Total of Columns (1) Plus (2) Plus (3)	Distribution of Amounts in Column 1				
					By Type of Borrower			By Maturity	
					Banks	Public Sector Entities	Other	One Year and Under	Over One Year
	(1)	(2)	(3)	(4)	(5)	(6)	(7)	(8)	(9)

PART B—Information on exposure (as defined in Part A, Column 4) to any country *not* listed in Part A, where exposure exceeds 0.75 percent but does not exceed 1 percent of the reporting institution's assets or is between 15 percent and 20 percent of its total capital, whichever is less.

Names of countries where exposures meet the reporting criteria stated for Part B

_____

_____

_____

Total amount of exposure to all of the countries listed in Part B $ [   ]

Statement by management of the reporting institution concerning the information reported above. (OPTIONAL)

16. 2006 Country Exposure Report (FFIEC 009/009a).

Data Architecture

Data quality: Data collection and management tasks present the single greatest BASEL II challenge. For the first time, banks are required to pull data together from disparate financial systems, risk systems, and manual processes, each processing proprietary databases with minimal levels of standardization.

To ensure a solid foundation for the new support systems needed to support the revised and new credit risk guidelines, financial institutions will see paybacks from developing a robust functional architecture. Here, we will briefly outline several of the subsystems that the functional architecture for Credit Risk should have.

Data Supply Infrastructure

The new Capital Accord calls for one common data infrastructure to collect, aggregate, validate, and reconcile enterprisewide credit data. Some of the requirements, which this credit data architecture must satisfy, include product coverage, building block, and risk mitigation data.

Exposure Computation

The Credit Exposure Module will have to be built on the common credit data infrastructure. Banks using the Advanced IRB approach can supply their own exposure at default (EAD) estimates. The other two methods will need other functionalities supported.

Risk Mitigation

Some of the techniques and mechanisms that Basel II recognizes for credit risk mitigation include netting, guarantees, credit derivatives, and collateral. Support for both on- and off-balance netting needs to be provided. Guarantees and credit derivatives and their risk transfer effects should be modeled as given in the new Accord. Lastly, the collateral module should have a mechanism of applying pools of collateral to pools of facilities. It should be flexible enough to define the eligibility criteria of various collateral types and the application of haircuts based on volatility of collateral value, maturity mismatches, currency translation risks, and exposure value volatility.

Ratings Allocation

The ratings allocation module will have to manage and store risk ratings for all three approaches, as well as for purposes of regulatory audit under Pillar II. It should provide support for multiple ratings (internal and external) per obligor, per issue, and per country. Probability of default (PD), whether internally derived or externally acquired, must be captured for each rating grade or for specific obligors and facilities. User-defined logic needs to be supported in order to select the correct rating bucket in the event of multiple ratings and hence to determine the appropriate PD.

Risk Weight and Capital Computation

This module should provide risk-weighted assets on every exposure on a stand-alone basis after the application of adjustments for credit mitigation. It should support inputs from Credit Risk Models and adjustments using collateral, credit derivatives, guarantees, and netting arrangements.

Credit Capital Reporting Facility

The solution must have a reporting infrastructure with a complete range of Web-based reporting tools that will allow risk analysis to be performed along multiple dimensions. Furthermore, the reporting infrastructure must be flexible enough to support multiple reporting technologies and user reporting requirements.

Data Warehousing

A data warehouse is architecture for organizing data: a subject-oriented, integrated, time-variant, nonvolatile collection of data in support of information systems. A data warehouse stores tactical information answering the questions "who?" and "what?" A query submitted to a data warehouse might be: "What were aggregate construction loan outstandings between February 3 and April 14 for the ten largest branches in the third lending district?" Typically, data warehouse systems contain a set of programs that feed data from exposure positions through the bank (the global exposure environment). Three attributes of data warehouses are time-series data, data administration, and systems architecture:

1. *Time-Series Data*: A bank's data warehouse will support analysis of loan trends over time and compare data, current vs. historical.
2. *Data Administration*: Another critical factor is senior management commitment to maintenance of the quality of exposure data. Data administrators proactively manage how data is applied in tracking family exposures.
3. *Systems Architecture*: Databases should be able to retrieve large sets of aggregate and historical data within a quick response time, as mentioned earlier. A defining characteristic of data warehousing is the separation of operational and decision support functionality. By separating these two very different processing patterns, the data warehouse architecture enables both operational and decision support applications to focus on what they do best and therefore provide better performance and functionality.

Architecture is a design completed early in a project that encompasses (but does not necessarily detail) all aspects of the finished product. It includes:

- A description of the credit-related, exposure-related problem(s) that the system is designed to address.
- Local and global (bankwide) objectives, constraints, and critical success factors for the system.
- Project participants and the role of each participant—relationship bankers, family unit responsibility and senior-level facility approvals, and portfolio management described earlier.
- Major system components and the interfaces, connections, or communication paths among the components.
- Anticipated GES system enhancements, migration paths, and modifications.
- Individuals charged with developing the system on schedule and maintaining it over the long term.

Data Mining

Although some institutions have constructed large data warehouses that hold vast amounts of data, database solutions are often buried under mounds of data/statistics. Data mining technology is used to unlock the intelligence hidden in the databases by making predictions like forecasting "family" exposures, or by providing raw data senior bankers use to set guidelines: for example, exposure limits, limits on loan to deposit ratios, limits on loan to capital ratios, or general limits on the relationship between anticipated funding needs and funding sources. If banks really expect good paybacks from the large investments that are being made in creating data warehouses or data marts, they may need to turn to data mining technology in order to find effective database solutions. The characteristics associated with a data mining system include:

- *Response speed*: a major factor in any GES—the time it takes for the system to complete analysis or submit data at a desired level of accuracy. *Real time* is standard response speed, not the exception.

- *Compactness:* For smaller banks facing budget constraints, an exposure system's compactness can be a key budgetary issue. Compactness refers to how small bytewise the system can function without compromising portfolio objectives. In addition, compactness means the ease with which the system can be encoded into a compact portable format, whether embedded in a spreadsheet, coded into a specific computer language like Visual Basic, or carved on a silicon chip. If a system is too "bulky" to easily embed itself into a format making it usable where and when needed, the system itself may not be very useful.

- *Flexibility:* This is another concern GES designers face: the ease with which the relationships among the variables or their domains can be changed, or the goals of the system modified.

- *Embedability*: This additional attribute refers to the ease with which the bank's exposure system can be coupled with the infrastructure of the organization, particularly when banks merge or divest operations. After a reorganization or merger, for example, a formally localized system may be drafted as a component within a larger system or form part of other databases. In this case, the localized system must be able communicate with other components within the larger infrastructure. If the original system was outsourced, it may contain proprietary hardware/software that could result in time delays or the additional cost of renegotiated license agreements.

- *Friendliness*: Related to the idea of embedability is the system's "friendliness" and tolerance or noise. Friendliness—ease of use—refers to how complicated a GES's mining appears to users: line officers to senior bankers. A mining system's tolerance for data noise is a measure of its overall proficiency and accuracy.

- *Tolerance for complexity*: This refers to the degree to which a system is affected by interactions among various components of the process (e.g., the prodigious GES information network). Complex processes involve many, often nonlinear, interactions between variables. A quintessential example is default prediction involving a host of nonlinear systematic and unsystematic factors: industry growth/decline rates, macroeconomic factors, financial and operating leverage, market demographics, and so on. These variables interact in complex ways, which is why default prediction is high art and science, often requiring the service of specialists like KMV.

On-line Analytical Processing

In contrast to a data warehouse, on-line analytical processing takes a multidimensional view of aggregate data to provide quick access to strategic information for further analysis. On-line analytical processing is a software technology that allows users to gain insight from information transformed from raw data into real dimensionality.

A data warehouse stores and manages data for data access, whereas on-line analytical processing (OLAP) metamorphoses warehouse data into tactical information. OLAP ranges from basic navigation and browsing (often known as "slice and dice") to calculations and to more serious analyses such as time series and complex modeling. One important characteristic is multidimensional analysis: analysis reaching beyond conventional two-dimensional scrutiny to different dimensions of the same data, thus allowing for analyses across boundaries. For example, one possible query coming from a credit area VP might be: "What is the effect on the covariance–family exposure with respect to the general loan portfolio if operating segment 'A' reduced its outstanding loan by $45 million while the portfolio's standard deviation increased by 'X' basis points?" Or from a producer's perspective: "What will be the change in widget production cost if metal prices increased by $.25/pound and transportation costs went down by $.15/mile?"

OLAP's analytical and navigational activities include but are not limited to:

1. Calculations and modeling applied across dimensions, through hierarchies and/or across members
2. Trend analysis over sequential time periods
3. Slicing subsets for on-screen viewing
4. Drill-down to deeper levels of consolidation
5. Reach-through to underlying detail data
6. Rotation to new dimensional comparisons in the viewing area

Data Marts

A data mart is a simple form of a data warehouse that locks onto a single subject (or functional area), such as accountants in metropolitan district XYZ, who rendered clean opinions on deals that turned out bad, or the number of loan facilities a banker approved this quarter over $4 million. Data marts are often built and controlled by a single department within an organization. Given its single-subject focus, a data mart typically draws data from limited sources. The information flow could come from internal operational systems, a central data warehouse, or external data. In contrast, a *data warehouse* deals with multiple subject areas and is typically implemented and controlled by a central organizational unit such as Unit Family Coordinators which we reviewed earlier. Typically, a data warehouse assembles data from multiple-source systems.

Data marts are typically smaller and less complex than data warehouses; hence, they are easier to build and maintain. Table 13-1 summarizes the basic differences between a data warehouse and a data mart.

The three types of data marts are *dependent*, *independent*, and *hybrid*. Categorization is based primarily on the data source feeding into the data mart. Dependent data marts draw data from a central data warehouse that has already been created. Independent data marts, in contrast, are stand-alone systems built by drawing data directly

Table 13-1   Fundamental Differences Between Data Warehouses and Data Marts

	Data Warehouse	Data Mart
Realm	Senior-level Loan Risk Management—Global	Small Bank Letters of Credit Department
Fields	Multiple	Single Field/Subject
Data Sources	Numerous	Sparse
Normal Size	100 gigabytes to over a trillion bytes	Less than 100 gigabytes
Time to Realization	Months to Years	Weeks to Months

from operational or external sources of data or both. Hybrid data marts can draw data from operational systems or data warehouses.

A *dependent* data mart allows an operating unit, say a local bank's Department "D," to combine its data into one data warehouse, providing all the advantages that arise from centralization. An *independent* data mart can be created without the use of a central data warehouse to, say, smaller units within department "D." A *hybrid* data mart allows Department "D" to combine input from sources other than a data warehouse. This could be useful if the department required ad hoc integration—for example, if a new loan product were added to the Department "D" product mix.

Neural Networks

A neural network is thus a statistical technique that calculates weights (score points) for predictor characteristics (such as age and income) by self-learning from data examples (such as good and bad loans). A neural network can be trained to detect fraud by reviewing examples of good and fraudulent transactions on a bank's portfolio. Banks can set different thresholds on the transaction to determine the type and severity of the follow-up action they will take on the account. A key contributor to the neural network's accurate detection is its ability to factor in loan history to determine probabilities that an exposure will migrate 3, 4, and 5 credit grades. Neural networks adopt as they are inherently learning systems that adjust to changes in loan behavior patterns that match up to credit deterioration criterion. Different neural network models are in place to help financial institutions acquire, service, maintain, and manage portfolios.

Rule Induction

Rule induction is another approach used to reveal patterns in the data. This approach may be applied to the same data analyzed by neural networks. The data should include both positive and negative examples—such as a borrower table, where each record refers to another borrower, and the fields are various features, such as income, profit, address, industry, key ratios, and whether the firm paid the loan on time. If the last field is selected as the dependent variable, the rule induction software will reveal if-then rules such as: "If the firm's cash flow coverage ratio is between 15 and 25 percent, and the industry credit grade is below 5, the probability that the loan is not paid is 0.8. (There are 1,500 customers.)"

In addition to revealing if-then rules, a system may find if-and-only-if rules, such as: If the profit is less than 200, or industry is food manufacturing, the probability that the loan is not paid is 0.9, and if these two conditions do not hold (that is, the profit is at least 200, and the field of business is not food manufacturing), then the probability that the loan is paid is 0.85." Contrary to if-then rules, those sufficient conditions, if-and-only-if rules present necessary and sufficient conditions. Obviously, when an if-and-only-if rule such as the above-mentioned is discovered, we can say that we found a theory explaining almost all the cases in the data. Either the if-then rules or the if-then-only-if rules can then be used for the following purposes:

1. Issuing predictions for new cases: For example, when a new customer asks for a loan, the software calculates the probability that the customers will not pay the loan by applying the rules on the customer's data.
2. Revealing cases to be audited: Cases in the data that deviate from strong rules might be data errors or cases of fraud.
3. Revealing interesting phenomena: Unexpected rules denote interesting phenomena in the data.

Conclusion

There should be effective internal control systems and reliable information systems covering all significant activities of the institution.[17]

a. A critical component of an institution's activities is the establishment and maintenance of management information systems that cover the full range of its activities. This information is typically provided through both electronic and nonelectronic means. Institutions must be particularly aware of the organizational and internal control requirements related to processing information in an electronic form, and of the necessity to have an adequate audit trail. Management decision making could be adversely affected by unreliable or misleading information provided by systems that are poorly designed and controlled.

b. Information systems, including those that hold and use data in electronic form, must be secure, independently monitored, and supported by adequate contingency arrangements.

---

17. Guidelines on the Application of the Supervisory Review Process under Pillar 2 (CP03 revised) IG 18 25, January 2006.

CHAPTER 14

Credit Risk Rating and Debt Analysis (Credit Premium and Debt Options)

This chapter discusses applications of credit and debt valuation and analysis. Specifically, we look at the computations of credit spread or the risk premium that should be charged beyond a standard interest rate depending on the obligor's probability of default, valuing the effects of credit spreads on bond and debt prices, simulating and computing credit spreads of a firm, creating a credit shortfall risk and risk ratings table, running a cost-benefit analysis on new credit issues, determining the market value of risky debt, generating a debt amortization table, and valuing the price and yield on risky debt where the underlying interest rates are mean-reverting and stochastic, using the Merton and Vasicek models. As usual, the underlying theories and algorithms are not discussed. Rather, the hands-on applications are presented, inasmuch as this is an applications handbook for bankers on Basel II requirements. We forgo the detailed technical theories for the sake of brevity and instead focus on the pragmatic applications.

Illustrative Example: Credit Analysis—Credit Premium

File Name: *Credit Analysis—Credit Premium*
Location: *Modeling Toolkit | Credit Analysis | Credit Premium*
Brief Description: *Used to determine the credit risk premium that should be charged beyond any standard interest rates depending on the default probability of the debt holder*
Requirements: *Modeling Toolkit*

Credit Risk Premium Based on Default Probability

		Increasing Default Probability Increases Risk Premium				
		Default Probability	1.00%	0.25%	0.50%	2.00%	4.00%

| Standard Interest Rate | 5.00% |
| Default Probability | 1.00% |

| | | Default Risk Premium | 0.14% | 0.04% | 0.07% | 0.29% | 0.59% |

NPV	1386.09

				Adjusted Cash Flows	Adjusted Cash Flows	Adjusted Cash Flows	Adjusted Cash Flows	Adjusted Cash Flows
Year	Cash Flows	PVCF	Compute!					
1	100.00	95.24		94.42	95.03	94.83	93.59	91.94
2	100.00	90.70		90.04	90.54	90.37	89.38	88.05
3	100.00	86.38		85.87	86.26	86.13	85.36	84.33
4	100.00	82.27		81.90	82.18	82.08	81.52	80.77
5	100.00	78.35		78.11	78.29	78.23	77.86	77.35
6	100.00	74.62		74.49	74.59	74.56	74.36	74.08
7	100.00	71.07		71.04	71.06	71.05	71.01	70.95
8	100.00	67.68		67.75	67.70	67.72	67.82	67.95
9	100.00	64.46		64.61	64.50	64.54	64.77	65.08
10	1100.00	675.30		677.85	675.94	676.57	680.41	685.58

Figure 14-1   A simple credit spread premium computation given default probabilities.

This model is used to determine the credit risk premium that should be charged above the standard interest rate given the default probability of this debt or credit's anticipated cash flows. Enter the *years* and relevant *cash flows* in the model as well as the *interest rate* and anticipated *default probability* and click on **Compute** to determine the credit spread required (Figure 14-1). All values should be positive, and the default probability input can be determined using any of the Modeling Toolkit's default probability models. For instance, in Figure 14-1, assuming a regular 10-year bond with a $1,000 face value paying a 10 percent coupon rate, where the prevailing interest rate is 5 percent, a 1 percent default probability means that the default risk premium spread is 0.14 percent, making the total interest charge 5.14 percent.

Illustrative Example: Credit Analysis—Credit Risk Analysis and Effects on Prices

File Name: *Risk Analysis—Credit Risk and Effects on Prices*
Location: *Modeling Toolkit | Risk Analysis | Credit Risk and Effects on Prices*
Brief Description: *Values the effects of credit spreads as it applies to bond and debt prices*
Requirements: *Modeling Toolkit, Risk Simulator*

Banks selling fixed income products and vehicles need to understand interest rate risks. This model is used to analyze the effects of a credit spread as it is applied to the price of a bond or debt. The worse the credit rating, the higher the required credit spread and the lower the market value of the bond or debt. This model also allows you to determine what effects a change in credit rating has on the price of debt. (See Figure 14-2.)

Illustrative Example: Credit Analysis—External Debt Ratings and Spread

File Name: *Credit Analysis—Debt Rating and Spreads*
Location: *Modeling Toolkit | Credit Analysis | Debt Rating and Spreads*

CREDIT RISK ANALYSIS

Face Value	$100.00
Coupon Rate	5.50%
Maturity	10.00
Current Interest Rate	5.00%
Credit Spread	2.39%

Banks selling fixed income products and vehicles need to understand the interest rate risks. This model is used to analyze the effects of a credit spread applied to the price of a bond or debt. The worse the credit rating, the higher the required credit spread and the lower the market value of the bond or debt. This model also allows you to determine the effects of a change in credit rating.

Bond Price Original	$103.86
Bond Price with Spread	$86.96
Reduction in Value	-16.27%

Function Used: B2BondPriceDiscrete

Cash Flow	Interest Rates	Year	Rates with Spread		Credit Spreads	
$5.50	5.00%	1	7.39%			
$5.50	5.00%	2	7.39%		**Credit Spreads**	
$5.50	5.00%	3	7.39%		AAA	0.54%
$5.50	5.00%	4	7.39%		AA	0.64%
$5.50	5.00%	5	7.39%		A	0.90%
$5.50	5.00%	6	7.39%		BBB	1.23%
$5.50	5.00%	7	7.39%		BB	2.39%
$5.50	5.00%	8	7.39%		B+	2.86%
$5.50	5.00%	9	7.39%		B	3.40%
$105.50	5.00%	10	7.39%		B-	4.33%

Figure 14-2   Credit risk analysis.

Brief Description: *Simulating and computing the credit risk spread of a particular firm based on industry standards (EBIT and interest expenses of the debt holder), to determine the risk-based spread*

Requirements: *Modeling Toolkit, Risk Simulator*

This model is used to run a risk-based Monte Carlo simulation on a company's creditworthiness given that its earnings are uncertain. The goal is to determine this firm's credit category, given its financial standing and the industry in which it operates. Assuming we have a prespecified credit category for various industries (see the various Credit Risk Rating Models in the Basel II Modeling Toolkit for examples of how to determine the creditworthiness of a customer or company using internal and external risk-based models and how the credit category and scoring table is obtained), we can then determine what interest rate to charge the company for a new loan.

Figure 14-3 illustrates a manufacturing firm's earnings before interest and taxes (EBIT) as well as its current interest expenses, and benchmarked against some long-term government bond rate. On the basis of industry standards, the debt is then rated appropriately using a predefined credit ratings table, and the default spread and total interest charge are then computed.

Each of the inputs can be simulated using Risk Simulator to determine the statistical confidence of the cost of debt or interest rate to charge the client. For instance, Figure 14-4 shows that the 90 percent confidence interval has the cost of debt at between 5.07 and 7.43 percent, indicating the optimal rate to charge this obligor for the debt, based on the simulation of its EBIT and interest expense levels, and the resulting benchmark ratios.

Debt Rating and Spreads Analysis Under Uncertainty

Type of firm   Manufacturing Firm ▾
Earnings before interest and taxes $10,000
Current interest expenses $1,000
Current long term government bond rate   6.00%

Interest coverage ratio   **10.00**
Estimated Bond Rating   **AAA**
Estimated Default Spread   **0.20%**
Estimated Cost of Debt   **6.20%**

| For large manufacturing firms | | | | For financial service firms | | | | |
| *If interest coverage ratio is* | | | | *If long term interest coverage ratio is* | | | | |
>	≤ to	Rating is	Spread is	greater than	≤ to	Rating is	Spread is	EBIT Decline
-100000	0.199999	D	10.00%	-100000	0.049999	D	10.00%	-50.00%
0.2	0.649999	C	7.50%	0.05	0.099999	C	7.50%	-40.00%
0.65	0.799999	CC	6.00%	0.1	0.199999	CC	6.00%	-40.00%
0.8	1.249999	CCC	5.00%	0.2	0.299999	CCC	5.00%	-40.00%
1.25	1.499999	B-	4.25%	0.3	0.399999	B-	4.25%	-25.00%
1.5	1.749999	B	3.25%	0.4	0.499999	B	3.25%	-20.00%
1.75	1.999999	B+	2.50%	0.5	0.599999	B+	2.50%	-20.00%
2	2.499999	BB	2.00%	0.6	0.799999	BB	2.00%	-20.00%
2.5	2.999999	BBB	1.50%	0.8	0.999999	BBB	1.50%	-20.00%
3	4.249999	A-	1.25%	1	1.49999	A-	1.25%	-17.50%
4.25	5.499999	A	1.00%	1.5	1.99999	A	1.00%	-15.00%
5.5	6.499999	A+	0.80%	2	2.49999	A+	0.80%	-10.00%
6.5	8.499999	AA	0.50%	2.5	2.99999	AA	0.50%	-5.00%
8.50	100000	AAA	0.20%	3	100000	AAA	0.20%	0.00%

Figure 14-3   Simulating debt rating and spreads.

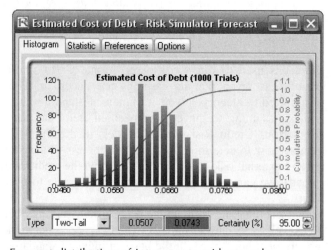

Figure 14-4   Forecast distribution of interest rate with spreads.

Illustrative Example: Credit Analysis—Internal Credit Risk Rating Model

File Name: *Credit Analysis—Internal Credit Risk Rating Model*
Location: *Modeling Toolkit | Credit Analysis | Internal Credit Risk Rating Model*

INTERNAL CREDIT RISK RATING MODEL
RATING OF CREDIT RISK

Probability of Default   1.00%
Recovery Rate   25.00%
Interest Charged   7.00%

Computed Credit Shortfall Risk 0.77%
Computed Risk Rating   B

Function: CreditRiskShortfall

Assumptions for Creating of a Risk Rating Table

Total Categories   12
Base Level (Requires Calibration) 2.0000

Functions: B2CreditRatingWidth

This is an internal credit rating model similar to the ones used by Moody's or other rating agencies. Obtain the Probability of Default from other probability of default models in the Basel II Toolkit, and use this model to determine the rating of this company or debt holder. To further enhance the model, the category widths of the Rating Table can be further refined through additional parameter width estimates given actual data.

Example Internal Rating Table

Category	Width	Min	Max	Rating
1	0.0244%	0.0000%	0.0244%	AAA
2	0.0488%	0.0244%	0.0733%	AA
3	0.0977%	0.0733%	0.1709%	A
4	0.1954%	0.1709%	0.3663%	BBB
5	0.3907%	0.3663%	0.7570%	BB
6	0.7814%	0.7570%	1.5385%	B
7	1.5629%	1.5385%	3.1013%	CCC
8	3.1258%	3.1013%	6.2271%	CC
9	6.2515%	6.2271%	12.4786%	C
10	12.5031%	12.4786%	24.9817%	DDD
11	25.0061%	24.9817%	49.9878%	DD
12	50.0122%	49.9878%	100.0000%	D

Figure 14-5   Internal credit risk rating model and risk table generation.

Brief Description: *Applying credit rating models like the ones used by Moody's to determine the credit shortfall risk and alphabetical risk rating given the probability of default*

Modeling Toolkit Function Used: *B2CreditRatingWidth*

This is an internal credit rating model similar to those used by Moody's or other rating agencies. The required *probability of default* input is obtained from other probability of default models in the Modeling Toolkit, and this model is used to determine the rating of this company or debt holder. To further enhance the model, the category widths of the rating table can be further refined through additional parameter width estimates given actual data. For instance, Figure 14-5 illustrates how a ratings table can be generated; this model shows how the previous model, the *External Debt Ratings and Spreads* example, is created. That is, by entering the desired number of total categories for the risk ratings table and the base level (which requires calibration with actual data, and typically ranges between 1.1 and 3.0), one can develop the ratings table and determine the risk rating and credit risk shortfall, given some probability of default, recovery rate, and interest charged to a company. In some instances, the base level can be calibrated using a backcasting approach where several base-level values are tested using various probabilities of default, and the resulting risk rating is used to benchmark against other industry standards.

Illustrative Example: Credit Analysis—Profit-Cost Analysis of New Credit

File Name: *Credit Analysis—Profit Cost Analysis of New Credit*
Location: *Modeling Toolkit | Credit Analysis | Profit Cost Analysis of New Credit*

Brief Description: *Analyzes the cost and profit from a potential credit issue based on the possibilities of nonpayment by the debt holder*

Requirements: *Modeling Toolkit, Risk Simulator*

Modeling Toolkit Function Used: *B2CreditAcceptanceCost, B2CreditRejection Cost*

This model is used to decide if new credit should be granted to a new applicant based on the requisite costs of opening the new account, as well as other incremental costs. In addition, the cost of funds and average time to receive payments, as well as the probability of nonpayment or default (use the various probability of default models in the Modeling Toolkit, which are also explained in previous chapters, to determine the cost of funds), we can then determine the cost of accepting and rejecting this new line of credit and the probability of breakeven. By using this model, a bank or credit-issuing firm can decide if it is more profitable to accept or reject the application, as well as compute the probability of breakeven on this line of credit by applying Monte Carlo risk-based simulation with Risk Simulator. (See Figure 14-6.)

Illustrative Example: Debt Analysis— Asset-Equity Parity Model

File Name: *Credit Analysis—Profit Cost Analysis of New Credit*
Location: *Modeling Toolkit | Debt Analysis | Asset-Equity Parity Model*

CREDIT ACCEPTANCE VS. REJECTION PROFIT/COST MODEL

Inputs

Acceptance Costs

Clerical Costs Associated With Opening Account	$30
Credit Investigation Cost	$40
Collection Costs	$130
Dollars Tied Up In Receivables (Sale Price)	$100,000
Probability of Non Payment	3.00%
Incremental Cost of Production and Selling	$60,000
Average Time in Days between Sale and Payment	45
Cost of Funds	15.00%

Rejection Costs

Marginal Profit From Sale	$40,000
Probability of Payment	97.00%

Outputs

Acceptance Cost	$3,849
Rejection Cost	$38,800
Accept/Reject Credit:	ACCEPT CREDIT
Probability B/E	37.98%

Figure 14-6   Credit acceptance and rejection profit and cost model.

ASSET-EQUITY PARITY MODEL
PRICING DEBT USING AN OPTIONS APPROACH

Input Assumptions

Book Value of Asset	$141.0000
Book Value of Debt	$31.0000
Time to Maturity (Years)	3.0000
Riskfree Rate	5.00%
Volatility of Equity	40.00%
Market Value of Equity	$141.0000

Market Value of Risky Debt	$26.5729
Required Return on Risky Debt	13.2192%
Market Value of Asset	$167.5729
Implied Volatility of Asset	43.2046%

Compute Implied Volatility!

Figure 14-7   Asset-equity options model.

Brief Description: *Applying the asset-equity parity relationship to determine the market value of risky debt and its required return, as well as the market value of asset and its volatility*

Requirements: *Modeling Toolkit*

Modeling Toolkit Function Used: *B2AEPMarketValueDebt, B2AEPMarketValue-Asset, B2AEPMarketValueAsset*

This model applies the Asset-Equity Parity (AEP) assumptions, whereby given the company's book values of debt and asset, as well as the market value of equity and its corresponding volatility, we can determine the company's market value of risky debt, the required return on the risky debt in the market, and the market value of the company's assets and the asset's volatility. Using the model, enter the relevant inputs and click on **Compute Implied Volatility** to determine the implied volatility of the asset (Figure 14-7).

This model also applies the basic parity assumption that the assets of a company equal any outstanding equity plus its liabilities. In publicly traded companies, the equity value and equity volatility can be computed using available stock prices, while the liabilities of the firm can be readily quantified based on financial statements. However, the market value and volatility of the firm's assets are not available or easily quantified (contrary to the book value of asset, which can be readily obtained through financial records). These values are required in certain financial, options, and credit analyses and can be obtained only through this asset-equity parity model. In addition, using the equity volatility and book value of debt, we can also impute the market value of debt and the required return on risky debt.

Illustrative Example: Debt Analysis—Cox Model on Price and Yield of Risky Debt with Mean Reverting Rates

File Name: *Debt Analysis—Cox Model on Price and Yield of Risky Debt with Mean Reverting Rates*

COX INGERSOLL ROSS MODEL
PRICING RISKY DEBT WITH MEAN-REVERTING INTEREST RATES

Input Assumptions

Time to Maturity of the Bond or Debt (Years)	1.0000
Riskfree Rate (Short Rate)	3.50%
Long-run Mean Rate	5.00%
Annualized Volatility of Interest Rate	20.00%
Market Price of Interest Rate Risk	5.00%
Rate of Mean Reversion	10.00%
Price of Zero Coupon Bond	**$0.9659**
Yield of Zero Coupon Bond	**3.47%**

Figure 14-8 Cox model with underlying mean-reverting interest rates.

Location: *Modeling Toolkit | Debt Analysis | Cox Model on Price and Yield of Risky Debt with Mean Reverting Rates*
Brief Description: *Applying the Cox model to price risky debt as well as to model the yield curve, assuming that interest rates are stochastic and follow mean-reverting rates*
Requirements: *Modeling Toolkit, Risk Simulator*
Modeling Toolkit Function Used: *B2CIRBondPrice, B2CIRBondYield*

The Cox-Ingersoll-Ross (CIR) stochastic model of mean-reverting interest rates is modeled here to determine the value of a zero-coupon bond as well as reconstructing the yield curve. This model assumes a stochastic and mean-reverting term structure of interest rates with a rate of reversion as well as long-run rate that the interest reverts to in time. There is also a Yield Curve CIR model in a later section that is used to generate the yield curve and term structure of interest rates using this CIR model.

You may also use Risk Simulator to run simulations on the inputs to determine the price and yield of debt, or to determine the input parameters such as the long-run mean rate and rate of mean reversion (use Risk Simulator's Statistical Analysis Tool to determine these stochastic input parameters when calibrated on historical data, and the Forecasting–Data Diagnostics model has examples of how to calibrate these stochastic input parameters based on historical data).

Illustrative Example: Debt Analysis—Debt Repayment and Amortization

File Name: *Debt Analysis—Debt Repayment and Amortization*
Location: *Modeling Toolkit | Debt Analysis | Debt Repayment and Amortization*
Brief Description: *Simulating interest rates on a mortgage and amortization schedule to determine the potential savings on interest payments if additional payments are made each period and when the interest rates can become variable and unknown over time*
Requirements: *Modeling Toolkit, Risk Simulator*

This is an amortization model examining a debt repayment schedule. In this example, we look at a 30-year mortgage with a portion of that period based on a fixed interest

	A	B	C	D	E	F	G	H	I	J	K	L
1												
2							Debt Repayment and Amortization Schedule					
3												
4		Mortgage at Initiation:		$550,000		Additional Payments:		$500				
5		Years to Maturity:		30		Once a month						
6		Interest Rate (Fixed):		4.50%								
7						Fixed Rate for the first		5		years		
8		Required Payment:		$2,786.77								
9		Variable Rate:		4.50%			With Minimum	Additional				
10							Payments	Payments	Savings			
11		Max Rate	4.50%			Total Checks Written:	$1,003,237	$867,182	$136,055			
12		Likely Rate	5.50%			Total Interest Paid:	$453,237	$317,192	$136,045	22.00	years	
13		Min Rate	6.50%			Total Principal Paid:	$550,000	$550,000	**30 Years to payoff if paying minimum**			
14												
15			Period	Start	Payment	Principal	Interest	Left	Rate	Years	Extras	
16			1	$550,000	$2,787	$724	$2,063	$549,276	Fixed	0.08 Years	$500	
17			2	$549,276	$2,787	$727	$2,060	$548,549	Fixed	0.17 Years	$500	
18			3	$548,549	$2,787	$730	$2,057	$547,819	Fixed	0.25 Years	$500	
19			4	$547,819	$2,787	$732	$2,054	$547,087	Fixed	0.33 Years	$500	
20			5	$547,087	$2,787	$735	$2,052	$546,351	Fixed	0.42 Years	$500	
21			6	$546,351	$2,787	$738	$2,049	$545,613	Fixed	0.5 Years	$500	
22			7	$545,613	$2,787	$741	$2,046	$544,873	Fixed	0.58 Years	$500	
23			8	$544,873	$2,787	$743	$2,043	$544,129	Fixed	0.67 Years	$500	
24			9	$544,129	$2,787	$746	$2,040	$543,383	Fixed	0.75 Years	$500	
25			10	$543,383	$2,787	$749	$2,038	$542,634	Fixed	0.83 Years	$500	
26			11	$542,634	$2,787	$752	$2,035	$541,882	Fixed	0.92 Years	$500	
27			12	$541,882	$2,787	$755	$2,032	$541,127	Fixed	1 Years	$500	
28			13	$541,127	$2,787	$758	$2,029	$540,370	Fixed	1.08 Years	$500	
29			14	$540,370	$2,787	$760	$2,026	$539,609	Fixed	1.17 Years	$500	
30			15	$539,609	$2,787	$763	$2,024	$538,846	Fixed	1.25 Years	$500	
31			16	$538,846	$2,787	$766	$2,021	$538,080	Fixed	1.33 Years	$500	
32			17	$538,080	$2,787	$769	$2,018	$537,311	Fixed	1.42 Years	$500	
33			18	$537,311	$2,787	$772	$2,015	$536,539	Fixed	1.5 Years	$500	
34			19	$536,539	$2,787	$775	$2,012	$535,764	Fixed	1.58 Years	$500	
35			20	$535,764	$2,787	$778	$2,009	$534,987	Fixed	1.67 Years	$500	

Figure 14-9   Debt amortization table.

rate and a subsequent period of variable rates with minimum and maximum caps. This model illustrates how the mortgage or debt is amortized and paid off over time, resulting in a final value of zero at the end of the debt's maturity (Figure 14-9). Furthermore, this model allows for some additional periodic (monthly, quarterly, semiannually, annually) payment, which will reduce the total amount of payments, the total interest paid, and the length of time it takes to pay off the loan. Notice that, initially, the principal paid off is low but increases over time. As a result, the initial interest portion of the loan is high but decreases over time as the principal is paid off.

The required input parameters are highlighted in boxes, and an assumption on the uncertain interest rate is set in cell D9, with a corresponding forecast cell at I12. By entering additional payments per period, you can significantly reduce the term of the mortgage (i.e., pay it off faster) and with much fewer total payments (the obligor ends up saving a lot on interest payments). A second forecast cell is set on J12 in order to find out the number of years it takes to pay off the loan if additional periodic payments are made. The mortgage holder can therefore use this model to determine the length of payoff and interest saved if making additional payments, and the bank can use it to determine the risk of early prepayment options on debt or credit.

Procedure

You may either change the assumptions or keep the existing assumptions and run the simulation:

1. Click on **Risk Simulator** | **Change Profile** and select the *Debt Repayment and Amortization* profile and click on **OK**.
2. Run the simulation by clicking on **Risk Simulator** | **Run Simulation**.

Interpretation

The resulting forecast chart on the example inputs indicates that the least amount of money that can be saved by paying an additional $500 per month can potentially save the mortgage holder $136,985 (minimum), and at most $200,406 (maximum) given the assumed uncertainty fluctuations of interest rates during the variable rate period. The 90 percent confidence level can also be obtained, meaning that 90 percent of the time, the total interest saved is between $145,749 and $191,192 (Figure 14-10).

In addition, the Payoff Year with Extra Payment forecast chart shows that, given the expected fluctuations of interest rates and the additional payments made per period, there is a 90 percent chance that the mortgage will be paid off between 20.9 and 21.8 years, with an average of 21.37 years (mean value). In addition, the quickest payoff is 20.67 years (minimum) and, if interest rates are on the high end, may take up to 22 years (maximum), as seen in Figures 14-10 to 14-13.

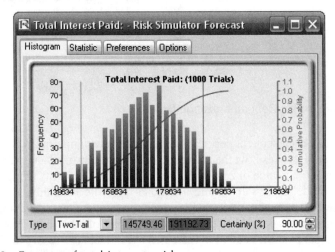

Figure 14-10   Forecast of total interest paid.

Statistics	Result
Number of Trials	1000
Mean	1.690514E+005
Median	1.692578E+005
Standard Deviation	1.359216E+004
Variance	1.847468E+008
Average Deviation	1.114806E+004
Maximum	2.004062E+005
Minimum	1.369855E+005
Range	6.342076E+004
Skewness	-0.0645
Kurtosis	-0.6164
25% Percentile	1.592768E+005
75% Percentile	1.787881E+005
Percentage Error Precision at 95% Confidence	0.4983%

Figure 14-11   Forecast statistics of total interest paid.

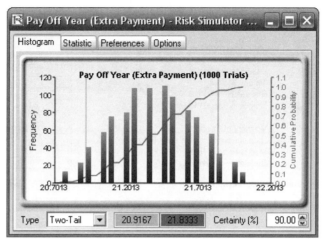

Figure 14-12   Forecast of payoff year.

Statistics	Result
Number of Trials	1000
Mean	21.3694
Median	21.3333
Standard Deviation	0.2818
Variance	0.0794
Average Deviation	0.2317
Maximum	22.0000
Minimum	20.6667
Range	1.3333
Skewness	0.0041
Kurtosis	-0.5953
25% Percentile	21.1667
75% Percentile	21.5833
Percentage Error Precision at 95% Confidence	0.0817%

Figure 14-13   Forecast statistics of total interest paid.

Illustrative Example: Debt Analysis—Merton Price of Risky Debt with Stochastic Asset and Interest

File Name: *Debt Analysis—Merton Price of Risky Debt with Stochastic Asset and Interest*

Location: *Modeling Toolkit | Debt Analysis | Merton Price of Risky Debt with Stochastic Asset and Interest*

Brief Description: *Computes the market value of risky debt using the Merton option approach assuming that interest rates are mean-reverting and volatile, while further assuming that the company's internal assets are also stochastic and changing over time*

Requirements: *Modeling Toolkit, Risk Simulator*

Modeling Toolkit Function Used: *B2MertonBondPrice*

MERTON MODEL OF RISKY DEBT
PRICING DEBT WITH STOCHASTIC ASSET AND STOCHASTIC INTEREST

Input Assumptions

Asset Book Value	$110.0000
Debt Book Value	$36.9940
Time to Maturity	20.00
Riskfree Rate	8.00%
Long-Run Interest Rate	8.00%
Volatility of Interest Rate	16.00%
Volatility of Asset	16.00%
Rate of Reversion of Interest Rate	15.00%
Market Price of Risk	1.00%
Correlation (Market to Asset)	0.00

Price of Debt	**$11.4392**

Figure 14-14 Merton model of risky debt assuming stochastic interest and asset movements.

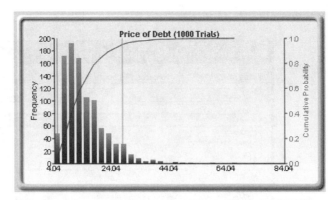

Type: Two-Tail, Lower: 4.9892, Upper: 27.7442, Certainty: 90.0000%

Figure 14-15 Simulation results on the Merton model.

The Merton model for risky debt computes the market value of debt while taking into account the book values of asset and debt in a company as well as the volatility of interest rates and asset value over time, where the interest rate is assumed to be stochastic in nature and is mean-reverting at some rate of reversion, to a long-term value (Figure 14-14). Furthermore, the market price of risk and the correlation of the company's asset value to the market are also imputed in the model. You can set the correlation and market price of risk to zero for indeterminable conditions, while the rate of reversion and long-run interest rates can be determined and modeled using Risk Simulator's Statistical Analysis tool. Simulation on any of the inputs can also be run using Risk Simulator, to determine the risk and statistical confidence of the market price of risky debt.

Illustrative Example: Debt Analysis—Vasicek Debt Option Valuation

File Name: *Debt Analysis—Vasicek Debt Option Valuation*
Location: *Modeling Toolkit | Debt Analysis | Vasicek Debt Option Valuation*

VASICEK MODEL
PRICING DEBT OPTIONS WITH MEAN-REVERTING INTEREST RATES

Input Assumptions

Face Value of Debt	$100.0000
Strike Price	$90.0000
Time to Bond Maturity (Years)	3.0000
Time to Option Expiration (Years)	2.0000
Interest Rate	8.00%
Long-Run Mean Reversion Level	9.00%
Rate of Mean Reversion	5.00%
Annualized Volatility	25.00%

Call Option Value   **$18.0134**
Put Option Value   **$8.0134**

Figure 14-16   Vasicek model of debt options with mean-reverting rates.

Brief Description: *Applies the Vasicek model of debt options assuming that the interest rates are stochastic, volatile, and mean-reverting*
Requirements: *Modeling Toolkit, Risk Simulator*
Modeling Toolkit Function Used: *B2VasicekBondCallOption, B2VasicekBondPutOption*

This is the Vasicek model (Figure 14-16) on bond or debt options, where the underlying debt issue changes in value based on the level of prevailing interest rates, which follows a mean-reverting tendency where the interest rate at any future period approaches a long-run mean interest rate with a rate of reversion and volatility around this reversion trend. Both options are European and can be executed only at termination. To determine other types of options such as American and Bermudan options, use the Modeling Toolkit's *Options on Debt* modules to build lattices on mean-reverting interest rates and their respective option values.

Illustrative Example: Debt Analysis—Vasicek Price and Yield of Risky Debt

File Name: *Debt Analysis—Vasicek Price and Yield of Risky Debt*
Location: *Modeling Toolkit | Debt Analysis | Vasicek Price and Yield of Risky Debt*
Brief Description: *Used to price risky debt and to compute the yield on risky debt, where the underlying interest rate structure is stochastic, volatile, and mean-reverting (also often used to compute and forecast yield curves)*
Requirements: *Modeling Toolkit, Risk Simulator*
Modeling Toolkit Function Used: *B2VasicekBondPrice, B2VasicekBondYield*

The Vasicek stochastic model of mean-reverting interest rates is modeled here to determine the value of a zero-coupon bond as well as the yield curve. This model assumes a mean-reverting term structure of interest rates with a rate of reversion as well as a long-run rate that the interest reverts to in time. Use the Yield Curve Vasicek

VASICEK & VAN DEVENTER MODEL
PRICING DEBT AND YIELD WITH MEAN-REVERTING INTEREST RATES

Input Assumptions

Time to Maturity of the Bond or Debt (Years)	1.00
Riskfree Rate (Short Rate)	5.00%
Long-run Mean Rate	8.00%
Annualized Volatility of Interest Rate	10.00%
Market Price of Interest Rate Risk	0.00%
Rate of Mean Reversion	1.00%

Price of Zero Coupon Bond	**$0.9527**
Yield of Zero Coupon Bond	**4.8495%**

Figure 14-17   Price and yield of risky debt.

model to generate the yield curve and term structure of interest rates using this model. You may also use Risk Simulator to run simulations on the inputs to determine the price and yield of the zero-coupon debt, or to determine the input parameters such as the long-run mean rate and rate of mean reversion (use Risk Simulator's Statistical Analysis Tool to determine these values based on historical data). See Figure 14-17.

CHAPTER 15

Interest Rate Risk, Foreign Exchange Risk, Volatility Estimation, Risk Hedging, Yield Curve Forecasting, and Advanced Forecasting Techniques

A handbook on Basel II risk analysis is not complete without a discussion of risk hedging, specifically, looking at the effects of interest rate risk, the risk return profiles of a portfolio and the effects of correlation on portfolio risk, foreign exchange risk, volatilities, and the construction of the yield curve. In addition, the topic of financial and economic forecasting techniques is also included at the end of the chapter because every banker and financial analyst should understand the various concepts of advanced analytical forecasting (used in forecasting an obligor's financial conditions, interest rates, inflation rates, stock performance, pro forma statements, and revenues or cash flows in the future, and many other applications). These topics are discussed in this chapter through the use of several hands-on example models.

Illustrative Example: Risk Analysis—Interest Rate Risk

File Name: *Risk Analysis—Interest Rate Risk*
Location: *Modeling Toolkit | Risk Analysis | Interest Rate Risk*
Brief Description: *Applies duration and convexity measures to account for a bond's sensitivity and how interest rate shifts can affect the new bond price, and how this new bond price can be approximated using these sensitivity measures*
Requirements: *Modeling Toolkit, Risk Simulator*

Modeling Toolkit Functions Used: *B2BondPriceDiscrete, B2ModifiedDuration, B2ConvexityDiscrete*

Banks that sell fixed income products and vehicles need to understand interest rate risks. This model uses duration and convexity to show how fixed income products react under various market conditions. To compare the effects of interest rate and credit risks on fixed income investments, this model uses modified duration and convexity (discrete discounting) to analyze the effects of a change in interest rates on the value of a bond or debt (Figure 15-1).

Duration and convexity are sensitivity measures that describe exposure to parallel shifts in the spot interest rate yield curve, applicable to individual fixed income instruments or entire fixed income portfolios. These sensitivities cannot warn of exposure to more complex movements in the spot curve, including tilts and bends, only parallel shifts. The idea behind duration is simple. Suppose a portfolio has a duration measure of 2.5 years. This means that the portfolio's value will decline about 2.5 percent for each 1 percent increase in interest rates—or rise about 2.5 percent for each 1 percent decrease in interest rates. Typically, a bond's duration will be positive, but exotic instruments such as mortgage-backed securities may have negative durations, or portfolios that short fixed income instruments or pay fixed for floating on an interest rate swap. Inverse floaters tend to have large positive durations. Their values change significantly for small changes in rates. Highly leveraged fixed income portfolios tend to have very large (positive or negative) durations.

In contrast, convexity summarizes the second most significant piece of information, or the nonlinear curvature of the yield curve, whereas duration measures the linear or

INTEREST RATE RISK

Face Value	$100.00
Coupon Rate	5.50%
Maturity	30.00
Current Interest Rate	5.50%
Interest Rate Shift	0.25%

Original Bond Price	$100.00	
Modified Duration	14.5337	
Convexity	321.0265	
	Duration and Convexity	**Using New Rates**
New Price After Shift	$96.47	$96.46
Price Change After Shift	-3.53%	-3.54%

Cash Flow	**Interest Rates**	**Year**	**Shifted Interest Rates**
$5.50	5.50%	1	5.75%
$5.50	5.50%	2	5.75%
$5.50	5.50%	3	5.75%
$5.50	5.50%	4	5.75%
$5.50	5.50%	5	5.75%
$5.50	5.50%	6	5.75%
$5.50	5.50%	7	5.75%
$5.50	5.50%	8	5.75%
$5.50	5.50%	9	5.75%
$5.50	5.50%	10	5.75%

Figure 15-1   Interest rate risk.

first-approximation sensitivity. Duration and convexity have traditionally been used as tools for immunization or asset-liability management. To avoid exposure to parallel spot curve shifts, an organization (such as an insurance company or defined benefit pension plan) with significant fixed income exposures might perform duration matching by structuring its assets so that their duration matches the duration of its liabilities, thereby allowing the two to offset each other. Even more effective (but less frequently practical) is duration-convexity matching, in which assets are structured so that durations and convexities match.

Illustrative Example: Risk Analysis—Portfolio Risk Return Profiles

File Name: *Risk Analysis—Portfolio Risk and Return Profile*
Location: *Modeling Toolkit | Risk Analysis | Portfolio Risk and Return Profile*
Brief Description: *Computes the risk and return on a portfolio of multiple assets given each asset's own risk and return as well as their respective pairwise covariances*
Requirements: *Modeling Toolkit*
Modeling Toolkit Functions Used: *B2PortfolioReturns, B2PortfolioVariance, B2PortfolioRisk*

This model (see Figure 15-2) computes the portfolio level's returns and risks given the percent allocated on various assets, the expected returns and risks on individual assets, and variance-covariance matrix of the asset mix. (You can use the Variance-Covariance tool in the Modeling Toolkit to compute this matrix if you have the raw stock returns data.)

For instance, if raw data on various assets exists (Figure 15-3), simply select the data area and run the Variance-Covariance Matrix tool under the **Modeling Toolkit | Statistical Tools** menu item. The generated results are shown in the computed Variance-Covariance worksheet. This is a very handy tool, and the portfolio risk return functions are very powerful as the portfolio risk σ_p (computed as volatility) is

PORTFOLIO RISK-RETURN PROFILE USING VARIANCE-COVARIANCE MATRIX

Variance Covariance Matrix	S&P 500	High-Yield Bonds	Leveraged Loans	Corporate Bonds	7-10 Year Treasuries	3-5 Year Treasuries	International Equities
S&P 500	0.0001549	0.0000164	-0.0000001	0.0000299	0.0000374	0.0000189	0.0000970
High-Yield Bonds	0.0000164	1.0000000	0.0000012	0.0000147	0.0000179	0.0000106	0.0000145
Leveraged Loans	-0.0000001	0.0000012	1.0000000	0.0000008	0.0000009	0.0000008	0.0000003
Corporate Bonds	0.0000299	0.0000147	0.0000008	0.0000449	0.0000516	0.0000303	0.0000263
7-10 year Treasuries	0.0000374	0.0000179	0.0000009	0.0000516	0.0000686	0.0000408	0.0000345
3-5 year Treasuries	0.0000189	0.0000106	0.0000008	0.0000303	0.0000408	0.0000266	0.0000209
International Equities	0.0000970	0.0000145	0.0000003	0.0000263	0.0000345	0.0000209	0.0001721

	Asset Allocation	Returns			
S&P 500	14.29%	11.07%			
High-Yield Bonds	14.29%	11.52%			
Leveraged Loans	14.29%	7.61%			
Corporate Bonds	14.29%	7.56%	Portfolio Expected Returns	8.430%
7-10 year Treasuries	14.29%	7.09%	Portfolio Variance	4.084%
3-5 year Treasuries	14.29%	6.04%	Portfolio Risk	20.210%
International Equities	14.29%	8.11%		
TOTAL	100.00%	8.43%		

Figure 15-2 Portfolio risk return profile.

Dates	S&P 500	High-Yield Bonds	Leveraged Loans	Corporate Bonds	7-10 Year Treasuries	3-5 Year Treasuries	International Equities
1/3/1992	-1.011%	1.309%	-0.062%	0.098%	-0.096%	-0.169%	-2.226%
1/10/1992	0.906%	0.528%	0.111%	-0.836%	-1.349%	-0.662%	-0.378%
1/17/1992	-0.807%	0.640%	0.285%	-0.143%	-0.491%	-0.097%	0.543%
1/24/1992	-1.613%	0.651%	0.362%	0.014%	0.009%	0.013%	-0.310%
1/31/1992	0.565%	0.639%	0.131%	0.528%	0.667%	0.500%	0.690%
2/7/1992	0.338%	0.654%	0.125%	-0.759%	-1.074%	-0.829%	-2.883%
2/14/1992	-0.255%	0.526%	0.156%	-0.117%	-0.262%	-0.253%	-0.346%
2/21/1992	0.309%	0.403%	0.479%	0.995%	1.239%	0.841%	0.597%
2/28/1992	-2.001%	0.681%	0.240%	-0.573%	-1.143%	-0.864%	-2.727%
3/6/1992	0.346%	0.214%	0.140%	-0.774%	-1.160%	-0.848%	-1.689%
3/13/1992	1.333%	0.311%	0.073%	0.334%	0.549%	0.255%	0.123%
3/20/1992	-1.884%	0.323%	0.138%	0.641%	0.768%	0.665%	-0.649%
3/27/1992	-0.483%	0.203%	0.127%	1.020%	0.919%	0.960%	-2.460%
4/3/1992	0.682%	0.183%	0.218%	0.441%	0.498%	0.675%	0.543%
4/10/1992	2.906%	0.178%	0.126%	-0.253%	-0.384%	-0.321%	2.116%
4/17/1992	-1.687%	0.133%	0.003%	-0.305%	-0.184%	0.038%	-0.623%
4/24/1992	0.858%	0.178%	0.182%	0.299%	0.018%	0.226%	1.035%
5/1/1992	0.853%	0.329%	0.126%	0.668%	0.839%	0.503%	1.956%
5/8/1992	-1.433%	0.448%	0.265%	0.778%	0.835%	0.614%	-0.340%
5/15/1992	0.958%	0.291%	0.126%	-0.001%	-0.144%	-0.178%	1.349%
5/22/1992	0.321%	0.406%	0.126%	0.363%	0.354%	0.410%	0.897%
5/29/1992	-0.450%	0.297%	0.144%	0.215%	0.345%	0.276%	-0.813%
6/5/1992	-0.900%	0.312%	0.065%	0.307%	0.334%	0.403%	-1.176%
6/12/1992	-1.486%	0.343%	0.127%	0.356%	0.435%	0.335%	-2.126%
6/19/1992	-0.054%	0.234%	0.112%	0.504%	0.640%	0.528%	-0.391%

Figure 15-3   Raw stock returns data.

$$\sigma_P = \sqrt{\sum_{k=1}^{N} w_k^2 \sigma_k^2 + \sum_{i=1}^{m}\sum_{j=1}^{n} 2w_i w_j \rho_{i,j} \sigma_i \sigma_j}$$ where each asset's (k) volatility is squared and multiplied by its weight squared, summed, and added to the summation of all pairwise correlations among the assets (ρ), by their respective weights (w) and volatilities (σ). For the example model, this equation expands to 21 cross terms and 7 squared terms, creating a relatively complicated equation to compute manually. By using the single *B2PortfolioRisk* equation in Modeling Toolkit, the process is greatly simplified.

Illustrative Example: Risk Hedging— Delta-Gamma Hedging

File Name: *Risk Analysis—Delta Gamma Hedge*

Location: *Modeling Toolkit | Risk Analysis | Delta Gamma Hedge*

Brief Description: *Sets up a delta-gamma riskless and costless hedge in determining the number of call options to sell and buy, the number of common stocks to buy, and the borrowing amount required, to set up a perfect arbitrage-free hedge*

Requirements: *Modeling Toolkit*

Modeling Toolkit Functions Used: *B2DeltaGammaHedgeCallSold, B2DeltaGammaHedgeSharesBought, B2DeltaGammaHedgeMoneyBorrowed*

DELTA-GAMMA HEDGE

Asset	$100.00
Strike for Call Sold	$95.00
Strike for Call Bought	$100.00
Maturity for Call Sold	0.50
Maturity for Call Bought	0.75
Riskfree	8.00%
Volatility	20.00%
DividendRate	3.00%
Sell Calls	**$9.7258**
Shares to Buy	**($6.9058)**
Buy Calls	**($9.1991)**
Borrow This Amount	**$6.3791**
Delta-Gamma-Neutral Position Sum	**$0.0000**

Figure 15-4   Delta-gamma hedging.

The Delta-Gamma hedge provides a hedge against larger changes in the asset value. This is done by buying some equity shares and a call option, which are funded by borrowing some amount of money and selling a call option at a different strike price. The net amount is a zero-sum game, making this hedge completely effective in generating a zero delta and zero gamma for the portfolio. Just as in a delta hedge, where the total portfolio's delta is zero (e.g., to offset a positive delta of some underlying assets), call options are sold to generate sufficient negative delta to completely offset the existing deltas to generate a zero delta portfolio. The problem associated with delta neutral portfolios is that secondary changes (i.e., larger shocks) are not hedged. Delta-gamma hedged portfolios, on the contrary, hedge both delta and gamma risk, making it a lot more expensive to generate. The typical problem with such a hedging vehicle is that in larger quantities, buying and selling additional options or underlying assets may change the market value and prices of the same instruments used to perform the hedge. Therefore, typically, a dynamic hedge, or continuously changing hedge portfolios, might be required.

Illustrative Example: Risk Hedging—Delta Hedging

File Name: *Risk Analysis—Delta Hedge*

Location: *Modeling Toolkit | Risk Analysis | Delta Hedge*

Brief Description: *Sets up a delta riskless and costless hedge in determining the number of call options to sell, the number of common stocks to buy, and the borrowing amount required, to set up a delta-neutral hedge*

Requirements: *Modeling Toolkit*

Modeling Toolkit Functions Used: *B2DeltaHedgeCallSold, B2DeltaHedgeShares-Bought, B2DeltaHedgeMoneyBorrowed*

The Delta hedge (Figure 15-5) provides a hedge against small changes in the asset value by buying some equity shares of the asset and financing it through selling a call option and borrowing some money. The net should be a zero-sum game to provide a hedge where the portfolio's delta is zero. For instance, an investor computes the portfolio delta of some underlying asset and offsets this delta through buying or selling

DELTA HEDGE

Asset	$100.00
Strike	$95.00
Maturity	0.50
Riskfree	8.00%
Volatility	20.00%
DividendRate	3.00%
Sell 1 Call	**$9.7258**
Shares to Buy	**($71.8275)**
Borrow This Amount	**$62.1018**
Delta-Neutral Position Sum	**$0.0000**

Figure 15-5   Delta hedging.

some additional instruments, such that the new instruments will offset the delta of the existing underlying assets. Typically, an investor holds some stocks or commodity like gold in the long position, creating a positive delta for the asset. To offset this, he or she sells some calls to generate negative delta, such that the amount of the call options sold on the gold is sufficient to offset the delta in the portfolio.

Illustrative Example: Risk Hedging—Effects of Fixed versus Floating Rates (Swaps)

File Name: *Risk Hedging—Effects of Fixed versus Floating Rates*
Location: *Modeling Toolkit | Risk Hedging | Effects of Fixed versus Floating Rates*
Brief Description: *Sets up various levels of hedging to determine the impact on earnings per share*
Requirements: *Modeling Toolkit*

This model illustrates the impact to financial earnings and earnings before interest and taxes (EBIT) on a hedged versus unhedged position (Figure 15-6). The hedge is done through an interest rate swap payments. Various scenarios of swaps (different combinations of fixed rate versus floating rate debt are tested and modeled) can be generated in this model to determine the impact to earnings per share (EPS) and other financial metrics.

The foreign exchange cash flow hedge model (shown next) goes into more detail on the hedging aspects of foreign exchange through the use of risk simulation.

Illustrative Example: Risk Hedging—Foreign Exchange Cash Flow Model

File Name: *Risk Hedging—Foreign Exchange Cash Flow Model*
Location: *Modeling Toolkit | Risk Hedging | Foreign Exchange Cash Flow Model*
Brief Description: *Illustrates how to use Risk Simulator for simulating foreign exchange rates to determine if the value of a hedged fixed exchange rate or floating unhedged rate is worth more*
Requirements: *Modeling Toolkit, Risk Simulator*

IMPACTS OF FIXED VERSUS FLOATING RATE INTEREST PAYMENTS

Assumptions

EBIT	$3,000,000
Shares Outstanding	$500,000
Tax Rate	40.00%
Total Debt	$8,000,000
Fixed Interest Rate	7.00%
LIBOR	6.00%
10-Year Swap Rate	5.00%

		Scenarios		
Initial Debt Structure (before swap)	**Current**	**1**	**2**	**3**
% of Total Debt in Fixed-rate Debt	50.00%	50.00%	50.00%	50.00%
% of Total Debt in Floating-rate Debt	50.00%	50.00%	50.00%	50.00%
Desired Debt Structure (after swap)				
% of Total Debt in Fixed-rate Debt	50.00%	30.00%	100.00%	0.00%
% of Total Debt in Floating-rate Debt	50.00%	70.00%	0.00%	100.00%
Change in Interest Rates	0.00%	1.00%	0.50%	0.10%
Financials				
Fixed-rate Debt	7.00%	7.00%	7.00%	7.00%
Floating-rate Debt	8.00%	9.00%	8.50%	8.10%
EBIT	3,000,000	3,000,000	3,000,000	3,000,000
Interest Expense	(600,000)	(672,000)	(560,000)	(648,000)
Net Income before Taxes	2,400,000	2,328,000	2,440,000	2,352,000
Earnings	1,440,000	1,396,800	1,464,000	1,411,200
EPS	2.8800	2.7936	2.9280	2.8224
Change in Interest Expense		72,000	(40,000)	48,000
Change in Earnings		(43,200)	24,000	(28,800)

Figure 15-6 Impacts of an unhedged versus hedged position.

This is a cash flow model used to illustrate the effects of hedging foreign exchange rates (Figure 15-7). The tornado sensitivity analysis illustrates that foreign exchange rate, or forex, has the highest effects on the profitability of the project (shown in the Excel model). Suppose for the moment that the project undertaken is in a foreign country (FC) and the values obtained are denominated in FC currency, and that the parent company is in the United States (U.S.) and requires that the net revenues be repatriated back to the U.S. The questions we try to ask here are, what is the appropriate forex rate to hedge at, and what are the appropriate costs for that particular rate? Banks will be able to provide your firm with the appropriate pricing structure for various exchange forward rates, but by using the model here, we can determine the added value of the hedge and hence, can decide if the value added exceeds the cost to obtain the hedge. This model is already preset for you to run a simulation.

The *Forex Data* worksheet shows historical exchange rates between the FC and U.S. Dollar. Using these values, we can create a *custom* distribution (we simply used the rounded values in our illustration), which is already preset in this example model. However, should you wish to replicate creating the simulation model, you can follow these steps:

1. Start a new profile (**Risk Simulator | New Profile**) and give it an appropriate name.

2. Go to the *Forex Data* worksheet, select the data in cells **K6:K490,** and click on **Edit | Copy** or **Ctrl + C**.
3. Select an empty cell (e.g., cell **K4**), click on **Risk Simulator | Set Input Assumption,** and select **Custom Distribution**.
4. Click on **Paste** to paste the data into the custom distribution, then **Update Chart** to view the results on the chart. Then, **File | Save** and save the newly created distribution to your hard drive. Close the set assumption dialog.
5. Go to the *Model* worksheet, select the **Forex** cell (**J9**), click on **Risk Simulator | Set Input Assumption**, and choose **Custom**; then, click on **Open** a distribution and select the previously saved custom distribution.
6. You may continue to set assumptions across the entire model, and set the **NPV** cell (**G6**) as a forecast (**Risk Simulator | Set Output Forecast**).
7. **RUN** the simulation with the custom distribution to denote an unhedged position. You can then rerun the simulation, but this time delete the custom distribution (use the *Delete Simulation Parameter* icon and not Excel's delete function, nor should you hit the keyboard's delete key) and enter in the relevant hedged exchange rate, indicating a fixed rate. You may create a report after each simulation to compare the results.

From the sample analysis, we see the following:

Table 15-1 Simulated results on hedging risk and returns

	Mean ($000)	Stdev ($000)	90% Confidence ($000)	CV (%)
Unhedged	2292.82	157.94	2021 to 2550	6.89%
Hedged at 0.85	2408.81	132.63	2199 to 2618	5.51%
Hedged at 0.83	2352.13	129.51	2147 to 2556	5.51%
Hedged at 0.80	2267.12	124.83	2069 to 2463	5.51%

From Table 15-1, several things are evident:

- The higher the hedged exchange rate is, the more profitable the project (e.g., 0.85 USD/FC is worth more than 0.80 USD/FC).
- The relative risk ratio, computed as the coefficient of variation (CV, or the standard deviation divided by the mean) is the same regardless of the exchange rate, as long as it is hedged.
- The CV is lower for hedged positions than for unhedged positions, indicating that the relative risk is reduced by hedging.

Cash Flow Model

Base Year	2006	Sum PV Net Benefits	FC 3,809.62		
Start Year	2006	Sum PV Investments	FC 1,389.08		
Discount Rate	15.00%	Net Present Value	FC 2,420.54		
Private-Risk Discount Rate	5.00%	Internal Rate of Return	54.64%		
Terminal Period Growth Rate	2.00%	Return on Investment	174.25%		
Tax Rate	40.00%	Profitability Index	2.74	Forex Rate (USD/FC)	0.85000

	2006	2007	2008	2009	2010	2011	2012	2013	2014	2015
Prod A Price	FC 10.00	FC 10.50	FC 11.00	FC 11.50	FC 12.00	FC 12.00	FC 12.00	FC 12.00	FC 12.00	FC 12.00
Prod B Price	FC 12.25	FC 12.50	FC 12.75	FC 13.00	FC 13.25	FC 13.25	FC 13.25	FC 13.25	FC 13.25	FC 13.25
Prod C Price	FC 15.15	FC 15.30	FC 15.45	FC 15.60	FC 15.75	FC 15.75	FC 15.75	FC 15.75	FC 15.75	FC 15.75
Prod A Quantity	50	50	50	50	50	50	50	50	50	50
Prod B Quantity	35	35	35	35	35	35	35	35	35	35
Prod C Quantity	20	20	20	20	20	20	20	20	20	20
Total Revenues (Local Currency)	FC 1,231.75	FC 1,268.50	FC 1,305.25	FC 1,342.00	FC 1,378.75	FC 1,378.75	FC 1,378.75	FC 1,378.75	FC 1,378.75	FC 1,378.75
Direct Cost of Goods Sold	FC 184.76	FC 190.28	FC 195.79	FC 201.30	FC 206.81	FC 206.81	FC 206.81	FC 206.81	FC 206.81	FC 206.81
Gross Profit	FC 1,046.99	FC 1,078.23	FC 1,109.46	FC 1,140.70	FC 1,171.94	FC 1,171.94	FC 1,171.94	FC 1,171.94	FC 1,171.94	FC 1,171.94
Operating Expenses	FC 157.50	FC 157.50	FC 157.50	FC 157.50	FC 157.50	FC 157.50	FC 157.50	FC 157.50	FC 157.50	FC 157.50
Sales, General and Admin. Costs	FC 15.75	FC 15.75	FC 15.75	FC 15.75	FC 15.75	FC 15.75	FC 15.75	FC 15.75	FC 15.75	FC 15.75
Operating Income (EBITDA)	FC 873.74	FC 904.98	FC 936.21	FC 967.45	FC 998.69	FC 998.69	FC 998.69	FC 998.69	FC 998.69	FC 998.69
Depreciation	FC 10.00	FC 10.00	FC 10.00	FC 10.00	FC 10.00	FC 10.00	FC 10.00	FC 10.00	FC 10.00	FC 10.00
Amortization	FC 3.00	FC 3.00	FC 3.00	FC 3.00	FC 3.00	FC 3.00	FC 3.00	FC 3.00	FC 3.00	FC 3.00
EBIT	FC 860.74	FC 891.98	FC 923.21	FC 954.45	FC 985.69	FC 985.69	FC 985.69	FC 985.69	FC 985.69	FC 985.69
Interest	FC 2.00	FC 2.00	FC 2.00	FC 2.00	FC 2.00	FC 3.00	FC 4.00	FC 5.00	FC 6.00	FC 7.00
EBT	FC 858.74	FC 889.98	FC 921.21	FC 952.45	FC 983.69	FC 982.69	FC 981.69	FC 980.69	FC 979.69	FC 978.69
Taxes	FC 343.50	FC 355.99	FC 368.49	FC 380.98	FC 393.48	FC 393.08	FC 392.68	FC 392.28	FC 391.88	FC 391.48
Net Income	FC 515.24	FC 533.99	FC 552.73	FC 571.47	FC 590.21	FC 589.61	FC 589.01	FC 588.41	FC 587.81	FC 587.21
Depreciation/Amort	FC 13.00	FC 13.00	FC 13.00	FC 13.00	FC 13.00	FC 13.00	FC 13.00	FC 13.00	FC 13.00	FC 13.00
Net Working Capital	FC 0.00	FC 0.00	FC 0.00	FC 0.00	FC 0.00	FC 0.00	FC 0.00	FC 0.00	FC 0.00	FC 0.00
Capital Expenditures	FC 0.00	FC 0.00	FC 0.00	FC 0.00	FC 0.00	FC 0.00	FC 0.00	FC 0.00	FC 0.00	FC 0.00
Free Cash Flow	FC 528.24	FC 546.99	FC 565.73	FC 584.47	FC 603.21	FC 602.61	FC 602.01	FC 601.41	FC 600.81	FC 4,709.36
Investments	FC 500.00		FC 1,500.00							
Net Free Cash Flow	-FC 1,105.97	FC 546.99	FC 565.73	FC 584.47	FC 603.21	FC 602.61	FC 602.01	FC 601.41	FC 600.81	FC 4,709.36

Figure 15-7   Hedging foreign exchange risk cash flow model.

- It seems that the exchange rate hedge should be above 0.80, such that the hedged position is more profitable than the unhedged.
- In comparing a hedged versus unhedged position, we can determine the amount of money the hedging is worth. For instance, going with a 0.85 USD/FC means that on average, the hedge is worth $115,990,000 (computed as $2,408.81 − $2,292.82 denominated in thousands). This means that as long as the cost of the hedge is less than this amount, it is a good idea to pursue the hedge.

Illustrative Example: Risk Hedging—Hedging Foreign Exchange Exposure

File Name: *Risk Hedging—Hedging Foreign Exchange Exposure*
Location: *Modeling Toolkit | Risk Hedging | Hedging Foreign Exchange Exposure*
Brief Description: *Illustrates how to use Risk Simulator for simulating foreign exchange rates to determine the value of a hedged currency option position*
Requirements: *Modeling Toolkit, Risk Simulator*

This model is used to simulate possible foreign exchange spot and future prices and the effects on the cash flow statement of a company under a freely floating exchange rate versus using currency options to hedge the foreign exchange exposure (Figure 15-8).

Figure 15-9 shows the effects of the Value at Risk (VaR) of a hedged versus unhedged position. Clearly, the right-tailed VaR of the loss distribution is higher without the currency options hedge. Figure 15-10 shows that there is a lower risk,

Hedging Foreign Exchange Exposure with Currency Options

Months	Jan	Feb	Mar	April	May	June	July
FX Spot Rate (HKD/USD)	7.80	7.40	7.60	7.30	7.10	7.20	7.40
FX Strike Rate (HKD/USD)	7.80	7.80	7.80	7.80	7.80	7.80	7.80
Maturity (Years)	0.5833	0.5000	0.4167	0.3333	0.2500	0.1667	0.0833
Risk Free Rate US	6.08%	6.08%	6.08%	6.08%	6.08%	6.08%	6.08%
Risk Free Rate HK	5.06%	5.06%	5.06%	5.06%	5.06%	5.06%	5.06%
Volatility	15.00%	15.00%	15.00%	15.00%	15.00%	15.00%	15.00%
Quantity of Options Hedge Position	10,000,000	10,000,000	10,000,000	10,000,000	10,000,000	10,000,000	10,000,000
Currency Put Option Value (HKD/USD)	0.3229	0.5191	0.3795	0.5533	0.7012	0.6034	0.4102
Market Value of Hedge	3,229,135	5,191,009	3,794,813	5,532,845	7,012,229	6,034,435	4,102,320
Intrinsic Value	0	4,000,000	2,000,000	5,000,000	7,000,000	6,000,000	4,000,000
Time Value	3,229,135	1,191,009	1,794,813	532,845	12,229	34,435	102,320

FINANCIAL STATEMENTS IMPACTS - MARK TO MARKET

Balance Sheet (in 000's)	Jan	Feb	Mar	April	May	June	July
Option Contract	3,229,135	5,191,009	3,794,813	5,532,845	7,012,229	6,034,435	4,102,320
Other Comp Income (SE)		4,000,000	2,000,000	5,000,000	7,000,000	6,000,000	4,000,000

Income Statement (in 000's)							
Hedge Effectiveness gain or loss per period		(2,038,126)	603,805	(1,261,969)	(520,615)	22,206	67,884
Hedge Effectiveness sum of all periods							(3,126,816)
Market Cost of Hedge (Current Period)							3,229,135
Income from Option Exercise							4,000,000
Net Valuation of Hedging							770,865
Income from Hedging							74,770,865
Income from No Hedge							74,000,000
Loss Distribution from Hedging							3,229,135
Loss Distribution from No Hedge							4,000,000

Figure 15-8   Hedging currency exposures with currency options.

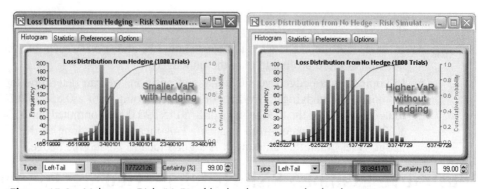

Figure 15-9   Values at Risk (VaR) of hedged versus unhedged positions.

Figure 15-10   Forecast statistics of the loss distribution.

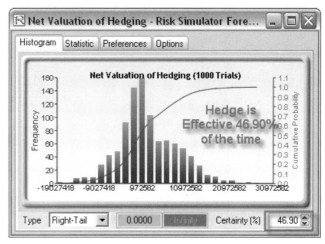

Figure 15-11   Hedging effectiveness.

lower risk to returns ratio, higher returns, and less swing in the outcomes of a currency hedged position than an exposed position. Finally, Figure 15-11 shows the hedging effectiveness, that is, how often the hedged is in the money and becomes usable.

Illustrative Example: Volatility—Implied Volatility

File Name: *Volatility—Implied Volatility*
Location: *Modeling Toolkit | Volatility | Implied Volatility*
Brief Description: *Computes the implied volatilities using an internal optimization routine, given the values of a call or put option, as well as all their required inputs*
Requirements: *Modeling Toolkit, Risk Simulator*
Modeling Toolkit Function Used: *B2ImpliedVolatilityCall, B2ImpliedVolatilityPut*

This implied volatility computation is based on an internal iterative optimization, which means it will work under typical conditions (without extreme volatility values, i.e., too small or too large). It is always good modeling technique to recheck the imputed volatility using an options model to make sure the answers coincide with each other before adding more sophistication to the model. That is, given all the inputs in an option analysis as well as the option value, the volatility can be imputed (Figure 15-12).

Illustrative Example: Volatility—Volatility Computations

File Name: *Volatility—Volatility Computations*
Location: *Modeling Toolkit | Volatility | Volatility Computations*
Brief Description: *Uses Risk Simulator to apply Monte Carlo simulation in order to compute a project's volatility measure*
Requirements: *Modeling Toolkit, Risk Simulator*

IMPLIED VOLATILITY FUNCTION

Asset	$100.00
Strike	$95.00
Maturity	0.50
Riskfree	8.00%
Volatility	25.00%
DividendRate	3.00%

Call Option	$10.9126
Put Option	$3.6764

Implied Volatility Calculation

Call Option	25.00%
Put Option	25.00%

Figure 15-12 Getting the implied volatility from options.

The volatility used in the option models can be estimated in several ways; the most common and valid approaches are:

Logarithmic Cash Flow Returns Approach or Logarithmic Stock Price Returns Approach: This method is used mainly for computing the volatility on liquid and tradable assets such as stocks in financial options; however, it is sometimes used for other traded assets such as price of oil and price of electricity. The drawback is that discounted cash flow models with only a few cash flows will generally overstate the volatility and this method cannot be used when negative cash flows occur. This means that this volatility approach is only applicable for financial instruments and not for real options analysis. The benefits include its computational ease, transparency, and modeling flexibility of the method. In addition, no simulation is required to obtain a volatility estimate. The approach is simply to take the annualized standard deviation of the logarithmic relative returns of the time-series data as the proxy for volatility. The Modeling Toolkit function **B2Volatility** is used to compute this volatility, where the time series of stock prices is arranged in time series (can be chronological or reverse chronological). See the **Log Cash Flow Returns** example model under the Volatility section of Modeling Toolkit for details.

Exponentially Weighted Moving Average (EWMA) Models: This approach is similar to the previous approach of logarithmic cash flow returns approach, using the **B2Volatility** function, to compute the annualized standard deviation of the natural logarithms of relative stock returns. The difference here is that the most recent value will have a higher weight than values further in the past. A **lambda** or weight variable is required (typically, industry standards set this at 0.94), where the most recent volatility is weighted at this lambda value, and the period before that is $(1 - \text{lambda})$, and so forth. See the **EWMA** example model under the Volatility section of Modeling Toolkit for details.

Logarithmic Present Value Returns Approach: This approach is used mainly when computing the volatility on assets with cash flows. A typical application is in real options. The drawback of this method is that simulation is required to obtain a single volatility and is not applicable for highly traded liquid assets such as stock prices. The benefit includes the ability to accommodate certain negative cash flows and applies more rigorous analysis than the logarithmic cash flow returns approach, providing a more accurate and conservative estimate of volatility when assets are analyzed. In addition, within say, a cash flow model, multiple simulation assumptions can be set up (we can insert any types of risks and uncertainties, such as related assumptions, correlated distributions, and nonrelated inputs, multiple stochastic processes, and so forth). We allow the model to distill all the interacting risks and uncertainties in these simulated assumptions, and we obtain the single value volatility, which represents the integrated risk of the project. See the **Log Asset Returns** example model under the Volatility section of Modeling Toolkit for details.

Management Assumptions and Guesses: This approach is used for both financial options and real options. The drawback is that the volatility estimates are very unreliable and are only subjective best guesses. The benefit of this approach is its simplicity—this method is very easy to explain to management the concept of volatility, and this approach is simplistic in both execution and interpretation. That is, most people understand what probability is but have a hard time understanding what volatility is. Using this approach, we can impute one from another. See the **Probability to Volatility** example model under the Volatility section of Modeling Toolkit for details.

Generalized Autoregressive Conditional Heteroskedasticity (GARCH) Models: These models are used mainly for computing the volatility on liquid and tradable assets such as stocks in financial options. This model is sometimes used for other traded assets such as price of oil and price of electricity. The drawback is that a lot of data and advanced econometric modeling expertise are required, and this approach is highly susceptible to user manipulation. The benefit is that rigorous statistical analysis is performed to find the best-fitting volatility curve, providing different volatility estimates over time. The EWMA or exponentially weighted moving average model is a simple weighting model, whereas the GARCH model is a more advanced analytical and econometric model that requires advanced algorithms such as generalized method of moments to obtain the volatility forecasts. See the GARCH model example in the Modeling Toolkit's Volatility section.

This chapter only provides a high-level review of all these methods as it pertains to hands-on applications. For detailed technical details on volatility estimates, please refer to Chapter 7A of Dr. Johnathan Mun's *Real Options Analysis*, Second Edition (Wiley, 2005). The section of this book goes into the theory and step-by-step interpretation of the method, whereas this chapter only describes the approach on a very superficial level, focusing on the application rather than the theory.

Procedure

For the **Log Cash Flow Approach**, make sure that your data are all positive (this approach cannot apply negative values). The Log Cash Flow Approach worksheet illustrates an example computation of downloaded Microsoft stock prices (Figure 15-13). The stock price is first converted into relative returns; then the natural logarithm is applied. The standard deviation of 52 weeks' log relative returns are computed and multiplied by the square root of 52 to annualize it. You can perform **Edit | Copy** and **Edit | Paste Special | Values Only** using your own stock closing prices to compute the volatility using the existing model, or you can use the Modeling Toolkit's **B2Volatility** function. If your periodicity changes (e.g., if you are using monthly or daily data), make sure the standard deviation is on the appropriate number of periods

Downloaded Weekly Historical Stock Prices of Microsoft | **Volatility Computations**

Date	Open	High	Low	Close	Volume	Adj. Close*	LN Relative Returns	Moving Average Volatilities		
27-Dec-04	27.01	27.10	26.68	26.72	52388840	26.64	-0.0108	17.87%		
20-Dec-04	27.01	27.17	26.78	27.01	77413174	26.93	0.0019	17.84%		
13-Dec-04	27.10	27.40	26.80	26.96	108628300	26.88	-0.0045	17.85%		
6-Dec-04	27.10	27.44	26.91	27.08	83312720	27.00	-0.0055	18.00%	*One-Year Annualized Volatility Analysis*	
29-Nov-04	26.64	27.44	26.61	27.23	83103200	27.15	0.0235	18.13%		
22-Nov-04	26.75	26.82	26.10	26.60	61834599	26.52	-0.0098	18.03%	Average	21.89%
15-Nov-04	27.34	27.50	26.84	26.86	75375960	26.78	-0.0011	18.10%	Median	22.30%
8-Nov-04	29.18	30.20	29.13	29.97	109385736	26.81	0.0223	18.20%		
1-Nov-04	28.16	29.36	27.96	29.31	85044019	26.22	0.0468	18.28%		
25-Oct-04	27.67	28.54	27.55	27.97	70791679	25.02	0.0084	17.71%		
18-Oct-04	28.07	28.89	27.58	27.74	74671318	24.81	-0.0092	17.80%		
11-Oct-04	28.20	28.27	27.80	27.99	48396360	25.04	0.0000	19.68%		
4-Oct-04	28.44	28.59	27.97	27.99	52998320	25.04	-0.0091	19.69%		
27-Sep-04	27.17	28.32	27.04	28.25	61783760	25.27	0.0346	19.68%		
20-Sep-04	27.44	27.74	27.07	27.29	59162520	24.41	-0.0082	19.62%		
13-Sep-04	27.53	27.57	26.74	27.51	51599880	24.61	0.0008	20.52%		
7-Sep-04	27.29	27.51	27.14	27.49	51935175	24.59	0.0139	21.30%		
30-Aug-04	27.30	27.68	26.85	27.11	45125980	24.25	-0.0127	21.25%		
23-Aug-04	27.27	27.67	27.09	27.46	40526880	24.56	0.0123	22.29%		
16-Aug-04	27.03	27.50	26.89	27.20	52571740	24.26	0.0066	22.29%		
9-Aug-04	27.26	27.75	26.86	27.02	51244080	24.10	-0.0041	22.42%		
2-Aug-04	28.27	28.55	27.06	27.14	56739100	24.20	-0.0488	22.42%		
26-Jul-04	28.36	28.81	28.13	28.49	65555220	25.41	0.0163	21.97%		
19-Jul-04	27.62	29.89	27.60	28.03	114579322	25.00	0.0198	22.11%		
12-Jul-04	27.67	28.36	27.25	27.48	57970740	24.51	-0.0138	22.02%		
6-Jul-04	28.32	28.33	27.55	27.86	61197249	24.85	-0.0250	22.04%		
28-Jun-04	28.60	28.84	28.17	28.57	66214339	25.48	0.0000	22.07%		
21-Jun-04	28.22	28.66	27.81	28.57	82202478	25.48	0.0079	22.30%		
14-Jun-04	26.55	28.50	26.53	28.35	97727643	25.28	0.0574	22.48%		
7-Jun-04	26.02	26.79	25.97	26.77	55540250	23.87	0.0311	22.71%		
1-Jun-04	26.13	26.28	25.86	25.95	49284475	23.14	-0.0107	22.86%		
24-May-04	26.05	26.35	25.60	26.23	51927460	23.39	0.0129	23.19%		
17-May-04	25.47	26.27	25.42	25.89	56652040	23.09	0.0013	23.21%		
10-May-04	25.63	26.19	25.43	25.86	58864200	23.06	0.0030	23.87%		
3-May-04	26.19	26.60	25.75	25.78	60847680	22.99	-0.0134	24.07%		
26-Apr-04	27.45	27.55	25.96	26.13	77381899	23.30	-0.0527	24.05%		
19-Apr-04	25.08	27.72	25.06	27.54	102244677	24.56	0.0903	23.67%		
12-Apr-04	25.48	25.77	25.10	25.16	56472679	22.44	-0.0124	21.92%		
5-Apr-04	25.81	25.98	25.35	25.48	52838950	22.72	-0.0144	22.50%		
29-Mar-04	25.25	25.90	24.85	25.85	69704180	23.05	0.0322	22.76%		
22-Mar-04	24.48	25.51	24.01	25.03	92829802	22.32	0.0158	22.59%		

Figure 15-13   Historical stock prices and volatility estimates.

that covers a year (e.g., 252 trading days per year or 12 months per year), and then multiply the result by the square root of the number of periods per year to obtain the annualized volatility.

For the **Log Present Value Approach**, negative cash flows are allowed. In fact, this approach is preferred to the first approach when modeling volatilities in a real options world. First, set some assumptions in the model or use the preset assumptions as is. The *Intermediate X Variable* is used to compute the project's volatility (Figure 15-14). Run the simulation and view the Intermediate Variable X's forecast chart. Go to the **Statistics** tab and obtain the **Standard Deviation** (Figure 15-15); annualize it by multiplying the value with the square root of the number of periods per year. In this case, the annualized volatility is 11.64 percent as the periodicity is annual; otherwise, multiply the standard deviation by square root of 4 if quarterly data is used, or square root of 12 if monthly data is used, and so on.

For the **Volatility to Probability** approach, rough estimates of volatility can be obtained, or the approach can be used to explain to senior management the concept of volatility (Figure 15-16). To illustrate, say your model has an expected value of $100M, and the best-case scenario as modeled or expected or anticipated by subject matter experts or senior management is $150M with a 10 percent chance of exceeding this value; we compute the implied volatility as 39.02%.

Although this is a rough estimate, it is nonetheless a good start if you do not wish to perform elaborate modeling and simulation to obtain a volatility measure. Furthermore, this approach can be reversed. That is, instead of getting volatility from proba-

Log Present Value Approach

Input Parameters		Results	
Discount Rate (Cash Flow)	15.00%	Present Value (Cash Flow)	**$286.66**
Discount Rate (Impl. Cost)	5.00%	Present Value (Impl. Cost)	**$189.58**
Tax Rate	10.00%	Net Present Value	**$97.09**

	2002	2003	2004	2005	2006
Revenue	$100.00	$200.00	$300.00	$400.00	$500.00
Cost of Revenue	$40.00	$80.00	$120.00	$160.00	$200.00
Gross Profit	$60.00	$120.00	$180.00	$240.00	$300.00
Operating Expenses	$22.00	$44.00	$66.00	$88.00	$110.00
Depreciation Expense	$5.00	$10.00	$15.00	$20.00	$25.00
Interest Expense	$3.00	$6.00	$9.00	$12.00	$15.00
Income Before Taxes	$30.00	$60.00	$90.00	$120.00	$150.00
Taxes	$3.00	$6.00	$9.00	$12.00	$15.00
Income After Taxes	$27.00	$54.00	$81.00	$108.00	$135.00
Non-Cash Expenses	$12.00	$12.00	$12.00	$12.00	$12.00
Cash Flow	$39.00	$66.00	$93.00	$120.00	$147.00
Implementation Cost	$25.00	$25.00	$50.00	$50.00	$75.00

Volatility Estimates (Logarithmic PV Approach)

PV (0)	$39.00	$57.39	$70.32	$78.90	$84.05
PV (1)	N/A	$66.00	$80.87	$90.74	$96.65
Static PV (0)	$39.00	$63.65	$81.21	$93.10	$100.51
Variable X	-0.1216				
Volatility	Simulate to obtain volatility				

Figure 15-14   Using the PV Asset approach to model volatility.

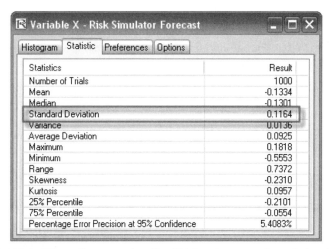

Figure 15-15   Volatility estimates using the PV Asset approach and simulation.

bility, we can get probability from volatility. This reversed method is very powerful in explaining the concept of volatility to senior management. To illustrate, we use the *worst-case scenario* model next.

Suppose you run a simulation model and obtain an annualized volatility of 35 percent and need to explain what this means to management. Well, 35 percent volatility does not mean that there is a 35 percent chance of something happening. Nor does it mean that the expected value can go up 35 percent, and so forth. Management has a hard time understanding volatility, but probability is a simple concept. For instance, if you state that there is a 10 percent chance of something happening (like a product being successful in the market), management understands this to mean that 1 out of 10 products will be a superstar. So, we take advantage of this fact and impute the probability from the analytically computed volatility to explain the concept in a simplified manner. Using the *probability to volatility worst-case scenario* model and assuming that the worst-case is defined as the 10 percent left tail (you can change this if you wish) and that your analytical model provides a 35 percent estimate of volatility, in Excel, simply click on **Tools | Goal Seek** and set the cell as **F24** (the volatility cell) to change to the value 35 percent (your computed volatility) by *changing the cell alternate worst-case scenario* (**F21**). Clicking on **OK** returns the value $55.15 in cell F21. This means that a 35 percent volatility can be described as a project with an expected NPV of $100M but is risky enough such that the worst-case scenario, which can occur less than 10 percent of the time, will reduce the project's NPV to $55.15M. In other words, there is a 1 in 10 chance the project will be below $55.15M or 9 out of 10 times will make at least $55.15M (Figure 15-17).

For the **EWMA and GARCH** approaches, multiple volatility forecasts that are time specific are obtained. That is, a term structure of volatility can be determined

Probability to Volatility (Best-Case Scenario)

Expected NPV of the Asset:	$100.00
Alternate Best-Case Scenario NPV:	$150.00
Percentile of Best-Case Scenario:	90.00%
Implied Volatility Estimate:	39.02%

Figure 15-16   Probability to volatility approximation approach.

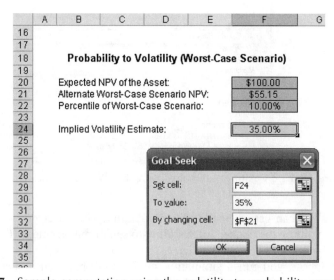

Figure 15-17   Sample computation using the volatility to probability approach.

using these approaches. GARCH models are used mainly in analyzing financial time-series data, in order to ascertain their conditional variances and volatilities. These volatilities are then used to value the options as usual, but the amount of historical data necessary for a good volatility estimate remains significant. Usually, several dozen—and even up to hundreds—of data points are required to obtain good GARCH estimates. In addition, GARCH models are very difficult to run and interpret and require great facility with econometric modeling techniques. GARCH is a term that incorporates a family of models that can take on a variety of forms, known as GARCH(p,q), where p and q are positive integers that define the resulting GARCH model and its forecasts. In most cases for financial instruments, a GARCH(1,1) is sufficient and is most generally used.

For instance, a GARCH (1,1) model takes the form of

$$y_t = x_t \gamma + \varepsilon_t$$
$$\sigma_t^2 = \omega + \alpha \varepsilon_{t-1}^2 + \beta \sigma_{t-1}^2$$

where the first equation's dependent variable (y_t) is a function of exogenous variables (x_t) with an error term (ε_t). The second equation estimates the variance (squared volatility σ_t^2) at time t, which depends on a historical mean (ω), news about volatility from the previous period, measured as a lag of the squared residual from the mean equation (ε_{t-1}^2), and volatility from the previous period (σ_{t-1}^2). The exact modeling specification of a GARCH model is beyond the scope of this book and is not discussed. Suffice it to say that detailed knowledge of econometric modeling (model specification tests, structural breaks, and error estimation) is required to run a GARCH model, making it less accessible to the general analyst. The other problem with GARCH models is that the model usually does not provide a good statistical fit. That is, it is impossible to predict the stock market, and of course equally, if not harder, to predict a stock's volatility over time. Figure 15-18 shows a GARCH(1,1) on a sample set of historical stock prices using the B2GARCH model in the Modeling Toolkit software.

In order to create GARCH forecasts, start the Modeling Toolkit and open the **Volatility | GARCH** model. You will see a model that resembles Figure 15-19. Follow these procedures to create the volatility estimates. Note that Risk Simulator has an automated GARCH module that is much simpler to apply and use.

- Enter in the Stock Prices in chronological order (e.g., cells I6:I17).
- Use the B2GARCH function call in the Modeling Toolkit. For instance, cell K3 has the function call: "B2GARCH($I$6:$I$17,$I$19,1,3)" where the stock price inputs are in cells I6:I17, the periodicity is 12 (i.e., there are 12 months in a year, to obtain the annualized volatility forecasts), predictive base is 1, and we forecast for a sample of 3 periods into the future. Because we will copy and paste the function down the column, make sure that absolute addressing is used (i.e., $I$6 and not relative addressing of I6).
- Copy cell K3 and paste the function on cells K3:K20 (select cell K3 and drag the fill handle to copy the function down the column). This is because the first three values are the GARCH estimated parameters of Alpha, Beta, and Gamma, and at the bottom (e.g., cells K18:K20) are the forecast values.
- With the entire column selected (cells K3:K20 selected), hit F2 on the keyboard, and then hold down Shift+Ctrl and hit Enter. This will update the entire matrix with GARCH forecasts.

	A	B	I	J
1			Computed Alpha	0.082019894
2	User Data		Couted Beta	0.914890346
3	Period	Inputs	Computed Omega	0.000000968
4	1	459.11		0.00%
5	2	460.71	Periods/Year	0.00%
6	3	460.34	252	17.80%
7	4	460.68		17.10%
8	5	460.83		16.44%
9	6	461.68		15.80%
10	7	461.66		15.22%
11	8	461.64		14.64%
12	9	465.97		14.09%
13	10	469.38		14.21%
14	11	470.05		14.08%
15	12	469.72		13.57%
16	13	466.95		13.08%
17	14	464.78		12.89%
18	15	465.81		12.61%
19	16	465.86		12.20%
20	17	467.44		11.78%

Figure 15-18 Sample GARCH(1,1) model.

			GARCH (1,1)
		Alpha	0.1939450
		Beta	0.0000000
Periods (Months)	Stock Price	Omega	0.0013381
Jan	10.25		0.00%
Feb	13.25		0.00%
Mar	15.36		41.16%
Apr	15.95		25.86%
May	16.15		13.92%
Jun	15.45		12.81%
Jul	14.55		14.36%
Aug	15.50		15.63%
Sep	16.00		15.93%
Oct	16.20		13.57%
Nov	16.90		12.81%
Dec	17.50		14.22%
			13.74%
Periodicity	12		13.74%
			13.74%

Figure 15-19 Setting up a GARCH model.

Note that the GARCH function has several inputs, as follows:

Stock Prices

This is the time series of stock prices, where typically dozens of data points are required for a decent volatility forecast.

Periodicity

This is a positive integer indicating the number of periods per year (e.g., 12 for monthly data, 252 for daily trading data, and so forth), assuming you wish to annualize the volatility. For getting periodic volatility, enter 1.

Predictive Base

This is the number of periods (the time-series data) back to use as a base to forecast volatility. The higher this number, the longer the historical base is used to forecast future volatility.

Forecast Period

This is a positive integer indicating how many future periods beyond the historical stock prices you wish to forecast.

Variance Targeting

This variable is set as False by default (even if you do not enter anything here) but can be set as True. False means that the omega variable is automatically optimized and computed. The suggestion is to leave this variable empty. If you wish to create mean-reverting volatility with variance targeting, set this variable as True.

P

This is the number of previous lags on the mean equation.

Q

This is the number of previous lags on the variance equation.

Illustrative Example: Yield Curve—CIR Model

File Name: *Yield Curve—CIR Model*

Location: *Modeling Toolkit | Yield Curve | CIR Model*

Brief Description: *The CIR model for estimating and modeling the term structure of interest rates and yield curve approximation assuming the interest rates are mean-reverting*

Requirements: *Modeling Toolkit, Risk Simulator*

Modeling Toolkit Function Used: *B2CIRBondYield*

The yield curve is the time-series relationship between interest rates and the time to maturity of the debt. The more formal mathematical description of this relationship is called the term structure of interest rates. The yield curve can take on various shapes. The normal yield curve means that yields rise as maturity lengthens and the yield curve is positively sloped, reflecting investor expectations for the economy to grow in the future (and hence, an expectation that inflation rates will rise in the future). An inverted yield curve occurs when the opposite occurs, where the long-term yields fall below short-term yields, and long-term investors will settle for lower yields now if they think the economy will slow or even decline in the future, indicative of a worsening economic situation in the future (and hence, an expectation that inflation will remain low in the future). Another potential situation is a flat yield curve, signaling uncertainty in the economy. The yield curve can also be humped or show a smile or a frown. The yield curve over time can change in shape through a twist or bend, a parallel shift, or a movement on one end versus another.

Because the yield curve is related to inflation rates as discussed earlier, and central banks in most countries have the ability to control monetary policy to target inflation rates, inflation rates are mean-reverting in nature. This also implies that interest rates are mean-reverting, as well as stochastically changing over time.

This section shows the Cox-Ingersoll-Ross (CIR) model, which is used to compute the term structure of interest rates and yield curve (Figure 15-20). The CIR model assumes a mean-reverting stochastic interest rate. The rate of reversion and long-run mean rates can be determined using Risk Simulator's statistical analysis tool. If the

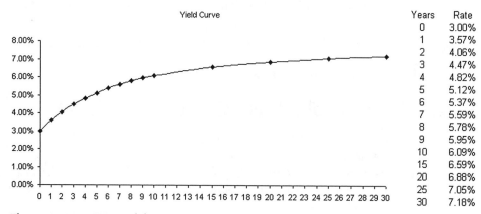

CIR MODEL
YIELD CURVE CONSTRUCTION

Input Assumptions

Time to Maturity of the Bond or Debt (Years)	1.00
Riskfree Rate (Short Rate)	3.00%
Long-run Mean Rate	8.00%
Annualized Volatility of Interest Rate	6.00%
Market Price of Interest Rate Risk	0.00%
Rate of Mean Reversion	25.00%

Yield of Zero Coupon Bond　　　　　**3.5744%**

Years	Rate
0	3.00%
1	3.57%
2	4.06%
3	4.47%
4	4.82%
5	5.12%
6	5.37%
7	5.59%
8	5.78%
9	5.95%
10	6.09%
15	6.59%
20	6.88%
25	7.05%
30	7.18%

Figure 15-20   CIR model.

long-run rate is higher than the current short rate, the yield curve is upward sloping, and vice versa.

Illustrative Example: Yield Curve—Curve Interpolation BIM Model

File Name: *Yield Curve—Curve Interpolation BIM*
Location: *Modeling Toolkit | Yield Curve | Curve Interpolation BIM*
Brief Description: *The BIM model for estimating and modeling the term structure of interest rates and yield curve approximation using a curve interpolation method*
Requirements: *Modeling Toolkit, Risk Simulator*
Modeling Toolkit Function Used: *B2YieldCurveBIM*

A number of alternative methods exist for estimating the term structure of interest rates and the yield curve. Some are fully specified stochastic term structure models, whereas others are simply interpolation models. The former are models such as the CIR and Vasicek models (illustrated in other sections in this book), and the latter are interpolation models such as the Bliss or Nelson approach. This section examines the Bliss interpolation model (Figure 15-21) for generating the term structure of interest rates and yield curve estimation. This model requires several input parameters whereby their estimations require some econometric modeling techniques to calibrate their

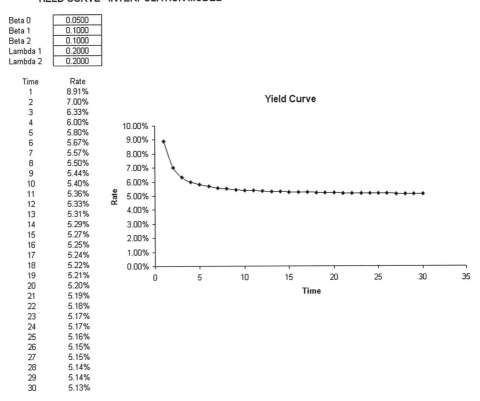

Figure 15-21 BIM model.

values. The Bliss approach is a modification of the Nelson-Siegel method by adding another generalized parameter. Virtually any yield curve shape can be interpolated using these models, which are widely used at banks around the world.

Illustrative Example: Yield Curve—Curve Spline Interpolation and Extrapolation Model

File Name: *Yield Curve—Spline Interpolation and Extrapolation*
Location: *Modeling Toolkit | Yield Curve | Spline Interpolation and Extrapolation*
Brief Description: *The multidimensional cubic spline model for estimating and modeling the term structure of interest rates and yield curve approximation using a curve interpolation and extrapolation methods*
Requirements: *Modeling Toolkit, Risk Simulator*
Modeling Toolkit Function Used: *B2CubicSpline*

The cubic spline polynomial interpolation and extrapolation model is used to "fill in the gaps" of missing spot yields and term structure of interest rates whereby the model can be used to both interpolate missing data points within a time series of interest rates (as well as other macroeconomic variables such as inflation rates and commodity prices or market returns) and to extrapolate outside of the given or known range, useful

Years	Spot Yields
0.0833	4.55%
0.2500	4.47%
0.5000	4.52%
1.0000	4.39%
2.0000	4.13%
3.0000	4.16%
5.0000	4.26%
7.0000	4.38%
10.0000	4.56%
20.0000	4.88%
30.0000	4.84%

These are the yields that are known and are used as inputs in the Cublic Spline Interpolation and Extrapolation model

Spline Interpolation and Extrapolation Results

Years	Yield	Notes
0.5	4.52%	Interpolate
1.0	4.39%	Interpolate
1.5	4.21%	Interpolate
2.0	4.13%	Interpolate
2.5	4.13%	Interpolate
3.0	4.16%	Interpolate
3.5	4.19%	Interpolate
4.0	4.22%	Interpolate
4.5	4.24%	Interpolate
5.0	4.26%	Interpolate
5.5	4.29%	Interpolate
6.0	4.32%	Interpolate
6.5	4.35%	Interpolate
7.0	4.38%	Interpolate
7.5	4.41%	Interpolate
8.0	4.44%	Interpolate
8.5	4.47%	Interpolate
9.0	4.50%	Interpolate
9.5	4.53%	Interpolate
10.0	4.56%	Interpolate
10.5	4.59%	Interpolate
11.0	4.61%	Interpolate
11.5	4.64%	Interpolate
12.0	4.66%	Interpolate
12.5	4.68%	Interpolate
13.0	4.70%	Interpolate
13.5	4.72%	Interpolate
14.0	4.74%	Interpolate

INTEREST RATE STATISTICS

Daily Treasury Yield Curve Rates

Get e-mail updates when this information changes.

This data is also available in XML format by clicking on the XML icon

September 2007

Date	1 mo	3 mo	6 mo	1 yr	2 yr	3 yr	5 yr	7 yr	10 yr	20 yr	30 yr
09/04/07	4.55	4.47	4.52	4.39	4.13	4.16	4.26	4.38	4.56	4.88	4.84
09/05/07	4.41	4.36	4.41	4.26	4.03	4.05	4.16	4.29	4.48	4.82	4.78
09/06/07	4.28	4.29	4.42	4.30	4.08	4.09	4.20	4.32	4.51	4.84	4.79
09/07/07	4.03	4.07	4.20	4.10	3.90	3.92	4.03	4.17	4.38	4.73	4.70
09/10/07	3.93	3.96	4.20	4.09	3.87	3.89	4.00	4.13	4.34	4.68	4.65
09/11/07	4.13	4.11	4.27	4.16	3.95	3.97	4.07	4.19	4.37	4.68	4.65
09/12/07	4.00	4.03	4.20	4.12	3.95	3.99	4.11	4.23	4.41	4.72	4.68
09/13/07	4.04	4.08	4.27	4.20	4.08	4.11	4.22	4.33	4.49	4.79	4.75
09/14/07	3.85	4.01	4.22	4.18	4.05	4.07	4.18	4.30	4.47	4.77	4.72
09/17/07	3.82	4.15	4.31	4.23	4.08	4.11	4.21	4.32	4.48	4.76	4.72
09/18/07	3.87	4.01	4.12	4.08	4.00	4.04	4.19	4.32	4.50	4.81	4.77

Daily Treasury Yield Curve Rates
Daily Treasury Bill Rates
Historical Data
Daily Treasury Long-Term Rates
Daily Treasury Real Yield Curve Rates
Daily Treasury Real Long-Term Rates

Figure 15-22 NS model.

for forecasting purposes. In Figure 15-22, the actual U.S. Treasury risk-free rates are shown and entered into the model as known values. The timing of these spot yields are entered as Years (the known X value inputs), whereas the known risk-free rates are the known Y values. Using the "B2Cubicspline" function, we can now interpolate the in-between risk-free rates that are missing as well as the rates outside of the given input dates. For instance, the risk-free Treasury rates given include 1-month, 3-month, 6-month, 1-year, and so forth, until the 30-year rate. Using these data, we can interpolate the rates for say, 5 months or 9 months, and so forth, as well as extrapolate beyond the 30-year rate. You can also use Risk Simulator's cubic spline tool to automatically run the model.

Illustrative Example: Yield Curve—Forward Rates from Spot Rates

File Name: *Yield Curve—Forward Rates from Spot Rates*
Location: *Modeling Toolkit | Yield Curve | Forward Rates from Spot Rates*
Brief Description: *A bootstrap model used to determine the implied forward rate given two spot rates*
Requirements: *Modeling Toolkit, Risk Simulator*
Modeling Toolkit Function Used: *B2ForwardRate*

Given two spot rates (from Year 0 to some future time periods), you can determine the implied forward rate between these two time periods. For instance, if the spot rate

FORWARD RATES
COMPUTING FORWARD RATES FROM SPOT RATES

Input Assumptions	
Spot Rate 1	8.00%
Spot Rate 2	7.00%
Time of Spot Rate 1	1.00
Time of Spot Rate 2	2.00

Forward Rate	6.00%

Figure 15-23   Forward rate extrapolation.

from Year 0 to Year 1 is 8% and the spot rate from Year 0 to Year 2 is 7% (both yields are known currently), the implied forward rate from Year 1 to Year 2 (that will occur based on current expectations) is 6%. This is simplified by using the B2ForwardRate function in Modeling Toolkit (Figure 15-23).

Illustrative Example: Yield Curve—Term Structure of Volatility

File Name: *Yield Curve—Term Structure of Volatility*

Location: *Modeling Toolkit | Yield Curve | Term Structure of Volatility*

Brief Description: *Not only are the interest rates themselves critical but its underlying volatility is also key, and this model illustrates the term structure of volatilities of interest rates.*

Requirements: *Modeling Toolkit, Risk Simulator*

This model illustrates the term structure of volatility of interest rates. In fact, interest rate volatilities change over time and, depending on the maturity, are also different during the same time period. So, which are more volatile: shorter term or long-term rates? The answer of course depends on the liquidity preference, trading market depth, economic outlook, and so forth. Using multiple years of historical data, we can analyze spot interest rates and tabulate their respective volatilities in the model. The results are shown in Figures 15-24 and 15-25.

Notice that longer-term yields tend to have smaller volatilities than shorter-term, more liquid and highly traded instruments (Figure 15-25), such as 1-year Treasury bills.

Illustrative Example: Yield Curve—U.S. Treasury Risk-free Rates

File Name: *Yield Curve—U.S. Treasury Risk-free Rates*

Location: *Modeling Toolkit | Yield Curve | U.S. Treasury Risk-free Rates*

Brief Description: *Illustrates how to use Risk Simulator for applying distributional fitting and computing volatilities of risk-free rates*

Requirements: *Modeling Toolkit, Risk Simulator*

This model shows the daily historical yield of the U.S. Treasury securities, from 1 month to 30 years, for the years 1990 to 2006. The volatilities of these time-series

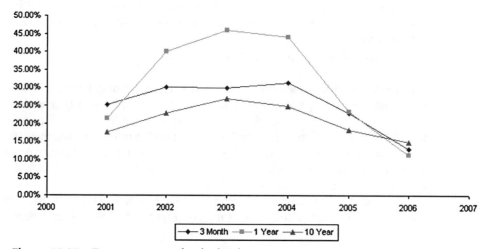

Term Structure of Volatility

	3 Month	6 Month	1 Year	2 Year	3 Year	5 Year	7 Year	10 Year	20 Year
Average	8.65%	8.58%	9.29%	13.06%	13.39%	13.79%	13.62%	12.80%	12.12%

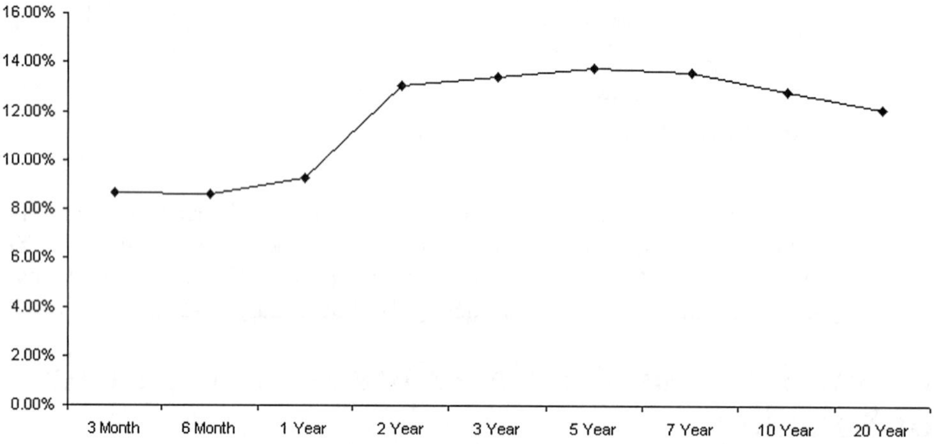

Figure 15-24 Term structure of average volatility.

Figure 15-25 Term structure of volatility by maturity.

yields are also computed, and they are then put through a distributional fitting routine in Risk Simulator to determine whether volatilities can be fitted to a particular distribution and hence used in a model elsewhere (Figure 15-26).

The *Risk-Free Rate Volatility* worksheet shows the computed annualized volatilities for each term structure, together with the average, median, minimum and maximum values. These volatilities are also fitted to continuous distributions, and the results are shown in the *Fitting Volatility* worksheet. Notice that longer-term yields tend to have smaller volatilities than shorter-term, more liquid and highly traded instruments.

Multiple Variable Distributional Fitting

Statistical Summary

Variable Name	3 Month		Variable Name	6 Month		Variable Name	1 Year	
Best-Fit Assumption	0.32		Best-Fit Assumption	0.30		Best-Fit Assumption	0.33	
Fitted Distribution	**Lognormal**		Fitted Distribution	**Triangular**		Fitted Distribution	**Gumbel (Maximum)**	
Mu	-1.36		Minimum	-0.05		Alpha	0.23	
Sigma	0.70		Most Likely	0.08		Beta	0.22	
			Maximum	0.84				
Kolmogorov-Smirnov Statistic	0.11		Kolmogorov-Smirnov Statistic	0.15		Kolmogorov-Smirnov Statistic	0.15	
P-Value for Test Statistic	**0.9853**		P-Value for Test Statistic	**0.8181**		P-Value for Test Statistic	**0.8180**	

	Actual	Theoretical		Actual	Theoretical		Actual	Theoretical
Mean	0.32	0.33	Mean	0.30	0.29	Mean	0.33	0.36
Standard Deviation	0.22	0.26	Standard Deviation	0.21	0.20	Standard Deviation	0.20	0.29
Skewness	1.28	2.87	Skewness	1.05	0.52	Skewness	0.46	1.14
Excess Kurtosis	1.51	17.51	Excess Kurtosis	0.98	-0.60	Excess Kurtosis	-0.48	2.40

Variable Name	2 Year		Variable Name	3 Year		Variable Name	5 Year	
Best-Fit Assumption	0.34		Best-Fit Assumption	0.31		Best-Fit Assumption	0.26	
Fitted Distribution	**Lognormal**		Fitted Distribution	**Lognormal**		Fitted Distribution	**Lognormal**	
Mu	-1.21		Mu	-1.31		Mu	-1.51	
Sigma	0.76		Sigma	0.66		Sigma	0.52	

Correlation Matrix

	3 Month	6 Month	1 Year	2 Year	3 Year	5 Year	7 Year	10 Year
3 Month	1							
6 Month	0.986068	1						
1 Year	0.907243	0.958162	1					
2 Year	0.578518	0.684161	0.8539608	1				
3 Year	0.449018	0.56911	0.7588623	0.981742	1			
5 Year	0.201037	0.337348	0.5485411	0.869494	0.944104	1		
7 Year	0.137761	0.273914	0.472691	0.789994	0.881749	0.983872	1	
10 Year	0.085105	0.217716	0.3945755	0.684885	0.788038	0.931852	0.9798362	1

Figure 15-26 P-values and cross correlations of fitting routines.

Procedure

The volatilities and their distributions have already been determined in this model. To review them, follow these instructions:

1. Select any of the worksheets (1990 to 2006) and look at the historical risk-free rates as well as how the volatilities are computed using the logarithmic returns approach.

2. Go to the *Fitting Volatility* worksheet and view the resulting fitted distributions, their p-values, theoretical vs. empirical values, and their cross-correlations.

3. Notice that in most cases, the p-values are pretty high. For example, the p-value for the 3-month volatilities for the past 17 years is 0.9853, or roughly, about 98.53 percent of the fluctuations in the actual data can be accounted for by the fitted lognormal distribution, indicative of an extremely good fit. We can now use this information to robustly model and simulate short-term volatilities. In addition, the cross-correlations indicate that yields of closely related terms are highly correlated but the correlated decreases over time. For instance, the 3-month volatilities tend to be highly correlated to the 6-month volatilities, but only have negligible correlations to longer term yields' (e.g., 10-year) volatilities. This is highly applicable

for simulating and modeling options embedded instruments such as options adjusted spreads that require the term structure if interest rates and term structure of volatility.

To replicate the distributional fitting routine, follow the instructions given next. You can perform a single-variable fitting and replicate the steps for multiple variables or you can perform a multiple fitting routine once. To perform individual fits:

1. Start a new profile by clicking on **Risk Simulator | New Simulation Profile** and give it a name.
2. Go to the *Risk-Free Rate Volatility* worksheet and select a data column (e.g., select cells **K6:K22**).
3. Start the single-fitting procedure by clicking on **Risk Simulator | Tools | Distributional Fitting (Single-Variable)**.
4. Select **Fit to Continuous Distributions** and make sure all distributions are checked (by default) and click on **OK**.
5. Review the resulting fits. Note that the best-fitting distribution is listed or ranked first, complete with the p-value (Figure 15-27). A high p-value is considered statistically to be a good fit. That is, the null hypothesis that the fitted distribution is the right distribution cannot be rejected; therefore, we can conclude that the distribution fitted is the best fit. Thus, the higher the p-value, the better the fit. Alternatively, you can roughly think of the p-value as the percentage fit for example, the Gumbel Maximum Distribution fits the 10-year volatilities at about 95.77 percent. You can also review the theoretical versus empirical statistics to see how closely the theoretical distribution matches the actual empirical data. If you click on **OK**, a single-fit report will be generated together with the assumption.

Alternatively, you can perform a multiple-variable fitting routine to fit multiple variables at the same time. The problem here is that the data must be complete. In other words, there must be no gaps in the area selected. Looking at the *Risk-Free Rate Volatility* worksheet, there are gaps because in certain years the 1-month Treasury Bill, 20-year Treasury Note, and 30-year Treasury Bond are not issued, hence the empty cells. So, you may have to perform a multi-variable fitting routine on the 3-month to 10-year volatilities and perform single-variable fits on the remaining 1-month, 20-year, and 30-year issues. To perform a multi-variable fit, follow these instructions:

1. Make sure you have already created a simulation profile. Then, select the cells **D6: K22** and start the multi-fit routine: **Risk Simulator | Tools | Distributional Fitting (Multi-Variable)**.
2. You can rename each of the variables if desired, and make sure that the distribution types are all set to **Continuous**. Click on **OK** when ready (Figure 15-28). A multiple-distribution fitting report will then be generated (see the *Fitting Volatility* spreadsheet).

Illustrative Example: Yield Curve—Vasicek Model

File Name: *Yield Curve—Vasicek Model*
Location: *Modeling Toolkit | Yield Curve | Vasicek Model*

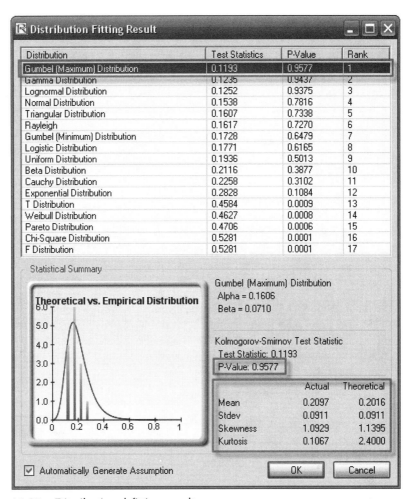

Figure 15-27   Distributional fitting results.

Brief Description: *Used to create the term structure of interest rates and to reconstruct the yield curve assuming the underlying interest rates are mean-reverting and stochastic*
Requirements: *Modeling Toolkit, Risk Simulator*
Modeling Toolkit Function Used: *B2VasicekBondYield*

This is the Vasicek model used to compute the term structure of interest rates and yield curve. The Vasicek model assumes a mean-reverting stochastic interest rate (Figure 15-29). The rate of reversion and long-run mean rates can be determined using Risk Simulator's statistical analysis tool. If the long-run rate is higher than the current short rate, the yield curve is upward sloping, and vice versa.

The yield curve is the time-series relationship between interest rates and the time to maturity of the debt. The more formal mathematical description of this relationship is called the term structure of interest rates. As discussed previously, the yield curve can take on various shapes. The normal yield curve means that yields rise as maturity lengthens and the yield curve is positively sloped, reflecting investor expectations for

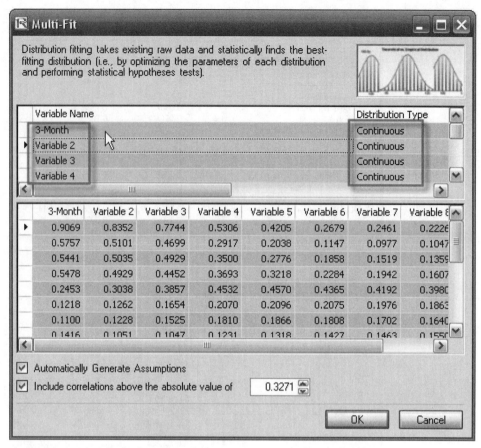

Figure 15-28   Multiple fitting result.

the economy to grow in the future (and hence, an expectation that inflation rates will rise in the future). An inverted yield curve occurs when the opposite occurs, where the long-term yields fall below short-term yields, and long-term investors will settle for lower yields now if they think the economy will slow or even decline in the future, indicative of a worsening economic situation in the future (and hence, an expectation that inflation will remain low in the future). Another potential situation is a flat yield curve, signaling uncertainty in the economy. The yield curve can also be humped or show a smile or a frown. The yield curve over time can change in shape through a twist or bend, a parallel shift, or a movement on one end versus another.

As the yield curve is related to inflation rates as discussed earlier and central banks in most countries have the ability to control monetary policy to target inflation rates, inflation rates are mean-reverting. This also implies that interest rates are mean-reverting, as well as stochastically changing over time.

A Czech mathematician, Oldrich Vasicek, in a 1977 paper, proved that bond prices on a yield curve over time and various maturities are driven by the short end of the yield curve, or the short-term interest rates, using a risk-neutral martingale measure. In his work the mean-reverting Ornstein-Uhlenbeck process was assumed. Hence, the resulting Vasicek model requires that a mean-reverting interest rate process be modeled (rate of mean reversion and long-run mean rates are both inputs in the Vasicek model).

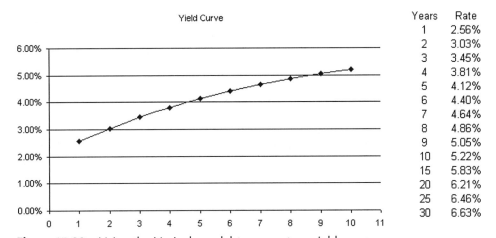

VASICEK MODEL
YIELD CURVE CONSTRUCTION

Input Assumptions

Time to Maturity of the Bond or Debt (Years)	1.00
Riskfree Rate (Short Rate)	2.00%
Long-run Mean Rate	8.00%
Annualized Volatility of Interest Rate	2.00%
Market Price of Interest Rate Risk	0.00%
Rate of Mean Reversion	20.00%

Yield of Zero Coupon Bond   **2.5562%**

Years	Rate
1	2.56%
2	3.03%
3	3.45%
4	3.81%
5	4.12%
6	4.40%
7	4.64%
8	4.86%
9	5.05%
10	5.22%
15	5.83%
20	6.21%
25	6.46%
30	6.63%

Figure 15-29 Using the Vasicek model to generate a yield curve.

Illustrative Example: Stochastic Forecasting of Interest Rates and Stock Prices

File Name: *Forecasting—Stochastic Processes*
Location: *Modeling Toolkit | Forecasting | Stochastic Processes*
Brief Description: *Illustrates how to simulate Stochastic Processes (Brownian Motion Random Walk, Mean-Reversion, Jump-Diffusion, and Mixed Models)*
Requirements: *Modeling Toolkit, Risk Simulator*

A stochastic process is a sequence of events or paths generated by probabilistic laws. That is, random events can occur over time but are governed by specific statistical and probabilistic rules. The main stochastic processes include Random Walk or Brownian Motion, Mean-Reversion, and Jump-Diffusion. These processes can be used to forecast a multitude of variables that seemingly follow random trends but yet are restricted by probabilistic laws. We can use Risk Simulator's *Stochastic Process* module to simulate and create such processes. These processes can be used to forecast a multitude of time-series data, including stock prices, interest rates, inflation rates, oil prices, electricity prices, and commodity prices.

Stochastic Process Forecasting

To run this model, simply:

1. Select **Risk Simulator | Forecasting | Stochastic Processes**.
2. Enter a set of relevant inputs or use the existing inputs as a test case (Figure 15-30).
3. Select the relevant process to simulate.
4. Click on **Update Chart** to view the updated computation of a single path or click on **OK** to create the process.

Model Results Analysis

For your convenience, the analysis report sheet is included in the model. A stochastic time-series chart and forecast values are provided in the report as well as each step's time period, mean, and standard deviation of the forecast (Figure 15-31). The mean values can be used as the single-point estimate, or assumptions can be manually generated for the desired time period. That is, finding the appropriate time period, create an assumption with a normal distribution with the appropriate mean and standard deviation computed. A sample chart with 10 iteration paths is included to graphically illustrate the behavior of the forecasted process.

The key is to calibrate the inputs to a stochastic process forecast model. The input parameters can be obtained very easily through some econometric modeling of historical

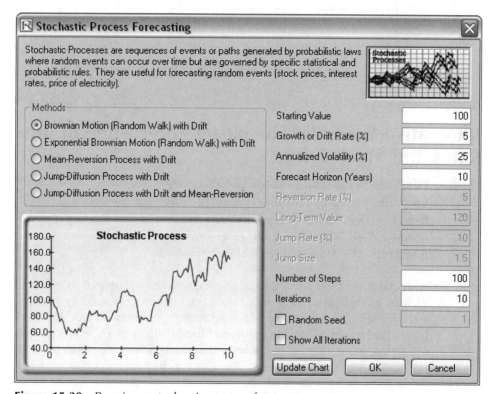

Figure 15-30 Running a stochastic process forecast.

Stochastic Process Forecasting

Statistical Summary

A stochastic process is a sequence of events or paths generated by probabilistic laws. That is, random events can occur over time but are governed by specific statistical and probabilistic rules. The main stochastic processes include Random Walk or Brownian Motion, Mean-Reversion, and Jump-Diffusion. These processes can be used to forecast a multitude of variables that seemingly follow random trends but yet are restricted by probabilistic laws.

The Random Walk Brownian Motion process can be used to forecast stock prices, prices of commodities, and other stochastic time-series data given a drift or growth rate and a volatility around the drift path. The Mean-Reversion process can be used to reduce the fluctuations of the Random Walk process by allowing the path to target a long-term value, making it useful for forecasting time-series variables that have a long-term rate such as interest rates and inflation rates (these are long-term target rates by regulatory authorities or the market). The Jump-Diffusion process is useful for forecasting time-series data when the variable can occasionally exhibit random jumps, such as oil prices or price of electricity (discrete exogenous event shocks can make prices jump up or down). Finally, these three stochastic processes can be mixed and matched as required.

The results on the right indicate the mean and standard deviation of all the iterations generated at each time step. If the Show All Iterations option is selected, each iteration pathway will be shown in a separate worksheet. The graph generated below shows a sample set of the iteration pathways.

Time	Mean	Stdev
0.0000	100.00	0.00
0.1000	99.10	7.47
0.2000	96.03	7.22
0.3000	94.97	13.59
0.4000	97.39	15.57
0.5000	99.50	17.01
0.6000	97.79	20.92
0.7000	102.23	25.54
0.8000	106.54	26.54
0.9000	102.34	21.16
1.0000	102.77	20.86
1.1000	103.30	22.41
1.2000	103.27	19.23
1.3000	103.02	23.61
1.4000	97.78	19.65
1.5000	96.84	20.53
1.6000	100.92	25.22
1.7000	105.18	26.90
1.8000	100.75	30.33
1.9000	101.20	29.71
2.0000	103.67	36.95
2.1000	108.09	42.76
2.2000	111.58	42.61
2.3000	111.25	41.54
2.4000	108.47	35.22
2.5000	107.13	32.56
2.6000	108.95	32.95
2.7000	114.64	38.78
2.8000	114.13	36.61
2.9000	114.97	35.91
3.0000	114.33	39.90
3.1000	112.69	39.94
3.2000	115.11	39.89
3.3000	117.64	42.82
3.4000	114.70	39.91
3.5000	115.52	43.45
3.6000	117.60	49.89
3.7000	120.21	51.94
3.8000	116.64	53.52
3.9000	118.70	56.12
4.0000	113.19	56.71
4.1000	109.09	58.33
4.2000	103.70	52.23
4.3000	108.41	53.12
4.4000	108.67	56.30
4.5000	105.96	52.42
4.6000	106.12	55.80
4.7000	107.70	55.11
4.8000	109.43	58.43
4.9000	114.50	59.64
5.0000	110.44	53.91

Stochastic Process: Brownian Motion (Random Walk) with Drift

Start Value	100	Steps	100.00	Jump Rate	N/A	
Drift Rate	5.00%	Iterations	10.00	Jump Size	N/A	
Volatility	25.00%	Reversion Rate	N/A	Random Seed	1431155157	
Horizon	10	Long-Term Value	N/A			

Figure 15-31   Stochastic process forecast results.

data, and examples of using Risk Simulator to compute these input parameters are seen in the data diagnostic and statistical analysis model examples. See Dr. Johnathan Mun's *Modeling Risk* (Wiley, 2006) for the technical details on obtaining these parameters.

Illustrative Example: Econometric Forecasting using Box-Jenkins ARIMA

File Name: *Forecasting—Time-Series ARIMA*

Location: *Modeling Toolkit | Forecasting | ARIMA*

Brief Description: *Illustrates how to run an econometric model called the Box-Jenkins ARIMA, which stands for autoregressive integrated moving average, an advanced forecasting technique taking into account historical fluctuations, trends, seasonality, cycles, prediction errors, and nonstationarity of the data*

Requirements: *Modeling Toolkit, Risk Simulator*

The *Data* worksheet in the ARIMA sample model contains some historical time-series data on the money supply in the United States, denoted M1, M2, and M3. M1 is the most liquid form of money (cash, coins, savings accounts, and so forth), while M2 and M3 are less liquid forms (bearer bonds, certificates of deposit, and so forth). These datasets are useful examples of long-term historical time-series data where ARIMA can be applied.

For technical details on ARIMA modeling, refer to Dr. Johnathan Mun's *Modeling Risk: Applying Monte Carlo Simulation, Real Options Analysis, Forecasting, and Optimization*, (Wiley, 2006). As a quick summary, the ARIMA econometric modeling technique takes into account historical data and decomposes it into an *Autoregressive* (AR) process, where there is a memory of past events (e.g., the interest rate this month is related to the interest rate last month, and so forth, with a decreasing memory lag); *Integrated* (I) process, which accounts for stabilizing or making the data stationary and ergodic, making it easier to forecast; and a *Moving Average* (MA) of the forecast errors, such that the longer the historical data, the more accurate the forecasts will be, as it learns over time. ARIMA models therefore have three model parameters—one for the AR(p) process, one for the I(d) process, and one for the MA(q) process—all combined and interacting among each other and recomposed into the ARIMA (p,d,q) model.

Running a Monte Carlo Simulation

To run this model simply:

1. Go to the *Data* worksheet and select **Risk Simulator | Forecasting | ARIMA**
2. Click on the link icon beside the *Time-Series Variable* input box, and link in **C7: C442**.
3. Enter in the relevant *P, D, Q* inputs, forecast periods, maximum iterations, and so forth (Figure 15-32).

Illustrative Example: Time-Series Forecasting

File Name: *Forecasting—Time-Series Analysis*
Location: *Modeling Toolkit | Forecasting | Time-Series Analysis*
Brief Description: *Illustrates how to run time-series analysis forecasts, which take into account historical base values, trends, and seasonalities to project the future*
Requirements: *Modeling Toolkit, Risk Simulator*

The historical sales revenue data are located in the *Time-Series Data* worksheet in the model. The data are quarterly sales revenue from Q1 2000 to Q4 2004. The data exhibits quarterly seasonality, which means that the seasonality is 4 (there are 4 quarters in 1 year or 1 cycle).

Time-series forecasting decomposes the historical data into the baseline, trend, and seasonality, if any. The models then apply an optimization procedure to find the *alpha*, *beta*, and *gamma* parameters for the baseline, trend, and seasonality coefficients, and then recompose them into a forecast. In other words, this methodology first applies a *backcast* to find the best-fitting model and best-fitting parameters of the model that minimizes forecast errors, and then proceeds to *forecast* the future based on the historical data that exist. This of course assumes that the same baseline growth, trend, and seasonality hold going forward. Even if they do not, say when there exists a

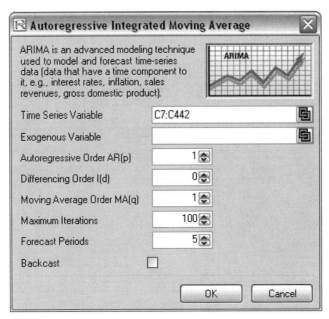

Figure 15-32   Running a Box-Jenkins ARIMA model.

structural shift (e.g., the company goes global, has a merger, spin-off, and so forth), the baseline forecasts can be computed, and then the required adjustments can be made to the forecasts.

Procedure

To run this model, simply:

1. Select the historical data (cells **H11:H30**).
2. Select **Risk Simulator | Forecasting | Time-Series Analysis**.
3. Select *Auto Model Selection*, **Forecast 4 Periods** and **Seasonality 4 Periods** (Figure 15-34).

Note that you can only select *Create Simulation Assumptions* if an existing Simulation Profile exists (if not, click on **Risk Simulator**, **New Simulation Profile**, and then run the time-series forecast per the steps above, but remember to check the *Create Simulation Assumptions* box).

Model Results Analysis

For your convenience, the analysis Report and Methodology sheets are included in the model. A fitted chart and forecast values are provided in the report as well as the error measures and a statistical summary of the methodology (Figure 15-35). The Methodology sheet provides the statistical results from all eight time-series methodologies. Refer to *Modeling Risk* (Wiley, 2006) by Dr. Johnathan Mun for more detailed discussions of how to interpret the statistics and analysis results.

ARIMA (Autoregressive Integrated Moving Average)

Regression Statistics

R-Squared (Coefficient of Determination)	0.9999	Akaike Information Criterion (AIC)	4.6213
Adjusted R-Squared	0.9999	Schwarz Criterion (SC)	4.6632
Multiple R (Multiple Correlation Coefficient)	1.0000	Log Likelihood	-1005.1340
Standard Error of the Estimates (SEy)	297.5246	Durbin-Watson (DW) Statistic	1.8588
Number of Observations	435	Number of Iterations	5

Autoregressive Integrated Moving Average or ARIMA(p,d,q) models are the extension of the AR model that use three components for modeling the serial correlation in the time-series data. The first component is the autoregressive (AR) term. The AR(p) model uses the p lags of the time series in the equation. An AR(p) model has the form: y(t)=a(1)*y(t-1)+...+a(p)*y(t-p)+e(t).The second component is the integration (d) order term. Each integration order corresponds to differencing the time series. I(1) means differencing the data once. I(d) means differencing the data d times. The third component is the moving average (MA) term. The MA(q) model uses the q lags of the forecast errors to improve the forecast. An MA(q) model has the form: y(t)=e(t)+b(1)*e(t-1)+...+b(q)*e(t-q).Finally, an ARIMA(p,q) model has the combined form: y(t)=a(1)*y(t-1)+...+a(p)*y(t-p)+e(t)+b(1)*e(t-1)+...+b(q)*e(t-q).

The R-Squared, or Coefficient of Determination, indicates the percent variation in the dependent variable that can be explained and accounted for by the independent variables in this regression analysis. However, in a multiple regression, the Adjusted R-Squared takes into account the existence of additional independent variables or regressors and adjusts this R-Squared value to a more accurate view the regression's explanatory power. However, under some ARIMA modeling circumstances (e.g., with nonconvergence models), the R-Squared tends to be unreliable.

The Multiple Correlation Coefficient (Multiple R) measures the correlation between the actual dependent variable (Y) and the estimated or fitted (Y) based on the regression equation. This correlation is also the square root of the Coefficient of Determination (R-Squared).

Regression Results

	Intercept	AR(1)	MA(1)
Coefficients	-0.0626	1.0055	0.4936
Standard Error	0.3108	0.0006	0.0420
t-Statistic	-0.2013	1691.1373	11.7633
p-Value	0.8406	0.0000	0.0000
Lower 5%	0.4498	1.0065	0.5628
Upper 95%	-0.5749	1.0046	0.4244

Degrees of Freedom		Hypothesis Test	
Degrees of Freedom for Regression	2	Critical t-Statistic (99% confidence with df of 432)	2.5673
Degrees of Freedom for Residual	432	Critical t-Statistic (95% confidence with df of 432)	1.9655
Total Degrees of Freedom	434	Critical t-Statistic (90% confidence with df of 432)	1.6484

Autocorrelation

Time Lag	AC	PAC	Lower Bound	Upper Bound	Q-Stat	Prob
1	0.9921	0.9921	(0.0958)	0.0958	431.1216	-
2	0.9841	(0.0105)	(0.0958)	0.0958	856.3037	-
3	0.9760	(0.0109)	(0.0958)	0.0958	1,275.4818	-
4	0.9678	(0.0142)	(0.0958)	0.0958	1,688.5499	-
5	0.9594	(0.0098)	(0.0958)	0.0958	2,095.4625	-
6	0.9509	(0.0113)	(0.0958)	0.0958	2,496.1572	-
7	0.9423	(0.0124)	(0.0958)	0.0958	2,890.5594	-
8	0.9336	(0.0147)	(0.0958)	0.0958	3,278.5669	-
9	0.9247	(0.0121)	(0.0958)	0.0958	3,660.1152	-
10	0.9156	(0.0139)	(0.0958)	0.0958	4,035.1192	-
11	0.9066	(0.0049)	(0.0958)	0.0958	4,403.6117	-
12	0.8975	(0.0068)	(0.0958)	0.0958	4,765.6032	-
13	0.8883	(0.0097)	(0.0958)	0.0958	5,121.0697	-
14	0.8791	(0.0087)	(0.0958)	0.0958	5,470.0032	-
15	0.8698	(0.0064)	(0.0958)	0.0958	5,812.4256	-
16	0.8605	(0.0056)	(0.0958)	0.0958	6,148.3694	-
17	0.8512	(0.0062)	(0.0958)	0.0958	6,477.8620	-
18	0.8419	(0.0038)	(0.0958)	0.0958	6,800.9622	-
19	0.8326	(0.0003)	(0.0958)	0.0958	7,117.7709	-
20	0.8235	0.0002	(0.0958)	0.0958	7,428.3952	-

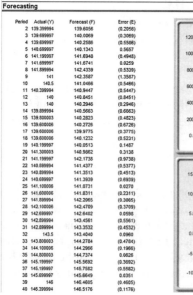

If autocorrelation AC(1) is nonzero, it means that the series is first order serially correlated. If AC(k) dies off more or less geometrically with increasing lag, it implies that the series follows a low-order autoregressive process. If AC(k) drops to zero after a small number of lags, it implies that the series follows a low-order moving-average process. Partial correlation PAC(k) measures the correlation of values that are k periods apart after removing the correlation from the intervening lags. If the pattern of autocorrelation can be captured by an autoregression of order less than k, then the partial autocorrelation at lag k will be close to zero. Ljung-Box Q-statistics and their p-values at lag k has the null hypothesis that there is no autocorrelation up to order k. The dotted lines in the plots of the autocorrelations are the approximate two standard error bounds. If the autocorrelation is within these bounds, it is not significantly different from zero at (approximately) the 5% significance level.

Forecasting

Period	Actual (Y)	Forecast (F)	Error (E)
2	139.399994	139.6056	(0.2056)
3	139.699997	140.0069	(0.3069)
4	139.699997	140.2586	(0.5586)
5	140.699997	140.1343	0.5657
6	141.199997	141.6948	(0.4948)
7	141.699997	141.6741	0.0259
8	141.899994	142.4339	(0.5339)
9	141	142.3587	(1.3587)
10	140.5	141.0468	(0.5466)
11	140.399994	140.9447	(0.5447)
12	140	140.8451	(0.8451)
13	140	140.2946	(0.2946)
14	139.899994	140.5663	(0.6663)
15	139.800003	140.2823	(0.4823)
16	139.600006	140.2726	(0.6726)
17	139.600006	139.9775	(0.3775)
18	139.600006	140.1232	(0.5231)
19	140.199997	140.0513	0.1487
20	141.300003	140.9862	0.3138
21	141.199997	142.1738	(0.9738)
22	140.899994	141.4377	(0.5377)
23	140.899994	141.3513	(0.4513)
24	140.699997	141.3939	(0.6939)
25	141.100006	141.0731	0.0270
26	141.600006	141.8311	(0.2311)
27	141.899994	142.2065	(0.3065)
28	142.100006	142.4709	(0.3709)
29	142.699997	142.6402	0.0598
30	142.899994	143.4561	(0.5561)
31	142.899994	143.3532	(0.4532)
32	143.5	143.4040	0.0960
33	143.800003	144.2784	(0.4784)
34	144.100006	144.2966	(0.1966)
35	144.800003	144.7374	0.0626
36	145.199997	145.5692	(0.3692)
37	145.199997	145.7582	(0.5582)
38	145.699997	145.6649	0.0351
39	146	146.4605	(0.4605)
40	146.399994	146.5176	(0.1176)

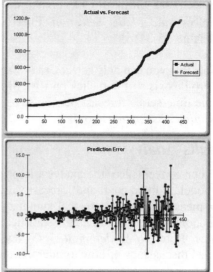

Figure 15-33 ARIMA results.

Historical Sales Revenues

Year	Quarter	Period	Sales
2000	1	1	$684.20
2000	2	2	$584.10
2000	3	3	$765.40
2000	4	4	$892.30
2001	1	5	$885.40
2001	2	6	$677.00
2001	3	7	$1,006.60
2001	4	8	$1,122.10
2002	1	9	$1,163.40
2002	2	10	$993.20
2002	3	11	$1,312.50
2002	4	12	$1,545.30
2003	1	13	$1,596.20
2003	2	14	$1,260.40
2003	3	15	$1,735.20
2003	4	16	$2,029.70
2004	1	17	$2,107.80
2004	2	18	$1,650.30
2004	3	19	$2,304.40
2004	4	20	$2,639.40

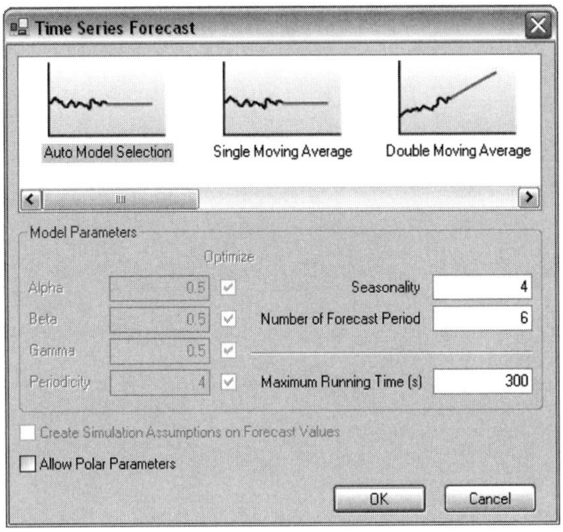

Time Series Forecast
Auto Model Selection
Single Moving Average
Double Moving Average
Model Parameters
Optimize
Alpha
0.5
Beta
0.5
Gamma
0.5
Periodicity
4
Seasonality
4
Number of Forecast Period
6
Maximum Running Time (s)
300
Create Simulation Assumptions on Forecast Values
Allow Polar Parameters
OK
Cancel

Figure 15-34 Running a time-series analysis forecast.

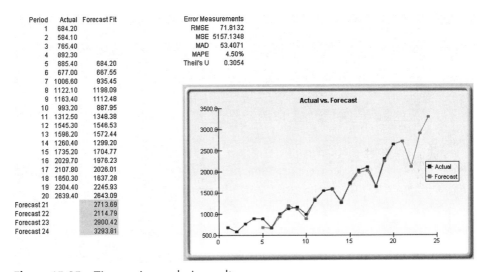

Period	Actual	Forecast Fit
1	684.20	
2	584.10	
3	765.40	
4	892.30	
5	885.40	684.20
6	677.00	667.55
7	1006.60	935.45
8	1122.10	1198.09
9	1163.40	1112.48
10	993.20	887.95
11	1312.50	1348.38
12	1545.30	1546.53
13	1596.20	1572.44
14	1260.40	1299.20
15	1735.20	1704.77
16	2029.70	1976.23
17	2107.80	2026.01
18	1650.30	1637.28
19	2304.40	2245.93
20	2639.40	2643.09
Forecast 21		2713.69
Forecast 22		2114.79
Forecast 23		2900.42
Forecast 24		3293.81

Error Measurements	
RMSE	71.8132
MSE	5157.1348
MAD	53.4071
MAPE	4.50%
Theil's U	0.3054

Actual vs. Forecast
3500.0
3000.0
2500.0
2000.0
1500.0
1000.0
500.0
0
5
10
15
20
25
Actual
Forecast

Figure 15-35 Time-series analysis results.

CHAPTER | 16

Exotic Options and Credit Derivatives

Valuing and analyzing exotic options, over-the-counter (OTC) exotic derivatives, and debt and credit-based derivatives are part of the Basel II requirements. The following provides quick excerpts of the required aspects of some of these derivatives, direct from the Basel Committee on Banking Supervision's June 2004 publication.

Section 112

The comprehensive approach for the treatment of collateral will also be applied to calculate the counterparty risk charges for *OTC derivatives* and repo-style transactions booked in the trading book.

Section 140

Where *guarantees or credit derivatives* are direct, explicit, irrevocable and unconditional, and supervisors are satisfied that banks fulfill certain minimum operational conditions relating to risk management processes they may allow banks to take account of such credit protection in calculating capital requirements.

Section 189

Other than non-payment by a protection purchaser of money due in respect of the credit protection contract it must be irrevocable; there must be no clause in the contract that would allow the protection provider unilaterally to cancel the credit cover or that would increase the effective cost of cover as a result of deteriorating credit quality in the *hedged exposure*. Paragraph 203 sets forth the treatment of *call options* in determining remaining maturity for credit protection.

Section 203

The maturity of the underlying exposure and the *maturity of the hedge* should both be defined conservatively. . . . *For the hedge, embedded options* which may reduce the term of the hedge should be taken into account so that the shortest possible effective maturity is used. Where a *call is at the discretion of the protection seller*, the maturity will always be at the first call date. If the call is at the discretion of the protection buying bank but the terms of the arrangement at origination of the hedge contain a positive incentive for the bank to call the transaction before contractual maturity, the remaining time to the first call date will be deemed to be the effective maturity.

Section 527 (e)

Institutions must use an internal model that is appropriate for the risk profile and complexity of their equity portfolio. Institutions with material holdings with values that are highly non-linear in nature (e.g., *equity derivatives, convertibles*) must employ an internal model designed to *capture appropriately the risks associated with such instruments*.

Section 702

Banks will be required to calculate the *counterparty credit risk charge for OTC derivatives*, repo-style and other transactions booked in the trading book, separate from the capital charge for general market risk and specific risk. The risk weights to be used in this calculation must be consistent with those used for calculating the capital requirements in the banking book.

Section 713

Specific *risk capital charges for positions hedged by credit derivatives*. . . . Full allowance will be recognised when the values of two legs (i.e., long and short) always move in the opposite direction and broadly to the same extent.

Section 733

Credit risk: Banks should have methodologies that enable them to assess the credit risk involved in exposures to individual borrowers or counterparties as well as at the portfolio level. For more sophisticated banks, the credit review assessment of capital adequacy, at a minimum, should cover four areas: *risk rating systems, portfolio analysis/aggregation, securitisation/complex credit derivatives, and large exposures and risk concentrations*.

As can be determined from these excerpts, exotic options are used in a variety of settings in a bank, including the applications of general risk hedging and credit risk hedging. This chapter provides several most commonly used derivates in a bank and their respective valuations. For details of other exotic options, please refer to the Basel

II Modeling Toolkit software and the Real Options SLS software. It is assumed at this point that the reader is somewhat familiar with the functionalities and use of these two software programs. If not, please first refer to Appendix 1 for a quick primer before proceeding.

Illustrative Example: Exotic Options—Accruals on Basket of Assets

File Name: *Exotic Options—Accruals on Basket of Assets*
Location: *Modeling Toolkit | Real Options Models | Accruals on Basket of Assets*
Brief Description: *Essentially financial portfolios of multiple underlying assets where the holder of the instrument receives the maximum of the basket of assets or some prespecified guarantee amount*
Requirements: *Modeling Toolkit, Real Options SLS*

The Accruals on Basket of Assets is an exotic option whereby there are several assets in a portfolio and the holder of the instrument receives the maximum of either the guaranteed amount or any one of the assets' value. This instrument can be modeled as either an American option, which can be executed at any time, or as a European option, which can only be exercised at maturity (and sometimes as Bermudan options with vesting and blackout periods where the option cannot be executed). Using the multiple assets and multiple phased module of the Real Options SLS software, we can model the value of an accrual option (Figure 16-1). The inputs are usual option inputs, while the terminal and intermediate equations are shown below.

The Terminal Node Equation is:

$$Max(FirstAsset, SecondAsset, ThirdAsset, FourthAsset, Guarantee)$$

While the Intermediate Node Equation is:

$$Max(FirstAsset, SecondAsset, ThirdAsset, FourthAsset, OptionOpen)$$

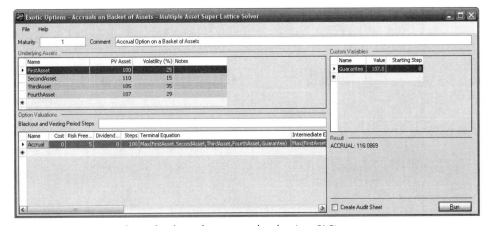

Figure 16-1 Accruals on basket of assets (solved using SLS).

Illustrative Example: Exotic Options—American Call Option on Foreign Exchange

File Name: *Exotic Options—American Call Option on Foreign Exchange*
Location: *Modeling Toolkit | Real Options Models | American Call Option on Foreign Exchange*
Brief Description: *Computation of American and European options on foreign exchange currencies*
Requirements: *Modeling Toolkit, Real Options SLS*

A Foreign Exchange Option (FX Option or FXO) is a derivative in which the owner has the right but not the obligation to exchange money denominated in one currency into another currency at a pre-agreed exchange rate on a specified date. The FX Options market is the deepest, largest, and most liquid market for options of any kind in the world. The valuation here uses the Garman-Kohlhagen model (Figure 16-2). You can use the *Exotic Options—Currency (Foreign Exchange) Options* model in the Modeling Toolkit software to compare the results of this Real Options SLS model.

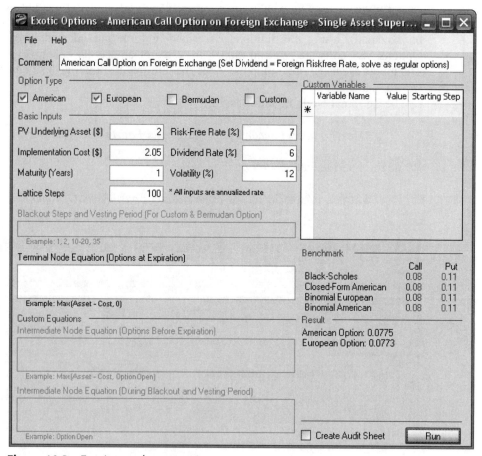

Figure 16-2 Foreign exchange option.

The former is used to compute the European version using closed-form models, while the latter, the example showcased in this chapter, computes the European and American options using a binomial lattice approach. The only caveat when using the binomial lattice approach in the Real Options SLS software is to remember to set the *Dividend Rate* as the foreign country's risk-free rate, the *PV Underlying Asset* as the spot exchange rate, and the *Implementation Cost* as the strike exchange rate.

As an example of a foreign exchange option, if we suppose the British pound (GBP) versus the U.S. dollar (USD) is USD2/GBP1, then the spot exchange rate is 2.0, and because the exchange rate is denominated in GBP (the denominator), then the domestic risk-free rate is the rate in the U.K. and the foreign rate is the rate in the U.S. This means that the foreign exchange contract allows the holder the option to call GBP and put USD.

To illustrate, suppose a U.K. firm is getting US$1M in six months, and the spot exchange rate is USD2/GBP1. Over time, if the GBP currency strengthens, the U.K. firm loses when it has to repatriate USD back to GBP, but gains if the GBP currency weakens. If the firm hedges the foreign exchange exposure with an FXO and gets a call on GBP (put on USD), then it hedges itself from any foreign exchange fluctuation risks. For discussion purposes, say the timing is short, interest rates are low, and volatility is low; getting a call option with a strike of 1.90 yields a call value approximately 0.10 (that is, the firm can execute the option and gain the difference of 2.00 − 1.90 or 0.10 immediately). This means that the rate now becomes USD1.90/GBP1, and it is cheaper to purchase GBP with the same USD, or the U.K. firm gets a higher GBP payoff.

Illustrative Example: Exotic Options—Barrier Options

File Name: *Exotic Options—Barrier Options*
Location: *Modeling Toolkit | Exotic Options | Barrier Options*
Brief Description: *Values various types of barrier options such as up and in, down and in, up and out, down and out call and put options*
Requirements: *Modeling Toolkit*
Modeling Toolkit Function Used: *B2Barrier functions*

Barrier options (Figure 16-3) become valuable or get knocked in-the-money only if a barrier (upper or lower barrier) is breached (or not), and the payout is in the form of the option on the underlying asset. Sometimes, as remuneration for the risk of not being knocked in, a specified cash rebate is paid at the end of the instrument's maturity (at expiration) assuming that the option has not been knocked in.

As an example, the *Up and In Call Option* implies that the instrument pays the specified cash amount at expiration if and only if the asset value does not breach the upper barrier (asset value does not go above the upper barrier), providing the holder of the instrument a safety net or a cash insurance. However, if the asset breaches the upper barrier, the option gets knocked in and becomes a live option. An *Up and Out* option means the option is live only as long as the asset does not breach the upper barrier, and so forth. *Monitoring Periodicities* means how often during the life of the option the asset or stock value will be monitored to see if it breaches a barrier. As an example, entering 12 implies monthly monitoring, 52 for weekly, 252 for daily trading, 365 for daily calendar, and 1,000,000 for continuous monitoring.

348   CHAPTER | 16 Exotic Options and Credit Derivatives

BARRIER OPTIONS

Input Assumptions

Asset Value or Stock Price	$100.00
Strike Price	$100.00
Barrier Price	$115.00
Cash Rebate Value	$3.00
Time to Maturity	0.50
Riskfree Rate	8.00%
Dividend Rate	4.00%
Annualized Volatility	20.00%
Monitoring Periodicities (Per Year)	365.00

Down and In Call Option	$39.52
Up and In Call Option	$7.27
Down and In Put Option	$2.16
Up and In Put Option	$2.03
Down and Out Call Option	$0.00
Up and Out Call Option	$2.12
Down and Out Put Option	$5.79
Up and Out Put Option	$5.42

Figure 16-3   Computing barrier options.

Illustrative Example: Exotic Options—Binary Digital Options

File Name: *Exotic Options—Binary Digital Options*
Location: *Modeling Toolkit | Exotic Options | Binary Digital Options*
Brief Description: *Instruments that get knocked in or out of the money depending on whether the asset value breaches or does not breach certain barriers*
Requirements: *Modeling Toolkit, Real Options SLS*
Modeling Toolkit Function Used: *B2Binary functions*

Binary exotic options (also known as *Digital*, *Accrual*, or *Fairway* options) become valuable only if a barrier (upper or lower barrier) is breached (or not), and the payout could be in the form of some prespecified cash amount or the underlying asset itself. The cash or asset exchanges hands either at the point when the barrier is breached or at the end of the instrument's maturity (at expiration), assuming that the barrier is breached at some point prior to maturity.

For instance, the *Down and In Cash at Expiration* option implies that the instruments pay the specified cash amount at expiration if and only if the asset value breaches the lower barrier (asset value goes below the lower barrier), providing the holder of the instrument with a safety net or a cash insurance in case the underlying asset does not perform well. The *Up and In* options are such that the cash or asset is provided if the underlying asset goes above the upper barrier threshold. The *Up and Out* or *Down and Out* options mean that the asset or cash are paid as long as the upper or lower barrier is not breached. The *At Expiration* options mean that cash and assets are paid at maturity, whereas the *At Hit* instruments are payable at the point when the barrier is breached. See Figure 16-4.

BINARY DIGITAL OPTIONS

Input Assumptions

Asset Value or Stock Price	$10.00
Strike Price	$10.00
Upper Barrier Price	$8.00
Lower Barrier Price	$12.00
Cash Value	$10.00
Time to Maturity	1.00
Riskfree Rate	3.00%
Dividend Rate	0.00%
Annualized Volatility	25.00%
Delta T	0.00

Down and In Cash at Expiration Call Option	**$9.96**
Up and In Cash at Expiration Call Option	**$3.80**
Down and In Asset at Expiration Call Option	**$14.76**
Up and In Asset at Expiration Call Option	**$4.87**
Down and Out Cash at Expiration Call Option	**$0.00**
Up and Out Cash at Expiration Call Option	**$1.03**
Down and Out Asset at Expiration Call Option	**$0.00**
Up and Out Asset at Expiration Call Option	**$1.10**
Down and In Cash at Expiration Put Option	**$4.87**
Up and In Cash at Expiration Put Option	**$0.70**
Down and In Asset at Expiration Put Option	**$4.03**
Up and In Asset at Expiration Put Option	**$0.63**
Down and Out Cash at Expiration Put Option	**$0.00**
Up and Out Cash at Expiration Put Option	**$4.17**
Down and Out Asset at Expiration Put Option	**$0.00**
Up and Out Asset at Expiration Put Option	**$3.40**

Figure 16-4   Binary digital options.

Illustrative Example: Exotic Options—Commodity Options

File Name: *Exotic Options—Commodity Options*

Location: *Modeling Toolkit | Exotic Options | Commodity Options*

Brief Description: *Models and values a commodity option where the spot and future values of a commodity are used to value the option, while the forward rates and convenience yields are assumed to be mean-reverting and volatile*

Requirements: *Modeling Toolkit*

Modeling Toolkit Function Used: *B2CommodityCallOptionModel, B2Commodity PutOptionModel*

This model computes the values of commodity-based European call and put options, where the convenience yield and forward rates are assumed to be mean-reverting and each has its own volatilities and cross-correlations. This is a complex multifactor model with interrelationships among each variable, as can be seen in Figure 16-5.

VALUE OF A COMMODITY OPTION

Price of Zero Coupon Bond	$0.9753
Futures Price	$95.0000
Strike Price	$95.0000
Maturity of the Option	0.5000
Maturity of the Futures Contract	1.0000
Volatility of the Spot Commodity Price	26.60%
Volatility of Future Convenience Yield	24.90%
Volatility of the Forward Interest Rate	0.96%
Correlation Commodity Price and Convenience Yield	0.8050
Correlation Commodity Price and Forward Rate	0.0964
Correlation Convenience Yield and Forward Rate	0.1243
Speed of Mean Reversion of the Convenience Yield	104.50%
Speed of Mean Reversion of the Forward Rates	20.00%

Commodity Call Option Value	**$4.7245**
Commodity Put Option Value	**$4.7262**

Figure 16-5 Commodity option.

Input Assumptions

Spot Exchange Rate	2.00
Strike Exchange Rate	2.05
Maturity	1.00
Domestic Riskfree Rate	7.00%
Foreign Riskfree Rate	6.00%
Volatility	12.00%

Foreign Currency Call Option	**$0.0775**
Foreign Currency Put Option	**$0.1054**

Figure 16-6 Foreign exchange option.

Illustrative Example: Exotic Options—Currency (Foreign Exchange) Options

File Name: *Exotic Options—Currency Options*

Location: *Modeling Toolkit | Exotic Options | Currency Options*

Brief Description: *Values a foreign exchange currency option, typically used in hedging foreign exchange fluctuations, and the key inputs are the spot exchange rate, the contractual purchase or sale price of the foreign exchange currency for delivery in the future*

Requirements: *Modeling Toolkit*

Modeling Toolkit Function Used: *B2CurrencyCallOption, B2CurrencyPutOption*

A Foreign Exchange Option (FX Option or FXO) is a derivative in which the owner has the right but not the obligation to exchange money denominated in one currency into another currency at a pre-agreed exchange rate on a specified date. The FX Options market is the deepest, largest, and most liquid market for options of any kind in the world. The valuation here uses the Garman-Kohlhagen model (Figure 16-6).

Illustrative Example: Exotic Options—Extreme Spreads Option

File Name: *Exotic Options—Extreme Spreads*

Location: *Modeling Toolkit | Exotic Options | Extreme Spreads*

Brief Description: *Computes extreme spread option values, where the vehicle is divided into two segments, and the option pays off the difference between the extreme values (min or max) of the asset during the two time segments*

Requirements: *Modeling Toolkit*

Modeling Toolkit Function Used: *B2ExtremeSpreadCallOption, B2Extreme SpreadPutOption, B2ExtremeSpreadReverseCallOption, B2ExtremeSpread ReversePutOption*

Extreme Spread Options have their maturities divided into two segments, starting from time zero to the *First Time Period* (first segment) and from the *First Time Period* to *Maturity* (second segment). An extreme spread call option pays the difference between the maximum asset value from the second segment and the maximum value of the first segment. Conversely, the put pays the difference between the minimum of the second segment's asset value and the minimum of the first segment's asset value. A reverse call pays the minimum from the first less the minimum of the second segment, whereas a reverse put pays the maximum of the first less the maximum of the second segments. These are all modeled in Figure 16-7.

EXTREME SPREAD OPTIONS

Input Assumptions

Asset Price	$100.00
Observed Minimum	$90.00
Observed Maximum	$110.00
First Time Period	0.25
Maturity	1.00
Riskfree Rate	5.00%
Dividend Rate	0.00%
Volatility	30.00%

Extreme Spread Call	**$14.4021**
Extreme Spread Put	**$7.3515**
Reverse Extreme Spread Call	**$4.4490**
Reverse Extreme Spread Put	**$4.2039**

Functions:
B2ExtremeSpreadCallOption
B2ExtremeSpreadPutOption
B2ExtremeSpreadReverseCallOption
B2ExtremeSpreadReversePutOption

Figure 16-7   Extreme spreads options.

Illustrative Example: Exotic Options—Foreign Equity Linked Foreign Exchange Options in Domestic Currency

File Name: *Exotic Options—Foreign Equity Linked Forex Options*

Location: *Modeling Toolkit | Exotic Options | Equity Linked Forex*

Brief Description: *Computes the option where the underlying asset is in a foreign market and the exchange rate is fixed in advanced to hedge the exposure risk and the strike price is set as a foreign exchange rate rather than a price*

Requirements: *Modeling Toolkit*

Modeling Toolkit Function Used: *B2EquityLinkedFXCallOptionDomesticValue, B2EquityLinkedFXPutOptionDomesticValue*

Equity Linked Foreign Exchange Options are options whose underlying asset is in a foreign equity market and the option holder can hedge the fluctuations of the foreign exchange risk by having a strike price on the foreign exchange rate (Figure 16-8). The resulting valuation is in the domestic currency. There are three closely related models in this section, and the following two sections (foreign equity linked foreign exchange option, foreign equity struck in domestic currency, and foreign equity with fixed exchange rate in domestic currency), but their similarities and differences can be summarized as:

- The underlying asset is denominated in a foreign currency.
- The foreign exchange rate is domestic currency to foreign currency.
- The option is valued in domestic currency.
- The strike prices are different where:
  - The exchange rate is the strike for the foreign equity linked foreign exchange option
  - The domestic currency is the strike for the foreign equity struck in domestic currency option
  - The foreign currency is the strike for the foreign equity with fixed exchange rate in domestic currency option

EQUITY LINKED FOREIGN EXCHANGE OPTIONS IN DOMESTIC CURRENCY

Input Assumptions

Fixed Exchange Rate	1.50
Asset Price	$70.00
Strike Price	1.25
Maturity	0.50
Domestic Risk Free Rate	5.00%
Foreign Risk Free	6.00%
Dividend Rate	1.00%
Volatility of Asset	25.00%
Volatility of Currency	15.00%
Correlation	0.25

Foreign Equity Linked Call Option	**$17.5633**
Foreign Equity Linked Put Option	**$0.1777**

Figure 16-8 Equity linked options.

**FOREIGN EQUITY OPTIONS STRUCK
IN DOMESTIC CURRENCY**

Input Assumptions

Exchange Rate (Domestic/Foreign)	1.50
Asset Price in Foreign Currency	70.00
Strike Price in Domestic Currency	80.00
Maturity	0.50
Domestic Risk Free Rate	5.00%
Dividend Rate	1.00%
Volatility of Asset	25.00%
Volatility of Currency	15.00%
Correlation (Asset and Currency)	0.25

Foreign Equity Struck in Domestic Currency Call	**$27.4203**
Foreign Equity Struck in Domestic Currency Put	**$0.9688**

Figure 16-9   Foreign equity with the strike in domestic currency.

Illustrative Example: Exotic Options—Foreign Equity Struck in Domestic Currency

File Name: *Exotic Options—Foreign Equity Struck in Domestic Currency*
Location: *Modeling Toolkit | Exotic Options | Foreign Equity Domestic Currency*
Brief Description: *Values the options on foreign equities denominated in foreign exchange currency while the strike price is in domestic currency*
Requirements: *Modeling Toolkit*
Modeling Toolkit Function Used: *B2ForeignEquityDomesticCurrencyCall, B2ForeignEquityDomesticCurrencyPut*

Foreign Equity Options Struck in Domestic Currency is an option on foreign equities in a foreign currency, but the strike price is in domestic currency (Figure 16-9). At expiration, assuming the option is in-the-money, its value will be translated back into the domestic currency. The Exchange Rate is the spot rate for domestic currency to foreign currency, the asset price is denominated in a foreign currency, and the strike price is in domestic currency.

Illustrative Example: Exotic Options—Foreign Equity with Fixed Exchange Rate

File Name: *Exotic Options—Foreign Equity with Fixed Exchange Rates*
Location: *Modeling Toolkit | Exotic Options | Foreign Equity Fixed Forex*
Brief Description: *Values foreign equity options where the option is in a currency foreign to that of the underlying asset but with a risk hedging on the exchange rate*
Requirements: *Modeling Toolkit*
Modeling Toolkit Function Used: *B2ForeignEquityFixedFXRateDomesticValueQuantoCall, B2ForeignEquityFixedFXRateDomesticValueQuantoPut*

Quanto options are traded on exchanges around the world and are also known as Foreign Equity Options (Figure 16-10). The options are denominated in another cur-

FOREIGN EQUITY QUANTO OPTIONS WITH FIXED
EXCHANGE RATES VALUED IN DOMESTIC CURRENCY

Input Assumptions

Fixed Exchange Rate	1.50
Asset Price	70.00
Strike Price	80.00
Maturity	0.50
Domestic Risk Free Rate	5.00%
Foreign Risk Free	6.00%
Dividend Rate	1.00%
Volatility of Asset	25.00%
Volatility of Currency	15.00%
Correlation	0.25

Quanto Call Option	**$3.0794**
Quanto Put Option	**$15.6076**

Figure 16-10 Foreign equity in domestic currency with fixed exchange rate (quanto options).

rency than that of the underlying asset. The option has an expanding or contracting coverage of the foreign exchange value of the underlying asset. The valuation of these options depends on the volatilities of the underlying assets and the currency exchange rate, as well as the correlation between the currency and the asset value.

Illustrative Example: Exotic Options—Perpetual Options

File Name: *Exotic Options—Perpetual Options*
Location: *Modeling Toolkit | Exotic Options | Perpetual Options*
Brief Description: *Computes the value of an American option that has a perpetual life where the underlying is a dividend-paying asset*
Requirements: *Modeling Toolkit*
Modeling Toolkit Function Used: *B2PerpetualCallOption, B2PerpetualPutOption*

The perpetual call and put options are American options with continuous dividends that can be executed at any time but have an infinite life (Figure 16-11). Clearly, a European option (exercisable only at termination) has a zero value; hence only American options are viable perpetual options. American closed-form approximations with 100-year maturities are also provided in the model to benchmark the results.

Illustrative Example: Exotic Options—Range Accruals (Fairway Options)

File Name: *Exotic Options—Range Accruals*
Location: *Modeling Toolkit | Exotic Options | Range Accruals*
Brief Description: *Computes the value of Fairway options or Range Accrual options, where the option pays a specified return if the underlying asset is within a range, but pays something else if it is outside the range, at any time during its maturity*
Requirements: *Modeling Toolkit*

PERPETUAL AMERICAN OPTION

Asset Price	$110.0000
Strike Price	$100.0000
Riskfree Rate	5.00%
Volatility	20.00%
Dividend Rate	5.00%

Perpetual Call Option	$27.6787
Perpetual Put Option	$20.1772
American Call Option	$27.6748
American Put Option	$20.1725

Figure 16-11   Perpetual American options.

A Range Accrual option is also called a Fairway option, whereby the option pays a certain return if the asset value stays within a certain range (between the upper and lower barriers), but pays a different amount or return if the asset value falls outside this range, during any time before and up to maturity. The name Fairway option is sometimes used because it is similar to the game of golf where if the ball stays within the fairway (a narrow path), then the ball is in play, and if it goes outside, a penalty might be imposed (in this case, a lower return). Such options and instruments can be solved using the Real Options SLS software as seen in Figure 16-12, using the Custom Option approach, where we enter the terminal equation as:

$$If(Asset > = LowerBarrier \ \& \ Asset < = Upper \ Barrier,$$

$$Asset*(1 + InsideReturn), \ Asset*(1 + OutsideReturn))$$

And if we wish to solve a European option, we enter the following as the intermediate equation:

OptionOpen

If we were solving an American option, then the intermediate equation would be:

$$If(Asset > = LowerBarrier \ \& \ Asset < = UpperBarrier, \ Max(Asset*(1$$
$$+ InsideReturn), OptionOpen), Max(Asset*(1 + OutsideReturn), OptionOpen))$$

Illustrative Example: Options Analysis—Binary Digital Instruments

File Name: *Options Analysis—Binary Digital Instruments*
Location: *Modeling Toolkit | Options Analysis | Binary Digital Instruments*
Brief Description: *Investment vehicles whereby the holder will be paid some cash amount or be provided the underlying asset as long as the value of the asset does not breach some specified barriers*
Requirements: *Modeling Toolkit*
Modeling Toolkit Functions Used: *B2Binary functions*

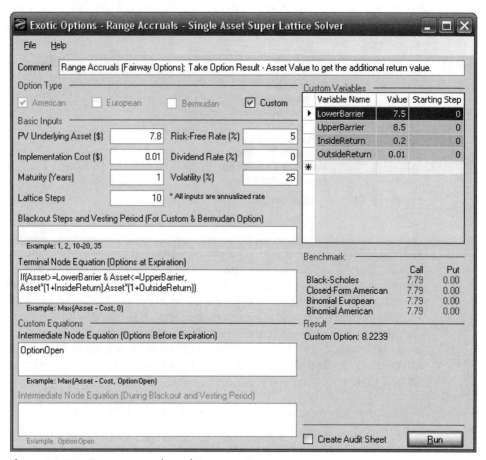

Figure 16-12 Range accruals or fairway options.

Binary exotic instruments (also known as *Digital*, *Accrual*, or *Fairway* instruments) become valuable only if a barrier (upper or lower barrier) is breached (or not), and the payout could be in the form of some prespecified cash amount or the underlying asset itself. The cash or asset exchanges hands either at the point when the barrier is breached, or at the end of the instrument's maturity (at expiration) assuming that the barrier is breached at some point prior to maturity.

For instance, the *Down and In Cash at Expiration* instrument implies that the instruments pay the specified cash amount at expiration if and only if the asset value breaches the lower barrier (asset value goes below the lower barrier), providing the holder of the instrument a safety net or a cash insurance in case the underlying asset does not perform well. The *Up and In* instruments are such that the cash or asset is provided if the underlying asset goes above the upper barrier threshold. The *Up and Out* or *Down and Out* instruments mean that the asset or cash is paid as long as the barrier is not breached. The *At Expiration* instruments mean that cash and assets are paid at maturity, whereas the *At Hit* instruments are payable at the point when the barrier is breached. Figure 16-13 shows a sample set of inputs in a binary digital instrument.

BINARY DIGITAL INSTRUMENTS

Input Assumptions

Asset Value or Stock Price	$10.00
Strike Price	$10.00
Upper Barrier Price	$8.00
Lower Barrier Price	$12.00
Cash Value	$10.00
Time to Maturity	1.00
Riskfree Rate	3.00%
Dividend Rate	0.00%
Annualized Volatility	25.00%
Delta T	0.00

Down and In Cash at Expiration	**$14.83**
Up and In Cash at Expiration	**$4.50**
Down and In Asset at Expiration	**$18.80**
Up and In Asset at Expiration	**$5.50**
Down and Out Cash at Expiration	**$0.00**
Up and Out Cash at Expiration	**$5.20**
Down and Out Asset at Expiration	**$0.00**
Up and Out Asset at Expiration	**$4.50**
Down and In Cash at Hit or Nothing	**$15.66**
Up and In Cash at Hit or Nothing	**$4.58**
Down and In Asset at Hit or Nothing	**$15.66**
Up and In Asset at Hit or Nothing	**$4.58**

Figure 16-13　Binary digital options.

Illustrative Example: Valuation of Debt and Interest Rate-Based Instruments with Options Embedded

Certain types of debt instruments come with an option-embedded provision, for instance, a bond might be callable if the market price exceeds a certain value (when prevailing interest rates drop, making it more profitable for the issuing company to call the debt and reissue new ones at the lower rate) or have a prepayment allowance of mortgages or lines of credit and debt. The option-adjusted spread, i.e., the additional premium that should be charged for the option provision, can be valued. Many other options embedded instruments exist or can be engineered. For instance, bond options, prepayment options on debt, inversely floating coupons, and many others, can be valued through the use of modified binomial lattices, where the short rate or spot interest rate can be simulated using a discrete step approach in a lattice. Please note that a regular binomial or trinomial lattice used to model stock prices and financial or exotic options cannot be used. These stock price lattices assume a Brownian motion process versus the modified lattices used in this section are calibrated to the term structure of interest rates with localized and changing volatilities over time. At each step in the lattice, the yield curve or term structure of interest rates is mirrored, through a series of interest rates and instantaneous volatilities changing over time.

For instance, Figure 16-14 shows the input parameters required for solving options-embedded debt instruments (e.g., face value of the bond or principal of the debt, maturity, total steps in the lattice, current spot risk-free interest rate, the current coupon

INVERSE FLOATER WITH YIELD CURVE AND VOLATILITY TERM STRUCTURE

Real Options Valuation
www.realoptionsvaluation.com

Face Value	$100.00	Market Price of Debt	$102.00	Delta T	0.4167
Maturity	5	Callable Price	$100.00	Value of Hedge	11.1989
Total Steps	12	Callable Step	5		
Current Rate (Yield)	1.50%				
Initial Coupon Rate	3.50%				

Stepped Up Coupon Payments		$1.50	$2.00	$2.00	$2.00	$2.00	$3.00	$3.00	$3.00	$3.00	$3.00	$4.00	$4.00
Periodic Interest Rates (Yields)	6.00%	6.00%	5.50%	5.50%	5.25%	5.25%	5.00%	5.00%	4.50%	4.50%	4.00%	4.00%	4.00%
Interest Volatilities	0.00%	25.00%	25.00%	25.00%	25.00%	25.00%	25.00%	25.00%	25.00%	25.00%	25.00%	25.00%	25.00%

Steps

	0	1	2	3	4	5	6	7	8	9	10	11	12

Short Rate Lattice

Step	0	1	2	3	4	5	6	7	8	9	10	11	12
0	6.00%	6.62%	5.49%	7.40%	6.32%	8.63%	6.35%	10.03%	1.11%	11.03%	0.01%	8.95%	13.22%
1		5.38%	4.45%	6.01%	5.13%	7.00%	5.16%	8.14%	0.90%	8.95%	0.01%	7.27%	10.73%
2			3.62%	4.88%	4.17%	5.69%	4.19%	6.61%	0.73%	7.27%	0.01%	5.90%	8.71%
3				3.96%	3.38%	4.62%	3.40%	5.37%	0.59%	5.90%	0.01%	4.79%	7.08%
4					2.75%	3.75%	2.76%	4.36%	0.48%	4.79%	0.01%	3.89%	5.75%
5						3.04%	2.24%	3.54%	0.39%	3.89%	0.00%	3.16%	4.66%
6							1.82%	2.87%	0.32%	3.16%	0.00%	2.56%	3.79%
7								2.33%	0.26%	2.56%	0.00%	2.08%	3.08%
8									0.21%	2.08%	0.00%	1.69%	2.50%
9										1.69%	0.00%	1.37%	2.03%
10											0.00%	1.11%	1.65%
11												0.91%	1.34%
12													1.09%

Floater Price Lattice   Using Modeling Toolkit Function: 108.7943

Step	0	1	2	3	4	5	6	7	8	9	10	11	12
0	108.7943	108.0641	107.1943	105.8311	105.4349	104.6346	104.0503	102.5540	102.9305	99.3574	100.3244	95.5588	94.6976
1		112.0328	110.9811	109.5144	108.8586	107.8621	106.8785	105.1301	104.9311	101.4562	101.7327	97.1018	95.6836
2			114.1615	112.6057	111.7256	110.5604	109.2349	107.2719	106.5863	103.1942	102.8917	98.3733	96.4918
3				115.1840	114.1127	112.8040	111.1887	109.0447	107.9507	104.6281	103.8432	99.4181	97.1530
4					116.0908	114.6612	112.8024	110.5067	109.0723	105.8075	104.6226	100.2748	97.6932
5						116.1930	114.1308	111.7090	109.9921	106.7752	105.2600	100.9758	98.1340
6							115.2217	112.6953	110.7451	107.5677	105.7806	101.5486	98.4933
7								113.5029	111.3606	108.2157	106.2053	102.0162	98.7861
8									111.8630	108.7448	106.5515	102.3974	99.0244
9										109.1763	106.8335	102.7080	99.2184
10											107.0630	102.9609	99.3761
11												103.1667	99.5044
12													99.6086

Price Lattice

Step	0	1	2	3	4	5	6	7	8	9	10	11	12
0	97.5954	96.7341	96.1846	95.1933	95.0709	94.5850	95.1972	95.0106	96.5852	94.5019	96.7383	94.4701	96.0604
1		100.3979	99.6968	98.6238	98.2804	97.6305	97.8968	97.4921	98.5459	96.5625	98.1511	96.0180	97.0607
2			102.6487	101.5050	100.9701	100.1784	100.1474	99.5562	100.1683	98.2694	99.3139	97.2936	97.8805
3				103.9095	103.2107	102.2981	102.0143	101.2654	101.5062	99.6779	100.2685	98.3419	98.5512
4					105.0683	104.0535	103.5568	102.6754	102.6062	100.8368	101.0505	99.2014	99.0991
5						105.5019	104.8270	103.8352	103.5085	101.7878	101.6901	99.9048	99.5463
6							105.8703	104.7868	104.2471	102.5667	102.2125	100.4797	99.9108
7								105.5661	104.8509	103.2036	102.6387	100.9489	100.2078
8									105.3439	103.7237	102.9861	101.3314	100.4495
9										104.1479	103.2691	101.6431	100.6462
10											103.4994	101.8969	100.8063
11												102.1035	100.9364
12													101.0421

Figure 16-14   Interest-based options lattice setup

rate, market price of the bond, and if the bond is callable at certain steps and at a certain predetermined callable price). Further, the period-specific coupon payments, risk-free or external interest rate and the interest rate volatilities can be entered as inputs. These three variables are entered as a time-series (creating different interest yield curves with specific shapes and localized volatilities) in rows 13 to 15 of the model.

The first step is to create the short rate lattice, that is, the fluctuations of the interest rates based on the term structure of interest rates and localized volatilities entered in rows 14 and 15. As a segue to the discussion, we can make sure that the interest rate lattice is built correctly by simply setting all the volatilities to zero and use some simple interest rates such as those seen in the first part of Figure 16-15. Here we see that step 1's lattice rate of 3% is the sum of step 0 and step 1's spot rates (1% and 2%), and step 2's lattice rate of 5% is the same as the sum of step 1 and step 2's rates (2% and 3%), and so forth. This indicates that the interest rate lattice is calibrated correctly for interest rates.

Finally, we can check that the interest rate lattice is calibrated correctly for the localized volatility by putting in nonzero annualized volatilities and make the number of years match the number of lattice steps (this means each step taken on the lattice is one year). The second part of Figure 16-15 shows this calibration (cell C5 = C6 = 12, row 15 are all nonzero volatilities, and the volatility checks on row 19 are simply

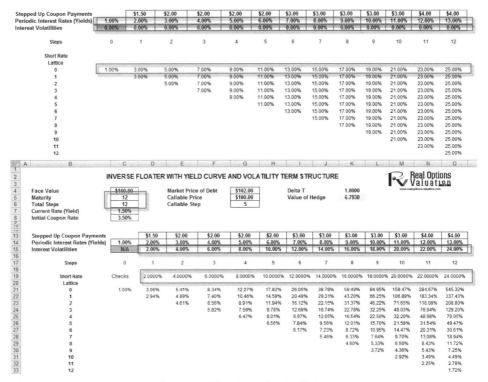

Figure 16-15 Interest rate lattice calibration of volatilities

the natural logarithmic ratios of the upper and lower values on the lattice divided by two). As an example, the formula in cell D19 is LN(D21/D22)/2, which yields 2%, the input local volatility for that step. The remaining columns in row 19 match the input volatilities, indicating that the interest rate lattice is calibrated correctly for the yield curve and its corresponding volatilities.

To create this interest rate lattice, use the *B2BDTInterestRateLattice* function and link the inputs to the relevant locations in the spreadsheet. Figure 16-16 shows the function used and the input links for cell C21, the first input in the interest rate lattice. Once this function is completed, copy this cell C21 and select the 13 × 13 matrix (we need a 13 × 13 matrix because we have a 12-step lattice starting at time 0, yielding a total of 13 steps) and paste the values in this area (C21:O33). Then, make sure the entire area is selected and click on *F2* and then hold down the *Shift + Control* keys and hit *Enter*. This will update the matrix to the results seen in Figure 16-14.

Replicate the steps above for the second matrix using the *B2BDTFloatingCoupon-PriceLattice* function, which computes the price of a bond with floating and changing coupon payments. Finally, generate the third lattice using *B2BDTNoncallableDebt-PriceLattice* for a non-callable straight bond value without any floating or changing coupons. The prices of these bonds are read directly off the lattices at step 0. For example, $108.79 and $97.59 for the two bonds respectively. The difference in price ($11.19 in cell K5) comes from the hedging effects of the floating coupons.

In addition, instead of having to build complete lattices, you can use the *B2BDT-FloatingCouponPriceValue* and *B2BDTNoncallableDebtPriceValue* functions to obtain the values of the bonds (see cells F35 and F51) and the difference is the value of the floating coupon hedge. These "value" functions come in really handy as the

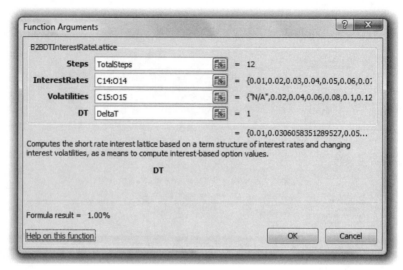

Figure 16-16 Modeling Toolkit function for cell C21

results can be obtained immediately without having to recreate cumbersome lattice models.

The following subsections briefly describe several most-commonly encountered options-embedded provisions in debt, for instance, inversely floating coupons, options adjusted spreads, callable bond options, and others. Each of these models applies the same techniques as described above, and the details can be viewed in the Modeling Toolkit software.

A. Inverse Floater Bond

File Name: *Options Analysis—Inverse Floater Bond Lattice*

Location: *Modeling Toolkit | Options Analysis | Inverse Floater Bond Lattice*

Brief Description: *An inverse floater bond or debt has a coupon payment that is inversely related to interest rates*

Requirements: *Modeling Toolkit*

Modeling Toolkit Functions Used: *B2BDTInterestRateLattice, B2BDTFloating-CouponPriceLattice, B2BDTNoncallableDebtPriceLattice, B2BDTFloatingCoupon-PriceValue, B2BDTNoncallableDebtPriceValue*

A floating coupon bond is a bond or other type of debt whose coupon rate has a direct or inverse relationship to short-term interest rates, and can be constructed using modified interest rate based binomial lattices. With an inverse floater, as interest rates rise, the coupon rate falls. When short-term interest rates fall, an inverse floater holder benefits in two ways: The bond appreciates in price and the yield increases. The opposite is true for a direct floater bond. Alternatively, coupons could be allowed to float based on some external benchmark. At each step in the lattice, the yield curve or term structure of interest rates is mirrored, through a series of interest rates and instantaneous volatilities changing over time. The inverse rate, or the amount of coupon rate decrease per percent increase in interest rate, is an input to compute this inverse floater. The result is the value of the inverse floater hedge. It is also assumed that this bond is callable, and the callable price and time step are also required inputs. For more details on the valuation, please review the Excel-based model *Inverse Floater Bond Lattice* in the Modeling Toolkit software.

B. Options Analysis—Options Adjusted Spreads Lattice

File Name: *Options Analysis—Options Adjusted Spreads on Debt*

Location: *Modeling Toolkit | Options Analysis | Options Adjusted Spreads on Debt*

Brief Description: *Options adjusted spreads or OAS, value the spread between a straight bond and a bond with some embedded options, such as callability covenants, and are used to create modified binomial lattices to value such instruments, assuming changing interest rates and volatilities over time*

Requirements: *Modeling Toolkit*

Modeling Toolkit Functions Used: *B2BDTInterestRateLattice, B2BDTNoncallableDebtPriceLattice, B2BDTCallableDebtPriceLattice*

Options adjusted spreads or OAS, value the spread between a straight bond and a bond with some embedded options, such as callability covenants or any other embedded options and covenants. Again, to value these types of instruments, we need to create modified binomial lattices, assuming changing interest rates and volatilities over time.

For specific modeling details, see Modeling Toolkit's *Options Adjusted Spreads* model. In the model, the interest rates are assumed to be changing over time, with changing instantaneous volatilities, as it is in real life, where the yield curve or term structure of interest rates changes over time and has different volatilities at different ends of the curve. The entire yield curve may shift, twist or bend, with higher maturity. Note that one of the key inputs in the model is the call price of the bond, and the time to call, translated into time steps. For instance, in a 4-year debt modeled using an 8-step lattice, if the bond is callable starting in the third year, then the callable step is set as 6. Be careful as the higher the number of steps, the longer it takes to generate and compute the lattices, depending on your computer's processor speed.

C. Illustrative Example: Options Analysis—Options on Debt

File Name: *Options Analysis—Options on Debt*

Location: *Modeling Toolkit | Options Analysis | Options on Debt*

Brief Description: *This model is used to compute options using the binomial lattice approach, assuming that the yield curve and term structure of interest rates change over time (both interest rates and volatility of interest rates are changing over time)*

Requirements: *Modeling Toolkit*

Modeling Toolkit Functions Used: *B2BDTInterestRateLattice, B2BDTZeroPriceLattice, B2BDTAmericanCallonDebtLattice, B2BDTAmericanPutonDebtLattice, B2BDTEuropeanCallonDebtLattice, B2BDTEuropeanPutonDebtLattice, B2BDTAmericanCallonDebtValue, B2BDTAmericanPutonDebtValue, B2BDTEuropeanCallonDebtValue, B2BDTEuropeanPutonDebtValue*

This example illustrates how to compute the American and European options on debt using a binomial lattice modified to account for changing volatilities and term structure of interest rates over the life of the option. This model provides a sample template for building interest rate pricing lattices using the Modeling Toolkit functions. Please review the *Options on Debt* model in the toolkit for more details.

The model example is set up to only compute up to 10 steps. Using this template, you can generate many additional steps as required, as well as create customized lattices to value any types of embedded-option debt instruments. Also, you can use the Real Options SLS software to value many types of options and options-embedded instruments. The modified lattices introduced in these last few sections are specific to financial instruments that depend on interest rates, where the underlying asset's fundamental values are driven by interest rate fluctuations. Note that in the model, the entire lattices can be built using the "lattice" functions or the value of the bond option can be computed simply by using the "value" functions in the model.

Illustrative Example: Options Analysis—Options Trading Strategies

File Name: *Options Analysis—Options Strategies*
Location: *Modeling Toolkit | Options Analysis | Options Trading Strategies*
Brief Description: *Illustrating various options trading strategies such as covered calls, protective puts, bull and bear spreads, straddles and strangles*
Requirements: *Modeling Toolkit*
Modeling Toolkit Functions Used: *B2OptionStrategyLongCoveredCall, B2OptionStrategyWriteCoveredCall, B2OptionStrategyLongProtectivePut, B2OptionStrategyWriteProtectivePut, B2OptionStrategyLongBullDebitSpread, B2OptionStrategyLongBearDebitSpread, B2OptionStrategyLongBullCreditSpread, B2OptionStrategyLongBearCreditSpread, B2OptionStrategyLongStraddle, B2OptionStrategyWriteStraddle, B2OptionStrategyLongStrangle, B2OptionStrategyWriteStrangle*

We will start by discussing a simple option example. Suppose ABC's stock is currently trading at $100, you can either purchase 1 stock of ABC for ABC or purchase an options contract on ABC. Let's see what happens. If you purchase the stock at $100 and in 3 months if the stock goes up to $110, you made $10 or 10%. And if it goes down to $90, you lost $10 of 10%. This is simple enough. Now, suppose you purchased a European call option with a strike price of $100 (at-the-money) for a 3-month expiration which costs $5 each, and if the underlying stock price goes up to $110, you execute the call option, buy the stock at $100 contractually, and sell the stock in the market at $110, and after the cost of the option, you net $110–$100–$5 = $5. The cost of the option was $5 and you made $5, the return was 100%. If the stock goes down to $90, you let the option expire worthless and lose the $5 payment to buy the option, and not a loss of $10 if you held the stock. In addition, if the stock goes to $0, you only lose $5 if you held the option versus losing $100 if you held the stock! This shows the limited downside of the option, and unlimited upside leverage, the concept of hedging. The problem is, you can purchase many options through the leverage power of options. For instance, if you bought 20 options at $5 each, it costs you $100, the same as holding one stock. If the stock stays at $100 at maturity, you lose nothing on the stock, but you would lose 100% or 100% of your option premium. This is the concept of speculation!

Now, let's complicate things. We can represent the payoffs on call and put options graphically as seen in Figure 16-17. For instance, take the call option with a strike price of $10 purchased when the stock price was also $10. The premium paid to buy the option was $2. Therefore, if at maturity, the stock price goes up to $15, the call option is executed (buy the stock at the contractual price of $10, turn around and sell the stock at the market price of $15, make $5 in gross profits, and deduct the cost of the option of $2, yields a net profit of $3). Following the same logic, the remaining payoff schedule can be determined as shown in Figure 16-17. Note that the breakeven point is when the stock price is $12 (strike price plus the option premium). If the stock price falls to $10 or below, the net is −$2 in losses because the option will never be exercised and the loss is the premium paid on the option. We can now chart the payoff schedules for buying (long) and selling (short) simple calls and puts. The "hockey stick" charts shown are the various option payoff schedules.

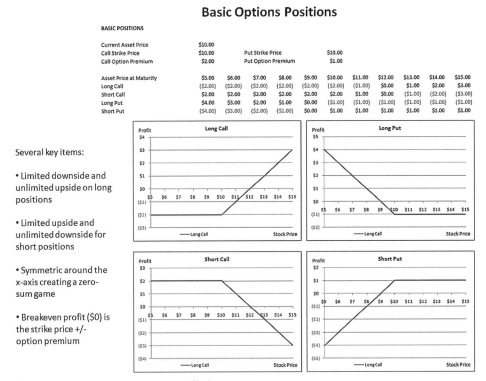

Figure 16-17   Basic option payoff chart

Next, we can use these simple calls and puts and put them in a portfolio or various combinations to create options trading strategies. Options trading strategy refers to the use of multiple investment vehicles, including call options, put options and the underlying stock. These vehicles can be purchased or sold at various strike prices to create strategies that will take advantage of certain market conditions. For instance, Figure 16-18 shows a Covered Call strategy, which comprises a long stock and short call combination. The position requires buying a stock and simultaneously selling a call option on that stock. The colored charts in the Excel model provide a better visual than those shown in this chapter. Please refer to the model for more details.

Just like in previous sections in this chapter, the functions used are matrices, where the first row is always the stock price at maturity, the second and third rows are the individual positions' net returns (e.g., in the case of the covered call, the second row represents the returns on the stock and the third row represents the short call position), and the fourth row is always the net total profit of the positions combined. As usual, apply the relevant Modeling Toolkit equations, copy and paste the cell's functions to a matrix comprising 4 rows by 18 columns, select the entire matrix area, hold down the ***Shift + Control*** keys and hit ***Enter*** to fill in the entire matrix. There are also two optional input parameters, the starting and ending points on the plot. These values refer to the starting and ending stock prices at maturity to analyze. If left empty, the software will automatically decide on these values.

The model also illustrates other options trading strategies. Figure 16-18 shows the graphical representation of these positions and the following lists these strategies and how they are obtained.

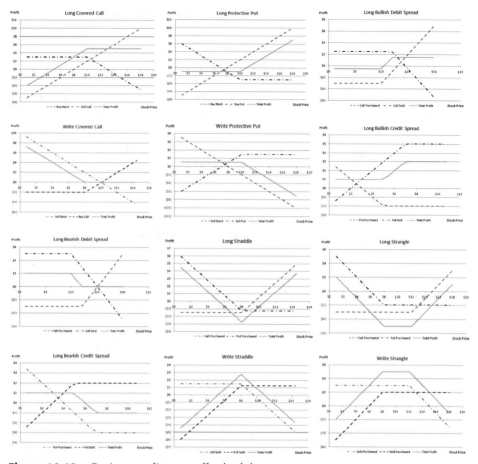

Figure 16-18 Options trading payoff schedule

- A long covered call position is a combination of buying the stock (underlying asset) and selling a call of the same asset, typically at a different strike price than the starting stock price.

- A writing a covered call is a combination of selling the stock (underlying asset) and buying a call of the same asset, typically at a different strike price than the starting stock price.

- A long protective put position is a combination of buying the stock (underlying asset) and buying a put of the same asset, typically at a different strike price than the starting stock price.

- Writing a protective put is a combination of selling the stock (underlying asset) and selling a put of the same asset, typically at a different strike price than the starting stock price.

- A long bull spread position is the same as writing a bearish spread, both of which are designed to be profitable if the underlying security rises in price. A bullish debit spread involves purchasing a call and selling a further out-of-the-money call. A bullish credit spread involves selling a put and buying further out-of-the money put.

- A long bearish spread takes advantage of a falling market and the strategy involves the simultaneous purchase and sale of options and both puts and calls can be used. Typically, a higher strike price option is purchased and a lower strike price option is sold. The options should have the same expiration date.

- A long bull spread position is the same as writing a bearish spread, both of which are designed to be profitable if the underlying security rises in price. A bullish debit spread involves purchasing a call and selling a further out-of-the-money call. A bullish credit spread involves selling a put and buying further out-of-the money put.

- A long bearish spread takes advantage of a falling market and the strategy involves the simultaneous purchase and sale of options and both puts and calls can be used. Typically, a higher strike price is purchased and a lower strike price is sold. The options should have the same expiration date.

- A long straddle position requires the purchase of an equal number of puts and calls with identical strike price and expiration. A straddle provides the opportunity to profit from a prediction about the future volatility of the market. Long straddles are used to profit from high volatility but the direction of the move is unknown.

- Writing a straddle position requires the sale of an equal number of puts and calls with identical strike price and expiration. A straddle provides the opportunity to profit from a prediction about the future volatility of the market. Writing a straddles is used to profit from low volatility but the direction of the move is unknown.

- A long strangle requires the purchase of an out-of-the-money call and the purchase of an out-of-the-money put for a similar expiration (or within the same month), and profits from significant volatility of either directional move of the stock.

- Writing a strangle strategy requires the sale of an out-of-the-money call and the sale of an out-of-the-money put for a similar expiration (or within the same month), and profits from low volatility of either directional move of the stock.

Illustrative Example: Options Analysis—Five Plain Vanilla Options

File Names: *Options Analysis—Plain Vanilla Call Options (I-IV) and Plain Vanilla Put Options*
Location: *Modeling Toolkit | Real Options | Plain Vanilla Options (I-IV and Put Options)*
Brief Description: *Plain vanilla call and put option examples solved using the Real Options SLS software by applying advanced binomial lattices*
Requirements: *Real Options SLS, Modeling Toolkit*

This section shows the five plain vanilla call and put options solved using Real Options SLS. These are plain vanillas, for they are the simplest call and put options, without any exotic add-ons. A simple European call option is computed in this example using SLS. To follow along, start this example file by selecting **Start | Programs | Real Options Valuation | Real Options SLS | Real Options SLS**. Then, click on the first icon, Create a New Single Asset Model, and when the single asset SLS opens, click on **File | Examples**. This is a list of the example files that come with the software for the single asset lattice solver. Start the Plain Vanilla Call Option I example. This example file will be loaded into the SLS software, as seen in Figure 16-19. Alternatively, you can start the *Modeling Toolkit* software, click on **Modeling Toolkit** in Excel, select *Real Options SLS*, and select the appropriate *Options Analysis* files. As this chapter uses the Real Options SLS software, it is recommended that readers who are not exposed to real options analysis or financial options analysis first familiarize him/herself with the introductory materials in Appendix 1 of this book before proceeding with this chapter.

The starting PV Underlying Asset or starting stock price is $100, and the Implementation Cost or strike price is $100 with a 5-year maturity. The annualized risk-free rate of return is 5%, and the historical, comparable, or future expected annualized volatility is 10%. Click on **RUN** (or Alt-R), a 100-step binomial lattice is computed, and the results indicate a value of $23.3975 for both the European and American call options. Benchmark values using Black-Scholes and Closed-Form American approximation models as well as standard plain vanilla Binomial American and Binomial European Call and Put Options with 1,000-step binomial lattices are also computed. Notice that only the American and European options are selected, and the computed results are for these simple plain vanilla American and European call options.

The benchmark results use both closed-form models (Black-Scholes and Closed-Form Approximation models) and 1,000-step binomial lattices on plain vanilla options.

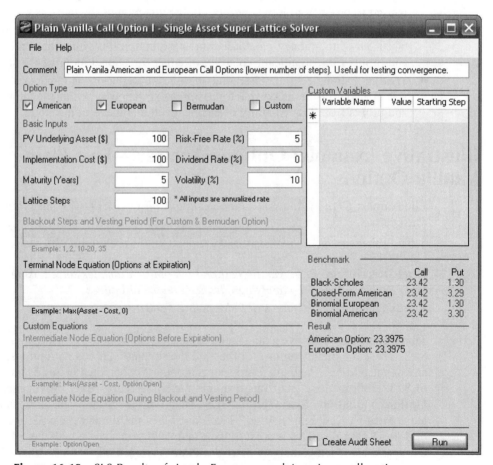

Figure 16-19 SLS Results of simple European and American call options.

You can change the steps to *1,000* in the basic inputs section (or open and use the *Plain Vanilla Call Option II* example model) to verify that the answers computed are equivalent to the benchmarks as seen in Figure 16-20. Notice that, of course, the values computed for the American and European options are identical to each other and identical to the benchmark values of $23.4187, as it is never optimal to exercise a standard plain vanilla call option early if there are no dividends. Be aware that the higher the lattice step, the longer it takes to compute the results. It is advisable to start with lower lattice steps to make sure the analysis is robust and then progressively increase lattice steps to check for results convergence. See Chapter 6 of *Real Options Analysis*, Second Edition (Wiley, 2006) by Dr. Johnathan Mun on convergence criteria on lattices for more details about binomial lattice convergence as to how many lattice steps are required for a robust option valuation. However, as a rule of thumb, the typical convergence occurs between 100 and 1,000 steps.

Alternatively, you can enter Terminal and Intermediate Node Equations for a call option to obtain the same results. Notice that using 100 steps and creating your own Terminal Node Equation of *Max(Asset-Cost,0)* and Intermediate Node Equation of *Max(Asset-Cost,OptionOpen)* will yield the same answer. When entering your own equations, make sure that Custom Option is first checked.

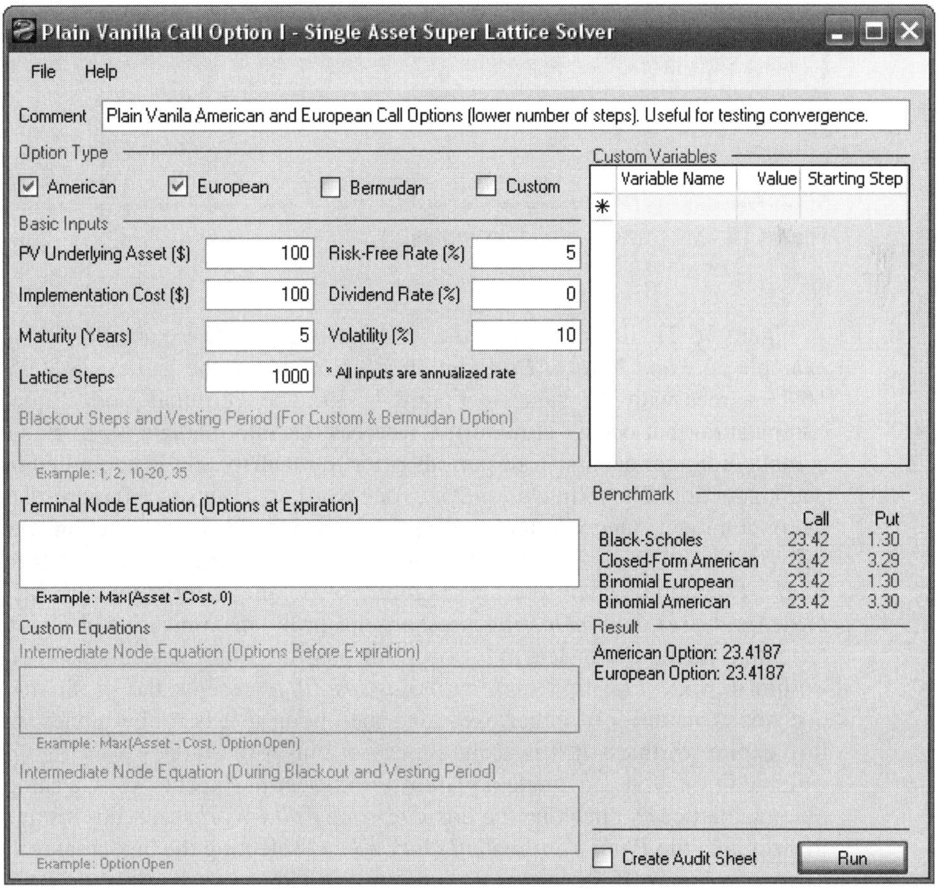

Figure 16-20   SLS Comparing results with benchmarks.

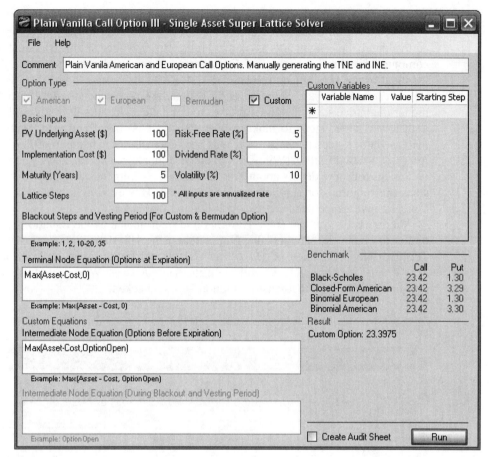

Figure 16-21   Custom equation inputs.

Figure 16-21 illustrates how the analysis is done. The example file used in this example is: *Plain Vanilla Call Option III*. Notice that the value $23.3975 in Figure 16-21 agrees with the value in Figure 16-19. The Terminal Node Equation is the computation that occurs at maturity, whereas the Intermediate Node Equation is the computation that occurs at all periods prior to maturity and is computed using backward induction. The term *OptionOpen* (one word, without spaces) represents "keeping the option open," and is often used in the Intermediate Node Equation when analytically representing the fact that the option is not executed but kept open for possible future execution. Therefore, in Figure 16-21, the Intermediate Node Equation *Max(Asset-Cost,OptionOpen)* represents the profit maximization decision of either executing the option or leaving it open for possible future execution. In contrast, the Terminal Node Equation of *Max(Asset-Cost,0)* represents the profit maximization decision at maturity of either executing the option if it is in-the-money, or allowing it to expire worthless if it is at-the-money or out-of-the-money.

In addition, you can create an Audit Worksheet in Excel to view a sample 10-step binomial lattice by checking the box *Generate Audit Worksheet*. For instance, loading the example file *Plain Vanilla Call Option I* and selecting the box creates a worksheet as seen in Figure 16-22. Several items on this audit worksheet are noteworthy:

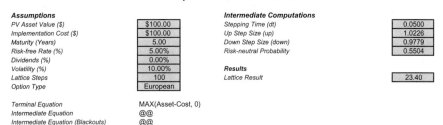

Option Valuation Audit Sheet

Assumptions

PV Asset Value ($)	$100.00
Implementation Cost ($)	$100.00
Maturity (Years)	5.00
Risk-free Rate (%)	5.00%
Dividends (%)	0.00%
Volatility (%)	10.00%
Lattice Steps	100
Option Type	European

Terminal Equation   MAX(Asset-Cost, 0)
Intermediate Equation   @@
Intermediate Equation (Blackouts)   @@

Intermediate Computations

Stepping Time (dt)	0.0500
Up Step Size (up)	1.0226
Down Step Size (down)	0.9779
Risk-neutral Probability	0.5504

Results

Lattice Result	23.40

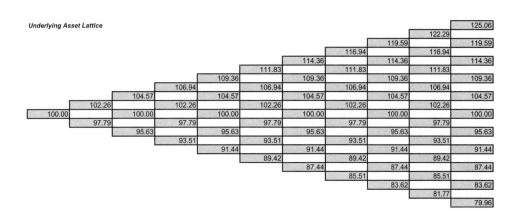

Underlying Asset Lattice

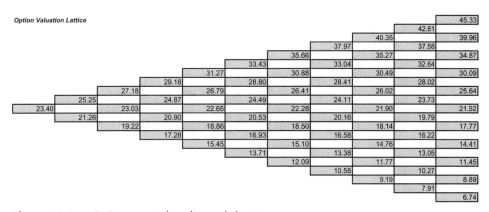

Option Valuation Lattice

Figure 16-22 SLS generated audit worksheet.

- The audit worksheet generated will show the first 10 steps of the lattice, regardless of how many you enter. That is, if you enter 1,000 steps, the first 10 steps will be generated. If a complete lattice is required, simply enter 10 steps in the SLS and the full 10-step lattice will be generated instead. The Intermediate Computations and Results are for the Super Lattice, based on the number of lattice steps entered, and not based on the 10-step lattice generated. To obtain the Intermediate Computations for 10-step lattices, simply rerun the analysis inputting 10 as the lattice steps. This way, the audit worksheet generated will be for a 10-step lattice, and the results from SLS will now be comparable (Figure 16-23).

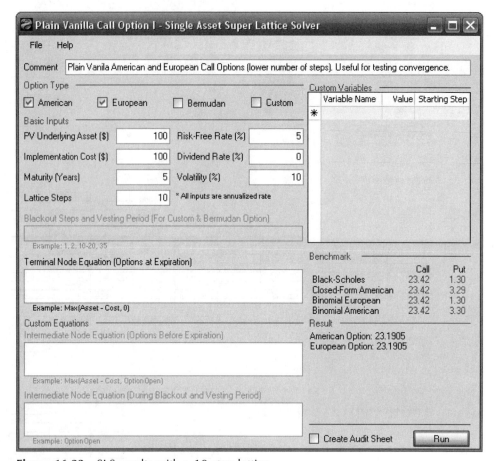

Figure 16-23 SLS results with a 10-step lattice.

- The worksheet only provides values as it is assumed that the user was the one who entered in the terminal and intermediate node equations. Hence there is really no need to re-create these equations in Excel again. The user can always reload the SLS file and view the equations or print out the form if required (by clicking on **File | Print**).

The software also allows you to save or open analysis files. That is, all the inputs in the software will be saved and can be retrieved for future use. The results will not be saved because you may accidentally delete or change an input, and the results will no longer be valid. In addition, rerunning the super lattice computations will only take a few seconds, and it is always advisable for you to rerun the model when opening an old analysis file.

You may also enter in Blackout Steps. These are the steps on the super lattice that will have different behaviors than the terminal or intermediate steps. For instance, you can enter *1,000* as the lattice steps, and enter *0–400* as the blackout steps, and some Blackout Equation (e.g., *OptionOpen*). This means that for the first 400 steps, the option holder can only keep the option open. Other examples include entering: *1, 3, 5, 10* if these are the lattice steps where blackout periods occur. You will have to calculate the relevant steps within the lattice where the blackout exists. For instance, if the blackout exists in years 1 and 3 on a 10-year, 10-step lattice, then steps 1, 3 will be the blackout dates. This blackout step feature comes in handy when analyzing options with holding periods, vesting periods, or periods where the option cannot be executed. Employee stock options have blackout and vesting periods, and certain contractual real options have periods during which the option cannot be executed (e.g., cooling-off periods, or proof of concept periods).

If equations are entered into the Terminal Node Equation box and American, European, or Bermudan Options are chosen, the Terminal Node Equation you entered will be the one used in the super lattice for the terminal nodes. However, for the intermediate nodes, the American option assumes the same Terminal Node Equation plus the ability to keep the option open; the European option assumes that the option can only be kept open and not executed; while the Bermudan option assumes that during the blackout lattice steps, the option will be kept open and cannot be executed. If you also enter the Intermediate Node Equation, the Custom Option should be first chosen (otherwise you cannot use the Intermediate Node Equation box). The Custom Option result uses all the equations you have entered in Terminal, Intermediate, and Intermediate with Blackout sections.

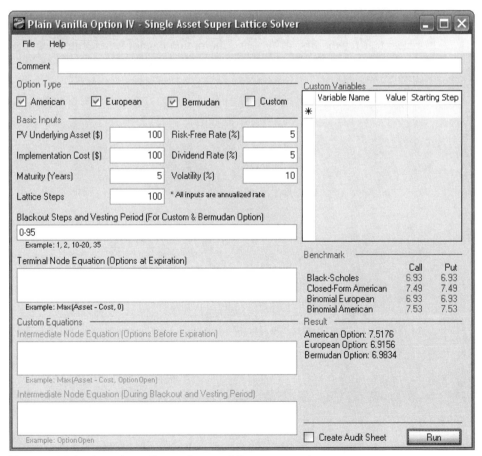

Figure 16-24 American, Bermudan, and European options.

The Custom Variables list is where you can add, modify, or delete custom variables, the variables that are required beyond the basic inputs. For instance, when running an abandonment option, you need the salvage value. You can add this in the Custom Variables list, provide it a name (a variable name must be a single word), the appropriate value, and the starting step when this value becomes effective. That is, if you have multiple salvage values (i.e., if salvage values change over time), you can enter the same variable name (e.g., *salvage*) several times, but each time, its value changes and you can specify when the appropriate salvage value becomes effective. For instance, in a 10-year, 100-step super lattice problem where there are two salvage values—$100 occurring within the first 5 years and increases to $150 at the beginning of Year 6—you can enter two salvage variables with the same name, $100 with a starting step of 0, and $150 with a starting step of 51. Be careful here as Year 6 starts at step 51 and not 61. That is, for a 10-year option with a 100-step lattice, we have: Steps 1–10 = Year 1; Steps 11–20 = Year 2; Steps 21–30 = Year 3; Steps 31–40 = Year 4; Steps 41–50 = Year 5; Steps 51–60 = Year 6; Steps 61–70 = Year 7; Steps 71–80 = Year 8; Steps 81–90 = Year 9; and Steps 91–100 = Year 10. Finally, incorporating *0* as a blackout step indicates that the option cannot be executed immediately.

Finally, using the example file, *Plain Vanilla Option IV*, we see that when a dividend exists, the American option with its ability for early exercise, is worth more than the Bermudan which has early exercise but blackout periods when it cannot be exercised (e.g., Blackout Steps of 0–95 for a 100-step lattice on a 5 year maturity model means that for the first 4.75 years, the option cannot be executed), which in turn is worth more than the European option, which can only be exercised at expiration (Figure 16-24).

Appendix 1: Getting Started with Real Options SLS Software Application on Modeling Customizable Exotic and Real Options

The **Real Options Super Lattice Software (SLS)** comprises several modules, including the **Single-Asset and Single-Phased SLS**, **Multiple-Asset or Multiple-Phased SLS**, **Multinomial Lattice Solver**, **SLS Excel Solution**, and **SLS Functions** (Figure A1-1). These modules are highly powerful and customizable binomial and multinomial lattice solvers and can be used to solve many types of options (including the three main families of options: *real options*, which deals with physical and intangible assets; *financial options*, which deals with financial assets and the investments of such assets; and *employee stock options*, which deals with financial assets provided to employees within a corporation). The power of this software is the ability to create and financially engineer your own customized options, as seen throughout this book. Specifically, this software can be used to solve exotic options that cannot be solved using closed-form models or equations. For instance, exotic instruments such as fairway options, basket of exotics, chooser options, options with specific blackout periods and vesting periods, and many other combinations and *a la carte* options that a bank or investment company can engineer, can be readily solved using this software. This Appendix is not meant as a detailed training for these exotic options; rather, it is designed as a getting started primer for using the SLS software. Please refer to the rest of the book for details on applying this software in solving exotic options, as well as the Basel II Modeling Toolkit for running and solving these exotics.

Briefly, the SLS software has several modules as seen in Figure A1-1:

- The **single-asset and single-phased module** is used primarily for solving options with a *single underlying asset* using binomial lattices. Even highly complex options with a single underlying asset can be solved using the SLS, such as options with vesting and blackouts, barrier options, options with exotic caveats and requirements, and many others.
- The **multiple-phased or multiple-asset module** is used for solving options with *multiple underlying assets* and sequential compound options with *multiple phases*

Figure A1-1   The SLS Software's main page.

using binomial lattices. Highly complex options with multiple underlying assets and phases can be solved using the MSLS, including the ability to choose from several underlying assets or benchmarks options (e.g., two asset correlation option, exchange of asset option, option that vests depending on the outcome of another asset or option, switching options, chooser options, and many others).

- The **multinomial lattice solver module** uses *multinomial lattices* (trinomial quadranomial, pentanomial) to solve specific options that cannot be solved using binomial lattices. These are exotics that depend on the underlying assets that follow mean-reverting processes (options tied to interest rates or inflation rates), jump-diffusion processes (options on commodity assets, or assets whose prices follow stochastic jumps such as the price of oil or electricity), and so forth.

- The **SLS Excel Solution** implements the SLS and MSLS computations within the Excel environment, allowing users to access the SLS and MSLS functions directly in Excel. This feature facilitates model building, formula and value linking and embedding, as well as running risk-based simulations with Risk Simulator, and provides the user sample templates to create such models.

- The **SLS Functions** are additional real options and financial options models accessible directly through Excel. This facilitates model building, linking and embedding, and running simulations.

The SLS software was created by Dr. Johnathan Mun, one of the authors of this book, and accompanies the materials presented at different training courses on real options simulation, and employee stock options valuation taught by Dr. Mun, including the Certified in Risk Management (CRM) seminars. While the software and its models are based on his books, the training courses cover the real options subject matter in more depth, including the solution of sample business cases, the solution of exotic options, and the framing of real options of actual cases. For real options applications, yet another vast area that is untapped in the banking industry, it is strongly recommended that the reader familiarize him- or herself with the fundamental concepts of real options by either watching some of the getting started videos in the accompanying CD or reading Chapters 1 to 7 of *Real Options Analysis*, Second Edition (Wiley, 2006), prior to attempting an in-depth real options analysis using this software.

Single-Asset and Single-Phased Module

Figure A1-2 illustrates the single-asset and single-phased SLS module. After installing the software, the user can access the SLS by clicking on **Start** | **Programs** | **Real Options Valuation** | **Real Options SLS** | **Real Options SLS** and choose the **Create**

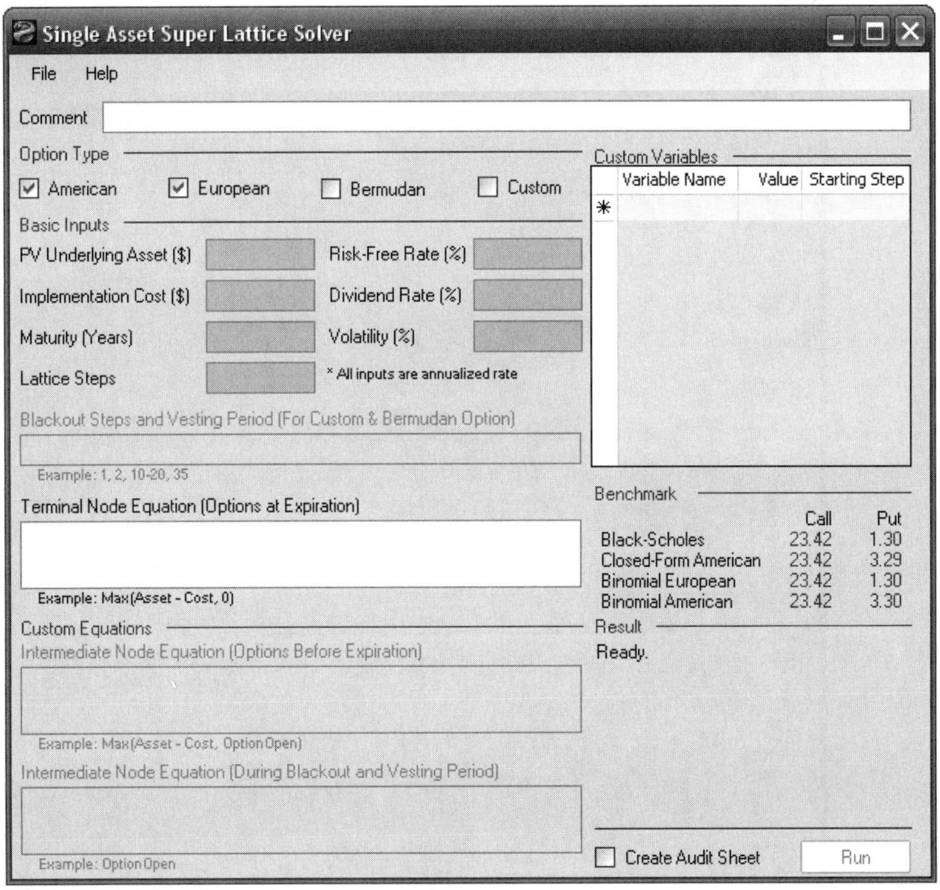

Figure A1-2   Single asset and single phase SLS.

a New Single Asset Option Model. The module has several sections: Option Type, Basic Inputs, Custom Equations, Custom Variables, Benchmark, Result, and Create Audit Worksheet.

To help you get started, several simple examples are in order. A simple European call option is computed in this example using SLS. To follow along, start this example file by selecting **Start | Programs | Real Options Valuation | Real Options SLS | Real Options SLS**. Then, click on the first icon, Create a New Single Asset Model (Figure A1-1) and when the single asset SLS opens (Figure A1-2), click on **File | Examples**. This is a list of the example files that come with the software for the single- asset lattice solver. Start the Plain Vanilla Call Option I example. This example file will be loaded into the SLS software as seen in Figure A1-3. The starting PV Underlying Asset or starting stock price is $100, and the Implementation Cost or strike price is $100 with a five-year maturity. The annualized risk-free rate of return is 5 percent, and the historical, comparable, or future expected annualized volatility is 10 percent. Click on **RUN** (or Alt-R) and a 100-step binomial lattice is computed, the results indicating a value of $23.3975 for both the European and American call options. Benchmark values using Black-Scholes and Closed-Form American approximation models, as well as standard plain vanilla Binomial American and Binomial

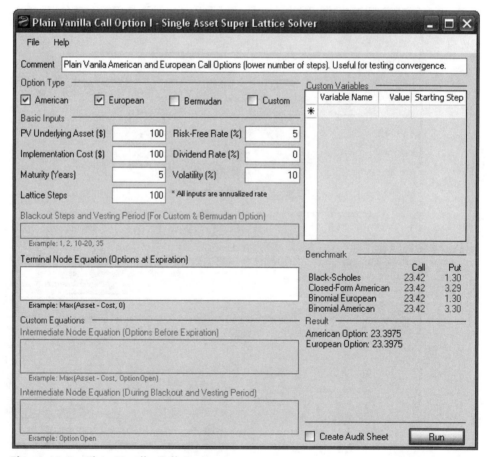

Figure A1-3 Plain Vanilla Call Option I.

European call and put options with 1,000-step binomial lattices are also computed. Notice that only the American and European options are selected and the computed results are for these simple plain-vanilla American and European call options.

The benchmark results use both closed-form models (Black-Scholes and Closed-Form Approximation models) and 1,000-step binomial lattices on plain vanilla options. You can change the steps to *1,000* in the basic inputs section to verify that the answers computed are equivalent to the benchmarks as seen in Figure A1-4. Notice that, of course, the values computed for the American and European options are identical to each other and identical to the benchmark values of $23.4187, as it is never optimal to exercise a standard plain vanilla call option early if there are no dividends. Be aware that the higher the lattice step, the longer it takes to compute the results. It is advisable to start with lower lattice steps to make sure the analysis is robust and then progressively increase lattice steps to check for results convergence. See Chapter 6 of *Real Options Analysis*, Second Edition (Wiley, 2006) by Dr. Mun for more details about binomial lattice convergence as to how many lattice steps are required for a robust option valuation. However, as a rule of thumb, the typical convergence occurs between 100 and 1,000 steps. It is important to note that it would be impossible to solve this manually, as a 1,000-step binomial lattice would take many, many years to compute

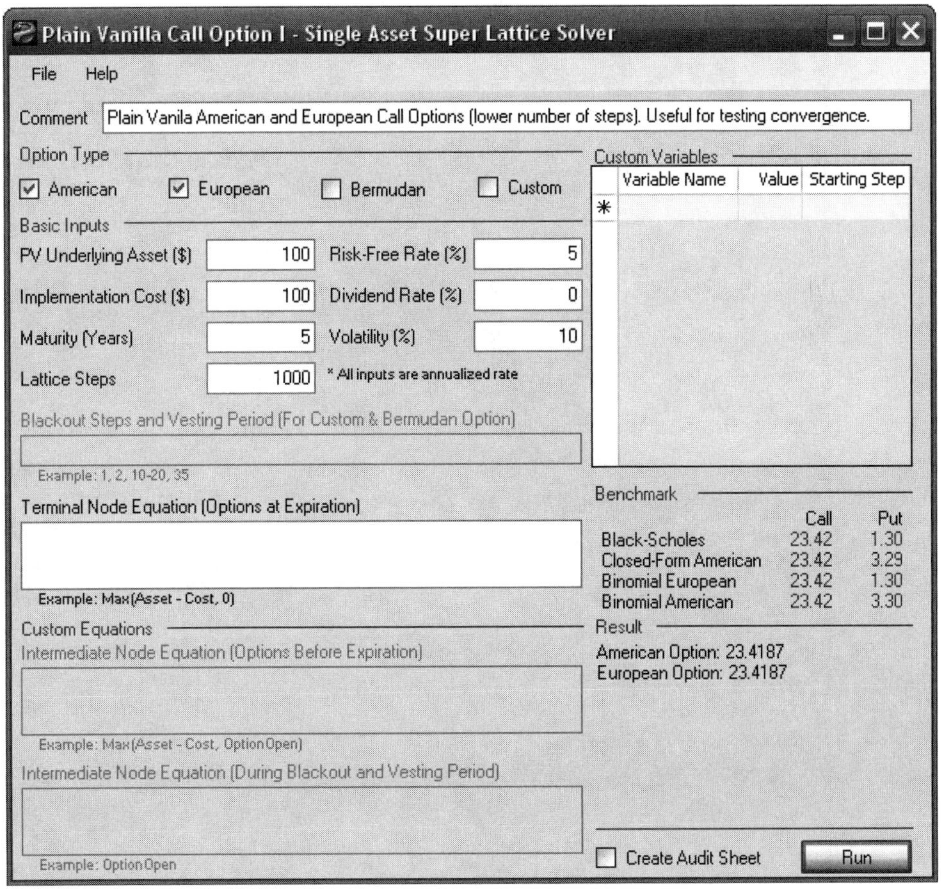

Figure A1-4   1,000-step lattice result.

and solve by hand. In comparison, the SLS software uses advanced algorithms to compute the results in seconds.

Alternatively, you can enter Terminal and Intermediate Node Equations for a call option to obtain the same results. Notice that using 100 steps and creating your own Terminal Node Equation of *Max(Asset-Cost,0)* and Intermediate Node Equation of *Max(Asset-Cost,OptionOpen)* will yield the same answer. When entering your own equations, make sure that Custom Option is first checked.

Figure A1-5 illustrates how the analysis is done. The example file used in this example is: *Plain Vanilla Call Option III*. Notice that the value $23.3975 in Figure A1-5 agrees with the value in Figure A1-3. The Terminal Node Equation is the computation that occurs at maturity, while the Intermediate Node Equation is the computation that occurs at all periods prior to maturity, and is computed using backward induction. The term *OptionOpen* (one word, without spaces) represents "keeping the option open" and is often used in the Intermediate Node Equation when analytically representing the fact that the option is not executed but kept open for possible future execution. Therefore, in Figure A1-5, the Intermediate Node Equation *Max(Asset-Cost,OptionOpen)* represents the profit maximization decision of either executing the option or leaving it open for possible future execution. In contrast, the Terminal Node

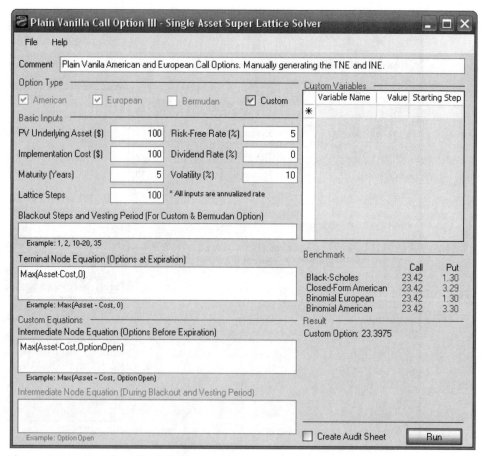

Figure A1-5   Plain Vanilla Call Option II.

Equation of *Max(Asset-Cost,0)* represents the profit maximization decision at maturity of either executing the option if it is in-the-money, or allowing it to expire worthless if it is at-the-money or out-of-the-money.

Note that the customizable feature of these equations is the power of this software, where in the hands of the expert user, one can financially engineer any type of exotic options and price them accordingly, as is seen in examples throughout this book, and where the Modeling Toolkit provides an abundance of examples.

In addition, you can create an Audit Worksheet in Excel to view a sample 10-step binomial lattice by checking the box *Generate Audit Worksheet.* For instance, loading the example file *Plain Vanilla Call Option I* and selecting the box creates a worksheet as seen in Figure A1-6. Several items on this audit worksheet are noteworthy:

- The audit worksheet generated will show the first 10 steps of the lattice, regardless of how many you enter. That is, if you enter 1,000 steps, the first 10 steps will be generated. If a complete lattice is required, simply enter 10 steps in the SLS and the full 10-step lattice will be generated instead. The Intermediate Computations and Results are for the Super Lattice, based on the number of lattice steps entered, and not on the 10-step lattice generated. To obtain the Intermediate Computations for 10-step lattices, simply rerun the analysis inputting 10 as the lattice steps. This way, the audit worksheet generated will be for a 10-step lattice, and the results from SLS will now be comparable (Figure A1-7).
- The worksheet only provides values as it is assumed that the user was the one who entered in the terminal and intermediate node equations. Hence there is really no need to re-create these equations in Excel again. The user can always reload the SLS file and view the equations or print out the form if required (by clicking on **File | Print**).

The software also allows you to save or open analysis files. That is, all the inputs in the software will be saved and can be retrieved for future use. The results will not be saved because you may accidentally delete or change an input and the results will no longer be valid. In addition, rerunning the super lattice computations will only take a few seconds, and it is always advisable for you to rerun the model when opening an old analysis file.

You may also enter in Blackout Steps. These are the steps on the super lattice that will have different behaviors than the terminal or intermediate steps. For instance, you can enter *1,000* as the lattice steps, and enter *0–400* as the blackout steps, and some Blackout Equation (e.g., *OptionOpen*). This means that for the first 400 steps, the option holder can only keep the option open. Other examples include entering: *1, 3, 5, 10* if these are the lattice steps where blackout periods occur. You will have to calculate the relevant steps within the lattice where the blackout exists. For instance, if the blackout exists in years 1 and 3 on a 10-year, 10-step lattice, then steps 1, 3 will be the blackout dates. This blackout step feature comes in handy when analyzing options with holding periods, vesting periods, or periods where the option cannot be executed. Employee stock options have blackout and vesting periods, and certain contractual real options have periods during which the option cannot be executed (e.g., cooling-off periods, or proof of concept periods).

If equations are entered into the Terminal Node Equation box and American, European, or Bermudan options are chosen, the Terminal Node Equation you entered will be the one used in the super lattice for the terminal nodes. However, for the intermedi-

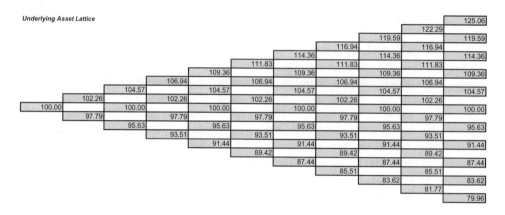

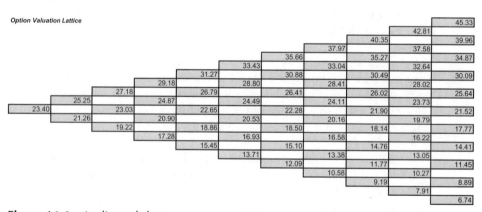

Figure A1-6 Audit worksheet.

ate nodes, the American option assumes the same Terminal Node Equation plus the ability to keep the option open; the European option assumes that the option can only be kept open and not executed; while the Bermudan option assumes that during the blackout lattice steps, the option will be kept open and cannot be executed. If you also enter the Intermediate Node Equation, the Custom Option should be first chosen (otherwise you cannot use the Intermediate Node Equation box). The Custom Option result uses all the equations you have entered in Terminal, Intermediate, and Intermediate with Blackout sections.

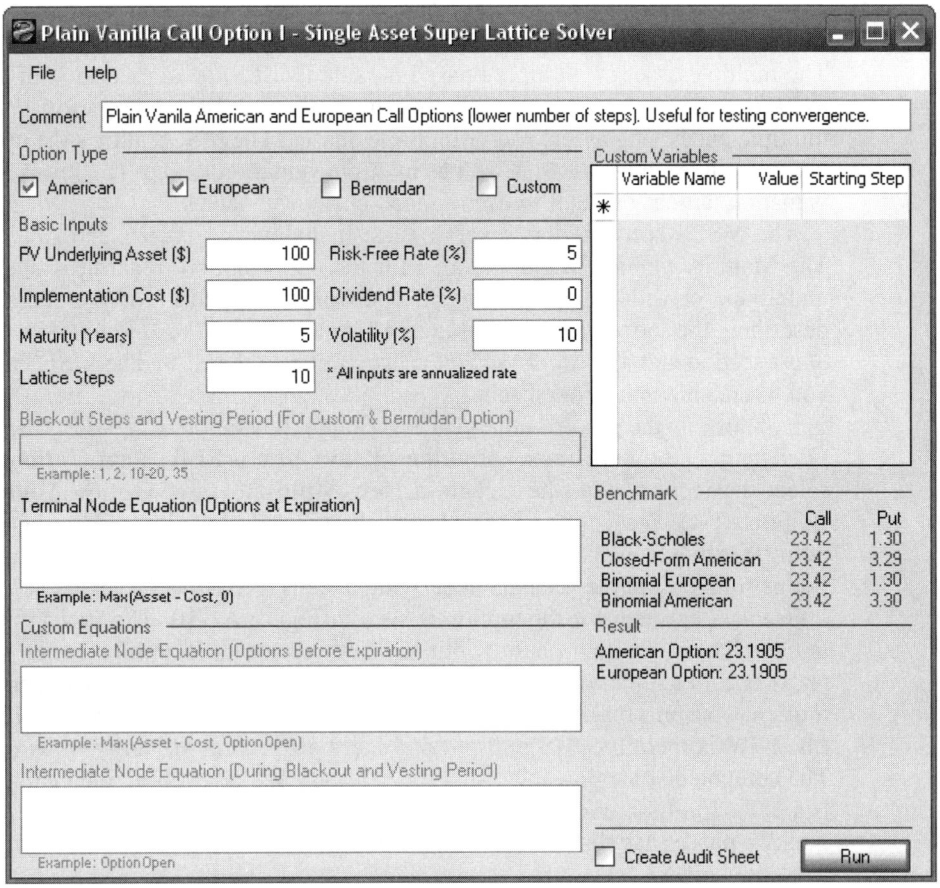

Figure A1-7   10-step lattice model.

The Custom Variables list is where you can add, modify, or delete custom variables, the variables that are required beyond the basic inputs. For instance, when running an abandonment option, you need the salvage value. You can add this in the Custom Variables list, give it a name (a variable name must be a single word), the appropriate value, and the starting step when this value becomes effective. That is, if you have multiple salvage values (i.e., if salvage values change over time), you can enter the same variable name (e.g., *salvage*) several times, but each time, its value changes and you can specify when the appropriate salvage value becomes effective. For instance, in a 10-year, 100-step super lattice problem where there are two salvage values—$100 occurring within the first five years and increases to $150 at the beginning of Year 6—you can enter two salvage variables with the same name, $100 with a starting step of 0 and $150 with a starting step of 51. Be careful here as Year 6 starts at step 51 and not 61. That is, for a 10-year option with a 100-step lattice, we have: Steps 1–10 = Year 1; Steps 11–20 = Year 2; Steps 21–30 = Year 3; Steps 31–40 = Year 4; Steps 41–50 = Year 5; Steps 51–60 = Year 6; Steps 61–70 = Year 7; Steps 71–80 = Year 8; Steps 81–90 = Year 9; and Steps 91–100 = Year 10. Finally, incorporating *0* as a blackout step indicates that the option cannot be executed immediately.

Multiple-Asset or Multiple-Phased SLS Module

The multiple-asset or multiple-phased module (MSLS) is an extension of the single-asset and single-phased module in that the MSLS can be used to solve options with multiple underlying assets and/or multiple phases. The MSLS allows the user to enter multiple underlying assets as well as multiple valuation lattices (Figure A1-8). These valuation lattices can call to user-defined custom variables.

The MSLS software has several areas, including a *Maturity* and *Comment* area. The Maturity value is a global value for the entire option, regardless of how many underlying or valuation lattices exist. The Comment field is for your personal notes describing the model you are building. There are also a *Blackout and Vesting Period Steps* section and a *Custom Variables* list similar to the SLS. The MSLS also allows you to create Audit Worksheets.

To illustrate the power of the MSLS, a simple illustration is in order. Click on **Start | Programs | Real Options Valuation | Real Options SLS | Real Options SLS** and select the second icon, the **Create a New Multiple Asset Option Model** module (Figure A1-1). Then, click on **File | Examples | Simple Two Phased Sequential Compound Option** to load our first example. Figure A1-9 shows the MSLS example loaded. In this simple example, a single underlying asset is created with two valuation phases.

The strategy tree for this option is seen in Figure A1-10. The project is executed in two phases—the first phase within the first year costs $5 million, while the second phase occurs within two years but only after the first phase is executed, and costs $80 million, both in present value dollars. The PV Asset of the project is $100 million (the NPV is therefore $15 million) and faces 30 percent volatility in its cash flows. The computed strategic value using the MSLS is $27.67 million, indicating that there is a $12.67 million in option value. That is, spreading out and staging the investment into two phases has significant value (an expected value of $12.67 million to be exact).

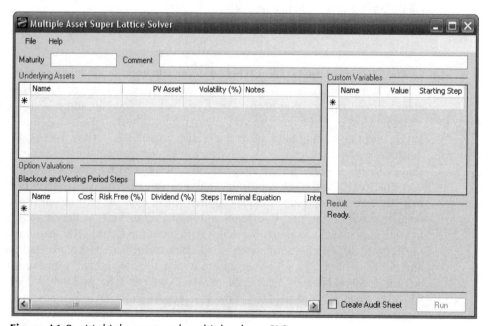

Figure A1-8   Multiple asset and multiple phase SLS.

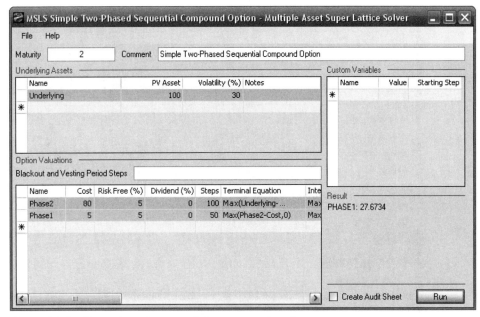

Figure A1-9 Two phased sequential compound option.

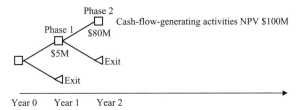

Figure A1-10 Decision or strategy tree of a two phased option.

See the sections on compound options in Chapter 10 of *Real Options Analysis*, Second Edition (Wiley, 2006) for more examples and interpretation of results.

Multinomial SLS Module

The *Multinomial Lattice Solver* (MNLS) is the third module of the Real Options Valuation's SLS software. The MNLS applies multinomial lattices—where multiple branches stem from each node—such as trinomials (three branches), quadranomials (four branches), and pentanomials (five branches). Figure A1-11 illustrates the MNLS module. The module has a Basic Inputs section, where all of the common inputs for the multinomials are listed. Then, there are four sections with four different multinomial applications complete with the additional required inputs and results for both American and European call and put options.

Figure A1-12 shows an example call and put option computation using trinomial lattices. To follow along, start the third module from the Real Options SLS software main screen (click on the third icon, **Create a New Multinomial Option Model**) and open the example file *Simple Calls and Puts Using Trinomial Lattices* under the **File | Examples** menu. Note that the results shown in Figure A1-12 using a 50-step lattice is equivalent to the results shown in Figure A1-3 using a 100-step binomial lattice. In

Figure A1-11   Multinomial SLS.

fact, a trinomial lattice or any other multinomial lattice provides identical answers to the binomial lattice at the limit, but convergence is achieved faster at lower steps. To illustrate, Table A1-1 shows how the trinomial lattice of a certain set of input assumptions yields the correct option value with fewer steps than it takes for a binomial lattice. Because both yield identical results at the limit but trinomials are much more difficult to calculate and take a longer computation time, the binomial lattice is usually used instead. However, a trinomial is required only under one special circumstance: when the underlying asset follows a mean-reverting process.

With the same logic, quadranomials and pentanomials yield identical results as the binomial lattice, with the exception that these multinomial lattices can be used to solve the following different special limiting conditions:

- *Trinomials*: Results are identical to binomials and are most appropriate when used to solve mean-reverting underlying assets.
- *Quadranomials*: Results are identical to binomials and are most appropriate when used to solve options whose underlying assets follow jump-diffusion processes.

Table A1-1   Binomial versus Trinomial Lattices

Steps	5	10	100	1,000	5,000
Binomial Lattice	$30.73	$29.22	$29.72	$29.77	$29.78
Trinomial Lattice	$29.22	$29.50	$29.75	$29.78	$29.78

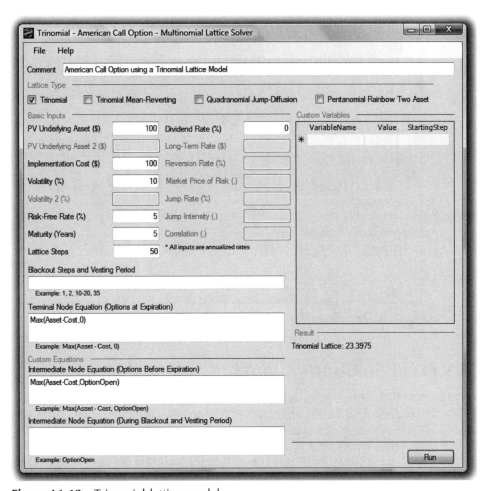

Figure A1-12   Trinomial lattice model.

- *Pentanomials*: Results are identical to binomials and are most appropriate when used to solve two underlying assets that are combined, called rainbow options (e.g., price and quantity are multiplied to obtain total revenues, but price and quantity each follows a different underlying lattice with its own volatility, but both underlying parameters could be correlated to one another). Other applications include solving for exchange of assets option or options with multiple underlying assets and phases.

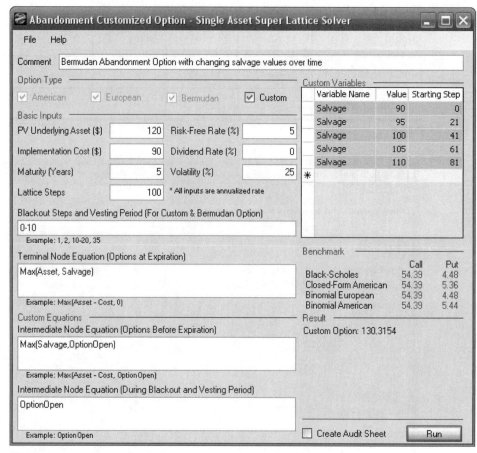

Figure A1-13   Customized abandonment option.

SLS Excel Solution Module

The SLS software also allows you to create your own models in Excel using customized functions. This is an important functionality because certain models may require linking from other spreadsheets or databases, run certain Excel macros and functions, or certain inputs need to be simulated, or inputs may change over the course of modeling your options. This Excel compatibility allows you the flexibility to innovate within the Excel spreadsheet environment. Specifically, the sample worksheet included in the software solves the SLS, MSLS, and Changing Volatility model.

To illustrate, Figure A1-13 shows a Customized Abandonment Option solved using SLS. The same problem can be solved using the *SLS Excel Solution* by clicking on **Start | Programs | Real Options Valuation | Real Options SLS | SLS Functions** and then start the **Excel Solution**. If using Excel XP or 2003, make sure to set Excel's macro security to medium or below (**Tools | Macro | Security | Medium**), whereas if using Excel 2007, make sure the security settings are turned off; otherwise the functions will not work properly (to reset your security settings when in Excel 2007, by clicking on the **Office** button located at the top left of the screen and selecting **Excel Options | Trust Center | Trust Center Settings | Macro Settings | Enable**

SUPER LATTICE SOLVER (SINGLE ASSET)

Option Type	0		Custom Variables List		
PV Underlying Asset	$120.00		Variable Name	Value	Starting Steps
Annualized Volatility	25.00%		Salvage	90.00	0
Maturity (Years)	5.00		Salvage	95.00	21
Implementation Cost	$0.00		Salvage	100.00	41
Risk-Free Rate	5.00%		Salvage	105.00	61
Dividend Yield	0.00%		Salvage	110.00	81
Lattice Steps	100				
Terminal Equation	MAX(Asset, Salvage)				
Intermediate Equation	MAX(Salvage, @@)				
Intermediate Equation During Blackout	@@				
Blackout Steps	0-10				

Super Lattice Solver Result	$130.3154

Note: This is the Excel version of the Super Lattice Solver, useful when running simulations or when linking to and from other spreadsheets.
Use this sample spreadsheet for your models. You can simply click on File, Save As to save as a different file and start using the model.
For the option type, set 0 = American, 1 = European, 2 = Bermudan, 3 = Custom

Figure A1-14   SLS solutions file.

All Macros). The sample solution is seen in Figure A1-14. Notice the same results using the SLS versus the SLS Excel Solution file. You can use the template provided by simply clicking on **File | Save As** in Excel and use the new file for your own modeling needs.

Similarly, the MSLS can also be solved using the SLS Excel Solver. Figure A1-15 shows a complex multiple-phased sequential compound option solved using the SLS Excel Solver. The results shown here are identical to the results generated from the MSLS module (example file: *Multiple Phased Complex Sequential Compound Option*). One small note of caution here is that if you add or reduce the number of option valuation lattices, make sure you change the function's link for the *MSLS Result* to incorporate the right number of rows; otherwise the analysis will not compute properly. For example, the default shows three option valuation lattices. By selecting the *MSLS Results* cell in the spreadsheet and clicking on **Insert | Function**, you will see that the function links to cells A24:H26 for these three rows for the *OVLattices* input in the function. If you add another option valuation lattice, change the link to A24:H27, and so forth. You can also leave the list of custom variables as is. The results will not be affected if these variables are not used in the custom equations.

Finally, Figure A1-16 shows a Changing Volatility and Changing Risk-free Rate Option. In this model, the volatility and risk-free yields are allowed to change over time, and a nonrecombining lattice is required to solve the option. In most cases, it is recommended that you create option models without the changing volatility term structure because getting a single volatility is difficult enough, let alone a series of changing volatilities over time. If different volatilities that are uncertain need to be modeled, run a Monte Carlo simulation using the *Risk Simulator* software on volatilities instead. This model should only be used when the volatilities are modeled robustly and the volatilities are rather certain and change over time. The same advice applies to a changing risk-free rate term structure.

SLS Excel Functions Module

The software also provides a series of SLS functions that are directly accessible in Excel. To illustrate its use, start the SLS Functions by clicking on **Start | Programs**

MULTIPLE SUPER LATTICE SOLVER (MULTIPLE ASSET & MULTIPLE PHASES)

MSLS Result $134.0802

Maturity (Years)	5.00
Blackout Steps	0-20
Correlation*	

Underlying Asset Lattices

Lattice Name	PV Asset	Volatility	Riskfree	Dividend
Underlying	100.00	25.00		

Custom Variables

Name	Value	Starting Steps
Salvage	100.00	31
Salvage	90.00	11
Salvage	80.00	0
Contract	0.90	0
Expansion	1.50	0
Savings	20.00	0

Option Valuation Lattices

Lattice Name	Cost	Riskfree	Dividend	Steps	Terminal Equation	Intermediate Equation	Intermediate Equation for Blackout
Phase3	50.00	5.00	0.00	50	Max(Underlying*Expansion-Cost,Underlying,Salvage)	Max(Underlying*Expansion-Cost,Salvage,@@)	@@
Phase2	0.00	5.00	0.00	30	Max(Phase3,Phase3*Contract+Savings,Salvage,0)	Max(Phase3*Contract+Savings,Salvage,@@)	@@
Phase1	0.00	5.00	0.00	10	Max(Phase2,Salvage,0)	Max(Salvage,@@)	@@

Note: This is the Excel version of the Multiple Super Lattice Solver, useful when running simulations or when linking to and from other spreadsheets. Use this sample spreadsheet for your models. You can simply click on File, Save As to save as a different file and start using the model.
*Because this is an Excel solution, the correlation function is not supported and is linked to an empty cell.

Figure A1-15   MNLS Solutions file.

Changing Volatility and Risk-Free Rates

Assumptions

PV Asset ($)	$100.00
Implementation Cost ($)	$100.00
Maturity in Years (.)	10.00
Vesting in Years (.)	4.00
Dividend Rate (%)	0.00%

Results

Generalized Black-Scholes	$48.78
10-Step Super Lattice	$49.15
Super Lattice Steps	10 Steps

Additional Assumption:

Year	Risk-free %		Year	Volatility %
1.00	5.00%		1.00	20.00%
2.00	5.00%		2.00	20.00%
3.00	5.00%		3.00	20.00%
4.00	5.00%		4.00	20.00%
5.00	5.00%		5.00	20.00%
6.00	5.00%		6.00	30.00%
7.00	5.00%		7.00	30.00%
8.00	5.00%		8.00	30.00%
9.00	5.00%		9.00	30.00%
10.00	5.00%		10.00	30.00%

Please be aware that by applying multiple changing volatilities over time, a nonrecombining lattice is required, which increases the computation time significantly. In addition, only smaller lattice steps may be computed. The function used is: SLSBinomialChangingVolatility

Figure A1-16   Changing volatility and risk-free rates.

| **Real Options Valuation** | **Real Options SLS** | **SLS Functions**, and Excel will start. When in Excel, you can click on the function wizard icon or simply select an empty cell and click on **Insert** | **Function**. While in Excel's equation wizard, either select the **All** category or **Real Options Valuation**, the name of the company that developed the software. Here you will see a list of SLS functions (with SLS-prefixes) that are ready for use in Excel. Figure A1-17 shows the Excel equation wizard.

Suppose you select the first function, *SLSBinomialAmericanCall* and hit **OK**. Figure A1-18 shows how the function can be linked to an existing Excel model. The values in cells B1 to B7 can be linked from other models or spreadsheets; created using Excel's Visual Basic for Applications (VBA) macros; or dynamic and changing as in when running a simulation. Another quick note of caution here is that certain SLS functions require many input variables, and Excel's equation wizard can only show five variables at a time. Therefore, remember to scroll down the list of variables by clicking on the vertical scroll bar to access the rest of the variables. Note that the Modeling Toolkit also has a lot of exotic, financial, and options models available within Excel.

SLS Excel Lattice Maker Module

Finally, the full version of the software comes with an advanced binomial *Lattice Maker* module. This Lattice Maker is capable of generating binomial lattices and decision lattices with visible formulas in an Excel spreadsheet. Figure A1-19 illustrates an example option generated using this module. The illustration shows the module inputs (you can obtain this module by clicking on the **Create a Lattice** icon on the main Real Options SLS software screen; see Figure A1-1). Enter in the relevant

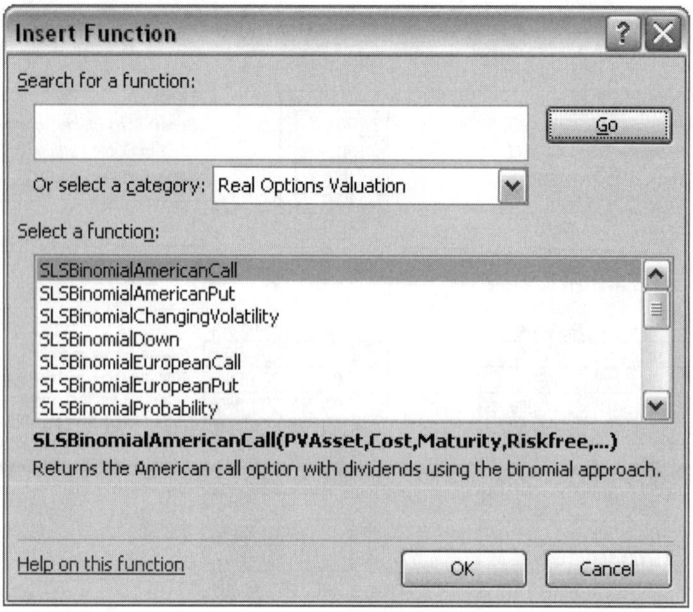

Figure A1-17 Excel's equation wizard.

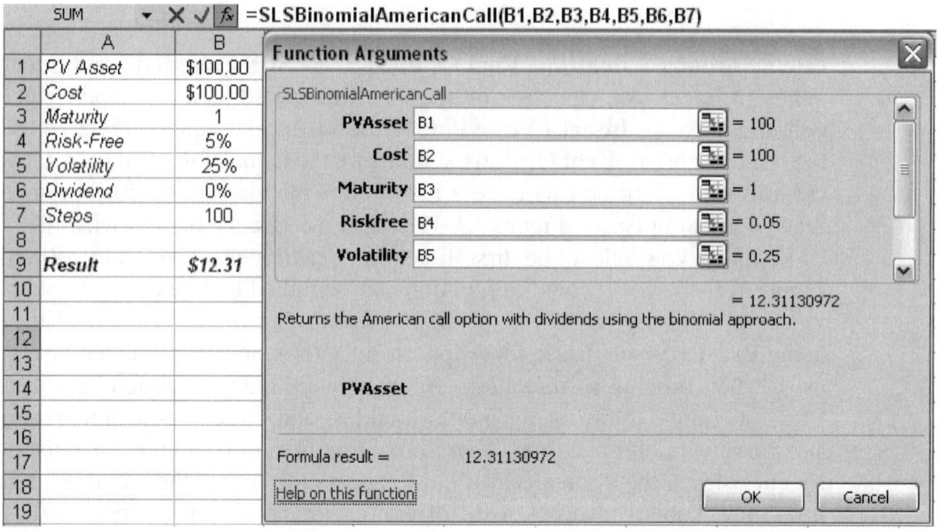

Figure A1-18 Linking the SLS functions.

inputs and click on **OK** to run the lattice maker (use the sample inputs as shown in Figure A1-19 as an example). Notice that the visible equations are linked to the existing spreadsheet, which means that this module will come in handy when running Monte Carlo simulations or when used to link to and from other spreadsheet models. The results can also be used as a presentation and learning tool to peep inside the analytical black box of binomial lattices. Last but not least, a decision lattice with

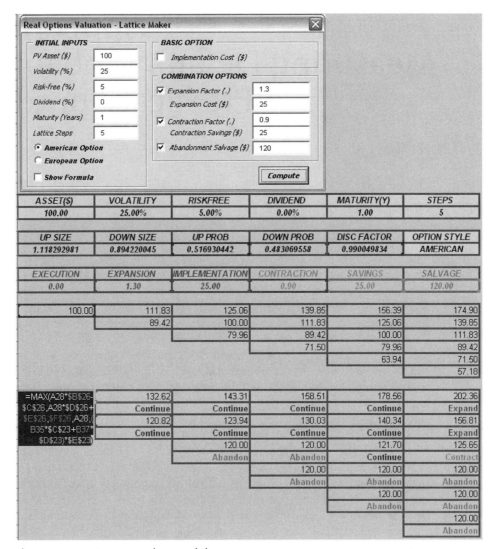

Figure A1-19   Lattice maker module.

specific decision nodes indicating expected optimal times of execution of certain options are also available in this module. The results generated from this module are identical to those generated using the SLS and Excel functions, but have the added advantage of a visible lattice (lattices of up to 200 steps can be generated using this module).

Appendix 2:
Measuring Default Probability:
A Practical Approach

Three basic types of information are relevant to the default probability of a firm: financial statements, market prices of the firm's debt and equity, and subjective appraisals of the firm's prospects and risk. Financial statements are inherently backward looking; they are reports of the past. Prices, in contrast, are inherently forward looking. Investors form debt and equity prices as they anticipate the firm's future. In determining the market prices, investors use, among many other things, subjective appraisals of the firm's prospects and risk, financial statements, and other market prices. This information is combined using their own analysis and synthesis and results in their willingness to buy and sell the firm's debt and equity securities. Market prices are the result of the combined willingness of many investors to buy and sell, and thus prices embody the synthesized views and forecasts of many investors.

The most effective default measurement, therefore, derives from models that utilize both market prices and financial statements. We do not mean here that markets are perfectly efficient in this synthesis. We assert only that it is difficult to do a better job than the markets. That is, it is very difficult to consistently beat the market. Consequently, where available, we want to utilize market prices to determine default risk because prices add considerably to the predictive power of the estimates.

Vasicek and Kealhofer have extended the Black-Scholes-Merton framework to produce a model of default probability known as the Vasicek-Kealhofer (VK) model. This model assumes that the firm's equity is a perpetual option with the default point acting as the absorbing barrier for the firm's asset value. When the asset value hits the default point, the firm is assumed to default. Multiple classes of liabilities are modeled: short-term liabilities, long-term liabilities, convertible debt, preferred equity, and common equity. When the firm's asset value becomes very large, the convertible securities are assumed to convert and dilute the existing equity. In addition, cash payouts such as dividends are explicitly used in the VK model. A default database is used to derive an empirical distribution relating the distance-to-default to a default probability. In this way, the relationship between asset value and liabilities can be captured without resorting to a substantially more complex model characterizing a firm's liability process.

Moody's KMV MKMV has implemented the VK model to calculate an Expected Default Frequency™ (EDF™) credit measure, which is the probability of default during the forthcoming year, or years, for firms with publicly traded equity. (This model can also be modified to produce EDF values for firms without publicly traded equity.) The EDF value requires equity prices and certain items from financial statements as inputs. EDF credit measures can be viewed and analyzed within the context of a software product called CreditEdge™ (CE). On a daily basis, CE calculates EDF values for years 1 through 5, allowing the user to see a term structure of EDF values. MKMV's EDF credit measure assumes that default is defined as the nonpayment of any scheduled payment, interest, or principal. A more recent extension to CE called CreditEdge Plus facilitates analysis across multiple markets. A probability of default estimated from the equity market can be compared (in the context of a sophisticated valuation model) to the spreads observed in the CDS and corporate bond markets. In this way, users of CE Plus can determine how the different markets are reflecting a particular firm's default probability, expected recovery in the event of default, and the risk premium implicit in the market. These tools highlight the strength of structural models of default risk in that multiple market views on the same firm can be reconciled in the context of an economically meaningful model framework. The remainder of this section describes the procedure MKMV employs to determine a public firm's probability of default.

The default probability of a firm can be determined through three steps:

- Estimate asset value and volatility: In this step, the asset value and asset volatility of the firm are estimated from the market value and volatility of equity, and the book value of liabilities.
- Calculate the distance-to-default: The distance-to-default (DD) is calculated from the asset value and asset volatility (estimated in the first step), and the book value of liabilities.
- Calculate the default probability: The default probability is determined directly from the distance-to-default and the default rate for given levels of distance-to-default.

Estimate Asset Value and Volatility

If the market price of equity is available, the market value and volatility of assets can be determined directly using an approach based on options pricing, which recognizes equity as a call option on the underlying assets of the firm. For example, consider a simplified case where there is only one class of debt and one class of equity, as in Figure A2-1.

The limited liability feature of equity means that the equity holders have the right, but not the obligation, to pay off the debt holders and take over the remaining assets of the firm. That is, the holders of the other liabilities of the firm essentially own the

Assets	Liabilities
100	80
	20

Figure A2-1   Simplified balance sheet.

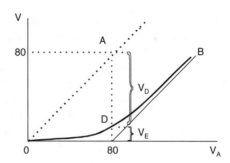

Figure A2-2 The VK model and the option framework.

firm until those liabilities are paid off in full by the equity holders. Thus, in the simplest case, equity is the same as a call option on the firm's assets with a strike price equal to the book value of the firm's liabilities.

The VK model uses this option nature of equity to derive the underlying asset value and asset volatility implied by the market value, volatility of equity, and book value of liabilities. This process is similar in spirit to the procedure that option traders use in determining the implied volatility of an option from the observed option price.

For example, assume that the firm is actually a type of levered mutual fund or unit trust. The assets of the firm are equity securities and thus can be valued at any time by observing their market prices. Furthermore, assume that our little firm is to be wound up after five years and that we can ignore the time value of money (discounting adds little to our understanding of the relationships and serves only to complicate the picture). That is, in five years time, the assets will be sold, and the proceeds divided between the debt and equity holders.

Initially, assume that we are interested in determining the market value of the equity from the market value of the assets. This is the reverse of the problem we face in practice, but provides a simpler perspective to initially understand the basic option relationships; Figure A2-2 illustrates this issue. To be specific, assume that we initially invest $20 in the firm and borrow $80 from a bank. The proceeds, $100, are invested in equities. At the end of five years, what is the value of equity? For example, if the market value of the assets at the end of year 5 is $60, then the value of equity will be zero. If the value of the assets is $110, then the value of the equity will be $30, and so on. Thus, in Figure A2-2, the lines from $0 to $80 and from $80 to point B represent the market value of the equity as a function of the asset value at the end of year 5.

Assume now that we are interested in valuing our equity prior to the final winding up of the firm. For example, assume that three years have passed since the firm was started and that there are two years remaining before we wind the firm up. Furthermore, we have marked the equities in our portfolio (not to be confused with the equity position in the structure that holds the equity securities; imagine that this firm is holding a mutual fund) to market, and their value is determined to be $80. What is the value of the firm's equity? Not zero. It is actually something greater than zero because it is the value of the assets two years hence that really matters, and there is still a chance that the asset value will be greater than $80 in two more years. In Figure A2-2, the value of the equity with two years to go is represented by the curve joining $0 and point B.

The higher the volatility of the assets, the greater the chance of high asset values after two years. For example, if we are dissatisfied with our fund's performance after three years because it has lost $20 in value, dropping from $100 to $80, we may be tempted to invest in higher-potential, higher-risk equities. If we do, what is the effect on the firm's equity value? It increases. The more volatile assets have higher probabilities of high values and, consequently, higher payouts for the equity. Of course, there are accompanying higher probabilities of lower asset values, because volatility works both ways, but with limited liability; very low asset values do not affect the equity value. At the end of the five years, it makes no difference to the equity if the final asset value is $79 or $9; its payout is the same, 0.

Assuming we did sell our existing equity securities and replaced them with the same total value of higher-potential, higher-risk equity securities, where did the increase in the firm's equity value come from? It did not come from an increase in the asset value. We simply sold our original portfolio for $80 and purchased a new portfolio of higher-risk equities for $80. No value was created there. The value, of course, came from the bank holding our firm's debt. In Figure A2-2, the value of the firm can be divided between the debt and equity holders along the line joining the points $80 and A, where the line 0 to A plots the asset value against itself. Thus, the only way the value of equity can increase while the asset value remains constant is to take the value from the market value of the debt. This should make sense. When we reinvested the firm's assets in higher-risk equities, we increased the default risk of the debt and consequently reduced this debt's market value.

The value of debt and equity are thus intimately entwined. Both are really derivative securities on the underlying assets of the firm. We can exploit the option nature of equity to relate the market value of equity and the book value of debt to determine the implied market value of the underlying assets. That is, we solve the reverse of the problem described in our simple example. We observe the market value of the equity and solve backwards for the market value of assets; see Figure A2-3.

In practice, we need to take account of the more complex capital structures and circumstances that exist in real life. For example, we need to consider the various terms and nature of debt (for example, long- and short-term debt, and convertible instruments), the perpetuity nature of equity, and the time value of money—and of course, we have to solve for the volatility of the assets at the same time. Thus, in practice, we solve[1] the following two relationships simultaneously:

$$\begin{bmatrix} \text{Equity} \\ \text{Value} \end{bmatrix} = OptionFunction\left(\begin{bmatrix} \text{Asset} \\ \text{Value} \end{bmatrix}, \begin{bmatrix} \text{Asset} \\ \text{Volatility} \end{bmatrix}, \begin{bmatrix} \text{Capital} \\ \text{Structure} \end{bmatrix}, \begin{bmatrix} \text{Interest} \\ \text{Rate} \end{bmatrix} \right)$$

$$\begin{bmatrix} \text{Equity} \\ \text{Volatility} \end{bmatrix} = OptionFunction\left(\begin{bmatrix} \text{Asset} \\ \text{Value} \end{bmatrix}, \begin{bmatrix} \text{Asset} \\ \text{Volatility} \end{bmatrix}, \begin{bmatrix} \text{Capital} \\ \text{Structure} \end{bmatrix}, \begin{bmatrix} \text{Interest} \\ \text{Rate} \end{bmatrix} \right)$$

1. For the more technically inclined: Simply inverting this system of equations and solving for the two unknown variables (asset value and asset volatility) are typically not possible in practice. Instead, the two unknown variables are determined by iteratively searching for quantities that make the equations hold for each date in a time series of equity returns. This iterative solution technique also allows for simple and straightforward implementation of robust estimation techniques that makes it easier to control for the influence of outliers. This estimation framework significantly improves the default predictive power of the EDF credit measure produced at MKMV. For more details on how EDF credit measures are estimated, please refer to the research papers available at www.moodyskmv.com.

Asset value and volatility are the only unknown quantities in these relationships, and thus the two equations can be solved to determine the values implied by the current equity value, volatility, and capital structure.

Calculate the Distance-to-Default

Six variables determine the default probability of a firm over some horizon, from now until time H (see Figure A2-4):

- The current asset value
- The distribution of the asset value at time H
- The volatility of the future assets value at time H
- The level of the default point, the book value of the liabilities
- The expected rate of growth in the asset value over the horizon
- The length of the horizon, H

The first four variables—asset value, future asset distribution, asset volatility, and level of the default point—are the critical variables. The expected growth in the asset value has little default discriminating power, and the analyst defines the length of the horizon.

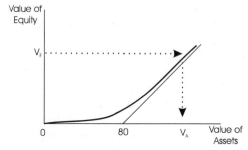

Figure A2-3   Market value of equity and assets.

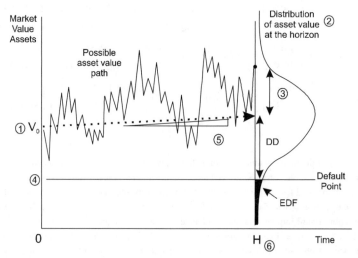

Figure A2-4   Distance to default.

If the value of the assets falls below the default point, the firm defaults. Therefore, the probability of default is the probability that the asset value will fall below the default point. This is the shaded area (EDF value) below the default point[2] in Figure A2-4. Figure A2-4 also illustrates the causative relationship and trade-off among the variables. This causative specification provides the analyst with a powerful and reliable framework in which he or she can ask what-if questions regarding the model's various inputs and examine the effects of any proposed capital restructuring. For example, the analyst can examine the effect of a large decrease in the stock price or the effects of an acquisition or merger.

If the future distribution of the distance-to-default were known, the default probability (expected default frequency, or EDF value) would simply be the likelihood that the final asset value was below the default point (the shaded area in Figure A2-4). However, in practice, the distribution of the distance-to-default is difficult to measure. Moreover, the usual assumptions of normal or lognormal distributions cannot be used. For default measurement, the likelihood of large adverse changes in the relationship of asset value to the firm's default point is critical to the accurate determination of the default probability. These changes may come about from changes in asset value or changes in the firm's leverage. In fact, changes in asset value and changes in firm leverage may be highly correlated. Consequently, MKMV first measures the distance-to-default as the number of standard deviations the asset value is away from default and then uses empirical data to determine the corresponding default probability. As discussed in a previous section, the distance-to-default is conceptually calculated[3] as:

$$[\text{Distance to Default}] = \frac{[\text{Market Value of Assets}] - [\text{Default Point}]}{[\text{Market Value of Assets}][\text{Asset Volatility}]}$$

and is marked as DD in Figure A2-4.

Calculate the Default Probability

One method of obtaining the relationship between distance-to-default and default probability requires data on historical default and bankruptcy frequencies. MKMV maintains a database that includes over 100,000 company-years of data and over 7,000 incidents of default or bankruptcy. From this data, a lookup or frequency table can be generated, which relates the likelihood of default to various levels of distance-to-default.

For example, assume that one is interested in determining the default probability over the next year for a firm that is 7 standard deviations away from default. To determine this EDF value, one would query the default history for the proportion of the firms, seven standard deviations away from default that defaulted over the next year. The answer from the MKMV data is about 5 basis points (bp), 0.05 percent, or an equivalent rating of AA.

2. *Strictly speaking, the shaded area in Figure A2-4 is the default probability if we assume that the default point is not an absorbing barrier. In other words, a firm whose asset value falls through the default point before the time horizon date H can still recover and end up above the default point by time H. In practice, MKMV uses an absorbing barrier model that more realistically models default as possible at any time. The default probability calculated out of an absorbing barrier model will be higher than the default probability characterized in Figure A2-4.*

3. *Refer to footnote 2 associated with distance-to-default for discussion of the actual formula.*

MKMV has tested the relationship between distance-to-default and default frequency for industry, size, time, and other effects and has found that the relationship is typically constant across all of these variables. This is not to say that there are no differences in default rates across industry, time, and size but only that it appears that these differences are captured by the distance-to-default measure. MKMV's studies of international default rates are continuing, but the preliminary results of these studies (as well as studies completed by some MKMV clients) indicate that the relationship is also invariant across most countries and regions.

In summary, three steps are required to calculate an EDF credit measure: (1) estimate the current market value and volatility of the firm's assets, (2) determine how far the firm is from default (i.e., determine its distance-to-default), and (3) transform the distance-to-default into a probability. For example, consider Philip Morris Companies Inc., which, at the end of April 2001, had a one-year EDF value of 25 bp, close to the median EDF value of firms with an A rating. Table A2-1 illustrates the relevant values and calculations for the EDF credit measure.

The Modeling Toolkit applies the same MKMV methodologies to obtain distance to default and probability of default for publicly and privately held companies using and iterative model. In addition, the toolkit also computes default probabilities for individuals. Please review the chapter on default probabilities for more details.

Table A2-1 Philip Morris Companies Statistics

Variable	Value	Notes
Market value of equity	$110.688 billion	(Share Price) × (Shares Outstanding).
Book liabilities	$64.062 billion	Balance sheet.
Market value of assets	$170.558 billion	Option-pricing model.
Asset volatility	21%	Option-pricing model.
Default point	$47.499 billion	Liabilities payable within one year.
Distance-to-default	3.5	Ratio: $\dfrac{72 - 37}{72 \times 10\%}$ (In this example we ignore the growth in the asset value between now and the end of the year.)
EDF (one year)	25 bp	Empirical mapping between distance-to-default and default frequency.

Appendix 3:
Server Based Applications for Running Data Intensive Basel II Credit and Market Risk Models

Throughout the book, we looked at individual Excel-based models to simplify the discussions and explanations. Nonetheless, these Excel models are limited in that they can only run on a limited set of data (e.g., Excel has a maximum number of rows and columns per worksheet) and might be much slower than a bank would consider optimal (this is due to the Excel computational overhead of including graphics, equations, and cell-by-cell platform). Banks typically have thousands if not millions of transactions per day across all its branches, and some of these credit and market risk analyses have to be done frequently and quickly. In this Appendix, we introduce the server-based applications of the Modeling Toolkit and Risk Simulator, where millions of data points and computations can be run within seconds on a server. The same analytics and models in these two software programs described throughout this book are now run in pure mathematical software codes, making the computations blazing fast and capable of handling large data sets.

This server-based software is called *Rov Risk Modeler* and it is divided into a few application modules:

- **Rov Risk Modeler for Credit Risk and Market Risk**—Risk Modeler is a simulation and analytical module which focuses on Credit Risk and Market Risk for Basel II based on a bank's existing data tables. It provides many models to simulate, fit, forecast, value, and reports the results to the user. Existing data tables are based on the user's requirements such as linking to an existing database (e.g., Oracle OFDM, SQL, CSV, DSN, ODBC, Excel, flat text files, and other proprietary database systems), manually inputting data, or setting simulation assumptions, and so forth. This module is used for computing PD, LGD, VAR, EAD, and other key metrics as well as for forecasting and simulating market risk variables using historical back-fitting, time-series forecasts (ARIMA), volatility computations (GARCH), and other applications.

- **Rov Risk Optimizer**—Risk Optimizer is an advanced optimization module that can be used to optimize large portfolios and to find optimal investment decisions for a bank. The decision variables can be discrete, continuous, integer, or binary, and the objective function can be linear or nonlinear. In addition, Risk Optimizer allows the user to link to existing data tables to run simulations, find the best-fitting models, and couple these techniques with optimization.

- **Rov Risk Valuator**—Risk Valuator is the application of over 600+ Basel II Modeling Toolkit functions. Users can input the required data for the selected model and this application will return the computed results very quickly. This module is useful for valuing derivative instruments, debt instruments, exotic options, options-embedded instruments, as well as multiple types of financial models.

  The 600+ advanced models are categorized into the following groups of applications:
  - Advanced Math Functions
  - Basic Finance Models
  - Basic Options Models
  - Bond Math, Options, Pricing, and Yields
  - Credit Risk Analysis
  - Delta Gamma Hedging
  - Exotic Options and Derivatives
  - Financial Ratios
  - Forecasting, Extrapolation and Interpolation
  - Probability Distributions
  - Put-Call Parity and Option Sensitivities
  - Real Options Analysis
  - Value at Risk, Volatility, Portfolio Risk and Return

System Architecture

The entire system architecture of this server-based application can be divided into three parts: the first level is the product's main application which is the user interface; the second level is the data map which is used to input the data to compute from various methods such as linking to existing databases or manually inputting the data, and so forth; the last level is the lowest level, which links the database to a *query*, *insert*, and *get* value function to and from data tables. Figure A3-1 illustrates the system architecture.

Figure A3-2 illustrates the first level of the system architecture, the user interface. A user can create new profiles for saving the data that will be used in the procedure (***File → New Profile***). There are two types of risk areas: Credit Risk and Market Risk. When selecting the risk analysis type, Risk Modeler will list the items in *Step 1* to *Step 3*. In *Step 1*, the user can select the type of credit or market risk analysis to perform, and in *Step 2,* a list of applicable models for the analysis type selected will be listed and shown. User can then ***ADD*** as many models as required, which will then appear in the *Created Models* list box for updating and editing. In *Step 3,* the list of required input assumptions and parameters will be listed. The user can then map, clear or reset the parameter values by clicking the ***MAP***, ***CLEAR*** or ***RESET*** buttons (short descriptions for each step are provided). Clicking on the ***SAVE*** button will save all the data to the Profile that the user had previously created. When all the required inputs have been populated, clicking ***RUN*** will compute the models selected.

When selecting a parameter in the *Step* 3 list box in the main application, and clicking the ***MAP*** button, the *Input Parameter Mapping* dialog will display. There are five methods afforded to the user, as seen in Figure A3-3. Selecting ***Data Link*** will allow the user to link to an existing database or Excel to access existing data. Selecting ***Manual Input*** will show a dialog requiring manual input of a specific variable. Selecting ***Data Compute*** shows a variable and data calculator to compute the parameter's value by incorporating other parameters or constants. Selecting ***Set Assumption***

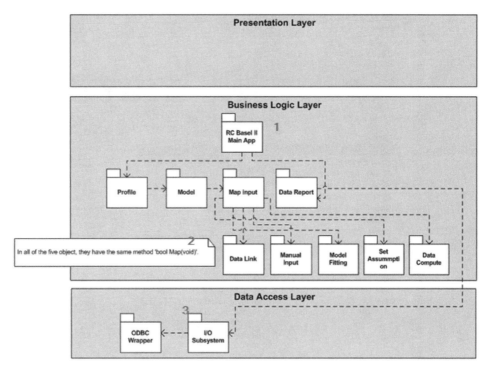

Figure A3-1   System architecture of Risk Modeler.

will provide the user the ability to choose the simulation distribution and input the risk simulation assumption values. Selecting *Model Fitting* will fit some existing data to 24 potential relevant distributions for that parameter.

There are seven types of ODBC data connect for accessing existing data (Figure A3-4). For instance, in the Oracle data connect, the user needs to setup the required login inputs such as User and Password to access the database. When clicking on the *OK* button, the software will call the database connect method to connect the specified database. For different types of ODBC applications, the software codes are wrapped with popular calling methods such as *CONNECT*, *QUERY*, and so forth.

Other types of database and software connections are also possible, for example, through Excel worksheets and plain text files like comma-delimited settings files (CSV), as well as other proprietary software databases.

For the *Risk Optimizer* modules, users can input values directly or use the same three-level approach described above to link input variables and output results with existing databases. User only needs to select the required model and input the required parameters' values, and run the analysis.

Rov Risk Modeler

The following is a very simple example showcasing how to use the *Risk Modeler* (Credit Risk and Market Risk) module. When Risk Modeler has been successfully installed, start the application. The application starts by showing the main user dialog. Click on *File → New Profile* to create a new profile. Then, select *Probability of Default (PD)* in the *Step 1* list box, and then select *PD for Publicly Traded Firms* in *Step 2*. Then, click on *Market Value Equity* in *Step 3* (Figure A3-5). Then, click on

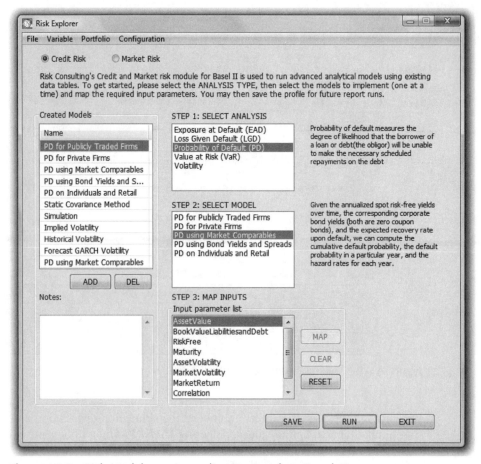

Figure A3-2   Risk Modeler main application interface (Level 1).

MAP and the program will open another dialog named *Input Parameter Mapping*. Click on the *Manual Input* radio button and hit *Next* (Figure A3-6).

When the *Manual Input* dialog opens (Figure A3-7), enter in a variable name such as *Var1* and click the third radio button to manually input 3000. Then, click on *Finish* to close this dialog. The program will return to the main application dialog. Using the same method, enter the following values to the required input parameters (enter any variable name as required):

Market Equity Volatility	0.45
Book Value Liabilities and Debt	10000
Risk-free	0.05
Growth Rate	0.07
Maturity	1.00

Alternatively, user can copy and paste multiple data points from an existing spreadsheet, a text file, or some other software application and paste these values directly into the data area. A flat text file can also be uploaded to populate this variable. Finally, for some special models, the input parameter to the selected variable might be constant

Figure A3-3   Input Parameter Mapping user interface (Level 2).

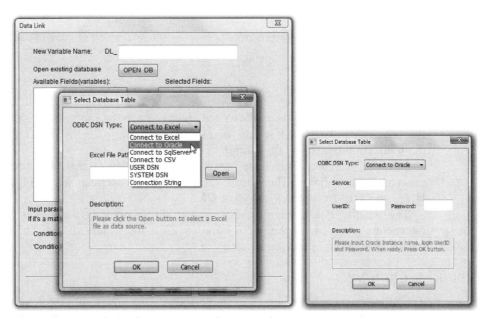

Figure A3-4   Link database user interface (Level 3).

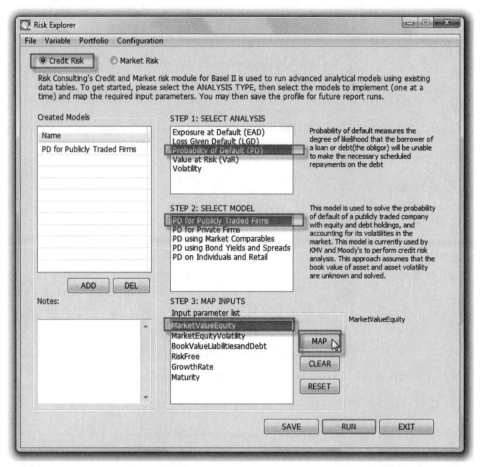

Figure A3-5   Using Risk Modeler.

for all cases and the software allows the ability to populate an entire data table with the same value (e.g., risk-free rate for a specific time period is the same regardless of the transaction type or credit listing).

When all the parameters have populated values, click on the **RUN** button in the main application dialog. There are several options the user can select (Figure A3-8). Here, select the first choice and click **OK**.

The Results dialog (Figure A3-9) shows the computed values using the input parameters specified. Click the **OK** button to close the Results dialog. The focus will return to the Main application dialog.

Rov Risk Optimizer

The following is another simple example showcasing how to use the **Risk Optimizer** module. When Risk Explorer has been successfully installed, start the Risk Optimizer application. The user interface has several tabs, *Method*, *Decision Variables*, *Constraints*, *Statistics*, and *Objective* (Figure A3-10). To get started, select the *Method* tab and click on *Static Optimization*.

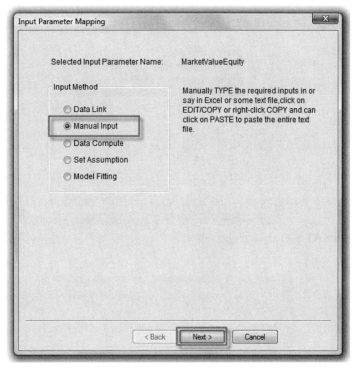

Figure A3-6   Parameter mapping.

Figure A3-7   Manual inputs.

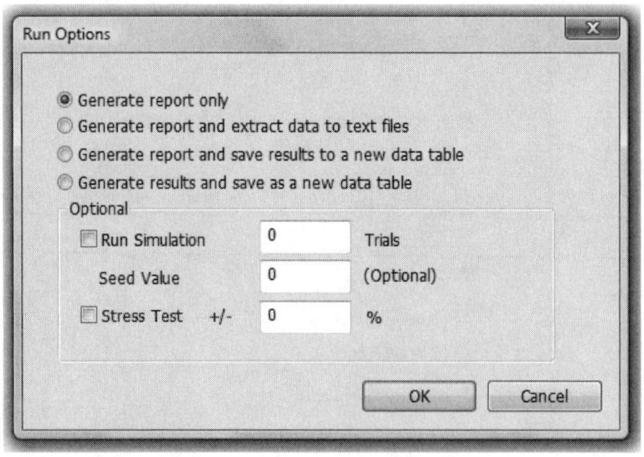

Figure A3-8 Running the report.

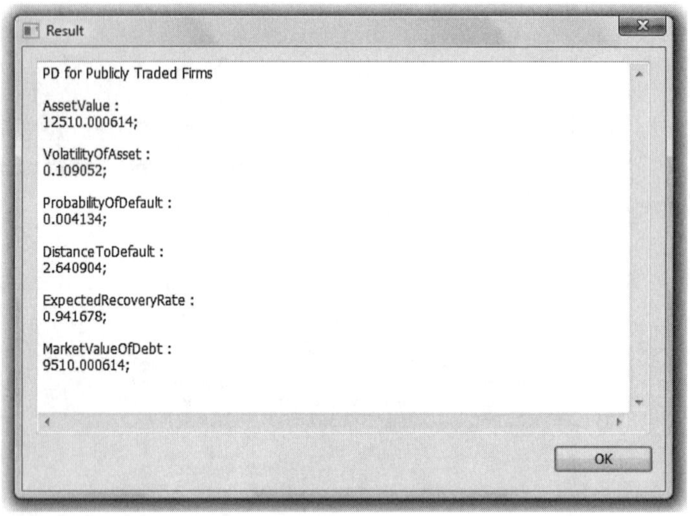

Figure A3-9 Results.

Next, click on the *Decision Variables* tab and **ADD** to add some variables. For instance, we have 4 different variables (*Asset1* to *Asset4*), and each asset can be set to take continuous, integer, binary, or discrete values. For our simple illustration, set the variables to all be *Continuous* between 0.10 and 0.40 (i.e., only asset allocations between 10% and 40% are allowed). Keep adding 4 different asset classes as decision variables as shown in Figure A3-11.

Next, click on the *Constraints* tab and **ADD** (Figure A3-12). Then, in the expressions input box, enter in the constraints (you can double click on the list of variables and the variable string will be transferred up to the expressions box). In our simple example, the sum of the decision variables must equal 1.0 (i.e., the total allocation of asset classes must total 100% in an investment portfolio).

Next, select the *Objective* tab and decide if you wish to run **Maximization** or **Minimization** on your objective. In addition, enter in the relevant objective expression

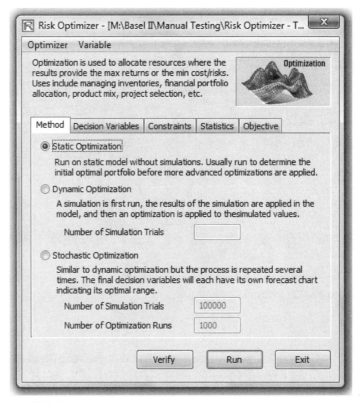

Figure A3-10   Risk Optimizer.

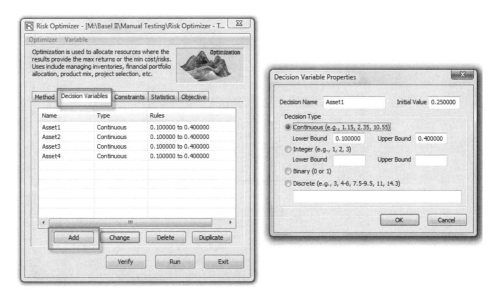

Figure A3-11   Setting decision variables.

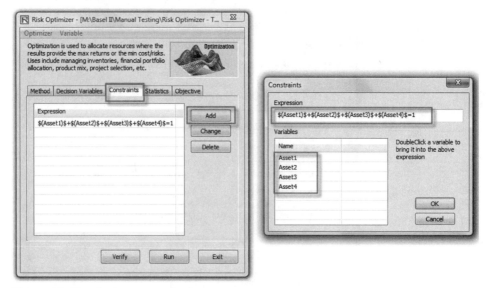

Figure A3-12 Setting constraints

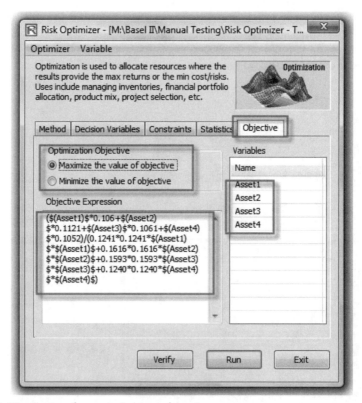

Figure A3-13 Setting the optimization objective.

as outlined in Figure A3-13. You can double click on the list of *Variables* to bring the variable name string to the objective expression input box.

When completed, click on **RUN** to obtain the results of your optimization.

You may also use Risk Optimizer to link to an existing database like Oracle or generate your own data tables to optimize. For instance, clicking on the **Variable →Variable Management** menu accesses the Variable Management tool, which will in turn allow you to **Add**, **Edit** or **Delete** variables. For instance, by clicking on **ADD**, the familiar *Input Parameter Mapping* tool appears (Figure A3-6), allowing you to link, compute, paste, simulate, or fit existing data for use in the optimization process.

Finally, if Dynamic or Stochastic Optimization is selected (Figure A3-10), and if the variables have risk simulation assumptions associated with them, you can then access the *Statistics* tab, whereby you can make use of the simulated statistical properties to run stochastic optimization on.

Rov Risk Valuator

Risk Valuator is used to perform quick computations from simple and basic models to advanced analytical models, and can handle single point values or a series of values. After installing the software, start Risk Valuator. Simply select the model type in the *Model Category* box and select the model of interest in the *Model Selection* box (Figure A3-16). The required input parameters will then be listed. Single point inputs (e.g., 10 or 10.4532) will be in the *single input parameters* area, whereas multiple data requirements will be shown in the *multiple series input parameters* area. When entering a single series of multiple data points, use commas or spaces to separate the

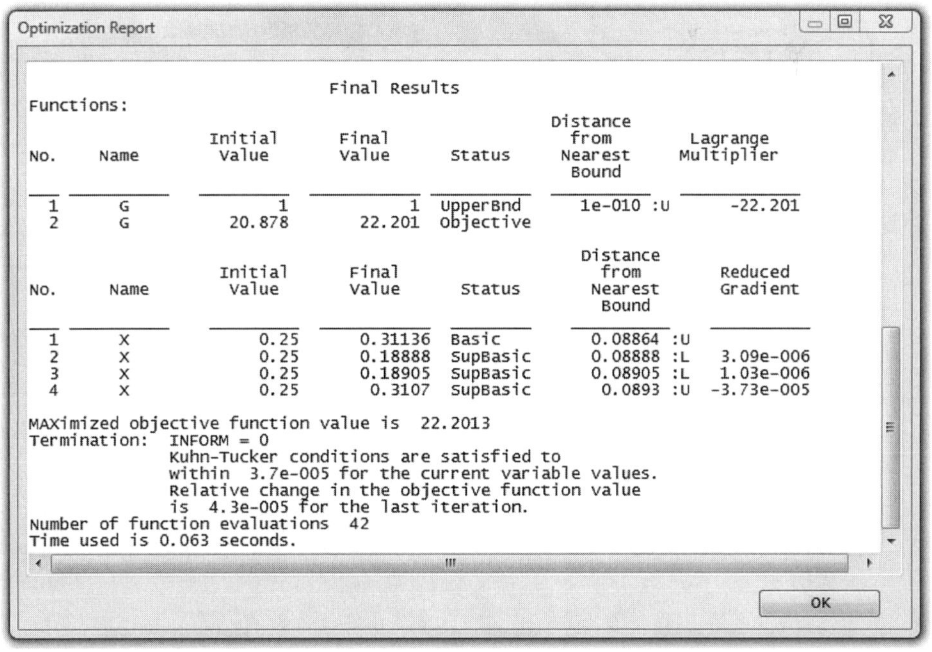

Figure A3-14   Optimization results.

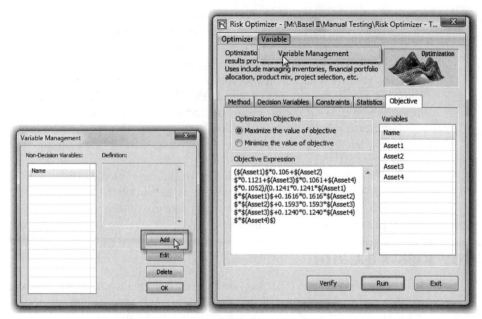

Figure A3-15   Variable management.

BASEL II MODELING TOOLKIT ANALYTICAL MODELS

MODEL CATEGORY:

Exotic Options and Derivatives
Financial Ratios
Forecasting Extrapolation and Interpolation
Inventory Analysis
Probability Distribution CDF, ICDF, PDF
Probability Distribution Theoretical Moments
Put-Call Parity and Option Sensitivity
Queuing Models
Real Options Analysis
Six Sigma Models
test temp
Value at Risk, Volatility, Portfolio Risk and Returns

MODEL SELECTION:

B2ImpliedVolatilityBestCase
B2ImpliedVolatilityCall
B2ImpliedVolatilityPut
B2ImpliedVolatilityWorstCase
B2PortfolioReturns
B2PortfolioRisk
B2PortfolioVariance
B2VaRCorrelationMethod
B2VarOptions
B2Volatility
B2VolatilityImpliedforDefaultRisk

MODEL DESCRIPTION:

Computes the Value at Risk using the Variance-Covariance and Correlation method, accounting for a specific VaR percentile and holding period

SINGLE INPUT PARAMETERS:

HorizonDays	10.00	Percentile	0.90	Input3:	0
Input4:	0	Input5:	0	Input6:	0
Input7:	0	Input8:	0	Input9:	0
Input10:	0	Input11:		Input12:	
Input13:		Input14:		Input15:	

MULTIPLE SERIES INPUT PARAMETERS (VALUES ARE COMMA SEPARATED):

Amounts	Daily Volatility	Correlations	Input4	Input5
1000 1200 2345	0.01 0.03 0.02	1.0,0.2,0.3 0.2,1,0.2 0.3,0.2,1.0		

RESULTS:

277.726447

COMPUTE   EXIT

Figure A3-16   Portfolio Value at Risk model solved using Risk Valuator.

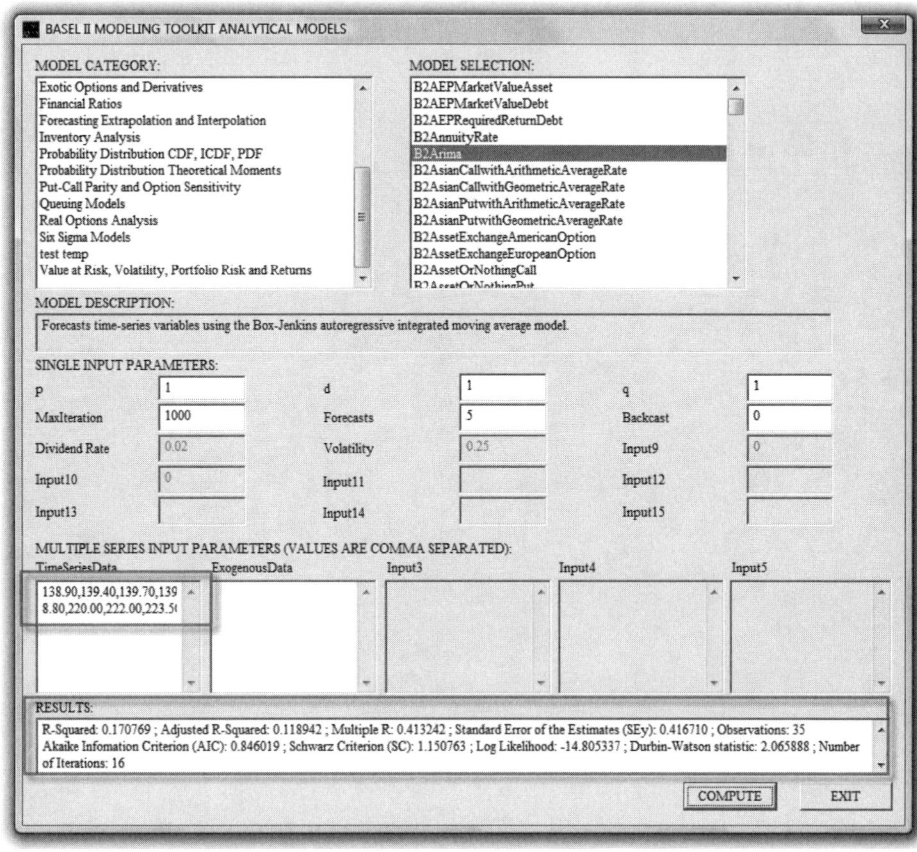

Figure A3-17   Complex ARIMA model solution.

values (e.g., a time-series of 6 months of interest rates can be entered either as 0.12, 0.124, 0.112, 0.1, 0.09, 0.16 or simply as 0.12 0.124 0.112 0.1 0.09 0.16).

Sometimes, certain models such as the Value at Risk (VaR) model using the standard correlation method, requires different columns of data and a correlation matrix. For instance, the goal is to compute the portfolio VaR using this model, where there are 3 asset classes, each with its own amounts, specific daily volatility for each asset class, and a square correlation matrix among these asset classes. In such a situation, the amounts and volatility inputs will have to be entered as a single column (hit **ENTER** at the end of entering a value, to create a new line, designating a new asset class) and the correlation matrix will be separated by commas for the same row with different columns, and semi-colons for different rows. This Risk Valuator module does not allow the user to link to various databases or simulate. To do so, use the Risk Modeler module instead. Many of the same models exist in both places. The Risk Valuator module is used to quickly obtain results without having to link to databases and so forth. Risk Valuator can also be used to compute more advanced models such as the Box-Jenkins ARIMA forecast (Figure A3-17). In summary, Risk Modeler can be used to run highly data intensive models as well as allows the user to link to existing databases, and yet run forecasting, simulation, and optimization algorithms, coupled with the advanced analytical models for credit and market risks as specified by Basel II.

Index